# INDEX TO
# DISTRICT OF COLUMBIA
# WILLS

1801 – 1920

Office of Public Records
Office of the Secretary

District of Columbia Government
Sharon Pratt Kelly, Mayor

# INDEX TO
# DISTRICT OF COLUMBIA
# WILLS

## 1801 – 1920

Prepared by
Dorothy S. Provine
District of Columbia Archives

CLEARFIELD

Published by Genealogical Publishing Co., Inc.
Baltimore, Maryland
1992

Library of Congress Catalogue Card Number 92-72714

Reprinted for Clearfield Company by
Genealogical Publishing Company
Baltimore, Maryland
2011

ISBN 978-0-8063-1354-2

*Made in the United States of America*

# INTRODUCTION

This book consists of an alphabetical name listing of more than 22,700 wills filed in the District of Columbia Orphans' Court (Probate Court) during the period 1801-1920. The D.C. Register of Wills transferred the records to the D.C. Archives in the summer of 1990 and the Archives assigned the records to Record Group 2, Records of Superior Court.

The documents are arranged by year of filing and thereunder alphabetically by name of person making the will. The entries in this finding aid give name of person, year the will was filed (which was usually, but not always, a short time after the death of the individual), and the number of the archives box that contains the document. Wills dated 1921-1953 are also in the District of Columbia Archives, but there is not yet any consolidated list for these items.

This series of records contains wills for a variety of people, some of whom were quite famous (or notorious). There are original wills for Dolley Madison, Francis Scott Key, Stephen Decatur, John H. Eaton, Frederick Douglass, Blanche K. Bruce, Charles J. Guiteau, Salmon P. Chase, Edward M. Stanton, Charles Francis Adams, Henry Adams, Carry Nation, Adm. George Dewey, Robert E. Peary, and William Crawford Gorgas. In addition, there are notarized copies of wills for other notable persons in the files including George Washington, John Quincy Adams, James Monroe, Thaddeus Kosuiszko, Andrew Jackson, Jerome Napoleon Bonaparte, Clara Barton, Benjamin F. Butler, Franklin Pierce, and others.

The vast bulk of the wills, of course, were created by the local middle and upper class property owners to ensure that the distribution of their possessions was carried out according to their wishes. Although most of the wills were penned by whites, a substantial number were created by Washington's prosperous African Americans: Eli Nugent, George Bell, Alice Grymes, Minty Hoban, William Costin, Rachel Shorter, Milly Gantt, Stepney Forrest, Nathaniel Herbert, Rosetta Dison, Leathe Hill, Basil Lancaster, Jeremiah Dant, Murray Barker, Alethe Tanner, Richmond Posey, Anthony Bowen, and many others.

Some of the documents are fragile and in poor condition. In cases where use of the item might result in further damage to the article, the researcher will be directed to volumes that contain verbatim transcriptions of the wills.

If you have any questions about the records described in this publication, please write the District of Columbia Archives, 1300 Naylor Court, N.W., Washington, D.C. 20001-4225, or call 202-727-2054.

# ACKNOWLEDGEMENTS

*I wish to thank the Register of Wills, Constance G. Evans, and her staff and summer interns for preparing the wills for transfer to the D.C. Archives and compiling the preliminary list of testators. I also want to thank Larry Baume for his overseeing of the will project for D.C. Archives and Philip Ogilvie for his general encouragement and practical assistance in getting the work into print.*

| | | | | | | |
|---|---|---|---|---|---|---|
| Abbe, Edward H. | 1915 | Box 508 | | Adams, Benjamin B. | 1897 | Box 167 |
| Abbe, Frances Martha | 1908 | Box 337 | | Adams, Catharine | 1854 | Box 22 |
| Abbot, Ann Taylor Gilman | 1861 | Box 29 | | Adams, Catharine Jane | 1880 | Box 71 |
| Abbot, Butler F. | 1918 | Box 589 | | Adams, Charles | 1890 | Box 117 |
| Abbot, Elizabeth | 1875 | Box 56 | | Adams, Charles Francis | 1915 | Box 508 |
| Abbot, George D. | 1874 | Box 53 | | Adams, Charles H. | 1908 | Box 337 |
| Abbot, George J. | 1886 | Box 95 | | Adams, Cornelius B. | 1858 | Box 26 |
| Abbot, Martha D. | 1915 | Box 508 | | Adams, Daniel I. | 1811 | Box 3 |
| Abbott, Joseph | 1861 | Box 29 | | Adams, Ed | 1918 | Box 589 |
| Abbott, Thomas J. | 1883 | Box 81 | | Adams, Eleanor | 1847 | Box 18 |
| Abbott, William E. | 1917 | Box 562 | | Adams, Elizabeth | 1882 | Box 78 |
| Abel, Jacob W. | 1902 | Box 219 | | Adams, Elizabeth J. | 1878 | Box 65 |
| Abel, John Frederick | 1897 | Box 167 | | Adams, Ella De Mott | 1915 | Box 508 |
| Abell, Alice R. Cornwell | 1919 | Box 618 | | Adams, Elvira Frances | 1905 | Box 275 |
| Abell, Arunah | 1901 | Box 203 | | Adams, Fanny Louisa | 1918 | Box 589 |
| Abell, Edwin F. | 1904 | Box 258 | | Adams, George | 1834 | Box 12 |
| Abell, Fannie A. | 1906 | Box 294 | | Adams, George | 1844 | Box 16 |
| Abell, George | 1901 | Box 203 | | Adams, George | 1902 | Box 219 |
| Abell, Sabra Philinda | 1885 | Box 90 | | Adams, George F. | 1913 | Box 460 |
| Abell, Walter | 1901 | Box 203 | | Adams, Hamilton | 1911 | Box 408 |
| Abert, John James | 1910 | Box 382 | | Adams, Hannah | 1902 | Box 219 |
| Abner, Edward | 1913 | Box 460 | | Adams, Henry | 1918 | Box 589 |
| Abner, Edward F. | 1910 | Box 382 | | Adams, Henry M. | 1910 | Box 382 |
| Abraham, Elizabeth | 1917 | Box 562 | | Adams, Henry T. | 1919 | Box 618 |
| Abraham, Hetty | 1919 | Box 618 | | Adams, James | 1877 | Box 62 |
| Abraham, Levi | 1876 | Box 60 | | Adams, James Bradley | 1892 | Box 129 |
| Abraham, Walter S. | 1917 | Box 562 | | Adams, James Osgood | 1908 | Box 337 |
| Abrams, William S. | 1917 | Box 562 | | Adams, James T. | 1877 | Box 62 |
| Acfield, Robert William | 1911 | Box 408 | | Adams, Jeremiah Sr. | 1920 | Box 650 |
| Achman, John | 1825 | Box 8 | | Adams, Jesse Lee | 1919 | Box 618 |
| Achstetter, Charles | 1920 | Box 649 | | Adams, John | 1855 | Box 23 |
| Achterkirchen, Henry F. W. | 1914 | Box 483 | | Adams, John | 1909 | Box 359 |
| Acker, Caroline C. | 1892 | Box 129 | | Adams, John George | 1879 | Box 67 |
| Acker, Elizabeth T. | 1919 | Box 618 | | Adams, John P. | 1869 | Box 40 |
| Acker, Nicholas | 1877 | Box 62 | | Adams, John Q. | 1848 | Box 19 |
| Ackley, Seth Mitchell | 1908 | Box 337 | | Adams, John R. | 1914 | Box 483 |
| Acosta, Mary C. | 1902 | Box 219 | | Adams, Joseph M. | 1860 | Box 28 |
| Acton, Ann M. | 1878 | Box 65 | | Adams, Joseph Thorton | 1878 | Box 65 |
| Acton, George | 1892 | Box 129 | | Adams, Josiah | 1888 | Box 106 |
| Acton, John C. | 1920 | Box 649 | | Adams, Julia M. | 1906 | Box 294 |
| Acton, Joseph | 1913 | Box 460 | | Adams, Margaret | 1883 | Box 81 |
| Acton, Osborn | 1870 | Box 42 | | Adams, Margaret | 1906 | Box 294 |
| Adam, William | 1883 | Box 81 | | Adams, Mary | 1892 | Box 129 |
| Adams, Ada C. | 1890 | Box 117 | | Adams, Mary C. | 1870 | Box 42 |
| Adams, Addie D. | 1877 | Box 62 | | Adams, Mary E. | 1914 | Box 483 |
| Adams, Adelaide Gilbert | 1919 | Box 618 | | Adams, Mary Jane | 1909 | Box 359 |
| Adams, Alden J. | 1919 | Box 618 | | Adams, Mary L. Edelin | 1911 | Box 408 |
| Adams, Alexander | 1859 | Box 27 | | Adams, Mary O. D. | 1910 | Box 382 |
| Adams, Alice M. | 1920 | Box 650 | | Adams, Mason P. | 1887 | Box 101 |
| Adams, Amanda | 1918 | Box 589 | | Adams, Milo R. | 1909 | Box 359 |
| Adams, Anna K. | 1914 | Box 483 | | Adams, Newton H. | 1869 | Box 40 |
| Adams, Annie M. | 1893 | Box 136 | | Adams, Priscilla L. | 1871 | Box 44 |

1

| | | | | | | |
|---|---|---|---|---|---|---|
| Adams, Robert | 1914 | Box 483 | Aiken, Matthew | 1909 | Box 360 |
| Adams, Robert S. | 1897 | Box 167 | Aiken, Prudence S. | 1867 | Box 37 |
| Adams, Sallie | 1912 | Box 434 | Akerman, John N. | 1917 | Box 562 |
| Adams, Sally G. | 1914 | Box 483 | Akers, Albert | 1914 | Box 483 |
| Adams, Samuel | 1873 | Box 50 | Alber, Catherine | 1897 | Box 167 |
| Adams, Samuel F. | 1910 | Box 382 | Albers, John Henry | 1886 | Box 95 |
| Adams, Sarah (Susannah) | 1823 | Box 7 | Albert, Allen D. | 1913 | Box 460 |
| Adams, Sarah Brent | 1871 | Box 44 | Albert, John | 1918 | Box 589 |
| Adams, Sydnie M. | 1905 | Box 275 | Albert, Silvanus Thayer | 1903 | Box 239 |
| Adams, Thomas Dunn | 1911 | Box 408 | Albrecht, Leonhard | 1892 | Box 129 |
| Adams, Thomas J. | 1900 | Box 190 | Albrecht, William F. | 1912 | Box 434 |
| Adams, Thomas N. | 1873 | Box 50 | Albrittain, Susannah | 1908 | Box 337 |
| Adams, Walter | 1811 | Box 3 | Alburger, Adam | 1848 | Box 19 |
| Adams, William | 1816 | Box 4 | Alcorn, John | 1899 | Box 181 |
| Adamson, Margaret | 1881 | Box 74 | Alden, Emily Josephine | 1913 | Box 460 |
| Adamson, Roger | 1861 | Box 29 | Alden, James | 1878 | Box 65 |
| Addison, Charles G. | 1917 | Box 562 | Alden, Louise W. | 1919 | Box 618 |
| Addison, Dunmore | 1848 | Box 19 | Alden, William H. | 1917 | Box 562 |
| Addison, Elizabeth H. | 1913 | Box 460 | Alden, William P. | 1895 | Box 151 |
| Addison, Hannibal Clagett | 1908 | Box 337 | Alder, Margaret F. | 1920 | Box 650 |
| Addison, James C. | 1910 | Box 382 | Alder, Mary C. | 1898 | Box 174 |
| Addison, John | 1905 | Box 275 | Alderman, Addie S. | 1893 | Box 136 |
| Addison, Katherine D. | 1917 | Box 562 | Aldis, Asa Owen | 1891 | Box 123 |
| Addison, Margaretta | 1901 | Box 203 | Aldis, Mary T. | 1909 | Box 360 |
| Addison, Maria E. | 1902 | Box 219 | Aldrich, Anna M. | 1913 | Box 460 |
| Addison, Martha E. | 1876 | Box 60 | Aldrich, Jessie S. | 1904 | Box 258 |
| Addison, Mary A. | 1917 | Box 562 | Aldridge, Clifford B. | 1915 | Box 508 |
| Addison, Mary N. | 1911 | Box 409 | Aldridge, John | 1834 | Box 12 |
| Addison, Murray | 1910 | Box 382 | Aler, Samuel | 1915 | Box 508 |
| Addison, Olivia Clagett | 1905 | Box 275 | Alexander, Aclelaide | 1894 | Box 143 |
| Addison, Paca | 1873 | Box 50 | Alexander, Charles | 1842 | Box 15 |
| Addison, Rebecca | 1828 | Box 9 | Alexander, Charles Armistead | 1870 | Box 42 |
| Addison, Reson | 1904 | Box 258 | Alexander, Charles Jerome | 1912 | Box 434 |
| Addison, Thomas | 1826 | Box 8 | Alexander, Charles Louis | 1881 | Box 74 |
| Addison, Thomas Grafton | 1896 | Box 159 | Alexander, Charles T. | 1918 | Box 589 |
| Addison, Walter D. | 1866 | Box 35 | Alexander, Columbus | 1898 | Box 174 |
| Adee, Ellen S. | 1918 | Box 589 | Alexander, Edward | 1886 | Box 96 |
| Adie, Patrick | 1887 | Box 101 | Alexander, Eliza J. | 1910 | Box 382 |
| Adler, Gertrude H. | 1913 | Box 460 | Alexander, Fendall E. | 1896 | Box 159 |
| Adler, Maurice J. | 1912 | Box 434 | Alexander, Finnella M. | 1904 | Box 258 |
| Adler, Morris | 1873 | Box 50 | Alexander, Jane E. | 1883 | Box 81 |
| Adlum, John | 1836 | Box 13 | Alexander, Mary R. | 1911 | Box 409 |
| Adlum, Margaret | 1852 | Box 21 | Alexander, Moses | 1872 | Box 46 |
| Adt, Alexis | 1907 | Box 315 | Alexander, Robert | 1811 | Box 3 |
| Agg, John | 1855 | Box 23 | Alexander, Russell | 1920 | Box 650 |
| Aguilar, Ygnacio | 1919 | Box 618 | Alexander, Sallie Kennedy | 1912 | Box 434 |
| Ahern, Johanna | 1869 | Box 40 | Alexander, Sandy | 1902 | Box 219 |
| Ahern, Mary | 1917 | Box 562 | Alexander, Sophia B. | 1920 | Box 650 |
| Aigler, Andrew | 1869 | Box 40 | Alexander, Susie | 1912 | Box 434 |
| Aigler, Sophia | 1901 | Box 203 | Alexander, Thomson H. | 1919 | Box 618 |
| Aiken, Eliza | 1907 | Box 315 | Alexander, William | 1909 | Box 360 |
| Aiken, Joseph D. | 1910 | Box 382 | Algate, John B. | 1918 | Box 589 |

| | | | | | | |
|---|---|---|---|---|---|---|
| Alig, Matthias L. | 1882 | Box 78 | Allyn, Lucius B. | 1876 | Box 60 |
| Allan, Edgar | 1904 | Box 258 | Allyn, Mary J. | 1906 | Box 294 |
| Allderdice, William Hillary | 1912 | Box 434 | Allyn, William H. | 1883 | Box 81 |
| Alleman, Hiram C. | 1908 | Box 337 | Almarode, John William | 1913 | Box 460 |
| Alleman, John S. | 1906 | Box 294 | Almarolia, Mary | 1904 | Box 258 |
| Allen, Aaron C. | 1913 | Box 460 | Almoore, Benjamin | 1918 | Box 589 |
| Allen Abby S. | 1917 | Box 562 | Almy, Alida Gardner | 1911 | Box 409 |
| Allen, Alexander T. | 1865 | Box 33 | Almy, John J. | 1895 | Box 151 |
| Allen, Amanda D. | 1907 | Box 315 | Alschwee, Emma | 1919 | Box 618 |
| Allen, Ann Rebecca | 1911 | Box 409 | Alschwee, Henry | 1918 | Box 589 |
| Allen, Charles E. | 1898 | Box 174 | Alsop, Benjamin H. | 1893 | Box 136 |
| Allen, Claude Joseph | 1915 | Box 508 | Altemus, Elizabeth A. | 1915 | Box 508 |
| Allen, Dewitt C. | 1884 | Box 85 | Altmansperger, Margaret | 1902 | Box 219 |
| Allen, Dora Z. | 1917 | Box 562 | Altrup, Frederick | 1902 | Box 219 |
| Allen, Edward K. | 1871 | Box 44 | Altschuh, Martin | 1905 | Box 275 |
| Allen, Eleanor | 1886 | Box 95 | Alvey, Elizabeth S. | 1909 | Box 360 |
| Allen, Ella Frances Reyburn | 1912 | Box 434 | Alvord, Benjamin | 1885 | Box 90 |
| Allen, Emily | 1893 | Box 136 | Alvord, Emily L. | 1885 | Box 90 |
| Allen, Ethan | 1913 | Box 460 | Alvord, Henry E. | 1904 | Box 258 |
| Allen, George W. | 1911 | Box 409 | Alvord, Julie | 1915 | Box 508 |
| Allen, Harrison | 1905 | Box 275 | Alworth, Daniel | 1912 | Box 434 |
| Allen, Henry A. | 1916 | Box 536 | Amberg, Regina | 1913 | Box 460 |
| Allen, James | 1874 | Box 53 | Amberger, Annie J. | 1915 | Box 508 |
| Allen, Jeremiah | 1901 | Box 203 | Amberger, Catharina M. | 1908 | Box 338 |
| Allen, Johana N. | 1916 | Box 536 | Ambler, Augustin Irel | 1897 | Box 167 |
| Allen, John Ethan | 1908 | Box 338 | Ambler, Roseline N. | 1903 | Box 239 |
| Allen, John F. | 1909 | Box 360 | Ambrose, Nathaniel M. | 1919 | Box 618 |
| Allen, Juliana | 1901 | Box 203 | Ambrose, Persis A. | 1910 | Box 382 |
| Allen, Lorinda A. | 1914 | Box 483 | Ambush, Andrew | 1911 | Box 409 |
| Allen, Lydia | 1856 | Box 24 | Ambush, Edward | 1865 | Box 33 |
| Allen, Martha | 1909 | Box 360 | Ambush, Enoch | 1876 | Box 60 |
| Allen, Mary E. | 1865 | Box 33 | Ameden, Nancy S. | 1895 | Box 151 |
| Allen, Nellie Louise | 1908 | Box 338 | Amende, Mollie E. | 1913 | Box 460 |
| Allen, Robert | 1918 | Box 589 | Amer, John W. | 1889 | Box 111 |
| Allen, Roberta Zimmerman | 1918 | Box 589 | Amery, Emma D. | 1918 | Box 589 |
| Allen, Samuel E. | 1911 | Box 409 | Amery, Robert L. | 1900 | Box 190 |
| Allen, Sarah | 1903 | Box 239 | Ames, Alfred H. | 1910 | Box 382 |
| Allen, Thomas | 1910 | Box 382 | Ames, Anna Seymour | 1910 | Box 382 |
| Allen, Thomas D. | 1876 | Box 60 | Ames, Delano | 1899 | Box 181 |
| Allen, Timothy | 1911 | Box 409 | Ames, Elizabeth Delano | 1905 | Box 275 |
| Allen, Victoria E. | 1918 | Box 589 | Ames, Horatio | 1871 | Box 44 |
| Allen, William H. | 1867 | Box 37 | Ames, John C. | 1875 | Box 56 |
| Allen, William P. | 1913 | Box 460 | Ames, John Griffith | 1910 | Box 382 |
| Allison, Catharine Craig | 1830 | Box 10 | Ames, Oliver | 1878 | Box 65 |
| Allison, James | 1901 | Box 203 | Amidon, Hollis | 1889 | Box 111 |
| Allison, Mary N. | 1893 | Box 136 | Ammon, Walter E. | 1913 | Box 460 |
| Allison, William B. | 1909 | Box 360 | Amoso, Anna Louise | 1902 | Box 219 |
| Allison, William H. | 1904 | Box 258 | Amrein, John | 1868 | Box 38 |
| Allman, Daniel | 1915 | Box 508 | Andermann, Elizabeth | 1907 | Box 315 |
| Allsop, Caroline | 1884 | Box 85 | Andermann, Phillip | 1903 | Box 239 |
| Allwine, Catharine L. | 1919 | Box 618 | Anderson, Alexander K. | 1919 | Box 618 |
| Allwine, Florence E. | 1920 | Box 650 | Anderson, Alfred J. | 1906 | Box 294 |

| | | | | | | |
|---|---|---|---|---|---|---|
| Anderson, Alice Thomas | 1910 | Box 382 | Anderson, Thomas Henry | 1916 | Box 536 |
| Anderson, Andrew | 1910 | Box 382 | Anderson, Thomas J. | 1910 | Box 382 |
| Anderson, Andrew E. A. | 1912 | Box 434 | Anderson, Victor | 1910 | Box 382 |
| Anderson, Ashland C. | 1881 | Box 74 | Anderson, William | 1881 | Box 74 |
| Anderson, Barbara | 1916 | Box 536 | Anderson, William | 1901 | Box 203 |
| Anderson, Blanche C. | 1920 | Box 650 | Andrews, Annie E. I. | 1904 | Box 258 |
| Anderson, Charles | 1901 | Box 203 | Andrews, Benjamin | 1909 | Box 360 |
| Anderson, Charles C. | 1899 | Box 181 | Andrews, Byron | 1911 | Box 409 |
| Anderson, Charles Finley | 1914 | Box 483 | Andrews, Celia E. | 1894 | Box 143 |
| Anderson, Cora B. | 1917 | Box 562 | Andrews, Eliphalet F. | 1915 | Box 508 |
| Anderson, David B. | 1920 | Box 650 | Andrews, Eliza H. | 1876 | Box 60 |
| Anderson, Edward E. | 1883 | Box 81 | Andrews, Ella C. | 1910 | Box 382 |
| Anderson, Edward Willoughby | 1916 | Box 536 | Andrews, Emily Kemble | 1920 | Box 650 |
| Anderson, Eleanor | 1877 | Box 62 | Andrews, Emma S. | 1890 | Box 117 |
| Anderson, Eliza Bayard | 1905 | Box 275 | Andrews, Fannie E. | 1912 | Box 434 |
| Anderson, Elizabeth Kilgour | 1917 | Box 562 | Andrews, Frank W. | 1903 | Box 239 |
| Anderson, Emma | 1901 | Box 203 | Andrews, Gardiner K. | 1892 | Box 129 |
| Anderson, Garret | 1853 | Box 22 | Andrews, George | 1910 | Box 382 |
| Anderson, George Burgwin | 1910 | Box 382 | Andrews, George L. | 1920 | Box 650 |
| Anderson, George C. | 1905 | Box 275 | Andrews, Henrietta M. | 1878 | Box 65 |
| Anderson, George Ross | 1920 | Box 650 | Andrews, Jane M. | 1830 | Box 10 |
| Anderson, George W. | 1873 | Box 50 | Andrews, Mary Lord | 1919 | Box 618 |
| Anderson, Griselda | 1887 | Box 101 | Andrews, Oliveira | 1914 | Box 483 |
| Anderson, Harry R. | 1919 | Box 618 | Andrews, Robert | 1903 | Box 239 |
| Anderson, Henrietta | 1901 | Box 203 | Andrews, Timothy P. | 1868 | Box 38 |
| Anderson, Hezekiah | 1868 | Box 38 | Andrus, Caroline A. H. | 1900 | Box 190 |
| Anderson, Isabel A. | 1912 | Box 434 | Andrus, Helen M. | 1904 | Box 258 |
| Anderson, James | 1892 | Box 129 | Andrus, Jonathan M. | 1897 | Box 167 |
| Anderson, John E. | 1918 | Box 589 | Angell, Maud M. S. | 1907 | Box 315 |
| Anderson, John P. | 1882 | Box 78 | Angermann, John | 1908 | Box 338 |
| Anderson, John W. | 1904 | Box 258 | Anibal, Calvin P. | 1919 | Box 618 |
| Anderson, Joseph | 1839 | Box 14 | Annadale, Martha E. | 1908 | Box 338 |
| Anderson, Joseph | 1880 | Box 71 | Annen, Caspar | 1894 | Box 143 |
| Anderson, Joseph H. | 1912 | Box 434 | Anthony, James H. | 1885 | Box 90 |
| Anderson, Laura R. | 1906 | Box 294 | Anthony, Joseph | 1899 | Box 181 |
| Anderson, Lavinia | 1913 | Box 460 | Antisell, Thomas | 1893 | Box 136 |
| Anderson, Lewis C. | 1918 | Box 589 | Antisell, Thomasina | 1919 | Box 619 |
| Anderson, Lucy A. | 1886 | Box 95 | Antrim, Mary Vincent | 1902 | Box 219 |
| Anderson, Lybrun | 1917 | Box 562 | Appel, Charles A. | 1911 | Box 409 |
| Anderson, Martha Ann | 1876 | Box 60 | Appich, Caroline | 1911 | Box 409 |
| Anderson, Martha R. | 1890 | Box 117 | Appich, Jacob J. | 1906 | Box 294 |
| Anderson, Mary | 1904 | Box 258 | Apple, Deborah J. | 1920 | Box 650 |
| Anderson, Mary E. | 1912 | Box 434 | Appleby, George F. | 1903 | Box 239 |
| Anderson, Nicholas L. | 1892 | Box 129 | Appleby, Martha | 1910 | Box 382 |
| Anderson, Notley | 1918 | Box 589 | Appleby, William | 1873 | Box 50 |
| Anderson, Robert | 1813 | Box 4 | Appler, Helen M. | 1909 | Box 360 |
| Anderson, Rose V. | 1909 | Box 360 | Appler, Mary | 1901 | Box 203 |
| Anderson, Samuel I. | 1854 | Box 22 | Appleton, Eben D. | 1919 | Box 619 |
| Anderson, Sarah Jane | 1893 | Box 136 | Appley, James D. | 1914 | Box 483 |
| Anderson, Thomas | 1872 | Box 46 | Applich, John | 1916 | Box 536 |
| Anderson, Thomas | 1887 | Box 101 | April, Mollie | 1916 | Box 536 |
| Anderson, Thomas F. | 1864 | Box 32 | Arbuckle, Sarah Ann | 1838 | Box 14 |

| | | | | | | |
|---|---|---|---|---|---|---|---|
| Arbuckle, Thomas | 1838 | Box 14 | Arnold, Henry | 1911 | Box 409 |
| Archer, Andrew | 1911 | Box 409 | Arnold, James E. | 1910 | Box 382 |
| Archer, Helen | 1894 | Box 143 | Arnold, John | 1916 | Box 536 |
| Archer, James E. | 1916 | Box 536 | Arnold, Lucy Louisa | 1890 | Box 117 |
| Archer, Mary Ringgold | 1890 | Box 129 | Arnold, Mary | 1873 | Box 50 |
| Archer, Samuel B. | 1825 | Box 8 | Arnold, Regin | 1871 | Box 44 |
| Archer, Simon | 1915 | Box 508 | Arnold, Richard A. | 1905 | Box 275 |
| Arctander, Emil | 1881 | Box 74 | Arnold, Sarah Jane | 1897 | Box 167 |
| Ardeeser, Henry | 1913 | Box 460 | Arnold, Teresa | 1911 | Box 409 |
| Ardeeser, John | 1917 | Box 562 | Arnold, William B. | 1881 | Box 74 |
| Ardeeser, John P. | 1910 | Box 382 | Arnold, William R. | 1913 | Box 460 |
| Ardeeser, Kathareena | 1902 | Box 219 | Arny, Adeline L. | 1899 | Box 181 |
| Arduser, Christian | 1887 | Box 101 | Arny, Charles W. | 1911 | Box 409 |
| Arendes, Elizabeth M. | 1907 | Box 315 | Arny, Louis C. | 1911 | Box 409 |
| Arendes, Joseph M. | 1912 | Box 434 | Arrick, William T. | 1891 | Box 123 |
| Arendes, Sophia | 1907 | Box 315 | Artes, Henry | 1899 | Box 181 |
| Arendes, William | 1902 | Box 219 | Arth, Christopher | 1901 | Box 203 |
| Arendes, William H. | 1920 | Box 650 | Arth, Jacob | 1880 | Box 71 |
| Argo, Margie Welker | 1914 | Box 483 | Arth, Katherine | 1904 | Box 258 |
| Argue, William L. | 1913 | Box 460 | Arthur, Caroline C. | 1887 | Box 101 |
| Arkward, Annie | 1919 | Box 619 | Arthur, Mary Jane | 1910 | Box 382 |
| Arlow, Robert T. | 1893 | Box 136 | Arthur, Patrick H. | 1905 | Box 275 |
| Armes, Charles H. | 1916 | Box 536 | Arundell, Charles A. | 1895 | Box 151 |
| Armes, George A. | 1920 | Box 650 | Asbury, Kate D. W. | 1915 | Box 508 |
| Armes, Josiah O. | 1879 | Box 67 | Aschenbach, John Valentine | 1878 | Box 65 |
| Armiger, William L. | 1907 | Box 315 | Aschenbach, George H. | 1893 | Box 136 |
| Armistead, Howard M. | 1904 | Box 258 | Ash, Sallie Hebb | 1905 | Box 275 |
| Armistead, Mary Margaret | 1904 | Box 258 | Ashburn, Martha A. | 1900 | Box 190 |
| Armistead, William A. | 1908 | Box 338 | Ashby, Bertrand S. | 1890 | Box 117 |
| Arms, Amorett | 1912 | Box 435 | Ashby, William T. | 1908 | Box 338 |
| Arms, John Taylor | 1912 | Box 435 | Ashdown, William Lemon | 1918 | Box 589 |
| Arms, Kate Watkins | 1904 | Box 258 | Ashe, Julia | 1904 | Box 258 |
| Armstead, George | 1890 | Box 117 | Ashe, Julia A. | 1898 | Box 174 |
| Armstead, Robert | 1913 | Box 460 | Ashford, Craven | 1877 | Box 62 |
| Armstrong, Anthony S. | 1903 | Box 239 | Ashford, Francis A. | 1883 | Box 81 |
| Armstrong, Charlotte C. | 1910 | Box 382 | Ashford, Francis M. | 1909 | Box 360 |
| Armstrong, Francis D. | 1902 | Box 219 | Ashford, Mahlon | 1901 | Box 203 |
| Armstrong, James W. | 1891 | Box 123 | Ashford, Mary | 1909 | Box 360 |
| Armstrong, Mary W. | 1909 | Box 360 | Ashford, Philip M. | 1918 | Box 589 |
| Armstrong, Robert | 1906 | Box 294 | Ashford, Sidney L. | 1919 | Box 619 |
| Armstrong, Sallie | 1913 | Box 460 | Ashford, William F. | 1917 | Box 562 |
| Armstrong, Sarah Matilda | 1914 | Box 483 | Ashley, Charles W. | 1920 | Box 650 |
| Armstrong, William | 1825 | Box 8 | Ashmun, Jehudi | 1828 | Box 9 |
| Armstrong, William Henry | 1914 | Box 483 | Ashton, Celia | 1835 | Box 12 |
| Armstrong, William J. | 1919 | Box 619 | Ashton, Hannah R. | 1906 | Box 294 |
| Armstrong, William W. | 1917 | Box 562 | Ashton, J. Hubley | 1907 | Box 315 |
| Arnold, Alfred J. | 1914 | Box 483 | Ashton, John N. | 1919 | Box 619 |
| Arnold, Alice | 1919 | Box 619 | Ashton, Roberta | 1920 | Box 650 |
| Arnold, Aquilla K. | 1871 | Box 44 | Ashton, Winnie Ann | 1903 | Box 239 |
| Arnold, Cleo A. Jones | 1919 | Box 619 | Ashwood, Mary J. | 1848 | Box 19 |
| Arnold, Enoch | 1829 | Box 10 | Askins, Bushrod W. | 1890 | Box 117 |
| Arnold, Frank | 1896 | Box 159 | Askins, Jacob B. | 1920 | Box 650 |

| | | | | | | |
|---|---|---|---|---|---|---|
| Asmussen, Augusta | 1884 | Box 85 | | Austin, Fred H. | 1919 | Box 619 |
| Asmussen, George W. B. | 1895 | Box 151 | | Austin, Jane | 1891 | Box 123 |
| Aspinwall, John Abel | 1913 | Box 460 | | Austin, Manville A. | 1911 | Box 409 |
| Aspinwall, Martha H. | 1920 | Box 650 | | Austin, Mary R. | 1918 | Box 589 |
| Asserson, Mary A. | 1910 | Box 382 | | Austin, Thomas H. | 1911 | Box 409 |
| Asserson, Peter C. | 1907 | Box 315 | | Auth, Regina | 1915 | Box 508 |
| Atchison, Eliza A. | 1920 | Box 650 | | Auth, Santus | 1910 | Box 383 |
| Atchison, Harris Lanham | 1909 | Box 360 | | Averill, John W. | 1916 | Box 536 |
| Athey, George | 1823 | Box 7 | | Avery, James D. | 1917 | Box 562 |
| Athey, John M. | 1895 | Box 151 | | Avery, Richard W. | 1899 | Box 181 |
| Atkins, Addison B. | 1905 | Box 275 | | Avery, Robert Stanton | 1895 | Box 151 |
| Atkins, David | 1866 | Box 35 | | Avery, William | 1901 | Box 203 |
| Atkins, David Alexander | 1897 | Box 167 | | Ayer, Sarah S. | 1895 | Box 151 |
| Atkins, George F. | 1891 | Box 123 | | Ayers, Alice C. | 1909 | Box 361 |
| Atkins, Joseph | 1907 | Box 315 | | Ayers, Annie Clark | 1895 | Box 151 |
| Atkins, Kate | 1901 | Box 203 | | Aylmer, Henry | 1854 | Box 22 |
| Atkins, Mary A. | 1916 | Box 536 | | Aylmer, Margaret | 1901 | Box 203 |
| Atkins, Sarah E. | 1912 | Box 434 | | Aylmer, Robert R. | 1868 | Box 38 |
| Atkinson, Elizabeth J. | 1894 | Box 144 | | Ayres, Edward W. | 1902 | Box 219 |
| Atwater, Grace E. | 1909 | Box 361 | | Ayres, Gustav | 1916 | Box 536 |
| Atwell, William P. | 1911 | Box 409 | | Baar, Lewis | 1906 | Box 294 |
| Atwood, Isaac Morgan | 1918 | Box 589 | | Babbington, Bridget | 1915 | Box 508 |
| Atwood, Louisa E. | 1919 | Box 619 | | Babbington, Joseph A. | 1918 | Box 589 |
| Atzel, John F. | 1900 | Box 190 | | Babbington, Thomas A. | 1912 | Box 435 |
| Au, William | 1909 | Box 361 | | Babbitt, Emma A. | 1918 | Box 589 |
| Au, William | 1910 | Box 383 | | Babcock, Anne Johns | 1891 | Box 123 |
| Aubere, Jewell Howard | 1909 | Box 361 | | Babcock, Charles P. | 1877 | Box 62 |
| Audenried, John T. | 1885 | Box 90 | | Babcock, Daniel A. | 1914 | Box 483 |
| Audenried, Mary C. | 1912 | Box 435 | | Babcock, George W. | 1912 | Box 435 |
| Aue, John H. | 1899 | Box 181 | | Babcock, Henrietta V. P. | 1917 | Box 562 |
| Auerbach, Carl | 1910 | Box 383 | | Babcock, Joseph W. | 1909 | Box 361 |
| Auerochs, John M. F. | 1880 | Box 71 | | Babcock, Lillian M. | 1907 | Box 315 |
| Aufrecht, Carl Gottlob | 1920 | Box 650 | | Babcock, Orville E. | 1884 | Box 85 |
| Augenstein, Theresia | 1912 | Box 435 | | Babe, Joseph W. | 1894 | Box 144 |
| Aughinbaugh, William Larimer | 1911 | Box 409 | | Babe, Mary A. | 1897 | Box 167 |
| Augur, Christopher C. | 1898 | Box 174 | | Babson, James A. | 1892 | Box 129 |
| Augur, Kate Dodge | 1920 | Box 650 | | Babson, John Walker | 1906 | Box 294 |
| August, James A. | 1914 | Box 483 | | Bache, Alfred T. | 1917 | Box 562 |
| Augusta, Alexander J. | 1891 | Box 123 | | Bache, Eliza C. | 1884 | Box 85 |
| Augusterfer, Harvey G. | 1918 | Box 589 | | Bache, Emma C. | 1896 | Box 159 |
| Aukward, Henry | 1842 | Box 15 | | Bache, Emma C. Shane | 1916 | Box 536 |
| Auld, James | 1885 | Box 90 | | Bache, George M. | 1896 | Box 159 |
| Auld, James | 1833 | Box 14 | | Bacigaluppi, John | 1912 | Box 435 |
| Auld, Mary | 1902 | Box 219 | | Backus, Armstead | 1919 | Box 619 |
| Auldridge, Sarah C. | 1919 | Box 619 | | Bacon, Delilah | 1906 | Box 294 |
| Aulick, John H. | 1873 | Box 50 | | Bacon, Elizabeth | 1861 | Box 29 |
| Aulick, Ralph J. | 1873 | Box 50 | | Bacon, Harry A. | 1917 | Box 562 |
| Aulick, Richmond Ogston | 1897 | Box 167 | | Bacon, Josephine C. | 1881 | Box 74 |
| Ault, Henry | 1840 | Box 15 | | Bacon, Margaret L. | 1919 | Box 619 |
| Aumann, Ottilie | 1905 | Box 275 | | Bacon, Mary E. | 1915 | Box 508 |
| Auracher, Christian C. | 1916 | Box 536 | | Bacon, Mary R. | 1890 | Box 117 |
| Austin, Edwin Forrest | 1913 | Box 460 | | Bacon, Peter F. | 1900 | Box 190 |

| | | | | | | |
|---|---|---|---|---|---|---|
| Bacon, Reuben A. | 1885 | Box 90 | Bainbridge, William P. | 1912 | Box 435 |
| Bacon, Samuel | 1887 | Box 101 | Bair, George W. | 1917 | Box 562 |
| Bacon, Samuel | 1912 | Box 435 | Baird, Cornelia M. Smith | 1883 | Box 81 |
| Bacon, Samuel H. | 1918 | Box 589 | Baird, Julia | 1916 | Box 536 |
| Bacon, Washington | 1872 | Box 46 | Baird, Lucy Hunter | 1913 | Box 460 |
| Baden, Eleanor | 1867 | Box 37 | Baird, Mary Helen Churchill | 1892 | Box 129 |
| Badger, Margaret J. | 1908 | Box 338 | Baird, Spencer F. | 1887 | Box 101 |
| Badger, Oscar C. | 1899 | Box 181 | Bairstow, William Henry | 1904 | Box 258 |
| Baefsky, Isaac | 1920 | Box 650 | Baker, Albert | 1920 | Box 650 |
| Baer, Karl | 1920 | Box 650 | Baker, Albert B. | 1888 | Box 106 |
| Baessell, Charles Frederick | 1918 | Box 590 | Baker, Annie Millard | 1900 | Box 190 |
| Bagg, George W. | 1909 | Box 361 | Baker, Arthur Heaton | 1896 | Box 159 |
| Bagger, André Louis | 1895 | Box 151 | Baker, Caroline A. | 1905 | Box 275 |
| Bagger, William | 1918 | Box 590 | Baker, Charles | 1877 | Box 62 |
| Bagley, William O. | 1920 | Box 650 | Baker, Charles C. | 1910 | Box 383 |
| Bagnam, William | 1887 | Box 101 | Baker, Charles Henry | 1896 | Box 159 |
| Baier, Albert | 1893 | Box 136 | Baker, Clara Lucinda | 1908 | Box 338 |
| Baier, Dorothea | 1901 | Box 203 | Baker, Daniel W. | 1919 | Box 619 |
| Baier, George K. | 1881 | Box 74 | Baker, Dora G. | 1891 | Box 123 |
| Baier, John | 1894 | Box 144 | Baker, Euphemia C. | 1920 | Box 651 |
| Baier, Sophie V. | 1919 | Box 619 | Baker, Fannie A. | 1910 | Box 383 |
| Baier, William | 1904 | Box 258 | Baker, Francis A. | 1893 | Box 136 |
| Bailey, Ada L. | 1915 | Box 508 | Baker, Frank | 1919 | Box 619 |
| Bailey, Adam | 1850 | Box 20 | Baker, Henrietta | 1907 | Box 315 |
| Bailey, Anne | 1853 | Box 22 | Baker, Henry | 1839 | Box 14 |
| Bailey, Arabelle | 1899 | Box 181 | Baker, Henry | 1910 | Box 383 |
| Bailey, Eileen A. | 1904 | Box 258 | Baker, Henry M. | 1912 | Box 435 |
| Bailey, Elizabeth | 1906 | Box 294 | Baker, Ira J. | 1918 | Box 590 |
| Bailey, Gamaliel | 1859 | Box 27 | Baker, J. Milton | 1911 | Box 409 |
| Bailey, George A. | 1878 | Box 65 | Baker, John | 1875 | Box 56 |
| Bailey, Ida S. | 1908 | Box 338 | Baker, John B. | 1918 | Box 590 |
| Bailey, John | 1897 | Box 167 | Baker, Katharine E. | 1919 | Box 619 |
| Bailey, John A. | 1905 | Box 275 | Baker, Laura A. C. | 1902 | Box 219 |
| Bailey, Leonard C. | 1918 | Box 590 | Baker, Lewis H. | 1878 | Box 65 |
| Bailey, Lucinda | 1905 | Box 275 | Baker, Marcus | 1903 | Box 239 |
| Bailey, Lucy | 1901 | Box 203 | Baker, Mary D. | 1908 | Box 338 |
| Bailey, Mary A. | 1908 | Box 338 | Baker, Mary E. | 1906 | Box 294 |
| Bailey, Miranda | 1898 | Box 174 | Baker, Mary E. | 1912 | Box 435 |
| Bailey, Rice W. | 1915 | Box 508 | Baker, Mary F. | 1920 | Box 651 |
| Bailey, Richard | 1919 | Box 619 | Baker, Nancy H. | 1839 | Box 14 |
| Bailey, Sarah A. | 1881 | Box 74 | Baker, Samuel | 1807 | Box 2 |
| Bailey, Theodorus | 1877 | Box 62 | Baker, Sidney S. | 1896 | Box 159 |
| Bailey, William H. | 1886 | Box 95 | Baker, Susannah | 1906 | Box 294 |
| Baillieux, Louis | 1912 | Box 435 | Baker, Thomas | 1866 | Box 35 |
| Baily, Julia E. | 1873 | Box 50 | Baker, William M. | 1889 | Box 111 |
| Baily, Mary | 1853 | Box 22 | Baker, William S. | 1911 | Box 409 |
| Bain, Alexander | 1911 | Box 409 | Bakersmith, George H. | 1907 | Box 315 |
| Bain, Andrew | 1898 | Box 174 | Balch, Mary L. | 1899 | Box 181 |
| Bain, John | 1874 | Box 53 | Balck, Coorde | 1853 | Box 22 |
| Bain, Julia E. | 1902 | Box 219 | Baldwin, Aaron | 1903 | Box 239 |
| Bain, Margaret | 1885 | Box 90 | Baldwin, Abraham | 1807 | Box 2 |
| Bain, Martha R. | 1912 | Box 435 | Baldwin, Almon | 1876 | Box 60 |

| | | | | | | |
|---|---|---|---|---|---|
| Baldwin, Annie M. | 1910 | Box 383 | Baltimore, John H. | 1886 | Box 95 |
| Baldwin, Barbara | 1913 | Box 460 | Baltz, John H. | 1919 | Box 619 |
| Baldwin, Brenton L. | 1896 | Box 159 | Baltzell, John | 1899 | Box 181 |
| Baldwin, Clara B. | 1911 | Box 409 | Baltzer, Mary Ann | 1898 | Box 174 |
| Baldwin, George B. | 1920 | Box 651 | Bancroft, Elizabeth | 1886 | Box 95 |
| Baldwin, Henry Clay | 1864 | Box 32 | Bancroft, George | 1891 | Box 123 |
| Baldwin, Honora | 1878 | Box 65 | Bancroft, George | 1896 | Box 159 |
| Baldwin, Isabel | 1918 | Box 590 | Bancroft, Matilda A. | 1916 | Box 536 |
| Baldwin, James D. | 1870 | Box 42 | Bancroft, Sarah | 1886 | Box 95 |
| Baldwin, Jeremiah | 1899 | Box 181 | Bancroft, William S. | 1885 | Box 90 |
| Baldwin, John H. | 1894 | Box 144 | Bane, Moses M. | 1898 | Box 174 |
| Baldwin, Kate I. | 1919 | Box 619 | Banes, Charles E. | 1919 | Box 619 |
| Baldwin, Lena Shay | 1895 | Box 151 | Banes, Elizabeth L. | 1912 | Box 435 |
| Baldwin, Mary E. | 1916 | Box 536 | Banes, Samuel P. | 1893 | Box 136 |
| Baldwin, Virginia B. | 1865 | Box 33 | Banf, John | 1897 | Box 167 |
| Baldwin, William Birth | 1895 | Box 151 | Bangs, Eleanor Evans | 1899 | Box 181 |
| Baldwin, William Dickson | 1915 | Box 508 | Bangs, George Pemberton | 1896 | Box 159 |
| Baldy, James | 1899 | Box 181 | Banke, Thomas | 1913 | Box 461 |
| Balinger, George William | 1910 | Box 383 | Bankett, Irving | 1919 | Box 619 |
| Balistier, Joseph | 1858 | Box 26 | Banks, David | 1905 | Box 275 |
| Ball, Ada V. | 1919 | Box 619 | Banks, Julia B. | 1902 | Box 219 |
| Ball, Catharine J. | 1913 | Box 461 | Banks, Mary Isabella | 1916 | Box 536 |
| Ball, Dabney | 1857 | Box 25 | Banks, Melvinia | 1918 | Box 590 |
| Ball, Ebenezer | 1900 | Box 190 | Banks, Sam | 1895 | Box 151 |
| Ball, Frances H. | 1904 | Box 258 | Barbadoes, Frederick G. | 1899 | Box 181 |
| Ball, Franklin | 1886 | Box 95 | Barbarin, Jane Oliver | 1907 | Box 315 |
| Ball, James N. | 1875 | Box 56 | Barber, Alice | 1911 | Box 410 |
| Ball, Jemima P. | 1915 | Box 508 | Barber, Amherst Willoughby | 1920 | Box 651 |
| Ball, Joseph J. G. | 1902 | Box 219 | Barber, Amzi L. | 1909 | Box 361 |
| Ball, Mary | 1845 | Box 17 | Barber, Casper | 1894 | Box 144 |
| Ball, Miriam | 1843 | Box 16 | Barber, Cornelius | 1853 | Box 22 |
| Ball, Richard Thomson Mason | 1913 | Box 461 | Barber, Elizabeth | 1898 | Box 174 |
| Ball, Robert | 1864 | Box 32 | Barber, Frank D. | 1918 | Box 590 |
| Ball, Robert | 1897 | Box 167 | Barber, George | 1878 | Box 65 |
| Ball, Virginia F. | 1919 | Box 619 | Barber, George E. | 1915 | Box 508 |
| Ball, William | 1855 | Box 23 | Barber, John T. | 1910 | Box 383 |
| Ballantine, Ann | 1889 | Box 111 | Barber, Joseph | 1877 | Box 62 |
| Ballantyne, William | 1906 | Box 294 | Barber, Julia Louise Langdon | 1912 | Box 435 |
| Ballard, William St. John | 1913 | Box 461 | Barber, Kimetta | 1901 | Box 203 |
| Ballauf, Daniel | 1914 | Box 484 | Barber, LeDroict Langdon | 1905 | Box 275 |
| Ballauf, Elisa | 1911 | Box 409 | Barber, Louis F. | 1878 | Box 65 |
| Ballbach, Margaretha | 1915 | Box 508 | Barber, Sarah E. | 1883 | Box 81 |
| Ballenger, Winfield S. | 1903 | Box 239 | Barber, Theodore C. | 1896 | Box 159 |
| Ballinger, Florence Fates | 1905 | Box 275 | Barber, Thomas S. | 1902 | Box 219 |
| Ballinger, Francis Marion | 1911 | Box 409 | Barbour, Anna M. | 1916 | Box 536 |
| Ballinger, Rebecca | 1911 | Box 410 | Barbour, Annie E. | 1900 | Box 190 |
| Ballman, Maria | 1904 | Box 258 | Barbour, Eliza | 1890 | Box 117 |
| Balloch, Elizabeth A. K. | 1914 | Box 484 | Barbour, James F. | 1916 | Box 536 |
| Balloch, George Williamson | 1907 | Box 315 | Barbour, Robert P. | 1889 | Box 111 |
| Ballock, George S. | 1909 | Box 361 | Barbour, Susan Sewall | 1886 | Box 95 |
| Balmain, Andrew | 1875 | Box 56 | Barbour, William | 1867 | Box 37 |
| Balster, Johannah | 1903 | Box 239 | Barclay, Catharine | 1880 | Box 71 |

| | | | | | | |
|---|---|---|---|---|---|---|
| Barclay, Charles F. | 1915 | Box 508 | Barnard, Rebekah A. | 1893 | Box 136 |
| Barclay, Frances Howard | 1904 | Box 258 | Barnard, Samuel John | 1847 | Box 18 |
| Barclay, John D. | 1870 | Box 42 | Barndollar, Elizabeth Hack | 1919 | Box 620 |
| Barclay, John M. | 1888 | Box 106 | Barnes, Benjamin F. | 1909 | Box 362 |
| Barclay, Mary Ann | 1825 | Box 8 | Barnes, Charles W. | 1903 | Box 239 |
| Barclay, Sophia D. | 1902 | Box 219 | Barnes, Elizabeth | 1917 | Box 563 |
| Barclay, Susan | 1866 | Box 35 | Barnes, George | 1913 | Box 461 |
| Barclay, William H. H. | 1872 | Box 46 | Barnes, George A. | 1837 | Box 13 |
| Barcroft, John W. | 1918 | Box 590 | Barnes, Hannah | 1905 | Box 275 |
| Barcroft, John W. (Sr.) | 1916 | Box 536 | Barnes, Hanson | 1854 | Box 22 |
| Barcroft, Maria | 1879 | Box 67 | Barnes, James J. | 1908 | Box 338 |
| Barcroft, Sarah W. | 1841 | Box 15 | Barnes, Johanna Mary | 1909 | Box 362 |
| Barden, Sarah M. | 1917 | Box 562 | Barnes, John | 1826 | Box 8 |
| Barker, Albert Smith | 1916 | Box 536 | Barnes, Joseph K. | 1883 | Box 81 |
| Barker, Ardella | 1897 | Box 167 | Barnes, Martha E. | 1900 | Box 190 |
| Barker, Blanche | 1893 | Box 136 | Barnes, Mary T. | 1912 | Box 435 |
| Barker, Charles Rowland | 1898 | Box 174 | Barnes, Mattie V. S. | 1917 | Box 563 |
| Barker, Eliza | 1897 | Box 167 | Barnes, Sarah A. L. Martin | 1887 | Box 101 |
| Barker, Fannie R. | 1914 | Box 484 | Barnes, Smith | 1910 | Box 383 |
| Barker, Francis C. | 1910 | Box 383 | Barnes, Thomas T. | 1873 | Box 50 |
| Barker, George | 1907 | Box 315 | Barnett, Claude L. | 1916 | Box 536 |
| Barker, George H. | 1892 | Box 129 | Barnette, Margaret E. | 1918 | Box 590 |
| Barker, George M. | 1889 | Box 111 | Barnette, William J. | 1909 | Box 362 |
| Barker, James W. | 1889 | Box 111 | Barney, Albert Clifford | 1903 | Box 239 |
| Barker, John H. | 1874 | Box 53 | Barney, Mary | 1872 | Box 46 |
| Barker, John H. | 1888 | Box 106 | Barnhill, Gabriel | 1867 | Box 37 |
| Barker, Julia A. | 1889 | Box 111 | Barns, Basil | 1845 | Box 17 |
| Barker, Julia S. | 1913 | Box 461 | Barnum, Horatio | 1920 | Box 651 |
| Barker, Margaret | 1876 | Box 60 | Barnum, Levi | 1896 | Box 159 |
| Barker, Martha J. | 1909 | Box 361 | Barnwell, Alice G. | 1920 | Box 651 |
| Barker, Mary H. | 1899 | Box 181 | Barnwell, R. Grant | 1917 | Box 563 |
| Barker, Murray | 1857 | Box 25 | Barotti, Felix | 1881 | Box 74 |
| Barker, Rebecca | 1883 | Box 81 | Barr, Ann Jane | 1904 | Box 258 |
| Barker, Richard W. | 1906 | Box 294 | Barr, Elizabeth | 1882 | Box 78 |
| Barker, Sarah C. | 1904 | Box 258 | Barr, Emma | 1908 | Box 338 |
| Barker, Susan A. | 1920 | Box 651 | Barr, Harriet C. | 1911 | Box 410 |
| Barker, William E. | 1919 | Box 619 | Barr, Henry D. | 1892 | Box 129 |
| Barklie, Francis | 1848 | Box 19 | Barr, James A. | 1882 | Box 78 |
| Barksdale, Noel W. | 1911 | Box 410 | Barr, John | 1902 | Box 219 |
| Barlow, Emeline C. | 1910 | Box 383 | Barret, John H. | 1915 | Box 508 |
| Barlow, Harry N. | 1884 | Box 85 | Barrett, Caroline Virginia Dulin | 1916 | Box 536 |
| Barlow, Joel | 1813 | Box 4 | Barrett, Catharine | 1877 | Box 62 |
| Barlow, Kate B. | 1914 | Box 484 | Barrett, Daniel | 1906 | Box 295 |
| Barlow, Ruth | 1818 | Box 5 | Barrett, Erastus B. | 1869 | Box 40 |
| Barnaby, Jerothmul B. | 1919 | Box 620 | Barrett, Hiram W. | 1917 | Box 563 |
| Barnard, Amelia | 1901 | Box 203 | Barrett, James | 1880 | Box 71 |
| Barnard, Erastus A. | 1919 | Box 620 | Barrett, James | 1915 | Box 508 |
| Barnard, George B. | 1889 | Box 111 | Barrett, Johannah | 1901 | Box 203 |
| Barnard, John H. | 1919 | Box 620 | Barrett, John C. | 1861 | Box 29 |
| Barnard, Katharine R. | 1895 | Box 151 | Barrett, Margaret A. | 1883 | Box 81 |
| Barnard, Margaret R. | 1917 | Box 563 | Barrett, Marion R. | 1916 | Box 536 |
| Barnard, Milton | 1901 | Box 203 | Barrett, Mary | 1901 | Box 203 |

| | | | | | | |
|---|---|---|---|---|---|
| Barrett, Mary | 1902 | Box 219 | Bartgis, Ann Rebecca | 1915 | Box 508 |
| Barrett, Mary | 1914 | Box 484 | Barth, William | 1874 | Box 53 |
| Barrett, Mary A. | 1913 | Box 461 | Barthel, John G. | 1906 | Box 295 |
| Barrett, Mary A. | 1916 | Box 536 | Barthel, Katharine G. | 1916 | Box 537 |
| Barrett, Michael | 1883 | Box 81 | Bartholomae, Emma | 1911 | Box 410 |
| Barrett, Oliver D. | 1902 | Box 219 | Bartholomae, William | 1917 | Box 563 |
| Barrett, Robert | 1893 | Box 136 | Bartholow, Isabella | 1920 | Box 651 |
| Barrett, Robert S. | 1902 | Box 219 | Bartle, George | 1899 | Box 181 |
| Barrett, Sallie Currie (Curry) | 1905 | Box 275 | Bartle, Howell | 1916 | Box 537 |
| Barrett, Thomas P. | 1892 | Box 129 | Bartle, Miranda | 1907 | Box 316 |
| Barrett, William Henry | 1914 | Box 484 | Bartlett, Clementine N. | 1908 | Box 338 |
| Barrick, Sarah A. | 1898 | Box 174 | Bartlett, Ellery C. | 1886 | Box 95 |
| Barrie, John | 1862 | Box 29 | Bartlett, George A. | 1906 | Box 295 |
| Barringer, Maria Massey | 1902 | Box 220 | Bartlett, Gertrude Richey | 1907 | Box 316 |
| Barringer, Victor C. | 1896 | Box 159 | Bartlett, Hannah Lavinia | 1905 | Box 275 |
| Barrington, Caroline G. | 1912 | Box 435 | Bartlett, Isaac Cook | 1864 | Box 32 |
| Barrington, William Leadbetter | 1903 | Box 239 | Bartlett, John H. | 1889 | Box 111 |
| Barron, Annaline S. | 1912 | Box 435 | Bartlett, John R. | 1904 | Box 259 |
| Barron, Henry | 1872 | Box 46 | Bartlett, Marcus M. | 1918 | Box 590 |
| Barron, James | 1839 | Box 14 | Bartley, Ellen Espy | 1905 | Box 275 |
| Barron, Patrick J. | 1918 | Box 590 | Bartley, Thomas Welles | 1886 | Box 95 |
| Barron, Samuel H. | 1918 | Box 590 | Bartol, Barnabas H. | 1889 | Box 111 |
| Barron, Sarah E. | 1902 | Box 220 | Barton, Clara (Clarissa Harlow) | 1914 | Box 484 |
| Barron, Wallace C. Sr. | 1909 | Box 362 | Barton, David L. | 1919 | Box 620 |
| Barry, Ann | 1891 | Box 123 | Barton, Elizabeth Sewell | 1902 | Box 220 |
| Barry, Ann C. | 1882 | Box 78 | Barton, George | 1866 | Box 35 |
| Barry, David | 1909 | Box 362 | Barton, J. William | 1870 | Box 42 |
| Barry, Edward P. | 1919 | Box 620 | Barton, Jonathan Q. | 1903 | Box 239 |
| Barry, Eliza | 1876 | Box 60 | Barton, Joseph | 1896 | Box 159 |
| Barry, Garrett P. | 1811 | Box 3 | Barton, Mary L. | 1917 | Box 563 |
| Barry, Henrietta Vermillion | 1909 | Box 362 | Bartscher, Christopher M. | 1914 | Box 484 |
| Barry, James | 1909 | Box 362 | Barwis, Richard | 1917 | Box 563 |
| Barry, James | 1811 | Box 3 | Bass, William M. | 1914 | Box 484 |
| Barry, Joanna | 1812 | Box 4 | Bassett, Amelia V. | 1874 | Box 53 |
| Barry, Joanna J. | 1907 | Box 316 | Bassett, Anna | 1901 | Box 203 |
| Barry, Johanna | 1840 | Box 15 | Bassett, Cora S. | 1917 | Box 563 |
| Barry, John N. | 1915 | Box 508 | Bassett, David | 1873 | Box 50 |
| Barry, Louisa | 1899 | Box 181 | Bassett, Euphemia | 1869 | Box 40 |
| Barry, Louisa Maria | 1872 | Box 46 | Bassett, George A. | 1885 | Box 90 |
| Barry, Margaret | 1912 | Box 435 | Bassett, George T. | 1908 | Box 338 |
| Barry, Margaret | 1914 | Box 484 | Bassett, Simeon | 1844 | Box 16 |
| Barry, Mary | 1915 | Box 508 | Bassford, John N. | 1890 | Box 117 |
| Barry, Mary | 1920 | Box 651 | Bastable, Charles | 1905 | Box 275 |
| Barry, Mary F. | 1920 | Box 651 | Baston, Carrie Larry | 1919 | Box 620 |
| Barry, Michael | 1904 | Box 259 | Bastress, Margaret F. | 1916 | Box 537 |
| Barry, Nicholas | 1852 | Box 21 | Batchelder, Richard | 1901 | Box 203 |
| Barry, Nora | 1896 | Box 159 | Batcheller, Emma W. | 1910 | Box 383 |
| Barry, Richard | 1813 | Box 4 | Batchelor, Charles | 1879 | Box 67 |
| Barry, Robert | 1885 | Box 90 | Bate, Elizabeth | 1905 | Box 276 |
| Barry, Sallie L. | 1910 | Box 383 | Bateman, Anna S. | 1871 | Box 44 |
| Barry, William F. | 1910 | Box 383 | Bateman, Annie C. | 1918 | Box 590 |
| Barstow, Maria Bedinger P. | 1894 | Box 144 | Bateman, Clara P. | 1905 | Box 276 |

| | | | | | | |
|---|---|---|---|---|---|---|
| Bateman, Nathaniel C. | 1900 | Box 190 | Baumgarten, Julius | 1915 | Box 508 |
| Bateman, Philena B. | 1895 | Box 151 | Baumgarten, Mathilde | 1915 | Box 508 |
| Bateman, Sebro | 1877 | Box 63 | Baumler, Johanna | 1872 | Box 46 |
| Bateman, William P. | 1906 | Box 295 | Baur, Fredericka | 1892 | Box 129 |
| Bates, Caroline E. | 1920 | Box 651 | Baurman, Augustus P. | 1900 | Box 190 |
| Bates, Catherine | 1865 | Box 33 | Baver, Horace | 1890 | Box 117 |
| Bates, Catharine S. | 1896 | Box 159 | Baxter, Florence T. | 1914 | Box 484 |
| Bates, Charles A. | 1918 | Box 590 | Baxter, Jedediah H. | 1890 | Box 117 |
| Bates, Charlotte J. | 1905 | Box 276 | Baxter, Judith P. | 1910 | Box 383 |
| Bates, David | 1821 | Box 6 | Baxter, Matthew C. | 1898 | Box 174 |
| Bates, Edward | 1857 | Box 25 | Baxter, Tillie A. | 1916 | Box 537 |
| Bates, Francis H. | 1895 | Box 151 | Baxtor, Samuel | 1905 | Box 276 |
| Bates, Frederick | 1889 | Box 111 | Bayard, Albert F. | 1913 | Box 461 |
| Bates, George W. | 1907 | Box 316 | Bayard, Thomas Francis | 1898 | Box 174 |
| Bates, Henry Hobart | 1916 | Box 537 | Bayler, Eliza A. | 1918 | Box 590 |
| Bates, Mary | 1882 | Box 78 | Bayles, Rosanna | 1916 | Box 537 |
| Bates, Mary E. Fields | 1914 | Box 484 | Bayley, George Henry | 1890 | Box 117 |
| Bates, Newton L. | 1897 | Box 167 | Bayley, James Roosevelt | 1880 | Box 71 |
| Bates, Sarah A. | 1900 | Box 190 | Baylor, Frances | 1892 | Box 129 |
| Bates, Sarah R. | 1897 | Box 167 | Baylor, William H. | 1906 | Box 295 |
| Bates, Stephen | 1907 | Box 316 | Bayly, Benjamin | 1869 | Box 40 |
| Bates, Thomas | 1856 | Box 24 | Bayly, Elise C. | 1890 | Box 117 |
| Batson, Helen | 1879 | Box 67 | Bayly, Maria | 1884 | Box 85 |
| Batten, Robert Grosvenor | 1911 | Box 410 | Bayly, Rafael A. | 1884 | Box 85 |
| Batters, John | 1896 | Box 159 | Bayly, William Hamilton | 1907 | Box 316 |
| Battiste, Josephine Melissa | 1904 | Box 259 | Bayne, Adelia T. | 1889 | Box 111 |
| Bauer, Agnes | 1915 | Box 508 | Bayne, Isaac N. | 1918 | Box 590 |
| Bauer, Anton | 1867 | Box 37 | Bayne, John | 1872 | Box 46 |
| Bauer, Christian | 1891 | Box 123 | Bayne, John F. | 1914 | Box 484 |
| Bauer, George | 1894 | Box 144 | Bayne, John W. | 1905 | Box 276 |
| Bauer, George W. | 1901 | Box 203 | Bayne, Thomas | 1886 | Box 95 |
| Bauer, Sophia | 1902 | Box 220 | Bayne, Thomas M. | 1894 | Box 144 |
| Bauerdorf, Josephine C. | 1896 | Box 159 | Bazurro, Andrew | 1893 | Box 136 |
| Baugher, Emma Catherine | 1912 | Box 435 | Beach, Edmund Leavenworth | 1918 | Box 590 |
| Baugher, Isaac | 1854 | Box 23 | Beach, Julia A. | 1912 | Box 435 |
| Baughton, Horace | 1899 | Box 181 | Beach, Julia M. | 1904 | Box 259 |
| Baum, Eliza | 1917 | Box 563 | Beacham, Anne | 1903 | Box 239 |
| Baum, Esther | 1911 | Box 410 | Beaird, Enoch G. | 1903 | Box 239 |
| Baum, Hattie | 1902 | Box 220 | Beale, Benjamin | 1891 | Box 123 |
| Baum, Henry | 1917 | Box 563 | Beale, Buchanan | 1909 | Box 362 |
| Baum, Jane A. | 1911 | Box 410 | Beale, Edward Fitzgerald | 1893 | Box 136 |
| Baum, Joseph | 1917 | Box 563 | Beale, George N. | 1912 | Box 435 |
| Baum, Louis | 1891 | Box 123 | Beale, George W. | 1898 | Box 174 |
| Baum, Margaret J. | 1917 | Box 563 | Beale, Helen M. | 1918 | Box 590 |
| Baum, William | 1919 | Box 620 | Beale, Mary D. | 1873 | Box 50 |
| Baum, William H. | 1906 | Box 295 | Beale, Mary Edwards | 1902 | Box 220 |
| Baumann, August | 1891 | Box 123 | Beale, Robert | 1866 | Box 35 |
| Baumann, Conrad | 1902 | Box 220 | Beall, Ann Truman | 1832 | Box 11 |
| Baumann, Paul | 1865 | Box 33 | Beall, Basil | 1892 | Box 129 |
| Baumbach, August | 1910 | Box 383 | Beall, Benjamin | 1891 | Box 123 |
| Baumgarten, Ada | 1913 | Box 461 | Beall, Beverly W. | 1855 | Box 23 |
| Baumgarten, Herman | 1905 | Box 276 | Beall, Charles | 1908 | Box 338 |

| | | | | | | |
|---|---|---|---|---|---|---|
| Beall, Clarence | 1920 | Box 651 | Beatty, Charles | 1804 | Box 1 |
| Beall, Cornelia | 1909 | Box 362 | Beatty, Charles Affordby | 1838 | Box 14 |
| Beall, Eleanor | 1821 | Box 6 | Beatty, Hugh Wilson | 1897 | Box 167 |
| Beall, Eliza | 1857 | Box 25 | Beatty, John M. | 1815 | Box 4 |
| Beall, Eliza B. | 1872 | Box 46 | Beatty, John R. | 1916 | Box 537 |
| Beall, Elizabeth W. | 1828 | Box 9 | Beatty, Mary Jane | 1919 | Box 620 |
| Beall, Frances | 1920 | Box 651 | Beatty, Robert L. | 1906 | Box 295 |
| Beall, George | 1807 | Box 2 | Beaumont, John C. | 1882 | Box 78 |
| Beall, George Ninian | 1919 | Box 620 | Beauregard, Joseph F. | 1918 | Box 590 |
| Beall, H. Virginia | 1873 | Box 50 | Beavans, Charles A. | 1895 | Box 151 |
| Beall, Howard | 1920 | Box 651 | Beavers, Edward C. | 1917 | Box 563 |
| Beall, James | 1821 | Box 6 | Beavers, Ernest S. | 1897 | Box 167 |
| Beall, James | 1875 | Box 56 | Beavers, Sarah H. | 1877 | Box 63 |
| Beall, John | 1901 | Box 204 | Beavers, Thomas R. | 1916 | Box 537 |
| Beall, Josephine R. | 1910 | Box 383 | Becht, John | 1905 | Box 276 |
| Beall, Joshua | 1903 | Box 239 | Beck, Jacob | 1918 | Box 591 |
| Beall, Margaret | 1823 | Box 7 | Beck, James B. | 1890 | Box 117 |
| Beall, Mary | 1806 | Box 2 | Beck, John | 1885 | Box 90 |
| Beall, Mary E. | 1920 | Box 651 | Beck, Kate | 1916 | Box 537 |
| Beall, Mary L. | 1893 | Box 136 | Beck, Mary | 1879 | Box 67 |
| Beall, Nannie Lewis | 1917 | Box 563 | Beck, Richard | 1810 | Box 3 |
| Beall, Richard J. | 1912 | Box 435 | Beck, Rosina K. | 1918 | Box 591 |
| Beall, Robert | 1899 | Box 181 | Beck, Theodore | 1912 | Box 435 |
| Beall, Robert A. | 1918 | Box 590 | Beck, Thomas | 1902 | Box 220 |
| Beall, Robert S. | 1852 | Box 21 | Beck, William H. | 1917 | Box 563 |
| Beall, Samuel | 1820 | Box 6 | Becker, Anton | 1897 | Box 167 |
| Beall, Sarah | 1823 | Box 7 | Becker, Benigne Pargny | 1888 | Box 106 |
| Beall, Seward | 1899 | Box 181 | Becker, Charles | 1880 | Box 71 |
| Beall, Thomas | 1819 | Box 5 | Becker, Dorothea | 1899 | Box 181 |
| Beall, Thomas B. | 1820 | Box 6 | Becker, Edward | 1920 | Box 651 |
| Beall, William D. | 1875 | Box 56 | Becker, George | 1904 | Box 259 |
| Beall, William Murdock | 1892 | Box 129 | Becker, George F. | 1919 | Box 620 |
| Beam, Lucretia S. | 1918 | Box 590 | Becker, Henry C. | 1907 | Box 316 |
| Beam, Samuel Orendorf | 1894 | Box 144 | Becker, Lydia | 1906 | Box 295 |
| Beaman, George Herbert | 1917 | Box 563 | Becker, Martin | 1895 | Box 151 |
| Beams, Susan H. | 1899 | Box 181 | Becker, Mary Eliza | 1897 | Box 167 |
| Bean, Ann | 1891 | Box 123 | Becker, Michael Henry | 1882 | Box 78 |
| Bean, Eliza | 1901 | Box 204 | Becker, Nicholas | 1891 | Box 123 |
| Bean, Thaddeus | 1918 | Box 590 | Becker, Sarah | 1901 | Box 204 |
| Bean, Thomas E. | 1872 | Box 46 | Becker, Vector | 1904 | Box 259 |
| Beanes, Colmore | 1860 | Box 28 | Becker, William Mathias | 1907 | Box 316 |
| Beans, Cecilia Ann | 1873 | Box 50 | Beckert, Charles | 1901 | Box 204 |
| Bear, Marvin W. | 1919 | Box 620 | Beckert, Francis Adolph | 1893 | Box 136 |
| Beard, Elizabeth B. | 1917 | Box 563 | Beckert, George | 1860 | Box 28 |
| Beard, Henry | 1894 | Box 144 | Beckert, George J. | 1918 | Box 591 |
| Beard, Lewis | 1868 | Box 38 | Beckert, Rosanna C. | 1899 | Box 181 |
| Beard, Martha A. | 1914 | Box 484 | Beckert, Theresia | 1889 | Box 111 |
| Beard, Nannie C. | 1909 | Box 362 | Beckett, Charlotte | 1906 | Box 295 |
| Beardmore, John | 1918 | Box 590 | Beckett, Frank O. | 1917 | Box 563 |
| Beardsley, Grove S. | 1906 | Box 295 | Beckett, James W. | 1905 | Box 276 |
| Beardsley, Joseph | 1894 | Box 144 | Beckett, John W. | 1906 | Box 295 |
| Beattey, George | 1834 | Box 12 | Beckett, Mary | 1894 | Box 144 |

| | | | | | | |
|---|---|---|---|---|---|---|
| Beckett, Sarah Jane | 1912 | Box 435 | | Bell, James | 1851 | Box 21 |
| Beckett, Trueman D. | 1905 | Box 276 | | Bell, James Lowrie | 1908 | Box 338 |
| Beckett, William | 1912 | Box 435 | | Bell, Jane A. | 1902 | Box 220 |
| Beckett, Wilton W. | 1913 | Box 461 | | Bell, John W. | 1913 | Box 461 |
| Beckley, John | 1807 | Box 2 | | Bell, Laura | 1868 | Box 38 |
| Beckley, Nancy | 1890 | Box 117 | | Bell, Lewis | 1895 | Box 151 |
| Beckmann, August | 1909 | Box 362 | | Bell, Libbie Josephine | 1917 | Box 563 |
| Becks, Chainey Elonzo | 1919 | Box 620 | | Bell, Mary E. | 1907 | Box 316 |
| Beckwith, Cornelia | 1911 | Box 410 | | Bell, Mary V. | 1870 | Box 42 |
| Beckwith, Edward G. | 1881 | Box 74 | | Bell, Robert A. | 1916 | Box 537 |
| Beckwith, Emma V. | 1910 | Box 383 | | Bell, Robert M. | 1893 | Box 136 |
| Beckwith, Hannah | 1855 | Box 23 | | Bell, Robert W. | 1890 | Box 117 |
| Beckwith, Maria J. | 1914 | Box 484 | | Bell, Roberta W. | 1885 | Box 90 |
| Becraft, William | 1854 | Box 23 | | Bell, Samuel | 1908 | Box 338 |
| Beddo, Harriet | 1886 | Box 95 | | Bell, Sarah E. | 1910 | Box 384 |
| Bedloe, Edward | 1915 | Box 508 | | Bell, Sophia | 1853 | Box 22 |
| Beebe, Bela W. | 1906 | Box 295 | | Bell, Susan | 1864 | Box 32 |
| Been, Henry | 1919 | Box 620 | | Bell, Thomas D. | 1870 | Box 42 |
| Beers, Isaac | 1864 | Box 32 | | Bell, Thomas P. | 1892 | Box 129 |
| Beers, Milly Ann | 1860 | Box 28 | | Bell, Virginia E. | 1918 | Box 591 |
| Beggs, Agnes U. | 1902 | Box 220 | | Bell, William H. | 1910 | Box 384 |
| Beha, John | 1892 | Box 129 | | Bell, William H. | 1917 | Box 563 |
| Beha, Wilhelmina | 1910 | Box 383 | | Bell, William S. | 1909 | Box 362 |
| Behrend, Amnon | 1916 | Box 537 | | Beller, James E. | 1920 | Box 651 |
| Behrend, Elise B. | 1884 | Box 85 | | Beller, Katherine | 1919 | Box 620 |
| Behrends, Isidor | 1895 | Box 151 | | Bellew, Margaret | 1915 | Box 508 |
| Behrends, Ulrike | 1899 | Box 181 | | Bellinger, Jacob B. | 1919 | Box 620 |
| Behrens, Charles | 1917 | Box 563 | | Bellows, Josiah | 1915 | Box 508 |
| Behrens, Frederick | 1880 | Box 71 | | Belmont, August | 1891 | Box 123 |
| Behrens, Frederick W. | 1915 | Box 508 | | Belmont, Hattie G. | 1912 | Box 435 |
| Behrens, John E. | 1873 | Box 50 | | Belrose, Louis | 1900 | Box 190 |
| Behrens, May B. | 1920 | Box 651 | | Belrose, Louis Jr. | 1894 | Box 144 |
| Beirne, Sally | 1893 | Box 136 | | Belt, Anna Eliza | 1912 | Box 435 |
| Belknap, Hiram W. | 1919 | Box 620 | | Belt, Charles D. | 1908 | Box 338 |
| Bell, Aileen A. | 1914 | Box 484 | | Belt, Edward Oliver | 1907 | Box 316 |
| Bell, Alexander M. | 1905 | Box 276 | | Belt, Ignatius | 1907 | Box 316 |
| Bell, Ann | 1876 | Box 60 | | Belt, John M. | 1880 | Box 71 |
| Bell, Carl Louise | 1911 | Box 410 | | Belt, Levi | 1822 | Box 7 |
| Bell, Charles | 1833 | Box 12 | | Belt, Martha | 1920 | Box 651 |
| Bell, Charles | 1845 | Box 17 | | Belt, Mary | 1828 | Box 9 |
| Bell, Charles M. | 1893 | Box 136 | | Belt, Mary A. Brown | 1908 | Box 338 |
| Bell, Daniel | 1877 | Box 63 | | Belt, Mary Anne | 1833 | Box 12 |
| Bell, David | 1879 | Box 68 | | Belt, Mary B. | 1917 | Box 563 |
| Bell, David Charles | 1903 | Box 239 | | Belt, Robert V. | 1910 | Box 384 |
| Bell, Edward Barber | 1913 | Box 461 | | Belt, Tobias | 1884 | Box 85 |
| Bell, Eliza Grace | 1897 | Box 167 | | Belt, William T. | 1909 | Box 362 |
| Bell, Ellen Adine | 1908 | Box 338 | | Bemon (McGraw), Catherine | 1825 | Box 8 |
| Bell, Enoch G. | 1878 | Box 65 | | Bender, Adeline | 1905 | Box 276 |
| Bell, George | 1845 | Box 17 | | Bender, George | 1865 | Box 33 |
| Bell, George | 1907 | Box 316 | | Bender, Harriet C. | 1908 | Box 338 |
| Bell, Henry | 1910 | Box 384 | | Bender, Robert E. | 1918 | Box 591 |
| Bell, Isabella | 1920 | Box 651 | | Bendire, Charles | 1897 | Box 167 |

| | | | | | | |
|---|---|---|---|---|---|
| Benedict, Virginia Coudert | 1913 | Box 461 | Berger, Henry | 1893 | Box 136 |
| Benerman, Emma M. | 1911 | Box 410 | Berger, William | 1885 | Box 90 |
| Benét, Laura | 1900 | Box 190 | Berghing, George | 1885 | Box 90 |
| Benét, Stephen V. | 1895 | Box 151 | Bergling, George | 1912 | Box 436 |
| Benjamin, Charles F. | 1915 | Box 509 | Bergman, Emma Bushby | 1920 | Box 651 |
| Benjamin, Clara S. | 1918 | Box 591 | Bergman, Gephart | 1858 | Box 26 |
| Benjamin, John Forbes | 1877 | Box 63 | Bergman, Lambert F. | 1912 | Box 436 |
| Benjamin, Rhuta-Louise | 1902 | Box 220 | Bergman, Lambert M. | 1910 | Box 384 |
| Benner, George L. | 1899 | Box 181 | Bergman, Peter | 1871 | Box 44 |
| Bennett, Clement Wells | 1896 | Box 159 | Bergman, William H. | 1888 | Box 106 |
| Bennett, Edward | 1887 | Box 101 | Bergmann, Catharine | 1888 | Box 106 |
| Bennett, Edwin | 1913 | Box 461 | Bergmann, Frederick W. | 1906 | Box 295 |
| Bennett, Eleanor R. | 1919 | Box 620 | Bergmann, Henry W. | 1869 | Box 40 |
| Bennett, Eva L. | 1916 | Box 537 | Bergmann, Wilhelmina | 1910 | Box 384 |
| Bennett, Harrison M. | 1919 | Box 620 | Bergmann, William | 1885 | Box 90 |
| Bennett, Hattie V. | 1883 | Box 81 | Berkley, Charles E. | 1883 | Box 81 |
| Bennett, James | 1914 | Box 484 | Berkley, Emelia C. | 1896 | Box 159 |
| Bennett, Joseph B. | 1913 | Box 461 | Berkley, Enos E. | 1859 | Box 27 |
| Bennett, Margaret M. | 1905 | Box 276 | Berkley, Matilda E. | 1913 | Box 461 |
| Bennett, Mary C. | 1910 | Box 384 | Berlin, William | 1901 | Box 204 |
| Bennett, Philo H. | 1886 | Box 95 | Berliner, Solomon | 1911 | Box 410 |
| Bennett, Richard A. | 1914 | Box 484 | Berman, Isaac | 1913 | Box 461 |
| Bennett, Sarah Jane | 1895 | Box 151 | Bermann, Isidor Sam Leopold | 1918 | Box 591 |
| Bennett, Susannah E. | 1897 | Box 167 | Berna, Charlotte | 1915 | Box 509 |
| Bennett, Thomas D. | 1912 | Box 435 | Bernau, Wilhelmine | 1893 | Box 136 |
| Bennett, William | 1905 | Box 276 | Bernaud, Clemence P. | 1894 | Box 144 |
| Benning, William | 1832 | Box 11 | Berner, Maria A. | 1887 | Box 101 |
| Bennit, Delia M. | 1896 | Box 159 | Bernhard, Charles E. | 1916 | Box 537 |
| Benson, Emma Josephine | 1912 | Box 436 | Bernhard, Grace C. | 1912 | Box 436 |
| Benson, Francis A. | 1909 | Box 362 | Bernhardt, Wilhelm | 1909 | Box 362 |
| Benson, Rebecca H. | 1917 | Box 563 | Bernheim, Hannah | 1920 | Box 651 |
| Benter, Maria | 1883 | Box 81 | Bernstein, Simon | 1913 | Box 461 |
| Bentley, Alexander J. | 1908 | Box 338 | Beron, John | 1915 | Box 509 |
| Bentley, Caleb | 1909 | Box 362 | Berrang, Catharine | 1917 | Box 563 |
| Bentley, Thomas | 1886 | Box 95 | Berret, James | 1901 | Box 204 |
| Benton, James Watson | 1897 | Box 167 | Berret, John J. | 1886 | Box 95 |
| Benton, John Hogan | 1914 | Box 484 | Berry, Ada Morton | 1919 | Box 620 |
| Benton, Thomas H. | 1858 | Box 26 | Berry, Augustus F. | 1868 | Box 38 |
| Benzler, Louisa M. | 1914 | Box 484 | Berry, Benjamin | 1877 | Box 63 |
| Beran, Franz | 1894 | Box 144 | Berry, Chloe Frances | 1918 | Box 591 |
| Berberich, Robert | 1918 | Box 591 | Berry, Emma C. | 1871 | Box 44 |
| Berckmann, John G. | 1917 | Box 563 | Berry, Emma J. | 1873 | Box 50 |
| Berdan, Hiram | 1894 | Box 144 | Berry, Engenia | 1883 | Box 81 |
| Berens, Bernhard | 1883 | Box 81 | Berry, Ferdinand V. | 1910 | Box 384 |
| Berens, William | 1897 | Box 167 | Berry, Frances E. | 1883 | Box 81 |
| Berens, William | 1915 | Box 509 | Berry, Georgeanna | 1907 | Box 316 |
| Beresford, Lillie | 1911 | Box 410 | Berry, Henrietta L. | 1907 | Box 316 |
| Beresford, Randolph | 1919 | Box 620 | Berry, James E. | 1917 | Box 564 |
| Bereton, Sarah E. | 1909 | Box 362 | Berry, Jerome C. | 1888 | Box 106 |
| Bergen, Gustav | 1889 | Box 111 | Berry, Margaret | 1876 | Box 60 |
| Berger, Adolphe | 1905 | Box 276 | Berry, Margaret A. | 1919 | Box 620 |
| Berger, Carl H. | 1872 | Box 46 | Berry, Mary A. | 1882 | Box 78 |

| | | | | | | |
|---|---|---|---|---|---|---|
| Berry, Mary Eliza | 1919 | Box 620 | Bianchi, Arthur | 1920 | Box 651 |
| Berry, Michael Mathew | 1913 | Box 461 | Bias, Nellie | 1913 | Box 461 |
| Berry, Philip T. | 1879 | Box 68 | Bibb, Mary Rebecca | 1881 | Box 74 |
| Berry, Sarah | 1858 | Box 26 | Bickford, Frederick True | 1903 | Box 239 |
| Berry, Sarah | 1883 | Box 81 | Bickford, Nathan | 1920 | Box 651 |
| Berry, Sarah B. | 1889 | Box 111 | Bickle, Aldine Begole | 1917 | Box 564 |
| Berry, Susan | 1888 | Box 106 | Biddis, John D. | 1909 | Box 362 |
| Berry, Thomas | 1877 | Box 63 | Biddis, Mary D. | 1920 | Box 652 |
| Berry, Thomas H. | 1872 | Box 46 | Biddle, Mary D. | 1910 | Box 384 |
| Berry, Washington | 1856 | Box 24 | Bieg, Frederick Charles | 1909 | Box 362 |
| Berry, Washington O. | 1911 | Box 410 | Biegler, John | 1888 | Box 106 |
| Berry, Zachariah | 1868 | Box 38 | Biegler, Phillip | 1888 | Box 106 |
| Berryman, Leroy H. | 1880 | Box 71 | Bien, Delia | 1910 | Box 384 |
| Berwanger, Abraham | 1904 | Box 259 | Bifield, John A. | 1913 | Box 461 |
| Berwick, William | 1920 | Box 651 | Bigalow, Olivia V. | 1903 | Box 239 |
| Bessler, George J. | 1917 | Box 564 | Bigelow, Charles H. | 1910 | Box 384 |
| Bessler, Rose L. | 1913 | Box 461 | Bigelow, Jessie C. | 1916 | Box 537 |
| Best, Absalah Carr | 1910 | Box 384 | Bigelow, Mary R. | 1913 | Box 461 |
| Best, Emory F. | 1912 | Box 436 | Bigelow, Otis | 1919 | Box 620 |
| Best, Mahlon H. | 1920 | Box 651 | Biggane, Michael | 1916 | Box 537 |
| Best, Roberta | 1901 | Box 204 | Biggins, James | 1891 | Box 123 |
| Best, Rosetta L. | 1872 | Box 46 | Biggins, Susan | 1910 | Box 384 |
| Bestor, Harvey B. | 1892 | Box 129 | Biggs, Levi | 1871 | Box 44 |
| Bestor, Norman | 1910 | Box 384 | Biggs, Lilly C. W. | 1909 | Box 362 |
| Bestor, Norman S. | 1904 | Box 259 | Bigly, William | 1857 | Box 25 |
| Bestor, Orson | 1901 | Box 204 | Bild, Rudolph | 1911 | Box 410 |
| Bestor, Selina | 1911 | Box 410 | Bildman, Joseph | 1907 | Box 316 |
| Bestor, Whitman C. | 1873 | Box 50 | Bill, Fred Will | 1907 | Box 316 |
| Bestor, Willie Jane | 1906 | Box 295 | Bill, Wilber W. | 1916 | Box 537 |
| Betout, Eugene | 1870 | Box 42 | Billing, Emily V. | 1897 | Box 167 |
| Bettes, Eugene | 1917 | Box 564 | Billing, Margaret M. | 1912 | Box 436 |
| Betts, Barzilla C. | 1865 | Box 33 | Billing, William | 1843 | Box 16 |
| Betts, Helen Maria | 1893 | Box 136 | Billings, Kate M. | 1912 | Box 436 |
| Betts, William H. | 1884 | Box 85 | Billingsley, Lucy Harris | 1916 | Box 537 |
| Betz, Caroline | 1899 | Box 181 | Billingsley, Mattie P. | 1910 | Box 384 |
| Betz, Lina | 1900 | Box 190 | Billson, Thomas Henry | 1919 | Box 620 |
| Beuchert, Agnes M. | 1905 | Box 276 | Bingham, Albert | 1901 | Box 204 |
| Beuchert, Edward | 1893 | Box 136 | Bingham, John | 1887 | Box 101 |
| Beuchert, John I. | 1914 | Box 484 | Bingham, Lafayette | 1898 | Box 174 |
| Beumer, Fred | 1916 | Box 537 | Bingham, Lina R. | 1892 | Box 129 |
| Bevans, Mary A. C. | 1917 | Box 564 | Bingham, Lucy J. | 1912 | Box 436 |
| Beveridge, Michael William | 1897 | Box 167 | Bingham, William | 1876 | Box 60 |
| Beveridge, Susan Jane | 1906 | Box 295 | Bingham, William | 1877 | Box 63 |
| Beverly, Virginia | 1903 | Box 239 | Binnix, Edward | 1901 | Box 204 |
| Bey, Jouseeff | 1864 | Box 32 | Birch, Bushrod | 1882 | Box 78 |
| Beyer, Harriet W. | 1890 | Box 117 | Birch, Charles E. | 1913 | Box 461 |
| Beyer, James M. | 1910 | Box 384 | Birch, Eliza J. | 1893 | Box 136 |
| Beyer, Louis | 1904 | Box 259 | Birch, Fannie | 1905 | Box 276 |
| Beyer, Mary | 1896 | Box 159 | Birch, Gertrude | 1918 | Box 591 |
| Beyer, Samuel B. | 1898 | Box 174 | Birch, John T. | 1900 | Box 190 |
| Beyer, Victor | 1915 | Box 509 | Birch, Joseph F. | 1891 | Box 123 |
| Beyer, Wilhelmina | 1905 | Box 276 | Birch, Joseph S. | 1889 | Box 111 |

| | | | | | | |
|---|---|---|---|---|---|---|
| Birch, Stephen | 1906 | Box 295 | Blackburn, Isaac Wright | 1911 | Box 411 |
| Birch, Susanna C. | 1883 | Box 81 | Blackburn, Joseph C. S. | 1918 | Box 591 |
| Birckhead, Amelia A. | 1878 | Box 65 | Blackburn, Mary E. | 1918 | Box 591 |
| Birckhead, Charles E. | 1895 | Box 151 | Blackford, Charles M. | 1912 | Box 436 |
| Bird, James C. | 1905 | Box 276 | Blackford, Edward | 1847 | Box 18 |
| Birdsong, Elizabeth Key | 1914 | Box 484 | Blackford, Frances T. | 1918 | Box 591 |
| Birge, Cyrus | 1871 | Box 44 | Blackford, Hannah | 1855 | Box 23 |
| Birkhimer, William E. | 1916 | Box 537 | Blackford, John S. | 1876 | Box 60 |
| Birney, Arthur A. | 1916 | Box 537 | Blackford, Launcelot Minor | 1914 | Box 484 |
| Birney, Catharine H. | 1891 | Box 123 | Blackford, Samuel S. | 1888 | Box 106 |
| Birney, Theodore W. | 1897 | Box 167 | Blackford, William D. | 1907 | Box 316 |
| Birney, William | 1907 | Box 316 | Blackistone, J. Chew | 1919 | Box 621 |
| Birnie, Clotworthy | 1872 | Box 46 | Blackley, R. Bassett | 1920 | Box 652 |
| Birnie, Harriet A. | 1882 | Box 78 | Blackmore, Lucinda | 1918 | Box 591 |
| Birth, Caroline E. | 1882 | Box 78 | Blackstone, Charles | 1911 | Box 411 |
| Birth, Henry | 1889 | Box 111 | Blackwell, Thomas | 1877 | Box 63 |
| Birth, William W. | 1907 | Box 316 | Bladen, William | 1886 | Box 95 |
| Bisbee, Horace V. | 1916 | Box 537 | Blagden, Anne | 1831 | Box 11 |
| Bischoff, John W. | 1909 | Box 362 | Blagden, George | 1826 | Box 8 |
| Biscoe, George W. | 1859 | Box 27 | Blagden, Laura Silliman | 1908 | Box 339 |
| Biscoe, Harry E. | 1913 | Box 461 | Blagrove, Martha | 1858 | Box 26 |
| Biscoe, Henry L. | 1905 | Box 276 | Blague, Elizabeth R. W. | 1900 | Box 190 |
| Biscoe, Jane E. | 1849 | Box 20 | Blague, Giles | 1898 | Box 174 |
| Bishop, Agnes I. A. | 1915 | Box 509 | Blain, Elizabeth | 1911 | Box 411 |
| Bishop, Augustus A. | 1913 | Box 462 | Blaine, Harriet Stanwood | 1907 | Box 316 |
| Bishop, Charles T. | 1914 | Box 484 | Blaine, James G. | 1894 | Box 144 |
| Bishop, David J. | 1906 | Box 295 | Blair, Ann Savage | 1918 | Box 591 |
| Bishop, E. Tracy | 1920 | Box 652 | Blair, Francis Preston | 1876 | Box 60 |
| Bishop, Francis B. | 1916 | Box 537 | Blair, Henry W. | 1913 | Box 462 |
| Bishop, Fred S. | 1918 | Box 591 | Blair, Herbert B. | 1906 | Box 295 |
| Bishop, H. H. | 1875 | Box 56 | Blair, Mary E. | 1887 | Box 101 |
| Bishop, Joshua | 1906 | Box 295 | Blair, Montgomery | 1883 | Box 81 |
| Bishop, Julia Ann | 1907 | Box 316 | Blair, Robert W. | 1914 | Box 484 |
| Bishop, Nancy D. | 1902 | Box 220 | Blaisdell, Albert | 1890 | Box 117 |
| Bishop, William Darius | 1905 | Box 276 | Blake, Anne | 1884 | Box 85 |
| Bispham, Charles | 1920 | Box 652 | Blake, George A. H. | 1884 | Box 85 |
| Bispham, Charles | 1920 | Box 652 | Blake, George Baty | 1887 | Box 101 |
| Bitner, Elizabeth | 1892 | Box 129 | Blake, Glorvina D. | 1853 | Box 22 |
| Bittenbender, Alvaretta | 1917 | Box 564 | Blake, James Heigh | 1819 | Box 5 |
| Bitter, Ferdinand | 1892 | Box 129 | Blake, Joseph | 1820 | Box 6 |
| Bittinger, Benjamin F. | 1913 | Box 462 | Blake, Joseph R. | 1831 | Box 11 |
| Bitz, John M. | 1879 | Box 68 | Blake, Kate K. | 1910 | Box 384 |
| Bivins, John T. | 1912 | Box 436 | Blake, Martha Tallulah | 1920 | Box 652 |
| Black, Caroline C. | 1911 | Box 411 | Blakelock, Richard James | 1888 | Box 106 |
| Black, Furman | 1852 | Box 21 | Blan, Herman | 1884 | Box 85 |
| Black, G. W. Z. | 1916 | Box 537 | Blanchard, Anne | 1871 | Box 44 |
| Black, J. Henry | 1893 | Box 136 | Blanchard, Benjamin W. | 1900 | Box 190 |
| Black, Jacob M. | 1915 | Box 509 | Blanchard, Emily J. | 1914 | Box 484 |
| Black, Jeremiah S. | 1883 | Box 81 | Blanchard, Ferdinand | 1893 | Box 136 |
| Black, Lavinia | 1888 | Box 106 | Blanchard, Philonzo A. | 1899 | Box 181 |
| Black, Owen | 1867 | Box 37 | Blanchard, Valentine | 1865 | Box 33 |
| Black, Thomas | 1899 | Box 181 | Bland, Charles W. | 1919 | Box 621 |

| | | | | | | |
|---|---|---|---|---|---|---|
| Bland, James A. | 1914 | Box 484 | Blumenthal, Michael | 1913 | Box 462 |
| Bland, William H. | 1890 | Box 117 | Blummer, Edward | 1901 | Box 204 |
| Blandy, Elizabeth B. | 1919 | Box 621 | Blundon, John Alexander | 1885 | Box 90 |
| Blaney, Johannah | 1887 | Box 101 | Blundon, John F. | 1905 | Box 276 |
| Blanford, Thomas L. | 1911 | Box 411 | Blundon, Sarah E. | 1903 | Box 240 |
| Blankman, John S. | 1900 | Box 190 | Blunt, Charles Edward | 1892 | Box 129 |
| Blaque, Theodore | 1870 | Box 42 | Blunt, Evelina | 1918 | Box 591 |
| Blasland, William | 1899 | Box 181 | Boardman, May Marriette E. | 1914 | Box 484 |
| Blatcher, William | 1916 | Box 537 | Boardman, William J. | 1915 | Box 509 |
| Blatchford, Samuel | 1907 | Box 316 | Boarman, Charles | 1819 | Box 6 |
| Blatchford, Samuel A. | 1907 | Box 316 | Boarman, Charles L. | 1872 | Box 46 |
| Blauvelt, Jane E. | 1916 | Box 538 | Boarman, Charles V. | 1901 | Box 204 |
| Blechynden, Alfred | 1899 | Box 181 | Boarman, Emily Elizabeth | 1920 | Box 652 |
| Bleifus, Rudolph | 1905 | Box 276 | Boarman, John B. | 1813 | Box 4 |
| Blenck, William | 1879 | Box 68 | Boarman, Mary E. | 1916 | Box 538 |
| Blett, Charles F. T. | 1913 | Box 462 | Boarman, Raphael H. | 1861 | Box 29 |
| Blincoe, Joseph T. | 1919 | Box 621 | Boarman, Richard | 1869 | Box 40 |
| Blincoe, William F. | 1896 | Box 159 | Boarman, Richard B. A. | 1811 | Box 3 |
| Bliss, Alexander | 1896 | Box 159 | Boarman, Susan | 1822 | Box 7 |
| Bliss, Alfred | 1900 | Box 190 | Boarman, Sylvester B. | 1890 | Box 117 |
| Bliss, Asoph L. | 1918 | Box 591 | Boarman, William W. | 1910 | Box 384 |
| Bliss, Dwight H. | 1869 | Box 40 | Bobinger, George | 1908 | Box 339 |
| Bliss, Edwin M. | 1919 | Box 621 | Bock, Max | 1901 | Box 204 |
| Bliss, Emerson William | 1911 | Box 411 | Boddington, James | 1809 | Box 3 |
| Bliss, Flora B. | 1907 | Box 317 | Bodfish, Sumner Homer | 1894 | Box 144 |
| Bliss, George H. | 1903 | Box 239 | Boernstein, Jennie E. | 1902 | Box 220 |
| Bliss, Henry C. | 1904 | Box 259 | Boettcher, Frederick | 1900 | Box 190 |
| Bliss, James E. | 1868 | Box 39 | Bogan, Charlie | 1895 | Box 151 |
| Bliss, Sylvia Longley | 1903 | Box 239 | Bogan, Ella D. | 1914 | Box 484 |
| Bliss, William W. | 1899 | Box 181 | Bogert, Mary C. | 1892 | Box 129 |
| Blodgett, James H. | 1916 | Box 538 | Boggis, James H. | 1900 | Box 190 |
| Blodgett, Sarah L. | 1907 | Box 317 | Boggs, Ellen M. | 1899 | Box 181 |
| Blodgett, William Hall Terry | 1906 | Box 295 | Boggs, Georgiana T. Elvans | 1917 | Box 564 |
| Bloesch (Blesh), George | 1854 | Box 23 | Boggs, Lawrence G. | 1916 | Box 538 |
| Blondheim, Elias | 1912 | Box 436 | Boggs, LeRoy J. | 1900 | Box 190 |
| Blood, Henry | 1901 | Box 204 | Boggs, William Brenton | 1897 | Box 167 |
| Bloom, William F. | 1920 | Box 652 | Boggs, William Brenton | 1875 | Box 56 |
| Bloomer, Arthur F. | 1908 | Box 339 | Bogia, Florida A. | 1911 | Box 411 |
| Bloomer, Caroline | 1889 | Box 111 | Bogue, Almos P. | 1915 | Box 509 |
| Bloss, Henry | 1918 | Box 591 | Bogus, George | 1896 | Box 159 |
| Bloss, John B. | 1914 | Box 484 | Bogus, Henry | 1909 | Box 362 |
| Bloss, Sarah G. | 1903 | Box 240 | Bohannon, William H. | 1908 | Box 339 |
| Blosser, John | 1867 | Box 37 | Bohannon, Willie C. | 1920 | Box 652 |
| Blount, Henry F. | 1918 | Box 591 | Bohler, Anna | 1892 | Box 129 |
| Blout, Isaac L. | 1917 | Box 564 | Bohn, Margaretha | 1919 | Box 621 |
| Blout, Rosa | 1919 | Box 621 | Bohrer, Abraham | 1864 | Box 32 |
| Bloxton, Robert Vinton | 1920 | Box 652 | Bohrer, Benjamin S. | 1862 | Box 30 |
| Blum, David | 1903 | Box 240 | Bohrer, Catherine | 1895 | Box 151 |
| Blum, Jeannette | 1890 | Box 117 | Bohrer, George A. | 1886 | Box 95 |
| Blum, Leonard | 1918 | Box 591 | Bohrer, Maria | 1870 | Box 42 |
| Blumenberg, Milton W. | 1916 | Box 538 | Bohrer, William | 1901 | Box 204 |
| Blumenthal, Abraham | 1898 | Box 174 | Bohrer, William H. | 1876 | Box 60 |

| | | | | | | |
|---|---|---|---|---|---|---|
| Boid, Eliza | 1883 | Box 81 | | Boone, Naomi | 1899 | Box 181 |
| Boland, Anthony | 1874 | Box 53 | | Boone, Nicholas Sansbury | 1825 | Box 8 |
| Boland, George | 1902 | Box 220 | | Boorman, Henry | 1890 | Box 117 |
| Boland, Nancy | 1880 | Box 71 | | Boose, Elijah | 1903 | Box 240 |
| Boland, Thomas M. | 1908 | Box 339 | | Boose, Henry | 1848 | Box 19 |
| Boland, Winifred | 1896 | Box 159 | | Boothe, Ann | 1853 | Box 22 |
| Bolen, William H. | 1915 | Box 509 | | Boothe, George | 1827 | Box 9 |
| Bolenius, Henry Carpenter | 1914 | Box 484 | | Boothe, Thomas | 1846 | Box 17 |
| Boll, Paul | 1891 | Box 123 | | Borches, Deidrich H. | 1910 | Box 385 |
| Bolles, Katherine Dix | 1894 | Box 144 | | Borden, Eugenia Reeve | 1918 | Box 591 |
| Bolles, Timothy Dix | 1892 | Box 129 | | Boreman, Sarah | 1870 | Box 42 |
| Bolling, Anna D. | 1919 | Box 621 | | Borer, Peter | 1900 | Box 190 |
| Bollinger, Christopher G. | 1903 | Box 240 | | Borland, Alexander | 1872 | Box 46 |
| Bolton, Elizabeth | 1865 | Box 33 | | Borland, Andrew J. | 1880 | Box 71 |
| Bolton, Henry Carrington | 1903 | Box 240 | | Borland, Charles Cook | 1914 | Box 485 |
| Bolway, Joseph S. | 1891 | Box 123 | | Borland, Margaret A. | 1881 | Box 74 |
| Boman, Mary Ellen | 1886 | Box 95 | | Borland, Maria C. | 1904 | Box 259 |
| Bomford, George C. | 1862 | Box 30 | | Borrows, Catherine G. | 1896 | Box 159 |
| Bonanni, Peter | 1821 | Box 6 | | Borrows, Joseph | 1889 | Box 112 |
| Bonaparte, Caroline Le Roy | 1912 | Box 436 | | Borrows, Mary V. | 1901 | Box 204 |
| Bonaparte, Jerome Napoleon | 1893 | Box 136 | | Borrows, Sarah Catharine | 1917 | Box 564 |
| Bonavedes, Paul | 1905 | Box 276 | | Boscow, Arthur | 1857 | Box 25 |
| Bond, Armstead | 1920 | Box 652 | | Boscow, Emma | 1866 | Box 35 |
| Bond, Cassandra | 1841 | Box 15 | | Bosley, Caroline M. | 1910 | Box 385 |
| Bond, Daniel | 1852 | Box 21 | | Bosley, Henry | 1915 | Box 509 |
| Bond, Elizabeth | 1909 | Box 362 | | Boss, Frances M. | 1916 | Box 538 |
| Bond, George W. | 1915 | Box 509 | | Bossie, Hyson I. | 1906 | Box 295 |
| Bond, Ignatius | 1876 | Box 60 | | Bostick, Maria M. | 1910 | Box 385 |
| Bond, Isaac | 1818 | Box 5 | | Boston, Emily | 1908 | Box 339 |
| Bond, Isaac | 1895 | Box 151 | | Boston, Isaac | 1892 | Box 129 |
| Bond, John | 1914 | Box 484 | | Boston, Rosetta | 1876 | Box 60 |
| Bond, John H. | 1896 | Box 159 | | Bostwick, Charlotte | 1899 | Box 181 |
| Bond, Josephine | 1898 | Box 174 | | Boswell, Allan T. | 1896 | Box 159 |
| Bond, Levi Sr. | 1863 | Box 31 | | Boswell, Frederick A. | 1878 | Box 65 |
| Bond, Robert V. | 1920 | Box 652 | | Boswell, George H. | 1911 | Box 411 |
| Bond, Samuel | 1891 | Box 123 | | Boswell, Otho | 1865 | Box 33 |
| Bond, Samuel S. | 1900 | Box 190 | | Boswell, Sarah | 1901 | Box 204 |
| Bond, Sarah | 1839 | Box 14 | | Bosworth, Ellen Zora | 1906 | Box 295 |
| Bond, William | 1876 | Box 60 | | Bosworth, John Stone | 1905 | Box 276 |
| Bone, Cary Ann | 1907 | Box 317 | | Boteler, C. W. | 1866 | Box 35 |
| Bonell, Ida Eugenia | 1900 | Box 190 | | Boteler, Charles | 1846 | Box 17 |
| Bonham, John M. | 1914 | Box 484 | | Boteler, Edward Mills | 1907 | Box 317 |
| Bonnet, Eugene | 1866 | Box 35 | | Boteler, Henry D. | 1892 | Box 129 |
| Bonnet, Peter Louis | 1902 | Box 220 | | Boteler, John D. | 1891 | Box 123 |
| Bonsal, Rebecca M. | 1914 | Box 485 | | Boteler, John L. | 1897 | Box 167 |
| Booker, Robert H. | 1874 | Box 53 | | Botsch, George L. | 1898 | Box 174 |
| Bool, Jacob | 1918 | Box 591 | | Botsche, William C. | 1903 | Box 240 |
| Boone, Charity | 1853 | Box 22 | | Botsford, Olive S. | 1902 | Box 220 |
| Boone, George S. | 1825 | Box 8 | | Botts, Jane | 1904 | Box 259 |
| Boone, George W. | 1913 | Box 462 | | Botts, Mary Virginia | 1920 | Box 652 |
| Boone, Isaac | 1896 | Box 159 | | Boude, John | 1901 | Box 204 |
| Boone, John B. | 1859 | Box 27 | | Boudin, Sarah Ellen | 1893 | Box 136 |

| | | | | | | |
|---|---|---|---|---|---|---|
| Boughton, Daniel Hall | 1914 | Box 485 | Bowman, Joseph | 1824 | Box 8 |
| Boughton, Horace | 1899 | Box 181 | Bowman, Lida | 1918 | Box 592 |
| Bouis, Eliza J. | 1913 | Box 462 | Bowman, Lucinda Ann | 1903 | Box 240 |
| Boulanger, Jane | 1871 | Box 44 | Bowman, Lucius | 1901 | Box 204 |
| Bouldin, Eliza Ann | 1915 | Box 509 | Bowman, Mary Eliz. Sinclair | 1917 | Box 564 |
| Bouquillon, Thomas | 1903 | Box 240 | Bowman, Newton H. | 1896 | Box 159 |
| Bourne, Thomas C. | 1892 | Box 129 | Bowne, Annie E. T. | 1913 | Box 462 |
| Boutelle, Charles O. | 1890 | Box 117 | Bowser, Anna Culver | 1916 | Box 538 |
| Boutwell, Samuel H. | 1894 | Box 144 | Bowsky, Charles | 1890 | Box 117 |
| Bouvet, Mathew | 1875 | Box 56 | Boxer, Joseph | 1901 | Box 204 |
| Bowbeer, George William | 1910 | Box 385 | Boyce, Ada F. | 1900 | Box 190 |
| Bowden, Elizabeth | 1893 | Box 136 | Boyce, Edward | 1862 | Box 30 |
| Bowe, Patrick | 1912 | Box 436 | Boyce, James | 1917 | Box 564 |
| Bowen, Amanda Riley (Mattie) | 1914 | Box 485 | Boyce, Mary McEwen | 1911 | Box 411 |
| Bowen, Anna B. | 1914 | Box 485 | Boyce, Sarah M. | 1913 | Box 462 |
| Bowen, Anna T. | 1905 | Box 276 | Boyce, William M. | 1855 | Box 23 |
| Bowen, Anthony | 1871 | Box 44 | Boyd, Agnes | 1877 | Box 63 |
| Bowen, Charles | 1901 | Box 204 | Boyd, Catharine | 1882 | Box 78 |
| Bowen, Charles M. | 1878 | Box 65 | Boyd, Charles | 1917 | Box 564 |
| Bowen, Esther Kirtley | 1919 | Box 621 | Boyd, Charles Heaton | 1893 | Box 136 |
| Bowen, Francis C. | 1920 | Box 652 | Boyd, Charles C. | 1909 | Box 362 |
| Bowen, George A. | 1919 | Box 621 | Boyd, Charles W. | 1909 | Box 362 |
| Bowen, James | 1884 | Box 85 | Boyd, George W. | 1905 | Box 277 |
| Bowen, James G. | 1912 | Box 436 | Boyd, George W. | 1914 | Box 485 |
| Bowen, Mary | 1847 | Box 18 | Boyd, James A. | 1911 | Box 411 |
| Bowen, Mary Jane | 1905 | Box 277 | Boyd, James McHenry | 1880 | Box 71 |
| Bowen, Paul | 1901 | Box 204 | Boyd, Jane | 1896 | Box 159 |
| Bowen, Sayles J. | 1898 | Box 174 | Boyd, John | 1917 | Box 564 |
| Bowen, Thomas H. | 1856 | Box 24 | Boyd, Joseph K. | 1851 | Box 21 |
| Bowen, Walter F. | 1918 | Box 591 | Boyd, Julia A. | 1918 | Box 592 |
| Bower, John | 1915 | Box 509 | Boyd, Larry W. | 1915 | Box 510 |
| Bower, Kitty | 1871 | Box 44 | Boyd, Mary A. | 1881 | Box 74 |
| Bowers, Henry V. | 1915 | Box 510 | Boyd, Mary R. A. | 1916 | Box 538 |
| Bowers, Joseph | 1868 | Box 39 | Boyd, Robert | 1903 | Box 240 |
| Bowers, Julia E. | 1913 | Box 462 | Boyd, Robert A. | 1913 | Box 462 |
| Bowers, Lloyd Wheaton | 1910 | Box 385 | Boyd, William | 1877 | Box 63 |
| Bowie, Anne Maria | 1905 | Box 277 | Boyd, William | 1878 | Box 65 |
| Bowie, Charity | 1910 | Box 385 | Boyd, William G. | 1918 | Box 592 |
| Bowie, Elizabeth | 1891 | Box 123 | Boyd, William H. | 1887 | Box 101 |
| Bowie, Elizabeth L. | 1886 | Box 95 | Boyd, William M. | 1904 | Box 259 |
| Bowie, Fannie | 1898 | Box 174 | Boyer, Frank | 1919 | Box 621 |
| Bowie, Francis | 1895 | Box 151 | Boyer, Herman Henry | 1902 | Box 220 |
| Bowles, Michael B. | 1891 | Box 123 | Boyer, John | 1894 | Box 144 |
| Bowles, Sophia Mary | 1891 | Box 123 | Boykin, Edwin T. | 1913 | Box 462 |
| Bowles, William L. | 1918 | Box 591 | Boyland, Andrew | 1870 | Box 42 |
| Bowling, John D. | 1895 | Box 151 | Boyle, Caroline Morselle | 1917 | Box 564 |
| Bowling, Mary M. | 1877 | Box 63 | Boyle, Francis E. | 1882 | Box 78 |
| Bowling, William Ignatius | 1828 | Box 9 | Boyle, J. I. | 1920 | Box 652 |
| Bowman, Adelaide | 1865 | Box 33 | Boynton, Charles A. | 1915 | Box 510 |
| Bowman, Hannah | 1863 | Box 31 | Boynton, Charles B. | 1883 | Box 81 |
| Bowman, Hannah S. | 1874 | Box 53 | Boynton, George | 1902 | Box 220 |
| Bowman, James H. | 1867 | Box 37 | Boynton, George W. | 1915 | Box 510 |

| | | | | | | |
|---|---|---|---|---|---|---|
| Boynton, Henry S. | 1907 | Box 317 | Bradley, Marc | 1919 | Box 621 |
| Boynton, Henry Van Ness | 1905 | Box 277 | Bradley, Margret | 1920 | Box 652 |
| Boynton, Jane L. | 1883 | Box 81 | Bradley, Mary | 1877 | Box 63 |
| Boyts, B. Frank | 1913 | Box 462 | Bradley, Mary | 1901 | Box 204 |
| Brace, Helen D. | 1909 | Box 362 | Bradley, Mary Ann | 1897 | Box 167 |
| Brace, Russell | 1882 | Box 78 | Bradley, Mary E. | 1917 | Box 564 |
| Brace, Sophia Kemp | 1913 | Box 462 | Bradley, Mary Grace Craig | 1832 | Box 11 |
| Brace, William D. | 1918 | Box 592 | Bradley, Phineas | 1845 | Box 17 |
| Brackenridge, John | 1841 | Box 15 | Bradley, Reed | 1856 | Box 24 |
| Brackett, Albert G. | 1896 | Box 159 | Bradley, Robert | 1849 | Box 20 |
| Brackett, John Ely | 1912 | Box 436 | Bradley, William A. | 1867 | Box 37 |
| Brackett, Rose F. | 1912 | Box 436 | Bradley, William A. | 1869 | Box 40 |
| Brackitt, Samuel B. | 1900 | Box 190 | Bradley, William P. | 1905 | Box 277 |
| Bradburn, Charles | 1821 | Box 6 | Brads, James | 1888 | Box 106 |
| Bradbury, John D. | 1899 | Box 181 | Bradshaw, Cornelius G. | 1906 | Box 296 |
| Bradbury, John W. | 1906 | Box 295 | Bradt, Edith Virginia | 1915 | Box 510 |
| Braddock, D. Scott | 1900 | Box 190 | Bradt, Jane Eliza | 1908 | Box 339 |
| Bradfield, Annie | 1914 | Box 485 | Bradt, Orlando W. | 1916 | Box 538 |
| Bradford, Ben B. | 1915 | Box 510 | Brady, Anna F. A. | 1902 | Box 220 |
| Bradford, Charles A. | 1907 | Box 317 | Brady, Arcinous Owen | 1915 | Box 510 |
| Bradford, Cornelia | 1911 | Box 411 | Brady, Catherine | 1919 | Box 621 |
| Bradford, Elisha H. | 1892 | Box 129 | Brady, Eleanor | 1830 | Box 10 |
| Bradford, Harriet C. | 1909 | Box 362 | Brady, Elizabeth M. | 1919 | Box 621 |
| Bradford, Isabel | 1899 | Box 181 | Brady, James | 1912 | Box 436 |
| Bradford, John Watt | 1894 | Box 144 | Brady, John W. S. | 1902 | Box 220 |
| Bradford, Mary C. | 1912 | Box 436 | Brady, Mary H. | 1918 | Box 592 |
| Bradford, Mary D. | 1907 | Box 317 | Brady, Mary Jane | 1914 | Box 485 |
| Bradford, Richard H. | 1835 | Box 12 | Brady, Ora A. | 1918 | Box 592 |
| Bradford, Winslow J. | 1870 | Box 42 | Brady, Peter | 1856 | Box 24 |
| Bradley, Abraham | 1824 | Box 8 | Brady, Randall | 1871 | Box 44 |
| Bradley, Abraham | 1838 | Box 14 | Brady, Sarita M. | 1884 | Box 85 |
| Bradley, Aditha D. | 1886 | Box 95 | Brady, Thomas | 1920 | Box 652 |
| Bradley, Andrew C. | 1902 | Box 220 | Bragdon, Mary L. | 1915 | Box 510 |
| Bradley, Catherine C. | 1895 | Box 151 | Bragunier, Daniel J. | 1908 | Box 339 |
| Bradley, Charles | 1881 | Box 74 | Brahler, William | 1892 | Box 129 |
| Bradley, Charles Smith | 1916 | Box 538 | Braid, Andrew | 1919 | Box 621 |
| Bradley, Elizabeth | 1866 | Box 35 | Brainard, Charles F. | 1881 | Box 74 |
| Bradley, George | 1886 | Box 95 | Brainard, Mark D. (Sr.) | 1904 | Box 259 |
| Bradley, George Lothrop | 1906 | Box 295 | Brainard, Norman | 1910 | Box 385 |
| Bradley, George W. | 1883 | Box 81 | Braitmayer, John E. | 1889 | Box 112 |
| Bradley, Henry | 1876 | Box 60 | Bramhall, Joseph Henry | 1910 | Box 385 |
| Bradley, Henry Clay (Mrs.) | 1917 | Box 564 | Bramlett, Annie Florence | 1920 | Box 652 |
| Bradley, Isaac | 1884 | Box 85 | Branan, Mary M. | 1902 | Box 221 |
| Bradley, Jane | 1909 | Box 362 | Brand, Adolph | 1919 | Box 621 |
| Bradley, John R. | 1917 | Box 564 | Brand, Mary E. | 1916 | Box 538 |
| Bradley, Joseph | 1868 | Box 39 | Brandebury, Samuel A. | 1909 | Box 362 |
| Bradley, Joseph F. | 1898 | Box 174 | Brandenburg, Edgar M. | 1885 | Box 90 |
| Bradley, Joseph H. (Jr.) | 1874 | Box 53 | Brandenburg, Emma M. | 1918 | Box 592 |
| Bradley, Joseph H. | 1887 | Box 101 | Brandenburg, F. Walter | 1920 | Box 652 |
| Bradley, Joseph P. | 1892 | Box 129 | Brandenburg, John W. | 1920 | Box 652 |
| Bradley, Katherine A. | 1893 | Box 137 | Brandes, Henry | 1899 | Box 181 |
| Bradley, Laura A. | 1914 | Box 485 | Brandes, Maria | 1912 | Box 436 |

| | | | | | | |
|---|---|---|---|---|---|---|
| Brandmann, Adolph | 1919 | Box 621 | Breeden, Joseph S. | 1913 | Box 462 |
| Brandon, Catharine A. | 1907 | Box 317 | Breen, Patrick | 1897 | Box 167 |
| Brandon, Elvira Bigler | 1883 | Box 81 | Breese, Samuel L. | 1899 | Box 181 |
| Brandt, Ernst | 1919 | Box 621 | Bremer, Christina | 1888 | Box 106 |
| Brandt, Gustavus A. | 1917 | Box 564 | Bremer, Eugenia J. | 1916 | Box 538 |
| Brandt, Louis | 1920 | Box 652 | Bremer, William | 1900 | Box 191 |
| Brannagan, Elizabeth | 1910 | Box 385 | Bremner, Margaret | 1901 | Box 204 |
| Brannagan, Julia | 1887 | Box 101 | Brengle, Laurence | 1822 | Box 7 |
| Brannagan, Patrick | 1913 | Box 462 | Brenizer, Margaret R. | 1918 | Box 592 |
| Brannan, Jackson | 1829 | Box 10 | Brennan, Catharine J. | 1911 | Box 411 |
| Brannan, John | 1888 | Box 106 | Brennan, Edward | 1891 | Box 123 |
| Brannan, Samuel | 1885 | Box 90 | Brennan, James | 1915 | Box 510 |
| Brannum, Kitty | 1873 | Box 50 | Brennan, Jane | 1887 | Box 101 |
| Branson, Benjamin | 1873 | Box 50 | Brennan, Mary A. | 1911 | Box 411 |
| Branson, Nancy H. | 1911 | Box 411 | Brennan, Matthew L. | 1871 | Box 44 |
| Branson, Serena M. | 1911 | Box 411 | Brennan, Patrick | 1897 | Box 167 |
| Brant, Benjamin T. | 1917 | Box 564 | Brennan, Patrick | 1904 | Box 259 |
| Brashear, William B. | 1891 | Box 123 | Brennan, Patrick H. C. | 1896 | Box 159 |
| Brass, Joseph P. | 1906 | Box 296 | Brennan, Patrick J. | 1909 | Box 362 |
| Bratenahl, Louisa Oakey | 1912 | Box 436 | Brennan, Thomas | 1901 | Box 204 |
| Bratt, Mary A. | 1895 | Box 151 | Brennon, John | 1877 | Box 63 |
| Brattan, Mary Martha | 1919 | Box 621 | Brent, Anna E. | 1872 | Box 46 |
| Bratton, Caroline | 1908 | Box 339 | Brent, Daniel | 1843 | Box 16 |
| Braumann, Wilhelmina | 1915 | Box 510 | Brent, Elizabeth | 1863 | Box 31 |
| Braun, Adolph | 1918 | Box 592 | Brent, Elizabeth | 1890 | Box 117 |
| Braunschweig, Dore | 1911 | Box 411 | Brent, James Anna | 1862 | Box 30 |
| Brawley, Mary A. | 1914 | Box 485 | Brent, James W. | 1886 | Box 95 |
| Brawley, William H. | 1919 | Box 621 | Brent, Jane R. | 1878 | Box 65 |
| Brawn, Charles T. | 1884 | Box 85 | Brent, John | 1885 | Box 90 |
| Brawner, Juliana E. | 1889 | Box 112 | Brent, John S. | 1917 | Box 564 |
| Brawner, Mary L. | 1884 | Box 85 | Brent, Julia C. | 1887 | Box 101 |
| Braxton, Carter | 1911 | Box 411 | Brent, Laurelia C. Brown | 1904 | Box 259 |
| Braxton, Carter B. | 1919 | Box 621 | Brent, Richard | 1815 | Box 4 |
| Braxton, Catherine | 1910 | Box 385 | Brent, Robert | 1821 | Box 6 |
| Braxton, John T. | 1866 | Box 35 | Brent, Robert Y. | 1904 | Box 259 |
| Bray, Ann E. | 1892 | Box 129 | Brent, Vivian | 1906 | Box 296 |
| Bray, Ellen A. | 1915 | Box 510 | Brent, William | 1848 | Box 19 |
| Bray, Rose | 1905 | Box 277 | Brereton, Samuel | 1854 | Box 23 |
| Brayton, Elizabeth P. | 1914 | Box 485 | Breslau, Ferdinand | 1905 | Box 277 |
| Brayton, George M. | 1911 | Box 411 | Bresnahan, Catharine | 1900 | Box 191 |
| Brazerol, Joseph | 1904 | Box 259 | Bresnahan, John | 1919 | Box 621 |
| Brech, John | 1872 | Box 46 | Bresnahan, John A. | 1908 | Box 339 |
| Breck, Samuel | 1809 | Box 3 | Breuninger, Henry F. | 1891 | Box 123 |
| Breckinridge, Edward | 1901 | Box 204 | Breuninger, Josephine | 1916 | Box 538 |
| Breckinridge, John S. | 1919 | Box 621 | Brevitt, John | 1872 | Box 46 |
| Breckinridge, Joseph Cabell | 1920 | Box 652 | Brewer, Anne M. | 1889 | Box 112 |
| Breckinridge, Louise Dudley | 1911 | Box 411 | Brewer, David J. | 1910 | Box 385 |
| Breckinridge, Mary Ashley | 1914 | Box 485 | Brewer, Florine Augusta | 1906 | Box 296 |
| Bredekamp, Herman | 1910 | Box 385 | Brewer, George J. | 1899 | Box 181 |
| Bredow, Frances von | 1909 | Box 362 | Brewer, Harrison G. | 1920 | Box 652 |
| Breed, Daniel | 1894 | Box 144 | Brewer, Hiram | 1886 | Box 95 |
| Breed, William J. | 1911 | Box 411 | Brewer, Johnathan | 1868 | Box 39 |

| | | | | | | |
|---|---|---|---|---|---|---|
| Brewer, Mark S. | 1915 | Box 510 | | Brinkman, August | 1909 | Box 363 |
| Brewer, Martha | 1913 | Box 462 | | Brinkman, Frederick | 1920 | Box 653 |
| Brewer, Wealthy Maria | 1899 | Box 181 | | Brinkman, Ivah Stella | 1907 | Box 317 |
| Brewer, William H. | 1920 | Box 652 | | Briscoe, George | 1886 | Box 95 |
| Brewster, Charles E. | 1918 | Box 592 | | Briscoe, Susan | 1894 | Box 144 |
| Brewster, Henry A. | 1873 | Box 50 | | Bristed, Charles Astor | 1890 | Box 117 |
| Brewster, Robert J. W. | 1920 | Box 652 | | Bristow, Pauline H. | 1914 | Box 485 |
| Brewster, Virginia | 1919 | Box 621 | | Britt, James | 1864 | Box 32 |
| Brewton, William W. | 1919 | Box 621 | | Britt, Mary A. | 1918 | Box 592 |
| Brian, Henry T. | 1917 | Box 564 | | Britt, William | 1899 | Box 181 |
| Brice, Ann | 1805 | Box 1 | | Brittingham, Eugenia | 1913 | Box 462 |
| Brice, Benjamin W. | 1893 | Box 137 | | Brittingham, Sarah W. | 1908 | Box 339 |
| Brice, Charles | 1857 | Box 25 | | Britton, Alexander T. | 1899 | Box 181 |
| Brice, Edward L. | 1919 | Box 621 | | Britton, Hiram S. | 1896 | Box 159 |
| Brickheimer, Moses | 1903 | Box 240 | | Britton, Julia A. | 1894 | Box 144 |
| Bride, Louise H. | 1912 | Box 436 | | Brixen, John | 1913 | Box 462 |
| Bridge, Charlotte M. | 1907 | Box 317 | | Broadfoot, Alexander D. | 1913 | Box 462 |
| Bridge, Horatio | 1895 | Box 151 | | Broadus, Daniel | 1917 | Box 564 |
| Bridges, John | 1819 | Box 6 | | Brock, Henry | 1903 | Box 240 |
| Bridget, John F. | 1886 | Box 95 | | Brock, Samuel | 1809 | Box 3 |
| Bridget, Mary E. | 1916 | Box 538 | | Brock, William S. | 1892 | Box 129 |
| Bridwell, Clementina | 1920 | Box 653 | | Brockenberry, Lizzie | 1898 | Box 174 |
| Briel, Michael | 1896 | Box 159 | | Brockenborough, Lizzie | 1898 | Box 174 |
| Briel, William Henry | 1912 | Box 436 | | Brocker, Bernard | 1892 | Box 129 |
| Brien, James F. | 1891 | Box 123 | | Brockman, John | 1916 | Box 538 |
| Brien, Mary | 1894 | Box 144 | | Brockwell, William N. | 1916 | Box 538 |
| Briggs, Edmund B. | 1917 | Box 564 | | Brodbeck, Jacob | 1852 | Box 21 |
| Briggs, Emily Edson | 1910 | Box 385 | | Broden, Patrick | 1899 | Box 181 |
| Briggs, Helen C. | 1909 | Box 362 | | Broderick, Catherine M. | 1909 | Box 363 |
| Briggs, John R. | 1873 | Box 50 | | Broderick, Ellen | 1891 | Box 123 |
| Briggs, Martha B. | 1889 | Box 112 | | Broderick, Thomas D. | 1907 | Box 317 |
| Briggs, Mary A. | 1896 | Box 159 | | Broderson, Otto | 1905 | Box 277 |
| Bright, Amelia Elizabeth | 1911 | Box 411 | | Brodhead, DeWitt Clinton | 1902 | Box 221 |
| Bright, George S. | 1875 | Box 56 | | Brodhead, John M. | 1880 | Box 71 |
| Bright, Henry J. | 1906 | Box 296 | | Brodhead, Josephine | 1900 | Box 191 |
| Bright, Jacob L. | 1919 | Box 622 | | Brodhead, Mark | 1906 | Box 296 |
| Bright, James | 1919 | Box 622 | | Brodrecht, Philip | 1881 | Box 74 |
| Bright, Jesse D. | 1876 | Box 60 | | Broeker, Mary M. | 1913 | Box 462 |
| Bright, Maria | 1914 | Box 485 | | Brogdon, Nancy | 1888 | Box 106 |
| Bright, Mary | 1879 | Box 68 | | Brolasky, Marie | 1918 | Box 592 |
| Bright, Mary E. | 1910 | Box 385 | | Brome, Elizabeth | 1852 | Box 21 |
| Bright, Rebecca | 1887 | Box 101 | | Bromwell, Alice B. | 1911 | Box 411 |
| Brightwell, Henrietta M. | 1920 | Box 653 | | Bromwell, Josiah R. | 1912 | Box 436 |
| Brightwell, John | 1846 | Box 17 | | Bronaugh, Frances P. T. | 1905 | Box 277 |
| Brightwell, Owen Hall | 1904 | Box 259 | | Bronson, Daniel D. | 1915 | Box 510 |
| Brightwell, Thomas Richard | 1902 | Box 221 | | Bronson, Rosetta Horn | 1906 | Box 296 |
| Brignole, Rocco | 1906 | Box 296 | | Brook, Samuel | 1828 | Box 9 |
| Briles, Georgiana | 1911 | Box 411 | | Brooke, Ann Eleanor | 1854 | Box 23 |
| Brinker, Josiah Henry | 1920 | Box 653 | | Brooke, Anne | 1854 | Box 23 |
| Brinkerhoff, Henry S. | 1916 | Box 538 | | Brooke, Benjamin C. | 1859 | Box 27 |
| Brinkerhoff, Margaret | 1920 | Box 653 | | Brooke, Clement H. | 1894 | Box 144 |
| Brinkley, John | 1913 | Box 462 | | Brooke, Edmund | 1835 | Box 12 |

| | | | | | | |
|---|---|---|---|---|---|---|
| Brooke, Jane E. | 1890 | Box 117 | | Brosman, Hugh | 1901 | Box 204 |
| Brooke, Joseph | 1828 | Box 9 | | Brosman, Margaret | 1907 | Box 317 |
| Brooke, Lucy Ann | 1853 | Box 22 | | Brosnahan, Martin J. | 1900 | Box 191 |
| Brooke, Margaret P. | 1909 | Box 363 | | Brosnahan, Timothy | 1916 | Box 538 |
| Brooke, Martha G. | 1903 | Box 240 | | Brosnan, Daniel A. | 1882 | Box 78 |
| Brooke, Mary A. | 1906 | Box 296 | | Brosnan, Edward J. | 1903 | Box 240 |
| Brooke, Mary C. | 1910 | Box 385 | | Brotherhead, Charles W. | 1915 | Box 510 |
| Brooke, Olivia C. | 1895 | Box 151 | | Brotzell, Virginia | 1919 | Box 622 |
| Brooke, Philip L. | 1903 | Box 240 | | Brough, John Hamilton | 1890 | Box 117 |
| Brooke, Thomas J. | 1919 | Box 622 | | Broughton, Almira | 1908 | Box 339 |
| Brooke, Walter T. | 1878 | Box 65 | | Broughton, Elizabeth | 1893 | Box 137 |
| Brooke, William | 1901 | Box 204 | | Brower, Frederick | 1829 | Box 10 |
| Brooke, William Irvin | 1918 | Box 592 | | Brown, Absalom | 1891 | Box 123 |
| Brookes, Ellen S. | 1885 | Box 90 | | Brown, Ada M. | 1920 | Box 653 |
| Brookes, Letticia | 1818 | Box 5 | | Brown, Adelaide J. | 1914 | Box 485 |
| Brooks, Amelia | 1919 | Box 622 | | Brown, Alice | 1900 | Box 191 |
| Brooks, Ann M. | 1876 | Box 60 | | Brown, Amanda E. | 1918 | Box 592 |
| Brooks, Anna Mary | 1918 | Box 592 | | Brown, Americus | 1870 | Box 42 |
| Brooks, Catherine S. | 1875 | Box 56 | | Brown, Anna E. | 1914 | Box 485 |
| Brooks, Charles | 1866 | Box 35 | | Brown, Annie V. | 1909 | Box 363 |
| Brooks, Charles H. | 1920 | Box 653 | | Brown, Archibald | 1877 | Box 63 |
| Brooks, Edwin F. | 1902 | Box 221 | | Brown, Augusta | 1870 | Box 42 |
| Brooks, Eliza Ann | 1918 | Box 592 | | Brown, Beatrice Wills | 1896 | Box 159 |
| Brooks, Emeline | 1903 | Box 240 | | Brown, Bedford | 1909 | Box 363 |
| Brooks, Emily | 1902 | Box 221 | | Brown, Bettina B. | 1912 | Box 437 |
| Brooks, Francis J. | 1879 | Box 68 | | Brown, Catharine | 1883 | Box 81 |
| Brooks, Hanson | 1873 | Box 50 | | Brown, Catharine E. | 1915 | Box 510 |
| Brooks, Harrison | 1910 | Box 383 | | Brown, Catherine | 1915 | Box 510 |
| Brooks, Horace | 1912 | Box 436 | | Brown, Catherine C. | 1876 | Box 60 |
| Brooks, James | 1873 | Box 50 | | Brown, Charles | 1901 | Box 204 |
| Brooks, James H. | 1916 | Box 538 | | Brown, Charles Baker | 1905 | Box 277 |
| Brooks, James J. | 1895 | Box 151 | | Brown, Charles Edwin | 1918 | Box 592 |
| Brooks, Janerio Virginia | 1918 | Box 592 | | Brown, Charles H. | 1899 | Box 181 |
| Brooks, John H. | 1891 | Box 123 | | Brown, Charles W. | 1918 | Box 592 |
| Brooks, John H. | 1893 | Box 137 | | Brown, Christabell | 1901 | Box 204 |
| Brooks, John H. | 1897 | Box 167 | | Brown, Clara L. | 1897 | Box 167 |
| Brooks, Joseph A. | 1916 | Box 538 | | Brown, Coluille | 1901 | Box 204 |
| Brooks, Judson | 1893 | Box 137 | | Brown, Commodore Perry | 1907 | Box 317 |
| Brooks, Levi | 1906 | Box 296 | | Brown, Cordelia A. | 1888 | Box 106 |
| Brooks, Lewis | 1869 | Box 40 | | Brown, Daniel | 1885 | Box 90 |
| Brooks, Madison | 1904 | Box 259 | | Brown, David Henry Porter | 1896 | Box 159 |
| Brooks, Margaret J. | 1919 | Box 622 | | Brown, David W. | 1904 | Box 259 |
| Brooks, Mary | 1909 | Box 363 | | Brown, Dennis | 1911 | Box 411 |
| Brooks, Richard | 1863 | Box 31 | | Brown, Eben G. | 1870 | Box 42 |
| Brooks, Walter L. | 1916 | Box 538 | | Brown, Edmund H. | 1920 | Box 653 |
| Brooks, William H. | 1822 | Box 7 | | Brown, Edward | 1907 | Box 317 |
| Brooks, William H. | 1903 | Box 240 | | Brown, Edward | 1910 | Box 385 |
| Brooks, William S. | 1903 | Box 240 | | Brown, Edward F. | 1908 | Box 339 |
| Broom, Elizabeth | 1851 | Box 21 | | Brown, Elbert B. | 1919 | Box 622 |
| Broom, Mary E. | 1872 | Box 46 | | Brown, Eliza E. S. | 1908 | Box 339 |
| Brophy, James E. | 1907 | Box 317 | | Brown, Elizabeth | 1842 | Box 15 |
| Brosenham, Richard | 1893 | Box 137 | | Brown, Elizabeth | 1871 | Box 44 |

| | | | | | | |
|---|---|---|---|---|---|---|
| Brown, Elizabeth | 1909 | Box 363 | Brown, Lorenzo S. | 1914 | Box 485 |
| Brown, Elizabeth Ellen | 1880 | Box 71 | Brown, Louise | 1918 | Box 592 |
| Brown, Elizabeth H. | 1887 | Box 101 | Brown, Lucie A. | 1900 | Box 191 |
| Brown, Elizabeth S. | 1917 | Box 564 | Brown, Margaret | 1826 | Box 8 |
| Brown, Elizabeth V. | 1915 | Box 510 | Brown, Margaret | 1914 | Box 485 |
| Brown, Ellis W. | 1905 | Box 277 | Brown, Margaret A. | 1920 | Box 653 |
| Brown, Eugene Price | 1896 | Box 159 | Brown, Margaret V. | 1893 | Box 137 |
| Brown, Eugene Vannoy | 1892 | Box 129 | Brown, Marshall | 1882 | Box 78 |
| Brown, F. D. | 1912 | Box 437 | Brown, Mary | 1913 | Box 463 |
| Brown, Fannie Harris | 1913 | Box 462 | Brown, Mary A. | 1907 | Box 317 |
| Brown, Francis F. | 1881 | Box 74 | Brown, Mary A. L. | 1887 | Box 101 |
| Brown, George | 1876 | Box 60 | Brown, Mary Ann | 1868 | Box 39 |
| Brown, George | 1903 | Box 240 | Brown, Mary B. | 1875 | Box 56 |
| Brown, George W. | 1891 | Box 123 | Brown, Mary E. | 1886 | Box 95 |
| Brown, George W. | 1894 | Box 144 | Brown, Mary E. | 1898 | Box 174 |
| Brown, Georgie G. | 1913 | Box 462 | Brown, Mary E. | 1908 | Box 339 |
| Brown, Hanson | 1884 | Box 85 | Brown, Mary H. | 1892 | Box 129 |
| Brown, Henry Billings | 1913 | Box 462 | Brown, Mary Louise | 1911 | Box 411 |
| Brown, Henry F. J. | 1889 | Box 112 | Brown, Mary T. | 1914 | Box 485 |
| Brown, Henry H. | 1909 | Box 363 | Brown, Micah R. | 1910 | Box 385 |
| Brown, Isaiah | 1920 | Box 653 | Brown, Nancy | 1874 | Box 53 |
| Brown, Jacob | 1828 | Box 9 | Brown, Obadiah B. | 1852 | Box 21 |
| Brown, James F. | 1906 | Box 296 | Brown, Oliphant B. | 1911 | Box 411 |
| Brown, Jeannie D. | 1897 | Box 167 | Brown, Patrick | 1881 | Box 74 |
| Brown, Jesse | 1847 | Box 18 | Brown, Patsey Diggs | 1891 | Box 123 |
| Brown, Jesse | 1904 | Box 259 | Brown, Percival M. | 1911 | Box 411 |
| Brown, Joanna R. | 1908 | Box 339 | Brown, Peter | 1843 | Box 16 |
| Brown, John | 1889 | Box 112 | Brown, Philip S. | 1915 | Box 510 |
| Brown, John | 1914 | Box 485 | Brown, Priscilla | 1893 | Box 137 |
| Brown, John | 1917 | Box 564 | Brown, Richard | 1859 | Box 27 |
| Brown, John A. | 1910 | Box 385 | Brown, Robert | 1821 | Box 6 |
| Brown, John Augustus | 1908 | Box 339 | Brown, Robert | 1849 | Box 20 |
| Brown, John B. | 1868 | Box 39 | Brown, Robert S. | 1911 | Box 411 |
| Brown, John B. | 1881 | Box 74 | Brown, Rosanna | 1853 | Box 22 |
| Brown, John H. | 1900 | Box 191 | Brown, Samuel | 1866 | Box 35 |
| Brown, John H. | 1912 | Box 437 | Brown, Samuel | 1868 | Box 39 |
| Brown, John M. | 1884 | Box 85 | Brown, Samuel | 1900 | Box 191 |
| Brown, John M. | 1888 | Box 106 | Brown, Samuel K. | 1908 | Box 339 |
| Brown, John Marshall | 1908 | Box 339 | Brown, Sarah | 1851 | Box 21 |
| Brown, John Mason | 1913 | Box 463 | Brown, Sarah | 1879 | Box 68 |
| Brown, John Mifflin | 1893 | Box 137 | Brown, Sarah | 1917 | Box 565 |
| Brown, John T. | 1858 | Box 26 | Brown, Sherman J. | 1899 | Box 181 |
| Brown, John W. | 1867 | Box 37 | Brown, Sopha Hollister | 1919 | Box 622 |
| Brown, Joseph Mansfield | 1915 | Box 510 | Brown, Sophia | 1920 | Box 653 |
| Brown, Julius | 1915 | Box 510 | Brown, Stephen | 1902 | Box 221 |
| Brown, Kate T. | 1915 | Box 510 | Brown, Stephen Thomas | 1913 | Box 463 |
| Brown, Lafayette J. | 1865 | Box 33 | Brown, Susan | 1910 | Box 385 |
| Brown, Laura | 1901 | Box 204 | Brown, Thomas | 1864 | Box 32 |
| Brown, Laura V. | 1895 | Box 151 | Brown, Thomas | 1873 | Box 50 |
| Brown, Lee | 1885 | Box 90 | Brown, Thomas A. | 1906 | Box 296 |
| Brown, Lewis | 1887 | Box 101 | Brown, Thomas A. | 1917 | Box 565 |
| Brown, Lewis Henry | 1860 | Box 28 | Brown, Thomas E. | 1904 | Box 259 |

| | | | | | | |
|---|---|---|---|---|---|---|
| Brown, Thomas J. | 1914 | Box 485 | Bruce, Clarissa | 1833 | Box 12 |
| Brown, Thomas James | 1915 | Box 510 | Bruce, Emma A. | 1919 | Box 622 |
| Brown, Walter | 1910 | Box 385 | Bruce, Eugene S. | 1920 | Box 653 |
| Brown, William | 1813 | Box 4 | Bruce, Hannah | 1903 | Box 240 |
| Brown, William | 1871 | Box 44 | Bruce, Harriot | 1824 | Box 8 |
| Brown, William | 1872 | Box 46 | Bruce, Henry C. | 1902 | Box 221 |
| Brown, William | 1902 | Box 223 | Bruce, Mary | 1891 | Box 123 |
| Brown, William | 1902 | Box 223 | Bruce, William H. | 1919 | Box 622 |
| Brown, William | 1917 | Box 565 | Bruce-Webster, Lou Belle | 1913 | Box 463 |
| Brown, William A. | 1917 | Box 565 | Bruden, Jesse E. | 1917 | Box 565 |
| Brown, William A. | 1920 | Box 653 | Brueckhauser, Theresa | 1914 | Box 485 |
| Brown, William Bedford | 1914 | Box 485 | Bruehl, Anna Clara | 1911 | Box 411 |
| Brown, William E. | 1909 | Box 363 | Bruehl, Emil G. | 1919 | Box 622 |
| Brown, William H. | 1887 | Box 101 | Bruen, Alexander | 1901 | Box 204 |
| Brown, William H. | 1904 | Box 259 | Bruett, Katharine C. | 1919 | Box 622 |
| Brown, William Jullien | 1912 | Box 437 | Brugess, Alexander | 1895 | Box 152 |
| Brown, William L. | 1874 | Box 53 | Bruggeman, Ellen Virginia | 1886 | Box 95 |
| Brown, William M. | 1890 | Box 117 | Brumidi, Constantino | 1881 | Box 74 |
| Brown, William R. | 1897 | Box 167 | Brumley, Mary | 1826 | Box 8 |
| Brown, William S. | 1913 | Box 463 | Brummel, Augustus Oliver | 1909 | Box 363 |
| Brown, William T. | 1917 | Box 565 | Brummett, Joseph | 1897 | Box 167 |
| Brown, William V. H. | 1914 | Box 485 | Brunet, Adolpho V. | 1919 | Box 622 |
| Browne, Aldis B. | 1914 | Box 485 | Brunet, Eliza | 1840 | Box 15 |
| Browne, Alice Key | 1905 | Box 277 | Brunett, Louis L. | 1895 | Box 151 |
| Browne, Andrew K. | 1892 | Box 129 | Brunner, Matilda E. | 1918 | Box 592 |
| Browne, Ann S. | 1897 | Box 167 | Brunor, Louise E. | 1918 | Box 592 |
| Browne, Cyrene E. | 1899 | Box 181 | Bruns, Christopher Leslie | 1918 | Box 592 |
| Browne, Elizabeth | 1892 | Box 129 | Brunthaver, Elizabeth A. | 1918 | Box 592 |
| Browne, John Mills | 1895 | Box 151 | Bruseke, Henry | 1902 | Box 221 |
| Browne, Louise Elizabeth | 1887 | Box 101 | Bruseke, Louisa | 1904 | Box 260 |
| Browne, Louise Wolcott K. | 1904 | Box 259 | Brush, Abner | 1864 | Box 32 |
| Browne, Marcia | 1858 | Box 26 | Brush, Harmon M. | 1909 | Box 363 |
| Browne, Robert W. | 1910 | Box 385 | Brush, John C. | 1822 | Box 7 |
| Browne, Samuel E. | 1917 | Box 565 | Bruun, Christian | 1919 | Box 622 |
| Browne, William | 1901 | Box 204 | Bryan, Augustus S. | 1907 | Box 317 |
| Browne, William B. | 1885 | Box 90 | Bryan, Bennete | 1918 | Box 592 |
| Browne, William Ross | 1895 | Box 151 | Bryan, Bernard | 1901 | Box 205 |
| Brownell, Charles | 1897 | Box 167 | Bryan, Charles C. | 1917 | Box 565 |
| Brownell, Polly Y. | 1888 | Box 106 | Bryan, Fannie | 1906 | Box 296 |
| Browner, Lewis | 1871 | Box 44 | Bryan, Frances H. | 1907 | Box 317 |
| Browning, Caroline | 1890 | Box 117 | Bryan, George D. | 1910 | Box 385 |
| Browning, Charles T. | 1910 | Box 385 | Bryan, Joseph | 1863 | Box 31 |
| Browning, Ella V. | 1917 | Box 565 | Bryan, Joseph | 1874 | Box 53 |
| Browning, George Pierce | 1903 | Box 240 | Bryan, Joseph B. | 1904 | Box 260 |
| Browning, Horatio | 1904 | Box 260 | Bryan, Marian | 1916 | Box 538 |
| Browning, John L. | 1915 | Box 510 | Bryan, Mary D. | 1896 | Box 159 |
| Browning, Livingston | 1904 | Box 260 | Bryan, Matthew | 1904 | Box 260 |
| Browning, Peregrine | 1901 | Box 204 | Bryan, Richard Thomas | 1897 | Box 167 |
| Brownwell, Frank E. | 1894 | Box 144 | Bryan, William | 1909 | Box 363 |
| Bruce, Aaron | 1859 | Box 27 | Bryant, Carolan O. B. | 1897 | Box 167 |
| Bruce, Blanche K. | 1898 | Box 174 | Bryant, Ella V. Bryant | 1905 | Box 277 |
| Bruce, Charles | 1876 | Box 60 | Bryant, George | 1863 | Box 31 |

| | | | | | | |
|---|---|---|---|---|---|
| Bryant, Isaac H. | 1919 | Box 622 | Buddecke, Philip William | 1909 | Box 363 |
| Bryant, James E. | 1909 | Box 363 | Budington, Thomas G. | 1905 | Box 277 |
| Bryant, John | 1822 | Box 7 | Budington, William G. | 1918 | Box 593 |
| Bryant, John Carlyle Herbert | 1916 | Box 538 | Buechler, Annetta F. | 1913 | Box 463 |
| Bryant, Levi J. | 1920 | Box 653 | Buehler, Caroline | 1906 | Box 296 |
| Bryant, Linn W. | 1919 | Box 622 | Buehler, Kate | 1913 | Box 463 |
| Bryant, Sallie P. | 1894 | Box 144 | Buese, Ferdinand | 1905 | Box 277 |
| Bryarly, Susan F. | 1909 | Box 363 | Buford, Blanche | 1920 | Box 653 |
| Bryerly, Mary | 1888 | Box 106 | Buford, Charlotte | 1918 | Box 593 |
| Bryson, Andrew | 1892 | Box 130 | Bugher, Aaron H. | 1889 | Box 112 |
| Buchanan, Eliza M. P. | 1919 | Box 622 | Bujac, Cora | 1897 | Box 167 |
| Buchanan, F. Selina | 1894 | Box 144 | Buker, James W. | 1887 | Box 101 |
| Buchanan, Irene S. | 1907 | Box 317 | Buley, Jane | 1897 | Box 167 |
| Buchanan, Israel | 1902 | Box 221 | Bulger, Margaret | 1874 | Box 53 |
| Buchanan, John | 1905 | Box 277 | Bulkley, Annie F. | 1895 | Box 151 |
| Buchanan, Rachel | 1812 | Box 4 | Bulkley, Isabella W. | 1904 | Box 260 |
| Buchanan, Roberdeau | 1917 | Box 565 | Bulkley, John W. | 1910 | Box 385 |
| Buchanan, Robert | 1908 | Box 339 | Bulkley, Virginia | 1916 | Box 538 |
| Buchanan, Robert C. | 1878 | Box 65 | Bullard, John B. | 1918 | Box 593 |
| Buchanan, William R. | 1920 | Box 653 | Bullard, Otis Brigham | 1905 | Box 277 |
| Bücheler, Christian C. | 1900 | Box 191 | Bulley, Eleanor C. | 1860 | Box 28 |
| Buchly, Anna Maria | 1897 | Box 167 | Bulley, William H. | 1915 | Box 509 |
| Buchly, Anthony | 1881 | Box 74 | Bullitt, John C. | 1904 | Box 260 |
| Buchly, Rudolph | 1875 | Box 56 | Bullock, James E. | 1890 | Box 118 |
| Buchly, William S. | 1883 | Box 81 | Bullock, Jason Leonidas | 1911 | Box 411 |
| Buck, Alonzo M. | 1906 | Box 296 | Bullock, Sarah Virginia | 1906 | Box 296 |
| Buck, C. Olivia | 1909 | Box 363 | Bumber, George | 1879 | Box 68 |
| Buck, Charles E. | 1918 | Box 593 | Bumbery, George | 1892 | Box 130 |
| Buck, Margaret | 1875 | Box 56 | Bumbry, William | 1885 | Box 90 |
| Buck, Sarah Augusta | 1902 | Box 221 | Bumpus, Lorenzo D. | 1909 | Box 363 |
| Buck, William Langdon | 1912 | Box 437 | Bundy, Armstead | 1882 | Box 78 |
| Buckelew, Margaret F. | 1908 | Box 339 | Bundy, James F. | 1915 | Box 510 |
| Buckelew, Mary Elliott | 1918 | Box 593 | Bunker, George W. | 1889 | Box 112 |
| Buckey, Charles A. | 1890 | Box 118 | Bunton, Peter | 1896 | Box 159 |
| Buckey, Elizabeth L. | 1918 | Box 593 | Bunyea, Seymour W. | 1913 | Box 463 |
| Buckhannan, Charles | 1830 | Box 10 | Bunzel, Matilda | 1919 | Box 622 |
| Buckingham, Caleb | 1872 | Box 46 | Burbage, William D. | 1918 | Box 593 |
| Buckingham, Elizabeth A. | 1902 | Box 221 | Burbank, Howard S. | 1912 | Box 437 |
| Buckingham, William E. | 1889 | Box 112 | Burbank, Sidney | 1909 | Box 363 |
| Buckler, Susan J. | 1917 | Box 565 | Burch, Ellen | 1867 | Box 37 |
| Buckler, Zachariah S. | 1917 | Box 565 | Burch, Fielder | 1858 | Box 26 |
| Buckley, Daniel | 1901 | Box 205 | Burch, Frederick A. | 1867 | Box 37 |
| Buckley, Edmond | 1868 | Box 39 | Burch, George D. | 1894 | Box 144 |
| Buckley, Emma | 1908 | Box 339 | Burch, Kezziah | 1831 | Box 11 |
| Buckley, James S. | 1874 | Box 53 | Burch, Marion G. | 1915 | Box 511 |
| Buckley, Jane | 1906 | Box 296 | Burch, Rebecca | 1848 | Box 19 |
| Buckley, John B. | 1915 | Box 510 | Burch, Sarah | 1862 | Box 30 |
| Buckley, John D. | 1907 | Box 317 | Burch, Susan | 1887 | Box 101 |
| Buckley, William | 1898 | Box 174 | Burch, Sylvester R. | 1910 | Box 385 |
| Buckman, Marcelina | 1891 | Box 123 | Burch, Thomas | 1847 | Box 18 |
| Buckman, Sallie A. | 1909 | Box 363 | Burch, Thomas Richard | 1899 | Box 181 |
| Budd, George T. | 1902 | Box 221 | Burch, Walter | 1804 | Box 1 |

| | | | | | | |
|---|---|---|---|---|---|---|
| Burch, William L. | 1869 | Box 40 | Burkhart, Herman | 1898 | Box 174 |
| Burchan, John | 1804 | Box 1 | Burkhart, Lottie M. | 1910 | Box 386 |
| Burchard, Carrie V. | 1900 | Box 191 | Burlew, Cornelius | 1899 | Box 182 |
| Burchard, William Metcalf | 1883 | Box 81 | Burley, Annie | 1901 | Box 205 |
| Burche, Benjamin Franklin | 1902 | Box 221 | Burmeister, Henry | 1911 | Box 411 |
| Burche, Samuel | 1846 | Box 17 | Burne, Theresa | 1850 | Box 20 |
| Burche, Samuel | 1901 | Box 205 | Burnell, William | 1918 | Box 593 |
| Burche, Susan M. | 1875 | Box 56 | Burnett, Aleathea | 1852 | Box 21 |
| Burchell, Noval W. | 1899 | Box 181 | Burnett, Bridget | 1885 | Box 90 |
| Burdett, Samuel S. | 1915 | Box 511 | Burnett, David L. | 1913 | Box 463 |
| Burdette, Susie E. | 1915 | Box 511 | Burnett, Ephraim | 1889 | Box 112 |
| Burdette, Walter Washington | 1906 | Box 296 | Burnett, Jerome C. | 1891 | Box 123 |
| Burdine, Reuben | 1860 | Box 28 | Burnett, Reuben | 1902 | Box 221 |
| Burgdorf, Carl E. | 1913 | Box 463 | Burnett, Ward B. | 1889 | Box 112 |
| Burgdorf, Ernest | 1919 | Box 622 | Burnett, William H. | 1912 | Box 437 |
| Burgdorf, Louis | 1895 | Box 151 | Burnett, William W. | 1918 | Box 593 |
| Burgess, Anna | 1912 | Box 437 | Burnham Minerva | 1899 | Box 182 |
| Burgess, Annie Louisa | 1910 | Box 386 | Burnham, Sallie M. | 1914 | Box 486 |
| Burgess, Charles | 1886 | Box 95 | Burnish, Hattie L. | 1903 | Box 240 |
| Burgess, Enoch N. | 1916 | Box 539 | Burns, Aida | 1918 | Box 593 |
| Burgess, Jane Ann E. | 1886 | Box 95 | Burns, Anne | 1883 | Box 81 |
| Burgess, Julia | 1900 | Box 191 | Burns, Arabella E. | 1912 | Box 437 |
| Burgess, Mary Gertrude Austin | 1896 | Box 159 | Burns, Benjamin F. | 1890 | Box 118 |
| Burgess, Mary Y. | 1906 | Box 296 | Burns, Catharine J. | 1917 | Box 565 |
| Burgess, Sarah E. | 1899 | Box 182 | Burns, Daniel | 1872 | Box 46 |
| Burghardt, Eliza J. | 1903 | Box 240 | Burns, Frank Harmon | 1920 | Box 653 |
| Burgher, John C. S. | 1912 | Box 437 | Burns, George | 1862 | Box 30 |
| Burgwin, Mildred C. | 1920 | Box 653 | Burns, George | 1901 | Box 205 |
| Burk, Catharine | 1911 | Box 411 | Burns, Harman | 1872 | Box 46 |
| Burk, Dennis | 1852 | Box 21 | Burns, James | 1896 | Box 159 |
| Burk, John | 1913 | Box 463 | Burns, Jennie T. | 1915 | Box 511 |
| Burk, Solomon | 1880 | Box 71 | Burns, John | 1864 | Box 32 |
| Burkart, Caroline | 1920 | Box 653 | Burns, John | 1893 | Box 137 |
| Burkart, Joseph William | 1890 | Box 118 | Burns, Margaret | 1902 | Box 221 |
| Burke, Anastasia | 1867 | Box 37 | Burns, Mary B. | 1914 | Box 486 |
| Burke, Annie M. | 1914 | Box 486 | Burns, Michael T. | 1911 | Box 412 |
| Burke, Caroline | 1896 | Box 159 | Burns, Theodore | 1893 | Box 137 |
| Burke, Catherine | 1915 | Box 511 | Burns, Thomas | 1879 | Box 68 |
| Burke, Frank P. | 1907 | Box 317 | Burns, William | 1889 | Box 112 |
| Burke, Hilliard H. | 1896 | Box 159 | Burns, William W. | 1892 | Box 130 |
| Burke, James | 1891 | Box 123 | Burnside, William H. | 1887 | Box 101 |
| Burke, Laurence F. | 1906 | Box 296 | Burnstein, Henry | 1896 | Box 159 |
| Burke, Margaret | 1883 | Box 81 | Burnstine, Bernard | 1903 | Box 241 |
| Burke, Mary E. | 1916 | Box 538 | Burnstine, Henry | 1874 | Box 53 |
| Burke, Michael | 1903 | Box 240 | Burnup, Martha Ann | 1904 | Box 260 |
| Burke, Michael | 1907 | Box 317 | Burr, Joseph F. | 1896 | Box 159 |
| Burke, Patrick | 1878 | Box 65 | Burr, Julia A. | 1896 | Box 159 |
| Burke, Robert W. | 1920 | Box 653 | Burr, Lizzie R. | 1895 | Box 152 |
| Burke, Thomas | 1903 | Box 240 | Burr, S. Augustine | 1888 | Box 106 |
| Burke, Thomas | 1877 | Box 63 | Burr, William Henry | 1908 | Box 339 |
| Burke, Thomas | 1912 | Box 437 | Burrell, Albert | 1873 | Box 50 |
| Burkhardt, Louisa | 1918 | Box 593 | Burrell, George Marshall | 1880 | Box 71 |

| | | | | | | |
|---|---|---|---|---|---|---|
| Burrell, Henry | 1888 | Box 106 | Busher, James M. | 1892 | Box 130 |
| Burrell, Jeremiah Murray | 1920 | Box 653 | Bushnell, John | 1896 | Box 160 |
| Burrell, Mary | 1896 | Box 160 | Bushrod, Sarah E. | 1919 | Box 622 |
| Burrell, Thomas J. | 1911 | Box 412 | Buss, Jacob | 1913 | Box 463 |
| Burress, Jane S. | 1869 | Box 40 | Bussard, Daniel | 1830 | Box 10 |
| Burris, William | 1891 | Box 123 | Bussey, Cyrus | 1915 | Box 511 |
| Burriss, Hester V. | 1893 | Box 137 | Busteed, Richard Jr. | 1867 | Box 37 |
| Burriss, Lemuel P. | 1906 | Box 296 | Busti, Paul | 1871 | Box 44 |
| Burritt, Anna Blanche | 1913 | Box 463 | Butcher, John H. | 1915 | Box 511 |
| Burritt, Ira N. | 1888 | Box 106 | Butler, A. E. | 1917 | Box 565 |
| Burritt, Payson | 1905 | Box 277 | Butler, Abraham | 1863 | Box 31 |
| Burritt, Payson | 1906 | Box 296 | Butler, Agnes | 1915 | Box 511 |
| Burroughs, Mary E. | 1918 | Box 593 | Butler, Amelia | 1891 | Box 123 |
| Burroughs, William | 1876 | Box 60 | Butler, Annie | 1897 | Box 167 |
| Burrows, Alexander | 1862 | Box 30 | Butler, Barbara | 1896 | Box 160 |
| Burrows, Cornelia A. | 1908 | Box 339 | Butler, Benjamin | 1887 | Box 101 |
| Burrows, Edward | 1811 | Box 3 | Butler, Benjamin F. | 1893 | Box 137 |
| Burrows, James Hamilton | 1917 | Box 565 | Butler, Charles H. | 1890 | Box 118 |
| Burrows, Julius C. | 1916 | Box 539 | Butler, Elizabeth | 1862 | Box 30 |
| Burrows, Samuel F. | 1898 | Box 174 | Butler, Ellen | 1901 | Box 205 |
| Burrus, John | 1843 | Box 16 | Butler, Ferdinand | 1876 | Box 60 |
| Burruss, John H. | 1911 | Box 412 | Butler, George | 1913 | Box 463 |
| Burt, Kate Ward | 1909 | Box 363 | Butler, George Washington | 1913 | Box 463 |
| Burton, Agnes E. | 1915 | Box 511 | Butler, Harriet | 1866 | Box 35 |
| Burton, Alphonse Joseph | 1920 | Box 653 | Butler, Harriet Ann | 1905 | Box 277 |
| Burton, Amelia Walton | 1918 | Box 593 | Butler, Henry | 1908 | Box 339 |
| Burton, Eddie Fizer | 1920 | Box 654 | Butler, Hiram Pitts | 1920 | Box 654 |
| Burton, George Correl | 1909 | Box 363 | Butler, James | 1902 | Box 221 |
| Burton, Henry H. | 1877 | Box 63 | Butler, Jane | 1863 | Box 31 |
| Burton, Lester W. | 1919 | Box 622 | Butler, Jarred | 1847 | Box 18 |
| Burtt, Ellery J. | 1912 | Box 437 | Butler, John | 1851 | Box 21 |
| Burwell, Armistead | 1879 | Box 68 | Butler, John Gazzam | 1914 | Box 486 |
| Bury, John | 1893 | Box 137 | Butler, John H. | 1902 | Box 221 |
| Bury, Nelson | 1873 | Box 50 | Butler, John S. | 1916 | Box 539 |
| Bury, William | 1857 | Box 25 | Butler, John W. | 1894 | Box 144 |
| Buschell, John Joseph Aloysius | 1917 | Box 565 | Butler, Ormond Hook | 1918 | Box 593 |
| Buscher, Henny | 1875 | Box 56 | Butler, Sarah | 1877 | Box 63 |
| Busey, Elizabeth | 1903 | Box 241 | Butler, Sarah | 1878 | Box 65 |
| Busey, Samuel | 1901 | Box 205 | Butler, Walter | 1876 | Box 60 |
| Busey, Sarah A. | 1887 | Box 101 | Butler, William H. | 1902 | Box 221 |
| Busey, William G. | 1881 | Box 74 | Butler, William H. | 1914 | Box 486 |
| Bush, Eleanore Adams Stanton | 1910 | Box 386 | Butler, William J. | 1864 | Box 32 |
| Bush, Esther | 1895 | Box 152 | Butt, Archibald Willingham | 1912 | Box 437 |
| Bush, George | 1906 | Box 296 | Butt, James D. | 1913 | Box 463 |
| Bush, Henry | 1805 | Box 1 | Butt, Margaret E. | 1897 | Box 167 |
| Bush, Henry | 1900 | Box 191 | Butt, William B. | 1877 | Box 63 |
| Bush, Lois I. | 1915 | Box 511 | Butter, William | 1821 | Box 6 |
| Bush, Samuel | 1916 | Box 539 | Butterfield, George | 1919 | Box 622 |
| Bush, William | 1861 | Box 29 | Butterfoss, Laura E. | 1917 | Box 565 |
| Bush, William Sharp | 1813 | Box 4 | Butterworth, Benjamin | 1898 | Box 174 |
| Bushby, William | 1810 | Box 3 | Butterworth, Mary E. | 1917 | Box 565 |
| Bushee, Recella J. | 1913 | Box 463 | Buttimore, Dennis | 1897 | Box 167 |

| | | | | | | |
|---|---|---|---|---|---|---|
| Buttner, Henry | 1911 | Box 412 | | Caffrey, Margaret | 1911 | Box 412 |
| Button, Lydia S. | 1888 | Box 106 | | Caffrey, Nicholas | 1901 | Box 205 |
| Button, Percy | 1915 | Box 511 | | Caffrey, Philip | 1916 | Box 539 |
| Butts, Frank A. | 1914 | Box 486 | | Cahill, Catherine | 1877 | Box 63 |
| Butts, Harry T. | 1910 | Box 386 | | Cahill, Margaret | 1913 | Box 463 |
| Buxman, John G. | 1899 | Box 182 | | Cahill, Margaret Theresa | 1920 | Box 654 |
| Buzby, Mary M. | 1914 | Box 486 | | Cahill, Nicholas | 1907 | Box 317 |
| Byers, Martha | 1917 | Box 565 | | Cahill, Patrick | 1881 | Box 74 |
| Byne, Charles | 1810 | Box 3 | | Cahill, Sarah A. | 1906 | Box 296 |
| Byng, George T. | 1891 | Box 123 | | Cahill, Thomas | 1920 | Box 654 |
| Byng, John | 1879 | Box 68 | | Cahill, William | 1885 | Box 90 |
| Byng, Maria | 1880 | Box 71 | | Cain, James | 1829 | Box 10 |
| Byram, James H. | 1908 | Box 339 | | Cain, Calvin | 1915 | Box 511 |
| Byrd, Adough M. | 1920 | Box 654 | | Cain, Cecilia | 1883 | Box 81 |
| Byrne, Charles | 1831 | Box 11 | | Cain, Edwardanna | 1891 | Box 123 |
| Byrne, Grace V. | 1909 | Box 363 | | Cain, George I. | 1836 | Box 13 |
| Byrne, James | 1892 | Box 130 | | Cain, Laura | 1896 | Box 160 |
| Byrne, John J. | 1913 | Box 463 | | Cain, Martha Mary | 1837 | Box 13 |
| Byrne, Margaret H. | 1884 | Box 85 | | Cain, Randall C. | 1914 | Box 486 |
| Byrne, Margaret M. C. | 1918 | Box 593 | | Cain, Richard H. | 1889 | Box 112 |
| Byrne, Martha C. | 1863 | Box 31 | | Cain, Richard S. | 1904 | Box 260 |
| Byrne, Mary E. | 1887 | Box 101 | | Caine, Alexander C. | 1909 | Box 363 |
| Byrne, Mathew | 1872 | Box 46 | | Cairns, Annie | 1899 | Box 182 |
| Byrne, Moriah | 1849 | Box 20 | | Cairns, Florence | 1919 | Box 623 |
| Byrne, Patrick | 1892 | Box 130 | | Calbert, Elizabeth G. | 1911 | Box 412 |
| Byrne, Patrick J. | 1919 | Box 622 | | Calder, Catharine | 1846 | Box 17 |
| Byrne, Peter | 1900 | Box 191 | | Caldwell, Caroline E. A. | 1894 | Box 144 |
| Byrne, Philip William | 1866 | Box 35 | | Caldwell, Elias C. | 1893 | Box 137 |
| Byrne, Theresa | 1850 | Box 20 | | Caldwell, Josiah F. | 1860 | Box 28 |
| Byrne, Thomas | 1868 | Box 39 | | Caldwell, Maria H. | 1878 | Box 65 |
| Byrne, William | 1870 | Box 42 | | Caldwell, Mary | 1901 | Box 205 |
| Byrnes, Emma | 1897 | Box 167 | | Caldwell, Thompson B. | 1873 | Box 50 |
| Byrnes, John | 1896 | Box 160 | | Calhoun, John T. | 1871 | Box 44 |
| Byrnes, Nellie G. | 1904 | Box 260 | | Call, Loren Heinlein | 1913 | Box 463 |
| Byron, George Hunt | 1895 | Box 152 | | Callaghan, Dennis | 1888 | Box 106 |
| Byron, Richard | 1888 | Box 106 | | Callaghan, George | 1894 | Box 144 |
| Byus, Annie Eccleston | 1905 | Box 277 | | Callaghan, John T. | 1918 | Box 593 |
| Byus, Stanley | 1805 | Box 1 | | Callaghan, Mary | 1908 | Box 340 |
| Cabaniss, George W. | 1920 | Box 654 | | Callaghan, Timothy | 1896 | Box 160 |
| Cabell, Annie | 1904 | Box 260 | | Callahan, Alice A. | 1920 | Box 654 |
| Cadden, Frances M. | 1916 | Box 539 | | Callahan, Ann | 1909 | Box 363 |
| Caden, James | 1860 | Box 28 | | Callahan, Bridget | 1914 | Box 486 |
| Caden, James F. | 1893 | Box 137 | | Callahan (Egan), Catharine | 1914 | Box 489 |
| Caden, Tomas | 1911 | Box 412 | | Callahan, John | 1804 | Box 1 |
| Cadwallader, Emma R. | 1895 | Box 152 | | Callahan, John | 1901 | Box 205 |
| Cady, Helen P. | 1895 | Box 152 | | Callahan, John | 1908 | Box 340 |
| Cady, Lucinda | 1890 | Box 118 | | Callahan, John | 1909 | Box 363 |
| Cady, Margaret | 1912 | Box 437 | | Callahan, John J. | 1885 | Box 90 |
| Cady, Martin | 1877 | Box 63 | | Callahan, Redmond | 1876 | Box 60 |
| Cady, Martin | 1918 | Box 593 | | Callahan, Thomas | 1909 | Box 363 |
| Cady, Mary | 1880 | Box 71 | | Callahan, Thomas | 1912 | Box 437 |
| Cady, Michael | 1886 | Box 95 | | Callan, Christina Van Ness | 1911 | Box 412 |

| | | | | | | |
|---|---|---|---|---|---|
| Callan, Cornelius Van Ness | 1911 | Box 412 | Campbell, Charles H. | 1915 | Box 511 |
| Callan, Lawrence | 1895 | Box 152 | Campbell, Clarisa | 1902 | Box 222 |
| Callan, Margaret | 1905 | Box 277 | Campbell, Daniel | 1857 | Box 25 |
| Callan, Mary Sophia | 1911 | Box 412 | Campbell, Ella C. | 1902 | Box 222 |
| Callan, Nicholas | 1847 | Box 18 | Campbell, Ellen J. | 1902 | Box 222 |
| Callanan, John | 1830 | Box 10 | Campbell, Emma J. | 1902 | Box 222 |
| Callanan, Julia | 1889 | Box 112 | Campbell, Frank L. | 1914 | Box 486 |
| Callanan, Patrick | 1889 | Box 112 | Campbell, Helen C. | 1905 | Box 277 |
| Callen, Bartholomew | 1912 | Box 437 | Campbell, Hugh A. | 1903 | Box 241 |
| Callis, Emma Lee | 1912 | Box 437 | Campbell, J. W. | 1920 | Box 654 |
| Callnan, John | 1830 | Box 10 | Campbell, Jabez Pitt | 1910 | Box 386 |
| Callow, William | 1899 | Box 182 | Campbell, James N. | 1871 | Box 44 |
| Calnan, Jeremiah | 1846 | Box 17 | Campbell, Jane | 1885 | Box 90 |
| Calnan, Mary | 1856 | Box 24 | Campbell, Jane S. | 1879 | Box 68 |
| Calver, Frances A. | 1914 | Box 486 | Campbell, Jerry | 1823 | Box 7 |
| Calver, Thomas | 1920 | Box 654 | Campbell, John | 1838 | Box 14 |
| Calvert, Edward | 1898 | Box 174 | Campbell, John | 1892 | Box 130 |
| Calvert, Edward H. | 1880 | Box 71 | Campbell, John | 1895 | Box 152 |
| Calvert, Elizabeth | 1912 | Box 437 | Campbell, John | 1914 | Box 486 |
| Calvert, Grace | 1881 | Box 74 | Campbell, John C. | 1898 | Box 174 |
| Calvert, Lucy Dorsey | 1910 | Box 386 | Campbell, John H. | 1915 | Box 511 |
| Calvert, Sadie A. | 1908 | Box 340 | Campbell, Joseph | 1892 | Box 130 |
| Calvert, William C. | 1919 | Box 623 | Campbell, Josephine B. | 1920 | Box 654 |
| Calvin, Margaret | 1904 | Box 260 | Campbell, Mary A. | 1886 | Box 95 |
| Cambell, Jane F. | 1849 | Box 18 | Campbell, Mary Adaline | 1889 | Box 112 |
| Cameron, Elizabeth | 1914 | Box 486 | Campbell, Mary I. | 1893 | Box 137 |
| Cameron, Gilbert | 1867 | Box 37 | Campbell, Mary J. | 1909 | Box 363 |
| Cameron, Gilbert | 1886 | Box 95 | Campbell, Mary J. | 1918 | Box 593 |
| Cameron, Ida | 1912 | Box 437 | Campbell, Mary K. | 1913 | Box 463 |
| Cameron, John | 1902 | Box 222 | Campbell, Mary P. | 1907 | Box 317 |
| Cameron, John S. | 1914 | Box 486 | Campbell, Mason | 1885 | Box 90 |
| Cameron, Margaret S. E. | 1920 | Box 654 | Campbell, Michael J. | 1899 | Box 182 |
| Cameron, Mary E. | 1874 | Box 53 | Campbell, Peter | 1888 | Box 106 |
| Cameron, Robert L. | 1904 | Box 260 | Campbell, Robert | 1883 | Box 81 |
| Cameron, Simon | 1901 | Box 205 | Campbell, Robert G. | 1903 | Box 241 |
| Cameron, Simon | 1901 | Box 205 | Campbell, Rosaline V. | 1909 | Box 363 |
| Camlin, Ann | 1848 | Box 19 | Campbell, Stewart | 1907 | Box 317 |
| Cammack, Christopher | 1872 | Box 46 | Campbell, Thomas A. | 1912 | Box 437 |
| Cammack, Edmund | 1889 | Box 112 | Campbell, Thomas B. | 1875 | Box 56 |
| Cammack, George C. | 1886 | Box 95 | Campbell, Thomas B. | 1902 | Box 222 |
| Cammack, Jeannette C. | 1900 | Box 191 | Campbell, Walter L. | 1905 | Box 277 |
| Cammack, John | 1908 | Box 340 | Campbell, William | 1860 | Box 28 |
| Cammack, William | 1871 | Box 44 | Campbell, William H. | 1881 | Box 74 |
| Camp, Francis Edward | 1903 | Box 241 | Campbell, William Shaw | 1904 | Box 260 |
| Camp, Herbert M. | 1908 | Box 340 | Cana, Frederick | 1822 | Box 7 |
| Campbell, Agnes Levina | 1919 | Box 623 | Cana, Mary Ann | 1835 | Box 12 |
| Campbell, Alcinda C. | 1853 | Box 22 | Canavan, John | 1901 | Box 205 |
| Campbell, Ann H. | 1886 | Box 95 | Caney, M. | 1900 | Box 191 |
| Campbell, Archibald | 1890 | Box 118 | Canfield, Charles I. | 1891 | Box 123 |
| Campbell, Blanche | 1901 | Box 205 | Canfield, Eunice A. | 1892 | Box 130 |
| Campbell, Catherine Elizabeth | 1911 | Box 412 | Canfield, Josephine L. | 1904 | Box 260 |
| Campbell, Charles A. | 1893 | Box 137 | Canfield, Mary Gross | 1915 | Box 511 |

| | | | | | | |
|---|---|---|---|---|---|
| Canisius, Arthur T. | 1916 | Box 539 | Carpenter, Joanna D. | 1920 | Box 654 |
| Cannon, Ann | 1913 | Box 463 | Carpenter, Laura A. | 1912 | Box 437 |
| Cannon, Lizzie | 1891 | Box 123 | Carpenter, Marguerite Louise B. | 1909 | Box 363 |
| Cannon, Michael J. | 1910 | Box 386 | Carpenter, Mary Lucille | 1908 | Box 340 |
| Cannon, Patrick | 1911 | Box 412 | Carpenter, Miriam H. | 1890 | Box 118 |
| Cantwell, James | 1907 | Box 317 | Carpenter, Otis A. | 1909 | Box 363 |
| Cantwell, Mary | 1898 | Box 174 | Carpenter, Patrick | 1896 | Box 160 |
| Cantwell, Simon | 1830 | Box 10 | Carpenter, Rachael | 1903 | Box 241 |
| Capehart, Baldy Ashbourne | 1905 | Box 277 | Carpenter, Sarah A. | 1920 | Box 654 |
| Capehart, Fanny | 1919 | Box 623 | Carpenter, Virginia S. | 1918 | Box 593 |
| Caperton, Eliza J. | 1873 | Box 50 | Carpenter, Zachary T. | 1891 | Box 123 |
| Caperton, Hugh | 1917 | Box 565 | Carr, Benjamin | 1886 | Box 95 |
| Caperton, Imogen | 1879 | Box 68 | Carr, David | 1920 | Box 654 |
| Caperton, Lizzie | 1911 | Box 413 | Carr, Eugene A. | 1915 | Box 511 |
| Caplan, Risha | 1917 | Box 565 | Carr, George W. | 1893 | Box 137 |
| Capron, Horace | 1885 | Box 90 | Carr, George W. | 1919 | Box 623 |
| Capron, Margaret | 1898 | Box 174 | Carr, John W. | 1901 | Box 205 |
| Capron, Mary | 1914 | Box 486 | Carr, Marie C. | 1893 | Box 137 |
| Carbaugh, Ethel | 1916 | Box 539 | Carr, Mary Carter | 1908 | Box 340 |
| Carbery, Eliza A. | 1918 | Box 593 | Carr, Solomon | 1912 | Box 437 |
| Carbery, James L. | 1891 | Box 123 | Carr, William K. | 1915 | Box 511 |
| Carbery, Ruth | 1869 | Box 40 | Carr, William P. | 1918 | Box 593 |
| Carbery, Sybilla | 1840 | Box 15 | Carraher, John V. | 1909 | Box 363 |
| Carbery, Thomas | 1863 | Box 31 | Carrick, Henry | 1867 | Box 37 |
| Card, Benjamin C. | 1916 | Box 539 | Carrick, Patrick | 1823 | Box 7 |
| Card, Isabel H. | 1917 | Box 565 | Carrico, James | 1864 | Box 32 |
| Cardella, Raymond F. | 1897 | Box 168 | Carrico, Margaret M. | 1900 | Box 191 |
| Carden, Margaret A. | 1900 | Box 191 | Carrico, William B. | 1858 | Box 26 |
| Carden, Thomas | 1898 | Box 174 | Carrier, Arthur J. | 1887 | Box 101 |
| Carey, Ellen | 1917 | Box 565 | Carriere, Caroline | 1911 | Box 413 |
| Carey, Joanna A. | 1910 | Box 386 | Carrigan, John | 1887 | Box 101 |
| Carey, John | 1843 | Box 16 | Carrington, Adeline M. | 1915 | Box 511 |
| Carey, John | 1888 | Box 106 | Carrington, Charles H. | 1908 | Box 340 |
| Carhart, Albert | 1898 | Box 174 | Carrington, Edmund | 1917 | Box 565 |
| Carl, Henry | 1858 | Box 26 | Carrington, Jacob | 1895 | Box 152 |
| Carleton, Joseph | 1812 | Box 4 | Carrington, William M. | 1916 | Box 539 |
| Carlichs, Francis | 1892 | Box 132 | Carroll, Ann C. | 1883 | Box 81 |
| Carlin, John | 1901 | Box 205 | Carroll, Daniel of Duddington | 1849 | Box 20 |
| Carlin, Martha J. | 1914 | Box 486 | Carroll, Edward C. | 1902 | Box 222 |
| Carlisle, John G. | 1910 | Box 386 | Carroll, Elizabeth | 1821 | Box 6 |
| Carlisle, James Mandeville | 1877 | Box 63 | Carroll, Elizabeth (Libby) A. | 1913 | Box 463 |
| Carlisle, Mildred E. | 1899 | Box 182 | Carroll, Emma A. | 1903 | Box 241 |
| Carll, John Henry | 1920 | Box 654 | Carroll, George H. | 1903 | Box 241 |
| Carmody, John | 1900 | Box 191 | Carroll, Harriet | 1861 | Box 29 |
| Carnes, John H. | 1909 | Box 363 | Carroll, Henry | 1886 | Box 95 |
| Carozzi, Giuseppe Napoleone | 1914 | Box 486 | Carroll, Henry | 1890 | Box 118 |
| Carpenter, Annie M. | 1895 | Box 152 | Carroll, Henry H. | 1855 | Box 23 |
| Carpenter, Claude S. | 1919 | Box 623 | Carroll, Jane | 1896 | Box 160 |
| Carpenter, Clementina H. | 1892 | Box 130 | Carroll, Jane Knowles | 1904 | Box 260 |
| Carpenter, Delos | 1873 | Box 50 | Carroll, John | 1884 | Box 85 |
| Carpenter, James | 1872 | Box 46 | Carroll, John H. | 1907 | Box 318 |
| Carpenter, Jesse | 1901 | Box 205 | Carroll, John J. | 1907 | Box 318 |

| | | | | | | |
|---|---|---|---|---|---|---|
| Carroll, Joseph H. | 1891 | Box 123 | Carter, James O. | 1910 | Box 386 |
| Carroll, Lewis O. | 1899 | Box 182 | Carter, John | 1850 | Box 20 |
| Carroll, Margaret | 1906 | Box 296 | Carter, John E. | 1886 | Box 95 |
| Carroll, Margaret E. | 1888 | Box 106 | Carter, John Thomas | 1905 | Box 278 |
| Carroll, Mary | 1911 | Box 413 | Carter, Joseph | 1918 | Box 593 |
| Carroll, Mary A. | 1875 | Box 56 | Carter, Lavinia | 1870 | Box 42 |
| Carroll, Mary A. | 1887 | Box 101 | Carter, Lee | 1919 | Box 623 |
| Carroll, Mary B. | 1915 | Box 511 | Carter, Lizzie | 1913 | Box 464 |
| Carroll, Mary F. | 1913 | Box 463 | Carter, Martha Custis | 1899 | Box 182 |
| Carroll, Mary H. | 1899 | Box 182 | Carter, Mary | 1906 | Box 296 |
| Carroll, Mary J. | 1918 | Box 593 | Carter, Mary Hannah | 1915 | Box 511 |
| Carroll, Mary M. | 1910 | Box 386 | Carter, Mary M. | 1909 | Box 363 |
| Carroll, Patrick | 1897 | Box 168 | Carter, Milly | 1897 | Box 168 |
| Carroll, Rebecca | 1887 | Box 101 | Carter, Richard W. | 1884 | Box 85 |
| Carroll, Rosanna | 1902 | Box 222 | Carter, Robert | 1887 | Box 101 |
| Carroll, Sally Sprigg | 1895 | Box 152 | Carter, Sarah J. | 1919 | Box 623 |
| Carroll, Sicely | 1886 | Box 95 | Carter, Thomas H. | 1911 | Box 413 |
| Carroll, Sophia Simms | 1900 | Box 191 | Carter, Violet | 1919 | Box 623 |
| Carroll, Thomas O. | 1908 | Box 340 | Carter, Walker | 1911 | Box 413 |
| Carroll, William | 1887 | Box 101 | Carter, William | 1917 | Box 566 |
| Carroll, William James | 1903 | Box 241 | Carter, William J. | 1907 | Box 318 |
| Carroll, William R. | 1875 | Box 56 | Carter, William W. | 1906 | Box 296 |
| Carroll, William S. | 1911 | Box 413 | Carter, Zachary | 1910 | Box 386 |
| Carroll, William Thomas | 1881 | Box 74 | Cartter, Nancy | 1896 | Box 160 |
| Carroll, Winfield | 1913 | Box 464 | Cartwright, Isaac | 1916 | Box 539 |
| Carrothers, Rose A. | 1915 | Box 511 | Cartwright, Julia Ann | 1901 | Box 205 |
| Carson, Anne S. | 1904 | Box 260 | Cartwright, Levin | 1841 | Box 15 |
| Carson, John Miller | 1912 | Box 437 | Cartwright, Levin T. | 1902 | Box 222 |
| Carson, Mary | 1907 | Box 318 | Cartwright, Rachel | 1869 | Box 40 |
| Carson, Perry H. | 1909 | Box 363 | Carusi, Lewis | 1872 | Box 46 |
| Carson, Susan Waugh | 1900 | Box 191 | Carusi, Nathaniel | 1878 | Box 65 |
| Carson, William A. | 1919 | Box 623 | Carusi, Samuel | 1878 | Box 65 |
| Carson, William H. | 1905 | Box 277 | Caruth, Henry Clay | 1913 | Box 464 |
| Carta, Angelo | 1920 | Box 654 | Carver, Minnie E. | 1920 | Box 654 |
| Carter, Abram | 1882 | Box 78 | Cary, Linton S. | 1893 | Box 137 |
| Carter, Ada Jane | 1897 | Box 168 | Cary, Mary Elizabeth | 1881 | Box 74 |
| Carter, Anna B. | 1914 | Box 486 | Casanave, Peter | 1860 | Box 28 |
| Carter, Charles H. | 1917 | Box 565 | Case, Ada B. | 1915 | Box 511 |
| Carter, Charles L. (Jr.) | 1891 | Box 123 | Case, Amanda R. B. | 1912 | Box 438 |
| Carter, Charles Monroe | 1909 | Box 363 | Case, Anna Rogers | 1892 | Box 130 |
| Carter, Edward Champ | 1910 | Box 386 | Case, Augustus | 1893 | Box 137 |
| Carter, Elizabeth S. | 1885 | Box 90 | Case, Augustus Ludlow | 1891 | Box 124 |
| Carter, Ella J. | 1917 | Box 566 | Case, Charles | 1883 | Box 81 |
| Carter, Ellen | 1860 | Box 28 | Case, Daniel Rogers | 1919 | Box 623 |
| Carter, Ellen Gertrude | 1916 | Box 539 | Case, Ida L. | 1908 | Box 340 |
| Carter, Emeline | 1883 | Box 81 | Case, John S | 1918 | Box 593 |
| Carter, Emily J. | 1889 | Box 112 | Casel, Sarah | 1915 | Box 511 |
| Carter, Emma J. | 1920 | Box 654 | Casey, Anastasia R. | 1906 | Box 297 |
| Carter, Fanny | 1855 | Box 23 | Casey, Charles C. | 1907 | Box 318 |
| Carter, Frank C. | 1920 | Box 654 | Casey, Daniel | 1901 | Box 205 |
| Carter, Henry | 1896 | Box 160 | Casey, Edmund | 1914 | Box 486 |
| Carter, James | 1875 | Box 57 | Casey, Emily White | 1902 | Box 222 |

| | | | | | | |
|---|---|---|---|---|---|---|
| Casey, John | 1864 | Box 32 | Catlin, Robert | 1904 | Box 260 |
| Casey, Joseph | 1879 | Box 68 | Caton, Edward | 1862 | Box 30 |
| Casey, Joseph | 1909 | Box 363 | Caton, James O. | 1909 | Box 363 |
| Casey, Lyman R. | 1914 | Box 486 | Caton, Julia A. | 1887 | Box 101 |
| Casey, Margaret | 1903 | Box 241 | Caton, Mary | 1914 | Box 486 |
| Casey, Mary A. | 1900 | Box 191 | Caton, Mary C. | 1907 | Box 318 |
| Casey, Silas | 1913 | Box 464 | Caton, Michael | 1858 | Box 26 |
| Casey, Thomas L. | 1896 | Box 160 | Caton, Michael | 1885 | Box 90 |
| Cash, Adale J. | 1906 | Box 297 | Cator, Joseph Thomas | 1912 | Box 438 |
| Cash, John F. | 1912 | Box 438 | Cattell, Beulah B. | 1918 | Box 594 |
| Cash, Leonard | 1860 | Box 28 | Cattell, Henry P. | 1916 | Box 539 |
| Cash, William | 1896 | Box 160 | Caughy, Samuel | 1855 | Box 23 |
| Cashell, Hazel B. | 1886 | Box 95 | Caulfield, Fillippa Estelle | 1910 | Box 386 |
| Casilear, George W. | 1912 | Box 438 | Caulk, Lucy A. | 1899 | Box 182 |
| Caspar, Caspar A. | 1918 | Box 593 | Causin, Nathaniel Pope | 1850 | Box 20 |
| Caspar, Christian | 1898 | Box 174 | Causten, James H. | 1856 | Box 24 |
| Caspar, John | 1882 | Box 78 | Causten, James H. | 1874 | Box 53 |
| Caspar, Josepha | 1899 | Box 182 | Cavanagh, Annie | 1918 | Box 594 |
| Caspari, Henry | 1892 | Box 130 | Cavanagh, Margaret | 1893 | Box 137 |
| Casper, Mary | 1895 | Box 152 | Cavanaugh, Mary E. | 1916 | Box 539 |
| Cassatt, Alexander J. | 1907 | Box 318 | Cavanaugh, Mathew | 1872 | Box 46 |
| Cassedy, Margaret | 1846 | Box 17 | Cavanaugh, Michael H. | 1920 | Box 654 |
| Cassedy, Nicholas | 1836 | Box 13 | Cavanaugh, Timothy | 1913 | Box 464 |
| Cassell, John T. | 1892 | Box 130 | Cavers, Adam | 1901 | Box 205 |
| Cassell, Mary A. | 1903 | Box 241 | Cavers, Caroline I. | 1918 | Box 594 |
| Cassels, Ellen F. | 1917 | Box 566 | Cavis, Adam T. | 1900 | Box 191 |
| Cassels, John | 1908 | Box 340 | Cawood, Hezekiah J. | 1914 | Box 486 |
| Cassidy, Caroline | 1890 | Box 118 | Cawood, Sarah E. | 1920 | Box 654 |
| Cassidy, Margaret | 1901 | Box 205 | Cays, Theodore A. | 1908 | Box 340 |
| Cassidy, Patrick | 1908 | Box 340 | Caywood, Aaron S. | 1918 | Box 594 |
| Cassin, E. Schley | 1919 | Box 623 | Caywood, Benjamin | 1891 | Box 124 |
| Cassin, Eliza | 1866 | Box 35 | Cecil, Edward Elias | 1914 | Box 486 |
| Cassin, Joseph R. | 1891 | Box 124 | Cecil (Cessil), Stewart | 1908 | Box 340 |
| Cassin, Sophia M. | 1858 | Box 26 | Center, Elizabeth M. | 1900 | Box 191 |
| Castell, Edward | 1895 | Box 152 | Center, Katharine M. | 1920 | Box 654 |
| Castella, Susie | 1900 | Box 191 | Cephas, John | 1892 | Box 130 |
| Castleman, Stephen D. | 1889 | Box 112 | Chadsey, Calvin H. | 1914 | Box 486 |
| Caswell, Caroline M. | 1895 | Box 152 | Chadwick, Julia H. | 1910 | Box 386 |
| Catalana, Martha | 1857 | Box 25 | Chadwick, Julia H. | 1914 | Box 486 |
| Catalano, Antonio | 1854 | Box 23 | Chalker, Adeline N. | 1907 | Box 318 |
| Catalano, Salvadore M. | 1846 | Box 17 | Chalmers, Anna M. | 1892 | Box 130 |
| Cate, Aaron B. | 1878 | Box 65 | Chalmers, Leigh | 1904 | Box 260 |
| Cate, Margaret W. | 1920 | Box 654 | Chalmers, Mary Ashbury | 1822 | Box 7 |
| Cate, Rae B. | 1920 | Box 654 | Chamberlain, Abbie M. | 1917 | Box 566 |
| Cathcart, Ellen Weir | 1916 | Box 539 | Chamberlain, Ann Maria | 1894 | Box 144 |
| Cathcart, James Leander | 1844 | Box 16 | Chamberlain, David B. | 1912 | Box 438 |
| Cathell, Jonathan Dennis | 1913 | Box 464 | Chamberlain, Georgia Anna | 1902 | Box 222 |
| Cathin, John R. | 1885 | Box 90 | Chamberlain, Henry B. | 1907 | Box 318 |
| Catilino, Julia | 1866 | Box 35 | Chamberlain, William | 1910 | Box 386 |
| Catlett, John H. | 1918 | Box 594 | Chamberlen, Isadora E. | 1903 | Box 241 |
| Catlin, Caroline | 1896 | Box 160 | Chamberlin, Edward | 1901 | Box 205 |
| Catlin, Charles M. | 1915 | Box 511 | Chamberlin, Edwina Pierpont | 1919 | Box 623 |

| | | | | | | |
|---|---|---|---|---|---|---|
| Chambers, Andrew | 1916 | Box 539 | Chapman, Jane W. | 1910 | Box 386 |
| Chambers, Bessie S. | 1919 | Box 623 | Chapman, Josephine B. | 1891 | Box 124 |
| Chambers, Boone | 1897 | Box 168 | Chapman, M. Velinda | 1916 | Box 539 |
| Chambers, David Abbot | 1907 | Box 318 | Chapman, Mary | 1849 | Box 20 |
| Chambers, Eliza Ann Bohle | 1910 | Box 386 | Chapman, Mary A. | 1919 | Box 623 |
| Chambers, Eliza Anne | 1910 | Box 386 | Chapman, Robert H. | 1918 | Box 594 |
| Chambers, Helen B. | 1916 | Box 539 | Chapman, Robert Hollister | 1920 | Box 655 |
| Chambers, Joana | 1870 | Box 42 | Chapman, Susannah A. | 1906 | Box 297 |
| Chambers, John | 1892 | Box 130 | Chapman, Vincent | 1919 | Box 623 |
| Chambers, Maria | 1920 | Box 654 | Chapman, William K. | 1895 | Box 152 |
| Chambers, Martha Ann | 1880 | Box 71 | Chappel, Maria | 1903 | Box 241 |
| Chambers, Michael | 1920 | Box 654 | Chappelear, James W. | 1919 | Box 623 |
| Chambers, Patrick | 1877 | Box 63 | Chappelear, William H. | 1909 | Box 364 |
| Chambers, William W. | 1911 | Box 413 | Chappell, Alcinda M. | 1915 | Box 512 |
| Champion, Charlotte Amelia | 1917 | Box 566 | Chappell, John | 1821 | Box 6 |
| Champion, Samuel | 1857 | Box 25 | Chappell, Thomas C. | 1916 | Box 539 |
| Champlin, Sarah J. | 1912 | Box 438 | Charles, Audason A. | 1910 | Box 386 |
| Chancey, John T. | 1914 | Box 487 | Charles, Emily Thornton | 1895 | Box 152 |
| Chandlee, Mabel Hurst | 1916 | Box 539 | Charles, Richard A. | 1917 | Box 566 |
| Chandlee, William E. | 1902 | Box 222 | Charlton, Benjamin | 1894 | Box 144 |
| Chandler, Florence Huntley | 1916 | Box 539 | Charlton, Sarah A. S. | 1875 | Box 57 |
| Chandler, Fred C. | 1916 | Box 539 | Chase, Buel B. | 1898 | Box 174 |
| Chandler, George | 1910 | Box 386 | Chase, Clara J. | 1916 | Box 539 |
| Chandler, John | 1902 | Box 222 | Chase, Constantine | 1902 | Box 222 |
| Chandler, Margaret | 1860 | Box 28 | Chase, Elizabeth | 1914 | Box 487 |
| Chandler, Mary | 1862 | Box 30 | Chase, Henry C. | 1914 | Box 487 |
| Chandler, Mary Frances | 1918 | Box 594 | Chase, Isaac McKim | 1903 | Box 241 |
| Chandler, Sallie F. | 1910 | Box 386 | Chase, Lucinda | 1893 | Box 137 |
| Chandler, Sarah E. | 1900 | Box 191 | Chase, Martha Elizabeth | 1913 | Box 464 |
| Chandler, Susan Robins | 1913 | Box 464 | Chase, May M. | 1918 | Box 594 |
| Chandler, William Eaton | 1911 | Box 413 | Chase, Sallie H. M. | 1911 | Box 413 |
| Chandler, Zachariah | 1880 | Box 71 | Chase, Salmon P. | 1873 | Box 50 |
| Chany, Jane Douglas Butler | 1914 | Box 487 | Chase, Samuel | 1841 | Box 15 |
| Chapin, Alvin M. | 1920 | Box 655 | Chase, Sarah A. | 1912 | Box 438 |
| Chapin, Anna S. M. | 1911 | Box 413 | Chase, Sarah E. | 1908 | Box 340 |
| Chapin, Catherine V. | 1893 | Box 137 | Chase, William H. | 1890 | Box 118 |
| Chapin, Erastus M. | 1903 | Box 241 | Chatfield, Alonzo B. | 1920 | Box 655 |
| Chapin, Helen M. | 1911 | Box 413 | Chatman, Roxey | 1903 | Box 241 |
| Chapin, Stephen | 1845 | Box 17 | Chauncey, Catherine | 1886 | Box 96 |
| Chapman, Catharine | 1901 | Box 205 | Chaves, Gregory G. | 1893 | Box 137 |
| Chapman, Charles | 1906 | Box 297 | Cheatham, Adelicia | 1889 | Box 112 |
| Chapman, Cyrus Durand | 1918 | Box 594 | Chedal, James D. | 1882 | Box 78 |
| Chapman, Daniel C. | 1895 | Box 152 | Cheesman, Roland C. | 1910 | Box 386 |
| Chapman, Edward | 1865 | Box 33 | Chelini, Elia | 1901 | Box 206 |
| Chapman, Ellen Thornton | 1916 | Box 539 | Cheney, James William | 1919 | Box 623 |
| Chapman, Etta Sperry | 1920 | Box 655 | Chenoweth, Frances A. | 1899 | Box 182 |
| Chapman, Fannie | 1906 | Box 297 | Cherry, Charles H. | 1918 | Box 594 |
| Chapman, George R. | 1905 | Box 278 | Cherry, George W. | 1856 | Box 24 |
| Chapman, Helen Mary | 1913 | Box 464 | Cherry, John | 1884 | Box 85 |
| Chapman, Henry B. | 1906 | Box 297 | Cherry, Mary A. | 1908 | Box 340 |
| Chapman, James | 1869 | Box 40 | Cheshire, Bessie Boone | 1909 | Box 364 |
| Chapman, James W. | 1900 | Box 191 | Cheshire, Laura | 1846 | Box 17 |

| | | | | | | |
|---|---|---|---|---|---|---|
| Cheshire, William W. | 1909 | Box 364 | Christie, Arthur | 1891 | Box 124 |
| Chesley, Charles | 1909 | Box 364 | Christie, Carrie C. | 1913 | Box 464 |
| Chesley, Katharine W. | 1894 | Box 144 | Christine, Cecilia | 1862 | Box 30 |
| Chester, James | 1903 | Box 241 | Christine, Josephine B. | 1911 | Box 413 |
| Chester, John | 1910 | Box 386 | Christlmiller, Mathias | 1882 | Box 78 |
| Chew, Amanda J. | 1911 | Box 413 | Christman, Byron | 1901 | Box 206 |
| Chew, Cassandra | 1811 | Box 3 | Christman, Emilie A. C. | 1876 | Box 60 |
| Chew, Elizabeth R. | 1899 | Box 182 | Christman, Hettie | 1909 | Box 364 |
| Chew, Harry L. | 1898 | Box 174 | Chubb, Charles St. J. | 1913 | Box 464 |
| Chew, John H. | 1885 | Box 90 | Chubb, Eliza Crane Warrington | 1909 | Box 364 |
| Chew, John Hamilton | 1916 | Box 540 | Chubb, Isaac Munroe | 1856 | Box 24 |
| Chew, John J. | 1916 | Box 540 | Chubb, Stedman C. | 1890 | Box 118 |
| Chew, Louis F. | 1918 | Box 594 | Church, Charles B. | 1908 | Box 340 |
| Chew, Sophia Genevieve | 1902 | Box 222 | Church, Joseph B. | 1914 | Box 487 |
| Chew, Thomas John | 1904 | Box 260 | Church, Margaret A. | 1913 | Box 464 |
| Chew, Walter | 1842 | Box 15 | Church, Margaret Woodward | 1915 | Box 512 |
| Chewning, William Samuel | 1911 | Box 413 | Churchill, William | 1920 | Box 655 |
| Chiaventoni, Giovanni B. | 1911 | Box 413 | Churchwell, Maria | 1901 | Box 206 |
| Chicester, Mary | 1872 | Box 46 | Cilley, Alice L. | 1905 | Box 278 |
| Chichester, Harry D. | 1911 | Box 413 | Ciscle, James | 1907 | Box 318 |
| Chickering, John White | 1888 | Box 106 | Cissel, Agnes C. | 1920 | Box 655 |
| Childs, Albert F. | 1902 | Box 222 | Cissel, George W. | 1904 | Box 260 |
| Childs, Charles H. | 1899 | Box 182 | Cissel, Thomas | 1908 | Box 340 |
| Childs, Eben L. | 1872 | Box 46 | Cissel, William Henry Harrison | 1914 | Box 487 |
| Childs, Elizabeth M. | 1905 | Box 278 | Cissell, Jeremiah | 1854 | Box 23 |
| Childs, Frank H. | 1919 | Box 623 | Clabaugh, Harry M. | 1914 | Box 487 |
| Childs, Jacob | 1891 | Box 124 | Claflin, Price C. | 1915 | Box 512 |
| Childs, Jane Lavenia Conover | 1909 | Box 364 | Clagett, Adele | 1920 | Box 655 |
| Childs, Margaret M. | 1912 | Box 438 | Clagett, Dorsey | 1899 | Box 182 |
| Childs, Mary | 1870 | Box 42 | Clagett, Hezekiah | 1894 | Box 144 |
| Childs, William E. | 1891 | Box 124 | Clagett, John Rozier | 1902 | Box 222 |
| Chinn, Caroline | 1898 | Box 174 | Clagett, Lucinda | 1912 | Box 438 |
| Chinn, Elizabeth Abbott | 1856 | Box 24 | Clagett, Mary A. | 1903 | Box 241 |
| Chipman, Amos James | 1915 | Box 512 | Clagett, Nathaniel | 1810 | Box 3 |
| Chipman, Emma A. | 1911 | Box 413 | Clagett, Susan A. | 1912 | Box 438 |
| Chipman, George | 1870 | Box 42 | Clagett, Thomas | 1876 | Box 60 |
| Chipman, Sarah Jane | 1885 | Box 90 | Clagett, William H. | 1892 | Box 130 |
| Chipp, Elizabeth | 1904 | Box 260 | Clagett, Willie Brice | 1891 | Box 124 |
| Chisholm, Catharine | 1873 | Box 50 | Claggett, David | 1863 | Box 31 |
| Chisholm, Emily | 1876 | Box 60 | Claggett, Harriet | 1888 | Box 106 |
| Chisholm, John A. | 1903 | Box 241 | Claggett, Hezekiah | 1888 | Box 106 |
| Chism, Elizabeth | 1902 | Box 222 | Clancy, Ann | 1892 | Box 130 |
| Chisolm, Emily S. M. | 1905 | Box 278 | Clancy, Daniel | 1915 | Box 512 |
| Chisolm, Frederic Fraser | 1911 | Box 413 | Clancy, John | 1908 | Box 340 |
| Chrisman, Dorothy Pauline | 1915 | Box 512 | Clancy, M. Agnes | 1913 | Box 464 |
| Chrisman, George W. | 1891 | Box 124 | Clancy, Michael A. | 1903 | Box 241 |
| Christian, Charles H. | 1907 | Box 318 | Clapham, Ann Maria | 1903 | Box 241 |
| Christian, Margaret | 1911 | Box 413 | Clapham, John | 1864 | Box 32 |
| Christian, Solomon | 1899 | Box 182 | Clapp, Almon W. | 1899 | Box 182 |
| Christiani, Antoinette DeSilver | 1911 | Box 413 | Clapp, Anna P. | 1911 | Box 413 |
| Christiani, Charles | 1899 | Box 182 | Clapp, Benjamin | 1897 | Box 168 |
| Christiansen, Bertha | 1918 | Box 594 | Clapp, Edward Dwight | 1916 | Box 540 |

| | | | | | | |
|---|---|---|---|---|---|---|
| Clapp, Emily B. | 1869 | Box 40 | Clark, Louisa M. | 1906 | Box 297 |
| Clapp, Emma Edmonston | 1918 | Box 594 | Clark, Mandamus | 1911 | Box 413 |
| Clapp, Henry H. | 1908 | Box 340 | Clark, Margaret | 1918 | Box 594 |
| Clapp, John M. | 1908 | Box 340 | Clark, Maria J. | 1891 | Box 124 |
| Clapp, Roland | 1828 | Box 9 | Clark, Martha M. L. | 1915 | Box 512 |
| Clapp, Woodbridge | 1919 | Box 623 | Clark, Mary | 1870 | Box 42 |
| Clark, A. Howard | 1919 | Box 623 | Clark, Mary | 1891 | Box 124 |
| Clark, Anna Maria | 1824 | Box 8 | Clark, Mary A. | 1874 | Box 53 |
| Clark, Annie E. | 1911 | Box 413 | Clark, Mary Ann | 1866 | Box 35 |
| Clark, Aurelia B. | 1920 | Box 655 | Clark, Mary F. | 1891 | Box 124 |
| Clark, Benjamin W. | 1915 | Box 512 | Clark, Mary H. Dorlon | 1903 | Box 241 |
| Clark, Charles B. | 1917 | Box 566 | Clark, Matilda | 1884 | Box 85 |
| Clark, Charles T. | 1819 | Box 6 | Clark, Nathan Beach | 1892 | Box 130 |
| Clark, Clara D. | 1917 | Box 566 | Clark, Otho | 1865 | Box 33 |
| Clark, Delilah | 1883 | Box 82 | Clark, Philip | 1919 | Box 623 |
| Clark, Edward Elmo | 1910 | Box 386 | Clark, Reuben B. | 1902 | Box 222 |
| Clark, Eliza | 1845 | Box 17 | Clark, Rosanna W. | 1913 | Box 464 |
| Clark, Eliza | 1918 | Box 594 | Clark, Samuel | 1865 | Box 33 |
| Clark, Ellen S. | 1878 | Box 65 | Clark, Samuel | 1873 | Box 50 |
| Clark, Emeline | 1888 | Box 106 | Clark, Sarah | 1884 | Box 85 |
| Clark, Emily A. | 1915 | Box 512 | Clark, Sarah | 1915 | Box 512 |
| Clark, George P. | 1920 | Box 655 | Clark, Sarah Pearce | 1910 | Box 386 |
| Clark, Gowen | 1872 | Box 46 | Clark, Seth L. | 1913 | Box 464 |
| Clark, Henrietta M. | 1912 | Box 438 | Clark, Susan | 1895 | Box 152 |
| Clark, Henry A. | 1908 | Box 340 | Clark, Susan V. | 1895 | Box 152 |
| Clark, Ignatius | 1881 | Box 74 | Clark, Thomas | 1862 | Box 30 |
| Clark, Jacob P. | 1911 | Box 413 | Clark, Thomas Fisher | 1892 | Box 130 |
| Clark, James | 1892 | Box 130 | Clark, William | 1837 | Box 13 |
| Clark, James | 1894 | Box 144 | Clark, William E. | 1895 | Box 152 |
| Clark, James | 1896 | Box 160 | Clark, William F. | 1903 | Box 241 |
| Clark, James | 1920 | Box 655 | Clark, William H. | 1913 | Box 464 |
| Clark, James Edwin | 1909 | Box 364 | Clark, William H. T. | 1874 | Box 53 |
| Clark, James J. | 1919 | Box 623 | Clark, William L. | 1919 | Box 623 |
| Clark, James S. | 1892 | Box 130 | Clarke, Albert | 1915 | Box 512 |
| Clark, Jane | 1888 | Box 106 | Clarke, Amorett J. | 1890 | Box 118 |
| Clark, Jane | 1893 | Box 137 | Clarke, Anna Maria | 1904 | Box 260 |
| Clark, John | 1805 | Box 1 | Clarke, Anna Rhea | 1850 | Box 20 |
| Clark, John | 1875 | Box 57 | Clarke, Annie Phillips | 1911 | Box 413 |
| Clark, John | 1877 | Box 63 | Clarke, Anthony J. | 1918 | Box 594 |
| Clark, John | 1890 | Box 118 | Clarke, Asaph M. | 1920 | Box 655 |
| Clark, John | 1916 | Box 540 | Clarke, Bernard A. | 1917 | Box 566 |
| Clark, John H. | 1900 | Box 191 | Clarke, Daniel B. | 1906 | Box 297 |
| Clark, John H. | 1900 | Box 191 | Clarke, Elizabeth | 1840 | Box 15 |
| Clark, John T. | 1897 | Box 168 | Clarke, Ellen | 1877 | Box 63 |
| Clark, John W. | 1918 | Box 594 | Clarke, Ephraim | 1872 | Box 46 |
| Clark, Joseph | 1835 | Box 12 | Clarke, Ethan C. | 1889 | Box 112 |
| Clark, Joshua | 1900 | Box 191 | Clarke, F. H. | 1870 | Box 42 |
| Clark, Julia B. | 1913 | Box 464 | Clarke, Francis G. | 1910 | Box 387 |
| Clark, June Hayden | 1915 | Box 512 | Clarke, Francis W. | 1873 | Box 50 |
| Clark, Lemuel F. | 1880 | Box 71 | Clarke, George T. | 1916 | Box 540 |
| Clark, Lena | 1920 | Box 655 | Clarke, George W. | 1905 | Box 278 |
| Clark, Letitia | 1870 | Box 42 | Clarke, Henry A. | 1898 | Box 174 |

| | | | | | | |
|---|---|---|---|---|---|---|
| Clarke, Henry D. | 1900 | Box 191 | | Clayton, John | 1916 | Box 540 |
| Clarke, Henry Francis | 1887 | Box 102 | | Clayton, John M. | 1857 | Box 25 |
| Clarke, Isaac | 1861 | Box 29 | | Clayton, Powell | 1915 | Box 512 |
| Clarke, J. Brainard | 1915 | Box 512 | | Clayton, Powell Jr. | 1917 | Box 566 |
| Clarke, James P. | 1911 | Box 413 | | Cleary, Elizabeth McCloskey | 1917 | Box 566 |
| Clarke, John | 1860 | Box 28 | | Cleary, John | 1905 | Box 278 |
| Clarke, John W. | 1904 | Box 260 | | Cleaveland, Frank Edward | 1910 | Box 387 |
| Clarke, Joseph | 1871 | Box 44 | | Cleaveland, Persis A. | 1908 | Box 340 |
| Clarke, Julia A. | 1887 | Box 102 | | Cleaver, Charles R. | 1912 | Box 438 |
| Clarke, Katherine Young | 1912 | Box 438 | | Cleaver, David W. | 1908 | Box 340 |
| Clarke, Lucian A. | 1919 | Box 623 | | Cleaver, Frank M. | 1918 | Box 594 |
| Clarke, M. Pauline | 1918 | Box 594 | | Cleaves, Elizabeth A. | 1915 | Box 512 |
| Clarke, Mary A. | 1909 | Box 364 | | Cleaves, Thomas P. | 1911 | Box 413 |
| Clarke, Mary A. | 1920 | Box 655 | | Clement, Elizabeth | 1917 | Box 566 |
| Clarke, Mary L. | 1920 | Box 655 | | Clement, Josephine A. | 1917 | Box 566 |
| Clarke, Michael F. | 1918 | Box 594 | | Clement, Sarah E. | 1920 | Box 655 |
| Clarke, Nancy | 1873 | Box 50 | | Clements, Alban | 1851 | Box 21 |
| Clarke, Nathan B. | 1888 | Box 106 | | Clements, Alexander | 1866 | Box 35 |
| Clarke, Nathaniel Stanley | 1899 | Box 182 | | Clements, Annie | 1916 | Box 540 |
| Clarke, Rachel | 1861 | Box 29 | | Clements, Arthur | 1903 | Box 242 |
| Clarke, Robert D. | 1891 | Box 124 | | Clements, Bennett | 1863 | Box 31 |
| Clarke, Rose L. | 1912 | Box 438 | | Clements, E. Marion | 1902 | Box 223 |
| Clarke, Sarah H. F. | 1908 | Box 340 | | Clements, Elizabeth | 1810 | Box 3 |
| Clarke, Sarah Robertina | 1905 | Box 278 | | Clements, Hester A. | 1888 | Box 106 |
| Clarke, Sarah Van Allen | 1904 | Box 260 | | Clements, Ignatius N. | 1857 | Box 25 |
| Clarke, Saterlee | 1849 | Box 20 | | Clements, James T. | 1911 | Box 413 |
| Clarke, Thomas | 1860 | Box 28 | | Clements, John T. | 1872 | Box 47 |
| Clarke, Walter M. | 1856 | Box 24 | | Clements, Joseph | 1913 | Box 464 |
| Clarke, William | 1807 | Box 2 | | Clements, Louisa | 1888 | Box 106 |
| Clarke, William | 1823 | Box 7 | | Clements, Martha | 1825 | Box 8 |
| Clarke, William | 1868 | Box 39 | | Clements, Mary Ann | 1834 | Box 12 |
| Clarke, William F. | 1895 | Box 152 | | Clements, Mary Ann | 1897 | Box 168 |
| Clarke, William Penniman | 1903 | Box 241 | | Clements, Mary E. | 1914 | Box 487 |
| Clarkson, Annie | 1910 | Box 387 | | Clements, Rachel | 1868 | Box 39 |
| Clarkson, Caroline | 1904 | Box 261 | | Clements, Richard | 1864 | Box 32 |
| Clarkson, Courtenaye Neville N. | 1918 | Box 594 | | Clements, Samuel | 1885 | Box 91 |
| Clarkson, Gertrude V. | 1920 | Box 655 | | Clements, Thomas | 1896 | Box 160 |
| Clarkson, Robert | 1909 | Box 364 | | Clemmer, Mary | 1885 | Box 90 |
| Clarridge, James A. | 1903 | Box 241 | | Clendening, James W. | 1909 | Box 364 |
| Clary, Ann T. | 1899 | Box 182 | | Clephane, Alan O. | 1918 | Box 594 |
| Clary, Annie A. | 1916 | Box 540 | | Clephane, Edith L. | 1919 | Box 624 |
| Clary, Clara J. | 1915 | Box 512 | | Clephane, Julia | 1903 | Box 242 |
| Clary, James D. | 1885 | Box 90 | | Clephane, Lewis | 1897 | Box 168 |
| Clary, Robert E. | 1890 | Box 118 | | Cleveland, David G. | 1913 | Box 464 |
| Clary, Wilbert | 1909 | Box 364 | | Cleveland, Grover | 1910 | Box 387 |
| Clary, William S. | 1863 | Box 31 | | Clevenger, John D. | 1919 | Box 624 |
| Claudy, Mary J. | 1896 | Box 160 | | Clevinger, Jacob A. | 1915 | Box 512 |
| Clay, George Henry | 1919 | Box 624 | | Clifford, Edwin A. | 1904 | Box 261 |
| Clayborn, Susan | 1904 | Box 261 | | Clifford, Eliza Geraldine | 1912 | Box 438 |
| Claybron, David | 1903 | Box 241 | | Clifford, Julia M. | 1905 | Box 278 |
| Clayton, Adeline | 1917 | Box 566 | | Clifton, Charles R. | 1885 | Box 90 |
| Clayton, Ella M. | 1919 | Box 624 | | Clifton, Frances A. | 1838 | Box 14 |

37

| | | | | | | |
|---|---|---|---|---|---|---|
| Cling, Ann M. | 1895 | Box 152 | Cochran, John | 1898 | Box 174 |
| Clinkins, Edward | 1906 | Box 297 | Cochran, Rosa M. | 1914 | Box 487 |
| Clinton, Anna M. | 1905 | Box 278 | Cochrane, John T. | 1866 | Box 35 |
| Clinton, Thomas G. | 1859 | Box 27 | Cock, Alfred | 1919 | Box 624 |
| Clipper, William | 1903 | Box 242 | Cocke, Edward | 1900 | Box 191 |
| Clitch, Frederick | 1847 | Box 18 | Cockerille, Hevila R. | 1911 | Box 413 |
| Clitch, Henrietta | 1873 | Box 50 | Cockerille, Samuel J. | 1903 | Box 242 |
| Cloe, Fannie | 1908 | Box 341 | Cockley, John A. | 1914 | Box 487 |
| Clokey, Susan R. | 1903 | Box 242 | Cockran, Rhoda E. | 1897 | Box 168 |
| Clomax, Jefferson | 1916 | Box 540 | Cockshutt, James George | 1886 | Box 96 |
| Clorivier, Joseph Pierre de | 1826 | Box 8 | Codman, Susan | 1888 | Box 107 |
| Close, Margarett | 1897 | Box 168 | Coe, Spencer A. | 1892 | Box 130 |
| Closs, Frank P. | 1904 | Box 261 | Coethen, Josephine Jost | 1880 | Box 71 |
| Closson, Henry W. | 1917 | Box 566 | Coeyman, William H. | 1895 | Box 152 |
| Closson, Julia W. | 1913 | Box 464 | Coffee, Patrick H. | 1895 | Box 152 |
| Clover, Elizabeth | 1915 | Box 512 | Coffey, Catharine | 1906 | Box 297 |
| Clover, Lewis Pierre | 1915 | Box 512 | Coffey, Mary Kerr | 1913 | Box 464 |
| Clover, Mary Eudora Miller | 1920 | Box 655 | Coffey, Patrick J. | 1907 | Box 318 |
| Clover, Richardson | 1919 | Box 624 | Coffey, Titian J. | 1897 | Box 168 |
| Clubb, John L. | 1875 | Box 57 | Coffin, George Y. | 1896 | Box 160 |
| Clubb, Miranda | 1897 | Box 168 | Coffin, Henry W. | 1916 | Box 540 |
| Clunie, Thomas J. | 1904 | Box 261 | Coffin, John H. C. | 1897 | Box 168 |
| Cluss, Adolf | 1905 | Box 278 | Coffin, Warren J. | 1915 | Box 512 |
| Clymer, George | 1881 | Box 74 | Coffin, William Harrison | 1912 | Box 438 |
| Clymer, Mary Shubrick | 1902 | Box 223 | Coflin, Harriet Buxton | 1909 | Box 364 |
| Coakley, Lucy | 1879 | Box 68 | Cogan, Edward T. | 1916 | Box 540 |
| Coakley, Mary E. | 1908 | Box 341 | Cogan, Gertrude | 1901 | Box 206 |
| Coakley, Thomas | 1906 | Box 297 | Cogan, James | 1908 | Box 341 |
| Coale, Charles R. | 1902 | Box 223 | Cogan, Loretta F. | 1917 | Box 566 |
| Coale, Edward J. | 1832 | Box 11 | Cogan, Mary | 1897 | Box 168 |
| Coale, John | 1894 | Box 144 | Cogan, Thomas | 1874 | Box 53 |
| Coale, Samuel | 1894 | Box 144 | Cogan, William J. | 1920 | Box 655 |
| Coates, Ann E. | 1906 | Box 297 | Coger, Ann | 1896 | Box 160 |
| Coates, Anthony | 1891 | Box 124 | Coger, Charles | 1896 | Box 160 |
| Coates, Charles Henry | 1910 | Box 387 | Coger, Frank | 1889 | Box 112 |
| Coates, Edwin Morton | 1913 | Box 464 | Coggins, Elizabeth | 1888 | Box 107 |
| Coates, James | 1920 | Box 655 | Coggins, Harry | 1908 | Box 341 |
| Coates, James E. | 1918 | Box 594 | Coggins, John | 1880 | Box 71 |
| Coates, John H. | 1901 | Box 206 | Cogswell, Benjamin S. | 1908 | Box 341 |
| Cobb, Mary C. | 1894 | Box 144 | Cogswell, Bertha T. | 1918 | Box 594 |
| Cobb, Nehemiah | 1894 | Box 144 | Cohan, Cornelius | 1883 | Box 82 |
| Coblenzer, Simon | 1899 | Box 182 | Cohen, Benjamin Julius | 1910 | Box 387 |
| Coblintz, Alta Z. | 1913 | Box 464 | Cohen, Edward | 1905 | Box 278 |
| Coburn, F. S. | 1902 | Box 223 | Cohen, Fannie | 1907 | Box 318 |
| Coburn, Joseph A. | 1870 | Box 42 | Cohen, Fannie | 1913 | Box 464 |
| Cochnower, Effie Hupert | 1915 | Box 512 | Cohen, George | 1906 | Box 297 |
| Cochnower, Frances | 1912 | Box 438 | Cohen, Henrietta | 1918 | Box 594 |
| Cochran, Anna | 1860 | Box 28 | Cohen, Mary E. | 1913 | Box 464 |
| Cochran, David | 1827 | Box 9 | Cohen, Philip | 1913 | Box 464 |
| Cochran, George Washington | 1899 | Box 182 | Cohen, Robert | 1880 | Box 71 |
| Cochran, Grace | 1825 | Box 8 | Cohen, Robert | 1909 | Box 364 |
| Cochran, Henry D. | 1909 | Box 364 | Cohill, Henry R. | 1900 | Box 191 |

| | | | | | | |
|---|---|---|---|---|---|---|
| Coker, John | 1907 | Box 318 | Colgate, Sarah R. | 1906 | Box 297 |
| Colbert, John | 1874 | Box 53 | Colhoun, Edmund R. | 1910 | Box 387 |
| Colbert, John | 1909 | Box 364 | Colhoun, J. Ross | 1919 | Box 624 |
| Colbert, Margaret C. | 1916 | Box 540 | Colhoun, Mary A. | 1916 | Box 540 |
| Colbert, Nicholas | 1915 | Box 512 | Colison, Charles C. | 1910 | Box 387 |
| Colbert, Pauline | 1917 | Box 566 | Colison, George Z. | 1914 | Box 487 |
| Colbrey, Agnes G. | 1917 | Box 566 | Coliston, Mary | 1915 | Box 512 |
| Colburn, Emily E. | 1889 | Box 112 | Coliston, Thomas | 1895 | Box 125 |
| Colburn, George F. J. | 1897 | Box 168 | Collamore, Andrew W. | 1898 | Box 174 |
| Colburn, Justin E. | 1879 | Box 68 | Collard, Eliza S. | 1873 | Box 50 |
| Colburn, Mary | 1896 | Box 160 | Collard, George | 1815 | Box 4 |
| Colby, Stoddard B. | 1867 | Box 37 | Collard, George | 1875 | Box 57 |
| Colclazier, Francis W. | 1892 | Box 130 | Collet, John | 1814 | Box 4 |
| Colclazier, Jacob | 1878 | Box 65 | Collins, Agnes Barton | 1916 | Box 540 |
| Coldwell, Laura Wilson | 1919 | Box 624 | Collins, Alfred | 1885 | Box 91 |
| Cole, Alvin B. | 1847 | Box 18 | Collins, Annie M. | 1912 | Box 438 |
| Cole, Annie | 1898 | Box 174 | Collins, Elizabeth | 1842 | Box 15 |
| Cole, Annie A. | 1914 | Box 487 | Collins, Elizabeth | 1884 | Box 85 |
| Cole, Barney | 1905 | Box 278 | Collins, Elizabeth | 1920 | Box 655 |
| Cole, Benjamin F. | 1911 | Box 413 | Collins, Ellen | 1915 | Box 512 |
| Cole, Bertha Elizabeth | 1916 | Box 540 | Collins, Ezra P. | 1916 | Box 540 |
| Cole, Elizabeth | 1824 | Box 8 | Collins, Frederick W. | 1904 | Box 261 |
| Cole, Elizabeth S. | 1920 | Box 655 | Collins, George W. | 1883 | Box 82 |
| Cole, Hiram | 1890 | Box 118 | Collins, Hannah | 1908 | Box 341 |
| Cole, Maria | 1891 | Box 124 | Collins, Harriet | 1909 | Box 364 |
| Cole, Mary Virginia | 1885 | Box 91 | Collins, Hezikiah | 1841 | Box 15 |
| Cole, William | 1886 | Box 96 | Collins, Jacob H. | 1900 | Box 191 |
| Cole, William P. | 1897 | Box 168 | Collins, John | 1873 | Box 50 |
| Cole, Wilson | 1904 | Box 261 | Collins, John | 1877 | Box 63 |
| Cole, Wyman L. | 1899 | Box 182 | Collins, John | 1884 | Box 85 |
| Colegate, Elizabeth M. | 1889 | Box 112 | Collins, John | 1907 | Box 318 |
| Colegate, James Hall | 1897 | Box 168 | Collins, John F. | 1913 | Box 464 |
| Colegate, Mary | 1868 | Box 39 | Collins, John J. | 1915 | Box 513 |
| Colegrove, James B. | 1909 | Box 364 | Collins, John P. | 1900 | Box 191 |
| Coleman, Aaron Samuel | 1888 | Box 107 | Collins, John W. | 1917 | Box 566 |
| Coleman, Alfred D. | 1911 | Box 413 | Collins, Joseph B. | 1889 | Box 112 |
| Coleman, Anna M. Stilwell | 1907 | Box 318 | Collins, Joseph F. | 1902 | Box 223 |
| Coleman, Anna Maria | 1904 | Box 261 | Collins, Kate | 1917 | Box 566 |
| Coleman, Bridget A. | 1915 | Box 512 | Collins, Lewis | 1897 | Box 168 |
| Coleman, Charles | 1865 | Box 33 | Collins, Mary | 1898 | Box 174 |
| Coleman, David E. | 1894 | Box 144 | Collins, Mary Amelia | 1917 | Box 566 |
| Coleman, Elender Adelaide | 1914 | Box 487 | Collins, Mary V. | 1913 | Box 465 |
| Coleman, Elias | 1874 | Box 53 | Collins, Maurice | 1915 | Box 513 |
| Coleman, Elizabeth F. | 1918 | Box 595 | Collins, Nellie | 1919 | Box 624 |
| Coleman, Henry | 1891 | Box 124 | Collins, Otto Harald | 1908 | Box 341 |
| Coleman, James | 1905 | Box 278 | Collins, Patrick J. | 1919 | Box 624 |
| Coleman, Jerry | 1885 | Box 91 | Collins, Richard | 1904 | Box 261 |
| Coleman, Mary | 1908 | Box 341 | Collins, Richard J. | 1896 | Box 160 |
| Coleman, Mary A. | 1917 | Box 566 | Collins, Robert | 1858 | Box 26 |
| Coleman, Philip W. | 1909 | Box 364 | Collins, Samuel A. | 1920 | Box 655 |
| Coleman, Sarah H. | 1893 | Box 137 | Collins, Samuel H. | 1916 | Box 540 |
| Coles, Mary Alverta | 1903 | Box 242 | Collins, Sarah | 1910 | Box 387 |

| | | | | | | |
|---|---|---|---|---|---|---|
| Collins, Sarah B. | 1920 | Box 655 | | Condict, Aretta G. | 1905 | Box 278 |
| Collins, Sarah D. | 1896 | Box 160 | | Condit-Smith, Sarah S. | 1908 | Box 341 |
| Collins, Thomas | 1851 | Box 21 | | Condon, Clarence M. | 1916 | Box 540 |
| Collins, Thomas | 1909 | Box 364 | | Condon, John R. | 1886 | Box 96 |
| Collins, Thomas | 1872 | Box 47 | | Condron, Abby N. | 1884 | Box 85 |
| Collins, Thomas H. | 1885 | Box 91 | | Conger, Stella B. | 1893 | Box 137 |
| Collins, Thomas P. | 1896 | Box 160 | | Congwer, Clara M. | 1919 | Box 628 |
| Collins, Varnum Daniel | 1900 | Box 191 | | Conine, William C. | 1884 | Box 85 |
| Collins, Walter F. | 1911 | Box 413 | | Conkling, Sarah B. | 1904 | Box 261 |
| Collins, William H. | 1903 | Box 242 | | Conlan, Maria F. | 1888 | Box 107 |
| Collins, William H. | 1907 | Box 318 | | Conlan, Peter | 1875 | Box 57 |
| Collison, Peter J. | 1869 | Box 40 | | Conlee, Augusta P. | 1910 | Box 387 |
| Colman, Charles D. | 1891 | Box 124 | | Conley, Catherine | 1917 | Box 566 |
| Colman, Clara | 1900 | Box 191 | | Conley, Elizabeth | 1896 | Box 160 |
| Colman, Jane E. | 1920 | Box 655 | | Conley, Elizabeth | 1912 | Box 438 |
| Colman, Moses | 1915 | Box 513 | | Conley, Helen M. | 1899 | Box 182 |
| Colman, Patrick | 1864 | Box 32 | | Conlon, John | 1906 | Box 297 |
| Colnan, John | 1915 | Box 513 | | Conlon, Michael | 1915 | Box 513 |
| Colquhoun, William S. | 1863 | Box 31 | | Connell, Dennis | 1891 | Box 124 |
| Colquitt, Mel R. | 1920 | Box 656 | | Connell, Dennis | 1898 | Box 174 |
| Coltman, Charles | 1861 | Box 29 | | Connell, John | 1907 | Box 318 |
| Coltman, Charles F. A. | 1866 | Box 35 | | Connell, Kate E. | 1912 | Box 438 |
| Coltman, Rebecca | 1894 | Box 144 | | Connell, Margaret | 1915 | Box 513 |
| Coltman, Sophia E. | 1871 | Box 44 | | Connell, Matthew | 1901 | Box 206 |
| Colton, Ellen M. | 1908 | Box 341 | | Connell, Robert | 1846 | Box 18 |
| Colton, Francis | 1913 | Box 465 | | Connelly, Bridget | 1832 | Box 11 |
| Colton, Harvey V. | 1910 | Box 387 | | Connelly, Michael C. | 1915 | Box 513 |
| Colton, Ida L. | 1908 | Box 341 | | Connelly, Sarah A. | 1907 | Box 318 |
| Columbus, Edward W. | 1895 | Box 152 | | Conner, George W. | 1916 | Box 540 |
| Colville, Alice J. | 1916 | Box 540 | | Conner, Harry | 1917 | Box 567 |
| Colvin, Jeremiah | 1881 | Box 74 | | Conner, Hattie Alma | 1907 | Box 318 |
| Colwell, Walter E. | 1914 | Box 487 | | Conner, Lendell A. | 1914 | Box 487 |
| Comalander, Jemima H. | 1914 | Box 487 | | Conner, Mary A. | 1907 | Box 318 |
| Combe, Sarah Lucile | 1918 | Box 595 | | Conner, Nelson | 1895 | Box 152 |
| Comber, John B. | 1915 | Box 513 | | Conner, Samuel W. | 1910 | Box 387 |
| Combs, Ann | 1848 | Box 19 | | Conner, William W. | 1866 | Box 35 |
| Combs, Annie E. | 1914 | Box 487 | | Connick, Ann R. | 1916 | Box 540 |
| Combs, Ignatius George | 1892 | Box 130 | | Connolly, Charles A. | 1895 | Box 152 |
| Combs, Joseph | 1879 | Box 68 | | Connolly, Charles M. | 1869 | Box 40 |
| Combs, Mary Emma | 1919 | Box 624 | | Connolly, John | 1901 | Box 206 |
| Combs, Robert M. | 1870 | Box 42 | | Connolly, Lavinia G. | 1889 | Box 112 |
| Commagere, Anita M. | 1896 | Box 160 | | Connolly, Margaret | 1902 | Box 223 |
| Commet, Mary Ann | 1813 | Box 4 | | Connolly, Margaret W. | 1893 | Box 137 |
| Compton, Alice E. | 1909 | Box 364 | | Connolly, Mary | 1908 | Box 341 |
| Comstock, Carolyn M. | 1919 | Box 624 | | Connolly, Mary Ann | 1910 | Box 387 |
| Comstock, Elsie W. | 1894 | Box 145 | | Connolly, Patrick | 1892 | Box 130 |
| Comstock, John M. | 1899 | Box 182 | | Connolly, Thomas C. | 1878 | Box 65 |
| Comstock, John Milton | 1885 | Box 91 | | Connoly, Laurence | 1805 | Box 1 |
| Comstock, Rosilla M. | 1910 | Box 387 | | Connor, Abigail | 1909 | Box 364 |
| Comstock, Sarah C. | 1919 | Box 624 | | Connor, Alice H. | 1916 | Box 540 |
| Conant, Charles A. | 1915 | Box 513 | | Connor, Catharine | 1908 | Box 341 |
| Conard, William | 1896 | Box 160 | | Connor, Catherine | 1902 | Box 223 |

| | | | | | | |
|---|---|---|---|---|---|---|---|
| Connor, Cathrine | 1873 | Box 50 | | Cook, Anna | 1906 | Box 297 |
| Connor, Charles E. | 1892 | Box 130 | | Cook, Anna E. | 1899 | Box 182 |
| Connor, Christopher | 1884 | Box 85 | | Cook, Betsey | 1888 | Box 107 |
| Connor, Hanna | 1916 | Box 540 | | Cook, Charles Ferguson | 1920 | Box 656 |
| Connor, Hugh Edward | 1888 | Box 107 | | Cook, Edward F. | 1920 | Box 656 |
| Connor, James | 1859 | Box 27 | | Cook, Elizabeth | 1890 | Box 118 |
| Connor, James A. | 1909 | Box 364 | | Cook, Elizabeth Ann | 1919 | Box 624 |
| Connor, Jemima B. | 1867 | Box 37 | | Cook, Emelia | 1909 | Box 364 |
| Connor, John | 1857 | Box 25 | | Cook, Emma P. | 1908 | Box 341 |
| Connor, John | 1884 | Box 85 | | Cook, Fenton | 1909 | Box 364 |
| Connor, John | 1912 | Box 438 | | Cook, Hattie C. | 1911 | Box 413 |
| Connor, John | 1916 | Box 540 | | Cook, Jane | 1914 | Box 487 |
| Connor, Louisa Gertrude | 1919 | Box 624 | | Cook, John | 1910 | Box 387 |
| Connor, Margaret | 1903 | Box 242 | | Cook, John | 1915 | Box 513 |
| Connor, Mary | 1904 | Box 261 | | Cook, John H. | 1879 | Box 68 |
| Connor, Michael | 1900 | Box 191 | | Cook, John H. | 1911 | Box 413 |
| Connor, Patrick | 1898 | Box 174 | | Cook, Lawrence H. A. | 1919 | Box 624 |
| Connor, Sarah A. | 1892 | Box 130 | | Cook, Lewellyn M. | 1920 | Box 656 |
| Connoway, Addison | 1854 | Box 23 | | Cook, Margaret A. | 1872 | Box 47 |
| Conover, Cornelius | 1901 | Box 206 | | Cook, Martin | 1833 | Box 12 |
| Conover, Emeline | 1902 | Box 223 | | Cook, Mary | 1853 | Box 22 |
| Conover, Samuel F. | 1885 | Box 91 | | Cook, Mary A. | 1907 | Box 318 |
| Conrad, Casper H. | 1899 | Box 182 | | Cook, Mary E. | 1906 | Box 297 |
| Conrad, Elizabeth J. | 1916 | Box 540 | | Cook, Mary L. | 1914 | Box 487 |
| Conrad, Michael H. | 1864 | Box 32 | | Cook, Milly | 1906 | Box 297 |
| Conrad, Monroe E. P. | 1897 | Box 168 | | Cook, Orlando | 1821 | Box 6 |
| Conrad, William | 1896 | Box 160 | | Cook, Peter W. | 1826 | Box 8 |
| Conradt, Frederick | 1907 | Box 318 | | Cook, Sarah Anna | 1917 | Box 566 |
| Conroy, Bernard | 1920 | Box 656 | | Cook, Sarah E. | 1891 | Box 124 |
| Conroy, Denis E. | 1910 | Box 387 | | Cook, Thomas | 1826 | Box 8 |
| Conroy, Dominick | 1860 | Box 28 | | Cook, Truman A. | 1881 | Box 74 |
| Conroy, James F. | 1899 | Box 182 | | Cook, William | 1882 | Box 78 |
| Conroy, Patrick | 1901 | Box 206 | | Cook, William A. | 1904 | Box 261 |
| Conroy, Theodosia | 1910 | Box 387 | | Cook, William H. | 1886 | Box 96 |
| Conroy, Thomas F. | 1904 | Box 261 | | Cook, William J. | 1919 | Box 624 |
| Constable, Susan M. | 1913 | Box 465 | | Cooke, Francis R. | 1912 | Box 438 |
| Constantine, Benedetto | 1910 | Box 387 | | Cooke, Henry D. | 1881 | Box 74 |
| Constantine, Thomas S. | 1896 | Box 160 | | Cooke, Joseph F. | 1897 | Box 168 |
| Constas, George | 1913 | Box 465 | | Cooke, Laura S. H. | 1904 | Box 261 |
| Contee, Elizabeth | 1868 | Box 39 | | Cooke, Margaret A. | 1916 | Box 541 |
| Contee, John | 1887 | Box 102 | | Cooke, Robert Randolph | 1918 | Box 595 |
| Contee, Jonathan R. | 1891 | Box 124 | | Cooksey, Albert G. | 1878 | Box 65 |
| Contillo, Rufus C. | 1916 | Box 541 | | Cooksey, Emma G. | 1910 | Box 387 |
| Converse, Eleanor M. | 1895 | Box 152 | | Cooksey, Joshua J. | 1915 | Box 513 |
| Converse, Jane A. | 1900 | Box 191 | | Cooley, Benjamin | 1892 | Box 130 |
| Conway, Melissa C. | 1907 | Box 318 | | Cooley, Blanche Idelle | 1920 | Box 656 |
| Conway, Nancy | 1915 | Box 513 | | Coolidge, Edmund | 1846 | Box 18 |
| Conway, Richard | 1811 | Box 3 | | Coolidge, Harriet B. | 1913 | Box 465 |
| Conway, Thomas | 1919 | Box 624 | | Coolidge, Richard H. | 1866 | Box 35 |
| Conway, William O. | 1904 | Box 261 | | Coolidge, Samuel Judson | 1812 | Box 4 |
| Cook, Abraham | 1865 | Box 33 | | Coombs, Griffith | 1845 | Box 17 |
| Cook, Alfred | 1858 | Box 26 | | Coombs, Louisa | 1843 | Box 16 |

| | | | | | | |
|---|---|---|---|---|---|
| Coombs, Samuel A. | 1906 | Box 297 | Corcoran, Edward E. | 1904 | Box 261 |
| Coomes, George E. | 1905 | Box 278 | Corcoran, Eliza | 1841 | Box 15 |
| Coon, Charlotte H. | 1914 | Box 487 | Corcoran, Emily | 1854 | Box 23 |
| Coon, Croswell | 1887 | Box 102 | Corcoran, James W. | 1912 | Box 438 |
| Coon, David L. | 1914 | Box 487 | Corcoran, John | 1919 | Box 624 |
| Coon, James | 1896 | Box 160 | Corcoran, Mary | 1890 | Box 118 |
| Coon, Mary E. | 1905 | Box 278 | Corcoran, Michael | 1888 | Box 107 |
| Cooney, Catharine M. | 1909 | Box 364 | Corcoran, Patrick | 1892 | Box 130 |
| Cooney, James | 1897 | Box 168 | Corcoran, Patrick Thomas | 1864 | Box 32 |
| Coons, Rosanna D. | 1864 | Box 32 | Corcoran, Thomas | 1830 | Box 10 |
| Cooper, Ann Eliza | 1913 | Box 465 | Corcoran, Thomas | 1846 | Box 18 |
| Cooper, Arthur | 1873 | Box 50 | Corcoran, Timothy | 1868 | Box 39 |
| Cooper, Eleanor J. | 1905 | Box 278 | Corcoran, Ursula | 1911 | Box 414 |
| Cooper, Elizabeth A. | 1899 | Box 182 | Corcoran, William D. | 1913 | Box 465 |
| Cooper, George H. | 1902 | Box 223 | Corcoran, William W. | 1888 | Box 107 |
| Cooper, George W. | 1893 | Box 137 | Cord, John William | 1905 | Box 278 |
| Cooper, Georgeanna J. | 1914 | Box 487 | Cord, Mary T. | 1911 | Box 414 |
| Cooper, Grenville C. | 1864 | Box 32 | Corey, Hattie V. | 1919 | Box 624 |
| Cooper, Harley | 1911 | Box 414 | Corish, Catherine | 1840 | Box 15 |
| Cooper, Harriet | 1891 | Box 124 | Corkery, John J. | 1913 | Box 465 |
| Cooper, James | 1885 | Box 91 | Corkhill, Helen B. | 1882 | Box 78 |
| Cooper, Jane Amanda | 1904 | Box 261 | Cornish, Ann A. | 1914 | Box 487 |
| Cooper, Lucy M. | 1909 | Box 364 | Cornish, George G. | 1910 | Box 387 |
| Cooper, Margaret | 1840 | Box 15 | Cornish, Louis Alexander | 1902 | Box 223 |
| Cooper, Rebecca | 1887 | Box 102 | Cornwall, Joseph W. | 1894 | Box 145 |
| Cooper, Rebecca H. | 1888 | Box 107 | Cornwell, Alice C. | 1917 | Box 567 |
| Cooper, Sarah | 1854 | Box 23 | Cornwell, Douglass | 1888 | Box 107 |
| Cooper, Susan | 1914 | Box 487 | Cornwell, George G. | 1892 | Box 130 |
| Cooper, Thomas | 1901 | Box 206 | Cornwell, Henry H. | 1900 | Box 191 |
| Cooper, William | 1871 | Box 44 | Cornwell, John | 1893 | Box 137 |
| Cooper, William | 1887 | Box 102 | Cornwell, Phoebe A. | 1918 | Box 595 |
| Cooper, William Wager | 1889 | Box 112 | Cornwell, Theodore D. | 1912 | Box 438 |
| Coover, Henry | 1864 | Box 32 | Corwine, Richard M. | 1876 | Box 60 |
| Cope, Henry | 1869 | Box 40 | Correll, Nora | 1912 | Box 438 |
| Cope, Jasper | 1881 | Box 74 | Corridon, James | 1906 | Box 297 |
| Copeland, Ann M. | 1895 | Box 152 | Corridon, James T. | 1915 | Box 513 |
| Copp, Amasa | 1887 | Box 102 | Corridon, Johanna Latitia | 1902 | Box 223 |
| Copp, Ellen | 1893 | Box 137 | Corridon, John | 1883 | Box 82 |
| Copp, Henry N. | 1912 | Box 438 | Corridon, Patrick | 1901 | Box 206 |
| Coppersmith, Henry | 1815 | Box 4 | Corridon, Thomas F. | 1906 | Box 297 |
| Coppinger, J. J. | 1910 | Box 387 | Corrigan, Catherine | 1892 | Box 130 |
| Coppinger, Martha A. M. | 1908 | Box 341 | Corrigan, Jennie M. | 1896 | Box 160 |
| Coquillette, Daniel W. | 1913 | Box 465 | Corson, Everett H. | 1918 | Box 595 |
| Corbet, Patrick | 1858 | Box 26 | Corson, William S. | 1867 | Box 37 |
| Corbett, Catherine | 1902 | Box 223 | Corwin, William Beson | 1918 | Box 595 |
| Corbett, Ellen | 1910 | Box 387 | Cosby, Frank Carvill | 1905 | Box 278 |
| Corbett, Frank E. | 1897 | Box 168 | Cosgray, Harry | 1919 | Box 624 |
| Corbett, Margaret | 1884 | Box 85 | Cosgrove, John | 1890 | Box 118 |
| Corbin, Henry | 1920 | Box 656 | Cosgrove, Priscilla | 1864 | Box 32 |
| Corbin, Mollie | 1920 | Box 656 | Coskery, Henry B. | 1876 | Box 60 |
| Corbit, William B. | 1882 | Box 78 | Costela, Francis | 1821 | Box 6 |
| Corby, Fannie L. | 1909 | Box 364 | Costello, John | 1898 | Box 174 |

| | | | | | | |
|---|---|---|---|---|---|---|
| Costello, Richard | 1904 | Box 261 | | Cox, Amanda | 1896 | Box 160 |
| Costello, Robert F. | 1908 | Box 341 | | Cox, Benjamin W. | 1910 | Box 387 |
| Costello, Thomas | 1876 | Box 60 | | Cox, Bessie O. | 1920 | Box 656 |
| Costello, Timothy | 1875 | Box 57 | | Cox, Charles Henry | 1914 | Box 488 |
| Costin, William | 1842 | Box 15 | | Cox, Christopher C. | 1893 | Box 137 |
| Costin, William C. | 1887 | Box 102 | | Cox, Clement | 1848 | Box 19 |
| Costin, William Custis | 1888 | Box 107 | | Cox, Elfrieda | 1893 | Box 137 |
| Costin, William G. | 1876 | Box 60 | | Cox, Ella M. | 1895 | Box 152 |
| Costinett, Paul | 1907 | Box 318 | | Cox, Francis Marcellus | 1910 | Box 388 |
| Coston, Martha J. | 1904 | Box 261 | | Cox, Frank C. | 1907 | Box 318 |
| Cotter, Martin | 1840 | Box 15 | | Cox, George G. | 1906 | Box 297 |
| Cotter, Mary | 1911 | Box 414 | | Cox, George W. | 1855 | Box 23 |
| Cottle, Albert | 1915 | Box 513 | | Cox, George W. | 1897 | Box 168 |
| Cotton, John B. | 1909 | Box 364 | | Cox, Gilbert | 1873 | Box 50 |
| Cotton, William H. | 1896 | Box 160 | | Cox, Jane P. | 1894 | Box 145 |
| Cottrell, Edward B. | 1909 | Box 364 | | Cox, John C. | 1909 | Box 364 |
| Cottrell, Joseph F. | 1894 | Box 145 | | Cox, John L. | 1898 | Box 174 |
| Coues, Elliott | 1900 | Box 191 | | Cox, Julia A. | 1911 | Box 414 |
| Coues, Mary Emily Bates | 1906 | Box 297 | | Cox, Margaretta | 1903 | Box 242 |
| Coughlan, John D. | 1917 | Box 567 | | Cox, Mark | 1916 | Box 541 |
| Coughlin, Johanna | 1916 | Box 541 | | Cox, Mary A. | 1898 | Box 175 |
| Coulson, Helena | 1901 | Box 206 | | Cox, Nancy F. | 1908 | Box 341 |
| Coumbe, Rachael | 1843 | Box 16 | | Cox, Sarah R. | 1905 | Box 278 |
| Counselman, Samuel | 1893 | Box 137 | | Cox, Susan G. | 1916 | Box 541 |
| Coursault, Edward | 1837 | Box 13 | | Cox, Walter S. | 1902 | Box 223 |
| Courtis, Frank | 1908 | Box 341 | | Cox, William | 1839 | Box 14 |
| Courts, Betsy | 1810 | Box 3 | | Coxe, Richard | 1841 | Box 15 |
| Courts, James C. | 1916 | Box 541 | | Coxe, Richard S. | 1865 | Box 33 |
| Courts, Nelly | 1843 | Box 16 | | Coxen, Millard F. | 1909 | Box 364 |
| Cousar, Robert M. | 1904 | Box 261 | | Coyle, Andrew | 1863 | Box 31 |
| Cousins, James Sr. | 1913 | Box 465 | | Coyle, Catherine | 1849 | Box 20 |
| Covert, George H. | 1915 | Box 513 | | Coyle, Catherine E. | 1886 | Box 96 |
| Covert, William E. | 1911 | Box 414 | | Coyle, Emma Frances | 1867 | Box 37 |
| Covington, Teco Mason | 1913 | Box 465 | | Coyle, Fitzhugh | 1877 | Box 63 |
| Covington, William H. | 1913 | Box 465 | | Coyle, Hannah | 1907 | Box 318 |
| Cowan, Bridget Ann | 1895 | Box 152 | | Coyle, Harriet L. | 1892 | Box 130 |
| Cowan, Mary E. | 1914 | Box 487 | | Coyle, Harriet L. | 1905 | Box 278 |
| Cowan, Pamela H. | 1904 | Box 261 | | Coyle, John | 1832 | Box 11 |
| Cowherd, Anna H. | 1920 | Box 656 | | Coyle, John | 1838 | Box 14 |
| Cowhick, O. Glenn | 1918 | Box 595 | | Coyle, John | 1860 | Box 28 |
| Cowie, George | 1891 | Box 124 | | Coyle, Laura Virginia | 1882 | Box 78 |
| Cowing, Frank Myrtle | 1894 | Box 145 | | Coyle, Leonidas | 1868 | Box 39 |
| Cowing, William | 1871 | Box 44 | | Coyle, Mary Eleanor | 1876 | Box 60 |
| Cowing, William J. | 1893 | Box 137 | | Coyne, Daniel | 1911 | Box 414 |
| Cowl, Alto V. | 1902 | Box 223 | | Coyne, John | 1883 | Box 82 |
| Cowling, Laura Virginia | 1917 | Box 567 | | Crabbe, Jennie H. | 1913 | Box 465 |
| Cowling, Mary | 1919 | Box 624 | | Craerin, Joseph | 1879 | Box 68 |
| Cowperthwait, Elizabeth T. | 1893 | Box 137 | | Craft, Brougham Henry | 1920 | Box 656 |
| Cowperthwait, Henrietta | 1899 | Box 182 | | Cragin, Charles H. | 1887 | Box 102 |
| Cowperthwait, Mary B. | 1910 | Box 387 | | Cragin, Harry W. | 1909 | Box 364 |
| Cowsill, James | 1896 | Box 160 | | Cragin, Isabelle | 1900 | Box 191 |
| Cox, Alexander S. | 1867 | Box 37 | | Craig, Ann M. | 1908 | Box 341 |

| | | | | | | |
|---|---|---|---|---|---|---|
| Craig, Annie B. M. | 1915 | Box 513 | Crawford, Joseph | 1919 | Box 624 |
| Craig, David P. | 1906 | Box 297 | Crawford, Margaret | 1916 | Box 541 |
| Craig, George | 1815 | Box 4 | Crawford, Margaret E. | 1917 | Box 567 |
| Craig, Henry C. | 1918 | Box 595 | Crawford, Samuel B. | 1913 | Box 465 |
| Craig, Henry K. | 1870 | Box 42 | Crawford, Sarah | 1832 | Box 11 |
| Craig, J. Watson | 1908 | Box 341 | Crawford, Sarah C. | 1864 | Box 32 |
| Craig, James M. | 1916 | Box 541 | Crawford, William | 1904 | Box 261 |
| Craig, John | 1908 | Box 341 | Creecy, Charles Eaton | 1909 | Box 365 |
| Craig Maria B. | 1888 | Box 107 | Creecy, Charles T. | 1916 | Box 541 |
| Craig, Mary E. | 1915 | Box 513 | Creecy, Sarah Caroline | 1916 | Box 541 |
| Craig, Moses | 1909 | Box 364 | Crehan, James | 1892 | Box 130 |
| Craig, Samuel | 1812 | Box 4 | Crenshaw, Elizabeth Ricarda | 1899 | Box 182 |
| Craige, John | 1879 | Box 68 | Creswell, Hannah J. R. | 1920 | Box 656 |
| Craigen, Phebe | 1915 | Box 513 | Creswell, John A. J. | 1892 | Box 130 |
| Craighead, Harriet Van Auken | 1909 | Box 364 | Crew, Fannie | 1895 | Box 152 |
| Craighead, James G. | 1895 | Box 152 | Crew, Samuel B. | 1888 | Box 107 |
| Craighill, James Brown | 1913 | Box 465 | Crews, John F. | 1892 | Box 131 |
| Craik, William | 1886 | Box 96 | Crews, William P. H. | 1910 | Box 388 |
| Craley, Annie A. | 1916 | Box 541 | Crichton, William | 1919 | Box 625 |
| Crall, Ellen | 1912 | Box 439 | Crider, Laura | 1902 | Box 223 |
| Cralle, Jefferson B. | 1920 | Box 656 | Crimmins, Elizabeth A. | 1904 | Box 261 |
| Cramer, Charles W. | 1909 | Box 365 | Crimmins, John P. | 1911 | Box 414 |
| Crampsey, William D. | 1904 | Box 261 | Crimmins, Mary | 1864 | Box 32 |
| Crampton, Catharine A. | 1912 | Box 439 | Crippen, Grace C. | 1894 | Box 145 |
| Crampton, Catherine Eliza | 1919 | Box 624 | Crippen, Ransom B. | 1868 | Box 39 |
| Crampton, Sarah | 1861 | Box 29 | Cripps, Ellen | 1876 | Box 60 |
| Crampton, William B. | 1864 | Box 32 | Cripps, William McL. | 1876 | Box 60 |
| Cranch, William | 1855 | Box 23 | Crise, John Franklin | 1910 | Box 388 |
| Crandall, Clark P. | 1893 | Box 137 | Crismond, Estelle Pauline | 1920 | Box 656 |
| Crandell, George | 1857 | Box 25 | Crissy, Sardis L. | 1906 | Box 298 |
| Crandell, Lucy S. | 1880 | Box 71 | Crist, Clarence | 1898 | Box 175 |
| Crandell, Lusanna Amies | 1907 | Box 318 | Crittenden, August W. | 1915 | Box 513 |
| Crane, A. Belden | 1894 | Box 145 | Crittenden, John E. | 1914 | Box 488 |
| Crane, Charles H. | 1883 | Box 82 | Crittenden, Thomas T. | 1905 | Box 278 |
| Crane, Eliza | 1861 | Box 29 | Crocker, Charlotte Helen | 1911 | Box 414 |
| Crane, James A. | 1874 | Box 53 | Crocker, Ellen H. | 1893 | Box 137 |
| Crane, John | 1906 | Box 297 | Crocker, Ellen Virginia | 1912 | Box 439 |
| Crane, Michael | 1896 | Box 160 | Crocker, Harriet E. | 1911 | Box 414 |
| Crane, William M. | 1846 | Box 18 | Crocker, John S. | 1890 | Box 118 |
| Cranford, Margaret J. | 1916 | Box 541 | Crocker, Mary G. | 1896 | Box 160 |
| Cranmer, David | 1915 | Box 513 | Crocker, Thomas S. | 1911 | Box 414 |
| Cratty, Helena M. | 1889 | Box 112 | Crockwell, M. M. | 1918 | Box 595 |
| Craven, John | 1829 | Box 10 | Croffut, Margaret M. | 1891 | Box 124 |
| Craven, Philip | 1858 | Box 26 | Croffut, William A. | 1915 | Box 513 |
| Crawford, Anna | 1893 | Box 137 | Croggon, Ellen H. | 1919 | Box 625 |
| Crawford, Edmonia S. | 1907 | Box 318 | Croggon, Henry B. | 1879 | Box 68 |
| Crawford, Hartley | 1863 | Box 31 | Croggon, Mary C. | 1912 | Box 439 |
| Crawford, Henry S. | 1896 | Box 160 | Croggon, Richard C. | 1872 | Box 47 |
| Crawford, Horace L. | 1919 | Box 624 | Croggon, William Newton | 1915 | Box 513 |
| Crawford, James | 1904 | Box 261 | Croghan, Luke J. | 1918 | Box 595 |
| Crawford, John D. | 1919 | Box 624 | Croghan, Patrick | 1874 | Box 53 |
| Crawford, John W. | 1908 | Box 341 | Croghan, Sarah | 1874 | Box 53 |

| | | | | | | |
|---|---|---|---|---|---|---|
| Croghan, Timothy | 1913 | Box 465 | Crowley, Patrick Henry | 1897 | Box 168 |
| Croissant, John Dempster | 1906 | Box 298 | Crowly, Ellen | 1886 | Box 96 |
| Crolly, Bernard P. | 1869 | Box 40 | Crown, Ann | 1868 | Box 39 |
| Crome, John | 1859 | Box 27 | Crown, Catharine | 1871 | Box 44 |
| Cromelien, Rowland | 1873 | Box 50 | Crown, Charles R. | 1916 | Box 541 |
| Cromelien, Sarah | 1902 | Box 223 | Crown, Elizabeth | 1918 | Box 595 |
| Cromelin, Roland F. | 1903 | Box 242 | Crown, Jeremiah | 1863 | Box 31 |
| Cromeline, William H. | 1895 | Box 152 | Crown, John F. | 1910 | Box 388 |
| Cromie, William | 1909 | Box 365 | Crown, John Owen | 1912 | Box 439 |
| Cromwell, Bartlett J. | 1917 | Box 567 | Crown, Percy S. | 1919 | Box 625 |
| Cromwell, John | 1835 | Box 12 | Crownen, Barney | 1873 | Box 50 |
| Cromwell, M. Evelyn | 1912 | Box 439 | Crowninshield, Caspar Schuyler | 1911 | Box 414 |
| Cromwell, Oliver E. | 1910 | Box 388 | Crowther, Richard | 1906 | Box 298 |
| Cronie, Henry R. | 1892 | Box 131 | Crowther, Sarah | 1915 | Box 513 |
| Cronie, William Henry | 1900 | Box 191 | Crowther, William H. | 1911 | Box 414 |
| Cronin, Margaret | 1870 | Box 42 | Crozier, Susan E. | 1902 | Box 223 |
| Cronin, Richard A. | 1890 | Box 118 | Cruikshank, Margaret A. | 1920 | Box 656 |
| Cronise, J. Calvin | 1909 | Box 365 | Cruikshank, Richard | 1898 | Box 175 |
| Crook, Alice | 1894 | Box 145 | Cruit, Alice A. | 1910 | Box 388 |
| Crook, Clara R. | 1911 | Box 414 | Cruit, Martha A. | 1905 | Box 278 |
| Crook, William H. | 1915 | Box 513 | Cruit, Mary | 1915 | Box 513 |
| Crooks, Robert C. | 1893 | Box 137 | Cruit, Mary A. | 1889 | Box 112 |
| Cropley, Elizabeth | 1890 | Box 118 | Cruit, Richard | 1886 | Box 96 |
| Cropley, Mary Lee | 1914 | Box 488 | Cruit, Robert | 1861 | Box 29 |
| Cropley, Robert B. | 1891 | Box 124 | Cruit, Susan | 1901 | Box 206 |
| Cropley, Samuel | 1869 | Box 40 | Crumbaugh, Daniel | 1919 | Box 625 |
| Cropper, John | 1907 | Box 318 | Crummell, Alexander | 1898 | Box 175 |
| Crosby, Hannah E. | 1913 | Box 465 | Crummell, Jennie Morris | 1903 | Box 242 |
| Crosby, Louisa Audenried | 1918 | Box 595 | Crump, Abner | 1847 | Box 18 |
| Crosby, Peirce | 1899 | Box 182 | Crump, Polly | 1891 | Box 124 |
| Croson, Ira | 1885 | Box 91 | Crumpton, William | 1895 | Box 152 |
| Croson, Mary E. | 1892 | Box 131 | Cruser, Maria L. | 1914 | Box 488 |
| Cross, Abraham V. | 1854 | Box 23 | Crush, B. A. | 1917 | Box 567 |
| Cross, Ann Maria | 1900 | Box 191 | Cruson, Washington | 1901 | Box 206 |
| Cross, Ebenezer P. | 1898 | Box 175 | Crutchet, John P. | 1883 | Box 82 |
| Cross, Eli | 1838 | Box 14 | Cruttenden, Harvey | 1868 | Box 39 |
| Cross, Elizabeth | 1868 | Box 39 | Cruttenden, Mary | 1869 | Box 40 |
| Cross, Frank W. | 1898 | Box 175 | Crux, Thomas | 1869 | Box 40 |
| Cross, Joseph | 1864 | Box 32 | Cryer, Elizabeth Jane | 1902 | Box 223 |
| Cross, Samuel | 1906 | Box 298 | Cuddy, Bridget | 1913 | Box 465 |
| Cross, Samuel | 1913 | Box 465 | Cudlipp, Agnes B. | 1896 | Box 160 |
| Cross, Thomas B. | 1891 | Box 124 | Cudlipp, Frederick | 1891 | Box 124 |
| Crossfield, Cornelia H. | 1889 | Box 112 | Cudmore, Bridget | 1908 | Box 341 |
| Crossman, Jacob H. | 1894 | Box 145 | Culbert, John | 1894 | Box 145 |
| Croswell, Michael | 1918 | Box 595 | Culhane, Catherine | 1912 | Box 439 |
| Crouch, Charles C. | 1919 | Box 625 | Culhane, Patrick | 1896 | Box 160 |
| Crounse, Amos | 1920 | Box 656 | Cull, John | 1829 | Box 10 |
| Crowe, Peter | 1908 | Box 341 | Cull, John | 1902 | Box 223 |
| Crowell, Henry S. | 1907 | Box 318 | Cull, Sarah A. | 1874 | Box 50 |
| Crowell, William H. | 1910 | Box 388 | Cullen, B. F. | 1903 | Box 242 |
| Crowley, Cornelius | 1883 | Box 82 | Cullen, Eliza Montgomery | 1920 | Box 656 |
| Crowley, Elizabeth A. | 1887 | Box 102 | Cullen, Margaret | 1908 | Box 342 |

| | | | | | | |
|---|---|---|---|---|---|---|
| Cullen, Mary J. | 1905 | Box 278 | Curry, Mary W. | 1903 | Box 242 |
| Cullen, Patrick | 1820 | Box 6 | Curry, Sarah | 1888 | Box 107 |
| Culley, Joseph | 1901 | Box 206 | Curser, Collin B. | 1904 | Box 262 |
| Culley, Theodore Perry | 1909 | Box 365 | Curtain, Ellen | 1902 | Box 223 |
| Cullinan, Andrew | 1907 | Box 319 | Curtain, Julia | 1891 | Box 124 |
| Cullinane, Bridget | 1919 | Box 625 | Curtin, Daniel | 1905 | Box 279 |
| Cullinane, John F. | 1897 | Box 168 | Curtin, Ellen | 1911 | Box 414 |
| Cullinane, Patrick | 1885 | Box 91 | Curtin, Honoria Kearin | 1916 | Box 541 |
| Culver, Abraham E. | 1910 | Box 388 | Curtin, John | 1904 | Box 262 |
| Culver, Frank E. | 1902 | Box 223 | Curtin, Mary E. | 1911 | Box 414 |
| Culver, Frederick B. | 1879 | Box 68 | Curtin, Mary Jane | 1890 | Box 118 |
| Culver, William E. | 1876 | Box 60 | Curtin, Patrick | 1905 | Box 279 |
| Cumberland, Albert | 1881 | Box 75 | Curtin, Richard | 1893 | Box 137 |
| Cumberland, Charles | 1871 | Box 44 | Curtis, Alfred | 1863 | Box 31 |
| Cumberland, Elizabeth S. | 1892 | Box 131 | Curtis, Benjamin F. | 1916 | Box 541 |
| Cumberland, John | 1884 | Box 85 | Curtis, Charles S. | 1919 | Box 625 |
| Cumberland, Margaret | 1879 | Box 68 | Curtis, Charles T. | 1893 | Box 137 |
| Cumberland, Robert C. | 1915 | Box 514 | Curtis, Edmund B. | 1907 | Box 319 |
| Cuming, Virginia A. | 1904 | Box 262 | Curtis, Elsy | 1888 | Box 107 |
| Cumming, Montgomery | 1917 | Box 567 | Curtis, Fanny Fassett | 1918 | Box 595 |
| Cummings, A. Boyd | 1891 | Box 124 | Curtis, George E. | 1866 | Box 35 |
| Cummings, Horace S. | 1912 | Box 439 | Curtis, George T. | 1885 | Box 91 |
| Cummings, Mary | 1818 | Box 5 | Curtis, George W. N. | 1917 | Box 567 |
| Cummings, Mary R. | 1887 | Box 102 | Curtis, Henry Adams | 1914 | Box 488 |
| Cummins, Ebenezer Harlow | 1834 | Box 12 | Curtis, Henry B. | 1880 | Box 71 |
| Cummins, Mary | 1895 | Box 152 | Curtis, James M. | 1917 | Box 567 |
| Cummins, Patrick | 1891 | Box 124 | Curtis, Jane L. | 1912 | Box 439 |
| Cumpston, Edward H. | 1885 | Box 91 | Curtis, John | 1905 | Box 279 |
| Cumpston, Mary Mitchell | 1891 | Box 124 | Curtis, John Jackson | 1908 | Box 342 |
| Cuneo, Maria | 1910 | Box 388 | Curtis, Josiah | 1883 | Box 82 |
| Cuneo, Michael | 1917 | Box 567 | Curtis, Mary | 1895 | Box 152 |
| Cunningham, Ephraim M. | 1852 | Box 21 | Curtis, Samuel Prentis | 1876 | Box 60 |
| Cunningham, Jane C. | 1917 | Box 567 | Curtis, William E. | 1911 | Box 414 |
| Cunningham, John | 1916 | Box 541 | Curtis, William L. | 1920 | Box 656 |
| Cunningham, Katherine | 1908 | Box 342 | Curtis, William Wallace | 1888 | Box 107 |
| Cunningham, Mary | 1917 | Box 567 | Curtis, Williamanna R. | 1892 | Box 131 |
| Cunningham, Peter | 1897 | Box 168 | Cusberd, Anne Maria | 1903 | Box 242 |
| Cunningham, William | 1909 | Box 365 | Cushing, Caleb | 1882 | Box 78 |
| Cunningham, William A. | 1915 | Box 514 | Cushing, Frank Hamilton | 1900 | Box 191 |
| Cuppy, Fletcher P. | 1887 | Box 102 | Cushing, Lyman F. W. | 1916 | Box 541 |
| Curgess, Charles H. | 1904 | Box 260 | Cushing, Samuel | 1901 | Box 206 |
| Curley, James | 1904 | Box 262 | Cushing, Thomas A. | 1903 | Box 242 |
| Curran, John J. | 1910 | Box 388 | Cushing, William B. | 1875 | Box 57 |
| Curran, John M. | 1918 | Box 595 | Cusick, Hester E. | 1917 | Box 567 |
| Curran, John W. | 1915 | Box 514 | Cusick, Patrick F. | 1920 | Box 656 |
| Currie, James M. | 1889 | Box 112 | Custard, William A. | 1914 | Box 488 |
| Currier, George Russell | 1911 | Box 414 | Custis, Elizabeth E. | 1907 | Box 319 |
| Currin, Hesther | 1859 | Box 27 | Custis, James B. Gregg | 1915 | Box 514 |
| Curry, Dorinda E. | 1884 | Box 85 | Cuthbert, James | 1900 | Box 191 |
| Curry, Hannah Ann | 1886 | Box 96 | Cuthbert, James | 1915 | Box 514 |
| Curry, J. L. M. | 1903 | Box 242 | Cutino, Edith M. | 1919 | Box 625 |
| Curry, Margaret | 1891 | Box 124 | Cutler, Hattie | 1918 | Box 595 |

| | | | | | | |
|---|---|---|---|---|---|
| Cutler, Lyman B. | 1903 | Box 242 | Daley, Annie | 1898 | Box 175 |
| Cutler, Martha | 1905 | Box 279 | Daley, Daniel J. | 1915 | Box 514 |
| Cutter, Benjamin F. | 1891 | Box 124 | Daley, Lawrence | 1875 | Box 57 |
| Cutter, George | 1915 | Box 514 | Daley, Uriah | 1893 | Box 138 |
| Cutter, George Francis | 1890 | Box 118 | Dall, Caroline H. | 1913 | Box 465 |
| Cutter, Marion | 1901 | Box 206 | Dallam, Jane J. | 1900 | Box 191 |
| Cutter, Mary Louisa | 1900 | Box 191 | Dallas, Frances Virginia | 1915 | Box 514 |
| Cutts, Dolly P. | 1839 | Box 14 | Dallas, Mary O. | 1918 | Box 595 |
| Cutts, Ellen E. | 1897 | Box 168 | Dallas, Stephen J. | 1883 | Box 82 |
| Cutts, Mary E. E. | 1856 | Box 24 | Dalrymple, Annie E. | 1914 | Box 488 |
| Cutts, Richard | 1845 | Box 17 | Dalton, Annie Kate | 1900 | Box 191 |
| Cutts, Richard D. | 1883 | Box 82 | Dalton, Francis | 1883 | Box 82 |
| Cuvillier, Jean Baptist | 1834 | Box 12 | Dalton, Robert | 1909 | Box 365 |
| Cuvillier, Marie J. | 1860 | Box 28 | Dalton, Thomas W. | 1920 | Box 656 |
| d'Astre, Frederick A. | 1914 | Box 488 | Daly, Annie A. | 1911 | Box 414 |
| d'Astre, Frederic A. | 1919 | Box 625 | Daly, Bartholomew | 1910 | Box 388 |
| D'Esterhazy, Sarah Virginia | 1918 | Box 595 | Daly, Eugene B. | 1913 | Box 465 |
| D'Lagnel, Juluis A. | 1847 | Box 19 | Daly, Frances P. | 1905 | Box 279 |
| Dabney, Albert | 1901 | Box 206 | Daly, Ida M. | 1912 | Box 439 |
| Dabney, Elizabeth | 1878 | Box 65 | Daly, James | 1870 | Box 42 |
| Dabney, Margaret M. | 1889 | Box 112 | Daly, James | 1908 | Box 342 |
| Dabney, William A. | 1890 | Box 118 | Daly, John | 1842 | Box 15 |
| Dacey, Ellen | 1887 | Box 102 | Daly, Josephine Esputa | 1909 | Box 365 |
| Daddysman, Emma H. C. | 1913 | Box 465 | Daly, Lucy E. Norman | 1894 | Box 145 |
| Dade, Adam | 1883 | Box 82 | Daly, Mary A. F. | 1909 | Box 365 |
| Dade, Betsy | 1828 | Box 9 | Daly, Patrick | 1894 | Box 145 |
| Dade, Henry H. | 1895 | Box 152 | Daly, Timothy D. | 1904 | Box 262 |
| Dade, Nannie M. | 1919 | Box 625 | Damm, Gertrude | 1907 | Box 319 |
| Dade, Virginia E. | 1906 | Box 298 | Dana, Francis E. | 1917 | Box 567 |
| Dadmun, Hannah | 1905 | Box 279 | Dana, George H. | 1913 | Box 465 |
| Daelen, Bernard V. | 1891 | Box 124 | Dana, James Jackson | 1898 | Box 175 |
| Daggs, Robert H. | 1905 | Box 279 | Dana, Julia B. | 1900 | Box 192 |
| Dahle, Ernst | 1908 | Box 342 | Dana, Napoleon J. T. | 1905 | Box 279 |
| Dahle, Henry | 1917 | Box 567 | Danaher, Daniel E. | 1913 | Box 465 |
| Dahle, John William | 1874 | Box 53 | Danaher, John J. | 1920 | Box 656 |
| Dahler, C. Louise | 1908 | Box 342 | Danels, Julia F. | 1896 | Box 160 |
| Dahler, John Frederick | 1898 | Box 175 | Danenhower, Elizabeth S. | 1920 | Box 656 |
| Dahlgren, John A. | 1870 | Box 42 | Danenhower, John W. | 1887 | Box 102 |
| Dahlgren, John Vinton | 1904 | Box 262 | Danenhower, William Weaver | 1894 | Box 145 |
| Dahlgren, Madeline S. Vinton | 1898 | Box 175 | Daneri, Giovanni | 1920 | Box 656 |
| Daiker, Hermann | 1906 | Box 298 | Danforth, Montgomery E. | 1919 | Box 625 |
| Dailey, Charlotte Throuston | 1917 | Box 567 | Danhakl, John | 1912 | Box 439 |
| Dailey, Charlotte Thruston | 1914 | Box 488 | Daniel, Joseph | 1897 | Box 168 |
| Dailey, Edward M. | 1891 | Box 124 | Daniel, Tacie A. | 1918 | Box 595 |
| Dailey, John | 1907 | Box 319 | Daniels, Ara M. | 1907 | Box 319 |
| Dailey, Margaret A. | 1916 | Box 541 | Daniels, Maria A. | 1914 | Box 488 |
| Dailey, Patrick R. | 1900 | Box 191 | Daniels, Rinaldo | 1901 | Box 206 |
| Daily, John L. | 1915 | Box 514 | Daniels, Robert J. | 1905 | Box 279 |
| Daily, Mary | 1918 | Box 595 | Daniels, William S. | 1904 | Box 262 |
| Daingerfield, Ellen C. | 1912 | Box 439 | Dankworth, Frederick | 1859 | Box 27 |
| Daish, John B. | 1918 | Box 595 | Dant, Jeremiah | 1857 | Box 25 |
| Daish, Silas S. | 1919 | Box 625 | Dant, Mary | 1898 | Box 175 |

| | | | | | |
|---|---|---|---|---|---|
| Dant, Mary L. | 1912 | Box 439 | Davidson, Samuel | 1810 | Box 3 |
| Dant, Thomas E. | 1898 | Box 175 | Davidson, Sarah S. | 1889 | Box 112 |
| Darby, Ralph | 1875 | Box 57 | Davidson, Susan V. | 1906 | Box 298 |
| Darby, Rufus Hilton | 1907 | Box 319 | Davidson, William A. | 1909 | Box 365 |
| Darden, Fred | 1901 | Box 206 | Davidson, William Hale | 1912 | Box 439 |
| Darden, James Dawley | 1900 | Box 192 | Davie, Ida K. | 1883 | Box 82 |
| Dare, Maria Jane Liggett | 1904 | Box 262 | Davies, Annie | 1894 | Box 145 |
| Dare, Maria P. | 1908 | Box 342 | Davies, Charles | 1907 | Box 319 |
| Darling, James H. | 1874 | Box 53 | Davies, David | 1907 | Box 319 |
| Darling, John A. | 1905 | Box 279 | Davies, Hannah B. | 1911 | Box 414 |
| Darlington, Joseph J. | 1920 | Box 656 | Davies, Thomas D. | 1919 | Box 625 |
| Darnal, Francis H. | 1856 | Box 24 | Davies, Walter R. | 1900 | Box 192 |
| Darnall, Fielder | 1858 | Box 26 | Davies, William | 1904 | Box 262 |
| Darnall, Henry | 1809 | Box 3 | Davis, Abel G. | 1872 | Box 47 |
| Darnall, John Carl | 1920 | Box 656 | Davis, Achsah C. | 1891 | Box 124 |
| Darne, Ann Eliza | 1880 | Box 71 | Davis, Alberta | 1915 | Box 514 |
| Darne, Richard H. | 1911 | Box 414 | Davis, Alice Strange | 1900 | Box 192 |
| Darneille, John D. | 1894 | Box 145 | Davis, Ann | 1896 | Box 160 |
| Darnell, Mary | 1886 | Box 96 | Davis, Anna B. | 1918 | Box 595 |
| Darragh, Ellen A. | 1870 | Box 42 | Davis, Anna H. | 1898 | Box 175 |
| Darrah, Andrew J. | 1913 | Box 465 | Davis, Anna Jane | 1920 | Box 656 |
| Darrall, John S. | 1915 | Box 514 | Davis, Annie E. | 1914 | Box 488 |
| Darrell, Oliver D. | 1915 | Box 514 | Davis, Benjamin Howard | 1917 | Box 567 |
| Dashiell, Elizabeth Camp | 1916 | Box 541 | Davis, Benjamin P. | 1906 | Box 298 |
| Dashiell, Robert B. | 1899 | Box 182 | Davis, Benjamin P. | 1908 | Box 342 |
| Daskam, Eugene B. | 1920 | Box 656 | Davis, Carmen A. | 1904 | Box 262 |
| Datcher, William | 1902 | Box 223 | Davis, Catharine | 1884 | Box 85 |
| Daughton, Burlington C. | 1916 | Box 541 | Davis, Catharine L. | 1906 | Box 298 |
| Daughton, Darius D. | 1907 | Box 319 | Davis, Catherine R. | 1920 | Box 656 |
| Dauterich, Henry L. | 1915 | Box 514 | Davis, Charles A. | 1916 | Box 541 |
| Davenport, Ann F. | 1886 | Box 96 | Davis, Charles Albert | 1882 | Box 78 |
| Davenport, Ira | 1906 | Box 298 | Davis, Charles B. | 1839 | Box 14 |
| Davenport, Isaac | 1890 | Box 118 | Davis, Charles H. | 1877 | Box 63 |
| Davenport, James L. | 1914 | Box 488 | Davis, Charles W. | 1870 | Box 42 |
| Davenport, Louise | 1910 | Box 388 | Davis, Clara R. | 1911 | Box 414 |
| Davidge, Charles H. | 1910 | Box 388 | Davis, E. C. (Mrs.) | 1872 | Box 47 |
| Davidge, Elizabeth E. | 1909 | Box 365 | Davis, Edward Wilson | 1900 | Box 192 |
| Davidge, Rezin | 1902 | Box 223 | Davis, Eldred Griffith | 1910 | Box 388 |
| Davidge, Walter | 1901 | Box 206 | Davis, Eli | 1897 | Box 168 |
| Davidson, Adelaide | 1914 | Box 488 | Davis, Elihu Thomas | 1920 | Box 656 |
| Davidson, Ann E. | 1905 | Box 279 | Davis, Eliza Ann | 1916 | Box 541 |
| Davidson, Clara Britannia | 1915 | Box 514 | Davis, Eliza Rankins | 1899 | Box 182 |
| Davidson, Delozier | 1885 | Box 91 | Davis, Elizabeth J. | 1912 | Box 439 |
| Davidson, Eleanor | 1866 | Box 35 | Davis, Esther | 1913 | Box 466 |
| Davidson, Falconer | 1901 | Box 206 | Davis, Evelina J. | 1888 | Box 107 |
| Davidson, George A. | 1919 | Box 625 | Davis, Frederica Gore | 1917 | Box 567 |
| Davidson, John | 1891 | Box 124 | Davis, George A. | 1862 | Box 30 |
| Davidson, John | 1807 | Box 2 | Davis, George B. | 1915 | Box 514 |
| Davidson, Joseph H. | 1885 | Box 91 | Davis, George W. | 1918 | Box 595 |
| Davidson, Kate | 1910 | Box 388 | Davis, Georgeanna | 1897 | Box 168 |
| Davidson, Margaret | 1852 | Box 21 | Davis, Gideon | 1833 | Box 12 |
| Davidson, Martha E. | 1914 | Box 488 | Davis, Hannah D. | 1912 | Box 439 |

| | | | | | | |
|---|---|---|---|---|---|---|
| Davis, Harold | 1917 | Box 567 | Davis, Thornton | 1903 | Box 242 |
| Davis, Harry Clay | 1913 | Box 466 | Davis, Virginia M. | 1914 | Box 488 |
| Davis, Henry | 1863 | Box 31 | Davis, Wilhelmina Baur | 1904 | Box 262 |
| Davis, Henry G. | 1919 | Box 625 | Davis, William | 1884 | Box 85 |
| Davis, Ignatius Thomas | 1891 | Box 124 | Davis, William | 1919 | Box 625 |
| Davis, Isabella | 1883 | Box 82 | Davis, William H. | 1914 | Box 488 |
| Davis, Jackson | 1891 | Box 124 | Davis, William L. | 1912 | Box 439 |
| Davis, Jacob | 1893 | Box 138 | Davis, William T. | 1909 | Box 365 |
| Davis, James B. | 1889 | Box 112 | Davis, Wirt | 1914 | Box 488 |
| Davis, James G. | 1871 | Box 44 | Davison, Henry L. | 1911 | Box 414 |
| Davis, James L. | 1907 | Box 319 | Davison, John | 1882 | Box 78 |
| Davis, James M. | 1855 | Box 24 | Davison, Joseph K. | 1919 | Box 625 |
| Davis, James T. | 1844 | Box 16 | Davison, Mary A. | 1891 | Box 124 |
| Davis, Jefferson William | 1917 | Box 567 | Davison, Mary E. | 1911 | Box 414 |
| Davis, Jennie A. | 1900 | Box 192 | Davison, Mary Elizabeth | 1885 | Box 91 |
| Davis, John | 1874 | Box 53 | Davisson, Harriet H. | 1908 | Box 342 |
| Davis, John | 1902 | Box 224 | Davy, Charles G. | 1903 | Box 242 |
| Davis, John Chandler Bancroft | 1908 | Box 342 | Daw, Frederick | 1897 | Box 168 |
| Davis, John Lee | 1889 | Box 112 | Daw, Reuben | 1891 | Box 124 |
| Davis, John M. K. | 1920 | Box 656 | Daw, William | 1901 | Box 206 |
| Davis, John of Abel | 1853 | Box 22 | Daw, William H. | 1918 | Box 595 |
| Davis, Jonah | 1838 | Box 14 | Dawes, Ann | 1864 | Box 32 |
| Davis, Joseph | 1901 | Box 206 | Dawes, Charles W. | 1911 | Box 414 |
| Davis, James N. | 1877 | Box 63 | Dawes, Charlotte M. | 1872 | Box 47 |
| Davis, Joshua | 1914 | Box 488 | Dawes, Elizabeth R. | 1912 | Box 439 |
| Davis, Julia | 1910 | Box 388 | Dawes, Frederick | 1852 | Box 21 |
| Davis, Kate C. | 1900 | Box 192 | Dawes, Richard M. | 1893 | Box 138 |
| Davis, Louisa Quackenbush | 1920 | Box 656 | Dawson, Edward M. | 1914 | Box 488 |
| Davis, Lucy Tasker | 1905 | Box 279 | Dawson, Ellen C. | 1909 | Box 365 |
| Davis, Madison | 1913 | Box 466 | Dawson, Gilbert Francis | 1894 | Box 145 |
| Davis, Margaret | 1895 | Box 152 | Dawson, John | 1814 | Box 4 |
| Davis, Margaret | 1903 | Box 242 | Dawson, Margaret | 1897 | Box 168 |
| Davis, Margaret Jane | 1916 | Box 541 | Dawson, Thomas Cleland | 1912 | Box 439 |
| Davis, Mary | 1920 | Box 656 | Day, Caroline | 1905 | Box 279 |
| Davis, Mary A. | 1911 | Box 414 | Day, David G. | 1872 | Box 47 |
| Davis, Mary Ann | 1876 | Box 60 | Day, Eliza J. | 1920 | Box 656 |
| Davis, Mitchell A. | 1919 | Box 625 | Day, Ira C. | 1916 | Box 541 |
| Davis, Moses | 1893 | Box 138 | Day, James | 1848 | Box 19 |
| Davis, Nannie G. | 1916 | Box 541 | Day, James H. | 1913 | Box 466 |
| Davis, Philip C. | 1854 | Box 23 | Day, James William | 1878 | Box 65 |
| Davis, Robert Stephen | 1900 | Box 192 | Day, John | 1911 | Box 414 |
| Davis, Sally | 1821 | Box 6 | Day, Leonora Freelove Hyde | 1916 | Box 541 |
| Davis, Samuel | 1867 | Box 37 | Day, Mary A. | 1917 | Box 567 |
| Davis, Samuel | 1900 | Box 192 | Dayton, Anna T. | 1898 | Box 175 |
| Davis, Samuel G. | 1911 | Box 414 | Dayton, Melville Emory | 1909 | Box 365 |
| Davis, Sarah | 1881 | Box 75 | De Atley, James C. | 1909 | Box 365 |
| Davis, Sarah E. | 1920 | Box 656 | De Badai, Louis | 1906 | Box 298 |
| Davis, Sidney H. | 1873 | Box 50 | De Batz, William | 1906 | Box 298 |
| Davis, Sophia | 1879 | Box 68 | De Caindry, Daniel | 1916 | Box 542 |
| Davis, Sophia Louisa | 1824 | Box 8 | De Carrè, Alfred | 1917 | Box 568 |
| Davis, Theodore E. | 1898 | Box 175 | de Cartaya, Adelaida Guiteras | 1918 | Box 595 |
| Davis, Thomas E. | 1906 | Box 298 | De Ford, John T. | 1892 | Box 131 |

| | | | | | | |
|---|---|---|---|---|---|---|
| de Gomar, Maria | 1918 | Box 595 | Dean, Jane | 1880 | Box 71 |
| De Graffenried, Mary Holt | 1902 | Box 224 | Dean, Mary E. J. | 1873 | Box 50 |
| De Grain, Reinhold F. | 1908 | Box 342 | Dean, Richard C. | 1910 | Box 388 |
| De Graw, Peter V. | 1914 | Box 488 | Dean, Sarai E. | 1904 | Box 262 |
| de Hart, Sarah Catharine | 1886 | Box 96 | Dean, William W. | 1905 | Box 279 |
| De Janon, Patrice | 1892 | Box 131 | Dear, Richard B. | 1911 | Box 414 |
| De Johnson, Elvira L. | 1908 | Box 342 | Deardoff, Paul C. | 1902 | Box 224 |
| De Klyn, Benjamin F. | 1919 | Box 625 | Deardoff, William S. | 1916 | Box 542 |
| De Knight, William F. | 1917 | Box 568 | Dearing, Elizabeth G. | 1917 | Box 567 |
| De Krafft, John W. | 1909 | Box 365 | Dearing, William | 1862 | Box 30 |
| De La Roche, George | 1860 | Box 29 | Dearth, Alice Southworth | 1902 | Box 224 |
| De La Roche, Jane J. | 1899 | Box 182 | Deasy, Jeremiah | 1908 | Box 342 |
| de'Lagnel, Julius A. | 1912 | Box 439 | DeBodisco, Alexander | 1855 | Box 24 |
| De Lamater, Jacob J. | 1886 | Box 96 | DeCaindry, William A. | 1915 | Box 514 |
| De Land, Theodore L. | 1911 | Box 414 | Decatur, Stephen | 1820 | Box 6 |
| de Lesdernier, Stafford G. | 1919 | Box 625 | Decatur, Susan | 1860 | Box 28 |
| De Loffre, Fannie E. | 1917 | Box 568 | Deck, William M. | 1915 | Box 514 |
| De Martini, Gianbatista | 1876 | Box 60 | Decker, Elizabeth | 1883 | Box 82 |
| De Moll, Theodore G. | 1911 | Box 414 | Decker, George W. | 1899 | Box 182 |
| De Monterville, Mary M. | 1911 | Box 414 | Decker, John | 1894 | Box 145 |
| De Montreville, Clarence | 1892 | Box 131 | Decker, William Henry | 1911 | Box 414 |
| de Rohan, William | 1891 | Box 124 | Deckman, Henry | 1871 | Box 44 |
| de Ronceray, H. Rosalie | 1914 | Box 489 | Deckman, William H. | 1913 | Box 466 |
| de Sibour, Mary L. | 1912 | Box 440 | Dedrick, William W. | 1897 | Box 168 |
| De Sibourg, Jean A. Gabriel | 1885 | Box 91 | Dee, James | 1831 | Box 11 |
| de Vado, Julia Dolores Johnson | 1918 | Box 595 | Dee, James | 1810 | Box 3 |
| De Valin, Charles E. | 1892 | Box 131 | Dee, Jeremiah | 1901 | Box 206 |
| De Valin, Ellen Appleby | 1910 | Box 388 | Dee, Maurice F. | 1908 | Box 343 |
| De Vere, Lucy Schele | 1898 | Box 175 | Deeble, Ann A. | 1904 | Box 262 |
| De Vere, Maximilian | 1898 | Box 175 | Deeble, James W. | 1887 | Box 102 |
| De Vincenty, Alfonso G. | 1906 | Box 298 | Deeble, Joseph A. | 1909 | Box 365 |
| De Vries, Mary Clement | 1919 | Box 626 | Deeble, William Riley | 1907 | Box 319 |
| de Wiechers, Margarita Boyer | 1916 | Box 542 | Deener, Josiah W. | 1878 | Box 66 |
| Deacon, Alice S. | 1920 | Box 656 | Deery, James P. | 1833 | Box 12 |
| Deakins, Eleanor | 1805 | Box 1 | Deery, Patrick | 1810 | Box 3 |
| Deakins, Francis | 1804 | Box 1 | Deevers, William H. | 1876 | Box 60 |
| Deakins, John E. | 1863 | Box 31 | Deford, Sarah | 1895 | Box 152 |
| Deakins, Nancy | 1834 | Box 12 | Degges, Ann E. | 1915 | Box 514 |
| Deakins, William Francis | 1913 | Box 466 | Degges, James A. | 1917 | Box 567 |
| Deakins, William J. | 1804 | Box 1 | Degges, John O. P. | 1847 | Box 18 |
| Deal, Bell W. | 1885 | Box 91 | DeGomez, Alfonso F. | 1881 | Box 75 |
| Deal, Virginia | 1893 | Box 138 | DeGroot, Henry B. | 1920 | Box 657 |
| Deale, Henry B. | 1912 | Box 439 | Deigenhart, Mary Anne | 1858 | Box 26 |
| Deale, John Summerfield | 1885 | Box 91 | Deis, Philip H. | 1908 | Box 343 |
| Dealy, Mary | 1909 | Box 365 | Deitz, Susan C. | 1908 | Box 343 |
| Dean, Amanda M. | 1906 | Box 298 | DeKnight, Roselia H. | 1918 | Box 595 |
| Dean, Charles | 1875 | Box 57 | DeKrafft, Edward | 1833 | Box 12 |
| Dean, Charles F. | 1917 | Box 567 | DeKrafft, Eleanor | 1835 | Box 12 |
| Dean, Edward Clark | 1890 | Box 118 | DeKrafft, Elizabeth S. | 1904 | Box 262 |
| Dean, Eliza Ashley | 1916 | Box 542 | DeKrafft, John Charles Philip | 1885 | Box 91 |
| Dean, Frederick I. | 1909 | Box 365 | Dela Roche, George F. | 1861 | Box 29 |
| Dean, Henry C. | 1899 | Box 182 | Delabar, Killian | 1919 | Box 625 |

| | | | | | | |
|---|---|---|---|---|---|---|
| Delafield, Richard | 1877 | Box 63 | Denison, James | 1910 | Box 388 |
| Delancey, John | 1896 | Box 160 | Denison, Jennie O. | 1912 | Box 439 |
| Deland, Francis S. | 1916 | Box 542 | Denison, Ruth C. | 1907 | Box 319 |
| Deland, Horace Carlile | 1912 | Box 439 | Denison, William | 1887 | Box 102 |
| Delaney, Gracie Ann | 1909 | Box 365 | Denison, William O. | 1907 | Box 319 |
| Delaney, Jane | 1909 | Box 365 | Denman, Hampton Y. | 1904 | Box 262 |
| Delaney, John | 1895 | Box 152 | Denman, Mary B. | 1898 | Box 175 |
| Delaney, Patrick | 1831 | Box 11 | Denney, Dorsey | 1893 | Box 138 |
| Delaney, Patrick | 1810 | Box 3 | Denney, Elizabeth A. | 1916 | Box 542 |
| Delano, Columbus | 1898 | Box 175 | Denney, Fannie W. | 1913 | Box 466 |
| Delano, Jane A. | 1919 | Box 625 | Denney, Francis | 1901 | Box 209 |
| Delany, Catharine | 1902 | Box 224 | Denney, Lucinda | 1898 | Box 175 |
| Delany, Susan | 1862 | Box 30 | Denney, Thomas | 1916 | Box 542 |
| Delany, Thomas | 1821 | Box 6 | Denning, Chester | 1862 | Box 30 |
| Delaplane, James Breathed | 1894 | Box 145 | Dennis, Jane E. | 1887 | Box 102 |
| Delaroche, Arabella W. Oliver | 1913 | Box 466 | Dennis, Jonathan (Jr.) | 1878 | Box 66 |
| Delarue, Leonide | 1916 | Box 542 | Dennis, Sarah Ann | 1879 | Box 68 |
| Delcher, Sarah | 1901 | Box 206 | Dennis, Thomas | 1908 | Box 343 |
| Delehanty, Patrick | 1897 | Box 168 | Dennis, William Henry | 1919 | Box 625 |
| Deleon, Edwin Demonet | 1900 | Box 192 | Dennis, William Hooper | 1912 | Box 439 |
| Dellett, Robert A. | 1914 | Box 488 | Dennison, Lewis | 1913 | Box 466 |
| Dellicker, L. B. | 1915 | Box 514 | Denny, Elizabeth F | 1882 | Box 78 |
| Dellinger, Elizabeth | 1911 | Box 414 | Denny, Frank L. | 1914 | Box 488 |
| Dellinger, Henry M. | 1911 | Box 414 | Denny, Jane | 1909 | Box 366 |
| DeLoffre, Augustus A. | 1899 | Box 182 | Densley, Hugh | 1822 | Box 7 |
| DeLongueville, Severe Charles | 1819 | Box 6 | Densmore, Edson S. | 1892 | Box 131 |
| Delphey, Ann Rebecca | 1858 | Box 26 | Dent, Abraham | 1876 | Box 60 |
| Demar, Charles H. | 1913 | Box 466 | Dent, Frances | 1890 | Box 118 |
| Demarest, Matilda Z. | 1914 | Box 488 | Dent, James Clinton | 1909 | Box 366 |
| Demas, Nicholas J. | 1919 | Box 625 | Dent, Rosina | 1878 | Box 66 |
| Dement, Frances R. | 1920 | Box 657 | Dent, Westley | 1906 | Box 298 |
| Dement, John D. | 1913 | Box 466 | Denton, Philip | 1870 | Box 42 |
| DeMeritt, John Henry | 1918 | Box 595 | Denton, Richard | 1904 | Box 262 |
| Deming, William | 1832 | Box 11 | Denty, L. A. | 1912 | Box 440 |
| Demmelman, David S. | 1890 | Box 115 | Denty, Samuel L. | 1905 | Box 279 |
| Demonet, Charles | 1868 | Box 39 | Denver, Arthur | 1895 | Box 152 |
| Demonet, Ida M. | 1900 | Box 192 | Depres, Maurice | 1912 | Box 440 |
| Dempsey, Honora | 1911 | Box 414 | Depue, George Morrison | 1918 | Box 595 |
| Dempsey, James | 1901 | Box 206 | Depue, Jacob | 1889 | Box 112 |
| Dempsie, John | 1809 | Box 3 | Derby, Louisa L. | 1886 | Box 96 |
| Deneale, William Young | 1884 | Box 85 | Derby, Mary Townsend | 1894 | Box 145 |
| DeNeale, Ann E. | 1913 | Box 466 | Derbyshire, Katharine Austin | 1920 | Box 657 |
| Denekas, Claas | 1906 | Box 298 | Dercourt, Alexander | 1910 | Box 388 |
| Denekas, John | 1908 | Box 343 | Dermody, John | 1898 | Box 175 |
| Dengler, Christiana | 1907 | Box 319 | Dermott, Anne Reed | 1860 | Box 28 |
| Denham, Charles S. | 1907 | Box 319 | Dermott, James Reed | 1803 | Box 1 |
| Denham, Columbus | 1905 | Box 279 | DeRochbrune, Lewis | 1803 | Box 1 |
| Denham, Emma | 1912 | Box 439 | Derrick, Edward | 1914 | Box 488 |
| Denham, John L. | 1902 | Box 224 | Derrick, Emma | 1897 | Box 168 |
| Denham, Oliver D. | 1913 | Box 466 | Derrick, George S. | 1912 | Box 440 |
| Denham, Thomas S. | 1907 | Box 319 | Derrick, William S. | 1852 | Box 21 |
| Denison, Henry Willard | 1915 | Box 514 | deSchweinitz, E. A. | 1914 | Box 489 |

| | | | | | | |
|---|---|---|---|---|---|---|
| DeShields, Matilda | 1898 | Box 175 | Dick, Thomas | 1803 | Box 1 |
| DeSilver, Elizabeth E. | 1914 | Box 489 | Dickas, Ernest | 1883 | Box 82 |
| Desmond, Dennis | 1857 | Box 25 | Dickens, Asbury | 1861 | Box 29 |
| Dessau, Andrew F. | 1871 | Box 44 | Dickens, Charles F. | 1918 | Box 595 |
| Dessez, Leon | 1896 | Box 160 | Dickerson, Ada G. | 1917 | Box 568 |
| Dessez, Mina | 1913 | Box 466 | Dickerson, Edward | 1891 | Box 124 |
| Detrick, Reuben B. | 1905 | Box 279 | Dickerson, Elizabeth | 1909 | Box 366 |
| Detrick, Susan E. | 1905 | Box 279 | Dickerson, Mary | 1918 | Box 595 |
| Dettrow, Thomas | 1840 | Box 15 | Dickerson, William | 1909 | Box 366 |
| Detweiler, Frederick M. | 1905 | Box 279 | Dickerson, William | 1909 | Box 366 |
| Detwiler, Edwin L. | 1917 | Box 568 | Dickey, Clarence W. | 1904 | Box 262 |
| Deufel, George | 1868 | Box 39 | Dickey, Lorenzo E. | 1894 | Box 145 |
| Deuringer, John | 1888 | Box 107 | Dickey, Mary | 1830 | Box 10 |
| Deutelin, Karl Herrmann | 1898 | Box 175 | Dickins, Francis W. | 1911 | Box 414 |
| DeVan, Joshua Benjamin | 1897 | Box 168 | Dickins, Marguerite | 1899 | Box 182 |
| DeVan, Susan B. | 1910 | Box 388 | Dickinson, George T. | 1890 | Box 118 |
| DeVaughan, Samuel | 1867 | Box 37 | Dickson (Dixon), John | 1826 | Box 8 |
| Devendorf, La Motte Kibby | 1917 | Box 568 | Dickson, Christopher | 1914 | Box 489 |
| Devereux, Maria G. | 1903 | Box 242 | Dickson, Elizabeth | 1828 | Box 9 |
| Devers, Lewis | 1876 | Box 60 | Dickson, Henry | 1907 | Box 319 |
| Devers, Louisa | 1878 | Box 66 | Dickson, John | 1870 | Box 42 |
| Devilliers, Eugene A. | 1900 | Box 192 | Dickson, John R. | 1907 | Box 319 |
| Devine, John T. | 1914 | Box 489 | Dickson, Mary E. | 1916 | Box 542 |
| Deviney, Julia | 1919 | Box 626 | Dickson, Sarah A. | 1888 | Box 107 |
| Devlin, John S. | 1857 | Box 25 | Diebitsch, Hermann H. | 1883 | Box 82 |
| Devlin, Mary A. J. | 1861 | Box 29 | Dieffenderfer, William E. | 1919 | Box 626 |
| Devoe, John F. L. | 1900 | Box 192 | Diehl, Margaret | 1916 | Box 542 |
| DeVos, Peter I. | 1844 | Box 16 | Dielger, Katharine | 1901 | Box 206 |
| Dewees, Eleanor | 1850 | Box 20 | Diemer, Jacob | 1912 | Box 440 |
| Dewees, William | 1836 | Box 13 | Diercks, Anna M. | 1912 | Box 440 |
| Deweese, Ella L. | 1909 | Box 366 | Diericks, John F. | 1903 | Box 242 |
| Deweese, John T. | 1914 | Box 489 | Dieste, Peter A. | 1902 | Box 224 |
| Dewey, George (Adm.) | 1917 | Box 568 | Dieterich, Christian P. | 1908 | Box 343 |
| Dewey, Lizzie | 1908 | Box 343 | Dieterich, Katherine | 1902 | Box 224 |
| DeWitt, Calvin | 1908 | Box 343 | Dietrich, Jacob | 1871 | Box 44 |
| Dexter, James Ewing | 1902 | Box 224 | Dietz, George T. | 1917 | Box 568 |
| Dexter, William H. | 1903 | Box 242 | Dietz, Irene Mae | 1917 | Box 568 |
| Dezmazures, Camille Augustin | 1889 | Box 113 | Dietz, Laura | 1911 | Box 414 |
| Di Marzo, Pasquale | 1914 | Box 489 | Dietz, Sydenham | 1911 | Box 414 |
| Diamond, Harry | 1914 | Box 489 | Dieudonne, Frank J. | 1910 | Box 388 |
| Dick, Alexander | 1841 | Box 15 | Diggan, John | 1884 | Box 85 |
| Dick, Christina | 1804 | Box 1 | Digges, Catherine | 1835 | Box 12 |
| Dick, Eliza E. W. | 1902 | Box 224 | Digges, John H. | 1871 | Box 44 |
| Dick, Elizabeth | 1859 | Box 27 | Digges, Julia Dulany | 1905 | Box 279 |
| Dick, Ewell A. | 1903 | Box 242 | Digges, Louisa | 1859 | Box 27 |
| Dick, George | 1901 | Box 206 | Digges, William Dudley | 1875 | Box 57 |
| Dick, George H. | 1893 | Box 138 | Diggins, Bartholomew | 1917 | Box 568 |
| Dick, John A. | 1891 | Box 124 | Diggs, Ann | 1850 | Box 20 |
| Dick, Louisa | 1898 | Box 175 | Diggs, Catherine | 1913 | Box 466 |
| Dick, Mary | 1916 | Box 542 | Diggs, Ewell | 1877 | Box 63 |
| Dick, Robert | 1871 | Box 44 | Diggs, Fannie Parker | 1915 | Box 515 |
| Dick, Robert | 1894 | Box 145 | Diggs, Isaac | 1893 | Box 138 |

| | | | | | | |
|---|---|---|---|---|---|---|
| Diggs, John | 1894 | Box 145 | | Docker, Gilbert | 1817 | Box 5 |
| Diggs, Mary | 1903 | Box 242 | | Docker, Jane | 1820 | Box 6 |
| Diggs, Mary J. | 1912 | Box 440 | | Dockett, Ellen H. | 1898 | Box 175 |
| Diggs, Mary Jane | 1910 | Box 388 | | Dockett, James H. | 1892 | Box 131 |
| Diggs, Norah | 1864 | Box 32 | | Dockett, Louisa | 1915 | Box 515 |
| Diggs, Samuel J. | 1875 | Box 57 | | Dodds, Joseph | 1852 | Box 21 |
| Diggs, Thomas J. | 1889 | Box 113 | | Dodek, Hyman | 1918 | Box 596 |
| Digmueller, Josephine | 1892 | Box 131 | | Dodge, Alexander | 1886 | Box 96 |
| Dikeman, Cornelia A. | 1882 | Box 78 | | Dodge, Allen | 1908 | Box 343 |
| Dikeman, Margaret G. | 1916 | Box 542 | | Dodge, Amasa T. C. | 1899 | Box 145 |
| Dikeman, William R. | 1874 | Box 53 | | Dodge, Clarence | 1916 | Box 542 |
| Dilger, Lorentz | 1891 | Box 124 | | Dodge, Ebenezer | 1901 | Box 206 |
| Dill, Elia Foulke | 1916 | Box 542 | | Dodge, Elizabeth A. | 1919 | Box 626 |
| Dill, Peter | 1902 | Box 224 | | Dodge, Ella S. | 1882 | Box 78 |
| Dillard, Emma | 1914 | Box 489 | | Dodge, Frances I. | 1876 | Box 60 |
| Dillard, James | 1910 | Box 388 | | Dodge, Francis | 1851 | Box 21 |
| Dille, Sophronia | 1885 | Box 91 | | Dodge, Francis S. | 1908 | Box 343 |
| Dillon, Margaret | 1903 | Box 243 | | Dodge, Henry H. | 1899 | Box 182 |
| Dillon, William J. | 1916 | Box 542 | | Dodge, J. Richards | 1906 | Box 298 |
| Diman, Frank M. | 1913 | Box 466 | | Dodge, Laura C. | 1906 | Box 298 |
| Dimick, Justin | 1871 | Box 44 | | Dodge, Laura Levin | 1908 | Box 343 |
| Dines, Mary Ann Maria | 1867 | Box 37 | | Dodge, Mary A. | 1912 | Box 440 |
| Dinger, Marie Rose Sadlier | 1910 | Box 388 | | Dodge, Mary Bolway | 1909 | Box 366 |
| Dinmore, Jane | 1804 | Box 1 | | Dodge, Mary Ellen | 1912 | Box 440 |
| Dinmore, Richard | 1811 | Box 3 | | Dodge, Robert P. | 1887 | Box 102 |
| Dinneen, Jeremiah | 1888 | Box 107 | | Dodge, Walter | 1895 | Box 152 |
| Dinwiddie, Cora L. | 1913 | Box 466 | | Dodge, William C. | 1914 | Box 489 |
| Dippel, Margareda | 1881 | Box 75 | | Dodge, Ysidora B. M. | 1904 | Box 262 |
| Dipple, Frederick Charles | 1849 | Box 20 | | Dodson, Harry | 1861 | Box 29 |
| Disher, Mary E. | 1918 | Box 595 | | Dodson, Margaret A. | 1916 | Box 542 |
| Disney, Lambert B. | 1911 | Box 414 | | Dodson, William | 1863 | Box 31 |
| Dison, Rosetta | 1859 | Box 27 | | Dodson, William | 1869 | Box 40 |
| Dittman, Gustav Adolph V. H. | 1909 | Box 366 | | Doehrer, August | 1885 | Box 91 |
| Dittrich, Rosa | 1906 | Box 298 | | Doering, Jonas | 1907 | Box 319 |
| Diven, Sisney L. | 1908 | Box 343 | | Doerner, Reinhold | 1901 | Box 206 |
| Diver, Jerome B. | 1909 | Box 366 | | Doherty, Annie | 1891 | Box 124 |
| Diver, Lucy H. | 1912 | Box 440 | | Doherty, Annie M. | 1901 | Box 206 |
| Divver, James Edward | 1888 | Box 107 | | Doherty, Ellen | 1883 | Box 82 |
| Dix, William C. | 1905 | Box 279 | | Doherty, John | 1913 | Box 466 |
| Dixon, Alice | 1910 | Box 389 | | Doherty, John T. | 1911 | Box 414 |
| Dixon, Carter | 1915 | Box 515 | | Doherty, Mary | 1900 | Box 192 |
| Dixon, David G. | 1910 | Box 389 | | Dohnea, Clara | 1907 | Box 319 |
| Dixon, David W. | 1888 | Box 107 | | Dohnea, Samuel | 1896 | Box 160 |
| Dixon, Ellen | 1901 | Box 206 | | Dolan, John | 1911 | Box 414 |
| Dixon, George A. | 1863 | Box 31 | | Dolan, John J. | 1900 | Box 192 |
| Dixon, Ira W. | 1916 | Box 542 | | Dolan, Mary M. | 1918 | Box 596 |
| Dixon, John E. | 1909 | Box 366 | | Dolan, Michael | 1911 | Box 414 |
| Dixon, William | 1886 | Box 96 | | Dolan, Patrick V. | 1915 | Box 515 |
| Dixon, William S. | 1919 | Box 626 | | Dolan, Sarah A. | 1900 | Box 192 |
| Dobbins, David | 1816 | Box 5 | | Dolbear, Caroline A. | 1883 | Box 82 |
| Dobbyn, James H. | 1892 | Box 131 | | Dolbear, Stillman F. | 1889 | Box 113 |
| Dobbyn, James R. | 1913 | Box 466 | | Dole, Elizabeth G. | 1900 | Box 192 |

| | | | | | | |
|---|---|---|---|---|---|---|
| Dole, William P. | 1889 | Box 113 | Donoho, Morgan | 1822 | Box 7 |
| Doley, Jonathan | 1825 | Box 8 | Donoho, Thomas | 1867 | Box 37 |
| Domer, Samuel | 1901 | Box 206 | Donohoe, Bridget | 1881 | Box 75 |
| Donaher, Patrick | 1904 | Box 262 | Donohoe, James | 1905 | Box 279 |
| Donahue, Timothy | 1903 | Box 243 | Donohoe, Margaret | 1907 | Box 319 |
| Donald, Sarah | 1913 | Box 466 | Donohoe, Olivia | 1898 | Box 175 |
| Donaldson, Andrew J. | 1896 | Box 160 | Donohoo, Harriet | 1876 | Box 60 |
| Donaldson, Charles | 1908 | Box 343 | Donohoo, William J. | 1899 | Box 182 |
| Donaldson, John T. | 1918 | Box 596 | Donohue, Matthew | 1909 | Box 366 |
| Donaldson, Kathinka | 1910 | Box 389 | Donohue, Thomas | 1908 | Box 343 |
| Donaldson, Laura | 1903 | Box 243 | Donovan, Catharine | 1905 | Box 280 |
| Donaldson, Mary Goodacre | 1918 | Box 596 | Donovan, Dennis | 1890 | Box 118 |
| Donaldson, Nancy L. | 1907 | Box 319 | Donovan, Jeremiah H. | 1907 | Box 319 |
| Donaldson, Robert B. | 1907 | Box 319 | Donovan, Margaret | 1897 | Box 168 |
| Donaldson, Walter F. | 1912 | Box 440 | Donovan, Margaret | 1919 | Box 626 |
| Donaldson, William | 1918 | Box 596 | Donovan, Mary | 1913 | Box 466 |
| Donaldson, William B. | 1912 | Box 440 | Donovan, Timothy | 1863 | Box 31 |
| Donath, August | 1913 | Box 466 | Donovan, William | 1853 | Box 22 |
| Donavin, Levi K. | 1916 | Box 542 | Donovan, William | 1887 | Box 102 |
| Donch, Henry | 1919 | Box 626 | Donovan, William J. | 1915 | Box 515 |
| Dondero, Bartolomeo | 1917 | Box 568 | Doody, Daniel | 1919 | Box 626 |
| Donelan, William C. | 1839 | Box 14 | Doolan, Margaret E. | 1909 | Box 366 |
| Dongal, William | 1895 | Box 125 | Dooley, Mary Janifer | 1892 | Box 131 |
| Donglan, Henry | 1873 | Box 50 | Dooley, Michael | 1856 | Box 24 |
| Doniphan, Edwin C. | 1909 | Box 366 | Doolittle, Lucy S. | 1908 | Box 343 |
| Doniphan, Mary Ann | 1888 | Box 107 | Doolittle, Myrick H. | 1913 | Box 466 |
| Doniphan, William T. | 1883 | Box 82 | Doran, John F. | 1903 | Box 243 |
| Donlevy, Christopher | 1832 | Box 11 | Dorges, August | 1868 | Box 39 |
| Donn, Annie McE. | 1905 | Box 279 | Dorian, Thomas H. | 1874 | Box 53 |
| Donn, Edward W. | 1915 | Box 515 | Dorman, Adele A. | 1878 | Box 66 |
| Donn, Francis Cookman | 1908 | Box 343 | Dorman, Johanna | 1891 | Box 124 |
| Donn, Francis W. | 1916 | Box 542 | Dorman, Julia E. | 1898 | Box 175 |
| Donn, George S. | 1897 | Box 168 | Dorman, Lottie | 1900 | Box 192 |
| Donn, John W. | 1905 | Box 279 | Dorman, Malvin | 1918 | Box 596 |
| Donn, Mary A. | 1884 | Box 85 | Dorn, Christina | 1887 | Box 102 |
| Donn, Oliver P. | 1896 | Box 160 | Dornoff, Mary Jane | 1915 | Box 515 |
| Donnally, Juliet | 1918 | Box 596 | Dorr, Andrew | 1904 | Box 262 |
| Donnelly, Annie | 1911 | Box 414 | Dorr, Anne Lodge | 1897 | Box 168 |
| Donnelly, Catharine | 1886 | Box 96 | Dorr, Clarence A. | 1897 | Box 168 |
| Donnelly, Delia F. | 1884 | Box 85 | Dörr, Louis | 1899 | Box 182 |
| Donnelly, Ellen | 1884 | Box 85 | Dorr, Samuel Hobart | 1913 | Box 466 |
| Donnelly, Francis P. | 1903 | Box 243 | Dorrance, Eliza B. | 1902 | Box 224 |
| Donnelly, John | 1904 | Box 262 | Dorrey, Frederick S. | 1911 | Box 414 |
| Donnelly, John (Jr.) | 1914 | Box 489 | Dorsett, Arabella | 1913 | Box 466 |
| Donnelly, Mary | 1885 | Box 91 | Dorsett, Harriet | 1898 | Box 175 |
| Donnelly, Mary | 1890 | Box 118 | Dorsey, Augustus | 1877 | Box 63 |
| Donnelly, Mary T. | 1884 | Box 85 | Dorsey, Clement | 1917 | Box 568 |
| Donnelly, Owen | 1904 | Box 262 | Dorsey, Cornelia L. | 1903 | Box 243 |
| Donnelly, Rose L. | 1902 | Box 224 | Dorsey, Dinah | 1882 | Box 78 |
| Donnelly, Sarah | 1889 | Box 113 | Dorsey, Edward | 1804 | Box 1 |
| Donnelly, Thomas | 1888 | Box 107 | Dorsey, Eliza | 1891 | Box 124 |
| Donoghue, Francis X. | 1917 | Box 568 | Dorsey, Henrietta S. | 1891 | Box 124 |

| | | | | | | |
|---|---|---|---|---|---|---|
| Dorsey, James | 1905 | Box 280 | Douglass, Henry | 1873 | Box 50 |
| Dorsey, James Owen | 1915 | Box 515 | Douglass, John Wesley | 1908 | Box 343 |
| Dorsey, Jane | 1897 | Box 168 | Douglass, Lloyd | 1905 | Box 280 |
| Dorsey, Jennie S. | 1918 | Box 596 | Douglass, Mary C. | 1897 | Box 168 |
| Dorsey, Katherine C. | 1893 | Box 138 | Douglass, Richard Henry | 1875 | Box 57 |
| Dorsey, Lucy J. | 1908 | Box 343 | Douglass, William Osman | 1899 | Box 182 |
| Dorsey, Lucy L. | 1917 | Box 568 | Dove, Charles B. | 1913 | Box 466 |
| Dorsey, Mary | 1892 | Box 131 | Dove, Eliza Jane | 1859 | Box 27 |
| Dorsey, Mary H. | 1885 | Box 91 | Dove, Joseph | 1841 | Box 15 |
| Dorsey, Mary M. | 1901 | Box 206 | Dove, Richard George | 1892 | Box 131 |
| Dorsey, Presley W. | 1871 | Box 44 | Dove, William F. | 1912 | Box 440 |
| Dorsey, Richard Albert | 1914 | Box 489 | Dover, Ariana (Aary Ann) | 1910 | Box 389 |
| Dorsey, Thomas Graham | 1897 | Box 168 | Dover, Judson | 1868 | Box 39 |
| Dorsey, Worthington | 1908 | Box 343 | Dovilliers, Philippa | 1902 | Box 224 |
| Dorsheimer, Isabella P. | 1907 | Box 319 | Dow, Jesse E. | 1891 | Box 124 |
| Dorwart, Jacob L. | 1883 | Box 82 | Dowde, Daniel | 1869 | Box 40 |
| Dos Passos, John R. | 1917 | Box 568 | Dowden, Benjamin Day | 1911 | Box 414 |
| Dos Passos, Lucy Sprigg | 1916 | Box 542 | Dowden, Edward | 1895 | Box 152 |
| Dosier, Catherine | 1873 | Box 50 | Dowell, Cynthia E. | 1916 | Box 542 |
| Doty, James H. | 1910 | Box 389 | Dowling, Amanda E. | 1910 | Box 389 |
| Doubleday, Charlotte | 1874 | Box 53 | Dowling, Edward J. | 1905 | Box 280 |
| Doubleday, Frances G. | 1910 | Box 389 | Dowling, Gertrude H. | 1918 | Box 596 |
| Doubleday, Henry Howell | 1899 | Box 182 | Dowling, James J. | 1897 | Box 168 |
| Doud, James | 1889 | Box 113 | Dowling, Michael | 1822 | Box 7 |
| Doud, Levi B. | 1906 | Box 298 | Dowling, Thomas | 1900 | Box 192 |
| Doud, Sidney W. | 1896 | Box 160 | Dowling, William | 1852 | Box 21 |
| Dougal, Mary Virginia | 1908 | Box 343 | Down, Patrick | 1891 | Box 124 |
| Dougherty, Ann E. | 1884 | Box 86 | Downer, John | 1901 | Box 206 |
| Dougherty, Emily Cooper | 1912 | Box 440 | Downes, Charlotte S. M. | 1891 | Box 124 |
| Dougherty, James | 1826 | Box 8 | Downes, John | 1882 | Box 78 |
| Dougherty, Mary | 1830 | Box 10 | Downey, Hugh | 1911 | Box 414 |
| Dougherty, Mary E. | 1919 | Box 626 | Downey, Jeremiah | 1891 | Box 124 |
| Doughty, Evalyn | 1905 | Box 280 | Downey, Jeremiah F. | 1904 | Box 262 |
| Doughty, William | 1859 | Box 27 | Downey, John M. | 1898 | Box 175 |
| Douglas, Anna J. | 1917 | Box 568 | Downey, Mary A. | 1913 | Box 466 |
| Douglas, August | 1894 | Box 145 | Downey, Michael | 1848 | Box 19 |
| Douglas, Harriet N. | 1914 | Box 489 | Downey, Patrick | 1909 | Box 366 |
| Douglas, Henry | 1904 | Box 262 | Downey, Timothy | 1868 | Box 39 |
| Douglas, Henry Clay | 1894 | Box 145 | Downey, William F. | 1914 | Box 489 |
| Douglas, John | 1881 | Box 75 | Downie, Lizzie | 1916 | Box 542 |
| Douglas, Lewis H. | 1909 | Box 366 | Downing, Joseph M. | 1869 | Box 40 |
| Douglas, Mary M. | 1887 | Box 102 | Downing, Patrick J. | 1885 | Box 91 |
| Douglas, Mary V. | 1908 | Box 343 | Downing, Robert | 1893 | Box 138 |
| Douglas, Richard Spencer | 1916 | Box 542 | Downing, William B. | 1884 | Box 86 |
| Douglas, Robert J. | 1885 | Box 91 | Downman, Mary A. Magruder | 1892 | Box 131 |
| Douglas, Sidney Virginia | 1909 | Box 366 | Downs, Ann | 1872 | Box 47 |
| Douglas, William | 1880 | Box 71 | Downs, Ellen Teresa | 1913 | Box 466 |
| Douglass, August Bernard | 1915 | Box 515 | Downs, John | 1901 | Box 206 |
| Douglass, Charles | 1895 | Box 152 | Downs, Martha C. | 1899 | Box 182 |
| Douglass, Daniel | 1861 | Box 29 | Downs, Mary | 1869 | Box 40 |
| Douglass, Frederick | 1895 | Box 152 | Downs, Mary | 1912 | Box 440 |
| Douglass, Helen | 1903 | Box 243 | Downs, Rose | 1916 | Box 542 |

| | | | | | | |
|---|---|---|---|---|---|---|
| Downs, Solomon | 1856 | Box 24 | | Dripps, John H. | 1916 | Box 542 |
| Dowson, Alfred R. | 1851 | Box 21 | | Driscoll, Catharine | 1892 | Box 131 |
| Dowty, Betsey | 1851 | Box 21 | | Driscoll, Daniel A. | 1915 | Box 515 |
| Doxon, Mary A. | 1913 | Box 466 | | Driscoll, Dennis | 1895 | Box 152 |
| Doyle, Anna Astatia | 1828 | Box 9 | | Driscoll, Jeremiah | 1874 | Box 53 |
| Doyle, Caroline | 1915 | Box 515 | | Driscoll, Johanna | 1909 | Box 366 |
| Doyle, Catherine | 1899 | Box 182 | | Driscoll, Mary | 1898 | Box 175 |
| Doyle, Francis | 1911 | Box 414 | | Driscoll, Patrick | 1884 | Box 86 |
| Doyle, Ida V. Slater | 1915 | Box 515 | | Driscoll, Patrick | 1889 | Box 113 |
| Doyle, John B. | 1914 | Box 489 | | Driscoll, Richard A. | 1914 | Box 489 |
| Doyle, John T. | 1906 | Box 298 | | Driver, George W. | 1918 | Box 596 |
| Doyle, Thomas | 1903 | Box 243 | | Driver, Margaret Ann | 1862 | Box 30 |
| Doyne, Jesse | 1805 | Box 1 | | Droop, Edward F. | 1908 | Box 343 |
| Drain, Rosannah | 1872 | Box 47 | | Drum, William F. | 1910 | Box 389 |
| Drake, Charles D. | 1902 | Box 224 | | Drummond, Francis | 1884 | Box 86 |
| Drake, George W. | 1904 | Box 263 | | Drummond, John C. | 1832 | Box 11 |
| Drake, Martha J. V. | 1913 | Box 467 | | Drummond, Matilda | 1848 | Box 19 |
| Draley, Joseph | 1881 | Box 75 | | Drummond, Nicholas | 1909 | Box 366 |
| Drane, Walter P. | 1912 | Box 440 | | Drury, Charles S. | 1902 | Box 224 |
| Draney, Felix Merritt | 1892 | Box 131 | | Drury, George A. | 1908 | Box 343 |
| Draper, Amos Galusha | 1917 | Box 568 | | Drury, George W. | 1918 | Box 596 |
| Draper, Daniel | 1904 | Box 263 | | Drury, John H. | 1914 | Box 489 |
| Draper, Florence D. | 1909 | Box 366 | | Drury, William L. | 1914 | Box 489 |
| Draper, Mary | 1901 | Box 206 | | Drury, Winifred | 1819 | Box 6 |
| Draper, Susan Preston | 1919 | Box 626 | | Dryer, Ellen A. | 1920 | Box 657 |
| Dravo, John F. | 1907 | Box 320 | | Du Barry, Laura | 1919 | Box 626 |
| Drawbaugh, Gertrude | 1904 | Box 263 | | Du Bois, Carrie L. | 1906 | Box 298 |
| Drawbaugh, John A. | 1898 | Box 175 | | Du Fief, Kate | 1910 | Box 389 |
| Dreier, Dorothea | 1871 | Box 44 | | Dubant, George G. | 1870 | Box 42 |
| Dreka, Augustus | 1913 | Box 467 | | Dubant, Peter M. | 1902 | Box 224 |
| Drescher, George F. C. | 1883 | Box 82 | | Dubant, Susan L. | 1915 | Box 515 |
| Dresel, Louise | 1913 | Box 467 | | DuBois, James T. | 1920 | Box 657 |
| Drew, Bernard | 1903 | Box 243 | | DuBois, Louise G. | 1902 | Box 224 |
| Drew, Edwardina | 1917 | Box 568 | | Dubois, William | 1910 | Box 389 |
| Drew, George J. | 1905 | Box 280 | | Ducat, Arthur C. | 1913 | Box 467 |
| Drew, George W. | 1877 | Box 63 | | Ducket, Lucy | 1853 | Box 22 |
| Drew, Solomon | 1854 | Box 23 | | Duckett, John | 1891 | Box 124 |
| Drew, William O. | 1917 | Box 568 | | Duckett, Lucy | 1917 | Box 568 |
| Drewes, Louis | 1908 | Box 343 | | Duckett, Martha Ann | 1911 | Box 415 |
| Drexel, Anthony J. | 1900 | Box 192 | | Duckett, Walter G. | 1909 | Box 366 |
| Dreyer, William L. | 1913 | Box 467 | | Dudley, Alice R. | 1920 | Box 657 |
| Dreyfuss, Babette | 1911 | Box 415 | | Dudley, Joseph | 1908 | Box 343 |
| Dreyfuss, David | 1888 | Box 107 | | Dudley, Sarah | 1903 | Box 243 |
| Drier, Henry | 1884 | Box 86 | | Dudley, Theresa F. | 1898 | Box 175 |
| Dries, Annie A. | 1909 | Box 366 | | Dudley, William W. | 1910 | Box 389 |
| Dries, John F. | 1911 | Box 415 | | Duff, John J. | 1918 | Box 596 |
| Dries, Marie E. | 1900 | Box 192 | | Duff, Robert J. | 1911 | Box 415 |
| Driggs, Mary Eddy | 1915 | Box 515 | | Duffie, Florence S. | 1913 | Box 467 |
| Drill, John | 1888 | Box 107 | | Duffie, John S. | 1917 | Box 568 |
| Drinkard, Mary F. | 1894 | Box 145 | | Duffin, James Thomas | 1906 | Box 298 |
| Drinkard, William B. | 1877 | Box 63 | | Duffy, Bryan | 1813 | Box 4 |
| Drinkhouse, Angeline | 1911 | Box 415 | | Duffy, Eleanor L. Burritt | 1916 | Box 542 |

| | | | | | | |
|---|---|---|---|---|---|---|
| Duffy, John | 1894 | Box 145 | | Dundas, Mary Y. | 1863 | Box 31 |
| Duffy, John | 1916 | Box 542 | | Dundas, William H. | 1861 | Box 29 |
| Duffy, Kate E. | 1902 | Box 224 | | Dungan, Elizabeth | 1917 | Box 568 |
| Duffy, Patrick | 1899 | Box 182 | | Dunham, Samuel C. | 1920 | Box 657 |
| Duffy, Rowena R. | 1919 | Box 626 | | Dunhoft, Bernard | 1889 | Box 113 |
| Duffy, Terrence A. | 1912 | Box 440 | | Dunkhorst, Elizabeth C. | 1897 | Box 168 |
| Dufour, Amanda L. | 1899 | Box 182 | | Dunkhorst, William H. | 1911 | Box 415 |
| Dufour, Oliver | 1891 | Box 124 | | Dunkins, Aaron | 1884 | Box 86 |
| Dugan, Emily C. | 1899 | Box 183 | | Dunlap, Alexander | 1820 | Box 6 |
| Dugan, Frederick I. | 1912 | Box 440 | | Dunlap, Andrew | 1914 | Box 489 |
| Dugan, John F. | 1911 | Box 415 | | Dunlap, Eliza Miller | 1913 | Box 467 |
| Dugan, Nora | 1908 | Box 343 | | Dunlap, Ellen Adams | 1918 | Box 596 |
| Dugan, Philip | 1869 | Box 40 | | Dunlop, Barbara L. | 1872 | Box 47 |
| Dugan, Sara V. | 1916 | Box 542 | | Dunlop, Ellen | 1907 | Box 320 |
| Dugger, Susan | 1912 | Box 440 | | Dunlop, Emily Redin | 1920 | Box 657 |
| Dugger, William Edwin | 1894 | Box 145 | | Dunlop, Fannie | 1917 | Box 568 |
| DuHamel, William J. C. | 1883 | Box 82 | | Dunlop, George T. | 1908 | Box 343 |
| Duhamel, William K. | 1893 | Box 138 | | Dunlop, George W. | 1858 | Box 26 |
| Duhey, Bridget | 1899 | Box 183 | | Dunlop, James | 1872 | Box 47 |
| Duhey, Timothy J. | 1903 | Box 243 | | Dunlop, John Henry | 1907 | Box 320 |
| Duke, Sarah D. | 1903 | Box 243 | | Dunlop, William L. | 1916 | Box 542 |
| Duke, Thomas | 1888 | Box 107 | | Dunmore, Frances | 1889 | Box 113 |
| Dukehart, Heinrich Wilhelm T. | 1905 | Box 280 | | Dunn, Bessie A. | 1907 | Box 320 |
| Dulaney, Caroline R. | 1893 | Box 138 | | Dunn, Elizabeth Lanier | 1910 | Box 389 |
| Dulaney, Jane S. | 1888 | Box 107 | | Dunn, James M. | 1910 | Box 389 |
| Dulany, Bladen | 1876 | Box 60 | | Dunn, John | 1831 | Box 11 |
| Dulany, Mary | 1808 | Box 3 | | Dunn, John | 1893 | Box 138 |
| Dulany, Walter | 1808 | Box 3 | | Dunn, John | 1894 | Box 145 |
| Dulenty, Patrick | 1897 | Box 168 | | Dunn, John J. | 1905 | Box 280 |
| Duley, Henry Brook | 1898 | Box 175 | | Dunn, John T. | 1915 | Box 515 |
| Duley, Jonathan | 1825 | Box 8 | | Dunn, Mary | 1832 | Box 11 |
| Dulhay, Charles R. | 1917 | Box 568 | | Dunn, Mary | 1918 | Box 596 |
| Dulin, Edward L. | 1854 | Box 23 | | Dunn, Orlando H. | 1870 | Box 42 |
| Dulin, Mary Bowie | 1917 | Box 568 | | Dunn, Patrick B. | 1890 | Box 118 |
| Dumaine, Auguste | 1920 | Box 657 | | Dunn, Robert W. | 1909 | Box 366 |
| Dumble, Mary E. | 1900 | Box 192 | | Dunn, Thomas | 1897 | Box 168 |
| Dummer, George | 1901 | Box 206 | | Dunn, William M. | 1887 | Box 102 |
| Dumn, Frances Anna | 1910 | Box 389 | | Dunne, William G. | 1908 | Box 343 |
| Dumont, Neill | 1906 | Box 298 | | Dunnigan, John | 1899 | Box 183 |
| Dumphreius, Thomas | 1852 | Box 21 | | Dunnigan, Marguerite C. | 1915 | Box 515 |
| Dunawin, Ellen A. | 1891 | Box 124 | | Dunning, Ralph | 1905 | Box 280 |
| Dunbar, Elizabeth A. | 1873 | Box 50 | | Dunnington, Alexznear M. | 1915 | Box 515 |
| Duncan, Joseph Wilson | 1912 | Box 440 | | Dunnington, E. B. Arbuckle | 1912 | Box 440 |
| Duncan, Mary Shields | 1907 | Box 320 | | Dunnington, Ella D. | 1910 | Box 389 |
| Duncan, Thomas | 1918 | Box 596 | | Dunnington, Mary E. | 1916 | Box 542 |
| Duncan, Thomas R. | 1909 | Box 366 | | Dunster, George | 1901 | Box 207 |
| Duncan, William A. | 1902 | Box 224 | | Dunton, Charles | 1915 | Box 515 |
| Duncanson, Henry A. | 1878 | Box 66 | | Dupree, Louis J. | 1893 | Box 138 |
| Duncanson, Martha D. | 1866 | Box 35 | | Dupuy, Catharine | 1816 | Box 5 |
| Duncanson, William M. | 1864 | Box 32 | | DuPuy, Eleanor Gertrude | 1920 | Box 658 |
| Duncanson, William Mayne | 1812 | Box 4 | | Durant, John H. | 1837 | Box 13 |
| Duncastle, Sarah | 1813 | Box 4 | | Durant, Thomas J. | 1882 | Box 78 |

| | | | | | | |
|---|---|---|---|---|---|---|
| Durebo, Zora B. | 1917 | Box 568 | Dyer, Thomas Baker | 1899 | Box 183 |
| Duren, John A. | 1876 | Box 60 | Dyett, James S. | 1915 | Box 515 |
| Durham, Catharine | 1912 | Box 440 | Dyett, Martha Marshall | 1910 | Box 389 |
| Durkin, Frances M. | 1920 | Box 658 | Dyott, Adeline T. | 1904 | Box 263 |
| Durkin, Patrick J. | 1885 | Box 91 | Dyrenforth, Robert G. | 1910 | Box 389 |
| Durnbaugh, Joseph A. | 1911 | Box 415 | Dyson, Charles | 1874 | Box 53 |
| Dutch, Anthony M. | 1883 | Box 82 | Dyson, Robert H. G. | 1896 | Box 160 |
| Duttamel, William J. C. | 1883 | Box 82 | Dzierozynski, Francis | 1855 | Box 24 |
| Dutton, George W. | 1913 | Box 467 | Eagan, John | 1893 | Box 138 |
| Dutton, Notley J. | 1909 | Box 366 | Eagan, Owen | 1893 | Box 138 |
| Dutton, Thomas | 1877 | Box 63 | Eakle, Edward Harmon | 1912 | Box 440 |
| Duval, Gabriella A. | 1887 | Box 102 | Eakle, Elias H. | 1864 | Box 32 |
| Duvall, Andrew B. | 1905 | Box 280 | Ealer, Eulalie | 1909 | Box 367 |
| Duvall, Anne Eliza | 1920 | Box 658 | Eames, Charles | 1867 | Box 37 |
| Duvall, Benjamin | 1904 | Box 263 | Eames, Fanny | 1890 | Box 118 |
| Duvall, Christina | 1899 | Box 183 | Earhart, Elizabeth C. | 1897 | Box 168 |
| Duvall, J. Albert | 1913 | Box 467 | Earl, Elizabeth F. | 1920 | Box 658 |
| Duvall, James A. | 1918 | Box 596 | Earl, Robert (Sr.) | 1874 | Box 53 |
| Duvall, James Walter | 1920 | Box 658 | Earl, Robert | 1918 | Box 596 |
| Duvall, Lewis E. | 1906 | Box 298 | Earl, Virginia Chew | 1916 | Box 543 |
| Duvall, Louisa | 1891 | Box 124 | Earle, George | 1899 | Box 183 |
| Duvall, Lucy | 1836 | Box 13 | Earle, Mary C. | 1906 | Box 299 |
| Duvall, Mathew E. | 1867 | Box 37 | Earle, Richard T. | 1891 | Box 124 |
| Duvall, Samuel | 1891 | Box 124 | Earle, William E. | 1894 | Box 145 |
| Duvall, Sarah | 1827 | Box 9 | Earley, James F. | 1906 | Box 299 |
| Duvall, Sarah Ann | 1861 | Box 29 | Earll, R. Edward | 1896 | Box 160 |
| Dwine, Hannora | 1901 | Box 207 | Early, Charles | 1914 | Box 489 |
| Dwire, Mary Isabel | 1916 | Box 542 | Early, Micajah | 1915 | Box 515 |
| Dwyer, Blanche F. | 1909 | Box 366 | Early, William | 1910 | Box 389 |
| Dwyer, Henry F. | 1896 | Box 160 | Earner, Michael J. | 1907 | Box 320 |
| Dwyer, John | 1920 | Box 658 | Earnshaw, Basil B. | 1916 | Box 543 |
| Dwyer, Mary Ellen | 1917 | Box 568 | Earnshaw, Richard Jackson | 1918 | Box 596 |
| Dyce, Robert | 1842 | Box 15 | Earnshaw, William F. | 1898 | Box 175 |
| Dye, Hobart S. | 1916 | Box 542 | Easby, Agnes A. M. | 1878 | Box 66 |
| Dye, John H. | 1903 | Box 243 | Easby, Fanny B. | 1919 | Box 626 |
| Dye, Peleg Edwin | 1907 | Box 320 | Easby, John W. | 1894 | Box 145 |
| Dyer, Alexander B. | 1874 | Box 53 | Easby, Rosa L. | 1917 | Box 569 |
| Dyer, Alford | 1891 | Box 124 | Easby, William | 1854 | Box 23 |
| Dyer, Edward | 1845 | Box 17 | East, Sarah | 1911 | Box 415 |
| Dyer, Edward C. | 1867 | Box 37 | Eastburn, Amelia | 1854 | Box 23 |
| Dyer, Elizabeth B. | 1892 | Box 131 | Eastburn, Jane | 1821 | Box 6 |
| Dyer, Ellen E. | 1899 | Box 183 | Eastburn, Samuel L. | 1900 | Box 192 |
| Dyer, George . | 1906 | Box 299 | Easterling, H. Virgil | 1920 | Box 658 |
| Dyer, George W. | 1889 | Box 113 | Eastman, J. R. | 1913 | Box 467 |
| Dyer, Giles | 1856 | Box 24 | Eastman, Mary Henderson | 1887 | Box 102 |
| Dyer, Henry Oswal | 1811 | Box 3 | Eastman, Mary J. | 1919 | Box 626 |
| Dyer, John T. | 1911 | Box 415 | Easton, John | 1808 | Box 3 |
| Dyer, Kate H. | 1902 | Box 224 | Easton, John W. | 1888 | Box 107 |
| Dyer, Margaret M. | 1883 | Box 82 | Easton, Sarah | 1844 | Box 16 |
| Dyer, Mary A. | 1889 | Box 113 | Eastwood, Julius C. | 1881 | Box 75 |
| Dyer, Mary E. | 1900 | Box 192 | Easty, Alice | 1917 | Box 569 |
| Dyer, Susan Cecilia | 1899 | Box 183 | Eatman, Meredith | 1900 | Box 192 |

| | | | | | | |
|---|---|---|---|---|---|---|
| Eaton, Alexander | 1901 | Box 207 | Edes, Margaret | 1905 | Box 280 |
| Eaton, Alonzo J. | 1906 | Box 299 | Edes, Samuel C. | 1866 | Box 35 |
| Eaton, Anna E. | 1920 | Box 658 | Edes, Samuel C. | 1906 | Box 299 |
| Eaton, Elizabeth L. | 1903 | Box 243 | Edes, William H. | 1865 | Box 33 |
| Eaton, John | 1906 | Box 299 | Edgar, Annie M. | 1911 | Box 415 |
| Eaton, John H. | 1856 | Box 24 | Edgar, Nora | 1915 | Box 515 |
| Eaton, Mary K. S. | 1897 | Box 168 | Edmond, Sarah Huntington | 1899 | Box 183 |
| Eaton, Susan | 1864 | Box 32 | Edmonds, George H. | 1866 | Box 35 |
| Eaton, Walter S. | 1903 | Box 243 | Edmonds, Henry Gordon | 1908 | Box 343 |
| Eaton, William | 1901 | Box 207 | Edmonds, James | 1901 | Box 207 |
| Ebaugh, Anna L. | 1894 | Box 145 | Edmonds, Lydia M. | 1913 | Box 467 |
| Ebaugh, Theodore Oliver | 1913 | Box 467 | Edmonds, Patsy | 1904 | Box 263 |
| Ebberts, Emma Frances | 1913 | Box 467 | Edmondston, Madeleinr H. | 1911 | Box 415 |
| Ebbs, Walter | 1905 | Box 280 | Edmonson, Alice E. | 1902 | Box 224 |
| Ebel, Catharine | 1909 | Box 367 | Edmonston, Amelia | 1874 | Box 53 |
| Ebel, Charles | 1893 | Box 138 | Edmonston, Brooke | 1820 | Box 6 |
| Ebeling, Theresia | 1884 | Box 86 | Edmonston, Caroline | 1905 | Box 280 |
| Eberly, Anton | 1907 | Box 320 | Edmonston, Charles | 1897 | Box 168 |
| Eberly, Daniel | 1876 | Box 60 | Edmonston, Decius W. | 1879 | Box 68 |
| Eberly, Frederick W. | 1902 | Box 224 | Edmonston, Dorothy | 1817 | Box 5 |
| Eberly, George F. | 1911 | Box 415 | Edmonston, Elijah | 1867 | Box 37 |
| Eberly, George Lewis | 1893 | Box 138 | Edmonston, Enoch | 1818 | Box 5 |
| Eberly, Margaret | 1909 | Box 367 | Edmonston, Enoch | 1913 | Box 467 |
| Eberly, Winifred E. | 1906 | Box 299 | Edmonston, Gabriel | 1918 | Box 596 |
| Ebert, Alexander | 1914 | Box 489 | Edmonston, Harriet Williss | 1887 | Box 102 |
| Ebert, Edward | 1916 | Box 543 | Edmonston, Jackson | 1872 | Box 47 |
| Ebert, Theresia | 1919 | Box 626 | Edmonston, James B. | 1816 | Box 5 |
| Eccleston, Samuel | 1860 | Box 28 | Edmonston, Margaret G. | 1832 | Box 11 |
| Echterman, Gerhard Henry | 1920 | Box 658 | Edmonston, Raphael A. | 1900 | Box 192 |
| Eckardt, John | 1830 | Box 10 | Edmonston, Richard A. | 1886 | Box 96 |
| Eckart, Herman T. | 1887 | Box 102 | Edmonston, Samuel H. | 1912 | Box 440 |
| Eckel, Charles E. | 1851 | Box 21 | Edmonston, Thomas | 1868 | Box 39 |
| Ecker, John Beard | 1915 | Box 515 | Edmunds, James | 1906 | Box 299 |
| Eckert, Leonhardt | 1911 | Box 415 | Edmundson, Adelia; Samuel P. | 1905 | Box 280 |
| Eckfeldt, Frederick | 1884 | Box 86 | Edmundson, Samuel Paul | 1907 | Box 320 |
| Eckhardt, Annie Laura | 1906 | Box 299 | Edmundson, W. B. | 1920 | Box 658 |
| Eckhardt, Johanna | 1901 | Box 207 | Edsall, John H. | 1915 | Box 515 |
| Eckhardt, Nicholas | 1920 | Box 658 | Edson, Mary | 1901 | Box 207 |
| Eckloff, Margaret | 1881 | Box 75 | Edson, Susan A. | 1898 | Box 175 |
| Eckloff, Martha J. | 1907 | Box 320 | Edwards, Alpheus L. | 1898 | Box 175 |
| Eckloff, Randolph J. | 1914 | Box 489 | Edwards, Ann | 1847 | Box 19 |
| Eddie, Emeline M. | 1874 | Box 53 | Edwards, Catherine McFee | 1879 | Box 68 |
| Eddins, Henry C. | 1913 | Box 467 | Edwards, Elizabeth | 1876 | Box 60 |
| Edds, Anna Maria | 1888 | Box 107 | Edwards, Elizabeth R. | 1891 | Box 124 |
| Eddy, Mary Houston | 1917 | Box 569 | Edwards, Ellen | 1883 | Box 82 |
| Edel, Ellen | 1903 | Box 243 | Edwards, Fannie | 1912 | Box 440 |
| Edel, Herman | 1889 | Box 113 | Edwards, George | 1853 | Box 22 |
| Edelen, Eva M. | 1917 | Box 569 | Edwards, George K. | 1897 | Box 168 |
| Edelen, Richard H. | 1902 | Box 224 | Edwards, Harriet E. | 1890 | Box 118 |
| Edelin, Charles | 1888 | Box 107 | Edwards, Henrietta | 1895 | Box 152 |
| Edelin, Judith T. | 1870 | Box 42 | Edwards, Henry | 1915 | Box 515 |
| Edelin, Susanna | 1813 | Box 4 | Edwards, James | 1901 | Box 207 |

| | | | | | | |
|---|---|---|---|---|---|---|
| Edwards, James Alexander | 1906 | Box 299 | Ela, Mary Henderson | 1913 | Box 467 |
| Edwards, James F. | 1916 | Box 543 | Elberfeld, John | 1911 | Box 415 |
| Edwards, James H. | 1911 | Box 415 | Eldredge, Albert G. | 1884 | Box 86 |
| Edwards, John | 1894 | Box 145 | Eldridge, Abigail R. | 1890 | Box 118 |
| Edwards, John S. | 1896 | Box 160 | Eldridge, William C. | 1908 | Box 343 |
| Edwards, Joseph | 1871 | Box 44 | Elgar, Ann | 1864 | Box 32 |
| Edwards, Lewis | 1912 | Box 441 | Elgin, Elizabeth | 1914 | Box 490 |
| Edwards, Margaret | 1876 | Box 60 | Elgin, Ernest T. | 1919 | Box 626 |
| Edwards, Mary Conger | 1916 | Box 543 | Eli, Daniel E. | 1912 | Box 441 |
| Edwards, Mary E. | 1863 | Box 31 | Eli, John W. | 1877 | Box 63 |
| Edwards, Mattie | 1916 | Box 543 | Eliot, Eugenia E. | 1884 | Box 86 |
| Edwards, Richard | 1905 | Box 280 | Eliot, Johnson | 1884 | Box 86 |
| Edwards, Sarah | 1909 | Box 367 | Eliot, Mary J. L. | 1915 | Box 516 |
| Edwards, Sarah M. | 1899 | Box 183 | Eliot, Randolph L. | 1906 | Box 299 |
| Edwards, Thomas J. | 1894 | Box 145 | Elkin, Lucy Victoria | 1876 | Box 60 |
| Edwards, William Wells B. | 1880 | Box 71 | Elkins, Philip Morgan | 1920 | Box 658 |
| Edwood, William A. | 1917 | Box 569 | Ellaby, Alfred | 1913 | Box 467 |
| Eells, Edward | 1897 | Box 168 | Ellery, Eleanor E. McL. | 1889 | Box 113 |
| Egan (Callahan), Catharine | 1914 | Box 489 | Ellet, Charles | 1862 | Box 30 |
| Egan, Amelia | 1906 | Box 299 | Ellicott, Charles J. F. | 1920 | Box 658 |
| Egan, Ben F. | 1908 | Box 343 | Ellicott, Virginia Gordon | 1909 | Box 367 |
| Egan, Eliza | 1899 | Box 183 | Ellinger, John A. | 1920 | Box 658 |
| Egan, Henry | 1902 | Box 224 | Elliot, George H. | 1900 | Box 192 |
| Egan, William | 1872 | Box 47 | Elliot, George P. | 1887 | Box 102 |
| Eggleston, Mary Alice | 1906 | Box 299 | Elliot, Jonathan | 1846 | Box 18 |
| Egleston, Elizabeth | 1901 | Box 207 | Elliot, Mary | 1897 | Box 168 |
| Egli, Maria | 1901 | Box 207 | Elliot, Robert K. | 1885 | Box 91 |
| Eglin, Charles | 1896 | Box 160 | Elliot, William | 1838 | Box 14 |
| Egloff, Balthasar | 1904 | Box 263 | Elliot, William B. | 1915 | Box 516 |
| Egloff, George | 1902 | Box 224 | Elliott, Alexander Jr. | 1906 | Box 299 |
| Egloff, Leonhard | 1910 | Box 389 | Elliott, Alfred H. | 1919 | Box 626 |
| Egloff, Martha | 1890 | Box 118 | Elliott, Elizabeth Darlington | 1916 | Box 543 |
| Egloff, Mary V. | 1920 | Box 658 | Elliott, Ezekiel B. | 1888 | Box 107 |
| Ehlers, Henry | 1920 | Box 658 | Elliott, George | 1834 | Box 12 |
| Ehlshlager, Adam Sr. | 1904 | Box 263 | Elliott, J. Wesley | 1919 | Box 626 |
| Ehnert, Caroline | 1918 | Box 596 | Elliott, Jared L. | 1881 | Box 75 |
| Eichholtz, Hugo G. | 1889 | Box 113 | Elliott, John H. | 1906 | Box 299 |
| Eichholtz, Juliusa | 1901 | Box 207 | Elliott, John Stuart | 1919 | Box 626 |
| Eichholz, Elizabeth | 1889 | Box 113 | Elliott, John Woods | 1913 | Box 467 |
| Eichhorn, Rudolph | 1907 | Box 320 | Elliott, Jehu W. | 1885 | Box 91 |
| Eichler, Wilhelmina | 1882 | Box 78 | Elliott, Juliet G. | 1887 | Box 102 |
| Eichman, Michael | 1895 | Box 152 | Elliott, Lina J. | 1914 | Box 490 |
| Eichner, Magdalena | 1908 | Box 343 | Elliott, Lucretia Ann | 1891 | Box 124 |
| Eider, Sarah Ratcliffe | 1914 | Box 489 | Elliott, Lucy Irland | 1903 | Box 243 |
| Eidier, Daniel Webster | 1914 | Box 489 | Elliott, Lynde | 1817 | Box 5 |
| Eimer, William G. | 1915 | Box 515 | Elliott, Maria | 1880 | Box 71 |
| Einolf, George | 1898 | Box 175 | Elliott, Mary Ann | 1904 | Box 263 |
| Einstein, Samuel | 1911 | Box 415 | Elliott, Matilda Moxley | 1910 | Box 389 |
| Eiseman, Bertha | 1904 | Box 263 | Elliott, Minnie J. | 1916 | Box 543 |
| Eisenbeise, Rosa Marie | 1909 | Box 367 | Elliott, R. Frank | 1908 | Box 343 |
| Eisenmann, Leonora | 1907 | Box 320 | Elliott, Stephen Habersham | 1917 | Box 569 |
| Eisinger, Annie C. | 1916 | Box 543 | Elliott, Virginius T. | 1898 | Box 175 |

| | | | | | | |
|---|---|---|---|---|---|---|
| Elliott-Bailey, Mabel Grey | 1911 | Box 415 | Emmerich, Frederick | 1882 | Box 78 |
| Ellis, Archie | 1910 | Box 389 | Emmerich, Katherine | 1888 | Box 107 |
| Ellis, Ebenezer | 1907 | Box 320 | Emmerich, George | 1892 | Box 131 |
| Ellis, Elizabeth | 1907 | Box 320 | Emmerick, John (Johannes) | 1845 | Box 17 |
| Ellis, Frank | 1917 | Box 569 | Emmert, Caroline H. | 1874 | Box 53 |
| Ellis, Henry | 1855 | Box 24 | Emmert, George | 1898 | Box 175 |
| Ellis, J. Frank | 1910 | Box 389 | Emmert, George | 1920 | Box 658 |
| Ellis, John Bartholomew | 1844 | Box 16 | Emmert, Henry | 1831 | Box 11 |
| Ellis, John F. | 1870 | Box 42 | Emmert, Henry W. | 1880 | Box 71 |
| Ellis, Lewis Y. | 1906 | Box 299 | Emmons, Clara L. P. | 1918 | Box 596 |
| Ellis, Lucinda A. | 1909 | Box 367 | Emmons, Jennie S. | 1915 | Box 516 |
| Ellis, Mary | 1891 | Box 124 | Emmons, Richard | 1908 | Box 343 |
| Ellis, Mary A. | 1907 | Box 320 | Emmons, Samuel Franklin | 1911 | Box 416 |
| Ellis, Mary A. | 1911 | Box 416 | Emmons, Weltha A. | 1888 | Box 107 |
| Ellis, Mary Dwyer | 1920 | Box 658 | Emory, Clara | 1918 | Box 596 |
| Ellis, Rosa H. | 1896 | Box 160 | Emory, George B. | 1888 | Box 107 |
| Ellis, Samuel H. | 1896 | Box 160 | Emory, Matilda W. | 1900 | Box 192 |
| Ellis, Thomas | 1915 | Box 516 | Emory, William H. | 1888 | Box 107 |
| Ellis, William H. | 1911 | Box 416 | Emrich, Henrietta C. | 1919 | Box 626 |
| Ellis, William K. | 1914 | Box 490 | Emrich, Maria Catharine | 1899 | Box 183 |
| Ellis, William Taylor | 1918 | Box 596 | Enderle, Joseph L. | 1915 | Box 516 |
| Ellis, Zabina | 1890 | Box 118 | Enders, Engelbert | 1905 | Box 280 |
| Ellison, Rodman B. | 1907 | Box 320 | Enders, John | 1903 | Box 243 |
| Ellyson, Onan | 1910 | Box 389 | Enders, Mary | 1905 | Box 280 |
| Elmes, Cornelia W. | 1912 | Box 441 | Endres, Adrian | 1884 | Box 86 |
| Elmes, Louisa Devereux | 1915 | Box 516 | Endres, Margaretha Amalia | 1902 | Box 224 |
| Elmore, Jerome | 1893 | Box 138 | Engel, Christian | 1881 | Box 75 |
| Elterich, William L. | 1905 | Box 280 | Engel, Christian | 1886 | Box 96 |
| Elton, Zaida M. | 1915 | Box 516 | Engel, Johanna | 1905 | Box 280 |
| Elvans, Frances | 1867 | Box 37 | Engel, William | 1920 | Box 658 |
| Elvans, Mary Ann | 1864 | Box 32 | Engels, Charles Ewald | 1912 | Box 441 |
| Ely, George | 1912 | Box 441 | Engels, Ewald | 1872 | Box 47 |
| Ely, George G. | 1894 | Box 145 | England, Sanford P. | 1870 | Box 42 |
| Ely, George S. | 1918 | Box 596 | Engle, J. F. | 1904 | Box 263 |
| Ely, Katharine | 1905 | Box 280 | Engle, James M. | 1919 | Box 626 |
| Elzey, Arnold | 1818 | Box 5 | English, Caroline V. | 1910 | Box 390 |
| Elzey, Henrietta | 1852 | Box 21 | English, Corrina Lee | 1896 | Box 160 |
| Embry, James H. | 1912 | Box 441 | English, David | 1862 | Box 30 |
| Emerson, George W. | 1873 | Box 50 | English, Emeline G. | 1916 | Box 543 |
| Emerson, Harrison A. | 1889 | Box 113 | English, Frederick | 1904 | Box 263 |
| Emerson, Robert P. | 1911 | Box 416 | English, Henry | 1919 | Box 626 |
| Emery, Amanda | 1914 | Box 490 | English, John R. | 1919 | Box 626 |
| Emery, Ernest William | 1914 | Box 490 | English, James | 1879 | Box 68 |
| Emery, George S. | 1920 | Box 658 | English, Julia | 1873 | Box 50 |
| Emery, Harriet Elizabeth | 1920 | Box 658 | English, Lydia S. | 1866 | Box 35 |
| Emery, John | 1801 | Box 1 | English, Minnie E. | 1911 | Box 416 |
| Emery, Lyman S. | 1900 | Box 192 | English, Patrick | 1869 | Box 40 |
| Emery, Mary G. | 1914 | Box 490 | English, Samuel S. | 1914 | Box 490 |
| Emery, Matthew G. (Jr.) | 1888 | Box 107 | English, Thomas W. | 1913 | Box 467 |
| Emery, Matthew G. | 1901 | Box 207 | English, William H. | 1896 | Box 160 |
| Emery, Samuel | 1916 | Box 543 | Ennis, Gregory | 1872 | Box 47 |
| Emmerich, Catherine C. | 1902 | Box 224 | Ennis, Gregory I. | 1899 | Box 183 |

| | | | | | | |
|---|---|---|---|---|---|---|
| Ennis, James A. | 1878 | Box 66 | Evans, Charlotte T. | 1920 | Box 658 |
| Ennis, John F. | 1896 | Box 160 | Evans, Daniel S. | 1907 | Box 320 |
| Ennis, Philip | 1851 | Box 21 | Evans, David | 1907 | Box 320 |
| Eno, Edward | 1812 | Box 4 | Evans, Edward C. | 1913 | Box 467 |
| Enright, Edward | 1891 | Box 124 | Evans, Ellen Allen | 1920 | Box 658 |
| Ensworth, Katharine | 1896 | Box 160 | Evans, Emily A. | 1845 | Box 17 |
| Enthoffer, Joseph | 1909 | Box 367 | Evans, Emily S. | 1912 | Box 441 |
| Entwisle, Isaac | 1886 | Box 96 | Evans, Evan | 1820 | Box 6 |
| Entwisle, Roberta S. | 1905 | Box 280 | Evans, Evan | 1848 | Box 19 |
| Entwisle, Thomas W. | 1881 | Box 75 | Evans, Frank D. | 1918 | Box 596 |
| Ergood, Jesse C. | 1916 | Box 543 | Evans, Frank Herbert | 1911 | Box 416 |
| Erhardt, John | 1911 | Box 416 | Evans, George | 1863 | Box 31 |
| Ermold, Henry | 1900 | Box 192 | Evans, George W. | 1913 | Box 467 |
| Erni, Gustave Adolph | 1899 | Box 183 | Evans, Harriett C. | 1919 | Box 626 |
| Erni, Henri | 1885 | Box 91 | Evans, Hattie A. | 1919 | Box 626 |
| Ernst, Margaret F. | 1914 | Box 490 | Evans, Henry | 1899 | Box 183 |
| Erwin, Frances G. | 1920 | Box 658 | Evans, Henry Cotheal | 1908 | Box 343 |
| Erwin, John B. | 1916 | Box 543 | Evans, Jane | 1905 | Box 280 |
| Erwin, Louisa F. | 1916 | Box 543 | Evans, John | 1850 | Box 20 |
| Esberg, Louis | 1905 | Box 280 | Evans, John | 1900 | Box 192 |
| Escher, Christina | 1905 | Box 280 | Evans, John William | 1882 | Box 78 |
| Eselhorst, Ernest L. | 1911 | Box 416 | Evans, Joseph T. | 1856 | Box 24 |
| Esher, George C. | 1920 | Box 658 | Evans, Julia E. | 1917 | Box 569 |
| Eshleman, Emma L. | 1901 | Box 207 | Evans, Lucy | 1830 | Box 10 |
| Eske, William | 1887 | Box 102 | Evans, Maria Matilda | 1894 | Box 145 |
| Eskridge, Ellen | 1912 | Box 441 | Evans, Martin N. | 1918 | Box 596 |
| Eskridge, John B. | 1900 | Box 192 | Evans, Mary | 1895 | Box 152 |
| Eslin, James | 1880 | Box 71 | Evans, Mary A. | 1915 | Box 516 |
| Espenshied, Laura | 1920 | Box 658 | Evans, Mary Jane | 1900 | Box 192 |
| Espey, Ferdinand | 1909 | Box 367 | Evans, Mary Mason | 1899 | Box 183 |
| Espinosa, Delores | 1908 | Box 343 | Evans, Philip | 1817 | Box 5 |
| Esputa, John | 1882 | Box 78 | Evans, Sarah T. | 1900 | Box 192 |
| Essex, James F. | 1867 | Box 37 | Evans, Susan | 1859 | Box 27 |
| Essex, John T. W. | 1875 | Box 57 | Evans, Thomas | 1884 | Box 86 |
| Essex, Josiah | 1883 | Box 82 | Evans, Thomas H. | 1885 | Box 91 |
| Estep, Rezin | 1855 | Box 24 | Evans, Thomas S. | 1908 | Box 343 |
| Estes, Julia W. | 1912 | Box 441 | Evans, Walter K. | 1920 | Box 658 |
| Estren, Samuel W. | 1894 | Box 145 | Evans, Warwick | 1915 | Box 516 |
| Esty, Warren B. | 1911 | Box 416 | Evans, Washington P. | 1917 | Box 569 |
| Etchberger, Charles Edwin Jr. | 1913 | Box 467 | Evans, William B. | 1887 | Box 102 |
| Etherington, Pernellar M. | 1916 | Box 543 | Evans, William C. | 1919 | Box 627 |
| Etka, William E. | 1909 | Box 367 | Evans, William Wilson | 1917 | Box 569 |
| Etting, Barnard G. | 1868 | Box 39 | Evans, Wilson Bruce | 1918 | Box 596 |
| Etting, Frances G. | 1868 | Box 39 | Eveleth, Harriet | 1891 | Box 124 |
| Etting, Solomon | 1854 | Box 23 | Eveleth, James | 1891 | Box 124 |
| Evans, Albert M. | 1892 | Box 131 | Eveleth, Mary W. | 1904 | Box 263 |
| Evans, Alexander H. | 1893 | Box 138 | Everard, Jane | 1872 | Box 47 |
| Evans, Andrew Wallace | 1910 | Box 390 | Everett, Frank M. | 1905 | Box 280 |
| Evans, Anthony W. W. | 1889 | Box 113 | Everett, James | 1834 | Box 12 |
| Evans, Arad | 1908 | Box 343 | Everett, Jane | 1901 | Box 207 |
| Evans, Bolden | 1901 | Box 207 | Everett, Mary E. | 1894 | Box 145 |
| Evans, Cecilia | 1874 | Box 53 | Everett, Rebecca | 1833 | Box 12 |

| | | | | | | |
|---|---|---|---|---|---|---|
| Everett, Thomas T. | 1873 | Box 50 | | Fallin, Elizabeth M. D. | 1909 | Box 367 |
| Eversfield, Charles | 1873 | Box 50 | | Fallon, Elizabeth E. | 1899 | Box 183 |
| Ewald, John | 1872 | Box 47 | | Fallon, John T. | 1887 | Box 102 |
| Ewell, John Louis | 1910 | Box 389 | | Fallon, Mary Ann | 1843 | Box 16 |
| Ewell, Thomas | 1848 | Box 19 | | Falls, Charlotte Armstrong | 1907 | Box 320 |
| Ewen, Clarence | 1919 | Box 627 | | Falls, Ella C. | 1881 | Box 75 |
| Ewers, George H. | 1912 | Box 441 | | Falls, Matilda M. C. | 1894 | Box 145 |
| Ewin, James Lithgow Sr. | 1915 | Box 516 | | Falls, Robert Wilson | 1907 | Box 320 |
| Ewing, George | 1909 | Box 367 | | Fanning, Alexander C. W. | 1846 | Box 18 |
| Ewing, Laura Creaser | 1912 | Box 441 | | Fanning, Caroline H. | 1853 | Box 22 |
| Exel, Elizabeth | 1918 | Box 596 | | Fanning, John | 1884 | Box 86 |
| Faber, John C. | 1872 | Box 47 | | Fanning, William H. | 1865 | Box 33 |
| Faber, Louis | 1909 | Box 367 | | Fanning, Williaminer | 1861 | Box 29 |
| Faber, Mary M. | 1872 | Box 47 | | Fardon, Abram P. | 1913 | Box 467 |
| Face, Eliza J. | 1899 | Box 183 | | Farish, Ellen D. | 1902 | Box 225 |
| Facius, Gustav | 1903 | Box 243 | | Farlee, Mary A. | 1906 | Box 300 |
| Facius, Leopoldine | 1917 | Box 569 | | Farlee, William A. | 1887 | Box 102 |
| Faehtz, Almira M. | 1897 | Box 169 | | Farlee, William A. | 1914 | Box 490 |
| Fagan, Ellen M. | 1914 | Box 490 | | Farless, Benjamin A. | 1899 | Box 183 |
| Fagan, Mary Ann | 1871 | Box 44 | | Farley, Annie P. | 1909 | Box 367 |
| Fagan, Mary E. | 1916 | Box 543 | | Farley, Edward W. | 1868 | Box 39 |
| Fague, Adeline W. | 1892 | Box 131 | | Farley, John | 1874 | Box 53 |
| Fague, Gilman Marston | 1897 | Box 169 | | Farmer, Ann | 1822 | Box 7 |
| Fague, Joseph R. | 1917 | Box 569 | | Farmer, Nancy | 1903 | Box 243 |
| Fahey, Patrick | 1911 | Box 416 | | Farnham, Arthur Boyle | 1911 | Box 416 |
| Fahnestock, Gibson | 1917 | Box 569 | | Farnham, Jane | 1891 | Box 125 |
| Fahnestock, Harris C. | 1917 | Box 569 | | Farnshaw, William | 1898 | Box 175 |
| Fahrenbruch, Charlotte M. | 1915 | Box 516 | | Farnsworth, John Franklin | 1897 | Box 169 |
| Fahrhkopf, John | 1910 | Box 390 | | Farquhar, Edward | 1905 | Box 281 |
| Fahrmeier, Magdalena | 1918 | Box 596 | | Farquhar, Edward Y. | 1871 | Box 44 |
| Fahrmeir, Peter | 1892 | Box 131 | | Farquhar, Emily W. | 1892 | Box 131 |
| Fair, George Washington | 1910 | Box 390 | | Farquhar, Rose Clark | 1882 | Box 78 |
| Fairall, Elizabeth Ann | 1851 | Box 21 | | Farr, Amelia | 1901 | Box 207 |
| Fairall, George Edwin | 1919 | Box 627 | | Farr, Walter P. | 1885 | Box 91 |
| Fairbank, Mary E. | 1911 | Box 416 | | Farrall, Elizabeth Ann | 1851 | Box 21 |
| Fairbank, Wilson H. | 1911 | Box 416 | | Farrar, Edward T. | 1904 | Box 263 |
| Fairbrother, Frances A. | 1878 | Box 66 | | Farrar, Mary | 1863 | Box 31 |
| Fairbrother, Frank L. | 1879 | Box 68 | | Farrar, Miranda M. | 1899 | Box 183 |
| Fairbrother, George W. | 1906 | Box 300 | | Farrar, Watson W. | 1899 | Box 183 |
| Fairbrother, Isaac | 1913 | Box 467 | | Farrar, William H. | 1874 | Box 53 |
| Fairfax, Arthur W. | 1920 | Box 659 | | Farrell, Edward | 1915 | Box 516 |
| Fairfax, George | 1893 | Box 138 | | Farrell, John | 1877 | Box 63 |
| Fairfax, Nancy | 1904 | Box 263 | | Farrell, John | 1894 | Box 145 |
| Falbush, Mary K. | 1914 | Box 490 | | Farrell, John S. | 1910 | Box 390 |
| Falconar, John H. | 1890 | Box 118 | | Farrell, Mary J. | 1915 | Box 516 |
| Falconer, Alfred | 1885 | Box 91 | | Farrell, Patrick | 1805 | Box 1 |
| Falconer, Mahlon | 1870 | Box 42 | | Farrell, Zephaniah | 1821 | Box 6 |
| Falconer, Ralph J. | 1871 | Box 44 | | Fastnaught, William H. | 1920 | Box 659 |
| Falconer, Sallie Clocker | 1920 | Box 659 | | Faulhaber, Elizabeth | 1891 | Box 125 |
| Falconer, William H. | 1890 | Box 118 | | Faulkner, Mollie | 1904 | Box 263 |
| Fales, Joseph Thomas | 1878 | Box 66 | | Faulkner, William H. | 1891 | Box 125 |
| Fallant, Elizabeth | 1873 | Box 51 | | Faunce, Agnes | 1910 | Box 390 |

| | | | | | | |
|---|---|---|---|---|---|---|
| Faunce, Margaret | 1905 | Box 281 | Fendall, Reginald | 1898 | Box 175 |
| Faunce, Mary L. | 1898 | Box 175 | Fender, John W. | 1919 | Box 627 |
| Faunce, Mary M. | 1895 | Box 153 | Fender, William J. | 1919 | Box 627 |
| Faunce, Mary Parkhurst | 1888 | Box 107 | Fendner, Christopher F. | 1909 | Box 367 |
| Faunce, Philip P. | 1909 | Box 367 | Fennell, Edward | 1809 | Box 3 |
| Fauntleroy, Brena | 1906 | Box 300 | Fennell, Margaret | 1816 | Box 5 |
| Fauth, Alfred Medford | 1920 | Box 659 | Fenner, Helen Lay | 1916 | Box 543 |
| Fauth, Julius | 1886 | Box 96 | Fenno, J. Brooks | 1894 | Box 145 |
| Fauth, Philip | 1915 | Box 516 | Fenton, Charles W. | 1918 | Box 596 |
| Faw, Abraham | 1889 | Box 113 | Fenton, Josephine W. | 1920 | Box 659 |
| Fawcett, Anna V. | 1920 | Box 659 | Fenton, Lillian L. | 1911 | Box 416 |
| Fawcett, Edwin C. | 1905 | Box 281 | Fenton, Mary | 1891 | Box 125 |
| Fawcett, Rachael R. | 1919 | Box 627 | Fenton, Michael | 1920 | Box 659 |
| Faxon, Charles | 1871 | Box 45 | Fenton, Michael J. | 1887 | Box 102 |
| Fay, Harriet H. | 1885 | Box 91 | Fenton, Sarah J. | 1904 | Box 263 |
| Fay, Harriett H. | 1890 | Box 118 | Fentress, Harriet | 1872 | Box 47 |
| Fay, Heman A. | 1911 | Box 416 | Fenwick, Ann | 1816 | Box 5 |
| Fay, John C. | 1913 | Box 467 | Fenwick, Benjamin I. | 1872 | Box 47 |
| Fay, John M. | 1897 | Box 169 | Fenwick, Edward | 1857 | Box 25 |
| Fazzi, Annie A. | 1914 | Box 490 | Fenwick, George | 1811 | Box 3 |
| Fealey, Patrick | 1906 | Box 300 | Fenwick, James | 1806 | Box 2 |
| Fealy, Mary | 1900 | Box 192 | Fenwick, James | 1872 | Box 47 |
| Fearson, Charles D. | 1885 | Box 91 | Fenwick, James Stewart | 1900 | Box 192 |
| Fearson, Joseph C. | 1883 | Box 82 | Fenwick, Julia | 1893 | Box 138 |
| Fearson, Joseph N. | 1867 | Box 37 | Fenwick, Mary | 1822 | Box 7 |
| Fearson, Laura A. | 1906 | Box 300 | Fenwick, Mary | 1873 | Box 50 |
| Fearson, Mary Ann | 1868 | Box 39 | Fenwick, Mary Caroline | 1865 | Box 33 |
| Feast, Howard D. | 1912 | Box 441 | Fenwick, Mary Helen | 1892 | Box 131 |
| Feast, Sarah A. | 1904 | Box 263 | Fenwick, Philip | 1863 | Box 31 |
| Fechtig, Annie M. | 1906 | Box 300 | Fenwick, Richard | 1829 | Box 10 |
| Fedarwisch, Kunigunda | 1905 | Box 281 | Fenwick, Robert W. | 1897 | Box 169 |
| Fedler, Anna | 1911 | Box 416 | Fenwick, Teresa | 1839 | Box 14 |
| Fee, Edward | 1886 | Box 96 | Fenwick, Thomas | 1847 | Box 19 |
| Feehan, Patrick | 1900 | Box 192 | Feran, Thomas | 1872 | Box 47 |
| Feeny, Nora | 1905 | Box 281 | Ferber, Johannes | 1911 | Box 416 |
| Feere, Elizabeth | 1899 | Box 183 | Ferguson, Agnes | 1896 | Box 161 |
| Fegan, John | 1895 | Box 153 | Ferguson, Aletia | 1905 | Box 281 |
| Fegan, Mary A. | 1919 | Box 627 | Ferguson, Andrew J. | 1897 | Box 169 |
| Fegan, Peter | 1886 | Box 96 | Ferguson, Benjamin S. | 1892 | Box 131 |
| Fegan, Teresa | 1912 | Box 441 | Ferguson, Henry | 1918 | Box 596 |
| Feig, Augusta | 1870 | Box 42 | Ferguson, James | 1859 | Box 27 |
| Feige, Herman | 1919 | Box 627 | Ferguson, Martha A. | 1906 | Box 300 |
| Felch, Abbie A. | 1913 | Box 467 | Ferguson, Mary B. | 1886 | Box 96 |
| Felka, Max E. | 1902 | Box 225 | Ferguson, Sarah E. | 1906 | Box 300 |
| Feller, Damion | 1858 | Box 26 | Ferguson, William M. | 1895 | Box 153 |
| Fellheimer, Moses | 1879 | Box 68 | Fernald, George W. | 1918 | Box 596 |
| Fellheimer, Myer | 1918 | Box 596 | Fernald, Maria | 1888 | Box 107 |
| Fellows, Augustus | 1905 | Box 281 | Fernandez, John M. | 1906 | Box 300 |
| Felter, Annie A. C. | 1909 | Box 367 | Fernandez, Ratie K. | 1918 | Box 596 |
| Fendall, Arthur | 1878 | Box 66 | Ferney, Harriet E. | 1892 | Box 131 |
| Fendall, Bessie | 1907 | Box 320 | Ferrall, Patrick | 1827 | Box 9 |
| Fendall, Mary Lee | 1911 | Box 416 | Ferrel, William | 1906 | Box 300 |

| | | | | | | |
|---|---|---|---|---|---|---|
| Ferrero, Joseph | 1920 | Box 659 | Finley, Jane T. | 1904 | Box 263 |
| Ferril, James | 1888 | Box 107 | Finley, William L. | 1894 | Box 145 |
| Ferris, Eliza V. | 1906 | Box 300 | Finley, William Wilson | 1913 | Box 467 |
| Ferris, Frank M. | 1911 | Box 416 | Finn, William | 1917 | Box 569 |
| Ferris, Margaret | 1859 | Box 27 | Finnacome, Mary Elizabeth | 1892 | Box 131 |
| Ferry, James | 1905 | Box 281 | Finnegan, Margaret | 1869 | Box 40 |
| Ferry, Mary | 1901 | Box 207 | Finney, John | 1879 | Box 68 |
| Ferry, Mary Elizabeth | 1908 | Box 344 | Finney, Leroy R. | 1915 | Box 516 |
| Ferry, Matilda | 1903 | Box 243 | Fischer, Anton | 1895 | Box 153 |
| Ferry, Hugh | 1871 | Box 45 | Fischer, Anton David | 1891 | Box 125 |
| Fersinger, Sophia | 1920 | Box 659 | Fischer, Bertha | 1900 | Box 192 |
| Fessenden, Mary Dunlevie | 1900 | Box 192 | Fischer, Charles | 1900 | Box 192 |
| Fessenden, Sarah A. | 1900 | Box 192 | Fischer, Harriot | 1859 | Box 27 |
| Fessenden, William | 1883 | Box 82 | Fischer, John | 1888 | Box 107 |
| Fetter, Henry | 1909 | Box 367 | Fischer, John George | 1888 | Box 107 |
| Fey, Adam | 1880 | Box 71 | Fischer, Julia Frances Lawson | 1916 | Box 543 |
| Fey, Adam | 1906 | Box 300 | Fischer, Phillippe | 1887 | Box 102 |
| Fey, George J. | 1915 | Box 516 | Fischer, William | 1852 | Box 21 |
| Ffoulke, Horace Cushing | 1903 | Box 243 | Fish, Amy | 1898 | Box 175 |
| Fickenscher, George William | 1916 | Box 543 | Fish, Ellen F. | 1914 | Box 490 |
| Fickenscher, Viola | 1914 | Box 490 | Fish, Emily E. | 1917 | Box 569 |
| Fickling, Jeremiah | 1913 | Box 467 | Fishback, Lucy Overton | 1904 | Box 263 |
| Field, Charles W. | 1892 | Box 131 | Fishbaugh, Charles H. | 1920 | Box 659 |
| Field, Hannah C. | 1919 | Box 627 | Fishel, Alexander | 1906 | Box 300 |
| Field, John W. | 1887 | Box 102 | Fisher, Abraham | 1855 | Box 24 |
| Field, Kate | 1896 | Box 161 | Fisher, Abraham | 1917 | Box 569 |
| Field, Mary J. | 1883 | Box 82 | Fisher, Andrew | 1867 | Box 37 |
| Field, Stephen J. | 1899 | Box 183 | Fisher, Anna | 1894 | Box 145 |
| Field, Sue V. | 1901 | Box 207 | Fisher, Catherine | 1914 | Box 490 |
| Field, Thomas | 1900 | Box 192 | Fisher, Charles B. | 1903 | Box 243 |
| Fields, Elizabeth | 1876 | Box 60 | Fisher, Charles Leonard | 1886 | Box 96 |
| Fields, Mary McElroy | 1889 | Box 113 | Fisher, Daniel W. | 1913 | Box 467 |
| Fields, Richard | 1873 | Box 50 | Fisher, Eliza Ann | 1908 | Box 344 |
| Fields, William | 1817 | Box 5 | Fisher, Elizabeth | 1885 | Box 91 |
| Fierer, Charles | 1861 | Box 29 | Fisher, Flavius J. | 1905 | Box 281 |
| Fietze, Louis A. G. | 1918 | Box 596 | Fisher, Frank W. | 1889 | Box 113 |
| Fifield, Joseph N. | 1919 | Box 627 | Fisher, George M. | 1899 | Box 183 |
| Figgins, James L. | 1889 | Box 113 | Fisher, George W. | 1909 | Box 367 |
| Fill, Frederick A. | 1883 | Box 82 | Fisher, Harriet T. | 1905 | Box 281 |
| Fillebrown, George B. | 1886 | Box 96 | Fisher, Henry | 1901 | Box 207 |
| Fillebrown, Thomas | 1873 | Box 50 | Fisher, Hironimus | 1890 | Box 118 |
| Filler, Charles W. | 1905 | Box 281 | Fisher, Isabella | 1911 | Box 416 |
| Fillette, St. Julian | 1894 | Box 145 | Fisher, John | 1914 | Box 490 |
| Finch, Ferris | 1913 | Box 467 | Fisher, Lester S. | 1898 | Box 175 |
| Finch, Helen M. | 1915 | Box 516 | Fisher, Louis H. | 1902 | Box 225 |
| Finckel, Samuel D. | 1873 | Box 50 | Fisher, Margareth | 1904 | Box 263 |
| Finckel, Sophie L. | 1916 | Box 543 | Fisher, Marvin P. | 1909 | Box 367 |
| Findley, Mary E. | 1908 | Box 344 | Fisher, Marvin W. | 1849 | Box 20 |
| Finkel, Samuel D. | 1873 | Box 50 | Fisher, Mary | 1915 | Box 516 |
| Finkmann, Conrad | 1878 | Box 66 | Fisher, Milton L. | 1911 | Box 416 |
| Finkmann, Wilhelmina | 1902 | Box 225 | Fisher, Samuel B. | 1885 | Box 91 |
| Finley, Francis H. | 1893 | Box 138 | Fisher, Samuel T. | 1911 | Box 416 |

| | | | | | | |
|---|---|---|---|---|---|---|
| Fisher, Sarah | 1903 | Box 243 | Fitzhugh, Maria Ringgold | 1917 | Box 569 |
| Fisher, Thomas J. | 1888 | Box 107 | Fitzhugh, Mary A. | 1920 | Box 659 |
| Fisher, Thomas J. | 1919 | Box 627 | Fitzhugh, Robert R. | 1853 | Box 22 |
| Fisher, William S. | 1913 | Box 468 | Fitzki, Edward | 1889 | Box 113 |
| Fishman, Solomon | 1902 | Box 225 | Fitzmorris, Richard | 1899 | Box 183 |
| Fisk, Charles B. | 1866 | Box 35 | Fitzpatrick, Alice | 1916 | Box 543 |
| Fisk, Harry C. | 1897 | Box 169 | Fitzpatrick, Bernard | 1892 | Box 131 |
| Fiske, Arthur W. | 1886 | Box 96 | Fitzpatrick, James | 1876 | Box 60 |
| Fitch, George K. | 1906 | Box 300 | Fitzpatrick, James | 1919 | Box 627 |
| Fitch, Henry W. | 1910 | Box 390 | Fitzpatrick, James N. | 1916 | Box 543 |
| Fitch, James E. | 1917 | Box 569 | Fitzpatrick, Minnie R. | 1894 | Box 145 |
| Fitch, Mary | 1913 | Box 468 | Fitzpatrick, Thomas | 1912 | Box 441 |
| Fitch, Sidney A. | 1914 | Box 490 | Fitzsimons, Edwin C. | 1915 | Box 516 |
| Fitch, William | 1896 | Box 161 | Fitzsimons, Paul | 1918 | Box 596 |
| Fithian, Annie E. | 1915 | Box 516 | Flack, George Raymond | 1915 | Box 516 |
| Fitnam, Isabella M. | 1915 | Box 516 | Fladung, Henry | 1873 | Box 50 |
| Fitnam, Rose | 1912 | Box 441 | Flagg, Arthur I. | 1898 | Box 175 |
| Fitnam, Thomas | 1878 | Box 66 | Flagler, Daniel W. | 1899 | Box 183 |
| Fitzgerald, Bridget | 1900 | Box 192 | Flagler, Mary | 1919 | Box 627 |
| Fitzgerald, Catharine | 1895 | Box 153 | Flagler, Mary M. | 1907 | Box 320 |
| Fitzgerald, Catherine T. | 1917 | Box 569 | Flahaven, Bridget | 1912 | Box 441 |
| Fitzgerald, David | 1850 | Box 20 | Flahaven, Michael | 1900 | Box 192 |
| Fitzgerald, David | 1868 | Box 39 | Flaherty, Bridget | 1892 | Box 131 |
| Fitzgerald, David | 1897 | Box 169 | Flaherty, Bridget | 1911 | Box 416 |
| Fitzgerald, Dennis | 1902 | Box 225 | Flaherty, John T. | 1908 | Box 344 |
| Fitzgerald, Edward | 1857 | Box 25 | Flanagan, Elizabeth | 1918 | Box 596 |
| Fitzgerald, Edward | 1899 | Box 183 | Flanagan, Hannah | 1886 | Box 96 |
| Fitzgerald, James | 1897 | Box 169 | Flanagan, James | 1871 | Box 45 |
| Fitzgerald, Johanna | 1902 | Box 225 | Flanagan, James J. | 1898 | Box 175 |
| Fitzgerald, John | 1887 | Box 102 | Flanagan, John | 1872 | Box 47 |
| Fitzgerald, John | 1889 | Box 113 | Flanagan, Patrick A. | 1914 | Box 490 |
| Fitzgerald, John | 1892 | Box 131 | Flannery, Nora | 1905 | Box 281 |
| Fitzgerald, John | 1901 | Box 207 | Flather, Alfred | 1914 | Box 490 |
| Fitzgerald, John | 1910 | Box 390 | Fleischhauer, Anna Maria | 1905 | Box 281 |
| Fitzgerald, John J. | 1906 | Box 300 | Fleishell, Jacob J. | 1885 | Box 91 |
| Fitzgerald, John J. | 1917 | Box 569 | Flemer, Charles | 1901 | Box 207 |
| Fitzgerald, Katherine | 1903 | Box 243 | Flemer, Martha | 1919 | Box 627 |
| Fitzgerald, Margaret | 1895 | Box 153 | Fleming, Lawrence | 1895 | Box 153 |
| Fitzgerald, Mary | 1903 | Box 243 | Fleming, Mary E. | 1902 | Box 225 |
| Fitzgerald, Michael | 1896 | Box 161 | Fleming, Mary Virginia | 1913 | Box 468 |
| Fitzgerald, Nora | 1920 | Box 659 | Fleming, Robert I. | 1907 | Box 321 |
| Fitzgerald, Susan | 1893 | Box 138 | Fleming, Thomas T. | 1907 | Box 321 |
| Fitzgerald, Willard Lyon | 1899 | Box 183 | Fleming, William | 1910 | Box 390 |
| Fitzgerald, William A. | 1868 | Box 39 | Flemming, Lorania Fairfax | 1907 | Box 321 |
| FitzGerald, Theophilus | 1916 | Box 543 | Flemming, Mary | 1889 | Box 113 |
| Fitzgibbens, William | 1909 | Box 367 | Flemming, Patrick F. | 1890 | Box 118 |
| Fitzhugh, Archer | 1873 | Box 50 | Flenner, George Cookman | 1916 | Box 543 |
| Fitzhugh, Daniel Carroll | 1917 | Box 569 | Flenner, Jesse Weirick | 1898 | Box 175 |
| Fitzhugh, Eliza M. | 1894 | Box 145 | Fletcher, Albert W. | 1914 | Box 490 |
| Fitzhugh, John T. | 1905 | Box 281 | Fletcher, Basil | 1867 | Box 37 |
| Fitzhugh, John W. | 1873 | Box 50 | Fletcher, Betsy P. | 1871 | Box 45 |
| Fitzhugh, Maria C. | 1883 | Box 82 | Fletcher, Christine P. | 1913 | Box 468 |

| | | | | | | |
|---|---|---|---|---|---|
| Fletcher, Edward Thomas | 1912 | Box 441 | Flynn, Michael | 1887 | Box 102 |
| Fletcher, Emma M. | 1916 | Box 543 | Flynn, Patrick | 1903 | Box 244 |
| Fletcher, Frank Herbert | 1917 | Box 569 | Flynn, Samuel Walter | 1911 | Box 416 |
| Fletcher, Hannah | 1897 | Box 169 | Flynn, Simon | 1867 | Box 37 |
| Fletcher, Henry | 1873 | Box 50 | Flynn, William | 1891 | Box 125 |
| Fletcher, Jesse | 1845 | Box 17 | Fobes, Edson | 1879 | Box 68 |
| Fletcher, John | 1865 | Box 33 | Foertsch, Mary Julia | 1898 | Box 175 |
| Fletcher, L. Fenn | 1894 | Box 146 | Fogarty, Johanna | 1915 | Box 516 |
| Fletcher, Louis C. | 1911 | Box 416 | Fogarty, John | 1908 | Box 344 |
| Fletcher, Louisa | 1884 | Box 86 | Fogarty, Mary | 1908 | Box 344 |
| Fletcher, Louisa M. | 1920 | Box 659 | Fogg, Lindley | 1913 | Box 468 |
| Fletcher, Lydia (Coyne) | 1904 | Box 263 | Fogle, George F. | 1903 | Box 244 |
| Fletcher, Mary E | 1908 | Box 344 | Foley, Ellen | 1913 | Box 468 |
| Fletcher, Mary Manning | 1913 | Box 468 | Foley, Ellen Josephine | 1919 | Box 627 |
| Fletcher, Noah | 1857 | Box 25 | Foley, Elmira | 1911 | Box 416 |
| Fletcher, Robert | 1912 | Box 441 | Foley, Mary | 1896 | Box 161 |
| Fletcher, Susan | 1902 | Box 225 | Foley, Mary | 1900 | Box 192 |
| Fletcher, William | 1911 | Box 416 | Foley, Michael | 1903 | Box 244 |
| Fletcher, William | 1914 | Box 490 | Foley, Timothy | 1883 | Box 82 |
| Fletcher, William H. | 1864 | Box 32 | Folger, Thomas C. | 1885 | Box 91 |
| Flewellen, Margaret Crawford | 1919 | Box 627 | Folk, Sarah W. | 1910 | Box 390 |
| Flinn, Michael P. | 1917 | Box 569 | Follain, Caroline | 1890 | Box 118 |
| Flint, Caroline | 1901 | Box 207 | Follansbee, Carrie M. | 1900 | Box 192 |
| Flint, James M. | 1920 | Box 659 | Follansbee, Charles | 1917 | Box 569 |
| Flint, Laura A. | 1898 | Box 175 | Follansbee, Joseph | 1867 | Box 37 |
| Flint, Lucy R. B. | 1905 | Box 281 | Follansbee, Lambert T. | 1893 | Box 138 |
| Flint, Weston | 1906 | Box 300 | Foller, Damian | 1858 | Box 26 |
| Flippin, Marie S. | 1889 | Box 113 | Föller, Elizabeth Louise | 1887 | Box 102 |
| Flitsch, Maria | 1892 | Box 131 | Foller, John | 1869 | Box 40 |
| Floeckher, Albert H. | 1913 | Box 468 | Foller, Mary | 1878 | Box 66 |
| Flohr, Martin C. | 1920 | Box 659 | Follmer, William L. | 1914 | Box 490 |
| Flood, Anne | 1889 | Box 113 | Folsom, Joseph L. | 1910 | Box 390 |
| Flood, John | 1884 | Box 86 | Folsom, Paris H. | 1904 | Box 263 |
| Flood, Maria | 1899 | Box 183 | Foos, John A. | 1898 | Box 175 |
| Flood, Mary Ann | 1896 | Box 161 | Foose, William | 1910 | Box 390 |
| Flood, William H. | 1911 | Box 416 | Foot, Rebecca L. Forster | 1915 | Box 516 |
| Florance, Matilda | 1886 | Box 96 | Foraker, Joseph B. | 1918 | Box 596 |
| Florence, Thomas B. | 1875 | Box 57 | Forbes, Hortense | 1907 | Box 321 |
| Florence, William J. | 1892 | Box 131 | Forbes, Mary P. | 1920 | Box 659 |
| Floyd, Charles M. | 1904 | Box 263 | Forbes, Sarah W. | 1888 | Box 107 |
| Floyd, Daphne Edwards | 1910 | Box 390 | Forbes, Theodore F. | 1917 | Box 570 |
| Floyd, Nannie Teackle | 1907 | Box 321 | Forbush, Almeda V. | 1902 | Box 225 |
| Fluger, Gustavus | 1913 | Box 468 | Force, Frances H. | 1900 | Box 192 |
| Flynn, Bridget | 1891 | Box 125 | Force, Georgianna L. | 1868 | Box 39 |
| Flynn, Elizabeth | 1896 | Box 161 | Force, Manning F. | 1899 | Box 183 |
| Flynn, Ellen | 1886 | Box 96 | Force, William Q. | 1880 | Box 71 |
| Flynn, Ellen | 1905 | Box 281 | Ford, Alfred | 1905 | Box 281 |
| Flynn, John | 1870 | Box 42 | Ford, Alice J. | 1916 | Box 543 |
| Flynn, Julia | 1915 | Box 516 | Ford, Anna L. | 1918 | Box 597 |
| Flynn, Margaret | 1902 | Box 225 | Ford, Charles | 1899 | Box 183 |
| Flynn, Mary | 1896 | Box 161 | Ford, Elizabeth E. | 1896 | Box 161 |
| Flynn, Michael | 1885 | Box 91 | Ford, Ellery C. | 1888 | Box 107 |

| | | | | | | |
|---|---|---|---|---|---|---|
| Ford, George | 1918 | Box 597 | Forteney, Edwin W. | 1873 | Box 50 |
| Ford, George Tod | 1912 | Box 441 | Fortier, Alexander Gaspe | 1917 | Box 570 |
| Ford, Harriet A. | 1898 | Box 175 | Fortuño, Manuel | 1897 | Box 169 |
| Ford, Isaac Henry | 1916 | Box 544 | Forwood, William Henry | 1915 | Box 517 |
| Ford, James | 1910 | Box 390 | Fosdick, Charles Raymond | 1897 | Box 169 |
| Ford, Jane Plowden | 1884 | Box 86 | Fosdick, Frances B. | 1918 | Box 597 |
| Ford, John G. | 1837 | Box 13 | Foskey, Eliza | 1896 | Box 161 |
| Ford, Josephine O. | 1915 | Box 517 | Foss, Cyrus K. | 1892 | Box 131 |
| Ford, Mary F. | 1917 | Box 570 | Foss, Lewe M. | 1914 | Box 490 |
| Ford, Michael H. | 1887 | Box 102 | Foss, Sarah A. | 1885 | Box 91 |
| Ford, Milton | 1894 | Box 146 | Foss, Sarah B. | 1919 | Box 627 |
| Ford, Milton E. | 1915 | Box 517 | Foster, Alice Gray Burch | 1903 | Box 244 |
| Ford, Patrick A. | 1919 | Box 627 | Foster, Anna J. | 1916 | Box 544 |
| Ford, Raymond L. | 1914 | Box 490 | Foster, Anthony | 1908 | Box 344 |
| Ford, Rebecca | 1857 | Box 25 | Foster, Arthur B. | 1910 | Box 390 |
| Ford, Roberta | 1904 | Box 263 | Foster, Catherine P. | 1900 | Box 192 |
| Ford, Telemachus | 1882 | Box 78 | Foster, Charlotte | 1873 | Box 51 |
| Ford, William | 1846 | Box 18 | Foster, David L. | 1907 | Box 321 |
| Ford, William | 1865 | Box 33 | Foster, Edward | 1874 | Box 53 |
| Ford, William | 1912 | Box 441 | Foster, Eunice L. | 1915 | Box 517 |
| Ford, William F. | 1891 | Box 125 | Foster, Fisher A. | 1883 | Box 82 |
| Foreble, Margaret | 1843 | Box 16 | Foster, Franklin J. | 1911 | Box 416 |
| Foreman, Edward | 1885 | Box 91 | Foster, John B. | 1894 | Box 146 |
| Foreman, Henrietta M. S. | 1894 | Box 146 | Foster, John W. | 1917 | Box 570 |
| Foreman, William S. | 1920 | Box 659 | Foster, Margaret E. | 1908 | Box 344 |
| Forney, Edward B. | 1913 | Box 468 | Foster, Martha | 1890 | Box 118 |
| Forney, Elizabeth Matilda | 1897 | Box 169 | Foster, Robert F. | 1873 | Box 51 |
| Forney, Pierre William | 1886 | Box 96 | Foster, Rose Adelaide | 1918 | Box 597 |
| Forney, Stehman | 1917 | Box 570 | Foster, Thomas | 1908 | Box 344 |
| Forrest, Albert Dulany | 1915 | Box 517 | Foster, Winthrop D. | 1919 | Box 627 |
| Forrest, Alexander | 1832 | Box 11 | Fouke, Emma M. | 1893 | Box 138 |
| Forrest, Alexander | 1886 | Box 96 | Foulk, Charles M. | 1918 | Box 597 |
| Forrest, Catharine | 1845 | Box 17 | Fountain, Aaron | 1880 | Box 71 |
| Forrest, Catharine | 1895 | Box 153 | Fountain, David C. | 1920 | Box 659 |
| Forrest, Douglas F. | 1902 | Box 225 | Fountain, Felix | 1906 | Box 300 |
| Forrest, Jane | 1862 | Box 30 | Fountain, Horace | 1911 | Box 416 |
| Forrest, Joseph | 1903 | Box 244 | Fountain, John | 1834 | Box 12 |
| Forrest, Mary | 1842 | Box 15 | Fouse, George | 1905 | Box 281 |
| Forrest, Rebecca | 1843 | Box 16 | Foushee, Francis | 1806 | Box 2 |
| Forrest, Samuel W. | 1913 | Box 468 | Foust, Judson | 1906 | Box 300 |
| Forrest, Sarah Jane | 1892 | Box 131 | Fowble, David | 1896 | Box 161 |
| Forrest, Stephney | 1855 | Box 24 | Fowke, Mary Harrison | 1879 | Box 68 |
| Forrest, Uriah | 1805 | Box 1 | Fowler, Caroline | 1883 | Box 82 |
| Forrest, Virginia | 1912 | Box 441 | Fowler, Edwin H. | 1904 | Box 264 |
| Forrest, William H. | 1898 | Box 175 | Fowler, Enoch S. | 1920 | Box 659 |
| Forrestal, James | 1852 | Box 21 | Fowler, Francis | 1903 | Box 244 |
| Forster, Frank | 1891 | Box 125 | Fowler, George W. | 1902 | Box 225 |
| Forster, Frank | 1892 | Box 131 | Fowler, Harvey | 1882 | Box 78 |
| Forster, Herman | 1911 | Box 416 | Fowler, Henderson | 1881 | Box 75 |
| Forster, Lena | 1898 | Box 176 | Fowler, Isabella R. | 1917 | Box 570 |
| Forsyth, James H. | 1906 | Box 300 | Fowler, James D. | 1916 | Box 544 |
| Forsyth, William | 1902 | Box 225 | Fowler, James F. | 1889 | Box 113 |

| | | | | | | |
|---|---|---|---|---|---|---|
| Fowler, James H. | 1884 | Box 86 | | Franc, Babette Rosenthal | 1912 | Box 441 |
| Fowler, James Hamilton | 1895 | Box 153 | | Franc, Henry | 1912 | Box 441 |
| Fowler, James W. | 1904 | Box 264 | | France, Kate | 1913 | Box 468 |
| Fowler, Jane S. | 1904 | Box 264 | | France, Maria | 1909 | Box 367 |
| Fowler, John | 1874 | Box 53 | | France, Mary E. | 1907 | Box 321 |
| Fowler, Joseph | 1871 | Box 45 | | France, Mary Jane | 1881 | Box 75 |
| Fowler, Joseph | 1891 | Box 125 | | France, Thomas E. | 1903 | Box 244 |
| Fowler, Marion E. | 1918 | Box 597 | | Frances, Carrie A. | 1901 | Box 207 |
| Fowler, Mary Ann | 1902 | Box 225 | | Francis, George | 1890 | Box 118 |
| Fowler, Mary C. | 1896 | Box 161 | | Francis, George W. | 1910 | Box 390 |
| Fowler, Mary H. | 1910 | Box 390 | | Francis, John R. | 1913 | Box 468 |
| Fowler, Mary W. | 1884 | Box 86 | | Francis, Lavinia C. | 1916 | Box 544 |
| Fowler, Mary W. | 1892 | Box 132 | | Francis, Richard | 1889 | Box 113 |
| Fowler, Samuel | 1900 | Box 193 | | Francis, Sarah | 1872 | Box 47 |
| Fowler, Sarah A. | 1890 | Box 118 | | Francis, Thomas | 1900 | Box 193 |
| Fowler, Susan W. | 1906 | Box 300 | | Francis, William Edwin | 1920 | Box 659 |
| Fowler, Susannah | 1917 | Box 570 | | Frank, Edward L. | 1916 | Box 544 |
| Fowler, T. Walter | 1920 | Box 659 | | Frank, Frederick | 1920 | Box 659 |
| Fowler, Wallace G. | 1917 | Box 570 | | Frank, J. H. | 1902 | Box 225 |
| Fowler, Walter E. | 1895 | Box 153 | | Frank, Jacob | 1887 | Box 102 |
| Fowler, William P. | 1887 | Box 102 | | Frank, Joseph | 1876 | Box 60 |
| Fowler, William T. | 1900 | Box 193 | | Frank, Julius Augs. | 1894 | Box 146 |
| Fox, Adam | 1888 | Box 107 | | Frank, Mary | 1868 | Box 39 |
| Fox, Bartleson | 1816 | Box 5 | | Frank, Mary Jane | 1869 | Box 40 |
| Fox, Charles | 1896 | Box 161 | | Frank, Royal T. | 1908 | Box 344 |
| Fox, Charles Eben | 1916 | Box 544 | | Frankenberger, Charles | 1857 | Box 25 |
| Fox, Elizabeth | 1819 | Box 6 | | Frankenberger, Margaret | 1861 | Box 29 |
| Fox, Elizabeth A. | 1903 | Box 244 | | Frankland, Henry William | 1899 | Box 183 |
| Fox, Fannie Kendall | 1914 | Box 490 | | Frankland, Mary E. | 1910 | Box 390 |
| Fox, George | 1918 | Box 597 | | Franklin, Ann | 1874 | Box 53 |
| Fox, Grace Ann | 1855 | Box 24 | | Franklin, Hannah J. | 1908 | Box 344 |
| Fox, Isaac N. | 1900 | Box 193 | | Franklin, James S. | 1896 | Box 161 |
| Fox, Jennie | 1918 | Box 597 | | Franklin, John P. | 1893 | Box 138 |
| Fox, Mary A. | 1909 | Box 367 | | Franklin, John S. | 1897 | Box 169 |
| Fox, Oscar C. | 1902 | Box 225 | | Franklin, Margaret R. | 1884 | Box 86 |
| Fox, Robert C. | 1891 | Box 125 | | Franklin, Margaret Virginia D. | 1913 | Box 468 |
| Fox, Virginia L. W. | 1908 | Box 344 | | Franklin, Marion | 1914 | Box 491 |
| Foxall, Catherine | 1847 | Box 19 | | Franklin, Mary M. | 1912 | Box 441 |
| Foxall, Henry | 1824 | Box 8 | | Franklin, Samuel | 1887 | Box 102 |
| Foxton, William | 1824 | Box 8 | | Franklin, Samuel R. | 1909 | Box 367 |
| Foy, John | 1855 | Box 24 | | Franklin, Sarah J. | 1907 | Box 321 |
| Foy, John T. | 1913 | Box 468 | | Franklin, Stephen P. | 1863 | Box 31 |
| Fracker, Harriet G. | 1903 | Box 244 | | Franklin, William | 1874 | Box 53 |
| Frailer, Charles | 1857 | Box 25 | | Franklin, William A. | 1868 | Box 39 |
| Frailey, Caroline L. | 1914 | Box 491 | | Franks, Barbara | 1890 | Box 118 |
| Frailey, Charles S. | 1857 | Box 25 | | Franks, Jane M. | 1892 | Box 132 |
| Frailey, Helen W. | 1915 | Box 517 | | Franz, Margaret | 1901 | Box 207 |
| Frailey, Leonard A. | 1914 | Box 491 | | Franzoni, Jane | 1872 | Box 47 |
| Frain, Ann M. | 1908 | Box 344 | | Fraser, Agnes Fulton | 1911 | Box 416 |
| Frain, Davis M. | 1906 | Box 300 | | Fraser, Anthony R. | 1881 | Box 75 |
| Frame, Agnes G. | 1902 | Box 225 | | Fraser, Cornelia | 1895 | Box 153 |
| Frame, James | 1905 | Box 281 | | Fraser, Ellen S. | 1911 | Box 417 |

| | | | | | | |
|---|---|---|---|---|---|---|
| Fraser, George S. | 1896 | Box 161 | French, Frances G. | 1919 | Box 627 |
| Fraser, James (Sr.) | 1865 | Box 33 | French, George | 1887 | Box 102 |
| Frawley, Katharine | 1906 | Box 300 | French, George H. | 1914 | Box 491 |
| Frawley, Michael J. | 1911 | Box 417 | French, George N. | 1909 | Box 367 |
| Frazer, Marshal | 1917 | Box 570 | French, George T. | 1915 | Box 517 |
| Frazer, Martha | 1883 | Box 82 | French, Isabella G. | 1894 | Box 146 |
| Frazier, Boutell W. | 1896 | Box 161 | French, John R. | 1907 | Box 321 |
| Frazier, Ellen | 1900 | Box 193 | French, John W. | 1873 | Box 51 |
| Frazier, Ernest D. | 1908 | Box 344 | French, Marianne Craik | 1849 | Box 20 |
| Frazier, Eugenia | 1915 | Box 517 | French, Mary | 1864 | Box 32 |
| Frazier, Frederick | 1892 | Box 132 | French, Mary Catharine | 1895 | Box 153 |
| Frazier, Harriet B. | 1918 | Box 597 | French, Mary E. | 1907 | Box 321 |
| Frazier, Margaret | 1878 | Box 66 | French, Mary Ellen | 1905 | Box 281 |
| Frazier, Robert Thomas | 1914 | Box 491 | French, Michael A. | 1898 | Box 176 |
| Frech, Elizabeth | 1911 | Box 417 | French, William B. | 1910 | Box 390 |
| Frederick, Mary | 1849 | Box 20 | Frere, Elizabeth | 1899 | Box 183 |
| Fredericks, Charles August | 1883 | Box 82 | Frere, Elizabeth | 1917 | Box 570 |
| Fredericks, Elizabeth | 1878 | Box 66 | Frere, James W. | 1882 | Box 78 |
| Freedman, Lizzie | 1915 | Box 517 | Frere, Mary C. | 1880 | Box 71 |
| Freeman, Ann | 1823 | Box 7 | Frere, Richard A. | 1911 | Box 417 |
| Freeman, Benjamin | 1890 | Box 118 | Freudenberg, Annie K. | 1888 | Box 107 |
| Freeman, Benjamin C. | 1866 | Box 35 | Freudenberg, Carl G. | 1885 | Box 91 |
| Freeman, Catherine | 1888 | Box 107 | Freudenthal, Mary | 1881 | Box 75 |
| Freeman, Charles P. | 1918 | Box 597 | Freudenthal, William H. | 1904 | Box 264 |
| Freeman, Ellen | 1911 | Box 417 | Freund, Elizabeth | 1908 | Box 344 |
| Freeman, Frank L. | 1907 | Box 321 | Freund, Frederick | 1897 | Box 169 |
| Freeman, George | 1915 | Box 517 | Freund, John Louis | 1916 | Box 544 |
| Freeman, John | 1839 | Box 14 | Freund, Justina | 1896 | Box 161 |
| Freeman, Joseph R. | 1911 | Box 417 | Frey, John A. | 1917 | Box 570 |
| Freeman, Malinda | 1865 | Box 33 | Frey, John J. | 1872 | Box 47 |
| Freeman, Margaret | 1843 | Box 16 | Frey, Joseph | 1856 | Box 24 |
| Freeman, Margaret C. | 1894 | Box 146 | Frey, William | 1890 | Box 118 |
| Freeman, Mary Jane | 1912 | Box 441 | Freyhold, Edward Von | 1892 | Box 132 |
| Freeman, Olive | 1880 | Box 71 | Freyre, Don Manuel de | 1878 | Box 66 |
| Freeman, Richard | 1815 | Box 4 | Freyre, Rosa | 1878 | Box 66 |
| Freeman, Susannah | 1911 | Box 417 | Frick, Mary M. | 1897 | Box 169 |
| Freeman, William C. | 1911 | Box 417 | Frickey, Laura A. | 1907 | Box 321 |
| Freeman, William G. | 1866 | Box 35 | Fridy, Sam Matt | 1911 | Box 417 |
| Freeman, William N. | 1906 | Box 300 | Friebus, M. Olivia | 1889 | Box 113 |
| Freewalt, Louis G. | 1900 | Box 193 | Friederich, Ludolph | 1888 | Box 107 |
| Freewalt, Rosa Barbara | 1900 | Box 193 | Friedlander, Harry | 1914 | Box 491 |
| Frehner, John | 1907 | Box 321 | Friedmann, Louise | 1907 | Box 321 |
| Freirick, Babette | 1907 | Box 321 | Friedrich, Bernhardina | 1914 | Box 491 |
| Freitag, Henry C. | 1916 | Box 544 | Friedrich, Henry | 1909 | Box 368 |
| Freitag, Henry Louis | 1920 | Box 659 | Friedrich, Leon Ludolph | 1915 | Box 517 |
| French, Adele B. | 1890 | Box 118 | Friedrich, William | 1899 | Box 183 |
| French, Agnes L. C. | 1908 | Box 344 | Friedrick, Albert A. | 1902 | Box 225 |
| French, Annie Elizabeth | 1915 | Box 517 | Friel, Elizabeth | 1863 | Box 31 |
| French, Benjamin B. | 1870 | Box 42 | Fries, Aaron | 1906 | Box 300 |
| French, D. McComas | 1918 | Box 597 | Fries, Elizabeth Ann | 1910 | Box 390 |
| French, Edward A. | 1914 | Box 491 | Fries, Eva | 1917 | Box 570 |
| French, Edwin | 1869 | Box 40 | Friess, Christopher | 1868 | Box 39 |

| | | | | | | |
|---|---|---|---|---|---|---|
| Frink, Emma A. | 1919 | Box 627 | Fulmer, Mary N. | 1865 | Box 33 |
| Fripp, Theodore Eugene | 1918 | Box 597 | Fulton, Henry H. | 1906 | Box 300 |
| Frisby, Catherine R. | 1898 | Box 176 | Fulton, Henry K. | 1892 | Box 132 |
| Frisby, Mary M. | 1896 | Box 161 | Fulton, Rosa Belle | 1918 | Box 598 |
| Frisby, Thomas | 1879 | Box 68 | Fulton, William | 1879 | Box 68 |
| Frischholz, Christoph | 1893 | Box 138 | Fultz, Herman C. | 1917 | Box 570 |
| Frissell, John C. | 1867 | Box 37 | Fulwood, Charles Edward | 1899 | Box 183 |
| Fritz, Joseph W. | 1915 | Box 517 | Funk, George | 1917 | Box 570 |
| Froley, J. W. | 1913 | Box 468 | Funk, Kate H. | 1894 | Box 146 |
| Frost, Charles C. | 1917 | Box 570 | Funk, William L. | 1920 | Box 660 |
| Frost, Harriet C. | 1916 | Box 544 | Furgerson, Joseph | 1855 | Box 24 |
| Frost, Horace J. | 1891 | Box 125 | Furlong, Moses | 1886 | Box 97 |
| Frost, John W. | 1908 | Box 344 | Furmage, Annie M. | 1899 | Box 183 |
| Frost, Mildred C. | 1896 | Box 161 | Fuss, Henrietta | 1872 | Box 47 |
| Frothingham, Catherine J. | 1919 | Box 627 | Fuss, J. Frederick | 1920 | Box 660 |
| Frothingham, Georgiana | 1901 | Box 207 | Fuss, William H. | 1917 | Box 570 |
| Frush, William | 1854 | Box 23 | Fussell, Jacob | 1912 | Box 441 |
| Fry, Catherine | 1896 | Box 161 | Fussell, Richard Thomas | 1898 | Box 176 |
| Fry, Gertrude May | 1891 | Box 125 | Gaddis, Adam | 1867 | Box 37 |
| Fry, Henry D. | 1919 | Box 627 | Gaddis, Adam | 1916 | Box 544 |
| Fry, Mary Louise | 1885 | Box 91 | Gaddis, Lemuel | 1909 | Box 368 |
| Frye, Katie D. | 1917 | Box 570 | Gadsby, James EAkin | 1919 | Box 627 |
| Frye, Thomas B. I. | 1890 | Box 118 | Gadsby, John | 1844 | Box 16 |
| Fuger, Margaret Tennant | 1918 | Box 598 | Gadsby, Provey | 1858 | Box 26 |
| Fugitt, Francis I. | 1886 | Box 97 | Gadsden, Edward Miles | 1900 | Box 193 |
| Fugitt, George B. | 1907 | Box 321 | Gaegler, John | 1898 | Box 176 |
| Fugitt, Harriet A. | 1919 | Box 627 | Gaegler, John Jr. | 1896 | Box 161 |
| Fugitt, Joseph | 1834 | Box 12 | Gaffard, Catharine H. | 1910 | Box 390 |
| Fugitt, Joseph | 1870 | Box 42 | Gaffard, William H. | 1910 | Box 390 |
| Fugitt, Magdalena | 1905 | Box 281 | Gaffney, Annie | 1917 | Box 570 |
| Fullalove, James | 1867 | Box 37 | Gaffney, Michael | 1865 | Box 33 |
| Fullalove, Richard | 1891 | Box 125 | Gage, Mary E. | 1890 | Box 118 |
| Fullalove, William | 1871 | Box 45 | Gahagan, Kate Sullivan | 1900 | Box 193 |
| Fuller, Benjamin C. | 1890 | Box 118 | Gaillard, Joseph d'E. | 1898 | Box 176 |
| Fuller, Benjamin F. | 1896 | Box 161 | Gain, Carl | 1917 | Box 570 |
| Fuller, Edward H. | 1866 | Box 35 | Gaines, Frances | 1899 | Box 183 |
| Fuller, Hannah | 1911 | Box 417 | Gaines, Frank | 1912 | Box 441 |
| Fuller, Harry W. | 1911 | Box 417 | Gaines, Frank | 1920 | Box 660 |
| Fuller, Henry | 1911 | Box 417 | Gainey, Daniel | 1903 | Box 244 |
| Fuller, Luther | 1919 | Box 627 | Gainey, Teresa R. | 1904 | Box 264 |
| Fuller, Miles | 1902 | Box 225 | Gaisberg, William Conrad | 1919 | Box 627 |
| Fuller, Miles | 1916 | Box 544 | Gaiser, Gesine | 1891 | Box 125 |
| Fuller, Perry | 1879 | Box 68 | Gaither, Catharine K. | 1862 | Box 30 |
| Fuller, Susan E. | 1907 | Box 321 | Gaither, Eugene C. | 1906 | Box 301 |
| Fuller, William D. | 1888 | Box 107 | Gaither, Francis S. | 1876 | Box 60 |
| Fullerton, David L. | 1907 | Box 321 | Gaither, Sallie S. | 1888 | Box 108 |
| Fullerton, Dixon | 1908 | Box 344 | Gaither, Sarah Ann | 1889 | Box 113 |
| Fullerton, James | 1899 | Box 183 | Gale, Anna Eliza | 1891 | Box 125 |
| Fullerton, Joseph Scott | 1897 | Box 169 | Gale, Elizabeth | 1850 | Box 20 |
| Fullerton, Margaret D. | 1915 | Box 517 | Gale, Ida M. | 1919 | Box 628 |
| Fullmore, Mary Ann | 1873 | Box 51 | Gale, Margaret E. | 1912 | Box 441 |
| Fulmer, George H. | 1859 | Box 27 | Gale, Thomas M. | 1920 | Box 660 |

| | | | | | | |
|---|---|---|---|---|---|---|
| Galer, Alice M. | 1897 | Box 169 | Gant, Bazil | 1833 | Box 12 |
| Gales, Joseph | 1860 | Box 28 | Gant, Benjamin J. | 1900 | Box 193 |
| Gales, Juliana Walker | 1908 | Box 344 | Gant, James | 1895 | Box 153 |
| Gales, Sarah J. M. | 1879 | Box 68 | Gant, James T. | 1901 | Box 207 |
| Gallagher, Albert A. | 1900 | Box 193 | Gant, Martha S. | 1920 | Box 660 |
| Gallagher, Catherine | 1879 | Box 68 | Gant, Minia | 1842 | Box 15 |
| Gallagher, Daniel | 1856 | Box 24 | Gant, Resin | 1884 | Box 86 |
| Gallagher, Elizabeth | 1908 | Box 344 | Gant, Thomas | 1820 | Box 6 |
| Gallagher, Eugenia M. | 1898 | Box 176 | Gantt, Ann | 1852 | Box 21 |
| Gallagher, Francis X. | 1915 | Box 517 | Gantt, Benjamin Stoddert | 1852 | Box 21 |
| Gallagher, James | 1911 | Box 417 | Gantt, Georgiann | 1913 | Box 468 |
| Gallagher, John | 1891 | Box 125 | Gantt, John Mackall | 1881 | Box 75 |
| Gallagher, Joseph D. | 1920 | Box 660 | Gantt, Margaret C. | 1891 | Box 125 |
| Gallagher, Louisa | 1903 | Box 244 | Gantt, Milly | 1841 | Box 15 |
| Gallagher, Michael | 1899 | Box 183 | Gantt, Sarah L. | 1872 | Box 47 |
| Gallagher, Richard J. | 1906 | Box 301 | Gantt, Thomas T. | 1889 | Box 113 |
| Gallagher, Timothy | 1895 | Box 153 | Gantt, Thomas Tasker | 1818 | Box 5 |
| Gallagher, Timothy A. | 1894 | Box 146 | Gantz, George M. | 1915 | Box 517 |
| Gallaher, Eliza A. | 1898 | Box 176 | Gantz, Ida S. | 1920 | Box 660 |
| Gallaher, Louisa Bernie | 1917 | Box 570 | Gapin, Washington Fort | 1902 | Box 225 |
| Gallant, Elizabeth | 1873 | Box 51 | Garden, Alexander | 1891 | Box 125 |
| Gallant, William G. | 1910 | Box 390 | Gardiner, John | 1839 | Box 14 |
| Gallaudet, Peter W. | 1843 | Box 16 | Gardner, Alexander | 1883 | Box 82 |
| Galligan, James | 1856 | Box 24 | Gardner, Ann Eliza | 1877 | Box 63 |
| Galligan, Thomas | 1891 | Box 125 | Gardner, Augustus P. | 1918 | Box 598 |
| Gallinger, Jacob H. | 1918 | Box 598 | Gardner, Caleb | 1885 | Box 91 |
| Gallion, Emmett D. | 1919 | Box 628 | Gardner, Charles K. | 1872 | Box 47 |
| Galloway, Anna Louisa | 1918 | Box 598 | Gardner, Charles T. | 1886 | Box 97 |
| Galloway, Charles Douglas | 1912 | Box 442 | Gardner, Charlotte | 1887 | Box 102 |
| Galloway, Elizabeth C. | 1906 | Box 301 | Gardner, David A. | 1881 | Box 75 |
| Galloway, John | 1810 | Box 3 | Gardner, Eliza C. | 1917 | Box 570 |
| Gallup, B. C. | 1919 | Box 628 | Gardner, Frank A. | 1903 | Box 244 |
| Galt, Charles E. | 1900 | Box 193 | Gardner, Fred W. | 1919 | Box 628 |
| Galt, James Howard | 1916 | Box 544 | Gardner, Harriet C. | 1918 | Box 598 |
| Galt, Mary A. | 1892 | Box 132 | Gardner, Kate | 1920 | Box 660 |
| Galt, Mary Jane | 1892 | Box 132 | Gardner, Lawrence | 1899 | Box 183 |
| Galt, Matthew W. | 1898 | Box 176 | Gardner, Marcellus | 1888 | Box 108 |
| Galt, Nancy | 1901 | Box 207 | Gardner, Margaret Sinclair | 1897 | Box 169 |
| Galt, Norman | 1908 | Box 344 | Gardner, Martha B. | 1903 | Box 244 |
| Galt, William | 1902 | Box 225 | Gardner, Mary J. | 1900 | Box 193 |
| Galt, William M. | 1889 | Box 113 | Gardner, Nellie | 1907 | Box 321 |
| Galt, William W. | 1904 | Box 264 | Gardner, Sarah Annie | 1912 | Box 442 |
| Galvin, Dorcas | 1850 | Box 20 | Gardner, Thomas I. | 1896 | Box 161 |
| Gangewer, Susan | 1908 | Box 344 | Gardner, Virginia Ott | 1912 | Box 442 |
| Gannett, Alfred | 1901 | Box 207 | Gardner, William Fowler | 1908 | Box 344 |
| Gannett, Henry | 1915 | Box 517 | Gardner, William Fowler | 1918 | Box 598 |
| Gannett, Sarah B. | 1895 | Box 153 | Gardner, William Franklin | 1898 | Box 176 |
| Gannon, Gilbert J. | 1917 | Box 570 | Gardner, William Henry | 1909 | Box 368 |
| Gannon, James P. | 1849 | Box 20 | Garges, Rebecca | 1920 | Box 660 |
| Gannon, Martin | 1907 | Box 321 | Garges, Susan | 1895 | Box 153 |
| Gannon, Mary | 1894 | Box 146 | Garland, Elcena M. | 1902 | Box 226 |
| Gans, Betty | 1909 | Box 368 | Garland, Jerome | 1916 | Box 544 |

| | | | | | | |
|---|---|---|---|---|---|---|
| Garland, Mary E. | 1919 | Box 628 | Gaskins, Thomas | 1903 | Box 244 |
| Garland, Mary T. | 1890 | Box 118 | Gaskins, William A. | 1895 | Box 153 |
| Garland, William H. | 1903 | Box 244 | Gass, Amelia A. | 1886 | Box 97 |
| Garlem, Peter H. | 1917 | Box 570 | Gass, Stuart J. | 1891 | Box 125 |
| Garlichs, Francis | 1892 | Box 132 | Gass, William | 1915 | Box 517 |
| Garner, Ann | 1854 | Box 23 | Gass, William Réa | 1887 | Box 102 |
| Garner, Catharine W. | 1858 | Box 26 | Gassaway, Lucinda | 1889 | Box 113 |
| Garner, Eliza H. | 1880 | Box 71 | Gassenheimer, Josephine | 1917 | Box 571 |
| Garner, James W. | 1877 | Box 63 | Gassmann, Adolf | 1903 | Box 244 |
| Garner, Martha A. | 1873 | Box 51 | Gaston, Catherine J. | 1889 | Box 113 |
| Garner, Millard F. | 1893 | Box 138 | Gaszynski, Tytus F. J. W. | 1874 | Box 53 |
| Garner, Patrick | 1906 | Box 301 | Gatchell, Delma J. | 1920 | Box 660 |
| Garner, Tristram H. | 1866 | Box 35 | Gatchell, Fred | 1911 | Box 417 |
| Garnett, Alex Y. P. | 1888 | Box 108 | Gatchell, William Forrest | 1912 | Box 442 |
| Garnett, Henry Wise | 1897 | Box 169 | Gately, James | 1904 | Box 264 |
| Garnett, Marian Morson | 1894 | Box 146 | Gately, John A. | 1873 | Box 51 |
| Garnett, Robert | 1870 | Box 42 | Gates, Charles L. | 1884 | Box 86 |
| Garnett, William Roane | 1906 | Box 301 | Gates, David Weston | 1912 | Box 442 |
| Garnier, Madeleine A. | 1917 | Box 570 | Gates, James | 1852 | Box 21 |
| Garratt, Harry P. | 1920 | Box 660 | Gates, John H. | 1913 | Box 468 |
| Garrett, Amanda E. | 1917 | Box 570 | Gates, Samuel | 1866 | Box 35 |
| Garrett, Ann Jane | 1878 | Box 66 | Gates, William H. | 1895 | Box 153 |
| Garrett, Augusta Browne | 1882 | Box 78 | Gatschet, Albert Louis Samuel | 1907 | Box 321 |
| Garrett, David | 1916 | Box 544 | Gatti, Stephen | 1919 | Box 628 |
| Garrett, David T. | 1920 | Box 660 | Gatto, Angela | 1888 | Box 108 |
| Garrett, Edward | 1913 | Box 468 | Gatto, Joseph | 1915 | Box 517 |
| Garrett, Jesse L. | 1904 | Box 264 | Gatton, Edward | 1895 | Box 153 |
| Garrett, Milton | 1869 | Box 40 | Gauges, Phillip | 1904 | Box 264 |
| Garrett, Rachel A. | 1900 | Box 193 | Gaunt, Fielder | 1807 | Box 2 |
| Garrett, Robert | 1905 | Box 281 | Gause, Cornelia B. | 1912 | Box 442 |
| Garrettson, Nimrod | 1882 | Box 79 | Gause, Isaac | 1920 | Box 660 |
| Garrigues, Charles | 1887 | Box 102 | Gause, John H. | 1913 | Box 468 |
| Garrison, George C. | 1883 | Box 82 | Gautron, Jean Baptiste | 1896 | Box 161 |
| Garrison, George H. | 1881 | Box 75 | Gautron, Therese Chaud | 1913 | Box 468 |
| Garrison, John R. | 1908 | Box 344 | Gavin, James | 1893 | Box 138 |
| Garrity, Catharine | 1876 | Box 61 | Gavin, John | 1883 | Box 82 |
| Garrity, Sarah | 1894 | Box 146 | Gavin, John J. | 1919 | Box 628 |
| Garst, Elizabeth Q. | 1916 | Box 544 | Gavin, Nora A. | 1915 | Box 517 |
| Gartrell, Thomas S. | 1909 | Box 368 | Gawler, Alfred H. | 1918 | Box 598 |
| Garvey (McGarvey), Annie | 1911 | Box 417 | Gawler, Charles J. | 1919 | Box 628 |
| Garvey, Patrick | 1872 | Box 47 | Gawler, Clara L. | 1909 | Box 368 |
| Garvin, Micheal | 1869 | Box 40 | Gawler, Joseph | 1910 | Box 390 |
| Garwood, Emma | 1901 | Box 207 | Gawler, Rosie H. | 1917 | Box 571 |
| Gary, Ann | 1835 | Box 13 | Gay, Ann | 1911 | Box 417 |
| Gary, Everard | 1815 | Box 4 | Gay, Elizabeth Jane | 1919 | Box 628 |
| Gary, William | 1815 | Box 4 | Gay, Ellen M. | 1915 | Box 517 |
| Gasaway, William | 1907 | Box 321 | Geary, Maggie L. | 1905 | Box 281 |
| Gasch, Herman | 1911 | Box 417 | Gebhart, Urban | 1904 | Box 264 |
| Gash, Otho | 1899 | Box 183 | Geddings, Henry D. | 1913 | Box 468 |
| Gaskin, John Thomas | 1913 | Box 468 | Gedney, Thomas R. | 1858 | Box 26 |
| Gaskin, William H. | 1918 | Box 598 | Gee, Fred A. | 1897 | Box 169 |
| Gaskins, James H. C. | 1917 | Box 571 | Gehr, Alice E. | 1920 | Box 660 |

| | | | | | | |
|---|---|---|---|---|---|
| Geier, Aloysius P. | 1905 | Box 281 | Geunther, Anglenica | 1876 | Box 61 |
| Geier, Bernard | 1899 | Box 183 | Gheen, Benedict W. | 1910 | Box 391 |
| Geier, Margaret | 1917 | Box 571 | Gheen, Edward H. | 1920 | Box 660 |
| Geier, Michael Anton | 1917 | Box 571 | Gheen, John H. | 1909 | Box 368 |
| Geier, Urban | 1907 | Box 321 | Gheen, Mary A. | 1890 | Box 118 |
| Geiger, Anna B. | 1912 | Box 442 | Ghegan, Philip | 1894 | Box 146 |
| Geiger, Martha | 1914 | Box 491 | Gherardi, Anna T. | 1891 | Box 125 |
| Geise, Charles | 1909 | Box 368 | Ghiselli, Alfred V. A. | 1917 | Box 571 |
| Gelletly, Celia | 1919 | Box 628 | Ghiselli, Angelo | 1914 | Box 491 |
| Gelston, Edward H. | 1886 | Box 97 | Giachetti, Peter | 1894 | Box 146 |
| Gelston, Florence B. | 1917 | Box 571 | Gibb, Helen | 1919 | Box 628 |
| Gelston, Hugh | 1875 | Box 57 | Gibbens, John A. | 1917 | Box 571 |
| Gelston, Victor De L. | 1883 | Box 82 | Gibbon, D. J. | 1907 | Box 321 |
| Gelt, Henry | 1875 | Box 57 | Gibbon, Marian E. | 1914 | Box 491 |
| Geneste, Bertie R. | 1918 | Box 598 | Gibbons, Benjamin | 1811 | Box 3 |
| Geneste, Leon D. | 1894 | Box 146 | Gibbons, John | 1889 | Box 113 |
| Geneste, Leonard | 1901 | Box 207 | Gibbons, John W. | 1854 | Box 23 |
| Gennet, Mary E. | 1908 | Box 344 | Gibbons, Mary Ann | 1909 | Box 368 |
| Gensler, Henry J. | 1920 | Box 660 | Gibbons, Patrick | 1863 | Box 31 |
| Gentner, John J. | 1889 | Box 113 | Gibbs, Andrew H. | 1908 | Box 345 |
| Genung, Frank S. | 1908 | Box 344 | Gibbs, Benjamin Franklin | 1887 | Box 102 |
| Geoghegan, Elvester | 1917 | Box 571 | Gibbs, Charles E. | 1899 | Box 183 |
| George, Charles | 1876 | Box 60 | Gibbs, Elizabeth B. | 1883 | Box 82 |
| George, Ellen M. | 1917 | Box 571 | Gibbs, Emma | 1879 | Box 68 |
| George, Henry Jr. | 1916 | Box 544 | Gibbs, George L. | 1905 | Box 281 |
| George, John J. | 1919 | Box 628 | Gibbs, Martha Custis | 1912 | Box 442 |
| George, P. C. | 1917 | Box 571 | Gibon, Richard | 1856 | Box 24 |
| Georgii, Fredericka | 1899 | Box 183 | Gibson, Amey | 1861 | Box 29 |
| Georgii, Robert | 1906 | Box 301 | Gibson, Annie H. | 1880 | Box 71 |
| Gerard, James W. | 1913 | Box 468 | Gibson, Annie V. H. | 1910 | Box 391 |
| Gerecke, Charles | 1893 | Box 138 | Gibson, Bessie L. | 1911 | Box 417 |
| Gerecke, John Frederick | 1862 | Box 30 | Gibson, Caleb J. | 1896 | Box 161 |
| Gerecke, Lisette | 1879 | Box 68 | Gibson, Carrie T. | 1906 | Box 301 |
| Gerecke, Margaret | 1911 | Box 417 | Gibson, Edward H. | 1907 | Box 321 |
| Gerhard, John | 1900 | Box 193 | Gibson, Flora A. | 1919 | Box 628 |
| Gerhard, Wilhelmina | 1910 | Box 391 | Gibson, Francis M. | 1920 | Box 660 |
| Gerhardt, Helena | 1893 | Box 138 | Gibson, George | 1861 | Box 29 |
| Gerhardt, Henry | 1915 | Box 517 | Gibson, George | 1913 | Box 468 |
| Gerhardt, Joseph | 1881 | Box 75 | Gibson, Irving | 1910 | Box 391 |
| Gerhold, John F. | 1918 | Box 598 | Gibson, James R. | 1900 | Box 193 |
| German, Philip | 1909 | Box 368 | Gibson, John | 1874 | Box 54 |
| Gernhardt, George | 1883 | Box 82 | Gibson, John | 1897 | Box 169 |
| Gerrish, Caroline P. | 1899 | Box 183 | Gibson, John | 1909 | Box 368 |
| Gertman, Jane C. | 1910 | Box 391 | Gibson, John F. | 1905 | Box 282 |
| Gessford, James W. | 1910 | Box 391 | Gibson, John H. | 1903 | Box 244 |
| Getchell, Everett T. | 1909 | Box 368 | Gibson, Margaret A. | 1918 | Box 598 |
| Gettier, Henry L. | 1899 | Box 183 | Gibson, Margaret Page | 1916 | Box 544 |
| Gettinger, Mary J. | 1890 | Box 118 | Gibson, Martha A. | 1892 | Box 132 |
| Getts, George H. | 1916 | Box 544 | Gibson, Mary A. | 1910 | Box 391 |
| Getty, Elizabeth G. | 1913 | Box 468 | Gibson, Minnie A. | 1913 | Box 468 |
| Getty, Matthew Clark | 1895 | Box 153 | Gibson, Montgomery | 1911 | Box 417 |
| Getz, Winonie | 1920 | Box 660 | Gibson, Randall Lee | 1893 | Box 138 |

| | | | | | | |
|---|---|---|---|---|---|---|
| Gibson, Rebecca R. | 1907 | Box 321 | Gillhuly, Philip H. | 1895 | Box 153 |
| Gibson, Richard | 1856 | Box 24 | Gilliam, Richard H. | 1914 | Box 491 |
| Gibson, Ruth A. | 1917 | Box 571 | Gilliam, William | 1875 | Box 57 |
| Gibson, Thomas | 1847 | Box 19 | Gilliard, Sarah | 1888 | Box 108 |
| Gibson, William | 1908 | Box 345 | Gilliland, George E. | 1914 | Box 491 |
| Gibson, William | 1903 | Box 244 | Gilliland, Sallie Lou | 1912 | Box 442 |
| Gibson, William | 1884 | Box 86 | Gillis, Elizabeth B. | 1896 | Box 161 |
| Gibson, William | 1888 | Box 108 | Gillis, James | 1898 | Box 176 |
| Gibson, William H. | 1869 | Box 40 | Gilliss, Rebecca S. | 1892 | Box 132 |
| Gibson, William M. | 1901 | Box 207 | Gillman, Emma H. | 1898 | Box 176 |
| Giddens, George W. S. | 1899 | Box 183 | Gillman, Z. D. | 1876 | Box 61 |
| Giddens, Margaret E. | 1915 | Box 517 | Gilmore, Charles D. | 1885 | Box 91 |
| Giddings, Alfred W. | 1919 | Box 628 | Gilmore, Charles F. | 1910 | Box 391 |
| Giddings, Dominick | 1916 | Box 544 | Gilmore, Julia F. | 1915 | Box 517 |
| Gideon, Catharine C. | 1909 | Box 368 | Gilmore, Mary J. | 1899 | Box 183 |
| Gideon, Jacob | 1864 | Box 32 | Gilmore, Robert | 1874 | Box 54 |
| Gies, Edward L. | 1918 | Box 598 | Gilmore, Thomas | 1890 | Box 118 |
| Gies, Jannett Berry | 1895 | Box 153 | Gilmore, Thomas Addison | 1877 | Box 63 |
| Gieseking, Caroline | 1877 | Box 63 | Gilmour, Allan | 1907 | Box 322 |
| Giesking, Frederick W. | 1870 | Box 42 | Gilmour, Helen | 1829 | Box 10 |
| Giesking, Henry N. | 1893 | Box 138 | Giltenan, Kittie | 1908 | Box 345 |
| Giesler, Gustav | 1893 | Box 138 | Gingell, James M. | 1905 | Box 282 |
| Giesy, Anna L. | 1889 | Box 114 | Gingell, Margaret Ann | 1912 | Box 442 |
| Giesy, Samuel H. | 1888 | Box 108 | Ginnaty, James | 1871 | Box 45 |
| Gihon, Mary A. | 1888 | Box 108 | Ginnaty, Mary A. | 1875 | Box 57 |
| Gilbert, Abbie P. | 1919 | Box 628 | Ginter, Catherine | 1902 | Box 226 |
| Gilbert, Abel | 1902 | Box 226 | Ginzer, Leonard | 1884 | Box 86 |
| Gilbert, Fannie M. | 1897 | Box 169 | Giovanini, Joseph | 1911 | Box 417 |
| Gilbert, Feroline M. | 1902 | Box 226 | Giovannetti, Angeline | 1917 | Box 571 |
| Gilbert, Grove Karl | 1918 | Box 598 | Giovannetti, Vincent | 1920 | Box 661 |
| Gilbert, James E. | 1909 | Box 368 | Girard, Alfred C. | 1914 | Box 491 |
| Gilbert, Julia Ann | 1899 | Box 183 | Girard, Julia A. | 1909 | Box 368 |
| Gilbert, Margaret A. | 1904 | Box 264 | Giraux, Joseph Placide | 1908 | Box 345 |
| Gilbert, Sarah Parker | 1906 | Box 301 | Gisburne, John R. | 1915 | Box 517 |
| Gilday, Edward J. | 1899 | Box 183 | Gist, George W. | 1892 | Box 132 |
| Giles, Ann | 1916 | Box 544 | Gist, Mary S. | 1902 | Box 226 |
| Giles, Monica | 1918 | Box 598 | Gitt, David L. | 1915 | Box 518 |
| Gilfillen, John Buchanan | 1904 | Box 264 | Gitt, Henry M. | 1915 | Box 518 |
| Gill, Charles | 1842 | Box 15 | Gittings, Christiann | 1863 | Box 31 |
| Gill, James | 1868 | Box 39 | Gitts, Michael | 1803 | Box 1 |
| Gill, Mary A. | 1920 | Box 660 | Giuliani, Achille | 1918 | Box 598 |
| Gill, Stephen F. | 1898 | Box 176 | Giusta, Alice D. | 1909 | Box 368 |
| Gill, Susan | 1907 | Box 322 | Giusta, Guiseppe | 1895 | Box 153 |
| Gill, Theodore N. | 1914 | Box 491 | Giusta (Guista), Mary | 1874 | Box 54 |
| Gill, William J. | 1894 | Box 146 | Giusta, Michael | 1872 | Box 47 |
| Gillem, James Nicholas | 1910 | Box 391 | Given, Thomas | 1835 | Box 13 |
| Gillem, Richard A. | 1888 | Box 108 | Giveny, Bernard | 1865 | Box 33 |
| Giller, Mary W. | 1909 | Box 368 | Glaab, George | 1900 | Box 193 |
| Gillespie, Joseph W. | 1918 | Box 598 | Gladman, John | 1838 | Box 14 |
| Gillet, Eleanor C. | 1881 | Box 75 | Gladman, Sylvester H. | 1906 | Box 301 |
| Gillett, Alfred S. | 1914 | Box 491 | Glaeser, Moritz | 1906 | Box 301 |
| Gillham, Robert | 1893 | Box 138 | Glascock, Alfred | 1918 | Box 598 |

| | | | | | | |
|---|---|---|---|---|---|---|
| Glascock, Cornelia | 1872 | Box 47 | Goddard, Honora A. | 1916 | Box 545 |
| Glascock, Hattie B. | 1889 | Box 114 | Goddard, James | 1887 | Box 102 |
| Glaser, Hannah | 1905 | Box 282 | Goddard, James D. | 1910 | Box 391 |
| Glasgow, Samuel L. | 1916 | Box 544 | Goddard, John B. | 1831 | Box 11 |
| Glasgow, Winona S. | 1916 | Box 544 | Goddard, John Baptist | 1809 | Box 3 |
| Glass, Charles David | 1919 | Box 628 | Goddard, John H. | 1886 | Box 97 |
| Glavin, Dorcas | 1850 | Box 20 | Goddard, Julia E. | 1895 | Box 153 |
| Glavis, George O. | 1898 | Box 176 | Goddard, Matthew | 1908 | Box 345 |
| Gleason, Bridget | 1906 | Box 301 | Goddard, Morgan R. | 1918 | Box 598 |
| Gleason, Catharine | 1915 | Box 518 | Goddard, Sarah | 1880 | Box 71 |
| Gleason, Dennis | 1893 | Box 138 | Goddard, Sarah | 1876 | Box 61 |
| Gleason, Edwin P. | 1894 | Box 146 | Goddard, William C. | 1887 | Box 102 |
| Gleason, Patrick | 1920 | Box 661 | Goddard, William H. | 1891 | Box 125 |
| Gleeson, Andrew | 1906 | Box 301 | Godden, James | 1886 | Box 97 |
| Gleeson, Bridget | 1909 | Box 368 | Godey, Caroline R. | 1913 | Box 468 |
| Gleeson, John A. | 1912 | Box 442 | Godey, John W. | 1887 | Box 102 |
| Glen, David | 1838 | Box 14 | Godey, William H. | 1872 | Box 47 |
| Glenn, Elizabeth | 1858 | Box 26 | Godron, William Henry | 1874 | Box 54 |
| Glenn, Joseph | 1901 | Box 207 | Goebel, J. Godfrey | 1919 | Box 628 |
| Glennan, Patrick | 1894 | Box 146 | Goell, Frank A. | 1880 | Box 71 |
| Glenny, Helen M. | 1916 | Box 544 | Goeppel, Elisabeth | 1895 | Box 153 |
| Glick, Eva Margaretha | 1917 | Box 571 | Goerner, Emil | 1877 | Box 63 |
| Glick, John H. | 1896 | Box 161 | Goethe, Kate W. McCowan | 1913 | Box 468 |
| Glick, Jonas | 1866 | Box 35 | Goetz, Barbara | 1904 | Box 264 |
| Glisan, Rodney T. | 1915 | Box 518 | Goetz, Herman H. | 1908 | Box 345 |
| Goetzinger, Ernst | 1898 | Box 176 | Goetz, Mina | 1915 | Box 518 |
| Gloetzner, Johanna | 1916 | Box 545 | Goetz, Susan | 1889 | Box 114 |
| Glorius, George | 1909 | Box 368 | Goff, John | 1809 | Box 3 |
| Glotzbach, Henry E. | 1907 | Box 322 | Goff, Mary R. | 1908 | Box 345 |
| Glover, Elizabeth T. | 1905 | Box 282 | Goines, Emma M. | 1912 | Box 442 |
| Glover, Jane | 1876 | Box 61 | Goings, Arthur | 1895 | Box 153 |
| Glover, Townsend | 1883 | Box 82 | Gold, Daniel | 1849 | Box 20 |
| Gloyd, John | 1901 | Box 207 | Goldberg, Moses | 1912 | Box 442 |
| Glynn, Mathias | 1914 | Box 491 | Golden, Alice F. | 1895 | Box 153 |
| Glynn, Patrick | 1897 | Box 169 | Golden, Caldwell D. | 1889 | Box 114 |
| Gmaehle, F. G. | 1870 | Box 42 | Golden, Catharine | 1865 | Box 33 |
| Goale, Edward J. | 1832 | Box 11 | Golden, Margaret | 1868 | Box 39 |
| Goble, Mary G. | 1908 | Box 345 | Golden, Maria E. | 1910 | Box 391 |
| Gobrecht, Harriet V. | 1906 | Box 301 | Golden, Robert A. | 1915 | Box 518 |
| Gochenour, William P. | 1916 | Box 545 | Golden, Stephen M. | 1894 | Box 146 |
| Gockeler, Christian G. | 1887 | Box 102 | Goldie, George | 1900 | Box 193 |
| Gockeler, George J. | 1889 | Box 114 | Goldin, John | 1825 | Box 8 |
| Gockeler, Henrietta Rempp | 1899 | Box 183 | Goldman, David | 1919 | Box 628 |
| Gockeler, Maria | 1901 | Box 207 | Goldman, Max | 1895 | Box 153 |
| Goddard, Charles B. | 1864 | Box 32 | Goldsborough, Alice B. | 1907 | Box 322 |
| Goddard, Charles H. | 1919 | Box 628 | Goldsborough, Catharine D. | 1851 | Box 21 |
| Goddard, Clark La Motte | 1905 | Box 282 | Goldsborough, Ellen Ray | 1907 | Box 322 |
| Goddard, Elisha | 1888 | Box 108 | Goldsborough, Hugh A. | 1890 | Box 118 |
| Goddard, Eliza R. | 1903 | Box 244 | Goldsborough, Isabel McCalla | 1912 | Box 442 |
| Goddard, Elizabeth | 1851 | Box 21 | Goldsborough, Jane | 1857 | Box 25 |
| Goddard, Elizabeth | 1893 | Box 138 | Goldsborough, John T. | 1910 | Box 391 |
| Goddard, Emma Attaway C. | 1860 | Box 28 | Goldsborough, Josephine | 1881 | Box 75 |

| | | | | | | |
|---|---|---|---|---|---|---|
| Goldsborough, Louis M. | 1877 | Box 63 | Gordon, David C. | 1917 | Box 571 |
| Goldsborough, Robert W. | 1811 | Box 3 | Gordon, Elizabeth R. | 1911 | Box 417 |
| Goldschmid, Rudolf | 1897 | Box 169 | Gordon, George | 1888 | Box 108 |
| Goldschmidt, Louis | 1918 | Box 598 | Gordon, Heningham | 1920 | Box 661 |
| Goldsmith, Anna Maria | 1909 | Box 368 | Gordon, Herbert W. | 1915 | Box 518 |
| Goldsmith, Clarence K. | 1919 | Box 628 | Gordon, James | 1864 | Box 32 |
| Goldsmith, Leopold | 1915 | Box 518 | Gordon, James H. | 1869 | Box 40 |
| Goldsmith, Max | 1906 | Box 301 | Gordon, James J. | 1911 | Box 417 |
| Gollnik, Frederick | 1889 | Box 114 | Gordon, John | 1888 | Box 108 |
| Gompers, Sophia | 1920 | Box 661 | Gordon, John H. | 1914 | Box 491 |
| Gonder, Sue F. | 1909 | Box 368 | Gordon, Malcolm B. | 1906 | Box 301 |
| Gonzales, Manuel J. | 1885 | Box 91 | Gordon, Manuel | 1902 | Box 226 |
| Gonzenbach, Frederick Adolph | 1875 | Box 57 | Gordon, Martha | 1835 | Box 13 |
| Gonzenbach, Louisa Catharine | 1892 | Box 132 | Gordon, Mary M. | 1918 | Box 598 |
| Gooch, Catherine E. | 1904 | Box 264 | Gordon, Mary T. G. | 1912 | Box 442 |
| Goodale, Josephine B. | 1892 | Box 132 | Gordon, Richard D. | 1913 | Box 469 |
| Goodall, Marcella K. | 1917 | Box 571 | Gordon, Sarah | 1909 | Box 368 |
| Goodall, Thomas | 1867 | Box 37 | Gordon, Sarah | 1910 | Box 391 |
| Goodchild, Martha A. | 1911 | Box 417 | Gordon, Sarah J. | 1900 | Box 193 |
| Goode, Francis C. | 1888 | Box 108 | Gordon, Susan E. | 1866 | Box 35 |
| Goode, George Brown | 1896 | Box 161 | Gore, Christopher | 1892 | Box 132 |
| Goode, Richard U. | 1903 | Box 244 | Gore, Lillian N. | 1913 | Box 469 |
| Goodell, James | 1864 | Box 32 | Gore, Mary M. | 1917 | Box 571 |
| Goodell, Raymond H. | 1884 | Box 86 | Gore, Rebecca T. | 1898 | Box 176 |
| Goodfellow, Julia | 1920 | Box 661 | Gore, Thomas H. | 1889 | Box 114 |
| Goodhart, Richard | 1904 | Box 264 | Gorgas, William Crawford | 1920 | Box 661 |
| Goodin, Elizabeth | 1864 | Box 32 | Gorham, George C. | 1909 | Box 368 |
| Goodin, Mary E. | 1902 | Box 226 | Gorham, Laura B. | 1915 | Box 518 |
| Gooding, Lizzie May | 1915 | Box 518 | Gorham, Mary E. | 1915 | Box 518 |
| Goodloe, Armstead | 1903 | Box 244 | Gorham, Sally Ann | 1879 | Box 68 |
| Goodloe, Bettie Beck | 1912 | Box 442 | Gorham, William H. H. | 1899 | Box 184 |
| Goodloe, Green Clay | 1917 | Box 571 | Gorman, Annie E. | 1902 | Box 226 |
| Goodman, Abraham | 1917 | Box 571 | Gorman, Arthur P. | 1906 | Box 301 |
| Goodman, Louisa C. | 1902 | Box 226 | Gorman, Catherine | 1903 | Box 244 |
| Goodman, William H. | 1919 | Box 628 | Gorman, Edward | 1805 | Box 1 |
| Goodrich, Henry N. | 1855 | Box 24 | Gorman, Edward M. | 1889 | Box 114 |
| Goodrich, Moses | 1908 | Box 345 | Gorman, Hannah D. | 1910 | Box 391 |
| Goodrick, Benjamin | 1887 | Box 102 | Gorman, Johanna A. | 1909 | Box 368 |
| Goodrick, John T. | 1907 | Box 322 | Gorman, John E. | 1883 | Box 82 |
| Goodrick, Sarah Margaret | 1896 | Box 161 | Gorman, Margaret | 1905 | Box 282 |
| Goodwin, Alice M. | 1905 | Box 282 | Gormley, Margaret | 1893 | Box 138 |
| Goodwin, Annie M. | 1912 | Box 442 | Gormley, Mary | 1875 | Box 57 |
| Goodwin, Mary E. | 1914 | Box 491 | Gosling, Henry L. | 1917 | Box 571 |
| Goodwin, Russell P. | 1917 | Box 571 | Goss, Thomas | 1899 | Box 184 |
| Goodwin, William C. | 1919 | Box 628 | Gossler, Catharine | 1883 | Box 82 |
| Goodyear, Charles | 1861 | Box 29 | Goszler, James | 1886 | Box 97 |
| Goose, William | 1897 | Box 172 | Gott, Delia | 1901 | Box 207 |
| Göppel, William | 1886 | Box 97 | Gotthardt, George | 1903 | Box 244 |
| Gorden, Louisa | 1853 | Box 22 | Gottsman, Anna C. | 1890 | Box 118 |
| Gordon, Amanda Elizabeth | 1917 | Box 571 | Gottsman, Margaret | 1918 | Box 598 |
| Gordon, Charles | 1916 | Box 545 | Gotz, Leonhard | 1902 | Box 226 |
| Gordon, Charles H. | 1915 | Box 518 | Goucher, Thomas | 1909 | Box 368 |

| | | | | | | |
|---|---|---|---|---|---|---|
| Gouges, Armand | 1810 | Box 3 | Graham, John | 1868 | Box 39 |
| Gough, Ann | 1812 | Box 4 | Graham, John A. | 1888 | Box 108 |
| Gough, Georgiana | 1892 | Box 132 | Graham, John C. | 1838 | Box 14 |
| Gould, Anna M. | 1892 | Box 132 | Graham, John E. | 1902 | Box 226 |
| Gould, Harry Lewis | 1919 | Box 628 | Graham, John M. | 1888 | Box 108 |
| Gould, Henrietta | 1916 | Box 545 | Graham, John R. | 1909 | Box 369 |
| Gould, Mary Ann | 1888 | Box 108 | Graham, Julia | 1903 | Box 244 |
| Gould, Sarah | 1919 | Box 628 | Graham, Lawrence Pike | 1906 | Box 301 |
| Gould, Sarah M. | 1902 | Box 226 | Graham, Louisa A. | 1893 | Box 138 |
| Goundie, Richard Moulton | 1895 | Box 153 | Graham, Mary Ann | 1888 | Box 108 |
| Gouverneur, Samuel L. | 1880 | Box 71 | Graham, Mary J. Wright | 1915 | Box 518 |
| Gove, William B. | 1885 | Box 91 | Graham, Ro. D. | 1905 | Box 282 |
| Gover, Temperance M. | 1904 | Box 264 | Graham, Robert H. | 1885 | Box 91 |
| Gowans, James | 1919 | Box 628 | Graham, Susan | 1860 | Box 28 |
| Gowans, Mary Ann | 1920 | Box 661 | Graham, William S. | 1892 | Box 132 |
| Goward, Gustavus | 1909 | Box 369 | Grahame, John M. | 1918 | Box 598 |
| Grace, Ann M. | 1908 | Box 345 | Grammer, Frederick | 1867 | Box 37 |
| Grace, Patrick | 1896 | Box 161 | Grammer, G. C. | 1864 | Box 32 |
| Gracie, Archibald | 1915 | Box 518 | Grammer, Gottlieb C. | 1857 | Box 25 |
| Grady, Daniel | 1909 | Box 369 | Grammer, Julius E. | 1907 | Box 322 |
| Grady, Julia | 1914 | Box 491 | Grammer, Louis M. | 1871 | Box 45 |
| Grady, Michael F. | 1909 | Box 369 | Granbery, James E. | 1920 | Box 661 |
| Grady, Patrick | 1906 | Box 301 | Grandin, Elijah Bishop | 1917 | Box 571 |
| Grady, Thomas | 1872 | Box 47 | Grandy, Thomas | 1911 | Box 417 |
| Graef, Mary E. Harnedy | 1914 | Box 491 | Graney, Michael | 1884 | Box 86 |
| Graer, James | 1920 | Box 661 | Granger, Harris W. | 1870 | Box 42 |
| Graff, Anna Maria | 1895 | Box 153 | Granger, James H. | 1898 | Box 176 |
| Graff, Charles | 1912 | Box 442 | Granger, John Tileston | 1916 | Box 545 |
| Graff, John | 1902 | Box 226 | Granger, Margaret A. | 1866 | Box 35 |
| Graff, Mary | 1892 | Box 132 | Granger, Pamelia | 1896 | Box 161 |
| Graff, Sophia | 1915 | Box 518 | Grant, Blanch | 1915 | Box 518 |
| Grafton, Benjamin F. | 1883 | Box 82 | Grant, Caroline Adelaide | 1919 | Box 629 |
| Grages, August | 1911 | Box 417 | Grant, Edwin H. | 1906 | Box 301 |
| Graham, Adaline R. | 1915 | Box 518 | Grant, Elisha C. | 1857 | Box 25 |
| Graham, Aloysia | 1863 | Box 31 | Grant, Elizabeth Arnold | 1903 | Box 245 |
| Graham, Amelia J. | 1909 | Box 369 | Grant, James | 1870 | Box 42 |
| Graham, Andrew B. | 1909 | Box 369 | Grant, James M. | 1894 | Box 146 |
| Graham, Ann S. | 1904 | Box 264 | Grant, Jesse F. | 1914 | Box 491 |
| Graham, Catharine | 1892 | Box 132 | Grant, Johanna | 1865 | Box 33 |
| Graham, Christopher C. | 1911 | Box 417 | Grant, Julia Dent | 1902 | Box 226 |
| Graham, Curtis B. | 1896 | Box 161 | Grant, Mary C. | 1917 | Box 571 |
| Graham, Eleanor Euphemia | 1919 | Box 629 | Grant, Richard Westly | 1919 | Box 628 |
| Graham, Elizabeth | 1865 | Box 33 | Grant, Robert E. | 1920 | Box 661 |
| Graham, Frank W. | 1914 | Box 491 | Grant, Sarah A. | 1910 | Box 391 |
| Graham, George R. | 1890 | Box 119 | Grant, Sarah T. | 1903 | Box 245 |
| Graham, George W. | 1872 | Box 47 | Grass, August | 1903 | Box 245 |
| Graham, James | 1892 | Box 132 | Grave, Herman H. | 1908 | Box 345 |
| Graham, James S. | 1915 | Box 518 | Graver, Ruth B. | 1920 | Box 661 |
| Graham, James T. | 1893 | Box 138 | Graves, Benjamin S. | 1915 | Box 518 |
| Graham, Jane (Jean) | 1818 | Box 5 | Graves, David Harrison | 1913 | Box 469 |
| Graham, Jane L. | 1870 | Box 42 | Graves, Edward | 1910 | Box 391 |
| Graham, John | 1820 | Box 6 | Graves, Emma Roxana | 1915 | Box 518 |

| | | | | | | |
|---|---|---|---|---|---|---|
| Graves, George E. | 1919 | Box 629 | Green, Fanny | 1869 | Box 40 |
| Graves, Herbert C. | 1919 | Box 629 | Green, Fanny | 1904 | Box 264 |
| Graves, Jane | 1896 | Box 161 | Green, Galen E. | 1919 | Box 629 |
| Graves, Mary E. S. | 1917 | Box 571 | Green, George F. | 1909 | Box 369 |
| Graves, Ralph C. | 1920 | Box 661 | Green, George W. | 1904 | Box 264 |
| Graves, Scott | 1907 | Box 322 | Green, Hannah Etta | 1898 | Box 176 |
| Gray, Amanda | 1917 | Box 572 | Green, Henry | 1897 | Box 169 |
| Gray, Annie M. | 1911 | Box 418 | Green, James | 1875 | Box 57 |
| Gray, Arthur S. | 1917 | Box 572 | Green, James G. | 1909 | Box 369 |
| Gray, Charles B. | 1912 | Box 442 | Green, John | 1879 | Box 68 |
| Gray, Cornelia T. | 1919 | Box 629 | Green, John | 1905 | Box 282 |
| Gray, Edward J. Sr. | 1912 | Box 442 | Green, John C. | 1876 | Box 61 |
| Gray, Eleanor | 1853 | Box 22 | Green, John F. | 1915 | Box 518 |
| Gray, Flora M. | 1910 | Box 391 | Green, John M. | 1878 | Box 66 |
| Gray, George W. | 1916 | Box 545 | Green, Lavinia | 1890 | Box 119 |
| Gray, Gilbert | 1914 | Box 491 | Green, Lucius | 1883 | Box 82 |
| Gray, Helen E. | 1917 | Box 572 | Green, Margaret | 1905 | Box 282 |
| Gray, Henrietta | 1916 | Box 545 | Green, Maria D. | 1891 | Box 125 |
| Gray, Horace | 1902 | Box 226 | Green, Martha D. | 1907 | Box 322 |
| Gray, Horace J. | 1908 | Box 345 | Green, Mary A. | 1919 | Box 629 |
| Gray, Isaac S. | 1907 | Box 322 | Green, Mary B. | 1867 | Box 37 |
| Gray, James | 1886 | Box 97 | Green, Meyer | 1909 | Box 369 |
| Gray, John W. | 1919 | Box 629 | Green, Michael | 1876 | Box 61 |
| Gray, Joseph Clagett | 1917 | Box 572 | Green, Michael | 1911 | Box 418 |
| Gray, Josiah | 1920 | Box 661 | Green, Nancy | 1911 | Box 418 |
| Gray, Marion E. | 1920 | Box 661 | Green, Nettie | 1909 | Box 369 |
| Gray, Mary A. | 1890 | Box 119 | Green, Oregon L. | 1893 | Box 138 |
| Gray, Thornton | 1905 | Box 282 | Green, Osceola C. | 1895 | Box 153 |
| Gray, William A. | 1911 | Box 418 | Green, Patrick | 1870 | Box 43 |
| Gray, Wilson H. | 1896 | Box 161 | Green, Richard M. | 1897 | Box 169 |
| Grayson, Henry T. | 1843 | Box 16 | Green, Robert | 1906 | Box 301 |
| Greason, William | 1881 | Box 75 | Green, Ruth | 1898 | Box 176 |
| Greaves, James T. | 1916 | Box 545 | Green, Sarah | 1857 | Box 25 |
| Greaves, Patrick | 1894 | Box 146 | Green, Sarah | 1901 | Box 207 |
| Greely, Henrietta C. H. Nesmith | 1918 | Box 598 | Green, Sarah | 1909 | Box 369 |
| Green, Adwin W. | 1909 | Box 369 | Green, Sarah | 1914 | Box 492 |
| Green, Alice C. | 1900 | Box 193 | Green, Sarah M. | 1896 | Box 161 |
| Green, Amelia M. | 1888 | Box 108 | Green, Stephen | 1871 | Box 45 |
| Green, Andrew M. | 1899 | Box 184 | Green, Susanna Rosina | 1889 | Box 114 |
| Green, Ann | 1870 | Box 42 | Green, Timothy F. | 1895 | Box 153 |
| Green, Anna Rebecca | 1908 | Box 345 | Green, William G. | 1918 | Box 598 |
| Green, Arthur L. | 1910 | Box 391 | Green, William M. B. | 1899 | Box 184 |
| Green, Bernard Richardson | 1914 | Box 491 | Greenawalt, Mary L. | 1918 | Box 598 |
| Green, Bryan | 1869 | Box 40 | Greene, Albert E. S. | 1899 | Box 184 |
| Green, David N. | 1876 | Box 61 | Greene, Columbus | 1892 | Box 132 |
| Green, David Y. | 1909 | Box 369 | Greene, E. Milton | 1919 | Box 629 |
| Green, Edward | 1911 | Box 418 | Greene, Eliza V. | 1908 | Box 345 |
| Green, Edwin | 1867 | Box 37 | Greene, John W. | 1908 | Box 345 |
| Green, Eleanor | 1817 | Box 5 | Greene, Louis | 1897 | Box 169 |
| Green, Eliza C. | 1909 | Box 369 | Greene, Mary A. | 1917 | Box 572 |
| Green, Elizabeth | 1893 | Box 138 | Greene, Samuel | 1851 | Box 21 |
| Green, Fannie | 1905 | Box 282 | Greene, Samuel H. | 1920 | Box 661 |

| | | | | | | |
|---|---|---|---|---|---|---|
| Greene, William B. | 1896 | Box 161 | Griesheimer, Helena E. | 1920 | Box 661 |
| Greenfield, Amelia | 1907 | Box 322 | Griffin, Augusta Price | 1913 | Box 469 |
| Greenfield, Elizabeth Ann | 1833 | Box 12 | Griffin, Caroline Hale | 1911 | Box 418 |
| Greenfield, Hattie M. | 1908 | Box 345 | Griffin, Carrie C. | 1916 | Box 545 |
| Greenfield, Mary E. | 1870 | Box 43 | Griffin, Catharine | 1910 | Box 391 |
| Greenfield, William W. | 1885 | Box 91 | Griffin, Celia E. | 1904 | Box 264 |
| Greenlees, Archibald | 1917 | Box 572 | Griffin, Charles T. | 1910 | Box 392 |
| Greenlees, Leonora | 1901 | Box 207 | Griffin, Ella M. | 1905 | Box 282 |
| Greenough, Ephraim A. | 1904 | Box 264 | Griffin, Ellen | 1865 | Box 33 |
| Greenwell, Alfred B. | 1913 | Box 469 | Griffin, Emma H. | 1907 | Box 322 |
| Greenwell, Benedict O. | 1892 | Box 132 | Griffin, Francis | 1920 | Box 662 |
| Greenwell, Combs | 1890 | Box 119 | Griffin, John W. | 1885 | Box 91 |
| Greenwell, Elizabeth | 1822 | Box 7 | Griffin, Julia | 1890 | Box 119 |
| Greenwell, Joseph B. | 1902 | Box 226 | Griffin, Margaret E. | 1910 | Box 392 |
| Greenwell, Robert | 1917 | Box 572 | Griffin, Mary | 1896 | Box 161 |
| Greenwell, William M. | 1897 | Box 169 | Griffin, Mary H. | 1821 | Box 6 |
| Greenwill, James B. | 1877 | Box 63 | Griffin, Robert G. | 1903 | Box 245 |
| Greenwood, Charles | 1916 | Box 545 | Griffin, Sarah | 1905 | Box 282 |
| Greer, Alexander A. | 1888 | Box 108 | Griffin, William | 1919 | Box 629 |
| Greer, James Augustin | 1904 | Box 264 | Griffin, William H. | 1903 | Box 245 |
| Greer, Marie Prince | 1916 | Box 545 | Griffin, William T. | 1885 | Box 91 |
| Greer, Mary R. | 1900 | Box 193 | Griffith, Addie | 1912 | Box 442 |
| Greer, Mary W. | 1885 | Box 91 | Griffith, Edwin W. W. | 1908 | Box 345 |
| Greer, Robert Jr. | 1894 | Box 146 | Griffith, Fleming R. | 1890 | Box 119 |
| Greeves, John | 1853 | Box 22 | Griffith, Frances C. | 1916 | Box 545 |
| Gregg, Samuel | 1888 | Box 108 | Griffith, Frances E. | 1900 | Box 193 |
| Gregg, Susan A. | 1916 | Box 545 | Griffith, John H. | 1870 | Box 43 |
| Gregorio, Anna Cascio | 1920 | Box 661 | Griffith, Margaret | 1895 | Box 153 |
| Gregory, Cora W. | 1915 | Box 518 | Griffith, Margaret M. | 1917 | Box 572 |
| Gregory, Eliza | 1891 | Box 125 | Griffith, Marnie V. | 1910 | Box 392 |
| Gregory, Eliza M. | 1902 | Box 226 | Griffith, Mary Catherine | 1905 | Box 282 |
| Gregory, Fannie N. | 1913 | Box 469 | Griffith, Michael | 1865 | Box 33 |
| Gregory, Fontaine Maury | 1905 | Box 282 | Griffith, Michael J. | 1919 | Box 629 |
| Gregory, George | 1885 | Box 91 | Griffith, Paul | 1919 | Box 629 |
| Gregory, John M. | 1899 | Box 184 | Griffith, Samuel Henderson | 1905 | Box 282 |
| Gregory, John Welch | 1920 | Box 661 | Griffith, Thomas A. | 1913 | Box 469 |
| Gregory, Louisa Catherine | 1920 | Box 661 | Griffith, Walter Scott | 1907 | Box 322 |
| Gregory, Maria L. | 1915 | Box 518 | Griffith, William B. | 1896 | Box 161 |
| Gregory, Mary Ann | 1897 | Box 169 | Griffith, Wilson W. | 1899 | Box 184 |
| Gregory, Wilson | 1905 | Box 282 | Griggs, David | 1901 | Box 207 |
| Grenacher, Charles H. | 1914 | Box 492 | Grigsby, Bushrod T. | 1910 | Box 392 |
| Gresham, Fanny W. | 1908 | Box 345 | Grigsby, Emily | 1914 | Box 492 |
| Grey, Margarett R. | 1894 | Box 146 | Grigsby, Mary Hellen | 1906 | Box 301 |
| Grey, William | 1868 | Box 39 | Grimes, Albert | 1910 | Box 392 |
| Grice, George | 1908 | Box 345 | Grimes, Alfred T. | 1867 | Box 37 |
| Grice, Mary C. | 1905 | Box 282 | Grimes, Ernest C. | 1920 | Box 662 |
| Gridley, Ann Eliza | 1909 | Box 369 | Grimes, George S. | 1920 | Box 662 |
| Gridley, James Hervey | 1895 | Box 153 | Grimes, John F. | 1888 | Box 108 |
| Grieb, William | 1918 | Box 598 | Grimes, Lucy Jane | 1891 | Box 125 |
| Grier, William | 1911 | Box 418 | Grimes, Margaret C. | 1868 | Box 39 |
| Griesbauer, Clara H. | 1914 | Box 492 | Grimes, Samuel J. | 1867 | Box 37 |
| Griesbauer, John A. | 1913 | Box 469 | Grimm, August | 1912 | Box 442 |

| | | | | | | |
|---|---|---|---|---|---|---|
| Grimm, Elizabeth | 1915 | Box 518 | | Grumley, Jeannette W. | 1893 | Box 138 |
| Grimm, Frederick | 1904 | Box 264 | | Grupe, Doris | 1902 | Box 226 |
| Grimstead, Marie L. | 1906 | Box 301 | | Gruser, Valentine | 1893 | Box 138 |
| Grindage, William | 1850 | Box 20 | | Grymes, Alice (Ellis) | 1851 | Box 21 |
| Grinder, Adam | 1874 | Box 54 | | Grymes, Craven Francis | 1872 | Box 47 |
| Grinder, John | 1892 | Box 132 | | Grymes, Thaddeus B. | 1881 | Box 75 |
| Grinder, Joseph | 1899 | Box 184 | | Gsantner, Otto Carl | 1915 | Box 519 |
| Grinstead, Amanda J. | 1918 | Box 598 | | Gudgin, Mary S. | 1902 | Box 226 |
| Grinstead, John | 1915 | Box 518 | | Gudgin, Richard | 1866 | Box 36 |
| Grinsted, Susannah A. | 1912 | Box 443 | | Guenther, Albert | 1882 | Box 79 |
| Grinsted, William | 1894 | Box 146 | | Guerdrum, Olaf Weis | 1902 | Box 226 |
| Gripp, Rose | 1915 | Box 519 | | Guerin, Michael | 1891 | Box 125 |
| Griswold, Ellen J. | 1888 | Box 108 | | Guernsey, William Henry | 1916 | Box 545 |
| Griswold, Henry A. | 1909 | Box 369 | | Guest, Anna Josephine | 1908 | Box 345 |
| Griswold, Mary Adelaide | 1906 | Box 301 | | Guest, John | 1919 | Box 629 |
| Griswold, Sarah B. | 1914 | Box 492 | | Guest, Nellie Reeves | 1920 | Box 662 |
| Griswold, Susanna | 1904 | Box 264 | | Guethler, Katharina | 1919 | Box 629 |
| Griswold, William A. | 1913 | Box 469 | | Guffin, Mary J. | 1902 | Box 226 |
| Groce, Susan M. | 1909 | Box 369 | | Guigon, Peter G. | 1897 | Box 169 |
| Groener, George | 1904 | Box 264 | | Guild, Alice P. | 1918 | Box 598 |
| Groener, George C. | 1913 | Box 469 | | Guild, Ellen | 1873 | Box 51 |
| Groener, William | 1917 | Box 572 | | Guild, Lucy W. | 1899 | Box 184 |
| Groesbeck, Daniel V. H. | 1919 | Box 629 | | Guilford, Harry H. | 1907 | Box 322 |
| Groff, Diller B. | 1910 | Box 392 | | Guista, Mary E. | 1910 | Box 391 |
| Gronberger, Sven Magnus | 1916 | Box 545 | | Guiteau, Charles J. | 1882 | Box 79 |
| Groot, John R. | 1869 | Box 40 | | Guiteras, Pedro J. | 1890 | Box 119 |
| Groot, Simon I. | 1907 | Box 322 | | Gulick, Elizabeth Milligan | 1894 | Box 146 |
| Grosh, Aaron Burt | 1884 | Box 86 | | Gulick, James H. | 1880 | Box 71 |
| Groshon, John H. T. | 1884 | Box 86 | | Gulick, John S. | 1884 | Box 86 |
| Grosjean, Johanna | 1916 | Box 545 | | Gulick, Mary Elizabeth | 1908 | Box 345 |
| Grosner, Isidor | 1920 | Box 662 | | Gullberg, Carl | 1904 | Box 265 |
| Gross, Andreas | 1919 | Box 629 | | Gullen, John R. | 1896 | Box 161 |
| Gross, Frank P. | 1904 | Box 264 | | Gullen, Mary Frances | 1890 | Box 119 |
| Gross, George | 1894 | Box 146 | | Gundling, Elisabeth | 1889 | Box 114 |
| Gross, Henry E. | 1894 | Box 146 | | Gundling, Louis | 1920 | Box 662 |
| Gross, John A. | 1910 | Box 392 | | Gunion, Zachariah P. | 1898 | Box 176 |
| Gross, John Michael | 1895 | Box 153 | | Gunnell, Helen M. | 1891 | Box 125 |
| Gross, John W. | 1906 | Box 301 | | Gunnell, Henry D. | 1875 | Box 57 |
| Gross, Sarah C. | 1916 | Box 545 | | Gunnell, James S. | 1907 | Box 322 |
| Grossman, Adolph | 1920 | Box 662 | | Gunnell, James S. | 1852 | Box 21 |
| Grouard, George M. | 1857 | Box 25 | | Gunnell, Mary Blakley | 1912 | Box 443 |
| Groux, Daniel E. | 1871 | Box 45 | | Gunnell, Mary Newbold | 1906 | Box 302 |
| Grove, Cornelius | 1920 | Box 662 | | Gunnell, Robert H. | 1902 | Box 226 |
| Grover, Cuvier | 1910 | Box 392 | | Gunning, Amos J. | 1918 | Box 598 |
| Grover, Cuvier | 1894 | Box 146 | | Gunning, Olive H. | 1916 | Box 545 |
| Grover, Cuvier | 1892 | Box 132 | | Gunnison, Caroline F. | 1912 | Box 443 |
| Grover, Elida A. | 1906 | Box 301 | | Gunnison, Sarah B. | 1920 | Box 662 |
| Grover, Frances H. | 1915 | Box 519 | | Gunsalus, Marietta | 1913 | Box 469 |
| Groves, James S. | 1916 | Box 545 | | Gunton, William | 1880 | Box 71 |
| Grubb, Laura J. | 1916 | Box 545 | | Gurley, Elizabeth Scott | 1892 | Box 132 |
| Gruber, Lucinda | 1919 | Box 629 | | Gurnnison, William H. | 1893 | Box 138 |
| Gruenke, Minna | 1898 | Box 176 | | Gury, Louis | 1901 | Box 207 |

| | | | | | | |
|---|---|---|---|---|---|---|
| Guss, Susan M. | 1917 | Box 572 | Hagmann, Victor | 1882 | Box 79 |
| Gusta, Charles | 1807 | Box 2 | Hagner, Alexander Burton | 1915 | Box 519 |
| Gustin, George Albert | 1907 | Box 322 | Hagner, Cora C. | 1918 | Box 599 |
| Gutekunst, Albert F. | 1919 | Box 629 | Hagner, Daniel R. | 1893 | Box 139 |
| Gutherz, Carl | 1909 | Box 369 | Hagner, Frances | 1863 | Box 31 |
| Gutherz, Kate | 1909 | Box 369 | Hagner, Frances Randall | 1920 | Box 662 |
| Guthridge, Jules | 1917 | Box 572 | Hagner, Francis R. | 1902 | Box 227 |
| Guthrie, Sophy W. | 1912 | Box 443 | Hagner, John R. | 1857 | Box 25 |
| Guthrie, Southwick | 1902 | Box 226 | Hagner, Louisa | 1905 | Box 282 |
| Guttensohn, John | 1902 | Box 207 | Hagner, Peter | 1850 | Box 20 |
| Guttenson, Amelia Caroline | 1898 | Box 176 | Hagner, Peter V. | 1893 | Box 139 |
| Guy, Franklin | 1892 | Box 132 | Hagner, Sarah A. | 1895 | Box 153 |
| Guy, John F. | 1892 | Box 132 | Hague, Arnold | 1917 | Box 572 |
| Guy, John M. | 1920 | Box 662 | Hague, John E. | 1920 | Box 662 |
| Guy, Margaret J. | 1901 | Box 208 | Hahn, Abram I. | 1919 | Box 629 |
| Guy, Susan Darnley | 1832 | Box 11 | Hahn, William | 1912 | Box 443 |
| Guy, William E. | 1904 | Box 265 | Hahn, William A. | 1908 | Box 346 |
| Gwathmey, Mary Eliza | 1902 | Box 226 | Hahne, Mella Gooch | 1910 | Box 392 |
| Gwynn, Walter | 1892 | Box 132 | Haight, Henry | 1908 | Box 346 |
| Gwynne, Maria O. | 1903 | Box 245 | Hailstock, Mary J. | 1916 | Box 546 |
| Haake, Ellen | 1888 | Box 108 | Haina, Josef F. | 1912 | Box 443 |
| Haarburger, Sarah | 1916 | Box 545 | Haines, Emily | 1908 | Box 346 |
| Haarsher, Abraham | 1903 | Box 245 | Haines, Sarah B. | 1907 | Box 322 |
| Haas, Anna B. | 1906 | Box 302 | Haines, Washington | 1895 | Box 153 |
| Haas, Edwin E. | 1915 | Box 519 | Haislett, Samuel Joseph | 1905 | Box 282 |
| Haas, Frederick | 1887 | Box 103 | Haislip, Thomas M. | 1903 | Box 245 |
| Haas, John | 1892 | Box 132 | Haislup, James B. | 1920 | Box 662 |
| Hackett, Michael J. | 1910 | Box 392 | Haldeman, Christiana | 1916 | Box 545 |
| Hackley, Harriet | 1860 | Box 28 | Halderman, John A. | 1908 | Box 346 |
| Hackman, David K. | 1908 | Box 346 | Haldman, Franklin L. | 1901 | Box 208 |
| Hadad, Mickael | 1919 | Box 629 | Hale, Grace | 1913 | Box 469 |
| Haddaway, Octavia S. | 1914 | Box 492 | Hale, John C. | 1918 | Box 599 |
| Haddaway, Samuel W. | 1893 | Box 139 | Hale, Mary Elizabeth | 1906 | Box 302 |
| Haddaway, Thomas D. | 1901 | Box 208 | Hale, Robert Joseph | 1903 | Box 245 |
| Haden, Charlotte | 1909 | Box 369 | Hale, William B. | 1886 | Box 97 |
| Hadfield, Charles F. | 1912 | Box 443 | Haley, William Aloysus | 1911 | Box 418 |
| Hadley, Maning | 1868 | Box 39 | Halford, Albert James | 1910 | Box 392 |
| Haenni, Rudolph | 1897 | Box 169 | Haliday, James F. | 1867 | Box 37 |
| Haerle, Bertha | 1895 | Box 153 | Haliday, Mary J. | 1919 | Box 629 |
| Hafle, Jacob (Mrs.) | 1910 | Box 392 | Haliday, William D. | 1917 | Box 572 |
| Hagan, Elizabeth | 1859 | Box 27 | Hall, Abby E. | 1874 | Box 54 |
| Hagan, Horatio | 1849 | Box 17 | Hall, Anna Elizabeth | 1910 | Box 392 |
| Hagan, Isabella | 1914 | Box 492 | Hall, Aquilla | 1899 | Box 184 |
| Hagan, John | 1893 | Box 139 | Hall, Catherine | 1861 | Box 29 |
| Hagan, Zachariah | 1889 | Box 114 | Hall, Charles | 1892 | Box 132 |
| Hagans, Mary C. | 1919 | Box 629 | Hall, Charles E. | 1901 | Box 208 |
| Hager, Christopher | 1885 | Box 91 | Hall, Clara B. Brooks | 1883 | Box 82 |
| Hager, Elijah W. | 1885 | Box 91 | Hall, Clarissa | 1858 | Box 26 |
| Hagerty, Daniel | 1875 | Box 57 | Hall, Cornelius D. | 1906 | Box 302 |
| Hagerty, Dennis | 1899 | Box 184 | Hall, Daniel W. | 1860 | Box 28 |
| Hagerty, Josephine R. | 1916 | Box 545 | Hall, Elizabeth | 1896 | Box 161 |
| Hagerty, Mary A. | 1911 | Box 418 | Hall, Elizabeth | 1915 | Box 519 |

| | | | | | | |
|---|---|---|---|---|---|---|
| Hall, Elizabeth M. | 1917 | Box 572 | Halley, Thomas F. | 1904 | Box 265 |
| Hall, Ellen S. | 1892 | Box 132 | Halley, William | 1906 | Box 302 |
| Hall, Elsie Ann | 1896 | Box 161 | Halliday, Edward C. | 1905 | Box 282 |
| Hall, Flora | 1914 | Box 492 | Hallman, George | 1913 | Box 469 |
| Hall, Francis | 1907 | Box 322 | Hallock, Charles | 1918 | Box 599 |
| Hall, Francis | 1916 | Box 546 | Hallock, Zerubbabel | 1877 | Box 63 |
| Hall, Frank A. | 1915 | Box 519 | Halloran, Mary Josephine | 1913 | Box 469 |
| Hall, Fred A. | 1904 | Box 265 | Halloran, William | 1839 | Box 14 |
| Hall, Frederick | 1843 | Box 16 | Halpine, Margaret G. | 1907 | Box 322 |
| Hall, George I. | 1907 | Box 322 | Halsey, Henry | 1817 | Box 5 |
| Hall, George R. | 1888 | Box 108 | Halstead, Annie B. | 1910 | Box 392 |
| Hall, Gervas | 1802 | Box 1 | Halstead, Emilie M. | 1907 | Box 322 |
| Hall, Goff Alfred | 1914 | Box 492 | Halstead, Eminel P. | 1912 | Box 443 |
| Hall, Harriet | 1910 | Box 392 | Halsted, Frances Louise | 1914 | Box 492 |
| Hall, Henry | 1888 | Box 108 | Halsted, John J. | 1905 | Box 282 |
| Hall, Henry | 1892 | Box 132 | Halsted, Mary | 1872 | Box 47 |
| Hall, Hillman A. | 1914 | Box 492 | Halsted, Pennington | 1913 | Box 469 |
| Hall, Ida M. G. | 1909 | Box 369 | Haltworth, Otto | 1910 | Box 392 |
| Hall, Ida M. G. | 1915 | Box 519 | Ham, Ann | 1879 | Box 68 |
| Hall, Isaac Newton | 1900 | Box 193 | Ham, Hiram Henry | 1874 | Box 54 |
| Hall, Isabelle M. | 1919 | Box 629 | Hamacher, Joseph | 1902 | Box 227 |
| Hall, James C. | 1880 | Box 71 | Hambleton, Benjamin E. | 1905 | Box 282 |
| Hall, John | 1903 | Box 245 | Hamden, William | 1814 | Box 4 |
| Hall, John Dean | 1920 | Box 662 | Hames, Henry | 1911 | Box 418 |
| Hall, John H. | 1896 | Box 161 | Hamill, C. A. | 1904 | Box 265 |
| Hall, John R. | 1899 | Box 184 | Hamill, John | 1838 | Box 14 |
| Hall, John W. | 1894 | Box 146 | Hamill, Samuel R. | 1881 | Box 75 |
| Hall, John W. | 1907 | Box 322 | Hamilton, Charles Beale | 1851 | Box 21 |
| Hall, Julia Rankin | 1918 | Box 599 | Hamilton, Christina | 1832 | Box 11 |
| Hall, Lavinia A. | 1904 | Box 265 | Hamilton, Eliza | 1861 | Box 29 |
| Hall, Mary E. | 1917 | Box 572 | Hamilton, Elizabeth | 1859 | Box 27 |
| Hall, Mary Frances | 1891 | Box 125 | Hamilton, Frances E. | 1884 | Box 86 |
| Hall, Nicholas | 1811 | Box 3 | Hamilton, Frances Rebecca | 1907 | Box 322 |
| Hall, Page | 1898 | Box 176 | Hamilton, George | 1909 | Box 369 |
| Hall, Richard | 1858 | Box 26 | Hamilton, Henry Weaver | 1917 | Box 572 |
| Hall, Ruth Adelle | 1900 | Box 193 | Hamilton, James H. | 1862 | Box 30 |
| Hall, Sarah | 1912 | Box 443 | Hamilton, John A. | 1915 | Box 519 |
| Hall, William B. | 1907 | Box 322 | Hamilton, Jonathan | 1906 | Box 302 |
| Hall, William G. | 1912 | Box 443 | Hamilton, Julia | 1919 | Box 629 |
| Hall, Winifred A. | 1830 | Box 10 | Hamilton, Letitia | 1817 | Box 5 |
| Halladay, Rowland P. | 1912 | Box 443 | Hamilton, Margaret | 1899 | Box 184 |
| Hallam, Henry C. | 1901 | Box 208 | Hamilton, Martha Morgan | 1904 | Box 265 |
| Hallaran, Elizabeth C. | 1907 | Box 322 | Hamilton, Mary A. | 1917 | Box 572 |
| Hallaran, William E. | 1876 | Box 61 | Hamilton, Mary Christina | 1846 | Box 18 |
| Halleck, Millard F. | 1895 | Box 153 | Hamilton, Merker R. | 1916 | Box 545 |
| Halleck, Walter F. | 1915 | Box 519 | Hamilton, William | 1889 | Box 114 |
| Halleck, William E. | 1897 | Box 169 | Hamilton, William T. | 1890 | Box 119 |
| Hallenbeck, Edgar | 1901 | Box 208 | Hamiter, David | 1882 | Box 79 |
| Haller, Maggie A. | 1915 | Box 519 | Hamlin, Frances B. | 1916 | Box 546 |
| Hallet, Elizabeth Caroline | 1904 | Box 265 | Hamlin, John P. | 1914 | Box 492 |
| Hallett, Margaret | 1869 | Box 40 | Hamlin, Joseph | 1886 | Box 97 |
| Halley, James Edward | 1909 | Box 369 | Hamlin, Teunis S. | 1907 | Box 322 |

| | | | | | | |
|---|---|---|---|---|---|
| Hamm, Allen B. | 1907 | Box 322 | Hanna, Robert | 1910 | Box 392 |
| Hammack, John D. | 1867 | Box 37 | Hannan, Bridget | 1912 | Box 443 |
| Hammack, Mary A. | 1903 | Box 245 | Hannan, Daniel P. | 1910 | Box 392 |
| Hammargren, Ernest L. | 1910 | Box 392 | Hannan, Edward J. | 1913 | Box 469 |
| Hammel, Ida | 1915 | Box 519 | Hannay, Peter | 1880 | Box 71 |
| Hammer, Charles A. | 1903 | Box 245 | Hannay, Sarah E. | 1908 | Box 346 |
| Hammer, George | 1915 | Box 519 | Hannon, Bartholomew | 1904 | Box 265 |
| Hammer, John G. | 1839 | Box 14 | Hannot, Victor | 1873 | Box 51 |
| Hammerly, Addie C. | 1902 | Box 227 | Hanscom, Isaiah | 1880 | Box 71 |
| Hammersley, Edward | 1883 | Box 82 | Hansell, Emerich W. | 1893 | Box 139 |
| Hammersley, William H. | 1904 | Box 265 | Hansell, Mary E. | 1894 | Box 146 |
| Hammett, Irene F. | 1917 | Box 572 | Hansen, Hans | 1907 | Box 323 |
| Hammill, James Henry | 1916 | Box 546 | Hansen, Johan | 1914 | Box 492 |
| Hammond, Deborah | 1879 | Box 69 | Hansen, John | 1915 | Box 519 |
| Hammond, Edward | 1902 | Box 227 | Hansford, Virginia | 1916 | Box 546 |
| Hammond, Edward A. | 1901 | Box 208 | Hanson, Amelia Campbell | 1887 | Box 103 |
| Hammond, Helen | 1877 | Box 63 | Hanson, Andrew | 1875 | Box 57 |
| Hammond, John B. | 1916 | Box 546 | Hanson, Ann | 1872 | Box 47 |
| Hammond, John E. | 1906 | Box 302 | Hanson, Grafton Dulany | 1903 | Box 245 |
| Hammond, Leonard L. | 1919 | Box 629 | Hanson, Julia | 1903 | Box 245 |
| Hammond, Mary | 1909 | Box 369 | Hanson, Maria Ingle | 1909 | Box 370 |
| Hammond, Richard E. | 1917 | Box 572 | Hanson, Mary | 1848 | Box 19 |
| Hammond, Sarah | 1883 | Box 82 | Hanson, Serena | 1895 | Box 153 |
| Hammond, William A. | 1900 | Box 193 | Hanson, Stephen Cantine | 1911 | Box 418 |
| Hamsher, William Reber | 1919 | Box 629 | Hanson, Thomas M. | 1889 | Box 114 |
| Hanaphy, Patrick | 1883 | Box 82 | Hantzmon, Mary Jane Arnold | 1905 | Box 283 |
| Hancock, Almira R. | 1893 | Box 139 | Happ, Nicholas | 1889 | Box 114 |
| Hancock, Andrew | 1881 | Box 75 | Haralson, Hugh A. | 1898 | Box 176 |
| Hancock, Mary Elizabeth | 1918 | Box 599 | Harang, Emily Willson | 1917 | Box 572 |
| Hand, Ann | 1826 | Box 8 | Harban, Edward | 1919 | Box 629 |
| Hand, Joseph W. | 1844 | Box 17 | Harban, James | 1891 | Box 125 |
| Handebeau, Ellen | 1899 | Box 184 | Harban, William T. | 1908 | Box 346 |
| Handley, Fanny H. | 1910 | Box 392 | Harbaugh, Adeline | 1871 | Box 45 |
| Handley, Margaret | 1913 | Box 469 | Harbaugh, Edgar G. | 1916 | Box 546 |
| Handley, William White | 1920 | Box 662 | Harbaugh, Joseph | 1862 | Box 30 |
| Handy, Edward G. | 1871 | Box 45 | Harbaugh, Maria W. | 1911 | Box 418 |
| Handy, Henrietta Dorsey | 1883 | Box 82 | Harbaugh, Valentine | 1871 | Box 45 |
| Handy, James H. | 1832 | Box 11 | Harbin, James | 1893 | Box 139 |
| Handy, Samuel Wilson Ker | 1897 | Box 169 | Harbin, Sarah P. | 1906 | Box 302 |
| Handy, Virginia | 1871 | Box 45 | Harbin, Thomas W. | 1885 | Box 92 |
| Hane, Christiana | 1901 | Box 208 | Hardell, John W. | 1913 | Box 469 |
| Hanfman, Catharina | 1912 | Box 443 | Hardell, Julia E. | 1906 | Box 302 |
| Hanfman, John Sebastian | 1912 | Box 443 | Harden, Frances | 1898 | Box 176 |
| Hange, Mary E. | 1919 | Box 629 | Harden, Richard J. | 1899 | Box 184 |
| Hanlon, Anthony | 1905 | Box 282 | Harden, Sarah C. | 1908 | Box 346 |
| Hanlon, Maurice | 1888 | Box 108 | Hardenbergh, Elizabeth | 1916 | Box 546 |
| Hanly, Annie L. | 1911 | Box 418 | Hardenbergh, Josiah F. | 1908 | Box 346 |
| Hanly, Edmund | 1843 | Box 16 | Hardesty, John W. | 1912 | Box 443 |
| Hanly, Thomas Smith | 1913 | Box 469 | Hardin, Helen H. | 1918 | Box 599 |
| Hann, Alvah R. | 1919 | Box 629 | Hardin, William L. | 1920 | Box 662 |
| Hanna, Edwin P. | 1909 | Box 369 | Harding, Alexander | 1919 | Box 629 |
| Hanna, Margaret | 1916 | Box 546 | Harding, Ann J. | 1912 | Box 443 |

| | | | | | | |
|---|---|---|---|---|---|---|
| Harding, James D. | 1912 | Box 443 | Harrington, George | 1893 | Box 139 |
| Harding, Josiah F. | 1873 | Box 51 | Harrington, George Dana | 1879 | Box 69 |
| Harding, Mary H. | 1877 | Box 64 | Harrington, James | 1870 | Box 43 |
| Harding, Mary S. | 1914 | Box 492 | Harrington, John | 1888 | Box 108 |
| Harding, Theodore A. | 1907 | Box 323 | Harrington, John C. | 1920 | Box 662 |
| Hardisty, Henry | 1872 | Box 47 | Harrington, Julia P. | 1908 | Box 346 |
| Hardmond, Sally | 1893 | Box 139 | Harrington, Mary | 1877 | Box 64 |
| Hardy, Robert W. | 1920 | Box 662 | Harrington, Mary S. | 1891 | Box 125 |
| Hare, Mary Louise | 1912 | Box 443 | Harrington, Michael | 1896 | Box 161 |
| Harford, Annie | 1908 | Box 346 | Harrington, Rachel | 1871 | Box 45 |
| Hargood, Margaret | 1819 | Box 6 | Harrington, William | 1887 | Box 103 |
| Harison, Laura Johnson | 1916 | Box 546 | Harriot, Samuel J. | 1919 | Box 629 |
| Harkness, Elizabeth Savington | 1885 | Box 92 | Harris, Ann | 1904 | Box 265 |
| Harkness, John C. | 1886 | Box 97 | Harris, Anna K. | 1868 | Box 39 |
| Harkness, John Williams | 1916 | Box 546 | Harris, Augusta | 1920 | Box 662 |
| Harkness, Maria L. | 1888 | Box 108 | Harris, Benjamin | 1900 | Box 193 |
| Harkness, Mary E. | 1891 | Box 125 | Harris, Caroline Jenkins | 1904 | Box 265 |
| Harkness, William | 1903 | Box 245 | Harris, Charles E. | 1920 | Box 662 |
| Harlan, Malvina French | 1919 | Box 629 | Harris, Edwin | 1908 | Box 346 |
| Harlan, Mary E. | 1899 | Box 184 | Harris, Elizabeth W. | 1898 | Box 176 |
| Harlan, Newton | 1877 | Box 64 | Harris, Eva Cobb | 1914 | Box 492 |
| Harley, Joseph Lafayette | 1913 | Box 469 | Harris, George E. | 1911 | Box 418 |
| Harley, William Evans | 1918 | Box 599 | Harris, Harriet Seaton | 1906 | Box 302 |
| Harlow, Fannie A. | 1920 | Box 662 | Harris, Hatton N. T. | 1905 | Box 283 |
| Harlow, Helen C. | 1915 | Box 519 | Harris, Henrietta | 1903 | Box 245 |
| Harman, John | 1900 | Box 193 | Harris, Henry Sutton T. | 1917 | Box 572 |
| Harman, Mary | 1903 | Box 245 | Harris, Henry Tudor B. | 1920 | Box 662 |
| Harmon, Henry C. | 1892 | Box 132 | Harris, Herbert | 1902 | Box 227 |
| Harmon, James L. | 1916 | Box 546 | Harris, James | 1846 | Box 18 |
| Harmon, Jennie D. | 1906 | Box 302 | Harris, Joel | 1882 | Box 79 |
| Harmon, Martha Frances | 1914 | Box 492 | Harris, John | 1845 | Box 17 |
| Harmony, David B. | 1918 | Box 599 | Harris, John B. | 1881 | Box 75 |
| Harner, Edwin H. | 1901 | Box 208 | Harris, John H. | 1918 | Box 599 |
| Harner, Roberta | 1911 | Box 418 | Harris, John T. | 1899 | Box 184 |
| Harnsberger, William Henry | 1915 | Box 519 | Harris, Joseph D. | 1885 | Box 92 |
| Harper, Edwin S. | 1915 | Box 519 | Harris, Joseph D. | 1899 | Box 184 |
| Harper, Elizabeth | 1910 | Box 392 | Harris, Leroy H. | 1912 | Box 443 |
| Harper, Grafton | 1887 | Box 103 | Harris, Louise H. | 1913 | Box 469 |
| Harper, James William | 1914 | Box 492 | Harris, Lucy H. | 1900 | Box 193 |
| Harper, Joseph | 1911 | Box 418 | Harris, Luke | 1823 | Box 7 |
| Harper, Kenton N. | 1914 | Box 492 | Harris, Maria M. | 1918 | Box 599 |
| Harper, Lettie M. | 1916 | Box 546 | Harris, Martha | 1918 | Box 599 |
| Harper, Nicholas | 1843 | Box 16 | Harris, Reuben | 1906 | Box 302 |
| Harper, Nicholas Columbus | 1919 | Box 629 | Harris, Robert | 1918 | Box 599 |
| Harper, Patrick | 1869 | Box 40 | Harris, Robert H. | 1917 | Box 572 |
| Harper, Thomas | 1883 | Box 82 | Harris, Robert Lewis | 1889 | Box 114 |
| Harr, John | 1903 | Box 245 | Harris, Samuel | 1825 | Box 8 |
| Harr, John F. | 1919 | Box 629 | Harris, Thomas DeKalb | 1873 | Box 51 |
| Harr, Peter | 1905 | Box 283 | Harris, Thomas DeKalb | 1875 | Box 57 |
| Harrigan, Ella | 1919 | Box 629 | Harris, William | 1901 | Box 208 |
| Harriman, Sarah A. | 1917 | Box 572 | Harris, William | 1865 | Box 33 |
| Harrington, Emma | 1902 | Box 227 | Harris, William A. | 1890 | Box 119 |

| | | | | | | |
|---|---|---|---|---|---|---|---|
| Harris, William C. | 1913 | Box 469 | | Hartgrove, William Bernard | 1918 | Box 599 |
| Harris, William Thompson | 1904 | Box 265 | | Hartig, Gustav F. L. | 1894 | Box 146 |
| Harrison, Benjamin | 1835 | Box 13 | | Hartigan, James F. | 1894 | Box 146 |
| Harrison, Caroline | 1892 | Box 132 | | Hartigan, Patrick J. | 1920 | Box 662 |
| Harrison, Elizabeth | 1916 | Box 546 | | Hartley, Edwin D. | 1887 | Box 103 |
| Harrison, Elizabeth G. | 1917 | Box 572 | | Hartley, Julia B. | 1920 | Box 662 |
| Harrison, George B. | 1898 | Box 176 | | Hartley, Mary L. | 1892 | Box 132 |
| Harrison, George Byrd | 1898 | Box 176 | | Hartman, Gustave A. | 1913 | Box 469 |
| Harrison, George F. E. | 1909 | Box 370 | | Hartman, Joseph | 1910 | Box 392 |
| Harrison, George L. | 1886 | Box 97 | | Hartman, Martin | 1918 | Box 599 |
| Harrison, James A. | 1898 | Box 176 | | Hartmann, Caroline | 1906 | Box 302 |
| Harrison, James T. | 1902 | Box 227 | | Hartmann, Charles | 1919 | Box 629 |
| Harrison, James W. | 1902 | Box 227 | | Hartnett, Ellen Mary | 1863 | Box 31 |
| Harrison, Jane Lenthall S. | 1908 | Box 346 | | Hartnett, Joanna | 1890 | Box 119 |
| Harrison, Joseph O. | 1914 | Box 492 | | Hartnett, William | 1885 | Box 92 |
| Harrison, Josephine A. | 1914 | Box 492 | | Hartogensis, Edward S. | 1905 | Box 283 |
| Harrison, Juliana | 1910 | Box 392 | | Hartogensis, Fannie | 1917 | Box 573 |
| Harrison, Marcus LaRue | 1890 | Box 119 | | Hartong, Helena | 1898 | Box 176 |
| Harrison, Margaret | 1906 | Box 302 | | Hartong, Sarach | 1900 | Box 194 |
| Harrison, Margaret | 1907 | Box 323 | | Hartshorn, George F. | 1868 | Box 39 |
| Harrison, Mary E. | 1898 | Box 176 | | Hartung, Elisabeth | 1895 | Box 153 |
| Harrison, Mildred | 1891 | Box 125 | | Hartung, Henry | 1891 | Box 125 |
| Harrison, Rachel | 1856 | Box 24 | | Hartwell, Mary E. | 1908 | Box 346 |
| Harrison, Rachel | 1866 | Box 36 | | Harvey, Alice Wheat | 1918 | Box 599 |
| Harrison, Richard | 1841 | Box 15 | | Harvey, Anna P. | 1867 | Box 37 |
| Harrison, Richard M. | 1864 | Box 32 | | Harvey, Annie E. | 1914 | Box 492 |
| Harrison, Samuel | 1905 | Box 283 | | Harvey, Arsenius I. | 1891 | Box 125 |
| Harrison, Thomas B. | 1907 | Box 323 | | Harvey, Arsenius T. | 1882 | Box 79 |
| Harrison, Virginia | 1914 | Box 492 | | Harvey, Eliza | 1907 | Box 323 |
| Harrison, William | 1885 | Box 92 | | Harvey, Frank Littleton | 1905 | Box 283 |
| Harrison, William A. | 1919 | Box 629 | | Harvey, George W. | 1909 | Box 370 |
| Harrison, William Henry | 1905 | Box 283 | | Harvey, Henry L. | 1860 | Box 28 |
| Harry, Francis A. | 1860 | Box 28 | | Harvey, Hugh F. | 1916 | Box 546 |
| Harry, Harriet Eliza | 1877 | Box 64 | | Harvey, James | 1876 | Box 61 |
| Harry, John | 1865 | Box 33 | | Harvey, James E. | 1894 | Box 146 |
| Harry, Philip | 1867 | Box 37 | | Harvey, James F. | 1856 | Box 24 |
| Harshman, Henry | 1813 | Box 4 | | Harvey, James S. | 1867 | Box 37 |
| Harshman, Susannah | 1834 | Box 12 | | Harvey, Joseph J. | 1905 | Box 283 |
| Hart, Alphonso | 1911 | Box 418 | | Harvey, Mary Ann | 1876 | Box 61 |
| Hart, Amos | 1878 | Box 66 | | Harvey, Rebecca | 1914 | Box 4 |
| Hart, Ellen L. | 1894 | Box 146 | | Harvey, Selina M. | 1900 | Box 194 |
| Hart, Henry | 1902 | Box 227 | | Harvey, Virginia K. | 1911 | Box 418 |
| Hart, James Morgan | 1916 | Box 546 | | Harwood, Mary Frances | 1893 | Box 139 |
| Hart, Joseph Edward | 1920 | Box 662 | | Hasbrouck, Adeline W. | 1911 | Box 418 |
| Hart, Josephine A. | 1877 | Box 64 | | Haskell, Edwin Bradbury | 1912 | Box 443 |
| Hart, Lelia Bertha | 1895 | Box 153 | | Haskell, Leonidas | 1873 | Box 51 |
| Hart, Mary | 1911 | Box 418 | | Haskell, Lydia P. | 1892 | Box 132 |
| Hart, Oliver J. | 1892 | Box 132 | | Haskins, Isiah W. | 1894 | Box 146 |
| Hartbrecht, Josephine | 1905 | Box 283 | | Hasler, Rudolph | 1908 | Box 346 |
| Hartbricht, Stephen | 1906 | Box 302 | | Haslup, Mary Ann | 1863 | Box 31 |
| Hartel, Charles | 1888 | Box 108 | | Hason, Mountjoy Barry | 1891 | Box 125 |
| Hartenstein, Alfred | 1917 | Box 572 | | Hassall, William J. | 1883 | Box 82 |

| | | | | | | |
|---|---|---|---|---|---|---|
| Hassel, Cora | 1915 | Box 519 | Hawkins, Alexander | 1913 | Box 469 |
| Hasselbusch, Charlotte | 1905 | Box 283 | Hawkins, Alfred | 1908 | Box 346 |
| Hasselfeldt, Charles | 1915 | Box 519 | Hawkins, Caleb | 1908 | Box 346 |
| Hasselman, Olive M. | 1915 | Box 519 | Hawkins, Earnest F. | 1910 | Box 393 |
| Hasson, Alexander B. | 1877 | Box 64 | Hawkins, Edward | 1896 | Box 162 |
| Hasson, Alexander R. | 1903 | Box 245 | Hawkins, H. C. | 1908 | Box 346 |
| Hastings, Margaret | 1916 | Box 546 | Hawkins, James F. | 1888 | Box 108 |
| Haswell, Jane E. | 1884 | Box 86 | Hawkins, John H. | 1900 | Box 194 |
| Hatch, Hannah Maria | 1907 | Box 323 | Hawkins, John J. | 1892 | Box 132 |
| Hatch, John S. | 1919 | Box 629 | Hawkins, Kate E. B. | 1899 | Box 184 |
| Hatch, Lorenzo James | 1920 | Box 662 | Hawkins, Lucy A. | 1918 | Box 599 |
| Hatch, Mary | 1913 | Box 469 | Hawkins, Mary Louise | 1918 | Box 599 |
| Hatch, Susan J. | 1914 | Box 492 | Hawkins, Matilda | 1856 | Box 25 |
| Hatcher, Floy | 1895 | Box 153 | Hawkins, Richard | 1871 | Box 45 |
| Hatcher, William | 1915 | Box 519 | Hawkins, Sarah H. | 1902 | Box 227 |
| Hathaway, Margaret L. | 1920 | Box 663 | Hawley, Caroline C. | 1908 | Box 346 |
| Hathaway, Maurice R. | 1917 | Box 573 | Hawley, Edwin H. | 1918 | Box 599 |
| Hatton, Frank | 1894 | Box 146 | Hawley, Marvin L. | 1908 | Box 346 |
| Hatton, William | 1906 | Box 302 | Hawley, William H. | 1917 | Box 573 |
| Hatzfeld, Amelia | 1915 | Box 519 | Hawley, William H. Jr. | 1917 | Box 573 |
| Hauer, Fred | 1899 | Box 184 | Hay, Clara S. | 1914 | Box 492 |
| Hauer, William | 1920 | Box 663 | Hay, Edwin B. | 1906 | Box 302 |
| Hauf, John George | 1917 | Box 573 | Hay, Elizabeth K. | 1841 | Box 15 |
| Hauf, John Lewis | 1898 | Box 176 | Hay, Henry P. | 1888 | Box 108 |
| Haufman, Joseph A. | 1874 | Box 54 | Hayden, Anna F. | 1892 | Box 132 |
| Hauge, Christian | 1908 | Box 346 | Hayden, Annie | 1919 | Box 630 |
| Hauke, Cindarilla Murray | 1891 | Box 125 | Hayden, Darby | 1884 | Box 86 |
| Haulein, Joseph H. | 1883 | Box 82 | Hayden, Jerome C. | 1915 | Box 519 |
| Haupt, Herman | 1906 | Box 302 | Hayden, Louise Anna | 1911 | Box 418 |
| Haupt, Mary Cecelia | 1911 | Box 418 | Hayden, Margaret T. | 1899 | Box 184 |
| Hauptman, Charles W. | 1900 | Box 194 | Hayden, Mary C. | 1920 | Box 663 |
| Hauptman, Daniel | 1874 | Box 54 | Hayden, Michael | 1917 | Box 573 |
| Hauptman, Francis E. | 1896 | Box 161 | Hayden, Nellie M. | 1908 | Box 346 |
| Hauptman, Martha | 1867 | Box 37 | Haydock, John | 1807 | Box 2 |
| Hauptman, Mary E. | 1899 | Box 184 | Hayes, Alexander | 1870 | Box 43 |
| Hauser, Fredericka E. | 1902 | Box 227 | Hayes, Catherine | 1911 | Box 419 |
| Hauser, Jacob | 1892 | Box 132 | Hayes, Charles Willard | 1916 | Box 546 |
| Hauslein, Anton | 1887 | Box 103 | Hayes, Edward | 1917 | Box 573 |
| Havenner, Thomas | 1871 | Box 45 | Hayes, Henry G. | 1903 | Box 245 |
| Haverfield, Samuel P. | 1886 | Box 97 | Hayes, Jacob | 1917 | Box 573 |
| Haviland, Abraham A. | 1864 | Box 32 | Hayes, James | 1905 | Box 283 |
| Haviland, Thomas G. | 1909 | Box 370 | Hayes, John | 1907 | Box 323 |
| Haw, John Stoddert | 1832 | Box 11 | Hayes, Lillie James | 1915 | Box 519 |
| Hawes, Benjamine N. | 1914 | Box 492 | Hayes, Margaret Marshall | 1907 | Box 323 |
| Hawes, Edward | 1911 | Box 418 | Hayes, Maria Louisa | 1903 | Box 245 |
| Hawes, George W. | 1882 | Box 79 | Hayes, Mary E. | 1908 | Box 346 |
| Hawes, James P. | 1915 | Box 519 | Hayes, Matilda | 1890 | Box 119 |
| Hawes, Mary J. | 1904 | Box 265 | Hayes, Sarah D. | 1881 | Box 75 |
| Hawes, William B. | 1879 | Box 69 | Hayes, Thomas | 1893 | Box 139 |
| Hawes, William H. H. | 1901 | Box 208 | Hayes, William | 1890 | Box 119 |
| Hawkes, Benjamin Franklin | 1906 | Box 302 | Hayghe, John L. | 1895 | Box 153 |
| Hawkes, Emma A. | 1919 | Box 629 | Hayghe, Mary J. | 1915 | Box 520 |

| | | | | | | |
|---|---|---|---|---|---|---|
| Haynes, Thomas | 1839 | Box 14 | | Heaton, Lucy A. | 1888 | Box 108 |
| Haynie, Elizabeth | 1890 | Box 119 | | Heazelton, George | 1910 | Box 393 |
| Haynie, Hancock Hiram | 1879 | Box 69 | | Hebb, Ellen C. | 1908 | Box 347 |
| Haynie, Henry Heath | 1903 | Box 245 | | Hebb, Priscilla B. | 1905 | Box 283 |
| Hayre, Catharine | 1879 | Box 69 | | Hebb, Wilhelmina G. | 1920 | Box 663 |
| Hayre, John | 1864 | Box 32 | | Hebbern, John | 1872 | Box 47 |
| Hayre, John F. | 1906 | Box 302 | | Hebner, Martin | 1897 | Box 169 |
| Hays, Charles Harrison | 1904 | Box 265 | | Hechinger, Amelia | 1917 | Box 573 |
| Hayward, Emma | 1885 | Box 92 | | Hechinger, Bettie | 1917 | Box 573 |
| Hayward, George M. | 1881 | Box 75 | | Heck, John J. | 1870 | Box 43 |
| Hayward, Harriot | 1815 | Box 4 | | Heck, John M. | 1882 | Box 79 |
| Haywood, Alfred | 1883 | Box 82 | | Heck, Philippine | 1889 | Box 114 |
| Haywood, Amanda | 1895 | Box 153 | | Heckman, Archimedes | 1892 | Box 132 |
| Haywood, William | 1907 | Box 323 | | Hedges, Agnes W. | 1908 | Box 347 |
| Hazard, Oliver Perry | 1920 | Box 663 | | Hedgman, Peter | 1869 | Box 40 |
| Hazel, Almira E. | 1904 | Box 265 | | Hedrick, Benjamin S. | 1886 | Box 97 |
| Hazel, Louisa | 1916 | Box 546 | | Heehan, Mary J. | 1914 | Box 493 |
| Hazel, William C. | 1900 | Box 194 | | Heenan, Catherine | 1917 | Box 573 |
| Hazel, Zachariah | 1851 | Box 21 | | Heenan, John A. | 1906 | Box 302 |
| Hazen, Abraham D. | 1902 | Box 227 | | Heffell, Ellen | 1890 | Box 119 |
| Hazen, Allen | 1898 | Box 176 | | Hefferman, Charles A. | 1912 | Box 443 |
| Hazen, Emma L. | 1920 | Box 663 | | Heffernan, Ellen | 1915 | Box 520 |
| Hazen, Mary Virginia | 1916 | Box 546 | | Heffner, Clara S. | 1911 | Box 419 |
| Hazen, William B. | 1887 | Box 103 | | Heiberg, Anna Howell Dodge | 1917 | Box 573 |
| Hazlett, Cunningham | 1873 | Box 51 | | Heiberger, Francis J. | 1901 | Box 208 |
| Hazlett, Isaac | 1919 | Box 630 | | Heiberger, Mary W. | 1917 | Box 573 |
| Head, George M. | 1878 | Box 66 | | Heid, Jacob | 1916 | Box 546 |
| Head, John Frazier | 1908 | Box 346 | | Heidenheimer, Fanny | 1904 | Box 265 |
| Head, Katharine A. | 1904 | Box 265 | | Heider, Charlotte | 1891 | Box 125 |
| Headley, Dovie | 1901 | Box 208 | | Heider, George D. | 1919 | Box 630 |
| Heald, Edwin | 1899 | Box 184 | | Heider, Henry W. | 1905 | Box 283 |
| Heald, Elizabeth Crosby | 1907 | Box 324 | | Heider, John F. | 1895 | Box 153 |
| Heald, Jane S. | 1875 | Box 57 | | Heider, Sophia | 1912 | Box 443 |
| Healey, Ellen A. | 1920 | Box 663 | | Heider, William D. | 1892 | Box 132 |
| Healey, Matthew | 1917 | Box 573 | | Heiges, David C. | 1898 | Box 176 |
| Heally, Dennis J. | 1907 | Box 324 | | Height, Sarah Jane | 1876 | Box 61 |
| Healy, Alice | 1917 | Box 573 | | Heil, Elizabeth | 1895 | Box 153 |
| Healy, Jeremiah J. | 1915 | Box 520 | | Heil, Elizabeth Bird | 1909 | Box 370 |
| Healy, Maurice D. | 1887 | Box 103 | | Heil, Henry | 1895 | Box 153 |
| Healy, Thomas A. | 1914 | Box 493 | | Heil, Henry J. | 1920 | Box 663 |
| Heany, Delia | 1914 | Box 493 | | Heil, John | 1896 | Box 162 |
| Heany, Thomas | 1914 | Box 493 | | Heil, Michael | 1876 | Box 61 |
| Heap, Samuel Davies | 1854 | Box 23 | | Heilman, Gottlieb | 1911 | Box 419 |
| Heard, Augustine | 1906 | Box 302 | | Heilprin, Isaac | 1900 | Box 194 |
| Heard, Minnie B. | 1892 | Box 132 | | Heimer, Augustus | 1916 | Box 546 |
| Hearn, Sarah | 1905 | Box 283 | | Heimerdinger, Dorothea | 1897 | Box 169 |
| Hearns, Indridge | 1905 | Box 283 | | Hein, Martha W. | 1920 | Box 663 |
| Heartman, John | 1870 | Box 43 | | Hein, Sophia S. | 1899 | Box 184 |
| Heaton, Augustus | 1919 | Box 630 | | Heine, Marie | 1920 | Box 663 |
| Heaton, Charles M. | 1899 | Box 184 | | Heine, William | 1887 | Box 103 |
| Heaton, E. Florence | 1910 | Box 393 | | Heinecke, Mary S. | 1911 | Box 419 |
| Heaton, Ella M. | 1913 | Box 469 | | Heiner, Helen G. | 1915 | Box 520 |

| | | | | | | |
|---|---|---|---|---|---|---|
| Heiner, Robert G. | 1891 | Box 125 | Henderson, Charles | 1900 | Box 194 |
| Heinlein, Jemima J. | 1911 | Box 419 | Henderson, Eli W. | 1915 | Box 520 |
| Heins, Catharine | 1908 | Box 347 | Henderson, Fannie | 1911 | Box 419 |
| Heintzelman, Charles | 1881 | Box 75 | Henderson, Hannah | 1902 | Box 227 |
| Heintzelman, Emily | 1902 | Box 227 | Henderson, Helen B. | 1904 | Box 265 |
| Heintzelman, Samuel P. | 1880 | Box 72 | Henderson, James | 1906 | Box 302 |
| Heinzerling, Christiane | 1908 | Box 347 | Henderson, John B. | 1913 | Box 469 |
| Heiskill, Henry L. | 1855 | Box 24 | Henderson, Julia | 1905 | Box 283 |
| Heisler, Frederick Dove | 1917 | Box 573 | Henderson, Kate C. | 1911 | Box 419 |
| Heisley, Jacob M. | 1914 | Box 493 | Henderson, Mary | 1912 | Box 443 |
| Heiss, Andrew | 1873 | Box 51 | Henderson, Richard | 1802 | Box 1 |
| Heiss, Catharine | 1887 | Box 103 | Henderson, Sarah B. | 1895 | Box 153 |
| Heiss, Clarissa | 1881 | Box 75 | Henderson, William A. | 1908 | Box 347 |
| Heiss, John Henry | 1885 | Box 92 | Hendley, Christiann | 1858 | Box 26 |
| Heiss, Martha Ann | 1907 | Box 324 | Hendley, Josephine | 1919 | Box 630 |
| Heissler, John | 1863 | Box 31 | Hendley, Josephine | 1920 | Box 663 |
| Heitmuller, Alfred | 1861 | Box 29 | Hendley, Mary A. | 1917 | Box 573 |
| Heitmuller, Anton | 1885 | Box 92 | Hendrick, David S. | 1902 | Box 227 |
| Heitmuller, Auguste | 1877 | Box 64 | Hendricks, Martin J. | 1896 | Box 162 |
| Heitmuller, Charlotte | 1893 | Box 139 | Hendrickson, Benjamin E. | 1903 | Box 245 |
| Heitmuller, Ferdinand A. | 1919 | Box 630 | Hendrickson, Hannah H. | 1906 | Box 302 |
| Heitmuller, Heinrich | 1893 | Box 139 | Heneberger, Lucien G. | 1919 | Box 630 |
| Heitzelman, Margaret L. | 1893 | Box 139 | Henecke, Heinrich | 1915 | Box 520 |
| Heizer, Sidney H. | 1901 | Box 208 | Henery, William | 1888 | Box 108 |
| Helbig, Amelia A. | 1916 | Box 546 | Henkel, Alice | 1916 | Box 546 |
| Helbig, Frederick W. | 1920 | Box 663 | Hennessey, Annie | 1907 | Box 324 |
| Helen, M. D. | 1909 | Box 370 | Hennessey, Martha | 1895 | Box 154 |
| Hellen, Adelaid | 1877 | Box 64 | Hennessy, Frances O'Reilly | 1916 | Box 547 |
| Hellen, Benjamin Johnson | 1864 | Box 32 | Hennig, Frederick | 1919 | Box 630 |
| Hellen, Eugene | 1898 | Box 176 | Hennige, Henry W. | 1917 | Box 573 |
| Hellen, Joseph | 1919 | Box 630 | Henning, Bennet | 1873 | Box 51 |
| Hellen, Virginia Edith | 1904 | Box 265 | Henning, Eliza | 1850 | Box 20 |
| Hellen, Walter | 1815 | Box 4 | Henning, Ellen | 1899 | Box 184 |
| Heller, Albert Sidney | 1916 | Box 546 | Henning, George | 1910 | Box 393 |
| Heller, Appolonia | 1891 | Box 125 | Henning, George C. | 1913 | Box 469 |
| Heller, Pauline | 1896 | Box 162 | Henning, Henry W. | 1890 | Box 119 |
| Heller, Simon | 1918 | Box 599 | Henning, James | 1895 | Box 154 |
| Hellmuth, Stephan (Stephen) | 1917 | Box 573 | Henning, Mary Ann | 1900 | Box 194 |
| Helm, Mornay D. | 1909 | Box 370 | Henning, Rebecca | 1913 | Box 470 |
| Helmuth, Matilda | 1904 | Box 265 | Henning, Sarah E. | 1916 | Box 547 |
| Hemm, Bartholomew | 1876 | Box 61 | Henning, Stephen | 1874 | Box 54 |
| Hemming, Dodge D. | 1919 | Box 630 | Hennings, Bernard J. | 1919 | Box 630 |
| Hemphill, John J. | 1912 | Box 443 | Hennings, Martha | 1914 | Box 493 |
| Hemstreet, Elizabeth | 1911 | Box 419 | Henriques, Bertha S. | 1918 | Box 599 |
| Henault, Jules Sebastian | 1877 | Box 64 | Henriques, Ellen | 1902 | Box 227 |
| Hendershott, Annebell | 1888 | Box 108 | Henriques, John A. | 1906 | Box 302 |
| Hendershott, Norman | 1902 | Box 227 | Henriques, John Philip | 1910 | Box 393 |
| Henderson, Alice | 1920 | Box 663 | Henriques, Semmy | 1895 | Box 154 |
| Henderson, Amanda | 1913 | Box 469 | Henry, Andrew A. | 1895 | Box 154 |
| Henderson, Ann M. | 1859 | Box 27 | Henry, Benjamin F. | 1919 | Box 630 |
| Henderson, Archibald | 1859 | Box 27 | Henry, Caroline | 1920 | Box 663 |
| Henderson, Bertha Louise | 1920 | Box 663 | Henry, Ellen D. | 1890 | Box 119 |

| | | | | | | |
|---|---|---|---|---|---|---|
| Henry, Grace Bell | 1898 | Box 176 | Herbert, William H. | 1883 | Box 83 |
| Henry, Harriet A. | 1882 | Box 79 | Herblin, Margaret | 1893 | Box 139 |
| Henry, Helen L. | 1912 | Box 443 | Herford, John | 1811 | Box 3 |
| Henry, James S. | 1912 | Box 444 | Herfurth, August | 1878 | Box 66 |
| Henry, John F. | 1872 | Box 47 | Herfurth, Emilie Augusta | 1871 | Box 45 |
| Henry, John F. | 1909 | Box 370 | Herfurth, Robert | 1873 | Box 51 |
| Henry, Kate | 1893 | Box 139 | Hergesheimer, Edwin | 1889 | Box 1141 |
| Henry, Margaretha | 1909 | Box 370 | Hergesheimer, Sarah Ann | 1908 | Box 347 |
| Henry, Mary A. | 1903 | Box 245 | Hering, Sophia | 1918 | Box 599 |
| Henry, Mary E. | 1920 | Box 663 | Hering, Thomas F. | 1915 | Box 520 |
| Henry, Sarah L. | 1868 | Box 39 | Herlihy, Daniel | 1837 | Box 13 |
| Henry, Sophia R. | 1893 | Box 139 | Herman, Abraham | 1905 | Box 283 |
| Henry, William D. | 1914 | Box 493 | Herman, Catherine | 1900 | Box 194 |
| Hense, Wilhelmine | 1913 | Box 470 | Herman, Charles | 1891 | Box 125 |
| Hensey, Alexander T. | 1920 | Box 663 | Herman, Joseph P. | 1897 | Box 169 |
| Hensey, Thomas G. | 1907 | Box 324 | Herman, Robert | 1915 | Box 520 |
| Henshaw, Caroline D. | 1903 | Box 245 | Herman, Samuel | 1919 | Box 630 |
| Henshaw, Charles W. | 1915 | Box 520 | Herman, Samuel Sr. | 1911 | Box 419 |
| Henshaw, Frances S. | 1912 | Box 444 | Hermann, Maria A. | 1915 | Box 520 |
| Hensley, James T. | 1913 | Box 470 | Hernandez, Enrique D. | 1918 | Box 599 |
| Henson, Agnes | 1920 | Box 663 | Herndon, Cumberland George | 1911 | Box 419 |
| Henson, Eli | 1891 | Box 125 | Herndon, William Sanford | 1918 | Box 599 |
| Henson, Mary Ann | 1873 | Box 51 | Herold, Adam George | 1866 | Box 36 |
| Henson, William Henry | 1907 | Box 324 | Herold, Clara | 1919 | Box 630 |
| Henze, Bernard | 1880 | Box 72 | Herold, E. Jane | 1903 | Box 246 |
| Hepburn, David | 1879 | Box 69 | Herold, Frederick | 1881 | Box 75 |
| Hepburn, Mary Ellen | 1912 | Box 444 | Heron, George H. | 1910 | Box 393 |
| Hepburn, Peter | 1900 | Box 194 | Herr, Samuel H. | 1897 | Box 169 |
| Hepburn, William P. | 1916 | Box 547 | Herrell, Eliza D. | 1910 | Box 393 |
| Hepburn, William P. | 1919 | Box 630 | Herrell, Henry A. | 1913 | Box 470 |
| Herbel, John | 1911 | Box 419 | Herrell, John E. | 1909 | Box 370 |
| Herberger, Frances | 1901 | Box 208 | Herriman, Ferdinand De Soto | 1911 | Box 419 |
| Herbert, Arthur | 1920 | Box 663 | Herrle, Gustave | 1902 | Box 228 |
| Herbert, Casper | 1887 | Box 103 | Herrmann, Friedrick M. | 1899 | Box 184 |
| Herbert, Catherina | 1907 | Box 324 | Herron, Henrietta V. | 1903 | Box 246 |
| Herbert, Catherine | 1907 | Box 324 | Herron, J. Whitley | 1910 | Box 393 |
| Herbert, Elizabeth | 1866 | Box 36 | Herron, Joseph B. | 1882 | Box 79 |
| Herbert, Elizabeth | 1881 | Box 75 | Herron, Lella J. | 1898 | Box 176 |
| Herbert, Gottlieb | 1897 | Box 169 | Herron, Mary Wilmina | 1842 | Box 15 |
| Herbert, Harriet S. | 1883 | Box 83 | Herron, Walter | 1867 | Box 37 |
| Herbert, Henry C. | 1919 | Box 630 | Hershey, Mary E. | 1919 | Box 630 |
| Herbert, Hilary A. | 1919 | Box 630 | Hershler, Nathaniel | 1919 | Box 630 |
| Herbert, James William | 1909 | Box 370 | Hershowitz, Annie | 1919 | Box 630 |
| Herbert, Janet | 1919 | Box 630 | Hertford, William E. | 1917 | Box 573 |
| Herbert, Katherine | 1909 | Box 370 | Hertrich, Anna | 1886 | Box 97 |
| Herbert, Montrey Taylor | 1912 | Box 444 | Herty, Mary Anne | 1837 | Box 13 |
| Herbert, Nathaniel | 1852 | Box 21 | Hervey, Robert | 1899 | Box 184 |
| Herbert, Samuel M. | 1867 | Box 37 | Herzberg, Isaac | 1871 | Box 45 |
| Herbert, Sarah E. | 1898 | Box 176 | Herzog, Joseph | 1919 | Box 630 |
| Herbert, Sidney W. | 1913 | Box 470 | Herzog, Lisette | 1920 | Box 663 |
| Herbert, Thomas | 1839 | Box 14 | Hess, George A. | 1919 | Box 630 |
| Herbert, William E. | 1908 | Box 347 | Hess, George H. | 1894 | Box 146 |

| | | | | | | |
|---|---|---|---|---|---|---|
| Hess, Jacob | 1882 | Box 79 | | Hickey, Katharine | 1920 | Box 663 |
| Hess, John | 1889 | Box 114 | | Hickey, Mary | 1892 | Box 132 |
| Hess, Louis | 1919 | Box 630 | | Hickman, Anthony | 1895 | Box 154 |
| Hess, Margaret C. | 1919 | Box 630 | | Hickman, Elizabeth D. | 1916 | Box 547 |
| Hess, Mary Elizabeth | 1870 | Box 43 | | Hickman, Mildred | 1902 | Box 228 |
| Hesse, Conrad E. | 1910 | Box 393 | | Hickman, William H. | 1904 | Box 265 |
| Hessel, Christina | 1917 | Box 573 | | Hickox, Chauncey | 1905 | Box 284 |
| Hessel, Rudolph | 1901 | Box 208 | | Hicks, Albert C. | 1835 | Box 13 |
| Hesselberger, Gustav A. | 1914 | Box 493 | | Hicks, Charles | 1890 | Box 119 |
| Hessler, Andrew | 1919 | Box 630 | | Hicks, Dorcas V. | 1915 | Box 520 |
| Hessler, Lorenz | 1881 | Box 75 | | Hicks, Edward | 1838 | Box 14 |
| Hessler, William | 1894 | Box 146 | | Hicks, Harriet | 1898 | Box 176 |
| Hester, Joseph G. | 1901 | Box 208 | | Hicks, John F. | 1893 | Box 139 |
| Hester, Josephine W. | 1917 | Box 573 | | Hicks, Louisa G. | 1917 | Box 573 |
| Hesterberg, Christopher | 1916 | Box 547 | | Hicks, Mary Caroline | 1901 | Box 208 |
| Hetfield, Charles K. | 1918 | Box 599 | | Hicks, Webster Manning | 1917 | Box 573 |
| Heth, Eva M. A. | 1916 | Box 547 | | Hicks, William | 1884 | Box 87 |
| Heth, Harriet S. | 1914 | Box 493 | | Hicks, William Cleveland | 1920 | Box 664 |
| Heth, Henry | 1914 | Box 493 | | Hieston, Alice V. | 1912 | Box 444 |
| Heth, Isabella | 1916 | Box 547 | | Higbee, George H. | 1919 | Box 630 |
| Hetrick, Emma K. | 1920 | Box 663 | | Higgins, Alice | 1915 | Box 520 |
| Hettinger, Johanna | 1894 | Box 146 | | Higgins, Christiana | 1897 | Box 169 |
| Heugh, Hariot | 1824 | Box 8 | | Higgins, John de Bree | 1918 | Box 600 |
| Heugh, Jane | 1829 | Box 10 | | Higgins, Julia A. | 1916 | Box 547 |
| Heugh, Mary | 1854 | Box 23 | | Higgins, Martin L. | 1892 | Box 132 |
| Heugh, Sarah | 1834 | Box 12 | | Higgins, William | 1919 | Box 630 |
| Heunsch, Johanna | 1906 | Box 303 | | Higginson, John Horn | 1815 | Box 4 |
| Heupel, John L. | 1920 | Box 663 | | Higgs, Thomas J. | 1908 | Box 347 |
| Heurich, Amelia | 1884 | Box 87 | | Higley, Eliza M. | 1905 | Box 284 |
| Hewett, Robert C. | 1888 | Box 108 | | Higley, Henry P. | 1912 | Box 444 |
| Hewitt, Alfred P. | 1867 | Box 37 | | Hiland, Thomas | 1907 | Box 324 |
| Hewitt, John J. | 1910 | Box 393 | | Hilbron, Mary Ann | 1874 | Box 54 |
| Hewitt, Sallie E. | 1908 | Box 347 | | Hilder, Frank Frederick | 1901 | Box 208 |
| Hewitt, William | 1839 | Box 14 | | Hildreth, Gertrude M. | 1912 | Box 444 |
| Hewlett, Stephen R. | 1918 | Box 599 | | Hildrup, Emma J. | 1919 | Box 630 |
| Hewlett, Susan | 1913 | Box 470 | | Hile, Joseph | 1882 | Box 79 |
| Heyburn, William | 1886 | Box 97 | | Hilferding, Henry M. | 1920 | Box 664 |
| Heydrick, Peter C. | 1920 | Box 663 | | Hilgard, Julius E. | 1891 | Box 125 |
| Heyl, Mary D. | 1902 | Box 228 | | Hilgard, Katherine | 1895 | Box 154 |
| Heywood, Charles | 1915 | Box 520 | | Hill, Alice | 1900 | Box 194 |
| Hibbert, Charles H. | 1916 | Box 547 | | Hill, Alice | 1912 | Box 444 |
| Hibbert, Susan E. | 1894 | Box 146 | | Hill, Alice S. | 1904 | Box 265 |
| Hichborn, Benjamin | 1888 | Box 108 | | Hill, Allen E. | 1919 | Box 630 |
| Hichborn, Philip | 1910 | Box 393 | | Hill, Amanda | 1915 | Box 520 |
| Hichborn, Samuel | 1888 | Box 108 | | Hill, Amanda | 1920 | Box 664 |
| Hickcox, John S. | 1911 | Box 419 | | Hill, Ann S. | 1863 | Box 31 |
| Hickcox, Sarah J. | 1916 | Box 547 | | Hill, Bennett H. | 1886 | Box 97 |
| Hickenlooper, George | 1907 | Box 324 | | Hill, Bridgett | 1916 | Box 547 |
| Hickerson, William T. | 1909 | Box 370 | | Hill, Catherine | 1885 | Box 92 |
| Hickey, Bridget | 1889 | Box 114 | | Hill, Charles | 1869 | Box 40 |
| Hickey, Elizabeth P. | 1918 | Box 600 | | Hill, Charles T. | 1919 | Box 630 |
| Hickey, George F. | 1908 | Box 347 | | Hill, Clement | 1807 | Box 2 |

| | | | | | | |
|---|---|---|---|---|---|
| Hill, Edward K. | 1912 | Box 444 | Hillmer, Freidrich | 1873 | Box 51 |
| Hill, Eleanor | 1872 | Box 47 | Hills, Thomas O. | 1903 | Box 246 |
| Hill, Elias J. | 1894 | Box 146 | Hills, Wallace H. | 1905 | Box 283 |
| Hill, Eliza | 1887 | Box 103 | Hillyer, Angeline | 1916 | Box 547 |
| Hill, Elizabeth M. | 1909 | Box 370 | Hillyer, Charles Sherman | 1913 | Box 470 |
| Hill, Florence A. | 1919 | Box 630 | Hillyer, Curtis J. | 1906 | Box 303 |
| Hill, Francis H. | 1906 | Box 303 | Hillyer, Mamie E. | 1917 | Box 574 |
| Hill, Frances Harriet | 1899 | Box 184 | Hillyer, Virgil | 1893 | Box 139 |
| Hill, Frank P. | 1882 | Box 79 | Hillyer, William Richards | 1916 | Box 547 |
| Hill, George | 1916 | Box 547 | Hiltman, Abraham B. | 1899 | Box 184 |
| Hill, George (Jr.) | 1898 | Box 176 | Hilton, Annie | 1908 | Box 347 |
| Hill, George Holden | 1911 | Box 419 | Hilton, Fannie A. | 1916 | Box 547 |
| Hill, George Roberts | 1905 | Box 283 | Hilton, James H. | 1919 | Box 630 |
| Hill, Georgina F. | 1917 | Box 573 | Hilton, James Molan | 1901 | Box 208 |
| Hill, Hariet | 1909 | Box 370 | Hilton, John P. | 1873 | Box 51 |
| Hill, Harriet | 1913 | Box 470 | Hilton, Mary | 1905 | Box 283 |
| Hill, Isaac | 1886 | Box 97 | Hilton, Samuel N. | 1899 | Box 184 |
| Hill, James G. | 1914 | Box 493 | Hilton, Uriah D. | 1886 | Box 97 |
| Hill, John | 1906 | Box 303 | Hiltzimer, Elizabeth | 1817 | Box 5 |
| Hill, Joseph | 1912 | Box 444 | Hindle, Thomas M. | 1911 | Box 419 |
| Hill, Joshua | 1892 | Box 132 | Hindmarsh, Walter B. | 1910 | Box 393 |
| Hill, Joshua | 1918 | Box 600 | Hinds, Cornelia | 1887 | Box 103 |
| Hill, Leathe | 1858 | Box 26 | Hinds, Sarah Barnum | 1914 | Box 493 |
| Hill, Louisa E. | 1902 | Box 228 | Hinds, Warren L. | 1912 | Box 444 |
| Hill, Martha Ellen | 1879 | Box 69 | Hine, Lemon G. | 1914 | Box 493 |
| Hill, Mary E. | 1898 | Box 176 | Hine, Robert B. | 1895 | Box 154 |
| Hill, Mary Georgiana | 1856 | Box 25 | Hines, Charles A. | 1915 | Box 520 |
| Hill, Mary H. | 1915 | Box 520 | Hines, Daniel | 1807 | Box 2 |
| Hill, Mary Jane | 1898 | Box 176 | Hines, David | 1866 | Box 36 |
| Hill, Nathaniel P. | 1912 | Box 444 | Hines, Edmund G. | 1920 | Box 664 |
| Hill, Peter H. | 1893 | Box 139 | Hines, Henry | 1854 | Box 23 |
| Hill, Richard | 1900 | Box 194 | Hines, Mary Lazenberry | 1911 | Box 419 |
| Hill, Robert A. | 1899 | Box 184 | Hines, Michael | 1891 | Box 125 |
| Hill, Robert H. | 1916 | Box 547 | Hingeley, Ezra | 1894 | Box 146 |
| Hill, Samuel | 1885 | Box 92 | Hinke, Henry | 1906 | Box 303 |
| Hill, Sarah A. | 1871 | Box 45 | Hinke, William | 1890 | Box 119 |
| Hill, Silas H. | 1860 | Box 28 | Hinkel, Fannie M. | 1905 | Box 283 |
| Hill, Stephen P. | 1884 | Box 87 | Hinkel, John G. | 1912 | Box 444 |
| Hill, Susan A. | 1905 | Box 283 | Hinkel, John P. | 1906 | Box 303 |
| Hill, Susan M. P. | 1874 | Box 54 | Hinman, Mary Ann | 1909 | Box 370 |
| Hill, Theresa | 1867 | Box 37 | Hinrichs, Christian | 1892 | Box 132 |
| Hill, William | 1889 | Box 114 | Hinrichs, Christina | 1907 | Box 324 |
| Hill, William C. | 1890 | Box 119 | Hinrichs, Oscar | 1892 | Box 132 |
| Hill, William E. | 1893 | Box 139 | Hinton, Charles B. | 1905 | Box 283 |
| Hill-Gough, A. C. | 1904 | Box 265 | Hinton, Charles Howard | 1907 | Box 324 |
| Hiller, John | 1873 | Box 51 | Hinton, Mary Ellen | 1908 | Box 347 |
| Hiller, Louisa | 1903 | Box 246 | Hinwood, William | 1871 | Box 45 |
| Hillery, Lewis | 1821 | Box 6 | Hirsh, Morris | 1915 | Box 520 |
| Hilliard, Agnes Lucinda | 1912 | Box 444 | Hirsh, Samuel | 1920 | Box 664 |
| Hilliard, Sidney A. | 1911 | Box 419 | Hirst, Eliza B. | 1906 | Box 303 |
| Hilliary, Theodore W. | 1907 | Box 324 | Hirst, Homer T. | 1920 | Box 664 |
| Hillman, Ann B. | 1902 | Box 228 | Hirst, William | 1908 | Box 347 |

| | | | | | | |
|---|---|---|---|---|---|---|
| Hiscock, Frank | 1915 | Box 521 | Hodgson, Henrietta | 1913 | Box 470 |
| Hiser (Haeusser), Paul | 1904 | Box 265 | Hodgson, Joseph | 1902 | Box 228 |
| Hisey, Lemuel M. | 1904 | Box 265 | Hodgson, Maria Louisa | 1912 | Box 444 |
| Hishley, Marinda | 1916 | Box 547 | Hodson, Elizabeth | 1892 | Box 132 |
| Hisser, Rudolf | 1901 | Box 208 | Hoebert, Charles | 1917 | Box 574 |
| Hitchcock, Martha R. | 1919 | Box 630 | Hoehling, Adolph A. | 1920 | Box 664 |
| Hite, Marguerite | 1846 | Box 18 | Hoeke, Elizabeth | 1912 | Box 444 |
| Hitt, Isaac R. | 1910 | Box 393 | Hoeke, William H. | 1912 | Box 444 |
| Hitt, Mary H. B. | 1909 | Box 370 | Hoelmann, Christine | 1912 | Box 444 |
| Hitte, Mary K. | 1895 | Box 154 | Hoelmann, Louis H. | 1913 | Box 470 |
| Hitz, Florian R. | 1920 | Box 664 | Hoepfner, Carl Heinrick W. | 1901 | Box 208 |
| Hitz, John | 1864 | Box 32 | Hoermann, Jacob | 1893 | Box 139 |
| Hitz, John | 1908 | Box 347 | Hoermann, Johanna | 1894 | Box 146 |
| Hitz, Susanna | 1906 | Box 303 | Hoey, Frances Sally | 1912 | Box 444 |
| Hoadley, John C. | 1890 | Box 119 | Hofer, Agatha Magdalena | 1907 | Box 324 |
| Hoban, Edward | 1836 | Box 13 | Hofer, Andrew Frank | 1892 | Box 132 |
| Hoban, Frederick H. Sr. | 1918 | Box 600 | Hofer, Robert | 1909 | Box 370 |
| Hoban, Henrietta | 1919 | Box 631 | Hoff, Almedia J. | 1906 | Box 303 |
| Hoban, Henry | 1866 | Box 36 | Hoff, John Van Rensselear | 1920 | Box 664 |
| Hoban, James | 1832 | Box 11 | Hoffliger, Philip J. | 1910 | Box 393 |
| Hoban, James | 1918 | Box 600 | Hoffman, Ann | 1859 | Box 27 |
| Hoban, Minty | 1838 | Box 14 | Hoffman, Elizabeth | 1903 | Box 246 |
| Hobbie, Selah R. | 1854 | Box 23 | Hoffman, Henry | 1854 | Box 23 |
| Hobbs, Christina | 1854 | Box 23 | Hoffman, Jarrett Francis | 1909 | Box 370 |
| Hobbs, Harriet N. | 1916 | Box 547 | Hoffman, John | 1892 | Box 132 |
| Hobbs, John W. | 1912 | Box 444 | Hoffman, Martha | 1907 | Box 324 |
| Hobbs, Lucretia | 1872 | Box 47 | Hoffman, Mary F. | 1910 | Box 393 |
| Hobbs, William C. | 1815 | Box 4 | Hoffman, Peter | 1881 | Box 75 |
| Hobson, Elizabeth C. | 1912 | Box 444 | Hoffman, Rosana | 1901 | Box 208 |
| Hobson, Matthew | 1912 | Box 444 | Hoffman, Samuel | 1886 | Box 97 |
| Hocheisen, Ferdinand | 1900 | Box 194 | Hoffman, Sarah C. | 1890 | Box 119 |
| Hockaday, Marie A. | 1909 | Box 370 | Hoffman, Susan A. | 1887 | Box 103 |
| Hockemeyer, John | 1899 | Box 184 | Hoffman, Teresa | 1867 | Box 37 |
| Hoddes, Rosie J. | 1916 | Box 547 | Hoffman, Wickham | 1900 | Box 194 |
| Hodermann, Henry | 1889 | Box 114 | Hoffman, William | 1918 | Box 600 |
| Hodes, Theodore | 1919 | Box 631 | Hoffman, Wolfgang | 1863 | Box 31 |
| Hodge, Allen T. | 1914 | Box 493 | Hoffmann, Wilhelmina | 1911 | Box 419 |
| Hodge, Andrew | 1857 | Box 25 | Hofmann, John T. | 1896 | Box 162 |
| Hodge, Eliza | 1843 | Box 16 | Hogan, John | 1904 | Box 265 |
| Hodge, Susan B. | 1918 | Box 600 | Hogan, John E. | 1919 | Box 631 |
| Hodge, Theodosia M. | 1894 | Box 146 | Hogan, Mary T. | 1912 | Box 444 |
| Hodge, William H. | 1869 | Box 41 | Hogan, Patrick | 1910 | Box 393 |
| Hodge, William L. | 1868 | Box 39 | Hogan, Patrick | 1910 | Box 393 |
| Hodges, Benanna | 1911 | Box 419 | Hogan, Peter | 1891 | Box 125 |
| Hodges, Charles L. | 1912 | Box 444 | Hogan, William | 1906 | Box 303 |
| Hodges, Eliza | 1890 | Box 119 | Hogans, Sarah | 1849 | Box 20 |
| Hodges, John G. | 1920 | Box 664 | Hoge, John Milton | 1914 | Box 493 |
| Hodges, Thomas C. | 1821 | Box 7 | Hoge, Maria | 1901 | Box 208 |
| Hodges, Virginia D. | 1897 | Box 169 | Hoge, Willie S. | 1920 | Box 664 |
| Hodges, William H. | 1918 | Box 600 | Hogner, Alexander | 1915 | Box 521 |
| Hodgman, Allen W. | 1913 | Box 470 | Hohmann, Frederick | 1908 | Box 347 |
| Hodgson, Frederick G. | 1918 | Box 600 | Holabird, Samuel Beckley | 1907 | Box 324 |

| | | | | | | |
|---|---|---|---|---|---|---|
| Holbrock, Edwin H. | 1916 | Box 547 | | Holmes, Mary | 1912 | Box 445 |
| Holbrook, Lillie B. | 1918 | Box 600 | | Holmes, Patrick C. | 1910 | Box 393 |
| Holbrook, Theodore Lewis | 1912 | Box 444 | | Holmes, Salome | 1895 | Box 154 |
| Holbrooks, Mary Eliza | 1920 | Box 664 | | Holmes, Silas | 1898 | Box 176 |
| Holcer, John A. | 1916 | Box 547 | | Holmes, Thomas E. | 1899 | Box 184 |
| Holcomb, Thomas W. | 1917 | Box 574 | | Holmes, Thomas J. | 1893 | Box 139 |
| Holcombe, Florence | 1878 | Box 66 | | Holmes, William O. | 1905 | Box 283 |
| Holcombe, Letitia L. | 1920 | Box 664 | | Holohan, Martin C. | 1907 | Box 324 |
| Holcombe, Sarah M. | 1886 | Box 97 | | Holroyd, John | 1879 | Box 69 |
| Holden, Gottfried Edward | 1911 | Box 419 | | Holschuh, John | 1898 | Box 176 |
| Holden, James M. | 1859 | Box 27 | | Holstein, George Wolfe | 1914 | Box 493 |
| Holdridge, Henry E. | 1918 | Box 600 | | Holt, Charles D. | 1907 | Box 324 |
| Holl, Eugene A. | 1906 | Box 303 | | Holt, George B. | 1918 | Box 600 |
| Holladay, Benjamin (Jr.) | 1887 | Box 103 | | Holt, John Henry | 1918 | Box 600 |
| Holland, George N. | 1910 | Box 393 | | Holt, Joseph | 1894 | Box 146 |
| Holland, Margaret | 1876 | Box 61 | | Holt, Joseph | 1895 | Box 154 |
| Holland, Milton M. | 1910 | Box 393 | | Holt, Joseph | 1902 | Box 228 |
| Holledge, James | 1852 | Box 21 | | Holt, William H. | 1911 | Box 419 |
| Holley, Caroline | 1905 | Box 283 | | Holtman, Catharine | 1895 | Box 154 |
| Holley, Carrie | 1920 | Box 664 | | Holtman, William | 1904 | Box 266 |
| Holliday, Eliza E. | 1908 | Box 347 | | Holton, Catharine S. | 1919 | Box 631 |
| Holliday, Lawrence | 1913 | Box 470 | | Holton, Israel P. | 1904 | Box 266 |
| Hollidge, James B. | 1911 | Box 419 | | Holton, Jerusha M. | 1908 | Box 347 |
| Hollidge, Phebe | 1881 | Box 75 | | Holton, John | 1903 | Box 246 |
| Hollidge, Thomas | 1869 | Box 41 | | Holton, Margaret F. | 1903 | Box 246 |
| Hollingsworth, Charles M. | 1916 | Box 547 | | Holtzclaw, Willie Baldwin | 1912 | Box 445 |
| Hollingsworth, John McH. | 1889 | Box 114 | | Holtzlander, Lorenzo | 1904 | Box 266 |
| Hollins, Joseph H. C. | 1909 | Box 370 | | Holtzman, George | 1835 | Box 13 |
| Hollins, Mary J. | 1901 | Box 208 | | Holtzman, Marie A. | 1910 | Box 393 |
| Hollohan, Simon A. | 1912 | Box 444 | | Holzbeierlein, Wolfgang | 1894 | Box 146 |
| Holloran, Mark | 1904 | Box 266 | | Homans, Daniel | 1850 | Box 20 |
| Holly, Eliza Hamilton | 1859 | Box 27 | | Homer, Mary J. | 1915 | Box 521 |
| Holman, Sarah M. | 1900 | Box 194 | | Homiller, Charles | 1888 | Box 108 |
| Holmead, Anthony | 1803 | Box 1 | | Homiller, Jacob | 1888 | Box 108 |
| Holmead, Charles H. | 1914 | Box 493 | | Homiller, Jenyev | 1906 | Box 303 |
| Holmead, Lottie F. | 1908 | Box 347 | | Homstead, Maria A. | 1914 | Box 493 |
| Holmead, Matilda S. | 1867 | Box 37 | | Honan, Mary Teresa | 1889 | Box 114 |
| Holmead, Sophia E. | 1894 | Box 146 | | Honey, Sarah | 1906 | Box 303 |
| Holmead, Susanna | 1806 | Box 2 | | Honeyman, Henry H. | 1919 | Box 631 |
| Holmead, William | 1904 | Box 266 | | Hood, Mary E. | 1906 | Box 303 |
| Holmes, Amanda A. | 1901 | Box 208 | | Hood, Thomas B. | 1900 | Box 194 |
| Holmes, Annie C. | 1911 | Box 419 | | Hooe, James C. | 1911 | Box 419 |
| Holmes, David | 1889 | Box 114 | | Hooe, Robert Arthur | 1908 | Box 347 |
| Holmes, David E. | 1899 | Box 184 | | Hooff, Jane H. | 1908 | Box 347 |
| Holmes, Edwin S. | 1914 | Box 493 | | Hoogs, Theresa Josephine | 1919 | Box 631 |
| Holmes, George M. | 1913 | Box 470 | | Hooker, Julias | 1913 | Box 470 |
| Holmes, Hugh | 1888 | Box 108 | | Hooker, Mary Osborne | 1919 | Box 631 |
| Holmes, James | 1907 | Box 324 | | Hooks, Charles E. | 1910 | Box 393 |
| Holmes, James H. | 1908 | Box 347 | | Hooks, Lorinda A. | 1914 | Box 493 |
| Holmes, James M. | 1912 | Box 445 | | Hooper, Elizabeth Ann | 1904 | Box 266 |
| Holmes, John | 1881 | Box 75 | | Hooper, Frances N. | 1905 | Box 284 |
| Holmes, Josephine V. A. | 1917 | Box 574 | | Hooper, Mary N. | 1904 | Box 266 |

| | | | | | | |
|---|---|---|---|---|---|---|
| Hooper, Samuel | 1875 | Box 57 | Horn, Henry J. | 1901 | Box 208 |
| Hooper, Samuel | 1880 | Box 72 | Horn, Julius | 1910 | Box 394 |
| Hooper, William E. | 1908 | Box 347 | Horn, Margaretta | 1918 | Box 600 |
| Hoops, Alpheus C. | 1905 | Box 284 | Horn, Wolf | 1896 | Box 162 |
| Hootee, Louis C. | 1898 | Box 176 | Hornbach, Barbara | 1910 | Box 394 |
| Hoover, Adam M. | 1910 | Box 393 | Hornbach, Valentine | 1878 | Box 66 |
| Hoover, Cecilia J. | 1909 | Box 370 | Hornblower, Caroline B. | 1885 | Box 92 |
| Hoover, Charles E. | 1896 | Box 162 | Hornblower, Joseph C. | 1908 | Box 347 |
| Hoover, Elizabeth Ann | 1881 | Box 75 | Hornblower, Matilda B. | 1895 | Box 154 |
| Hoover, George W. | 1900 | Box 195 | Hornblower, William H. | 1884 | Box 87 |
| Hoover, Helena | 1900 | Box 195 | Horner, Anna Stackhouse | 1915 | Box 521 |
| Hoover, John | 1889 | Box 114 | Horner, Annie E. | 1904 | Box 266 |
| Hoover, John W. | 1876 | Box 61 | Horner, Christoph | 1905 | Box 284 |
| Hoover, Jonah D. | 1871 | Box 45 | Horner, Clarence W. | 1918 | Box 600 |
| Hoover, Mary A. | 1906 | Box 303 | Horner, Jacob | 1881 | Box 75 |
| Hoover, Milton P. | 1887 | Box 103 | Horner, Sarah E. | 1914 | Box 494 |
| Hoover, Oliver H. | 1911 | Box 419 | Hornig, Peter F. | 1905 | Box 284 |
| Hoover, Samuel Lemon | 1915 | Box 521 | Horning, Elizabeth | 1916 | Box 547 |
| Hoover, Samuel S. | 1914 | Box 493 | Horning, George D. | 1879 | Box 69 |
| Hope, Randall | 1914 | Box 493 | Hornor, Charles W. | 1905 | Box 284 |
| Hope, William | 1914 | Box 493 | Hornsby, Isham | 1899 | Box 184 |
| Hopewell, Mary | 1838 | Box 14 | Hornsby, Rebekah Black | 1911 | Box 420 |
| Hopf, Frederick | 1850 | Box 20 | Hornung, Charles C. | 1911 | Box 420 |
| Hopfenmaier, Henrietta | 1919 | Box 631 | Horseman, George | 1862 | Box 30 |
| Hopfenmaier, Lewis | 1917 | Box 574 | Hörstman, Harriette Kelly | 1900 | Box 195 |
| Hopkins, California West | 1914 | Box 493 | Horstman, Matilda | 1909 | Box 370 |
| Hopkins, Cornelius | 1883 | Box 83 | Hort, Emily F. | 1903 | Box 246 |
| Hopkins, Emily N. | 1914 | Box 493 | Hort, Kate | 1861 | Box 29 |
| Hopkins, Emma L. | 1895 | Box 154 | Horton, Elias Quereau | 1919 | Box 631 |
| Hopkins, Frank T. | 1906 | Box 303 | Horton, Margaret E. | 1916 | Box 548 |
| Hopkins, George | 1881 | Box 75 | Horton, Sarah S. | 1905 | Box 284 |
| Hopkins, John | 1858 | Box 26 | Horton, William Edward | 1911 | Box 420 |
| Hopkins, Juliet A. | 1891 | Box 125 | Hosack, Mary J. | 1917 | Box 574 |
| Hopkins, Laura M. | 1898 | Box 176 | Hosch, August | 1876 | Box 61 |
| Hopkins, Lawrence H. | 1910 | Box 393 | Hosford, Elihu | 1890 | Box 119 |
| Hopkins, Louisa F. | 1880 | Box 72 | Hosier, Joseph C. | 1880 | Box 72 |
| Hopkins, Martha | 1898 | Box 176 | Hoskins, Isiah W. | 1894 | Box 146 |
| Hopkins, Mary | 1904 | Box 266 | Hosmer, Amanda Sturges | 1907 | Box 324 |
| Hopkins, Mary H. | 1910 | Box 393 | Hosmer, Mary E. | 1906 | Box 303 |
| Hopkins, Thaddeus | 1901 | Box 208 | Hoss, Alfred | 1892 | Box 132 |
| Hopkins, Thomas | 1888 | Box 108 | Hoss, Francina | 1902 | Box 228 |
| Hopping, Francis A. | 1902 | Box 228 | Hotaling, Albert S. | 1914 | Box 494 |
| Horan, Julia | 1916 | Box 547 | Hotaling, Gertrude A. | 1913 | Box 470 |
| Horan, Michael | 1895 | Box 154 | Hotaling, Steuben | 1911 | Box 420 |
| Hord, William T. | 1901 | Box 208 | Hotchkiss, Mary E. | 1902 | Box 228 |
| Horgan, Edmund | 1913 | Box 470 | Hottel, Martin V. | 1915 | Box 521 |
| Horgan, Johanna | 1905 | Box 284 | Houck, Samuel D. | 1917 | Box 574 |
| Horigan, Cornelius | 1915 | Box 521 | Hough, Bessie Ashley | 1911 | Box 420 |
| Horigan, Daniel | 1890 | Box 119 | Hough, Caroline A. | 1910 | Box 394 |
| Horigan, Dennis | 1910 | Box 394 | Hough, George J. | 1914 | Box 494 |
| Horigan, Mary F. | 1912 | Box 445 | Hough, Myron B. W. | 1884 | Box 87 |
| Horine, William T. | 1899 | Box 184 | Hough, William W. | 1895 | Box 154 |

| | | | | | | |
|---|---|---|---|---|---|---|
| Hough, Williston S. | 1912 | Box 445 | Howard, Sarah | 1853 | Box 22 |
| Houghton, Clara May Keys | 1920 | Box 664 | Howard, Theophilus | 1891 | Box 125 |
| Houghton, Josepha Headley | 1904 | Box 266 | Howard, Thomas | 1832 | Box 11 |
| Houlihan, Mary | 1916 | Box 548 | Howard, Thomas H. | 1881 | Box 75 |
| Hounschild, Maria | 1881 | Box 75 | Howard, Thomas P. | 1917 | Box 574 |
| House, Adelaide S. | 1919 | Box 631 | Howard, William E. | 1888 | Box 108 |
| House, Alice M. | 1898 | Box 176 | Howe, Chester | 1908 | Box 348 |
| House, Eliza M. | 1901 | Box 208 | Howe, Emma F. | 1901 | Box 208 |
| House, Helon Howard | 1918 | Box 600 | Howe, Harriet M. | 1910 | Box 394 |
| House, James | 1834 | Box 12 | Howe, Henry S. | 1910 | Box 394 |
| House, James Madison | 1905 | Box 284 | Howe, Myron W. | 1910 | Box 394 |
| Houser, Philip W. | 1916 | Box 548 | Howe, Sarah Bradley | 1905 | Box 284 |
| Houser, William Francis | 1916 | Box 548 | Howe, Walter | 1915 | Box 521 |
| Houston, Henry Warmoth | 1915 | Box 521 | Howell, Adelaide Caroline | 1918 | Box 600 |
| Houston, Thomas Truxton | 1860 | Box 28 | Howell, Amy Shepley | 1919 | Box 631 |
| Houston, William | 1872 | Box 47 | Howell, Annie E. | 1911 | Box 420 |
| Houston, William T. | 1918 | Box 600 | Howell, Edwin E. | 1911 | Box 420 |
| How, Robert F. | 1883 | Box 83 | Howell, George F. | 1909 | Box 370 |
| Howard, Addie M. | 1911 | Box 420 | Howell, John Cumming | 1894 | Box 154 |
| Howard, Adrian D. | 1834 | Box 12 | Howell, John H. | 1844 | Box 17 |
| Howard, Alexander S. | 1914 | Box 494 | Howell, Mary Stockton | 1889 | Box 114 |
| Howard, Angeline Lee | 1899 | Box 184 | Howell, Sarah C. | 1878 | Box 66 |
| Howard, Ann | 1920 | Box 664 | Howell, William P. | 1879 | Box 69 |
| Howard, Anna Brooks | 1882 | Box 79 | Howes, John | 1868 | Box 39 |
| Howard, Annie E. | 1902 | Box 228 | Howes, Sarah Lucy | 1905 | Box 284 |
| Howard, Annie Murray | 1882 | Box 79 | Howgate, Cordelia | 1908 | Box 348 |
| Howard, Beal | 1861 | Box 29 | Howison, Isabella B. | 1916 | Box 548 |
| Howard, Cecilia Riggs | 1908 | Box 347 | Howison, Julia F. | 1903 | Box 246 |
| Howard, Charlotte | 1915 | Box 521 | Howison, Samuel | 1914 | Box 494 |
| Howard, Edward | 1910 | Box 394 | Howison, William | 1805 | Box 1 |
| Howard, Elizabeth | 1863 | Box 31 | Howland, Frederica B. | 1902 | Box 228 |
| Howard, Emeline | 1874 | Box 54 | Howland, Jennie E. | 1915 | Box 521 |
| Howard, Flodoardo | 1888 | Box 108 | Howland, Marcus | 1906 | Box 303 |
| Howard, Francis | 1893 | Box 139 | Howland, Moses | 1907 | Box 324 |
| Howard, George | 1919 | Box 631 | Howland, William | 1917 | Box 574 |
| Howard, George Montgomerie | 1877 | Box 64 | Howlett, Jane E. | 1910 | Box 394 |
| Howard, George Thomas | 1866 | Box 36 | Howser, Jane A. | 1913 | Box 470 |
| Howard, H. P. | 1914 | Box 494 | Howser, Julia Virginia | 1911 | Box 420 |
| Howard, Hamilton | 1864 | Box 32 | Howser, Sallie T. | 1890 | Box 119 |
| Howard, Hannah E. | 1900 | Box 195 | Howser, Upton S. | 1902 | Box 228 |
| Howard, Hattie E. | 1902 | Box 228 | Hoy, Thomas | 1920 | Box 664 |
| Howard, Helen A. | 1916 | Box 548 | Hoye, John | 1877 | Box 64 |
| Howard, John | 1886 | Box 97 | Hoyle, Henry J. | 1896 | Box 162 |
| Howard, John G. | 1893 | Box 139 | Hoyle, William Jennings | 1887 | Box 103 |
| Howard, Katharine | 1910 | Box 394 | Hoyt, Alfred M. | 1905 | Box 284 |
| Howard, Lusiania (Luvinia) | 1901 | Box 208 | Hoyt, Florence Birney | 1896 | Box 162 |
| Howard, Mark | 1899 | Box 184 | Hoyt, Harriet B. | 1910 | Box 394 |
| Howard, Mary | 1889 | Box 114 | Hoyt, Henry M. | 1911 | Box 420 |
| Howard, Mary C. | 1893 | Box 139 | Hrdlicka, Marie | 1918 | Box 600 |
| Howard, Nannie | 1895 | Box 154 | Hubbard, Elizabeth | 1900 | Box 195 |
| Howard, Peter | 1821 | Box 7 | Hubbard, Elizabeth Boyd | 1904 | Box 266 |
| Howard, Robert A. | 1911 | Box 420 | Hubbard, Gardiner Greene | 1897 | Box 169 |

| | | | | | | |
|---|---|---|---|---|---|---|
| Hubbard, Gertrude M. | 1909 | Box 371 | Hughes, John | 1885 | Box 92 |
| Hubbard, Robert J. | 1905 | Box 284 | Hughes, John | 1886 | Box 97 |
| Hubbard, Solomon | 1876 | Box 61 | Hughes, John | 1898 | Box 176 |
| Hubbard, Stephen A. | 1898 | Box 176 | Hughes, Leanna | 1890 | Box 119 |
| Hubbert, Jesse | 1920 | Box 664 | Hughes, Lolita B. | 1894 | Box 146 |
| Hubble, William Wheeler | 1903 | Box 246 | Hughes, Louise Beauchamp | 1908 | Box 348 |
| Hubby, Frank W. | 1919 | Box 631 | Hughes, Lucinda | 1895 | Box 154 |
| Hubby, Leander M. | 1897 | Box 169 | Hughes, Marian Jane | 1917 | Box 574 |
| Huber, Louis | 1884 | Box 87 | Hughes, Nora M. | 1897 | Box 169 |
| Hubner, Catharine | 1892 | Box 132 | Hughes, Ophelia A. | 1910 | Box 394 |
| Huck, Emile | 1918 | Box 600 | Hughes, Sarah T. | 1863 | Box 31 |
| Hudders, Sarah | 1886 | Box 97 | Hughes, Thomas | 1837 | Box 13 |
| Huddleston, Joseph | 1818 | Box 5 | Hughes, Virginia M. | 1900 | Box 195 |
| Huddleston, Thomas | 1839 | Box 14 | Hughes, William | 1840 | Box 15 |
| Huder, Louis Xavier | 1839 | Box 14 | Hughes, William | 1853 | Box 22 |
| Hudnell, Beverly | 1912 | Box 445 | Hughes, William | 1865 | Box 33 |
| Hudnell, Delaware | 1898 | Box 176 | Hughes, William | 1879 | Box 69 |
| Hudson, Ann M. | 1913 | Box 470 | Hughes, William Louis | 1905 | Box 284 |
| Hudson, Carrie B. | 1901 | Box 208 | Hügle, Frederick | 1890 | Box 119 |
| Hudson, Charles Derius | 1895 | Box 154 | Hugle, Marie Antoinette | 1891 | Box 125 |
| Hudson, Harry | 1901 | Box 208 | Huguely, Charles W. | 1913 | Box 470 |
| Hudson, Henry A. | 1888 | Box 108 | Huguely, George W. | 1911 | Box 420 |
| Hudson, Maria | 1889 | Box 114 | Huguley, Harrison W. | 1913 | Box 470 |
| Hudson, Marion C. | 1897 | Box 169 | Huguley, James F. | 1920 | Box 664 |
| Hudson, Marion C. | 1900 | Box 195 | Huhn, George | 1900 | Box 195 |
| Hudson, William W. | 1886 | Box 97 | Huhn, Joseph | 1873 | Box 51 |
| Hudwell, Catharine | 1895 | Box 154 | Huhn, Mary A. | 1915 | Box 521 |
| Hues, John | 1875 | Box 57 | Huidekoper, Frederic W. | 1908 | Box 348 |
| Huestis, William H. | 1875 | Box 57 | Huidekoper, Virginia C. | 1914 | Box 494 |
| Hueter, Charles | 1879 | Box 69 | Hulburd, Rebecca C. | 1895 | Box 154 |
| Hueter, Christiana | 1894 | Box 146 | Hull, Alice Maud Mary | 1908 | Box 348 |
| Huey, Samuel C. | 1886 | Box 97 | Hull, Esther | 1888 | Box 108 |
| Huff, Burrell R. | 1920 | Box 664 | Hull, Mary | 1872 | Box 47 |
| Huff, Cathrine | 1919 | Box 631 | Hull, Maynard D. | 1920 | Box 664 |
| Huff, George F. | 1912 | Box 445 | Hull, Ransom | 1821 | Box 7 |
| Huff, Lloyd B. | 1920 | Box 664 | Hull, Stephen C. | 1908 | Box 348 |
| Huffington, William O. | 1909 | Box 371 | Hullett, Joseph | 1912 | Box 445 |
| Huffman, Allan F. | 1907 | Box 324 | Hulse, Charles | 1885 | Box 92 |
| Huggins, Edward F. | 1909 | Box 371 | Hulse, Margaret L. | 1892 | Box 132 |
| Huggins, Julia McComb | 1919 | Box 631 | Hume, Frank | 1906 | Box 303 |
| Hughes, Aaron Koukle | 1906 | Box 303 | Hume, Seward B. | 1892 | Box 132 |
| Hughes, Anne S. | 1891 | Box 125 | Humes, George C. | 1881 | Box 75 |
| Hughes, Edward B. | 1914 | Box 494 | Humes, John | 1839 | Box 14 |
| Hughes, Ella O. | 1893 | Box 139 | Humphrey, Elizabeth | 1858 | Box 26 |
| Hughes, Emily | 1911 | Box 420 | Humphrey, James Douglass | 1915 | Box 521 |
| Hughes, Ezekiel | 1883 | Box 83 | Humphrey, John | 1903 | Box 246 |
| Hughes, Harry R. | 1906 | Box 303 | Humphrey, Sarah C. | 1915 | Box 521 |
| Hughes, Henry | 1896 | Box 162 | Humphrey, William E. | 1906 | Box 303 |
| Hughes, James | 1873 | Box 51 | Humphreys, Andrew Atkinson | 1884 | Box 87 |
| Hughes, James | 1915 | Box 521 | Humphreys, Catharine M. | 1911 | Box 420 |
| Hughes, James Lyles | 1911 | Box 420 | Humphreys, Charles | 1907 | Box 324 |
| Hughes, John | 1859 | Box 27 | Humphreys, Eliza Jane | 1884 | Box 87 |

| | | | | | | |
|---|---|---|---|---|---|---|
| Humphreys, Rebecca H. | 1897 | Box 169 | | Hunter, Harriet M. | 1916 | Box 548 |
| Humphreys, Samuel | 1846 | Box 18 | | Hunter, Henrietta J. | 1912 | Box 445 |
| Humphreys, Thomas Henry | 1917 | Box 574 | | Hunter, Jane | 1869 | Box 41 |
| Humphries, Jannie A. | 1890 | Box 119 | | Hunter, Jessica Penn | 1910 | Box 394 |
| Humphries, Julia Anson | 1904 | Box 266 | | Hunter, John W. | 1905 | Box 284 |
| Humphys, Ann | 1917 | Box 574 | | Hunter, Larklin | 1896 | Box 162 |
| Humpton, Annie E. | 1920 | Box 664 | | Hunter, Lavinia Gertrude | 1902 | Box 228 |
| Humpton, Charles L. | 1920 | Box 664 | | Hunter, Louisa | 1865 | Box 33 |
| Hunaker, Harry | 1910 | Box 394 | | Hunter, Louisa Brooke | 1917 | Box 574 |
| Hundley, George A. | 1912 | Box 445 | | Hunter, Lucy L. | 1888 | Box 108 |
| Hundley, George S. | 1918 | Box 600 | | Hunter, Maria | 1887 | Box 103 |
| Hundley, Mariana | 1913 | Box 470 | | Hunter, Martha | 1897 | Box 169 |
| Hungerford, Carrie L. | 1905 | Box 284 | | Hunter, Mary Ann | 1898 | Box 177 |
| Hungerford, Daphne | 1883 | Box 83 | | Hunter, William | 1854 | Box 23 |
| Hungerford, Elizabeth C. | 1911 | Box 420 | | Hunter, William | 1886 | Box 97 |
| Hungerford, Philip C. | 1890 | Box 119 | | Hunter, William H. | 1912 | Box 445 |
| Hunley, Walter G. | 1900 | Box 195 | | Huntington, Adoniram Judson | 1903 | Box 246 |
| Hunnicut, Mildred | 1912 | Box 445 | | Huntington, Andrew Tyler | 1915 | Box 521 |
| Hunnicut, Willis | 1912 | Box 445 | | Huntington, David L. | 1900 | Box 195 |
| Hunt, Alice U. | 1920 | Box 664 | | Huntington, Ella B. | 1912 | Box 445 |
| Hunt, Amanda J. | 1894 | Box 146 | | Huntington, Emily S. | 1918 | Box 600 |
| Hunt, Anna G. | 1898 | Box 177 | | Huntington, Joshua | 1901 | Box 208 |
| Hunt, Anna Kellogg | 1910 | Box 394 | | Huntington, Sarah W. | 1917 | Box 574 |
| Hunt, Bridget | 1911 | Box 420 | | Huntington, Thomas | 1905 | Box 284 |
| Hunt, Ella G. | 1920 | Box 664 | | Huntley, Charlie C. | 1883 | Box 83 |
| Hunt, Emma E. | 1920 | Box 664 | | Huntley, Elias Dewitt | 1909 | Box 371 |
| Hunt, Franklin B. | 1900 | Box 195 | | Huntley, George | 1884 | Box 87 |
| Hunt, George E. | 1913 | Box 470 | | Huntley, Julian C. | 1918 | Box 600 |
| Hunt, Henry | 1838 | Box 14 | | Hunton, William A. | 1919 | Box 631 |
| Hunt, Henry J. | 1889 | Box 114 | | Huntress, Elizabeth | 1918 | Box 600 |
| Hunt, Henry J. | 1919 | Box 631 | | Huntt, Charles | 1875 | Box 57 |
| Hunt, Hiram | 1872 | Box 47 | | Huntt, Anna Maria | 1841 | Box 15 |
| Hunt, John Thomas | 1914 | Box 494 | | Huntt, Henry | 1838 | Box 14 |
| Hunt, John W. | 1913 | Box 470 | | Huntt, William A. L. | 1918 | Box 600 |
| Hunt, Lewis Cass | 1910 | Box 394 | | Hupert, George E. | 1915 | Box 521 |
| Hunt, Mary Bethune | 1911 | Box 420 | | Hurd, Lucy A. | 1910 | Box 394 |
| Hunt, Richard | 1891 | Box 125 | | Hurdle, James | 1862 | Box 30 |
| Hunt, Thomas F. | 1865 | Box 33 | | Hurdle, Leonard | 1806 | Box 2 |
| Hunt, William | 1857 | Box 25 | | Hurdle, Mary C. | 1899 | Box 184 |
| Hunt, William F. | 1910 | Box 394 | | Hurdle, Noble | 1874 | Box 54 |
| Hunt, William M. | 1907 | Box 324 | | Hurdle, Thomas T. | 1912 | Box 445 |
| Hunter, Alexander | 1849 | Box 20 | | Hurlbut, William J. | 1913 | Box 470 |
| Hunter, Alexander | 1914 | Box 494 | | Hurlebaus, George W. | 1915 | Box 521 |
| Hunter, Alfred | 1872 | Box 47 | | Hurlebaus, Gottlieb | 1900 | Box 195 |
| Hunter, Andrew | 1823 | Box 7 | | Hurley, Emily M. | 1911 | Box 420 |
| Hunter, Ann | 1865 | Box 33 | | Hurley, George E. | 1901 | Box 208 |
| Hunter, David | 1886 | Box 97 | | Hurley, John E. | 1918 | Box 601 |
| Hunter, Eliza B. | 1917 | Box 574 | | Hurley, Louise F. | 1910 | Box 394 |
| Hunter, Elizabeth A. | 1895 | Box 154 | | Hurley, Mary | 1872 | Box 47 |
| Hunter, Emma Eugenia | 1919 | Box 631 | | Hurley, Mary A. | 1907 | Box 324 |
| Hunter, Filah A. | 1915 | Box 521 | | Hurley, Maurice J. | 1878 | Box 66 |
| Hunter, H. Chadwick | 1919 | Box 631 | | Hurley, Washington S. | 1893 | Box 139 |

| | | | | | | |
|---|---|---|---|---|---|---|
| Hurlock, Henry Harrison | 1917 | Box 574 | Hyde, Elizabeth Neale | 1920 | Box 665 |
| Hurney, Hugh | 1905 | Box 284 | Hyde, Emily Farquhar | 1895 | Box 154 |
| Hurney, Mary | 1894 | Box 146 | Hyde, James | 1865 | Box 33 |
| Hurney, Mary E. | 1920 | Box 665 | Hyde, Josephine | 1899 | Box 184 |
| Hurst, John | 1903 | Box 246 | Hyde, Patrick | 1891 | Box 125 |
| Hurst, John F. | 1903 | Box 246 | Hyde, Thomas | 1841 | Box 15 |
| Hurst, Urias | 1879 | Box 69 | Hyde, Thomas | 1919 | Box 631 |
| Hurt, Henry | 1916 | Box 548 | Hyde, William | 1899 | Box 184 |
| Hurter, Kate | 1902 | Box 228 | Hyde, William H. | 1919 | Box 631 |
| Husband, Georgia C. | 1904 | Box 266 | Hyer, David | 1903 | Box 246 |
| Husband, Henry Morris | 1920 | Box 665 | Hyland, Eliza Jane | 1908 | Box 348 |
| Husband, Mary Morris | 1894 | Box 146 | Hyler, Oscar D. | 1916 | Box 548 |
| Huster, George | 1905 | Box 284 | Hynes, Thomas | 1901 | Box 208 |
| Huston, E. S. | 1916 | Box 548 | Iardella, Charles T. | 1897 | Box 169 |
| Hutcheson, Martha B. | 1895 | Box 154 | Ibach, Minnie | 1918 | Box 601 |
| Hutcheson, Martha Jane | 1877 | Box 64 | Ibarra, Marie F. | 1918 | Box 601 |
| Hutchingson, Apollonia | 1906 | Box 303 | Iddins, Frederick | 1877 | Box 64 |
| Hutchingson, Thomas | 1886 | Box 97 | Iddins, Henry | 1889 | Box 114 |
| Hutchins, Benedict | 1872 | Box 47 | Ide, George E. | 1917 | Box 574 |
| Hutchins, Dewitt C. | 1886 | Box 97 | Imbrie, Jeremiah R. | 1897 | Box 169 |
| Hutchins, Marion B. | 1917 | Box 574 | Imhof, Frederick | 1916 | Box 548 |
| Hutchins, Martha E. | 1856 | Box 25 | Imirie, Cecilia Daly | 1899 | Box 184 |
| Hutchins, Uriel H. | 1872 | Box 47 | Imirie, John | 1899 | Box 184 |
| Hutchinson, Eleanor J. | 1871 | Box 45 | Inch, Richard | 1911 | Box 420 |
| Hutchinson, Elias S. | 1913 | Box 470 | Indermauer, Jeremiah | 1869 | Box 41 |
| Hutchinson, Eliza C. | 1916 | Box 548 | Ingalls, Abbie Stimson | 1919 | Box 631 |
| Hutchinson, Hayward M. | 1883 | Box 83 | Ingalls, Melville Ezra | 1914 | Box 494 |
| Hutchinson, John | 1914 | Box 494 | Ingersoll, Charles M. | 1852 | Box 21 |
| Hutchinson, John T. | 1910 | Box 394 | Ingersoll, Henrietta C. | 1893 | Box 139 |
| Hutchinson, Joseph | 1863 | Box 31 | Ingersoll, Joseph R. | 1877 | Box 64 |
| Hutchinson, Louisa M. | 1886 | Box 97 | Ingersoll, Julia H. | 1898 | Box 177 |
| Hutchinson, Margaret A. | 1864 | Box 32 | Ingle, Edward | 1839 | Box 14 |
| Hutchinson, Mary J. | 1896 | Box 162 | Ingle, Edward Henry | 1920 | Box 665 |
| Hutchinson, Philip | 1896 | Box 162 | Ingle, Imogen | 1917 | Box 574 |
| Hutchinson, Thomas | 1873 | Box 51 | Ingle, John P. | 1863 | Box 31 |
| Hutchinson, William | 1896 | Box 162 | Ingle, Mary | 1844 | Box 17 |
| Hutchinson, William | 1904 | Box 266 | Ingle, Samuel S. | 1911 | Box 420 |
| Hutchinson, William E. | 1907 | Box 325 | Ingram, Clarance | 1915 | Box 521 |
| Hutchison, James | 1829 | Box 10 | Ingram, Mary | 1901 | Box 209 |
| Huth, Christian F. | 1911 | Box 420 | Ingram, Smith | 1870 | Box 43 |
| Huth, Frederick G. | 1893 | Box 139 | Ingram, William | 1912 | Box 445 |
| Huth, Herman F. | 1895 | Box 154 | Ingram, William B. | 1882 | Box 79 |
| Hutton, George W. | 1914 | Box 494 | Innes, Elizabeth A. | 1904 | Box 266 |
| Hutton, Harry Dubant | 1914 | Box 494 | Irby, George C. | 1893 | Box 139 |
| Hutton, Salome R. | 1874 | Box 54 | Ireland, Susannah | 1869 | Box 41 |
| Huyett, Margaret William | 1908 | Box 348 | Irving, Cortlandt | 1913 | Box 470 |
| Hyatt, Caroline A. | 1880 | Box 72 | Irving, Elise | 1920 | Box 665 |
| Hyatt, Elizabeth | 1871 | Box 45 | Irving, Henry | 1907 | Box 325 |
| Hyatt, Howard L. | 1888 | Box 108 | Irving, Henry Grant | 1915 | Box 521 |
| Hyatt, Rebecca E. | 1896 | Box 162 | Irving, John H. | 1890 | Box 119 |
| Hyatt, Seth | 1879 | Box 69 | Irving, Julia Granger | 1898 | Box 177 |
| Hyde, Anthony | 1892 | Box 132 | Irving, Louisa | 1904 | Box 266 |

| | | | | | |
|---|---|---|---|---|---|
| Irving, Priscilla | 1920 | Box 665 | Jackson, Harriet M. | 1900 | Box 195 |
| Irving, Sanders | 1884 | Box 87 | Jackson, Henry | 1885 | Box 92 |
| Irving, William | 1910 | Box 394 | Jackson, Henry | 1915 | Box 521 |
| Irwin, David | 1901 | Box 209 | Jackson, Howell E. | 1898 | Box 177 |
| Irwin, Harvey S. | 1917 | Box 574 | Jackson, Isaac N. | 1897 | Box 169 |
| Irwin, John | 1911 | Box 420 | Jackson, Jacob | 1841 | Box 15 |
| Irwin, Mary Elizabeth | 1910 | Box 394 | Jackson, Jasper M. | 1866 | Box 36 |
| Irwin, Nancy E. | 1915 | Box 521 | Jackson, Jasper M. | 1890 | Box 119 |
| Irwin, Walter R. | 1886 | Box 72 | Jackson, John H. | 1906 | Box 303 |
| Irwin, William | 1800 | Box 2 | Jackson, Joseph | 1831 | Box 11 |
| Irwin, William N. | 1911 | Box 420 | Jackson, Joseph H. | 1912 | Box 446 |
| Isaac, Henry Clay | 1887 | Box 103 | Jackson, Josephine | 1890 | Box 119 |
| Isaac, James Madison | 1887 | Box 103 | Jackson, Lemuel | 1915 | Box 521 |
| Ischinger, August | 1917 | Box 574 | Jackson, Lucy | 1903 | Box 246 |
| Isdell, Caroline | 1911 | Box 420 | Jackson, Lue | 1915 | Box 521 |
| Isdell, Nelson | 1885 | Box 92 | Jackson, Martha A. | 1900 | Box 195 |
| Isemann, Catharine | 1895 | Box 154 | Jackson, Martha A. | 1905 | Box 284 |
| Isemann, Emma | 1913 | Box 470 | Jackson, Mary Jane | 1899 | Box 184 |
| Isemann, George | 1901 | Box 209 | Jackson, Mary P. | 1869 | Box 41 |
| Isemann, Henry | 1885 | Box 92 | Jackson, Mary S. | 1896 | Box 162 |
| Isemann, John | 1902 | Box 228 | Jackson, Mary Voorhees | 1908 | Box 348 |
| Isherwood, Martha | 1869 | Box 41 | Jackson, Milley | 1850 | Box 20 |
| Isherwood, Robert | 1849 | Box 20 | Jackson, Millie | 1915 | Box 521 |
| Israel, Elizabeth S. C. | 1905 | Box 284 | Jackson, Nancy | 1866 | Box 36 |
| Itzel, Charles | 1908 | Box 348 | Jackson, Philip | 1848 | Box 19 |
| Ives, Amelia J. | 1899 | Box 184 | Jackson, Pompey | 1872 | Box 47 |
| Ives, Jennie H. | 1920 | Box 665 | Jackson, Rachel Ann | 1909 | Box 371 |
| Ivins, Robert S. | 1919 | Box 631 | Jackson, Richard | 1874 | Box 54 |
| Jackson, Albert L. | 1900 | Box 195 | Jackson, Richard P. | 1891 | Box 125 |
| Jackson, Alfred B. | 1897 | Box 169 | Jackson, Robert | 1914 | Box 494 |
| Jackson, Amelia | 1915 | Box 521 | Jackson, Samuel | 1905 | Box 284 |
| Jackson, Andrew | 1885 | Box 92 | Jackson, Samuel L. | 1895 | Box 154 |
| Jackson, Andrew | 1911 | Box 421 | Jackson, Sarah | 1920 | Box 665 |
| Jackson, Andrew A. | 1904 | Box 266 | Jackson, Sheldon | 1909 | Box 371 |
| Jackson, Angelo | 1878 | Box 66 | Jackson, Sojourner T. | 1914 | Box 494 |
| Jackson, Ann Eliza | 1903 | Box 246 | Jackson, Stephen | 1891 | Box 125 |
| Jackson, Annie E. | 1918 | Box 601 | Jackson, Susan Margaret | 1915 | Box 522 |
| Jackson, Arthur | 1913 | Box 471 | Jackson, Thomas | 1878 | Box 66 |
| Jackson, Basil | 1903 | Box 246 | Jackson, Thomas E. | 1879 | Box 69 |
| Jackson, Beverly | 1908 | Box 348 | Jackson, William B. | 1896 | Box 162 |
| Jackson, Blanche W. | 1918 | Box 601 | Jackson, William Joseph | 1919 | Box 631 |
| Jackson, Celeste T. | 1898 | Box 177 | Jackson, William L. | 1913 | Box 471 |
| Jackson, Cheney | 1854 | Box 23 | Jackson, William S. | 1894 | Box 146 |
| Jackson, Daniel | 1919 | Box 631 | Jackson, William W. | 1882 | Box 79 |
| Jackson, David | 1892 | Box 132 | Jacob, Christian M. | 1918 | Box 601 |
| Jackson, Dennis | 1919 | Box 631 | Jacob, Mary W. | 1920 | Box 665 |
| Jackson, Edward | 1876 | Box 61 | Jacobi, Adolph | 1858 | Box 26 |
| Jackson, Elihu E. | 1908 | Box 348 | Jacobs, Asbury Roszell | 1876 | Box 61 |
| Jackson, Elizabeth D. | 1891 | Box 125 | Jacobs, Augustus | 1900 | Box 195 |
| Jackson, Fannie | 1894 | Box 146 | Jacobs, Charles Porter | 1917 | Box 574 |
| Jackson, Frank H. | 1918 | Box 601 | Jacobs, David | 1876 | Box 61 |
| Jackson, Geneva Parker | 1914 | Box 494 | Jacobs, Elisha A. | 1915 | Box 522 |

| | | | | | | |
|---|---|---|---|---|---|---|
| Jacobs, Etta | 1920 | Box 665 | | Jaquette, Mary A. | 1910 | Box 394 |
| Jacobs, George | 1917 | Box 574 | | Jarboe, Francis M. | 1891 | Box 125 |
| Jacobs, Henry | 1854 | Box 23 | | Jarboe, John | 1842 | Box 15 |
| Jacobs, Jesse F. | 1900 | Box 195 | | Jarboe, Marcellina | 1900 | Box 195 |
| Jacobs, John C. | 1915 | Box 522 | | Jarboe, Mary | 1878 | Box 66 |
| Jacobsen, Elisabeth A. | 1906 | Box 303 | | Jarboe, Matthew | 1842 | Box 15 |
| Jacobsen, Herman | 1903 | Box 246 | | Jarboe, Matthew | 1917 | Box 574 |
| Jacobson, Herman | 1907 | Box 325 | | Jarboe, Thomas | 1855 | Box 24 |
| Jacoby, John | 1902 | Box 228 | | Jardin, Armand | 1886 | Box 97 |
| Jacques, Mary Emma | 1912 | Box 446 | | Jardin, Armand F. | 1914 | Box 494 |
| Jaeger, Anna Marie | 1907 | Box 325 | | Jardin, Honorine | 1909 | Box 371 |
| Jaeger, Hannah | 1907 | Box 325 | | Jarvis, Charles F. | 1886 | Box 97 |
| Jaeger, Henry | 1908 | Box 348 | | Jarvis, Cypriano | 1872 | Box 47 |
| Jaeger, Michael | 1909 | Box 371 | | Jarvis, Elizabeth | 1874 | Box 54 |
| Jaeschke, Charles | 1919 | Box 631 | | Jarvis, John | 1858 | Box 26 |
| Jakob, David C. | 1915 | Box 522 | | Jasper, Sarah E. | 1907 | Box 325 |
| James, Alice G. | 1910 | Box 394 | | Javins, Isabella A. | 1915 | Box 522 |
| James, Annie K. G. | 1912 | Box 446 | | Jay, Augustus | 1920 | Box 665 |
| James, Benjamin F. | 1882 | Box 79 | | Jayne, Joseph W. | 1892 | Box 132 |
| James, Caldwell W. | 1890 | Box 119 | | Jeffcott, Ann A. | 1905 | Box 285 |
| James, Charles A. | 1909 | Box 371 | | Jefferies, Emma | 1911 | Box 421 |
| James, Charles E. | 1899 | Box 184 | | Jeffers, William N. | 1883 | Box 83 |
| James, Eleanor H. | 1895 | Box 154 | | Jefferson, Emma J. | 1919 | Box 631 |
| James, Gertrude W. | 1899 | Box 184 | | Jefferson, Ferdinand | 1878 | Box 66 |
| James, Henry B. | 1892 | Box 132 | | Jefferson, James | 1885 | Box 92 |
| James, John Dawson | 1870 | Box 43 | | Jefferson, Margaret | 1882 | Box 79 |
| James, Joseph | 1897 | Box 170 | | Jefferson, Ralph | 1906 | Box 304 |
| James, Matilda | 1919 | Box 631 | | Jeffrey, Daisy E. | 1912 | Box 446 |
| James, Matilda V. | 1917 | Box 574 | | Jeffries, William | 1897 | Box 170 |
| James, Samuel | 1861 | Box 29 | | Jehle, Josephine | 1916 | Box 548 |
| James, William P. | 1916 | Box 548 | | Jenckes, Amos T. | 1882 | Box 79 |
| James, William R. | 1893 | Box 139 | | Jenckes, Emily J. | 1896 | Box 162 |
| Jameson, Albion B. | 1920 | Box 665 | | Jenifer, Caroline | 1893 | Box 139 |
| Jameson, John M. | 1884 | Box 87 | | Jenifer, Effie | 1906 | Box 304 |
| Jameson, Kate | 1915 | Box 522 | | Jenifer, George D. | 1917 | Box 574 |
| Jameson, Mary W. | 1875 | Box 58 | | Jenifer, Hermione | 1918 | Box 601 |
| Jameson, May Mildred | 1892 | Box 132 | | Jenifer, Thomas | 1878 | Box 66 |
| Jameson, Richard | 1824 | Box 8 | | Jenkins, Ada M. | 1915 | Box 522 |
| Jamieson, Bettie W. | 1912 | Box 446 | | Jenkins, Ann | 1857 | Box 25 |
| Jamison, Catharine C. | 1907 | Box 325 | | Jenkins, Calphernia | 1914 | Box 494 |
| Janey, Sarah | 1920 | Box 665 | | Jenkins, Elizabeth S. | 1913 | Box 471 |
| Janin, Edward | 1891 | Box 125 | | Jenkins, Fanny | 1847 | Box 19 |
| Janney, Anna | 1887 | Box 103 | | Jenkins, Frances L. Bogue | 1903 | Box 246 |
| Janney, Bernard T. | 1916 | Box 548 | | Jenkins, Harriet | 1842 | Box 16 |
| Janney, Edgar | 1898 | Box 177 | | Jenkins, Jesse | 1857 | Box 25 |
| Janney, Emma | 1919 | Box 631 | | Jenkins, John Zadock | 1896 | Box 162 |
| Janney, Henry | 1896 | Box 162 | | Jenkins, Joseph T. | 1891 | Box 125 |
| Jannus, Antony Habersak | 1916 | Box 548 | | Jenkins, Mary D. | 1899 | Box 184 |
| Jannus, Emeline C. Weightman | 1904 | Box 266 | | Jenkins, Mary Elizabeth | 1904 | Box 266 |
| Janus, Anthony H. | 1888 | Box 108 | | Jenkins, Robert R. | 1884 | Box 87 |
| Jaqua, Allen | 1906 | Box 304 | | Jenkins, Sarah E. | 1843 | Box 16 |
| Jaquette, Isaac G. | 1907 | Box 325 | | Jenkins, Sarah E. | 1918 | Box 601 |

| | | | | | | |
|---|---|---|---|---|---|---|
| Jenkins, Thomas | 1807 | Box 2 | | Johns, William B. | 1895 | Box 154 |
| Jenkins, Thomas | 1836 | Box 13 | | Johnson, A. Geary | 1920 | Box 665 |
| Jenkins, Thomas | 1886 | Box 97 | | Johnson, Albanus Stephenson | 1914 | Box 494 |
| Jenkins, Thorton Alexander | 1893 | Box 139 | | Johnson, Albert E. H. | 1909 | Box 371 |
| Jenkins, William Fairbanks | 1919 | Box 631 | | Johnson, Albert Eugene | 1912 | Box 446 |
| Jenks, Winfield S. | 1914 | Box 494 | | Johnson, Alexander H. | 1912 | Box 446 |
| Jennifer, Robert | 1870 | Box 43 | | Johnson, Allen S. | 1920 | Box 665 |
| Jennings, Hattie M. | 1898 | Box 177 | | Johnson, Alphus Franklin | 1920 | Box 665 |
| Jennings, Helen Augusta | 1916 | Box 548 | | Johnson, Amelia | 1919 | Box 632 |
| Jennings, James Hennen | 1920 | Box 665 | | Johnson, America Virginia | 1914 | Box 494 |
| Jennings, Katharine Sharpe | 1911 | Box 421 | | Johnson, Andrew Gill | 1894 | Box 146 |
| Jennings, M. H. | 1920 | Box 665 | | Johnson, Annie E. | 1905 | Box 285 |
| Jennings, Paul | 1874 | Box 54 | | Johnson, Annie E. | 1914 | Box 494 |
| Jennings, Sallie S. | 1916 | Box 548 | | Johnson, Annie M. | 1915 | Box 522 |
| Jennings, Sarah E. | 1907 | Box 325 | | Johnson, Asbury R. | 1905 | Box 285 |
| Jensen, Elenore L. | 1885 | Box 92 | | Johnson, Calvin R. | 1879 | Box 69 |
| Jenvey, George Kirton | 1919 | Box 631 | | Johnson, Caroline | 1893 | Box 139 |
| Jerome, Charles W. | 1918 | Box 601 | | Johnson, Catharine | 1884 | Box 87 |
| Jessup, Alfred D. | 1882 | Box 79 | | Johnson, Catherine M. | 1874 | Box 54 |
| Jester, John M. | 1913 | Box 471 | | Johnson, Cecelia A. | 1908 | Box 348 |
| Jesunofsky, Jacob | 1872 | Box 47 | | Johnson, Cecile D. de Lagarde | 1918 | Box 601 |
| Jesunofsky, Mary | 1890 | Box 119 | | Johnson, Charles | 1889 | Box 114 |
| Jesup, Thomas S. | 1860 | Box 28 | | Johnson, Charles A. | 1905 | Box 285 |
| Jett, Martha A. | 1915 | Box 522 | | Johnson, Charles A. | 1894 | Box 147 |
| Jett, Sarah | 1904 | Box 266 | | Johnson, Charles A. | 1914 | Box 494 |
| Jewell, Claudius B. | 1912 | Box 446 | | Johnson, Chauncey R. | 1856 | Box 25 |
| Jewell, Emma | 1899 | Box 184 | | Johnson, Clara | 1892 | Box 132 |
| Jewell, Eugene P. | 1917 | Box 574 | | Johnson, Clara A. D. | 1915 | Box 522 |
| Jewell, Jennie V. | 1919 | Box 631 | | Johnson, Cornelius | 1893 | Box 129 |
| Jewell, Jeremiah | 1901 | Box 209 | | Johnson, Cornelius W. | 1913 | Box 471 |
| Jewell, Louis W. | 1890 | Box 119 | | Johnson, Daniel | 1912 | Box 446 |
| Jewell, Thomas | 1893 | Box 139 | | Johnson, Daniel T. | 1890 | Box 119 |
| Jewell, William | 1856 | Box 25 | | Johnson, David G. | 1881 | Box 75 |
| Jewett, Richard Dickinson | 1919 | Box 631 | | Johnson, David R. A. | 1915 | Box 522 |
| Jidt, John P. | 1882 | Box 79 | | Johnson, Dennis | 1916 | Box 548 |
| Jinkins, Sarah | 1862 | Box 30 | | Johnson, E. Kurtz | 1894 | Box 147 |
| Jirdinston, James A. N. | 1904 | Box 266 | | Johnson, Edward | 1897 | Box 170 |
| Joachim, Jacob H. | 1874 | Box 54 | | Johnson, Eliza C. | 1917 | Box 574 |
| Joachim, John J. F. | 1876 | Box 61 | | Johnson, Elizabeth A. | 1905 | Box 285 |
| Joachim, Louisa | 1875 | Box 58 | | Johnson, Ellen Platt | 1918 | Box 601 |
| Joachim, Louisa | 1883 | Box 83 | | Johnson, Emily | 1883 | Box 83 |
| Jochum, Sarah | 1917 | Box 574 | | Johnson, Emily | 1895 | Box 154 |
| Johannes, John George | 1904 | Box 266 | | Johnson, Eunice S. | 1920 | Box 665 |
| Johansen, Herman P. T. | 1903 | Box 246 | | Johnson, Fannie | 1907 | Box 326 |
| Johansen, Mary Ann | 1920 | Box 665 | | Johnson, Fanny Valeda M. | 1919 | Box 632 |
| John, Bayard | 1919 | Box 632 | | Johnson, Frances Oliver | 1906 | Box 304 |
| Johnes, Mary J. | 1887 | Box 103 | | Johnson, Frank Warren | 1910 | Box 394 |
| Johnes, Timothy S. | 1887 | Box 103 | | Johnson, Frederick | 1906 | Box 304 |
| Johns, Franck D. | 1912 | Box 446 | | Johnson, Frederick | 1913 | Box 471 |
| Johns, Henry T. | 1906 | Box 304 | | Johnson, George J. | 1902 | Box 228 |
| Johns, Leonora R. | 1908 | Box 348 | | Johnson, George Robert | 1898 | Box 177 |
| Johns, Mary P. | 1831 | Box 11 | | Johnson, Hattie A. | 1907 | Box 326 |

| | | | | | | |
|---|---|---|---|---|---|---|
| Johnson, Hellen | 1867 | Box 37 | Johnson, Martha H. | 1884 | Box 87 |
| Johnson, Henry | 1896 | Box 162 | Johnson, Martha T. | 1919 | Box 632 |
| Johnson, Henry | 1917 | Box 574 | Johnson, Martin | 1865 | Box 34 |
| Johnson, Henry L. E. | 1916 | Box 548 | Johnson, Mary | 1892 | Box 132 |
| Johnson, Horace | 1897 | Box 170 | Johnson, Mary A. | 1918 | Box 601 |
| Johnson, Illinois | 1902 | Box 228 | Johnson, Mary A. Bridges | 1906 | Box 304 |
| Johnson, Isaac | 1896 | Box 162 | Johnson, Mary Ann | 1887 | Box 103 |
| Johnson, Isabella | 1897 | Box 170 | Johnson, Mary Anna | 1900 | Box 195 |
| Johnson, J. Harrison | 1907 | Box 326 | Johnson, Mary Augusta | 1916 | Box 548 |
| Johnson, J. Orville | 1915 | Box 522 | Johnson, Mary Frances | 1916 | Box 548 |
| Johnson, James | 1890 | Box 119 | Johnson, Mary Jane | 1896 | Box 162 |
| Johnson, James | 1895 | Box 154 | Johnson, Mary T. | 1881 | Box 75 |
| Johnson, James Bowen | 1899 | Box 185 | Johnson, Matilda L. | 1874 | Box 54 |
| Johnson, James D. | 1869 | Box 41 | Johnson, Max M. | 1915 | Box 522 |
| Johnson, Jane F. | 1901 | Box 209 | Johnson, Moses | 1912 | Box 446 |
| Johnson, Jennie E. | 1919 | Box 632 | Johnson, Noble | 1883 | Box 83 |
| Johnson, Jerome Fletcher | 1913 | Box 471 | Johnson, Noble William | 1920 | Box 665 |
| Johnson, John | 1863 | Box 31 | Johnson, Philip C. | 1887 | Box 103 |
| Johnson, John (of Bryant) | 1877 | Box 64 | Johnson, Philo Benjamin | 1850 | Box 21 |
| Johnson, John | 1900 | Box 195 | Johnson, Polly | 1884 | Box 87 |
| Johnson, John | 1903 | Box 246 | Johnson, Rachel | 1862 | Box 30 |
| Johnson, John | 1905 | Box 285 | Johnson, Rachel | 1883 | Box 83 |
| Johnson, John B. | 1893 | Box 139 | Johnson, Rachel | 1910 | Box 395 |
| Johnson, John H. | 1912 | Box 446 | Johnson, Rebecca | 1852 | Box 21 |
| Johnson, John J. | 1891 | Box 125 | Johnson, Reuben W. | 1920 | Box 666 |
| Johnson, John J. | 1909 | Box 371 | Johnson, Richard | 1878 | Box 66 |
| Johnson, John Lewis | 1910 | Box 394 | Johnson, Robert | 1867 | Box 37 |
| Johnson, John M. | 1883 | Box 83 | Johnson, Robert William | 1910 | Box 395 |
| Johnson, John T. | 1913 | Box 471 | Johnson, Roger | 1890 | Box 119 |
| Johnson, Joseph | 1843 | Box 16 | Johnson, Rudolph | 1917 | Box 574 |
| Johnson, Joseph J. | 1903 | Box 246 | Johnson, Ruth | 1899 | Box 185 |
| Johnson, Joseph L. | 1888 | Box 108 | Johnson, Samuel B. | 1915 | Box 522 |
| Johnson, Joseph R. | 1906 | Box 304 | Johnson, Sarah | 1913 | Box 471 |
| Johnson, Joseph R. | 1905 | Box 285 | Johnson, Sarah C. | 1885 | Box 92 |
| Johnson, Joseph S. | 1918 | Box 601 | Johnson, Sarah G. | 1909 | Box 371 |
| Johnson, Josephine | 1887 | Box 103 | Johnson, Sarah J. | 1898 | Box 177 |
| Johnson, Josephine R. | 1911 | Box 421 | Johnson, Simpson | 1914 | Box 495 |
| Johnson, Joshua | 1910 | Box 395 | Johnson, Stanley | 1906 | Box 304 |
| Johnson, Joshua | 1803 | Box 1 | Johnson, Susan B. | 1909 | Box 371 |
| Johnson, Laura Zea | 1907 | Box 326 | Johnson, Susan J. | 1910 | Box 395 |
| Johnson, Leathia | 1916 | Box 548 | Johnson, Sylvanus Elihu | 1908 | Box 348 |
| Johnson, Leonard | 1879 | Box 69 | Johnson, Theodore H. | 1917 | Box 574 |
| Johnson, Letitia Henson | 1914 | Box 495 | Johnson, Thomas | 1819 | Box 6 |
| Johnson, Lewis | 1872 | Box 47 | Johnson, Thomas | 1867 | Box 37 |
| Johnson, Lewis Thomas | 1911 | Box 421 | Johnson, Thomas | 1895 | Box 154 |
| Johnson, Louis E. | 1905 | Box 285 | Johnson, Thomas | 1896 | Box 162 |
| Johnson, Louisa | 1907 | Box 326 | Johnson, Thomas Baker | 1843 | Box 16 |
| Johnson, Lucretia E. | 1914 | Box 495 | Johnson, Tobias C. | 1891 | Box 125 |
| Johnson, Margaret A. | 1920 | Box 665 | Johnson, Townley | 1870 | Box 43 |
| Johnson, Maria F. | 1891 | Box 125 | Johnson, V. Baldwin | 1906 | Box 304 |
| Johnson, Martha | 1909 | Box 371 | Johnson, Walter T. | 1889 | Box 114 |
| Johnson, Martha Ann | 1899 | Box 185 | Johnson, Washington | 1901 | Box 209 |

| | | | | | | |
|---|---|---|---|---|---|---|
| Johnson, William | 1874 | Box 54 | Jones, David T. | 1894 | Box 147 |
| Johnson, William | 1881 | Box 75 | Jones, Deloss | 1906 | Box 304 |
| Johnson, William | 1896 | Box 162 | Jones, Edmonia Page | 1896 | Box 162 |
| Johnson, William | 1909 | Box 371 | Jones, Edward | 1829 | Box 10 |
| Johnson, William A. | 1903 | Box 246 | Jones, Edward P. | 1918 | Box 601 |
| Johnson, William Columbus | 1910 | Box 395 | Jones, Edward S. | 1907 | Box 326 |
| Johnson, William F. | 1902 | Box 228 | Jones, Edward William Jr. | 1913 | Box 471 |
| Johnson, William F. | 1908 | Box 348 | Jones, Edwin D. | 1910 | Box 395 |
| Johnson, William H. | 1885 | Box 92 | Jones, Edwin T. | 1914 | Box 495 |
| Johnson, William H. | 1912 | Box 446 | Jones, Eleanor Marguerite | 1919 | Box 632 |
| Johnson, William H. | 1915 | Box 522 | Jones, Eliza A. | 1894 | Box 147 |
| Johnson, William Morgan | 1919 | Box 632 | Jones, Elizabeth | 1885 | Box 92 |
| Johnston, Belle A. | 1910 | Box 395 | Jones, Elizabeth | 1890 | Box 119 |
| Johnston, Belle Jones | 1920 | Box 666 | Jones, Elizabeth Hartwell | 1899 | Box 185 |
| Johnston, Bernard H. | 1905 | Box 285 | Jones, Elizabeth Jane | 1900 | Box 195 |
| Johnston, Braxton B. | 1900 | Box 195 | Jones, Elizabeth M. | 1885 | Box 92 |
| Johnston, Charles E. | 1920 | Box 666 | Jones, Ellen | 1879 | Box 69 |
| Johnston, Charles H. | 1920 | Box 666 | Jones, Emily F. | 1871 | Box 45 |
| Johnston, Eleanor M. | 1905 | Box 285 | Jones, Fanny Lee | 1912 | Box 446 |
| Johnston, Emma T. | 1913 | Box 471 | Jones, Frances | 1908 | Box 348 |
| Johnston, Harriet Lane | 1903 | Box 246 | Jones, Frances Jane | 1892 | Box 132 |
| Johnston, Horace S. | 1888 | Box 108 | Jones, Frank H. | 1919 | Box 632 |
| Johnston, Isabella | 1897 | Box 170 | Jones, Fred C. | 1914 | Box 495 |
| Johnston, James M. | 1920 | Box 666 | Jones, Frederica Burckle | 1917 | Box 574 |
| Johnston, John | 1857 | Box 25 | Jones, Frederick W. | 1891 | Box 125 |
| Johnston, John G. | 1832 | Box 11 | Jones, George | 1884 | Box 87 |
| Johnston, Joseph E. | 1891 | Box 125 | Jones, George A. | 1908 | Box 348 |
| Johnston, Lydia McL. | 1887 | Box 103 | Jones, George F. | 1911 | Box 421 |
| Johnston, Mary M. | 1909 | Box 371 | Jones, George H. | 1857 | Box 25 |
| Johnston, Mildred | 1862 | Box 30 | Jones, George T. | 1890 | Box 119 |
| Johnston, Sarah Jane | 1896 | Box 162 | Jones, George W. | 1848 | Box 19 |
| Johnston, Thomas Jones | 1856 | Box 25 | Jones, George W. | 1920 | Box 666 |
| Johnston, William | 1910 | Box 395 | Jones, Gertrude | 1889 | Box 114 |
| Joice, Mary | 1846 | Box 18 | Jones, Gustavus | 1900 | Box 195 |
| Joice, William | 1900 | Box 195 | Jones, Hannah L. | 1916 | Box 548 |
| Jolly, Christiana A. | 1880 | Box 72 | Jones, Henry | 1890 | Box 119 |
| Jolly, Lydia | 1890 | Box 119 | Jones, Henry L. | 1916 | Box 548 |
| Jones, Alice C. | 1918 | Box 601 | Jones, Isaac B. | 1916 | Box 549 |
| Jones, Ann | 1888 | Box 108 | Jones, J. Edward | 1890 | Box 119 |
| Jones, Caroline E. | 1895 | Box 154 | Jones, Jacob Guest | 1898 | Box 177 |
| Jones, Caroline Eltinge | 1920 | Box 666 | Jones, Jacobus S. | 1917 | Box 574 |
| Jones, Caroline V. | 1917 | Box 574 | Jones, James Henry | 1915 | Box 522 |
| Jones, Catherine M. B. | 1912 | Box 446 | Jones, James I. | 1895 | Box 154 |
| Jones, Chalkley L. | 1898 | Box 177 | Jones, James Richard | 1910 | Box 395 |
| Jones, Charles Augustine | 1902 | Box 228 | Jones, James T. | 1920 | Box 666 |
| Jones, Charles Coates | 1911 | Box 421 | Jones, Jane Ann | 1877 | Box 64 |
| Jones, Charles E. | 1919 | Box 632 | Jones, Jeanie L. | 1920 | Box 666 |
| Jones, Charles H. | 1903 | Box 247 | Jones, Joel W. | 1883 | Box 83 |
| Jones, Charles M. | 1916 | Box 548 | Jones, John | 1813 | Box 4 |
| Jones, Clementia | 1901 | Box 209 | Jones, John | 1865 | Box 34 |
| Jones, David | 1850 | Box 21 | Jones, John | 1890 | Box 119 |
| Jones, David | 1890 | Box 119 | Jones, John Edward | 1918 | Box 601 |

| | | | | | | |
|---|---|---|---|---|---|---|
| Jones, John Godfrey | 1828 | Box 9 | Jones, William | 1902 | Box 228 |
| Jones, John Paul | 1907 | Box 326 | Jones, William Hemphill | 1880 | Box 72 |
| Jones, John S. | 1885 | Box 92 | Jones, William Marvin | 1919 | Box 632 |
| Jones, John W. | 1887 | Box 103 | Jones, William Thomas | 1884 | Box 87 |
| Jones, Julia Ann | 1899 | Box 185 | Jones, William Willis | 1920 | Box 666 |
| Jones, Julia G. | 1920 | Box 666 | Jones, Winfield S. | 1906 | Box 304 |
| Jones, Leon Teresa | 1894 | Box 147 | Jordan, Charles M. | 1899 | Box 185 |
| Jones, Letitia C. | 1869 | Box 41 | Jordan, Conrad | 1910 | Box 395 |
| Jones, Lettie Lee | 1916 | Box 549 | Jordan, Daniel | 1909 | Box 371 |
| Jones, Levi | 1896 | Box 162 | Jordan, Eliza | 1895 | Box 154 |
| Jones, Levin | 1856 | Box 25 | Jordan, Hattie E. | 1918 | Box 601 |
| Jones, Lewis | 1910 | Box 395 | Jordan, Hattie Eliza | 1919 | Box 632 |
| Jones, Lizzie | 1908 | Box 348 | Jordan, Henry C. | 1905 | Box 285 |
| Jones, Lottie M. | 1919 | Box 632 | Jordan, James Warren | 1917 | Box 574 |
| Jones, Louisa | 1840 | Box 15 | Jordan, Martha Althea | 1872 | Box 47 |
| Jones, Lucippia A. | 1905 | Box 285 | Jordan, Patrick | 1886 | Box 97 |
| Jones, Margaret Jane | 1905 | Box 285 | Jordan, Richard E. | 1918 | Box 601 |
| Jones, Maria | 1837 | Box 13 | Jordan, Robert H. | 1905 | Box 285 |
| Jones, Martha C. | 1917 | Box 574 | Jordan, Robert R. | 1918 | Box 601 |
| Jones, Martha E. | 1916 | Box 549 | Jordan, Robert Stewart | 1908 | Box 348 |
| Jones, Mary A. | 1908 | Box 348 | Jordon, Henry | 1896 | Box 162 |
| Jones, Mary A. | 1913 | Box 471 | Jorgensen, Edgar W. A. | 1891 | Box 126 |
| Jones, Mary A. | 1918 | Box 601 | Jorrin, Margarita | 1898 | Box 177 |
| Jones, Mary Ann Mason | 1873 | Box 51 | Jorry, Joseph | 1901 | Box 209 |
| Jones, Mary B. | 1891 | Box 126 | José, Jacob | 1916 | Box 549 |
| Jones, Mary H. | 1877 | Box 64 | Joseph, Isaac | 1837 | Box 13 |
| Jones, Mary Jane | 1895 | Box 154 | Joseph, Lizzie | 1896 | Box 162 |
| Jones, Mary T. | 1917 | Box 574 | Joseph, Richard | 1883 | Box 83 |
| Jones, Melville Emory | 1914 | Box 495 | Jost, Benedict | 1869 | Box 41 |
| Jones, Moses | 1905 | Box 285 | Jost, Conrad | 1897 | Box 170 |
| Jones, Nelson | 1918 | Box 601 | Jouvenal, Marie Margaretha | 1911 | Box 421 |
| Jones, Philip | 1892 | Box 133 | Jouvenal, Susanna | 1880 | Box 72 |
| Jones, Rachel L. | 1899 | Box 185 | Joy, Caroline Elizabeth | 1900 | Box 196 |
| Jones, Richard | 1862 | Box 30 | Joy, James | 1919 | Box 632 |
| Jones, Richard Isaac | 1848 | Box 19 | Joy, Jane E. | 1886 | Box 97 |
| Jones, Robert Charles | 1819 | Box 6 | Joyce, Andrew J. | 1882 | Box 79 |
| Jones, Robert L. | 1879 | Box 69 | Joyce, Ann | 1892 | Box 133 |
| Jones, Roger | 1889 | Box 114 | Joyce, Catharine M. | 1919 | Box 632 |
| Jones, Selwin (Selwyn) T. | 1894 | Box 147 | Joyce, Frances C. | 1918 | Box 601 |
| Jones, Singleton T. W. | 1891 | Box 126 | Joyce, George W. | 1895 | Box 154 |
| Jones, Sylvester F. | 1916 | Box 549 | Joyce, James W. | 1891 | Box 126 |
| Jones, Thomas G. | 1910 | Box 395 | Joyce, John A. | 1915 | Box 522 |
| Jones, Thomas J. | 1909 | Box 371 | Joyce, John J. | 1871 | Box 45 |
| Jones, Thomas O. | 1900 | Box 195 | Joyce, Katie M. | 1902 | Box 228 |
| Jones, Thomas P. | 1848 | Box 19 | Joyce, Lucy | 1884 | Box 87 |
| Jones, Thomas S. | 1863 | Box 31 | Joyce, Maurice | 1917 | Box 574 |
| Jones, Thomas W. | 1859 | Box 27 | Joyce, Susan | 1871 | Box 45 |
| Jones, Timothy | 1886 | Box 97 | Joyce, Thomas | 1849 | Box 20 |
| Jones, Violet | 1884 | Box 87 | Joyce, Thomas | 1902 | Box 228 |
| Jones, Walter | 1861 | Box 29 | Joynes, Louis G. | 1910 | Box 395 |
| Jones, William | 1867 | Box 37 | Judd, John G. | 1895 | Box 154 |
| Jones, William | 1882 | Box 79 | Judd, Sarah E. | 1898 | Box 177 |

| | | | | | |
|---|---|---|---|---|---|
| Judd, Theodore A. T. | 1918 | Box 601 | Kant, Gesine E. | 1893 | Box 139 |
| Judik, J. Henry | 1913 | Box 471 | Kappel, Frank | 1907 | Box 326 |
| Judson, Elnathan | 1829 | Box 10 | Kappeler, Alfred | 1887 | Box 103 |
| Juenemann, Barbara T. | 1904 | Box 266 | Kappler, Anton | 1892 | Box 133 |
| Juenemann, George | 1884 | Box 87 | Kappler, Gregor | 1886 | Box 97 |
| Juenemann, Jacob W. | 1904 | Box 266 | Kappler, Isabelle S. | 1912 | Box 446 |
| Juenemann, Julius E. | 1906 | Box 304 | Karr, Jacob | 1917 | Box 575 |
| Jullien, Caroline T. | 1915 | Box 522 | Karr, Julia | 1903 | Box 247 |
| Juneau, Margaret J. | 1919 | Box 632 | Karr, Margaret | 1887 | Box 103 |
| Junghans, Daniel | 1914 | Box 495 | Kaschka, Joseph A. | 1908 | Box 348 |
| Junhans, John M. | 1891 | Box 126 | Kasson, John A. | 1910 | Box 395 |
| Junken, Charles H. W. | 1893 | Box 139 | Kattlemann, Carl H. A. | 1913 | Box 471 |
| Junkin, George | 1902 | Box 228 | Katzenstein, Charles | 1909 | Box 371 |
| Just, Charles | 1873 | Box 51 | Kauffman, George | 1879 | Box 69 |
| Just, Stephen | 1880 | Box 72 | Kauffmann, Samuel Hay | 1906 | Box 304 |
| Justement, Louis | 1913 | Box 471 | Kauffmann, Sarah F. | 1900 | Box 196 |
| Kafka, Albert | 1910 | Box 395 | Kaufman, Caroline | 1887 | Box 103 |
| Kager, Isaiah | 1918 | Box 602 | Kaufman, Hanna | 1912 | Box 446 |
| Kahl, John George | 1906 | Box 304 | Kaufman, Marx | 1903 | Box 247 |
| Kahl, Sarah R. | 1911 | Box 421 | Kaufman, Niem | 1894 | Box 147 |
| Kahlert, August | 1915 | Box 523 | Kaufmann, Mathilda | 1907 | Box 326 |
| Kahlert, Elizabeth | 1911 | Box 421 | Kautzman, John V. | 1839 | Box 14 |
| Kahlert, Frederick Sr. | 1913 | Box 471 | Kavanaugh, Kate | 1918 | Box 602 |
| Kahlert, George Christopher | 1866 | Box 36 | Kavanaugh, Patrick | 1904 | Box 266 |
| Kahlert, Herman | 1913 | Box 471 | Kavrick, Rebecca | 1858 | Box 26 |
| Kahlert, Johanna | 1897 | Box 170 | Kay, Jacob S. | 1865 | Box 34 |
| Kain, Patrick | 1825 | Box 8 | Kayhoe, Matthias Elsworth | 1916 | Box 549 |
| Kaiser, Christine | 1907 | Box 326 | Kayser, Agnes | 1917 | Box 575 |
| Kaiser, Edward T. | 1909 | Box 371 | Kayser, John C. | 1874 | Box 54 |
| Kaiser, Elizabeth | 1895 | Box 154 | Keach, Eleanor W. | 1909 | Box 371 |
| Kaiser, Frederick J. | 1898 | Box 177 | Keadle, Wiseman G. | 1821 | Box 7 |
| Kaiser, Henry | 1882 | Box 79 | Keady, Daniel | 1887 | Box 103 |
| Kaiser, Henry | 1894 | Box 147 | Keady, John | 1916 | Box 549 |
| Kaiser, John | 1896 | Box 162 | Keady, Patrick | 1894 | Box 147 |
| Kaiser, John | 1903 | Box 247 | Keady, Thomas J. | 1899 | Box 185 |
| Kaiser, John L. | 1884 | Box 87 | Keahlor, Augustus | 1850 | Box 21 |
| Kaizer, John | 1872 | Box 47 | Kealey, Daniel E. | 1908 | Box 349 |
| Kalb, Isaac N. | 1892 | Box 133 | Kealey, Sarah A. | 1888 | Box 109 |
| Kalbfus, Thomas Bowman | 1920 | Box 666 | Kean, Bessie F. | 1903 | Box 247 |
| Kalk, Stanton F. | 1917 | Box 575 | Kean, Mary | 1917 | Box 575 |
| Kall, Isabel | 1895 | Box 154 | Kean, Thomas S. | 1916 | Box 549 |
| Kammerer, Frank W. | 1919 | Box 632 | Keane, Delia | 1904 | Box 267 |
| Kampfe, Frederick | 1915 | Box 523 | Keane, James | 1913 | Box 471 |
| Kandler, Hugh | 1889 | Box 83 | Keane, Maurice | 1920 | Box 666 |
| Kane, Bridget | 1914 | Box 495 | Keane, Patrick | 1903 | Box 247 |
| Kane, Daniel | 1912 | Box 446 | Keane, Thomas T. | 1904 | Box 267 |
| Kane, Dennis D. | 1884 | Box 87 | Keanes, John | 1909 | Box 371 |
| Kane, John | 1919 | Box 632 | Kearney, Blanche | 1910 | Box 395 |
| Kane, Julia | 1908 | Box 348 | Kearney, James | 1862 | Box 30 |
| Kane, Stephen | 1906 | Box 304 | Kearney, Katherine | 1894 | Box 147 |
| Kanode, Albert H. | 1918 | Box 602 | Kearney, Luke | 1917 | Box 575 |
| Kanouse, Helen M. | 1895 | Box 154 | Kearny, Thomas | 1897 | Box 170 |

| | | | | | | |
|---|---|---|---|---|---|---|
| Kearon, Robert | 1902 | Box 229 | | Keiningham, James L. | 1890 | Box 119 |
| Kearsley, Leslie Thomson | 1907 | Box 326 | | Keiser, Alice | 1901 | Box 209 |
| Keating, Bridget | 1891 | Box 126 | | Keiser, William Styne | 1913 | Box 471 |
| Keating, John T. | 1915 | Box 523 | | Keister, Richard | 1877 | Box 64 |
| Keating, Mary E. | 1908 | Box 349 | | Keith, Charles H. | 1918 | Box 602 |
| Keating, Michael | 1886 | Box 97 | | Keith, James | 1846 | Box 18 |
| Keating, Thomas | 1889 | Box 115 | | Keith, John L. | 1919 | Box 632 |
| Keck, Mary M. | 1917 | Box 575 | | Keith, Mary R. | 1915 | Box 523 |
| Kedglie, Ann | 1846 | Box 18 | | Keithley, John | 1883 | Box 83 |
| Kee, Susannah Shearman | 1889 | Box 115 | | Keleher, James | 1895 | Box 154 |
| Keefe, Blanche | 1919 | Box 632 | | Keleher, John W. | 1901 | Box 209 |
| Keefe, Jeremiah | 1887 | Box 103 | | Keliher, Ellen Ann | 1919 | Box 632 |
| Keefe, John | 1874 | Box 54 | | Keliher, James | 1902 | Box 229 |
| Keefe, John | 1883 | Box 83 | | Keliher, Johanna | 1880 | Box 72 |
| Keefe, John P. | 1890 | Box 119 | | Keliher, Mary | 1918 | Box 602 |
| Keefe, Theresa | 1915 | Box 523 | | Keliher, Thomas | 1902 | Box 229 |
| Keefer, Charles F. | 1914 | Box 495 | | Keller, Benjamin H. | 1888 | Box 109 |
| Keegan, Michael | 1913 | Box 471 | | Keller, Charles H. | 1902 | Box 229 |
| Keegin, William C. | 1912 | Box 446 | | Keller, Christine Barbara | 1871 | Box 45 |
| Keehn, Henry | 1917 | Box 575 | | Keller, Elizabeth | 1844 | Box 17 |
| Keeler, Anna | 1901 | Box 209 | | Keller, Frederick | 1839 | Box 14 |
| Keeler, Eben | 1873 | Box 51 | | Keller, Henrietta C. | 1900 | Box 196 |
| Keeley, Emma J. Rawlings | 1920 | Box 666 | | Keller, Jonas P. | 1871 | Box 45 |
| Keely, Bridget | 1894 | Box 147 | | Keller, Michael | 1854 | Box 23 |
| Keely, Michael | 1894 | Box 147 | | Kelley, Andrew W. | 1919 | Box 632 |
| Keen, Edwin S. | 1919 | Box 632 | | Kelley, Lizzie F. | 1917 | Box 575 |
| Keen, Ellen W. | 1904 | Box 267 | | Kelley, Mary J. | 1915 | Box 523 |
| Keen, George T. | 1909 | Box 371 | | Kelley, Peter | 1903 | Box 247 |
| Keenan, Charles | 1867 | Box 37 | | Kelley, Sarah C. | 1909 | Box 371 |
| Keenan, James | 1882 | Box 79 | | Kelley, Thomas | 1892 | Box 133 |
| Keenan, James F. | 1905 | Box 285 | | Kellog, Julia | 1897 | Box 170 |
| Keenan, John H. | 1894 | Box 147 | | Kellogg, Ansel N. | 1890 | Box 119 |
| Keene, Herbert Newton | 1919 | Box 632 | | Kellogg, Charles H. | 1919 | Box 632 |
| Keene, J. Everett | 1918 | Box 602 | | Kellogg, Edward B. | 1900 | Box 196 |
| Keene, James | 1908 | Box 349 | | Kellogg, Frances B. | 1919 | Box 632 |
| Keene, Joseph R. | 1920 | Box 666 | | Kellogg, Lucy W. | 1913 | Box 471 |
| Keep, Frederic A. | 1911 | Box 421 | | Kellogg, Mary E. | 1918 | Box 602 |
| Keese, Anna L. | 1917 | Box 575 | | Kellogg, Mary E. | 1911 | Box 421 |
| Keese, Augustus | 1902 | Box 229 | | Kellogg, Sanford Cobb | 1904 | Box 267 |
| Keese, Mary Catharine | 1916 | Box 549 | | Kellogg, William Pitt | 1918 | Box 602 |
| Keese, Mary F. | 1918 | Box 602 | | Kellum, Henry | 1898 | Box 177 |
| Keese, Samuel | 1901 | Box 209 | | Kellum, William C. | 1920 | Box 666 |
| Keese, Sophia Bertha | 1888 | Box 109 | | Kelly, Alice | 1909 | Box 371 |
| Keetch, Cloetilda | 1814 | Box 4 | | Kelly, Belle W. | 1917 | Box 575 |
| Kehl, John V. | 1890 | Box 119 | | Kelly, Bernard | 1846 | Box 18 |
| Kehl, Margaret C. | 1912 | Box 446 | | Kelly, Catherine | 1898 | Box 177 |
| Kehoe, Alice Slater | 1917 | Box 575 | | Kelly, Catherine | 1914 | Box 495 |
| Kehoe, William Joseph | 1918 | Box 602 | | Kelly, Columbia | 1892 | Box 133 |
| Kehrle, Albert | 1901 | Box 209 | | Kelly, Daniel James | 1920 | Box 666 |
| Keilholtz, William H. | 1900 | Box 196 | | Kelly, Edith Ray | 1920 | Box 666 |
| Keim, Morris | 1905 | Box 285 | | Kelly, Eliza | 1893 | Box 139 |
| Keiner, Christian | 1919 | Box 632 | | Kelly, Ella G. | 1913 | Box 471 |

| | | | | | | |
|---|---|---|---|---|---|---|
| Kelly, George | 1916 | Box 549 | Kengla, Jacob | 1848 | Box 19 |
| Kelly, Ida B. | 1911 | Box 421 | Kengla, Jacob H. | 1905 | Box 285 |
| Kelly, James | 1880 | Box 72 | Kengla, Lewis C. | 1909 | Box 371 |
| Kelly, Jane | 1875 | Box 58 | Kengla, Mary J. | 1914 | Box 495 |
| Kelly, Jane E. W. | 1883 | Box 83 | Kengla, Susan | 1888 | Box 109 |
| Kelly, Johanna | 1909 | Box 371 | Keniston, Ellen W. | 1920 | Box 666 |
| Kelly, John | 1912 | Box 446 | Kennard, Thomas A. | 1875 | Box 58 |
| Kelly, John F. | 1906 | Box 304 | Kennedy, Agnes | 1919 | Box 632 |
| Kelly, Julia A. | 1866 | Box 36 | Kennedy, Anna Felter | 1919 | Box 632 |
| Kelly, Kate | 1915 | Box 523 | Kennedy, Bridget | 1905 | Box 285 |
| Kelly, Mary L. | 1918 | Box 602 | Kennedy, Catharine M. | 1897 | Box 170 |
| Kelly, Michael | 1881 | Box 75 | Kennedy, Crammond | 1918 | Box 602 |
| Kelly, Richard S. | 1909 | Box 371 | Kennedy, Elizabeth A. | 1919 | Box 632 |
| Kelly, Samuel L. | 1905 | Box 285 | Kennedy, Elizabeth C. | 1913 | Box 471 |
| Kelly, Susannah F. | 1904 | Box 267 | Kennedy, George E. | 1900 | Box 196 |
| Kelly, Thomas | 1908 | Box 349 | Kennedy, Georgina | 1915 | Box 523 |
| Kelly, Thomas J. | 1917 | Box 575 | Kennedy, Harvey | 1890 | Box 119 |
| Kelly, William | 1898 | Box 177 | Kennedy, James A. | 1880 | Box 72 |
| Kelly, William | 1908 | Box 349 | Kennedy, James C. | 1873 | Box 51 |
| Kelly, Winifred | 1900 | Box 196 | Kennedy, Jane E. | 1902 | Box 229 |
| Kelsey, Edith L. | 1919 | Box 632 | Kennedy, John | 1882 | Box 79 |
| Kelsey, Mabel J. | 1904 | Box 267 | Kennedy, John C. | 1881 | Box 75 |
| Kelsey, Sherman S. | 1902 | Box 229 | Kennedy, Joseph C. G. | 1902 | Box 229 |
| Kelton, John C. | 1893 | Box 139 | Kennedy, Lauren O. | 1892 | Box 133 |
| Kemball, Marshall G. | 1904 | Box 267 | Kennedy, Margaret | 1887 | Box 103 |
| Kembel, Charles | 1881 | Box 75 | Kennedy, Margaret | 1897 | Box 170 |
| Kembel, Julia C. | 1873 | Box 51 | Kennedy, Marrianne A. B. | 1902 | Box 229 |
| Kemon, Solon C. | 1916 | Box 549 | Kennedy, Martin | 1908 | Box 349 |
| Kemp, Annie | 1917 | Box 575 | Kennedy, Mary | 1862 | Box 30 |
| Kemp, Christian | 1908 | Box 349 | Kennedy, Mary | 1905 | Box 285 |
| Kemp, Ezra L. | 1907 | Box 326 | Kennedy, Mary J. | 1908 | Box 349 |
| Kemp, Henry | 1908 | Box 349 | Kennedy, Thomas | 1901 | Box 209 |
| Kemp, Indiana | 1919 | Box 632 | Kennedy, William L. | 1894 | Box 147 |
| Kemp, Louisa R. | 1893 | Box 139 | Kennelly, Bridget M. | 1920 | Box 666 |
| Kemp, Ludwick | 1898 | Box 177 | Kenner, George D | 1890 | Box 119 |
| Kemp, Payton B. | 1912 | Box 446 | Kenner, Henry G. | 1894 | Box 147 |
| Kemp, William | 1909 | Box 371 | Kenney, Thomas | 1873 | Box 51 |
| Kenaday, Alexander McConnell | 1897 | Box 170 | Kenney, William | 1898 | Box 177 |
| Kendall, Amos | 1869 | Box 41 | Kennon, Beverley | 1844 | Box 17 |
| Kendall, Elizabeth Bright | 1889 | Box 115 | Kennon, Beverley | 1891 | Box 126 |
| Kendall, Henry Myron | 1912 | Box 446 | Kennon, Britannia W. | 1911 | Box 421 |
| Kendall, John | 1861 | Box 29 | Kenny, Elizabeth Behrens | 1905 | Box 285 |
| Kendall, John Blake | 1909 | Box 371 | Kenny, James J. | 1887 | Box 103 |
| Kendall, John E. | 1885 | Box 92 | Kenny, John | 1895 | Box 154 |
| Kendall, Samuel | 1840 | Box 15 | Kenny, Joseph E. | 1900 | Box 196 |
| Kendrick, Ann S. | 1875 | Box 58 | Kenny, Margaret | 1918 | Box 602 |
| Kendrick, William J. | 1864 | Box 32 | Kenshaw, Sarah | 1894 | Box 147 |
| Kenealy, Johanna | 1899 | Box 185 | Kent, Alexander | 1909 | Box 371 |
| Kenealy, Mary E. | 1909 | Box 371 | Kent, Carrie E. | 1918 | Box 602 |
| Kenealy, William C. | 1897 | Box 170 | Keobel, Jacob | 1892 | Box 133 |
| Kengla, Emma | 1909 | Box 371 | Keough, Johanna | 1890 | Box 119 |
| Kengla, Henry | 1905 | Box 285 | Keppler, John G. | 1899 | Box 185 |

| | | | | | | |
|---|---|---|---|---|---|---|
| Kerby, Francis A. | 1905 | Box 285 | Keyser, Charles M. | 1870 | Box 43 |
| Kerby, John Baptist | 1828 | Box 9 | Keyser, Edward Sage | 1911 | Box 421 |
| Kerens, Richard C. | 1917 | Box 575 | Keyser, Nicholas | 1920 | Box 666 |
| Kerlin, Charles W. | 1908 | Box 349 | Keyser, Peter L. | 1916 | Box 549 |
| Kerman, John | 1913 | Box 471 | Keyworth, John | 1897 | Box 170 |
| Kern, Frank Wesley | 1916 | Box 549 | Keyworth, Laura J. | 1887 | Box 103 |
| Kern, Frederick S. | 1899 | Box 185 | Keyworth, Mary | 1874 | Box 54 |
| Kern, George | 1900 | Box 196 | Keyworth, William Robert | 1898 | Box 177 |
| Kern, George W. | 1915 | Box 523 | Kiarbolling, William | 1918 | Box 602 |
| Kern, Johanna | 1905 | Box 285 | Kibbey, Elizabeth M. | 1894 | Box 147 |
| Kern, Josiah Quincy | 1914 | Box 495 | Kibbey, John B. | 1862 | Box 30 |
| Kernahan, William | 1900 | Box 196 | Kibbey, Sarah A. | 1883 | Box 83 |
| Kernan, Bernard | 1904 | Box 267 | Kibble, Alexander | 1870 | Box 43 |
| Kernan, Daniel | 1904 | Box 267 | Kibble, Elizabeth | 1892 | Box 133 |
| Kernan, Edward O. | 1916 | Box 549 | Kibley, William B. | 1881 | Box 75 |
| Kerr, Anne | 1850 | Box 21 | Kickham, Jane E. | 1907 | Box 326 |
| Kerr, Caroline J. | 1907 | Box 326 | Kickham, William | 1892 | Box 133 |
| Kerr, Denis | 1890 | Box 119 | Kickky, Elizabeth | 1907 | Box 326 |
| Kerr, Eliza | 1902 | Box 229 | Kidd, Harry J. | 1915 | Box 523 |
| Kerr, Henrietta | 1863 | Box 31 | Kidd, William | 1915 | Box 523 |
| Kerr, Henry | 1916 | Box 549 | Kidder, Byron A. | 1883 | Box 83 |
| Kerr, James K. Sr. | 1912 | Box 446 | Kidder, Jerome H. | 1889 | Box 115 |
| Kerr, Lily D. | 1913 | Box 471 | Kidrick, Harriet | 1895 | Box 154 |
| Kerr, Maggie | 1920 | Box 666 | Kidwell, Elizabeth J. | 1846 | Box 18 |
| Kerr, Mary Anne | 1875 | Box 58 | Kidwell, Jeremiah Leonard | 1876 | Box 61 |
| Kerr, Robert E. | 1851 | Box 21 | Kidwell, Marion F. | 1916 | Box 549 |
| Kerr, Thomas W. | 1916 | Box 549 | Kiefer, Conrad | 1918 | Box 602 |
| Kerr, Virginia | 1919 | Box 632 | Kiefer, Margaretha | 1897 | Box 170 |
| Kerr, William W. S. | 1855 | Box 24 | Kiefer, Rosa | 1918 | Box 602 |
| Kerry, Honora | 1898 | Box 177 | Kiefer, William G. | 1884 | Box 87 |
| Kersey, Melvina Washington | 1912 | Box 447 | Kieffer, Samuel S. | 1895 | Box 154 |
| Kervand, Ann E. | 1868 | Box 39 | Kierman, Philip | 1893 | Box 139 |
| Kessler, John | 1865 | Box 34 | Kierman, Sarah F. C. | 1890 | Box 119 |
| Ketcham, Augusta A. | 1915 | Box 523 | Kiernan, Catherine E. | 1918 | Box 602 |
| Ketcham, Ellis M. | 1910 | Box 395 | Kiesecker, Annie | 1909 | Box 371 |
| Ketcham, John H. | 1907 | Box 326 | Kiesecker, Johanna | 1909 | Box 371 |
| Ketchen, Jesse W. | 1877 | Box 64 | Kiesel, Theodore Adam | 1910 | Box 395 |
| Kettenring, Peter | 1920 | Box 666 | Kight, Thomas M. | 1916 | Box 549 |
| Kettler, J. H. William | 1914 | Box 495 | Kiichli, Joseph | 1915 | Box 523 |
| Keuchen, Elizabeth | 1913 | Box 471 | Kilerlane, Michael J. | 1916 | Box 549 |
| Keugh, Jane | 1830 | Box 10 | Kilfoyle, Martin | 1895 | Box 154 |
| Key, Francis Scott | 1843 | Box 16 | Kilgore, Nellie | 1909 | Box 372 |
| Key, Gillis | 1920 | Box 666 | Killafoyle, Nancy | 1889 | Box 115 |
| Key, Henry | 1873 | Box 51 | Kille, Anne M. | 1910 | Box 395 |
| Key, John F. | 1904 | Box 267 | Killeen, Mary J. | 1905 | Box 285 |
| Key, John J. | 1887 | Box 103 | Killian, John | 1874 | Box 54 |
| Keyes, Charles W. | 1906 | Box 304 | Killian, John | 1907 | Box 326 |
| Keyes, Hannah M. | 1892 | Box 133 | Killian, John G. | 1883 | Box 83 |
| Keyne, Bridget | 1827 | Box 9 | Killian, Leonhardt | 1899 | Box 185 |
| Keyne, Matthias | 1819 | Box 6 | Killigan, Mary E. | 1908 | Box 349 |
| Keys, Daniel | 1909 | Box 371 | Killigan, Timothy | 1895 | Box 154 |
| Keys, John | 1919 | Box 632 | Killin, Edward | 1808 | Box 3 |

| | | | | | | |
|---|---|---|---|---|---|---|
| Kilmartin, Bernard | 1909 | Box 372 | King, Hiram I. | 1885 | Box 92 |
| Kilmartin, Bridget | 1909 | Box 372 | King, Horatio | 1897 | Box 170 |
| Kilp, Anthony Joseph | 1918 | Box 602 | King, James M. | 1887 | Box 103 |
| Kilp, Fanny | 1902 | Box 229 | King, Jessie F. | 1907 | Box 326 |
| Kilpatrick, Jane | 1910 | Box 395 | King, John H. | 1855 | Box 24 |
| Kimball, Eva E. | 1916 | Box 549 | King, John J. | 1907 | Box 326 |
| Kimball, Helen L. McLean | 1911 | Box 421 | King, John L. | 1910 | Box 395 |
| Kimball, Israel | 1891 | Box 126 | King, John T. | 1918 | Box 602 |
| Kimball, Ivory G. | 1916 | Box 549 | King, Joseph | 1841 | Box 15 |
| Kimball, Nellie F. Pumphrey | 1896 | Box 162 | King, Laura A. | 1906 | Box 304 |
| Kimball, Olive H. | 1910 | Box 395 | King, Lavenia H. | 1909 | Box 372 |
| Kimberly, Susan Virginia | 1919 | Box 633 | King, Lou Y. | 1910 | Box 396 |
| Kimmel, Annie | 1908 | Box 349 | King, Margaret | 1904 | Box 267 |
| Kimmel, Ira W. | 1902 | Box 229 | King, Margaret | 1912 | Box 447 |
| Kimmel, Louis | 1910 | Box 395 | King, Margaret | 1912 | Box 447 |
| Kimmell, Obediah | 1888 | Box 109 | King, Margaretta | 1822 | Box 7 |
| Kincheloe, John W. | 1913 | Box 471 | King, Mary Anna | 1857 | Box 25 |
| Kinchy, Paul | 1852 | Box 22 | King, Mary E. | 1910 | Box 396 |
| King, Anna J. | 1905 | Box 285 | King, Mildred M. | 1903 | Box 247 |
| King, Annie Maria | 1910 | Box 395 | King, Norman Landon | 1919 | Box 633 |
| King, Betsey | 1894 | Box 147 | King, Norval W. | 1910 | Box 396 |
| King, Borrows W. | 1915 | Box 523 | King, Richard F. | 1899 | Box 185 |
| King, Caroline | 1893 | Box 139 | King, Robert | 1831 | Box 11 |
| King, Caroline | 1910 | Box 395 | King, Robert I. | 1908 | Box 349 |
| King, Catherine | 1891 | Box 126 | King, Samuel H. | 1920 | Box 666 |
| King, Charles | 1822 | Box 7 | King, Sarah | 1852 | Box 22 |
| King, Charles | 1885 | Box 92 | King, Sarah | 1917 | Box 575 |
| King, Charles | 1901 | Box 209 | King, Sarah A. | 1875 | Box 58 |
| King, Charles B. | 1862 | Box 30 | King, Sarah Elinor | 1886 | Box 97 |
| King, Charles J. | 1879 | Box 69 | King, Thomas | 1890 | Box 120 |
| King, Cora H. | 1911 | Box 421 | King, Thomas | 1901 | Box 209 |
| King, Cyrus S. | 1899 | Box 185 | King, Thomson M. | 1918 | Box 602 |
| King, Edward H. | 1879 | Box 69 | King, Virginia A. | 1907 | Box 326 |
| King, Eleanor F. | 1905 | Box 285 | King, Warrington C. | 1903 | Box 247 |
| King, Elizabeth | 1829 | Box 10 | King, William | 1854 | Box 23 |
| King, Elizabeth Ann | 1899 | Box 185 | King, William | 1888 | Box 109 |
| King, Elizabeth B. | 1907 | Box 326 | King, William | 1894 | Box 147 |
| King, Elizabeth M. | 1868 | Box 39 | King, William L. | 1913 | Box 471 |
| King, Endicott | 1909 | Box 372 | King, William R. | 1895 | Box 154 |
| King, Enoch | 1837 | Box 13 | King, Wilson | 1881 | Box 76 |
| King, Erin C. | 1887 | Box 103 | Kingman, Dan C. | 1916 | Box 549 |
| King, Florence | 1915 | Box 523 | Kingman, Eliab | 1883 | Box 83 |
| King, George | 1901 | Box 209 | Kingsford, Edward | 1859 | Box 27 |
| King, George | 1911 | Box 421 | Kinkead, Laura A. | 1872 | Box 47 |
| King, George W. | 1906 | Box 304 | Kinnahan, Peter | 1874 | Box 54 |
| King, Harry O. | 1895 | Box 154 | Kinnan, Arthur F. | 1913 | Box 471 |
| King, Helen W. | 1917 | Box 575 | Kinney, Addison D. | 1906 | Box 304 |
| King, Henrietta | 1890 | Box 120 | Kinney, Mary | 1901 | Box 209 |
| King, Henrietta L. | 1900 | Box 196 | Kinney, Theodore F. | 1913 | Box 472 |
| King, Henry | 1859 | Box 27 | Kinney, Thomas | 1905 | Box 285 |
| King, Henry | 1873 | Box 51 | Kinsell, James C. | 1905 | Box 285 |
| King, Henry | 1897 | Box 170 | Kinsey, Agnes J. | 1920 | Box 667 |

| | | | | | | |
|---|---|---|---|---|---|
| Kinsey, Edward J. | 1899 | Box 185 | Kleinhenz, Adam | 1892 | Box 133 |
| Kinsinger, William | 1911 | Box 421 | Klenk, George | 1901 | Box 209 |
| Kinsley, Benjamin | 1845 | Box 17 | Klimkowiz, Benvil H. L. | 1849 | Box 20 |
| Kinsley, Harriet Buchly | 1916 | Box 549 | Kline, Leila Cassel | 1919 | Box 633 |
| Kinsley, Samuel G. | 1904 | Box 267 | Kline, Mary Ayres | 1877 | Box 64 |
| Kinsley, William H. | 1895 | Box 154 | Kline, Peter | 1908 | Box 349 |
| Kinslow, Jennette | 1889 | Box 115 | Klinge, Henry | 1905 | Box 285 |
| Kinslow, Micheal | 1918 | Box 602 | Klingle, Joshua Pierce | 1892 | Box 133 |
| Kipp, Eden | 1913 | Box 472 | Klock, A. M. | 1918 | Box 602 |
| Kirby, Albert | 1912 | Box 447 | Kloman, Charles | 1879 | Box 69 |
| Kirby, Charles C. | 1893 | Box 139 | Kloman, Louisa | 1902 | Box 229 |
| Kirby, Eli E. | 1905 | Box 285 | Klopfer, Benjamin D. | 1899 | Box 185 |
| Kirby, Irene A. | 1917 | Box 575 | Klotz, Charles | 1893 | Box 139 |
| Kirby, Jennie | 1913 | Box 472 | Klotz, Louise | 1909 | Box 372 |
| Kirby, Samuel | 1883 | Box 83 | Klug, Brigitta | 1913 | Box 472 |
| Kirby, Thomas | 1873 | Box 51 | Klug, William B. | 1893 | Box 139 |
| Kirby, Thomas | 1917 | Box 575 | Knab, Frederick | 1919 | Box 633 |
| Kirby, William Wallace | 1905 | Box 285 | Knabe, Frederick | 1897 | Box 170 |
| Kirchner, J. K. Wilhelmina | 1906 | Box 304 | Knabe, Gustav Adolph | 1920 | Box 667 |
| Kirk, Charles | 1884 | Box 87 | Knapp, Ellen Theresa | 1890 | Box 120 |
| Kirk, Eleanor | 1836 | Box 13 | Knapp, Isabella M. | 1893 | Box 139 |
| Kirk, George E. | 1905 | Box 285 | Knapp, John J. | 1915 | Box 523 |
| Kirk, James B. | 1890 | Box 120 | Knapp, John R. | 1896 | Box 162 |
| Kirkland, Mary E. | 1920 | Box 667 | Knapp, Lafayette | 1910 | Box 396 |
| Kirkland, William | 1864 | Box 32 | Knapp, Mary E. | 1887 | Box 103 |
| Kirkley, Joseph W. | 1912 | Box 447 | Knapp, William Austin | 1910 | Box 396 |
| Kirkpatrick, Littleton | 1884 | Box 87 | Knatz, Conrad | 1904 | Box 267 |
| Kirkpatrick, Mary O'Connor | 1919 | Box 633 | Kneass, Camilla E. | 1891 | Box 126 |
| Kirkup, Amelia L. | 1913 | Box 472 | Kneessi, Emma Elizabeth | 1918 | Box 602 |
| Kirkus, Marion Weaver | 1910 | Box 396 | Kneessi, Kaspar | 1890 | Box 120 |
| Kirkwood, Jonathan | 1888 | Box 109 | Kneisley, Kate K. | 1916 | Box 550 |
| Kirkwood, Lola V. | 1919 | Box 633 | Kniffen, Louisa Jane | 1909 | Box 372 |
| Kirtley, William Bushrod | 1907 | Box 326 | Kniffin, Gilbert C. | 1917 | Box 575 |
| Kissner, Lorenz | 1920 | Box 667 | Knight, Ann C. | 1894 | Box 147 |
| Kitchen, Mary A. | 1894 | Box 147 | Knight, Anzolette H. | 1896 | Box 162 |
| Kitz, Francis | 1901 | Box 209 | Knight, Asa P. | 1900 | Box 196 |
| Klaine, Pierre | 1880 | Box 72 | Knight, Edward A. | 1862 | Box 30 |
| Kleiber, Henry C. | 1915 | Box 523 | Knight, George | 1866 | Box 36 |
| Kleiber, Rose | 1903 | Box 247 | Knight, Henry M. | 1910 | Box 396 |
| Kleiber, Rosina Margaret | 1888 | Box 109 | Knight, John | 1875 | Box 58 |
| Klein, Anna F. | 1899 | Box 185 | Knight, John G. D. | 1919 | Box 633 |
| Klein, Anne C. | 1916 | Box 549 | Knight, Lillie M. | 1912 | Box 447 |
| Klein, Bernhard | 1910 | Box 396 | Knight, Octavius | 1911 | Box 421 |
| Klein, Frederick | 1909 | Box 372 | Knightly, Robert | 1915 | Box 523 |
| Klein, Henry | 1882 | Box 79 | Knighton, Catherine T. | 1908 | Box 349 |
| Klein, Louis | 1919 | Box 633 | Knipe, Oscar A. | 1917 | Box 575 |
| Klein, Peter | 1910 | Box 396 | Knoblock, Frances E. | 1893 | Box 139 |
| Klein, Valentine | 1902 | Box 229 | Knode, Sallie | 1879 | Box 69 |
| Kleinberger, William | 1887 | Box 103 | Knoop, Frederick | 1911 | Box 421 |
| Kleindienst, Mary E. | 1916 | Box 549 | Knöppel, Daniel | 1886 | Box 97 |
| Kleinheim, August | 1911 | Box 421 | Knorr, Ernest R. | 1891 | Box 126 |
| Kleinhenn, Anna Elizabeth | 1916 | Box 550 | Knorr, Ernst August | 1917 | Box 575 |

| | | | | | | |
|---|---|---|---|---|---|---|
| Knorr, Mary | 1902 | Box 229 | | Konig, William | 1903 | Box 247 |
| Knorr, Rose | 1904 | Box 267 | | Koonce, Mary Anderson | 1911 | Box 422 |
| Knott, A. Leo | 1918 | Box 602 | | Koones, Albert L. | 1916 | Box 550 |
| Knott, George | 1858 | Box 26 | | Koones, Cecelia C. | 1869 | Box 41 |
| Knott, Ignatius McI. | 1893 | Box 139 | | Koones, Charles Montgomery | 1909 | Box 372 |
| Knott, Josias | 1884 | Box 87 | | Koones, Elizabeth S. K. B. | 1879 | Box 69 |
| Knott, Regina M. | 1912 | Box 447 | | Koones, Frederick | 1889 | Box 115 |
| Knott, Samuel | 1904 | Box 267 | | Koones, Inez B. | 1916 | Box 550 |
| Knott, William Jackson | 1905 | Box 285 | | Koons, Francis Mills | 1919 | Box 633 |
| Knowles, Ephraim | 1901 | Box 209 | | Koons, Henry | 1917 | Box 575 |
| Knowles, Henry | 1839 | Box 14 | | Koontz, Henry | 1886 | Box 97 |
| Knowles, Leonidas | 1885 | Box 92 | | Koontz, Irene E. | 1915 | Box 523 |
| Knowles, Thomas | 1822 | Box 7 | | Koontz, Jane | 1907 | Box 326 |
| Knowles, Thomas | 1895 | Box 154 | | Koontz, William | 1910 | Box 396 |
| Knowlton, John C. | 1888 | Box 109 | | Kopp, Franz W. | 1912 | Box 447 |
| Knox, Bartley | 1872 | Box 47 | | Korff, Herman G. | 1855 | Box 24 |
| Knox, George Vernon | 1911 | Box 421 | | Korman, Joseph W. | 1919 | Box 633 |
| Knox, George W. | 1892 | Box 133 | | Korte, Frederick | 1878 | Box 66 |
| Knox, Henry M. | 1904 | Box 267 | | Kosack, Eduard | 1920 | Box 667 |
| Knox, John J. | 1877 | Box 64 | | Kosciuszko, Thaddeus | 1847 | Box 19 |
| Knox, John O. | 1909 | Box 372 | | Koss, Frederick W. | 1889 | Box 115 |
| Knox, Lizzie E. | 1919 | Box 633 | | Koss, Herman | 1916 | Box 550 |
| Knox, Mary B. | 1903 | Box 247 | | Koss, Louise | 1907 | Box 326 |
| Knox, Mary C. | 1920 | Box 667 | | Kottman, Eberhardt | 1887 | Box 103 |
| Knox, Patrick | 1895 | Box 154 | | Kottmann, Barbara | 1910 | Box 396 |
| Knox, William S. | 1916 | Box 550 | | Kottmann, Henry | 1896 | Box 162 |
| Koblegard, Jacob | 1920 | Box 667 | | Kountze, Augustus | 1894 | Box 147 |
| Koch, August | 1883 | Box 83 | | Kowald, Adam | 1884 | Box 87 |
| Koch, Barbara | 1885 | Box 92 | | Kozel, George F. | 1907 | Box 327 |
| Koch, Gustav | 1911 | Box 421 | | Kraak, Henry | 1906 | Box 304 |
| Koch, Henry | 1907 | Box 326 | | Krackhardt, Minnie | 1915 | Box 523 |
| Koch, Josephine | 1907 | Box 326 | | Kraemer, Henry | 1909 | Box 372 |
| Koch, Maria Christine | 1885 | Box 92 | | Kraemer, John | 1890 | Box 120 |
| Koch, Valentine | 1916 | Box 550 | | Kraemer, Rose | 1910 | Box 396 |
| Koehler, George G. | 1884 | Box 87 | | Krafft, Sarah | 1912 | Box 447 |
| Koehler, John E. | 1888 | Box 109 | | Kraft, Christopher | 1879 | Box 69 |
| Koehler, Martha | 1904 | Box 267 | | Kraft, Conrad | 1911 | Box 422 |
| Koehler, Matilda | 1910 | Box 396 | | Kraft, John | 1901 | Box 209 |
| Koenicke, Charles J. | 1903 | Box 247 | | Kraft, John S. | 1890 | Box 120 |
| Koenig, George M. | 1899 | Box 185 | | Kraft, Maria | 1907 | Box 327 |
| Koenig, John M. | 1894 | Box 147 | | Kraft, Philip | 1872 | Box 47 |
| Koernicke, Sophie | 1913 | Box 472 | | Kraftholder, Ludwig | 1903 | Box 247 |
| Kohler, Elizabeth | 1908 | Box 349 | | Krake, Henry L. | 1905 | Box 285 |
| Kolar, John William | 1915 | Box 523 | | Kramer, Adam | 1885 | Box 92 |
| Kolb, Daniel | 1882 | Box 79 | | Kramer, Andrew | 1879 | Box 69 |
| Kolb, Edward W. | 1919 | Box 633 | | Kramer, August | 1918 | Box 602 |
| Kolb, George F. | 1909 | Box 372 | | Kramer, Bertha E. | 1896 | Box 162 |
| Kolb, John George | 1873 | Box 51 | | Kramer, James S. | 1912 | Box 447 |
| Kolipinski, Louis | 1915 | Box 523 | | Kramer, Margaret | 1918 | Box 602 |
| Kolkmeyer, Helen McK. | 1911 | Box 421 | | Kramer, Matilda | 1901 | Box 209 |
| Kondrup, Belinda | 1883 | Box 83 | | Kramer, Samuel | 1901 | Box 209 |
| Kondrup, John C. | 1875 | Box 58 | | Krantz, Mary Ward | 1919 | Box 633 |

| | | | | | | |
|---|---|---|---|---|---|
| Kratzenberg, Augusta | 1917 | Box 575 | Kyne, Mary | 1903 | Box 247 |
| Krauch, Elise | 1892 | Box 133 | Kyne, Patrick J. | 1904 | Box 267 |
| Krause, John | 1910 | Box 396 | La Garde, Louis A. | 1920 | Box 667 |
| Krause, Louis | 1896 | Box 162 | La Manna, Minerva Westafer | 1914 | Box 495 |
| Krause, Therese | 1905 | Box 285 | La Montagne, Kate | 1917 | Box 575 |
| Krauskopf, Charles G. | 1895 | Box 154 | Labbe, Francis C. | 1848 | Box 19 |
| Kreamer, George W. | 1915 | Box 523 | Lacavaro, Carmela | 1914 | Box 495 |
| Krebs, Charles G. | 1890 | Box 120 | Lacey, Anderson P. | 1895 | Box 155 |
| Kreis, Jacob | 1905 | Box 286 | Lacey, Blanche | 1899 | Box 185 |
| Kreis, John W. | 1917 | Box 575 | Lacey, Courtney A. | 1919 | Box 633 |
| Krentzlin, Julius A. | 1918 | Box 602 | Lacey, Margret M. | 1902 | Box 230 |
| Krepps, Marine T. | 1913 | Box 472 | Lacey, Robert A. | 1869 | Box 41 |
| Kretschmar, Emily S. | 1919 | Box 633 | Lachman, Martha Allen | 1884 | Box 87 |
| Kreuter, Johannetta | 1914 | Box 495 | Lackey, Elizabeth | 1917 | Box 575 |
| Kreuter, William | 1880 | Box 72 | Lackey, Milford F. | 1888 | Box 109 |
| Krey, Charles H. | 1908 | Box 349 | Lackey, Oscar H. | 1883 | Box 83 |
| Krichelt, Margaret | 1910 | Box 396 | Lacoppidan, Catherine A. | 1913 | Box 472 |
| Krieg, Catharine | 1898 | Box 177 | Lacy, Edward | 1868 | Box 39 |
| Krieg, George | 1887 | Box 103 | Lacy, Mary Louise | 1897 | Box 170 |
| Krieg, Gottfried | 1905 | Box 286 | Lacy, Minnie E. | 1901 | Box 210 |
| Kriner, George | 1915 | Box 523 | Lacy, Moses | 1903 | Box 247 |
| Kroehl, Sophia | 1916 | Box 550 | Ladd, Susan Lowell | 1889 | Box 115 |
| Kroell, Franz | 1906 | Box 304 | Ladde, Harriot V. | 1876 | Box 61 |
| Kroell, Frederick | 1879 | Box 69 | Ladson, Eliza E. Baxter | 1879 | Box 69 |
| Kroon, Elizabeth | 1920 | Box 667 | Lafayette, Emma | 1910 | Box 396 |
| Kropp, Barbara | 1917 | Box 575 | LaGrindeur, Romanus A. | 1920 | Box 667 |
| Kropp, Henry | 1907 | Box 327 | Laird, Anna Key | 1892 | Box 133 |
| Krouse, Ann | 1868 | Box 39 | Laird, Charles | 1910 | Box 396 |
| Krouse, T. J. | 1900 | Box 196 | Laird, James D. | 1897 | Box 170 |
| Krumke, Carl | 1914 | Box 495 | Laird, John | 1833 | Box 12 |
| Kryder, Fannie | 1917 | Box 575 | Laird, Margaret | 1858 | Box 26 |
| Kübel, Edward | 1896 | Box 162 | Laird, William | 1874 | Box 54 |
| Kughns, Catharine | 1849 | Box 20 | Laird, William (Jr.) | 1891 | Box 126 |
| Kuhblank, Emil | 1910 | Box 396 | Lake, Eliza J. | 1876 | Box 61 |
| Kuhn, Mary M. | 1903 | Box 247 | Lake, George W. | 1916 | Box 550 |
| Kuhns, William | 1823 | Box 7 | Lake, Mary B. | 1912 | Box 447 |
| Kuhns, William H. | 1878 | Box 66 | Lake, Moses | 1874 | Box 54 |
| Kullman, William Henry | 1912 | Box 447 | Lake, Samuel M. | 1912 | Box 447 |
| Kulp, John | 1876 | Box 61 | Lally, Sarah | 1911 | Box 422 |
| Kultz, Henry H. | 1888 | Box 109 | Lally, William | 1913 | Box 472 |
| Kumler, Jeremiah P. E. | 1909 | Box 372 | Lalor, Alice | 1846 | Box 18 |
| Kummell, Charles H. | 1897 | Box 170 | Lamar, Joseph Rucker | 1916 | Box 550 |
| Kuntz, Marie | 1919 | Box 633 | Lamasure, Edwin | 1910 | Box 396 |
| Künzig (Kinzig), Louisa | 1889 | Box 115 | Lamb, Annie | 1890 | Box 120 |
| Kurnitzki, Dora | 1901 | Box 209 | Lamb, Charles Miles | 1879 | Box 69 |
| Kurnitzki, Koppel | 1901 | Box 209 | Lamb, Francis Aubrey | 1896 | Box 163 |
| Kurtz, Elizabeth | 1882 | Box 79 | Lamb, J. Melvin | 1912 | Box 447 |
| Kurtz, Henry K. | 1920 | Box 667 | Lamb, Lizzie S. | 1895 | Box 155 |
| Kurtz, John D. | 1903 | Box 247 | Lambdin, Elizabeth Hines | 1896 | Box 163 |
| Kurtz, Louis Sr. | 1905 | Box 286 | Lambell, William | 1836 | Box 13 |
| Kurtz, Louise | 1896 | Box 162 | Lambert, Eugene F. | 1893 | Box 139 |
| Kurtz, Marie | 1919 | Box 633 | Lambert, Tallmadge A. | 1915 | Box 523 |

| | | | | | |
|---|---|---|---|---|---|
| Lamberton, Benjamin P. | 1912 | Box 447 | Lane, Mary R. | 1913 | Box 472 |
| Lamborn, William | 1906 | Box 304 | Lane, Samuel | 1822 | Box 7 |
| Lamm, Isaac L. | 1911 | Box 422 | Lane, Statius | 1881 | Box 76 |
| Lammond, Anna Brooke | 1901 | Box 210 | Lane, Susan M. | 1917 | Box 575 |
| Lamon, Sally L. | 1892 | Box 133 | Lane, Thomas F. | 1903 | Box 247 |
| Lamond, Angus | 1917 | Box 575 | Lane, Timothy T. | 1919 | Box 633 |
| Lamont, Eneas Neil | 1911 | Box 422 | Lane, William A. | 1882 | Box 79 |
| Lamparter, Pauline M. | 1920 | Box 667 | Lang, Eleanor R. | 1865 | Box 34 |
| Lampkin, Annie E. | 1901 | Box 210 | Lang, Emma A. M. | 1918 | Box 602 |
| Lamson, Harriet E. | 1903 | Box 247 | Lang, Ida M. | 1919 | Box 633 |
| Lamson, John R. | 1919 | Box 633 | Lang, John | 1869 | Box 41 |
| Lanahan, Bridget | 1915 | Box 524 | Langdale, John William | 1910 | Box 397 |
| Lanahan, Cornelius | 1886 | Box 98 | Lange, George W. | 1915 | Box 524 |
| Lanahan, Jeremiah | 1873 | Box 51 | Langer, Hugo A. | 1916 | Box 550 |
| Lanahan, John J. | 1912 | Box 447 | Langetti, Luciano | 1916 | Box 550 |
| Lanahan, Loretta M. | 1919 | Box 633 | Langford, Jane | 1886 | Box 98 |
| Lanahan, Mary | 1896 | Box 163 | Langford, John | 1879 | Box 69 |
| Lancaster, Basil | 1858 | Box 26 | Langhorne, John D. | 1916 | Box 550 |
| Lancaster, Catharine | 1825 | Box 8 | Langhorne, Mary Louise | 1906 | Box 305 |
| Lancaster, Catherine | 1876 | Box 61 | Langhorne, Mary Louise | 1909 | Box 372 |
| Lancaster, Catherine | 1897 | Box 170 | Langley, Hannah Elizabeth | 1920 | Box 667 |
| Lancaster, James M. | 1901 | Box 210 | Langley, Rose | 1911 | Box 422 |
| Lancaster, Katie | 1904 | Box 267 | Langley, Samuel Pierpont | 1906 | Box 305 |
| Lancaster, Mary Clare | 1845 | Box 17 | Langley, William B. | 1857 | Box 26 |
| Lander, Edward | 1907 | Box 327 | Langley, William H. | 1873 | Box 51 |
| Lander, Jean Margaret D. | 1903 | Box 247 | Langowska, Katherine | 1889 | Box 115 |
| Landgraf, Frederick | 1897 | Box 170 | Langran, Isobel | 1916 | Box 550 |
| Landic, Althea E. | 1893 | Box 139 | Langstaffe, John | 1890 | Box 120 |
| Landic, Isaac | 1891 | Box 126 | Langton, Rebecca Elizabeth | 1915 | Box 524 |
| Landon, Lyman D. | 1910 | Box 396 | Langtree, Mary R. | 1911 | Box 422 |
| Landrake, Sarah A. | 1913 | Box 472 | Langworthy, Emma F. | 1912 | Box 447 |
| Landrake, William H. | 1910 | Box 396 | Lanham, Elisha | 1822 | Box 7 |
| Landrick, John | 1849 | Box 20 | Lanham, Lenny | 1840 | Box 15 |
| Landrick, Louis | 1910 | Box 396 | Lanigan, Edward T. | 1914 | Box 495 |
| Landstreet, Caroline B. | 1914 | Box 495 | Lanigan, James M. | 1909 | Box 372 |
| Landvoigt, Edward | 1910 | Box 396 | Lanman, Charles | 1895 | Box 155 |
| Landvoigt, Elizabeth Arnold | 1912 | Box 447 | Lannan, Marcella | 1904 | Box 267 |
| Landvoigt, Lilly T. | 1916 | Box 550 | Lanning, Linda Caroline | 1903 | Box 247 |
| Lane, Charles H. | 1875 | Box 58 | Lansburgh, Gustave | 1911 | Box 422 |
| Lane, Charles M. | 1874 | Box 54 | Lansburgh, James | 1917 | Box 575 |
| Lane, Charles S. | 1911 | Box 422 | Lansdale, Anna E. | 1912 | Box 447 |
| Lane, Ellen D. | 1908 | Box 349 | Lansdale, Richard Henry | 1908 | Box 349 |
| Lane, Enoch Smith | 1805 | Box 1 | Lansdale, Thomas | 1805 | Box 1 |
| Lane, Helen B. | 1909 | Box 372 | Lanston, Beattie | 1908 | Box 349 |
| Lane, John | 1898 | Box 177 | Lanston, Tolbert | 1913 | Box 472 |
| Lane, John | 1907 | Box 327 | Lantz, Mary Lois Sherman | 1918 | Box 602 |
| Lane, John W. | 1919 | Box 633 | Lanza, Manfredi | 1896 | Box 163 |
| Lane, Jonathan Homer | 1880 | Box 72 | Lapp, Adam | 1914 | Box 495 |
| Lane, Maltby G. | 1890 | Box 120 | Larcombe, Catharine S. | 1891 | Box 126 |
| Lane, Mary E. | 1903 | Box 247 | Larcombe, J. Howard | 1906 | Box 305 |
| Lane, Mary E. | 1910 | Box 396 | Larcombe, James M. | 1903 | Box 247 |
| Lane, Mary F. | 1895 | Box 155 | Larcombe, John | 1901 | Box 210 |

| | | | | | | |
|---|---|---|---|---|---|---|
| Larcombe, Margaret E. | 1911 | Box 422 | | Lautner, Elizabeth | 1901 | Box 210 |
| Larguey, John P. | 1901 | Box 210 | | Lautner, George | 1904 | Box 267 |
| Larkin, Augustus J. B. | 1909 | Box 372 | | Lavalette, William Alexander | 1914 | Box 495 |
| Larkin, Mary Virginia | 1905 | Box 286 | | Lavering, Sarah | 1826 | Box 8 |
| Larkin, Patrick | 1900 | Box 196 | | Lavezzi, John | 1893 | Box 139 |
| Larkin, Sarah Jane | 1900 | Box 196 | | Lavigne, Adelaide | 1898 | Box 177 |
| Larman, Henry | 1919 | Box 633 | | Law, John George | 1860 | Box 28 |
| Larned, Elizabeth R. | 1856 | Box 25 | | Law, Thomas | 1834 | Box 12 |
| Larned, James | 1849 | Box 20 | | Lawrence, Alexander Hamilton | 1857 | Box 26 |
| Larner, Catherine E. | 1919 | Box 633 | | Lawrence, Annie E. | 1915 | Box 524 |
| Larner, Charles N. | 1895 | Box 155 | | Lawrence, David M. | 1879 | Box 69 |
| Larner, Fannie D. | 1917 | Box 575 | | Lawrence, DeWitt C. | 1892 | Box 133 |
| Larner, Mary V. | 1914 | Box 495 | | Lawrence, James | 1852 | Box 22 |
| Larner, Noble Danforth | 1903 | Box 247 | | Lawrence, John E. | 1901 | Box 210 |
| Larner, Rebecca G. | 1894 | Box 147 | | Lawrence, John Porter | 1913 | Box 472 |
| Larner, Robert M. | 1906 | Box 305 | | Lawrence, Joseph Henry | 1910 | Box 397 |
| Larrabee, Ephram F. | 1904 | Box 267 | | Lawrence, Margaret | 1863 | Box 31 |
| Larrobee, Jennie E. | 1901 | Box 210 | | Lawrence, Marvin H. | 1916 | Box 550 |
| Larry, Charles J. | 1900 | Box 196 | | Lawrence, Mary | 1882 | Box 79 |
| Larwill, Ann E. | 1918 | Box 602 | | Lawrence, Timothy Bigelow | 1890 | Box 120 |
| Larwill, Emma M. | 1914 | Box 495 | | Lawrence, William W. | 1917 | Box 575 |
| Larwill, Martha H. | 1918 | Box 602 | | Lawrie, Jane | 1891 | Box 126 |
| Lasselle, William P. | 1896 | Box 163 | | Lawrie, John W. | 1879 | Box 69 |
| Laster, Andrew | 1917 | Box 575 | | Laws, Ann Maria | 1917 | Box 575 |
| Latane, Marshall M. | 1887 | Box 103 | | Laws, Edward H. | 1916 | Box 550 |
| Latchford, William W. | 1897 | Box 170 | | Laws, James | 1905 | Box 286 |
| Latham, Ellen Hamilton | 1900 | Box 196 | | Laws, John | 1905 | Box 286 |
| Latham, Ephraim | 1893 | Box 139 | | Laws, William | 1898 | Box 177 |
| Lathrop, Mattie | 1884 | Box 88 | | Lawson, Alexander | 1904 | Box 267 |
| Latimer, Catherine | 1906 | Box 305 | | Lawson, Annie Ryland | 1917 | Box 575 |
| Latimer, Charles M. N. | 1912 | Box 447 | | Lawson, Gaines | 1906 | Box 305 |
| Latimer, Marcus Barron | 1903 | Box 247 | | Lawson, James H. | 1897 | Box 170 |
| LaTourrette, Annie M. | 1905 | Box 286 | | Lawson, Jennie | 1910 | Box 397 |
| Latterner, Anna | 1909 | Box 372 | | Lawson, John J. | 1919 | Box 633 |
| Latterner, Peter | 1900 | Box 196 | | Lawson, Kate Ashba | 1917 | Box 576 |
| Lattimore, Isabel | 1913 | Box 472 | | Lawson, Laura | 1894 | Box 147 |
| Laub, Ann Eliza | 1880 | Box 72 | | Lawson, Lewis | 1893 | Box 139 |
| Laub, John | 1837 | Box 13 | | Lawson, Mary E. | 1886 | Box 98 |
| Laub, William B. | 1846 | Box 18 | | Lawson, Thomas | 1861 | Box 29 |
| Laubscher, Peter | 1869 | Box 41 | | Lawton, Edwin M. | 1886 | Box 98 |
| Lauck, Henry Clay | 1869 | Box 41 | | Lawton, Salina | 1899 | Box 185 |
| Lauck, Susan Virginia | 1902 | Box 230 | | Lawton, Sarah E. | 1915 | Box 524 |
| Lauder, George | 1912 | Box 447 | | Lawton, William T. | 1907 | Box 327 |
| Lauer, Justina | 1906 | Box 305 | | Lay, Isabel E. | 1916 | Box 550 |
| Lauffer, Effie A. | 1888 | Box 109 | | Lay, Lillie W. | 1919 | Box 633 |
| Laughlin, Edgar R. | 1912 | Box 447 | | Lay, Mary B. | 1883 | Box 83 |
| Laughlin, Matthew J. | 1914 | Box 495 | | Lay, Mary Susan | 1873 | Box 51 |
| Laupp, Katherine | 1920 | Box 667 | | Lay, Norene B. | 1920 | Box 667 |
| Laurens, Mary J. | 1910 | Box 397 | | Lay, Thomas W. | 1913 | Box 472 |
| Laurenzi, Marco | 1912 | Box 447 | | Lay, William M. | 1894 | Box 147 |
| Laurie, Cranstoun | 1880 | Box 72 | | Layton, Lula S. | 1907 | Box 327 |
| Lautner, Catherine | 1904 | Box 267 | | Lazenby, Benjamin C. | 1901 | Box 210 |

| | | | | | | |
|---|---|---|---|---|---|
| Lazenby, Elisha | 1873 | Box 51 | Lee, Alfred S. | 1918 | Box 603 |
| Le Beau, Mabel A. | 1919 | Box 634 | Lee, Arthur | 1909 | Box 372 |
| Le Boutillier, James | 1914 | Box 495 | Lee, Bessie | 1911 | Box 422 |
| Le Compte, Victoria J. | 1910 | Box 397 | Lee, Cassandra | 1890 | Box 120 |
| Le Conte, Eva H. | 1911 | Box 422 | Lee, Catherine | 1895 | Box 155 |
| Lea, Gabriel M. | 1908 | Box 349 | Lee, David | 1905 | Box 286 |
| Leach, Eliza Jane | 1911 | Box 422 | Lee, Eleanor A. | 1891 | Box 126 |
| Leach, Ezra W. | 1900 | Box 196 | Lee, Elizabeth | 1860 | Box 28 |
| Leach, Hamilton E. | 1893 | Box 139 | Lee, Ellen | 1864 | Box 32 |
| Leach, Smith Stallard | 1909 | Box 372 | Lee, Everett | 1914 | Box 496 |
| Leach, Virginia Courtenay | 1912 | Box 447 | Lee, Fannie P. | 1889 | Box 115 |
| Leach, William | 1891 | Box 126 | Lee, Frances M. | 1916 | Box 551 |
| Leadingham, Alexander | 1892 | Box 133 | Lee, George | 1807 | Box 2 |
| Leadley, George W. | 1917 | Box 576 | Lee, Harriet V. | 1895 | Box 155 |
| Leahy, Anastasia | 1920 | Box 667 | Lee, Harriett | 1917 | Box 576 |
| Leahy, Honora | 1890 | Box 120 | Lee, Henry W. | 1910 | Box 397 |
| Leahy, Michael | 1856 | Box 25 | Lee, Jackson | 1892 | Box 133 |
| Lear, Benjamin L. | 1834 | Box 12 | Lee, James (Sr.) | 1885 | Box 92 |
| Lear, Frances D. | 1856 | Box 25 | Lee, James H. | 1916 | Box 551 |
| Lear, Joseph Henry | 1913 | Box 472 | Lee, Jennie E. | 1909 | Box 372 |
| Leary, John | 1872 | Box 47 | Lee, John F. | 1885 | Box 92 |
| Leary, Madison Small | 1904 | Box 267 | Lee, John Q. | 1905 | Box 286 |
| Leas, Stephen C. | 1915 | Box 524 | Lee, John T. | 1877 | Box 64 |
| Lease, Eliza | 1897 | Box 170 | Lee, John W. | 1914 | Box 496 |
| Leatherbury, Elizabeth | 1866 | Box 36 | Lee, John William | 1916 | Box 551 |
| Leatherman, Marshall E. | 1907 | Box 327 | Lee, Joseph D. | 1877 | Box 64 |
| Leathers, Annie R. | 1919 | Box 634 | Lee, Julia E. | 1910 | Box 397 |
| Leathers, B. Savilla | 1877 | Box 64 | Lee, Keturah | 1904 | Box 267 |
| Leathers, Robert B. | 1918 | Box 603 | Lee, Letitia V. | 1920 | Box 667 |
| Leaver, Henry K. | 1901 | Box 210 | Lee, M. Girard | 1915 | Box 524 |
| Leavey, Morris | 1893 | Box 139 | Lee, Maria L. Crawford | 1919 | Box 634 |
| Leavitt, Katherine Spencer | 1914 | Box 495 | Lee, Mary Augusta | 1895 | Box 155 |
| Leavy, Ellen B. | 1882 | Box 79 | Lee, Mary C. | 1892 | Box 133 |
| Leavy, Margaret | 1896 | Box 163 | Lee, Mary C. | 1898 | Box 177 |
| LeBarnes, John W. | 1898 | Box 177 | Lee, Mary Custis | 1919 | Box 634 |
| LeBrandt, Arthur | 1915 | Box 524 | Lee, Mary Lloyd | 1918 | Box 603 |
| Lechere, Eugenia | 1894 | Box 147 | Lee, Mary R. | 1920 | Box 667 |
| Leckie, A. E. L. | 1920 | Box 667 | Lee, Oscar | 1894 | Box 147 |
| Leckie, Robert | 1834 | Box 12 | Lee, Prather | 1867 | Box 37 |
| Leclerc, Louis | 1882 | Box 79 | Lee, Richard Henry | 1867 | Box 37 |
| LeConte, Harriet Nisbet | 1892 | Box 133 | Lee, Sanford | 1873 | Box 51 |
| Leddy, Charlotte F. | 1887 | Box 103 | Lee, Thacker E. | 1916 | Box 551 |
| Leddy, Owen | 1876 | Box 61 | Lee, Thomas (Sr.) | 1889 | Box 115 |
| Lederer, Charles William | 1912 | Box 447 | Lee, Thomas Sim | 1878 | Box 66 |
| Lederer, Christian G. | 1900 | Box 196 | Lee, William | 1893 | Box 139 |
| Lederer, Philip | 1911 | Box 422 | Lee, William B. | 1895 | Box 155 |
| Ledwith, Mary | 1895 | Box 155 | Lee, William E. | 1917 | Box 576 |
| Ledyard, L. Wolters | 1897 | Box 172 | Lee, William H. | 1893 | Box 139 |
| Ledyard, Lizzie V. | 1901 | Box 210 | Lee, William H. | 1896 | Box 163 |
| Lee, Alfred | 1868 | Box 39 | Leech, Abner Y. | 1906 | Box 305 |
| Lee, Alfred | 1882 | Box 79 | Leech, Margaretta Park | 1914 | Box 496 |
| Lee, Alfred H. | 1903 | Box 248 | Leech, Martha | 1871 | Box 45 |

| | | | | | | |
|---|---|---|---|---|---|---|
| Leech, Phoebe T. | 1882 | Box 79 | | Lenman, Mary E. | 1910 | Box 397 |
| Leech, Samuel V. | 1916 | Box 551 | | Lennan, Minnie | 1894 | Box 147 |
| Leecke, Christine | 1905 | Box 286 | | Lenoir, Charles E. | 1910 | Box 397 |
| Leehy, John | 1891 | Box 126 | | Lenoir, James J. | 1903 | Box 248 |
| Leeman, William E. | 1894 | Box 147 | | Lenox, Peter | 1832 | Box 11 |
| Leese, H. Watson | 1910 | Box 397 | | Lenox, Walter | 1874 | Box 54 |
| Leese, Mary A. | 1911 | Box 422 | | Lenox, William A. | 1837 | Box 13 |
| Leesmitzer, Ernst Julius | 1887 | Box 103 | | Lenthall, Jane | 1853 | Box 22 |
| Leetch, John | 1905 | Box 286 | | Lenthall, John | 1882 | Box 79 |
| Legare, Mary R. C. | 1914 | Box 496 | | Lenthall, Mary K. | 1892 | Box 133 |
| Legg, Aretas M. | 1915 | Box 524 | | Lentz, Ira B. | 1919 | Box 634 |
| Legge, John F. | 1907 | Box 327 | | Leonard, Araminta | 1910 | Box 397 |
| Legge, Julia | 1871 | Box 45 | | Leonard, Catherine | 1879 | Box 69 |
| Leggett, Aaron | 1860 | Box 28 | | Leonard, Elizabeth A. | 1916 | Box 551 |
| Leggo, Sarah J. | 1917 | Box 576 | | Leonard, Eva Spenser | 1910 | Box 397 |
| Legrand, Lucy B. | 1907 | Box 327 | | Leonard, Hannah Paulina | 1909 | Box 372 |
| Lehault, Marie Francis | 1840 | Box 15 | | Leonard, Hiram D. | 1870 | Box 43 |
| Lehman, Harriet P. | 1901 | Box 210 | | Leonard, Isabel | 1888 | Box 109 |
| Lehmann, Louis A. | 1918 | Box 603 | | Leonard, James C. | 1907 | Box 327 |
| Lehne, Henry | 1865 | Box 34 | | Leonard, John | 1836 | Box 13 |
| Lehnert, John | 1888 | Box 109 | | Leonard, John | 1886 | Box 98 |
| Lehnert, Philippina | 1916 | Box 551 | | Leonard, John A. B. | 1889 | Box 115 |
| Leib, Samuel D. | 1883 | Box 83 | | Leonard, Margaret E. | 1897 | Box 170 |
| Leibert, William W. | 1919 | Box 634 | | Leonard, Michael C. | 1916 | Box 551 |
| Leigh, Ellen V. | 1917 | Box 576 | | Leonard, Susan | 1919 | Box 634 |
| Leimbach, Adam | 1889 | Box 115 | | Leonhardt, Peter | 1920 | Box 667 |
| Leimbach, Louisa J. | 1916 | Box 551 | | Lepreau, Augustus | 1912 | Box 448 |
| Leimbach, Mathias | 1889 | Box 115 | | Lepreaux, Jane | 1867 | Box 37 |
| Leins, Bertran | 1875 | Box 58 | | Lepreux, Louis | 1917 | Box 576 |
| Leishear, William W. | 1902 | Box 230 | | Lerch, Caroline | 1907 | Box 327 |
| Leissring, Almira C. | 1895 | Box 155 | | Lerch, Henry F. Jr. | 1913 | Box 472 |
| Leitch, Eliza E. | 1872 | Box 47 | | Lescallett, Abraham B. | 1915 | Box 524 |
| Leitch, Mary | 1838 | Box 14 | | Lescallett, Maria | 1918 | Box 603 |
| Leiter, Levi Z. | 1904 | Box 268 | | Lesley, Susan Inches | 1910 | Box 397 |
| Leiter, Mary T. | 1913 | Box 472 | | Leslie, Robert | 1872 | Box 47 |
| Leith, Charles A. | 1911 | Box 422 | | Lester, Charles H. | 1912 | Box 448 |
| Leitzell, Stuart M. | 1920 | Box 667 | | Lester, Charles S. | 1913 | Box 472 |
| Leizear, Elijah | 1910 | Box 397 | | Lester, George W. | 1897 | Box 170 |
| Leland, Clara A. | 1917 | Box 576 | | Lester, Katharine G. | 1908 | Box 349 |
| Leleng, Sarah | 1918 | Box 603 | | Lester, Morgan H. | 1915 | Box 524 |
| Leman, Primus | 1868 | Box 39 | | Letts, Mary E. | 1905 | Box 286 |
| LeMerle, Aietta M. | 1916 | Box 550 | | Leupp, Francis E. | 1919 | Box 634 |
| Lemly, Samuel C. | 1909 | Box 372 | | Levely, Caroline M. | 1881 | Box 76 |
| Lemmer, Fred | 1882 | Box 79 | | Levely, John S. | 1880 | Box 72 |
| Lemon, Charity | 1873 | Box 51 | | Levely, William | 1822 | Box 7 |
| Lemon, George E. | 1897 | Box 170 | | Levering, Eugenia Helen | 1897 | Box 170 |
| Lemon, Hanson T. A. | 1919 | Box 634 | | Levering, Thomas H. | 1919 | Box 634 |
| Lemon, James H. M. | 1903 | Box 248 | | Leverone, David | 1908 | Box 349 |
| Lemon, John | 1900 | Box 196 | | Levi, Catharine | 1906 | Box 305 |
| Lenhart, Joseph M. | 1907 | Box 327 | | Levy, Daniel | 1915 | Box 524 |
| Lenihan, Michael | 1869 | Box 41 | | Levy, Esther Caroline | 1912 | Box 448 |
| Lenman, George B. | 1865 | Box 34 | | Levy, Hanna | 1907 | Box 327 |

| | | | | | | |
|---|---|---|---|---|---|---|
| Levy, Isaac | 1917 | Box 576 | | Lewis, Merritt | 1910 | Box 397 |
| Levy, Julius | 1890 | Box 120 | | Lewis, Mordecai | 1876 | Box 61 |
| Levy, Leopold F. | 1893 | Box 139 | | Lewis, Richard | 1907 | Box 327 |
| Levy, Martha S. | 1886 | Box 98 | | Lewis, Samuel | 1821 | Box 7 |
| Levy, Mary C. | 1896 | Box 163 | | Lewis, Samuel | 1849 | Box 20 |
| Lewellen, Mary Jane | 1919 | Box 634 | | Lewis, Samuel | 1879 | Box 69 |
| Lewellen, William Franklin | 1908 | Box 349 | | Lewis, Sarah J. | 1907 | Box 327 |
| Lewis, Anna | 1902 | Box 230 | | Lewis, Silas D. | 1920 | Box 667 |
| Lewis, Annie A. | 1917 | Box 576 | | Lewis, Stacy B. | 1876 | Box 61 |
| Lewis, Annie Johnstone | 1908 | Box 349 | | Lewis, Theodore | 1895 | Box 155 |
| Lewis, Arnold T. | 1918 | Box 603 | | Lewis, Therese | 1905 | Box 286 |
| Lewis, Bessie M. | 1902 | Box 230 | | Lewis, Thomas Jefferson | 1920 | Box 667 |
| Lewis, Carrie E. | 1919 | Box 634 | | Lewis, Virginia C. | 1910 | Box 397 |
| Lewis, Cassandra F. | 1907 | Box 327 | | Lewis, Walker | 1892 | Box 133 |
| Lewis, Clarence | 1914 | Box 496 | | Lewis, William C. | 1906 | Box 305 |
| Lewis, David W. | 1915 | Box 524 | | Lewis, William M. | 1908 | Box 350 |
| Lewis, Edwin C. | 1909 | Box 372 | | Leydane, Patrick | 1850 | Box 21 |
| Lewis, Elizabeth | 1916 | Box 551 | | Leyne, Mary A. | 1913 | Box 472 |
| Lewis, Elizabeth B. | 1899 | Box 185 | | Libbey, John Edward | 1908 | Box 350 |
| Lewis, Emma D. | 1912 | Box 448 | | Lichty, Martin B. | 1914 | Box 496 |
| Lewis, Eveline | 1891 | Box 126 | | Lieb, Bernhard | 1918 | Box 603 |
| Lewis, Frank J. | 1916 | Box 551 | | Lieb, William M. | 1887 | Box 103 |
| Lewis, Grenville | 1906 | Box 305 | | Lieber, Bettie A. | 1917 | Box 576 |
| Lewis, Harrison P. | 1860 | Box 28 | | Lieberman, Louisa Catharine | 1861 | Box 29 |
| Lewis, Henrietta A. | 1915 | Box 524 | | Liebermann, Charles H. | 1886 | Box 98 |
| Lewis, Herbert | 1914 | Box 496 | | Liebman, Alfred | 1916 | Box 551 |
| Lewis, James | 1889 | Box 115 | | Liebschutz, Eugénie | 1914 | Box 496 |
| Lewis, James F. | 1902 | Box 230 | | Liesch, Hattie C. | 1915 | Box 524 |
| Lewis, James P. | 1902 | Box 230 | | Liesmann, Julia | 1892 | Box 133 |
| Lewis, Jane | 1910 | Box 397 | | Light, Naasson M. | 1910 | Box 397 |
| Lewis, Jane | 1919 | Box 634 | | Lightbody, Louisa A. | 1903 | Box 248 |
| Lewis, John | 1871 | Box 45 | | Lighter, George W. | 1894 | Box 149 |
| Lewis, John A. | 1872 | Box 47 | | Lightfoot, Daniel | 1878 | Box 66 |
| Lewis, John T. | 1910 | Box 397 | | Lightfoot, Daniel M. | 1882 | Box 79 |
| Lewis, John W. | 1912 | Box 448 | | Lightfoot, John J. | 1914 | Box 496 |
| Lewis, Joseph C. | 1877 | Box 64 | | Lightfoot, Sarah Elizabeth | 1881 | Box 76 |
| Lewis, Julia | 1871 | Box 45 | | Lightfoot, Sophia | 1902 | Box 230 |
| Lewis, Lawrence | 1874 | Box 54 | | Lightner, Isaac | 1870 | Box 43 |
| Lewis, Lucinda | 1881 | Box 76 | | Lihault, Lewis I. | 1823 | Box 7 |
| Lewis, Margaret F. | 1859 | Box 27 | | Lihault, Mary Magdelaine | 1821 | Box 7 |
| Lewis, Margaret F. | 1919 | Box 634 | | Lilley, William | 1883 | Box 83 |
| Lewis, Margaret W. | 1919 | Box 634 | | Lillie, Maggie G. | 1909 | Box 373 |
| Lewis, Margaretina | 1915 | Box 524 | | Limeburner, Cornelia T. | 1915 | Box 524 |
| Lewis, Maria Louisa | 1893 | Box 139 | | Limerick, John A. | 1911 | Box 422 |
| Lewis, Marian | 1890 | Box 120 | | Limerick, Josephine | 1911 | Box 422 |
| Lewis, Mary E. | 1910 | Box 397 | | Limerick, William | 1903 | Box 248 |
| Lewis, Mary Francis | 1897 | Box 170 | | Lincoln, Margaret E. | 1910 | Box 397 |
| Lewis, Mary Hoskins | 1908 | Box 350 | | Lind, Samuel H. | 1893 | Box 139 |
| Lewis, Mary J. | 1919 | Box 634 | | Lind, William Musser | 1910 | Box 397 |
| Lewis, Mary M. | 1894 | Box 147 | | Lindawood, Rachel Grove | 1868 | Box 39 |
| Lewis, Mary P. | 1900 | Box 196 | | Lindenkohl, Adolphus | 1904 | Box 268 |
| Lewis, Mattie A. | 1919 | Box 634 | | Lindenkohl, Henry | 1920 | Box 667 |

| | | | | | | |
|---|---|---|---|---|---|
| Linderman, Jane S. | 1907 | Box 327 | Litchfield, Hiram S. | 1888 | Box 109 |
| Lindland, Ragna | 1919 | Box 634 | Litchfield, Martha A. | 1914 | Box 496 |
| Lindley, John M. | 1874 | Box 54 | Little, Elizabeth Jane | 1894 | Box 147 |
| Lindner, Katharina B. | 1902 | Box 230 | Little, Frank M. | 1907 | Box 327 |
| Lindner, Michael | 1897 | Box 170 | Little, Henrietta | 1911 | Box 422 |
| Lindsay, Adam | 1844 | Box 17 | Little, Israel W. | 1916 | Box 551 |
| Lindsay, George F. | 1857 | Box 26 | Little, John | 1847 | Box 19 |
| Lindsey, Absolum | 1905 | Box 286 | Little, Joseph | 1869 | Box 41 |
| Lindsey, Estella P. | 1920 | Box 667 | Little, Maria | 1916 | Box 551 |
| Lindsley, Anna | 1882 | Box 79 | Little, Martha E. | 1904 | Box 268 |
| Lindsley, Cleland | 1900 | Box 196 | Little, Martha H. | 1910 | Box 398 |
| Lindsley, Eleazer | 1864 | Box 32 | Little, Robert | 1827 | Box 9 |
| Lindsley, Lucy Harris | 1906 | Box 305 | Little, Samuel I. | 1855 | Box 24 |
| Lindsly, Harriet Le Roy | 1910 | Box 397 | Little, Sophia L. | 1901 | Box 210 |
| Lindsly, Harvey | 1889 | Box 115 | Little, William Agnew | 1920 | Box 667 |
| Lineaweaver, Kline C. | 1873 | Box 51 | Littler, Nathan | 1902 | Box 230 |
| Linehan, James Joseph | 1893 | Box 139 | Littleton, James | 1893 | Box 140 |
| Lines, Henry Fowler | 1882 | Box 79 | Littleton, Lawson | 1853 | Box 22 |
| Lines, Robert B. | 1895 | Box 155 | Littlewood, James B. | 1906 | Box 305 |
| Lingenfelter, Elizabeth | 1910 | Box 397 | Litz, Balthasar P. | 1908 | Box 350 |
| Linke, Gustave | 1918 | Box 603 | Litz, Frank J. | 1904 | Box 268 |
| Linker, Harrison S. | 1896 | Box 163 | Litz, Franziska | 1910 | Box 398 |
| Linkins, Daniel | 1889 | Box 115 | Litzenburg, John | 1887 | Box 103 |
| Linkins, Henry | 1832 | Box 11 | Livermore, Phebe Emma | 1917 | Box 576 |
| Linkins, Mary A. | 1919 | Box 634 | Livermore, William H. | 1918 | Box 603 |
| Linkins, Williams | 1892 | Box 133 | Liverpool, George | 1920 | Box 667 |
| Linn, Mary Knox | 1906 | Box 305 | Livings, Theodore | 1917 | Box 576 |
| Linscott, Ellen B. | 1909 | Box 373 | Livingston, Anne C. | 1915 | Box 524 |
| Linsey, Mary | 1884 | Box 88 | Livingston, La Rhett L. | 1903 | Box 248 |
| Linskey, James | 1902 | Box 230 | Livingstone, Anna Maria | 1865 | Box 34 |
| Linthicum, Edward Magruder | 1869 | Box 41 | Lloyd, Charles H. | 1912 | Box 448 |
| Linthicum, Harman R. | 1902 | Box 230 | Lloyd, Delos | 1905 | Box 286 |
| Linton, Jeannette H. | 1871 | Box 45 | Lloyd, Lucy Ann | 1913 | Box 472 |
| Linton, Maria L. | 1886 | Box 98 | Lloyd, Mary E. | 1906 | Box 305 |
| Lippert, John | 1888 | Box 109 | Lloyd, Richard B. | 1870 | Box 43 |
| Lippert, Magdalena | 1892 | Box 133 | Lloyd, Sarah | 1893 | Box 140 |
| Lipphard, John H. | 1917 | Box 576 | Lloyd, Sarah A. | 1912 | Box 448 |
| Lipphard, Loraine | 1906 | Box 305 | Loans, John T. L. | 1918 | Box 603 |
| Lipphardt, Adolphus F. | 1902 | Box 230 | Lobbie, Francis C. | 1848 | Box 19 |
| Lippincott, Benjamin | 1893 | Box 139 | Lochboehler, Caroline | 1906 | Box 305 |
| Lippincott, Carrie | 1911 | Box 422 | Lochboehler, Franz X. | 1911 | Box 422 |
| Lippincott, Frank P. | 1911 | Box 422 | Lochboehler, John H. | 1898 | Box 177 |
| Lippincott, Naomi R. | 1894 | Box 147 | Lochboehler, Joseph | 1891 | Box 126 |
| Lippitt, Eliza W. | 1903 | Box 248 | Lochboehler, Teresia M. | 1901 | Box 210 |
| Lippitt, Francis J. | 1902 | Box 230 | Lochery, Charles A. | 1915 | Box 524 |
| Lippoldt, Susanna Sophia | 1880 | Box 72 | Lochery, Eliza J. | 1915 | Box 524 |
| Lipscomb, Mary J. C. | 1912 | Box 448 | Locke, Joseph M. | 1917 | Box 576 |
| Lipscomb, William C. | 1880 | Box 72 | Locke, Laura Jane | 1901 | Box 210 |
| Liston, Michael | 1893 | Box 139 | Locke, Mary A. | 1894 | Box 147 |
| Liston, Patrick Joseph | 1918 | Box 603 | Locke, Mary F. | 1917 | Box 576 |
| Litchfield, Edward H. | 1898 | Box 177 | Locke, William R. | 1909 | Box 373 |
| Litchfield, Henry Percy | 1919 | Box 634 | Locker, Maria | 1919 | Box 634 |

| | | | | | | |
|---|---|---|---|---|---|
| Lockerman, Thomas G. | 1905 | Box 286 | Long, Elizabeth B. | 1918 | Box 603 |
| Lockie, John | 1907 | Box 327 | Long, Elizabeth W. | 1884 | Box 88 |
| Lockwood, Frances A. | 1885 | Box 92 | Long, Francis C. | 1908 | Box 350 |
| Lockwood, Henry A. | 1903 | Box 248 | Long, Jeremiah | 1895 | Box 155 |
| Lockwood, Homer N. | 1913 | Box 472 | Long, John G. | 1903 | Box 248 |
| Lockwood, Horace Hill | 1916 | Box 551 | Long, Margaret R. | 1918 | Box 603 |
| Lockwood, Julia | 1880 | Box 72 | Long, Mary | 1904 | Box 267 |
| Lockwood, Margaret M. | 1907 | Box 327 | Long, Mathew | 1821 | Box 7 |
| Lockwood, Mary | 1916 | Box 551 | Long, Michael | 1877 | Box 64 |
| Lockwood, Philo J. | 1905 | Box 286 | Long, Patrick | 1897 | Box 170 |
| Lockwood, Robert M. | 1906 | Box 305 | Long, William Clifford | 1919 | Box 634 |
| Lockwood, William A. | 1911 | Box 422 | Longan, Oliver W. | 1892 | Box 133 |
| Lockwood, William R. | 1896 | Box 163 | Longden, Mary A. | 1893 | Box 140 |
| Locraft, William | 1907 | Box 327 | Longley, Abner T. | 1896 | Box 163 |
| Lodge, Martha | 1902 | Box 230 | Longshaw, Annie F. | 1904 | Box 268 |
| Lodge, Miranda | 1903 | Box 248 | Loobey, Terence | 1852 | Box 22 |
| Lodge, Walter Harmon | 1916 | Box 551 | Looker, Katharine Earle | 1905 | Box 286 |
| Loeb, Jacob | 1897 | Box 170 | Looker, Thomas H. | 1910 | Box 398 |
| Loeffler, Ernst | 1885 | Box 92 | Loomis, Achsah Ashley | 1915 | Box 524 |
| Loeffler, Jacob | 1901 | Box 210 | Loomis, Lafayette Charles | 1905 | Box 286 |
| Loeffler, Mary E. | 1908 | Box 350 | Loomis, Mary Williams | 1910 | Box 398 |
| Loeliger, John | 1876 | Box 61 | Looney, Johanna | 1920 | Box 668 |
| Loew, Juliana | 1901 | Box 210 | Loovis, Asher M. | 1890 | Box 120 |
| Loffler, Andreas | 1905 | Box 286 | Lord, Francis B. | 1882 | Box 79 |
| Löffler, Ernest C. | 1919 | Box 634 | Lord, John H. | 1910 | Box 398 |
| Lofton, William S. | 1919 | Box 634 | Lord, Matilda D. | 1900 | Box 196 |
| Loftus, Austin | 1920 | Box 668 | Lord, Thomas W. | 1903 | Box 248 |
| Loftus, Dennis | 1908 | Box 350 | Lord, William | 1899 | Box 185 |
| Loftus, Edward | 1884 | Box 88 | Lorenz, Franziska | 1913 | Box 472 |
| Logan, Daniel J. | 1911 | Box 422 | Lorenz, Mary V. | 1912 | Box 448 |
| Logan, David | 1905 | Box 286 | Lorick, Julia | 1878 | Box 66 |
| Logan, George Wood | 1915 | Box 524 | Loring, Edward G. | 1891 | Box 126 |
| Logan, Henry | 1899 | Box 185 | Loring, Harriet B. | 1901 | Box 210 |
| Logan, Robert | 1912 | Box 448 | Loring, Mary B. | 1905 | Box 286 |
| Logsdon, Susan B. Pauline | 1919 | Box 634 | Losano, Francisco C. | 1899 | Box 185 |
| Lohs, Louisa | 1851 | Box 21 | Losano, Isabella | 1893 | Box 140 |
| Lomax, Aaron | 1882 | Box 79 | Lothrop, Alvin M. | 1912 | Box 448 |
| Lomax, Lucy | 1912 | Box 448 | Lothrop, John P. | 1901 | Box 210 |
| Lomax, Lunsford Lindsay | 1913 | Box 472 | Lott, Caroline | 1919 | Box 634 |
| Lomax, Mary | 1896 | Box 163 | Lott, Joseph R. | 1919 | Box 634 |
| Lomax, Peter Armstrong | 1914 | Box 496 | Lott, Katharina | 1920 | Box 668 |
| Lomax, Samuel F. | 1892 | Box 133 | Lotz, Jeremiah C. | 1910 | Box 398 |
| Lomax, Samuel F. | 1913 | Box 472 | Lotz, Thomas | 1910 | Box 398 |
| London, John H. | 1918 | Box 603 | Loucks, Phebe E. | 1904 | Box 268 |
| Long, August | 1912 | Box 448 | Loudin, Harriet C. | 1908 | Box 350 |
| Long, Catharine | 1893 | Box 140 | Loughborough, Hamilton | 1865 | Box 34 |
| Long, Catharine | 1911 | Box 422 | Loughran, Daniel | 1917 | Box 576 |
| Long, Catherine | 1920 | Box 668 | Loughran, Frances Marion | 1899 | Box 185 |
| Long, Charles | 1909 | Box 373 | Loughran, Joseph | 1897 | Box 170 |
| Long, Dennis | 1895 | Box 155 | Loughran, Joseph | 1911 | Box 423 |
| Long, Dennis J. | 1912 | Box 448 | Louis, Michael A. W. | 1910 | Box 398 |
| Long, Dora | 1920 | Box 668 | Loundes, Benjamin | 1810 | Box 3 |

| | | | | | | |
|---|---|---|---|---|---|---|
| Loussararian, Armenag H. | 1920 | Box 668 | Lowry, Fanny | 1892 | Box 133 |
| Louvrier, Hester M. | 1881 | Box 76 | Lowry, George | 1881 | Box 76 |
| Louwenthal, Jacob | 1866 | Box 36 | Lowry, Jane | 1914 | Box 496 |
| Love, Henry I. | 1888 | Box 109 | Lowry, Lily Jones | 1900 | Box 196 |
| Love, James Flavius | 1902 | Box 230 | Lowry, Margaret Jane | 1904 | Box 268 |
| Love, Mary Elizabeth | 1906 | Box 305 | Lucas, Eliza | 1864 | Box 32 |
| Love, Sarah S. | 1873 | Box 51 | Lucas, Harriet A. | 1891 | Box 126 |
| Lovejoy, John N. | 1890 | Box 120 | Lucas, Ignatuis | 1827 | Box 9 |
| Lovejoy, Maria N. | 1914 | Box 496 | Lucas, John | 1826 | Box 8 |
| Lovejoy, Susan E. | 1905 | Box 286 | Lucas, John P. | 1896 | Box 163 |
| Loveless, James H. | 1917 | Box 576 | Lucas, Louisa | 1871 | Box 45 |
| Loveless, Joseph E. | 1919 | Box 635 | Lucas, Mary | 1915 | Box 524 |
| Lovell, James | 1806 | Box 2 | Lucas, Mary Brown | 1894 | Box 147 |
| Lovell, Joseph | 1875 | Box 58 | Lucas, Philander | 1905 | Box 286 |
| Lovell, Joseph | 1836 | Box 13 | Lucas, William | 1893 | Box 140 |
| Loven, John W. | 1918 | Box 603 | Luchs, Fannie | 1905 | Box 286 |
| Lovett, Emeline Dore | 1903 | Box 248 | Luchs, Hannah | 1918 | Box 603 |
| Low, Elizabeth | 1818 | Box 5 | Luchs, Leopold | 1920 | Box 668 |
| Low, Robert | 1920 | Box 668 | Luchs, Max | 1897 | Box 170 |
| Lowdermilk, Temperance S. | 1920 | Box 668 | Lucke, Stephen | 1912 | Box 448 |
| Lowdermilk, William H. | 1898 | Box 177 | Luckel, Henry | 1896 | Box 163 |
| Lowe, Barbara | 1851 | Box 21 | Lückel, Margaret | 1910 | Box 398 |
| Lowe, Elizabeth | 1832 | Box 11 | Luckens, Charles | 1878 | Box 66 |
| Lowe, Elizabeth | 1888 | Box 109 | Luckett, Lucinde | 1911 | Box 423 |
| Lowe, Joseph F. | 1879 | Box 69 | Luckett, Regina M. | 1917 | Box 576 |
| Lowe, Mary B. | 1907 | Box 327 | Luckett, Samuel D. | 1913 | Box 472 |
| Lowe, Ralph P. | 1884 | Box 88 | Luckett, William F. | 1901 | Box 210 |
| Lowe, Ralph P. | 1894 | Box 147 | Ludgate, William | 1912 | Box 448 |
| Lowe, Samuel | 1897 | Box 170 | Ludlow, Mary McLean | 1915 | Box 524 |
| Lowe, Susanna | 1862 | Box 30 | Ludwig, Philip | 1879 | Box 69 |
| Lowe, Warren | 1869 | Box 41 | Luerssen, Hermann Gerhard | 1910 | Box 398 |
| Lowell, Delmar R. | 1912 | Box 448 | Lufborough, Nathan | 1887 | Box 103 |
| Loweree, George E. | 1903 | Box 248 | Lugenbeel, Pinkney | 1911 | Box 423 |
| Loweree, Margaret Anna | 1904 | Box 268 | Lugler, Joseph | 1902 | Box 230 |
| Lowery, Archibald H. | 1896 | Box 163 | Lüling, Theodore | 1885 | Box 92 |
| Lowery, Frances Woodbury | 1895 | Box 155 | Lulley, Anthony | 1918 | Box 603 |
| Lowery, Woodbury | 1906 | Box 305 | Lum, Joseph A. | 1898 | Box 177 |
| Lown, Warren Jesse | 1892 | Box 133 | Lumpkin, Thomas | 1871 | Box 45 |
| Lownd, William Richard | 1860 | Box 28 | Lumpkins, Rowena N. | 1915 | Box 524 |
| Lowndes, Benjamin | 1900 | Box 196 | Lumsdon, Mary A. | 1909 | Box 373 |
| Lowndes, Francis | 1815 | Box 4 | Lumsdon, William O. | 1868 | Box 39 |
| Lowndes, Francis | 1867 | Box 37 | Lundy, Thomas | 1873 | Box 51 |
| Lowndes, James | 1910 | Box 398 | Lurton, Horace H. | 1914 | Box 496 |
| Lowndes, Laura Wolcott | 1914 | Box 496 | Lusby, Ella E. | 1915 | Box 524 |
| Lowrey, Anne M. | 1874 | Box 54 | Lusby, Francis W. | 1912 | Box 448 |
| Lowrey, George H. | 1905 | Box 286 | Lusby, James A. | 1889 | Box 115 |
| Lowrey, Mary | 1840 | Box 15 | Lusby, Lemuel | 1902 | Box 230 |
| Lowrie, Margaret E. | 1903 | Box 248 | Lusby, Mary E. | 1904 | Box 268 |
| Lowrie, Randolph W. | 1913 | Box 472 | Lusby, Mary E. | 1916 | Box 551 |
| Lowry, Ann | 1862 | Box 30 | Lusby, Samuel | 1865 | Box 34 |
| Lowry, Caesar | 1807 | Box 2 | Lusk, Harriet S. | 1905 | Box 286 |
| Lowry, Elizabeth D. | 1888 | Box 109 | Luther, Daniel | 1889 | Box 115 |

| | | | | | | |
|---|---|---|---|---|---|
| Luther, Emil | 1911 | Box 423 | Lynch, Patrick J. | 1915 | Box 525 |
| Luther, Eugenia F. | 1909 | Box 373 | Lynch, Truman | 1868 | Box 39 |
| Luttrell, Harriet Lothrop | 1919 | Box 635 | Lynch, William | 1895 | Box 155 |
| Lutz, Blandina R. | 1914 | Box 496 | Lynch, William | 1914 | Box 496 |
| Lutz, Francis A. | 1885 | Box 92 | Lynch, William T. | 1920 | Box 668 |
| Lutz, Francis A. | 1903 | Box 248 | Lyndall, Thomas | 1834 | Box 12 |
| Lutz, John | 1841 | Box 15 | Lyne, Patrick | 1904 | Box 268 |
| Lutz, Mary A. | 1897 | Box 170 | Lynn, John | 1876 | Box 61 |
| Lutz, Samuel S. | 1918 | Box 603 | Lynn, Luther | 1901 | Box 210 |
| Lutz, William Frederick | 1904 | Box 268 | Lynn, Mary Ann | 1892 | Box 133 |
| Lybrand, Margaret E. | 1895 | Box 155 | Lynn, William F. | 1916 | Box 551 |
| Lycett, William C. | 1878 | Box 66 | Lyon, Ann J. | 1918 | Box 603 |
| Lydon, John | 1878 | Box 66 | Lyon, Elijah | 1843 | Box 16 |
| Lyle, Amelia J. | 1912 | Box 448 | Lyon, Harriet M. | 1905 | Box 286 |
| Lyles, Arianna J. | 1888 | Box 109 | Lyon, Henry G. | 1911 | Box 423 |
| Lyles, Eliza C. | 1854 | Box 23 | Lyon, Inez L. | 1912 | Box 448 |
| Lyles, Georgia T. | 1901 | Box 210 | Lyon, John M. | 1883 | Box 83 |
| Lyles, Harrison B. | 1911 | Box 423 | Lyon, Le Roy Springs | 1920 | Box 668 |
| Lyles, Martha | 1908 | Box 350 | Lyon, William A. | 1903 | Box 248 |
| Lyman, Charles | 1888 | Box 109 | Lyon, William F. | 1918 | Box 603 |
| Lyman, Maria Spalding | 1916 | Box 551 | Lyons, Annie | 1920 | Box 668 |
| Lynah, James | 1904 | Box 268 | Lyons, Catherine G. | 1918 | Box 603 |
| Lynch, Ambrose | 1862 | Box 30 | Lyons, Daniel B. | 1902 | Box 230 |
| Lynch, Amelia | 1908 | Box 350 | Lyons, Hugh | 1913 | Box 472 |
| Lynch, Augustus D. | 1908 | Box 350 | Lyons, Jacob | 1896 | Box 163 |
| Lynch, Cecilia | 1919 | Box 635 | Lysle, Caroline | 1915 | Box 525 |
| Lynch, Dominick | 1871 | Box 45 | Lytle, Robert S. | 1908 | Box 350 |
| Lynch, Edmund J. | 1905 | Box 286 | Lywood, Annie R. | 1913 | Box 472 |
| Lynch, Elizabeth | 1910 | Box 398 | Maack, Martha A. | 1904 | Box 268 |
| Lynch, Eugene M. | 1886 | Box 98 | Mabre, Benjamin | 1918 | Box 605 |
| Lynch, James Winslow | 1906 | Box 305 | Mac Vean, Margaret J. | 1913 | Box 473 |
| Lynch, Jane | 1900 | Box 196 | Macabee, William | 1859 | Box 27 |
| Lynch, Jeremiah | 1893 | Box 140 | Macalester, Charles | 1874 | Box 54 |
| Lynch, Jeremiah | 1897 | Box 170 | MacAllister, John F. | 1896 | Box 163 |
| Lynch, John | 1892 | Box 133 | MacAllister, Rebecca J. Ashby | 1888 | Box 109 |
| Lynch, John | 1892 | Box 133 | MacArthur, Arthur | 1896 | Box 163 |
| Lynch, John | 1900 | Box 196 | MacArthur, Mary E. | 1899 | Box 185 |
| Lynch, John | 1901 | Box 210 | Macartney, Elizabeth J. | 1907 | Box 328 |
| Lynch, John | 1920 | Box 668 | Macartney, Minerva | 1875 | Box 58 |
| Lynch, John P. | 1916 | Box 551 | Macarty, Daniel J. | 1910 | Box 399 |
| Lynch, Laura E. Thomas | 1915 | Box 525 | Macarty, Mary R. | 1914 | Box 497 |
| Lynch, Laura V. H. | 1911 | Box 423 | Maccubbin, Annie E. | 1901 | Box 211 |
| Lynch, Margaret | 1913 | Box 472 | Maccubbin, Mary G. | 1889 | Box 115 |
| Lynch, Martin | 1885 | Box 92 | Macdaniel, Mary | 1908 | Box 351 |
| Lynch, Mary | 1891 | Box 126 | Macdaniel, Norris | 1918 | Box 605 |
| Lynch, Mary | 1891 | Box 126 | Macdonald, Godfrey Harrison | 1918 | Box 605 |
| Lynch, Mary | 1908 | Box 350 | MacDonald, Charles Francis | 1902 | Box 230 |
| Lynch, Mary | 1918 | Box 603 | MacDonald, Sarah M. | 1911 | Box 423 |
| Lynch, Mary A. | 1913 | Box 472 | Mace, Thomas | 1884 | Box 88 |
| Lynch, Mary Josephine | 1910 | Box 398 | Macfarland, Horace Greeley | 1915 | Box 525 |
| Lynch, Patrick | 1852 | Box 22 | Macfarland, Isabelle Floyd | 1912 | Box 449 |
| Lynch, Patrick | 1889 | Box 115 | Macfarland, Joseph | 1876 | Box 61 |

| | | | | | | |
|---|---|---|---|---|---|
| Macfeely, Josephine B. | 1913 | Box 473 | MacMayo, Harry | 1895 | Box 155 |
| MacFeely, Robert | 1901 | Box 211 | MacNamara, Martin | 1862 | Box 30 |
| Macgill, Elizabeth | 1834 | Box 12 | Macomb, Alexander | 1841 | Box 15 |
| Macgill, Olivia E. | 1897 | Box 171 | Macomb, Harriet B. | 1869 | Box 41 |
| MacGreal, Wilburne P. | 1910 | Box 399 | Macomb, Jane | 1849 | Box 20 |
| MacGrotty, Edwin B. | 1899 | Box 185 | Macomb, John N. | 1889 | Box 115 |
| Machen, Arthur W. | 1916 | Box 552 | Macomb, Nannie Rodgers | 1916 | Box 552 |
| Machette, Adelaide Granet | 1904 | Box 268 | Macpherson, Mary E. | 1873 | Box 51 |
| Machette, Henry Clay | 1903 | Box 249 | Macrae, Nathaniel M. | 1914 | Box 497 |
| Machon, Margaret A. | 1911 | Box 423 | MacVeagh, Virginia R. Cameron | 1920 | Box 668 |
| Macias, Jose M. | 1894 | Box 147 | MacVeagh, Wayne | 1917 | Box 577 |
| Mack, Albert W. | 1899 | Box 185 | MacWilliam, James | 1868 | Box 39 |
| Mack, Augustus | 1917 | Box 577 | MacWilliams, Alex | 1898 | Box 177 |
| Mack, Caroline A. | 1916 | Box 552 | Madden, Antonia F. | 1887 | Box 104 |
| Mack, Frederick | 1897 | Box 171 | Madden, Matilda A. | 1909 | Box 373 |
| Mack, Frederick Otto | 1893 | Box 140 | Maddox, John F. | 1893 | Box 140 |
| Mack, George | 1903 | Box 249 | Maddox, Samuel | 1919 | Box 635 |
| Mack, Georgina M. | 1915 | Box 525 | Maddox, William F. | 1908 | Box 351 |
| Mack, Lorenz | 1914 | Box 497 | Madeira, Dorothy Joy | 1919 | Box 635 |
| Mack, Nellie M. | 1915 | Box 525 | Madeira, Julia P. | 1914 | Box 497 |
| Mackall, Benjamin | 1808 | Box 3 | Mader, Agnes Galvin | 1908 | Box 351 |
| Mackall, Benjamin | 1823 | Box 7 | Madert, Jacob | 1917 | Box 577 |
| Mackall, Benjamin F. | 1880 | Box 72 | Mades, Charles | 1915 | Box 525 |
| Mackall, Brooke | 1880 | Box 72 | Mades, Charles B. | 1919 | Box 635 |
| Mackall, Christiana | 1849 | Box 20 | Mades, Christopher | 1878 | Box 66 |
| Mackall, James McV. | 1909 | Box 373 | Madigan, John | 1917 | Box 577 |
| Mackall, Leonard | 1849 | Box 20 | Madigan, Kate | 1902 | Box 231 |
| Mackall, Louis | 1876 | Box 61 | Madigan, Margaret E. | 1920 | Box 669 |
| Mackall, Louis | 1906 | Box 305 | Madigan, Mary | 1917 | Box 577 |
| Mackall, Margaret Whann | 1910 | Box 399 | Madigan, Patrick | 1901 | Box 211 |
| Mackall, Martha | 1879 | Box 69 | Madigan, Thomas | 1917 | Box 577 |
| Mackay, George | 1917 | Box 577 | Madison, Catharine | 1886 | Box 98 |
| Mackboy, James | 1871 | Box 45 | Madison, Claiborn | 1896 | Box 163 |
| Mackenheimer, George L. | 1869 | Box 41 | Madison, Dolly | 1850 | Box 21 |
| Mackenzie, Catharine | 1908 | Box 351 | Madison, Francis | 1887 | Box 104 |
| Mackenzie, William Duncan | 1916 | Box 552 | Madison, Gracie A. | 1901 | Box 211 |
| MacKenzie, James B. | 1909 | Box 373 | Madison, Henry | 1914 | Box 497 |
| Mackey, Albert G. | 1881 | Box 76 | Madison, James | 1883 | Box 83 |
| Mackey, Edmund William M. | 1884 | Box 88 | Madison, Matilda E. | 1886 | Box 98 |
| Mackey, Franklin H. | 1905 | Box 287 | Madré (Madry), Charlotte | 1900 | Box 197 |
| Mackey, Hugh | 1916 | Box 552 | Madre, Helena B. | 1916 | Box 552 |
| Mackey, Mary E. | 1912 | Box 449 | Maedel, Julia W. | 1889 | Box 115 |
| Mackey, William | 1869 | Box 41 | Maegle, Jacob | 1860 | Box 28 |
| Mackkaus, Mary | 1917 | Box 577 | Maeias, Jose M. | 1894 | Box 147 |
| MacKnight, Arthur C. | 1901 | Box 211 | Maekel, Margaret | 1867 | Box 37 |
| Mackswell, Susan | 1913 | Box 474 | Maffit, Samuel | 1813 | Box 4 |
| MacLean, John | 1895 | Box 155 | Magaw, Alice D. | 1911 | Box 424 |
| Maclean, Mary T. | 1905 | Box 287 | Magee, Annie G. | 1894 | Box 147 |
| Macleod, Agnes | 1859 | Box 27 | Magee, Frank A. | 1919 | Box 636 |
| MacLeod, Elizabeth | 1888 | Box 109 | Magee, John | 1882 | Box 80 |
| MacLeod, Euphemia Helen | 1915 | Box 525 | Magee, James N. | 1884 | Box 88 |
| MacLeod, William | 1892 | Box 133 | Magee, Julia B. | 1916 | Box 552 |

| | | | | | | |
|---|---|---|---|---|---|---|
| Magee, Laura | 1891 | Box 126 | Maher, John T. | 1905 | Box 287 |
| Magee, Mary Ann | 1867 | Box 37 | Maher, Mary E. | 1905 | Box 287 |
| Magee, Mary S. | 1831 | Box 11 | Maher, Mary M. | 1919 | Box 636 |
| Magee, Matilda A. | 1911 | Box 424 | Maher, Michael | 1878 | Box 66 |
| Magee, Patrick | 1865 | Box 34 | Mahler, Rosie | 1911 | Box 424 |
| Magee, Samuel | 1883 | Box 83 | Mahon, Jane Owen | 1899 | Box 148 |
| Magee, William C. | 1876 | Box 61 | Mahon, Lizzie | 1890 | Box 120 |
| Magill, Catherine C. | 1891 | Box 126 | Mahon, Sophie I. | 1900 | Box 197 |
| Magill, William | 1843 | Box 16 | Mahoney, George | 1875 | Box 58 |
| Magoon, Charles E. | 1920 | Box 669 | Mahoney, Johannah | 1902 | Box 231 |
| Magrath, Owen F. | 1811 | Box 3 | Mahoney, John P. | 1913 | Box 474 |
| Magruder, Ann T. G. | 1894 | Box 148 | Mahoney, Julia | 1910 | Box 399 |
| Magruder, Catharine J. | 1884 | Box 88 | Mahoney, Lawrence A. | 1915 | Box 526 |
| Magruder, Denis | 1878 | Box 66 | Mahoney, Louisa | 1904 | Box 268 |
| Magruder, Eleanor A. H. | 1906 | Box 306 | Mahoney, Mary | 1893 | Box 140 |
| Magruder, Elizabeth | 1827 | Box 9 | Mahoney, Mary | 1913 | Box 474 |
| Magruder, Elizabeth O. | 1902 | Box 231 | Mahoney, Mary A. | 1919 | Box 636 |
| Magruder, Fielder | 1903 | Box 249 | Mahoney, Michael | 1887 | Box 104 |
| Magruder, George Lloyd | 1914 | Box 497 | Mahoney, Michael | 1898 | Box 177 |
| Magruder, James A. | 1897 | Box 171 | Mahoney, William L. | 1917 | Box 577 |
| Magruder, John H. T. | 1893 | Box 140 | Mahony, David | 1890 | Box 120 |
| Magruder, Joseph | 1904 | Box 268 | Mahood, Fontaine Watts | 1911 | Box 424 |
| Magruder, Lewis G. | 1907 | Box 328 | Mahorney, Mary E. | 1897 | Box 171 |
| Magruder, Mary | 1897 | Box 171 | Mahrer, Minnie Mary | 1876 | Box 61 |
| Magruder, Mary Blanche | 1918 | Box 605 | Maier, Dorothea | 1898 | Box 177 |
| Magruder, Mary E. | 1883 | Box 83 | Maier, George | 1917 | Box 577 |
| Magruder, Millicent A. B. | 1879 | Box 69 | Maillet, Jules | 1920 | Box 669 |
| Magruder, Ninian | 1823 | Box 7 | Main, Herschel | 1915 | Box 526 |
| Magruder, Sarah A. | 1917 | Box 577 | Main, Hial P. | 1894 | Box 148 |
| Magruder, Sarah H. B. | 1883 | Box 83 | Main, Lewis C. | 1905 | Box 287 |
| Magruder, Sarah Van Wyck | 1913 | Box 474 | Main, Nichol | 1917 | Box 577 |
| Magruder, Susanna | 1847 | Box 19 | Maitland, Ann | 1863 | Box 31 |
| Magruder, William B. | 1869 | Box 41 | Major, Elizabeth Ann | 1904 | Box 268 |
| Magruder, William Washington | 1917 | Box 577 | Major, John | 1853 | Box 22 |
| Maguire, Annastatia | 1869 | Box 41 | Major, John | 1864 | Box 32 |
| Maguire, Catharine | 1872 | Box 48 | Major, John R. | 1912 | Box 449 |
| Maguire, James F. | 1905 | Box 287 | Major, Mary E. | 1920 | Box 669 |
| Maguire, John | 1887 | Box 104 | Major, Sarah E. | 1881 | Box 76 |
| Maguire, John | 1897 | Box 171 | Major, Sarah E. | 1886 | Box 98 |
| Maguire, Joseph I. | 1908 | Box 351 | Major, Susannah | 1875 | Box 58 |
| Maguire, Kate | 1893 | Box 140 | Makinson, Augustus H. | 1920 | Box 669 |
| Maguire, Nannie Norris | 1903 | Box 249 | Malatesta, Giovanni | 1906 | Box 306 |
| Maguire, Nora | 1913 | Box 474 | Malby, George R. | 1915 | Box 526 |
| Maguire, Patrick | 1872 | Box 48 | Malcolm, Margaret | 1902 | Box 231 |
| Mahaney, John M. | 1912 | Box 449 | Mallery, Garrick | 1894 | Box 148 |
| Maher, Ann Elizabeth | 1918 | Box 605 | Mallery, Helen Marian | 1919 | Box 636 |
| Maher, Annie O'Brien | 1901 | Box 211 | Mallet, Edmond Sr. | 1907 | Box 328 |
| Maher, Eliza | 1913 | Box 474 | Mallett, Anna Smith | 1908 | Box 351 |
| Maher, Ellen | 1912 | Box 449 | Mallion, Vandora | 1857 | Box 26 |
| Maher, George W. | 1918 | Box 605 | Mallory, Alice A. | 1907 | Box 328 |
| Maher, James | 1859 | Box 27 | Mallory, W. E. | 1916 | Box 552 |
| Maher, James | 1869 | Box 41 | Malnati, Antonio | 1906 | Box 306 |

| | | | | | | |
|---|---|---|---|---|---|---|
| Malone, John | 1871 | Box 45 | | Manning, Mary | 1900 | Box 197 |
| Malone, John | 1886 | Box 98 | | Manning, Mary May | 1901 | Box 212 |
| Malone, Sarah | 1908 | Box 351 | | Manning, Rebecca V. | 1920 | Box 669 |
| Maloney, James | 1892 | Box 133 | | Manning, Robert | 1856 | Box 25 |
| Maloney, John P. | 1909 | Box 373 | | Manning, Sallie S. | 1867 | Box 37 |
| Maloney, Michael | 1880 | Box 72 | | Manning, Susan P. | 1912 | Box 449 |
| Maloney, Michael | 1906 | Box 306 | | Manning, William C. | 1901 | Box 212 |
| Maloney, Michael | 1918 | Box 605 | | Manning, William J. | 1909 | Box 373 |
| Maloney, Nannie B. | 1906 | Box 306 | | Mannix, D. Pratt | 1894 | Box 148 |
| Maloney, Patrick | 1912 | Box 449 | | Manogue, James K. | 1901 | Box 212 |
| Maloney, Thomas | 1901 | Box 211 | | Mansfield, Anna D. | 1903 | Box 249 |
| Malord, Jane C. | 1881 | Box 76 | | Mansfield, Charles D. | 1892 | Box 133 |
| Malord, Lillian B. | 1894 | Box 148 | | Mansfield, Charles M. | 1918 | Box 605 |
| Malvin, W. H. Judd | 1917 | Box 577 | | Mansfield, Joseph S. | 1867 | Box 37 |
| Mamreov, Anna F. | 1920 | Box 669 | | Mansfield, William Wallis | 1918 | Box 605 |
| Manchester, Catharine F. | 1913 | Box 474 | | Manson, Charles | 1920 | Box 669 |
| Mandeville, James H. | 1892 | Box 133 | | Mantegari, Bernardo | 1903 | Box 249 |
| Manduit, Hannah | 1815 | Box 4 | | Manton, Mary W. | 1903 | Box 249 |
| Manfred, Ethel | 1920 | Box 669 | | Mantz, Annie E. | 1919 | Box 636 |
| Mangan, Catharine | 1916 | Box 552 | | Mantz, Casper | 1875 | Box 58 |
| Mangan, John L. | 1916 | Box 552 | | Mantz, Peter | 1894 | Box 148 |
| Mangan, Maurice | 1911 | Box 424 | | Manuel, Rosa | 1919 | Box 636 |
| Mangan, Timothy | 1874 | Box 54 | | Marbury, Ann O. | 1847 | Box 19 |
| Mangold, John | 1913 | Box 474 | | Marbury, Elizabeth H. | 1909 | Box 374 |
| Mangold, Martin | 1905 | Box 287 | | Marbury, Harriet H. | 1887 | Box 104 |
| Mangum, James K. | 1901 | Box 212 | | Marbury, John | 1876 | Box 61 |
| Mangum, Luther | 1911 | Box 424 | | Marbury, John (Jr.) | 1905 | Box 287 |
| Mangum, Mary E. | 1901 | Box 212 | | Marbury, Nannie | 1892 | Box 133 |
| Manion, Kate A. | 1917 | Box 577 | | Marbury, William | 1835 | Box 13 |
| Mankin, George W. | 1918 | Box 605 | | Marbury, William | 1874 | Box 54 |
| Mankin, Lucy B. | 1880 | Box 72 | | Marbury, William | 1880 | Box 72 |
| Mankin, Thomas Edward | 1899 | Box 185 | | Marc, Charles J. | 1911 | Box 424 |
| Mankin, Valinda | 1905 | Box 287 | | Marceron, Annie E. | 1904 | Box 268 |
| Mann, Charles Addison | 1896 | Box 163 | | Marceron, Elizabeth E. | 1906 | Box 306 |
| Mann, George | 1917 | Box 577 | | Marcey, John Thomas | 1901 | Box 212 |
| Mann, Gertrude | 1920 | Box 669 | | Marche, Frances E. | 1904 | Box 268 |
| Mann, James T. | 1917 | Box 577 | | Marche, Mary de la | 1805 | Box 1 |
| Mann, Jesse F. | 1907 | Box 328 | | Marche, Peter | 1827 | Box 9 |
| Mann, Julia | 1910 | Box 399 | | Marden, Edwin R. | 1914 | Box 497 |
| Mann, Louisa C. F. | 1917 | Box 577 | | Marden, Martha D. | 1890 | Box 120 |
| Mann, Mary Elizabeth | 1913 | Box 474 | | Mardes, William | 1859 | Box 27 |
| Mann, William A. | 1907 | Box 328 | | Marean, Morell | 1902 | Box 231 |
| Mann, William M. | 1860 | Box 28 | | Marillion, Rebecca C. | 1906 | Box 307 |
| Manning, Anna J. | 1920 | Box 669 | | Marini, Louis G. | 1889 | Box 115 |
| Manning, Caroline E. T. | 1900 | Box 197 | | Mario, Virginia Stratton | 1915 | Box 526 |
| Manning, Catherine E. | 1909 | Box 373 | | Markell, Conrad | 1896 | Box 163 |
| Manning, Charles H. | 1885 | Box 93 | | Markell, Francis | 1896 | Box 163 |
| Manning, Euphermia | 1860 | Box 28 | | Markell, George | 1905 | Box 287 |
| Manning, Georgia Edith | 1893 | Box 140 | | Markell, Louis | 1896 | Box 163 |
| Manning, John S. | 1905 | Box 287 | | Markey, Thomas J. | 1918 | Box 605 |
| Manning, Joseph S. | 1919 | Box 636 | | Markland, Martha Louise | 1889 | Box 115 |
| Manning, Mary | 1846 | Box 18 | | Markley, Augusta | 1893 | Box 140 |

| | | | | | | |
|---|---|---|---|---|---|---|
| Markoe, Mary Galloway | 1907 | Box 328 | Marshall, John | 1802 | Box 1 |
| Markriter, John | 1883 | Box 83 | Marshall, Kate | 1919 | Box 636 |
| Markriter, Mary J. | 1917 | Box 577 | Marshall, Lydia | 1900 | Box 197 |
| Marks, Jacob | 1864 | Box 32 | Marshall, Rachael A. B. | 1917 | Box 577 |
| Marks, Julia Pierpont | 1878 | Box 66 | Marshall, Rebecca G. | 1915 | Box 526 |
| Marks, Julia S. | 1908 | Box 351 | Marshall, Rebecca S. | 1897 | Box 171 |
| Markward, Catharine M. | 1916 | Box 552 | Marshall, Roy E. | 1917 | Box 577 |
| Markward, Howard | 1905 | Box 287 | Marshall, Sally M. | 1855 | Box 24 |
| Markwood, Wesley | 1913 | Box 474 | Marshall, Sarah | 1918 | Box 605 |
| Marlatt, Florence L. | 1903 | Box 249 | Marshall, Sarah Ann | 1875 | Box 58 |
| Marlboro, Samuel | 1830 | Box 10 | Marshall, Stanley | 1893 | Box 140 |
| Marll, Elizabeth H. | 1879 | Box 69 | Marshall, Sydney F. | 1911 | Box 424 |
| Marll, William H. | 1872 | Box 48 | Marshall, Thomas J. | 1918 | Box 605 |
| Marlow, Alfred H. | 1904 | Box 268 | Marshall, William | 1870 | Box 43 |
| Marlow, Frank B. | 1905 | Box 287 | Marston, Hiram P. | 1919 | Box 636 |
| Marlow, Stuart Le Roy | 1919 | Box 636 | Marston, Julia F. | 1917 | Box 577 |
| Marlow, Walter H. | 1913 | Box 474 | Marthinson, Charles | 1913 | Box 474 |
| Marmaduke, Bettie C. | 1908 | Box 351 | Martin, Anna J. | 1920 | Box 669 |
| Marmion, Robert A. | 1907 | Box 328 | Martin, Artemas | 1918 | Box 605 |
| Maroney, John A. E. | 1901 | Box 212 | Martin, Arthur | 1911 | Box 424 |
| Marquand, Charles | 1875 | Box 58 | Martin, Catharine Miranda | 1902 | Box 231 |
| Marquis, Walter S. | 1908 | Box 351 | Martin, Celia S. | 1917 | Box 577 |
| Marr, Helen | 1918 | Box 605 | Martin, Charles C. | 1894 | Box 148 |
| Marr, James Donelan | 1914 | Box 497 | Martin, Charles X. | 1892 | Box 133 |
| Marr, James H. | 1893 | Box 140 | Martin, Charlotte A. | 1904 | Box 268 |
| Marr, Mary J. | 1917 | Box 577 | Martin, Elizabeth P. | 1890 | Box 120 |
| Marr, Rebecca | 1880 | Box 72 | Martin, Ella | 1901 | Box 212 |
| Marr, Samuel S. | 1915 | Box 526 | Martin, Ellen | 1896 | Box 163 |
| Marriott, Andrew | 1907 | Box 329 | Martin, Ellen | 1917 | Box 577 |
| Marriott, Rosa Ann | 1920 | Box 669 | Martin, Henrietta R. | 1913 | Box 474 |
| Marrow (Morrow), Mary | 1911 | Box 424 | Martin, Henry | 1884 | Box 88 |
| Marschalk, Christian | 1890 | Box 120 | Martin, Henry W. | 1917 | Box 577 |
| Marsh, Alonzo J. | 1891 | Box 126 | Martin, Hiram H. | 1919 | Box 636 |
| Marsh, Daniel D. | 1920 | Box 669 | Martin, John | 1875 | Box 58 |
| Marsh, George | 1915 | Box 526 | Martin, John W. | 1887 | Box 104 |
| Marsh, Maria Louisa | 1920 | Box 669 | Martin, Joseph S. | 1900 | Box 197 |
| Marsh, Ruth S. | 1916 | Box 552 | Martin, Luther | 1885 | Box 93 |
| Marsh, William P. | 1893 | Box 140 | Martin, Mary | 1871 | Box 45 |
| Marshal, Edward (Thomas) | 1894 | Box 148 | Martin, Mary E. S. | 1915 | Box 526 |
| Marshall, Ann E. | 1892 | Box 133 | Martin, Mary Emeline | 1915 | Box 526 |
| Marshall, Annie J. | 1903 | Box 249 | Martin, Mary Ross | 1880 | Box 72 |
| Marshall, Augusta | 1907 | Box 329 | Martin, Millard Fillmore | 1908 | Box 351 |
| Marshall, Charitz A. | 1873 | Box 51 | Martin, Nathan C. | 1908 | Box 351 |
| Marshall, Charles | 1913 | Box 474 | Martin, Noah H. | 1904 | Box 268 |
| Marshall, Dennis | 1887 | Box 104 | Martin, Patrick | 1914 | Box 497 |
| Marshall, Edward E. | 1918 | Box 605 | Martin, Rebecca A. | 1885 | Box 93 |
| Marshall, Eleanor A. H. | 1852 | Box 22 | Martin, Rhoda M. | 1920 | Box 669 |
| Marshall, George E. | 1900 | Box 197 | Martin, Robert L. | 1899 | Box 185 |
| Marshall, Harriet Ann | 1911 | Box 424 | Martin, Sarah A. | 1891 | Box 126 |
| Marshall, Isaac | 1874 | Box 54 | Martin, William | 1897 | Box 171 |
| Marshall, James | 1804 | Box 1 | Martyn, Francis | 1891 | Box 126 |
| Marshall, James Elger | 1812 | Box 4 | Martyn, John T. | 1896 | Box 163 |

| | | | | | | |
|---|---|---|---|---|---|---|
| Marvin, Julia R. | 1889 | Box 115 | | Massie, Fanny Ansley | 1920 | Box 669 |
| Marx, Clara | 1920 | Box 669 | | Massie, Henry | 1863 | Box 31 |
| Marx, George | 1895 | Box 155 | | Masson, Edmund E. | 1907 | Box 329 |
| Marye, William A. | 1903 | Box 249 | | Masson, Louisa | 1890 | Box 120 |
| Maschmeyer, Ann M. | 1918 | Box 605 | | Masson, Walter B. | 1886 | Box 98 |
| Masi, Francisco | 1857 | Box 26 | | Mastbrook, Catharine | 1898 | Box 177 |
| Masi, Philip Charles | 1907 | Box 329 | | Mastbrook, Henry J. | 1908 | Box 351 |
| Masi, Philip H. | 1894 | Box 148 | | Mastellos, Elephthenos | 1919 | Box 636 |
| Masi, Vincent | 1859 | Box 27 | | Masters, Margaret | 1806 | Box 2 |
| Mason, Anthony | 1916 | Box 552 | | Masterson, Hugh | 1904 | Box 268 |
| Mason, Beverley R. | 1910 | Box 399 | | Masterson, Mary Ann | 1882 | Box 80 |
| Mason, Caroline | 1919 | Box 636 | | Masterson, Mary Ann | 1884 | Box 88 |
| Mason, Daniel H. | 1920 | Box 669 | | Matchett, Thomas L. | 1912 | Box 449 |
| Mason, Ellen C. | 1891 | Box 126 | | Mateer, Annie E. | 1910 | Box 399 |
| Mason, Ellen V. | 1914 | Box 497 | | Mater, Savilla | 1895 | Box 156 |
| Mason, Emanuel | 1893 | Box 140 | | Mathers, James | 1811 | Box 3 |
| Mason, Emily V. | 1909 | Box 374 | | Mathers, Katherine D. | 1919 | Box 636 |
| Mason, Emma Josephine | 1896 | Box 163 | | Mathers, Mary Annie E. | 1900 | Box 197 |
| Mason, Eva Lee | 1915 | Box 526 | | Mathews, Andrew S. | 1891 | Box 126 |
| Mason, Eveline | 1886 | Box 98 | | Mathews, James | 1852 | Box 22 |
| Mason, Francis | 1895 | Box 155 | | Mathews, James H. | 1902 | Box 231 |
| Mason, Frank C. | 1914 | Box 497 | | Mathews, James L. | 1915 | Box 526 |
| Mason, George T. | 1882 | Box 80 | | Mathews, John Henry | 1900 | Box 197 |
| Mason, George W. | 1903 | Box 249 | | Mathews, Margaret | 1907 | Box 329 |
| Mason, Granville | 1895 | Box 155 | | Mathews, Morgan | 1877 | Box 64 |
| Mason, Henriette H. | 1915 | Box 526 | | Mathews, R. Stockett | 1891 | Box 126 |
| Mason, James | 1869 | Box 41 | | Mathews, Stanley | 1889 | Box 115 |
| Mason, John | 1866 | Box 36 | | Mathewson, Harriet Silliman | 1908 | Box 351 |
| Mason, John | 1894 | Box 148 | | Mathewson, Lucy M. Stickney | 1919 | Box 636 |
| Mason, John | 1907 | Box 329 | | Mathiot, Benjamin F. | 1920 | Box 669 |
| Mason, John Edwin | 1892 | Box 133 | | Mathiot, George | 1910 | Box 399 |
| Mason, Joseph | 1915 | Box 526 | | Mathiot, Martha E. | 1910 | Box 399 |
| Mason, James M. | 1879 | Box 69 | | Matile, George A. | 1881 | Box 76 |
| Mason, Kitty A. | 1920 | Box 669 | | Matile, James H. | 1911 | Box 424 |
| Mason, Mary Elizabeth | 1906 | Box 306 | | Matlock, Jeremiah G. | 1881 | Box 76 |
| Mason, Mattie E. | 1908 | Box 351 | | Matlock, Sarah Eleanor | 1917 | Box 577 |
| Mason, Milo | 1837 | Box 13 | | Matlock, Simeon | 1871 | Box 45 |
| Mason, Otis Tufton | 1908 | Box 351 | | Matlock, Simeon G. | 1899 | Box 185 |
| Mason, Rachael | 1912 | Box 449 | | Matsen, Andrew | 1908 | Box 351 |
| Mason, Serena | 1882 | Box 80 | | Mattern, Anna S. | 1891 | Box 126 |
| Mason, Theodorus B. M. | 1901 | Box 212 | | Mattern, Margaretha Seel | 1882 | Box 80 |
| Mason, Thomas | 1867 | Box 37 | | Mattes, Henry | 1920 | Box 669 |
| Mason, Thomas | 1890 | Box 120 | | Matteson, Lorenzo D. | 1898 | Box 177 |
| Mason, William C. | 1911 | Box 424 | | Matthews, Anna E. | 1878 | Box 66 |
| Mason, William L. | 1909 | Box 374 | | Matthews, Charity | 1876 | Box 61 |
| Mason, William M. | 1907 | Box 329 | | Matthews, Charles B. | 1919 | Box 636 |
| Mason, William T. T. | 1865 | Box 34 | | Matthews, Charles M. | 1894 | Box 148 |
| Massey, Ellen | 1838 | Box 14 | | Matthews, Eleanor Carr | 1920 | Box 669 |
| Massey, John H. | 1858 | Box 26 | | Matthews, Emily C. | 1912 | Box 449 |
| Massey, John L. | 1913 | Box 474 | | Matthews, Henry C. | 1862 | Box 30 |
| Massey, Walter S. | 1910 | Box 399 | | Matthews, John | 1887 | Box 104 |
| Massey, William | 1912 | Box 449 | | Matthews, John | 1891 | Box 126 |

| | | | | | | |
|---|---|---|---|---|---|---|
| Matthews, Lucinda | 1884 | Box 88 | | May, Edward H. | 1886 | Box 98 |
| Matthews, Mary K. | 1912 | Box 449 | | May, Frank P. | 1911 | Box 424 |
| Matthews, Matthew | 1866 | Box 36 | | May, Frederic | 1918 | Box 605 |
| Matthews, Robert Bowman | 1901 | Box 212 | | May, Frederick | 1847 | Box 19 |
| Matthews, Sophia | 1917 | Box 577 | | May, Frederick DeCourcey | 1893 | Box 140 |
| Matthews, Susan | 1900 | Box 197 | | May, George J. | 1911 | Box 424 |
| Matthews, Virginia R. | 1888 | Box 109 | | May, Heber J. | 1915 | Box 526 |
| Matthews, Washington | 1906 | Box 306 | | May, Henry C. | 1894 | Box 148 |
| Matthews, William | 1854 | Box 23 | | May, John Frederick | 1891 | Box 126 |
| Matthews, William Baynham | 1914 | Box 497 | | May, John M. | 1878 | Box 66 |
| Matthews, William E. | 1895 | Box 155 | | May, Juliana Gales | 1901 | Box 212 |
| Mattingly, Ann | 1855 | Box 24 | | May, Katie A. | 1919 | Box 636 |
| Mattingly, Ann | 1873 | Box 51 | | May, Mary | 1917 | Box 577 |
| Mattingly, Ella R. | 1876 | Box 61 | | May, Mary A. | 1902 | Box 231 |
| Mattingly, Eloysa | 1839 | Box 14 | | May, Mary Elizabeth | 1904 | Box 269 |
| Mattingly, Francis | 1889 | Box 115 | | May, Monroe E. | 1899 | Box 185 |
| Mattingly, George | 1884 | Box 88 | | May, Phebe M. | 1898 | Box 178 |
| Mattingly, Grace Agnes | 1907 | Box 329 | | May, Philip | 1899 | Box 185 |
| Mattingly, Joseph W. | 1908 | Box 351 | | May, Sarah Maria | 1920 | Box 669 |
| Mattingly, Julia | 1910 | Box 399 | | May, Thomas O. N. | 1845 | Box 17 |
| Mattingly, Lewis | 1856 | Box 25 | | Mayer, Mathilda | 1919 | Box 636 |
| Mattingly, Louisa | 1893 | Box 140 | | Mayer, Theodore J. | 1907 | Box 329 |
| Mattingly, Nancy | 1856 | Box 25 | | Mayes, Thomas A. | 1906 | Box 306 |
| Mattingly, Thomas Joseph | 1916 | Box 552 | | Mayfield, Benjamin | 1826 | Box 8 |
| Mattingly, William F. | 1919 | Box 636 | | Mayfield, Benjamin R. | 1900 | Box 197 |
| Mattingly, Zachariah | 1824 | Box 8 | | Mayfield, Charlotte L. | 1902 | Box 231 |
| Maulding, Theresa C. | 1919 | Box 636 | | Mayfield, Clifton | 1910 | Box 399 |
| Maulsby, Anna M. | 1892 | Box 133 | | Mayfield, Susanna | 1863 | Box 31 |
| Maulsby, Anna Matilda | 1896 | Box 163 | | Mayhew, Eliza | 1895 | Box 155 |
| Maupin, Hannah E. | 1884 | Box 88 | | Mayhew, Elizabeth | 1844 | Box 17 |
| Mauro, Lewis Johnson | 1915 | Box 526 | | Mayhew, John | 1890 | Box 120 |
| Maury, Elizabeth Herndon | 1903 | Box 249 | | Mayhew, Mary Etta | 1915 | Box 526 |
| Maury, Ellen | 1879 | Box 69 | | Maynadier, Elizabeth W. | 1898 | Box 178 |
| Maury, Isabel | 1890 | Box 120 | | Maynadier, William | 1871 | Box 45 |
| Maury, John W. | 1855 | Box 24 | | Maynard, George Colton | 1918 | Box 605 |
| Maury, Jourdan W. | 1883 | Box 83 | | Mayne, John | 1899 | Box 186 |
| Maury, Lucy E. | 1908 | Box 351 | | Mayo, Jennett P. | 1887 | Box 104 |
| Mauss, Richard G. | 1891 | Box 126 | | Mayo, Richard | 1906 | Box 306 |
| Mawrey, William A. | 1899 | Box 185 | | Mayo, Sarah B. | 1886 | Box 98 |
| Maxley, Lloyd | 1896 | Box 163 | | Mayo, William K. | 1900 | Box 197 |
| Maxson, Louis William | 1916 | Box 552 | | Mays, Benjamin F. | 1919 | Box 636 |
| Maxwell, Benjamin V. | 1915 | Box 526 | | Mays, Charles | 1913 | Box 474 |
| Maxwell, Charles A. | 1920 | Box 669 | | Mays, Margaret Blanch | 1913 | Box 474 |
| Maxwell, Charles D. | 1890 | Box 120 | | Mays, William | 1913 | Box 474 |
| Maxwell, Delia | 1877 | Box 64 | | Mazarakis, Stellios | 1920 | Box 669 |
| Maxwell, Hattie K. | 1908 | Box 351 | | Mazinger, Richard T. | 1915 | Box 526 |
| Maxwell, James | 1874 | Box 54 | | McAboy, Alice Bland | 1905 | Box 286 |
| Maxwell, Miriam K. | 1889 | Box 115 | | McAdoo, Julia W. | 1919 | Box 635 |
| Maxwell, William H. | 1886 | Box 98 | | McAleer, Mary J. | 1918 | Box 604 |
| May, Alfred J. | 1900 | Box 197 | | McAlister, James | 1858 | Box 26 |
| May, Alice | 1896 | Box 163 | | McAllister, Margaret | 1906 | Box 305 |
| May, Annie K. | 1919 | Box 636 | | McAllister, Michael | 1888 | Box 109 |

| | | | | | | |
|---|---|---|---|---|---|---|
| McAllister, Richard | 1897 | Box 170 | McCarthy, Charles | 1907 | Box 328 |
| McAllister, Sarah Elizabeth | 1884 | Box 88 | McCarthy, Charles S. | 1865 | Box 34 |
| McAlpine, Carrie Saunders | 1918 | Box 604 | McCarthy, Daniel | 1883 | Box 83 |
| McAlwee, Benjamin F. | 1918 | Box 604 | McCarthy, David K. | 1916 | Box 551 |
| McAndrews, Bartholomew | 1914 | Box 496 | McCarthy, Dennis J. | 1920 | Box 668 |
| McArdle, Stephen | 1893 | Box 140 | McCarthy, Ellen | 1912 | Box 448 |
| McAtee, Catharine E. | 1898 | Box 177 | McCarthy, Eugene | 1863 | Box 31 |
| McAuley, William | 1880 | Box 72 | McCarthy, Florence H. | 1902 | Box 230 |
| McAuliffe, Florence D. | 1920 | Box 668 | McCarthy, Florence J. | 1916 | Box 551 |
| McBath, Andrew M. | 1913 | Box 473 | McCarthy, James | 1854 | Box 23 |
| McBath, M. Isabella | 1916 | Box 551 | McCarthy, James | 1882 | Box 80 |
| McBee, Randolph | 1919 | Box 635 | McCarthy, Jane | 1913 | Box 473 |
| McBeth, William | 1896 | Box 163 | McCarthy, Jeremiah J. | 1906 | Box 306 |
| McBlain, Roberta H. | 1919 | Box 635 | McCarthy, John | 1844 | Box 17 |
| McBlair, Augusta | 1903 | Box 249 | McCarthy, John | 1874 | Box 54 |
| McBlair, John G. | 1899 | Box 185 | McCarthy, John | 1900 | Box 196 |
| McBride, Margaret Jane | 1907 | Box 327 | McCarthy, John | 1913 | Box 473 |
| McCabe, Alice | 1897 | Box 170 | McCarthy, John B. | 1916 | Box 551 |
| McCabe, Ann | 1884 | Box 88 | McCarthy, John J. | 1894 | Box 147 |
| McCabe, James M. | 1915 | Box 525 | McCarthy, Julia | 1917 | Box 576 |
| McCabe, Owen | 1911 | Box 423 | McCarthy, Julia E. | 1909 | Box 373 |
| McCafferty, Elizabeth | 1913 | Box 473 | McCarthy, Margaret | 1919 | Box 635 |
| McCaffray, George | 1906 | Box 305 | McCarthy, Margaret M. | 1913 | Box 473 |
| McCaffrey, Ellen | 1911 | Box 423 | McCarthy, Mary | 1907 | Box 328 |
| McCaffrey, Frank T. | 1898 | Box 177 | McCarthy, Mary E. | 1917 | Box 576 |
| McCaffrey, Hugh | 1901 | Box 210 | McCarthy, Mary Helena | 1916 | Box 551 |
| McCaffrey, R. Morriss | 1918 | Box 604 | McCarthy, Mary Helena | 1918 | Box 604 |
| McCaffrey, Terrence | 1900 | Box 196 | McCarthy, Michael | 1864 | Box 32 |
| McCalla, Elizabeth H. | 1920 | Box 668 | McCarthy, Mollie | 1920 | Box 668 |
| McCalla, Helen Hill | 1906 | Box 305 | McCarthy, Patrick | 1882 | Box 80 |
| McCalla, John M. | 1897 | Box 170 | McCarthy, Serena | 1872 | Box 48 |
| McCalla, Louisa G. | 1865 | Box 34 | McCarthy, Thomas | 1863 | Box 31 |
| McCalla, Maria F. | 1919 | Box 635 | McCarthy, Thomas | 1879 | Box 69 |
| McCalla, Maria Frances | 1860 | Box 28 | McCarthy, Timothy | 1897 | Box 170 |
| McCalla, Sarah H. | 1913 | Box 473 | McCarthy, William A. | 1910 | Box 398 |
| McCallan, John | 1918 | Box 604 | McCartin, Mary A. | 1911 | Box 423 |
| McCallum, Mary C. | 1908 | Box 350 | McCartney, Daniel Paul | 1903 | Box 249 |
| McCalmont, John S. | 1906 | Box 305 | McCarty, Cora | 1918 | Box 604 |
| McCammon, Joseph K. | 1907 | Box 328 | McCarty, Dennis | 1898 | Box 177 |
| McCane, Jacob R. | 1920 | Box 668 | McCarty, John | 1881 | Box 76 |
| McCann, Charles B. | 1913 | Box 473 | McCarty, Justus I. | 1881 | Box 76 |
| McCann, William | 1905 | Box 286 | McCarty, Mary E. | 1897 | Box 170 |
| McCardle, Annie E. | 1913 | Box 473 | McCarty, Thomas | 1899 | Box 185 |
| McCarrick, James | 1863 | Box 31 | McCatheran, Francis C. | 1917 | Box 576 |
| McCarten, Edward | 1895 | Box 155 | McCathran, Francis F. | 1907 | Box 328 |
| McCarteney, Charles M. | 1904 | Box 268 | McCathran, James A. | 1901 | Box 211 |
| McCarter, Archie | 1901 | Box 211 | McCathran, James R. | 1875 | Box 58 |
| McCarthy, Bartholomew | 1869 | Box 41 | McCathran, Maria V. | 1900 | Box 196 |
| McCarthy, Catherine | 1908 | Box 350 | McCauley, George | 1878 | Box 66 |
| McCarthy, Catherine | 1894 | Box 147 | McCauley, Henry C. | 1909 | Box 373 |
| McCarthy, Catherine | 1907 | Box 328 | McCauley, James | 1872 | Box 48 |
| McCarthy, Catherine | 1917 | Box 576 | McCauley, James A. | 1913 | Box 473 |

| | | | | | | |
|---|---|---|---|---|---|---|
| McCauley, James N. | 1881 | Box 76 | | McCormick, Hugh | 1873 | Box 51 |
| McCauley, Janie P. | 1896 | Box 163 | | McCormick, Joseph T. | 1890 | Box 120 |
| McCauley, John | 1858 | Box 26 | | McCormick, Martin J. | 1910 | Box 398 |
| McCauley, Joseph | 1904 | Box 268 | | McCormick, Patrick | 1873 | Box 51 |
| McCauley, Lucy | 1898 | Box 177 | | McCormick, Patrick | 1890 | Box 120 |
| McCauley, Susan | 1895 | Box 155 | | McCormick, Patrick | 1905 | Box 286 |
| McCauley, Theodore F. (Sr.) | 1895 | Box 155 | | McCormick, Patrick | 1912 | Box 448 |
| McCauley, Thomas | 1898 | Box 177 | | McCormick, Van Horn | 1914 | Box 496 |
| McCausland, Cora B. | 1918 | Box 604 | | McCorpen, John | 1895 | Box 155 |
| McCausland, James | 1809 | Box 3 | | McCortney, Edmonia R. | 1919 | Box 635 |
| McCay, Mary Emeline | 1901 | Box 211 | | McCortney, James R. | 1903 | Box 249 |
| McCeney, Henry C. | 1892 | Box 133 | | McCoy, Benjamin M. | 1884 | Box 88 |
| McCeney, Mary E. | 1912 | Box 448 | | McCoy, Joseph S. | 1916 | Box 551 |
| McChesney, Julia E. | 1908 | Box 350 | | McCoy, Mary Jane | 1895 | Box 155 |
| McCleary, Henry | 1878 | Box 66 | | McCoy, William | 1900 | Box 196 |
| McCleish, Aloysius | 1918 | Box 604 | | McCoy, William J. | 1907 | Box 328 |
| McClellan, John R. | 1896 | Box 163 | | McCrabb, Jane M. | 1911 | Box 423 |
| McClellan, Robert J. | 1906 | Box 306 | | McCracken, Mary A. | 1918 | Box 604 |
| McClellan, Sally Margaret | 1896 | Box 163 | | McCrea, Henry | 1908 | Box 350 |
| McClelland, John | 1896 | Box 163 | | McCreedy, Mary Alice | 1917 | Box 576 |
| McClelland, John | 1845 | Box 17 | | McCreery, Andrew B. | 1913 | Box 473 |
| McClelland, John W. | 1876 | Box 61 | | McCreery, John L. | 1906 | Box 306 |
| McClellen, Rose | 1910 | Box 398 | | McCrellis, James B. | 1901 | Box 211 |
| McClery, Elizabeth H. | 1914 | Box 496 | | McCristal, Edward J. | 1894 | Box 147 |
| McClosky, Mary Cecelia | 1919 | Box 635 | | McCubbin, Nicholas | 1877 | Box 64 |
| McClosky, Samuel H. | 1890 | Box 120 | | McCulloch, Frederick A. | 1910 | Box 398 |
| McClosky, William Richard | 1912 | Box 448 | | McCulloch, George M. D. | 1920 | Box 668 |
| McClurg, Edmonia Mason | 1909 | Box 373 | | McCulloch, Hugh | 1895 | Box 155 |
| McClurg, Walter Audubon | 1917 | Box 576 | | McCulloch, Mary A. | 1915 | Box 525 |
| McCollam, Edward F. | 1914 | Box 496 | | McCulloch, Susan | 1898 | Box 177 |
| McCollam, John J. | 1898 | Box 177 | | McCullough, Allen A. | 1914 | Box 496 |
| McComas, Florence A. | 1908 | Box 350 | | McCullough, Catharine R. | 1893 | Box 140 |
| McComas, John F. | 1902 | Box 230 | | McCullough, George | 1917 | Box 576 |
| McComas, Louis E. | 1907 | Box 328 | | McCullough, Harriet B. | 1919 | Box 635 |
| McCondach, Elizabeth E. | 1911 | Box 423 | | McCullough, James | 1876 | Box 61 |
| McCondach, James | 1899 | Box 185 | | McCullough, Marion | 1914 | Box 496 |
| McConnell, Ellen C. | 1899 | Box 185 | | McCullough, Martha S. | 1914 | Box 496 |
| McConnell, John A. | 1894 | Box 147 | | McCullough, Mary | 1907 | Box 328 |
| McConnell, Mary V. | 1907 | Box 328 | | McCullough, William W. | 1895 | Box 155 |
| McConville, William E. | 1918 | Box 604 | | McCullum, George Thomas | 1895 | Box 155 |
| McCooey, Joseph B. | 1898 | Box 177 | | McCully, Emma A. | 1917 | Box 576 |
| McCook, John | 1872 | Box 48 | | McCune, Herbert Austin | 1920 | Box 668 |
| McCormack, Henry P. | 1915 | Box 525 | | McCurdy, Lucy | 1912 | Box 448 |
| McCormick, Alexander | 1891 | Box 126 | | McCutchen, James | 1869 | Box 41 |
| McCormick, Alexander H. | 1917 | Box 576 | | McCutchen, Martha | 1890 | Box 120 |
| McCormick, Alice L. | 1916 | Box 551 | | McCutchen, Robert | 1901 | Box 211 |
| McCormick, Bridget | 1880 | Box 72 | | McCutchins, Genevieve C. | 1919 | Box 635 |
| McCormick, Bridget | 1900 | Box 196 | | McDaniel, George | 1890 | Box 120 |
| McCormick, Dorothea | 1914 | Box 496 | | McDaniel, Jesse | 1919 | Box 635 |
| McCormick, Edward | 1887 | Box 104 | | McDaniel, Leonard | 1817 | Box 5 |
| McCormick, Frances A. | 1899 | Box 185 | | McDaniel, Mary Ellen | 1894 | Box 147 |
| McCormick, Harriet P. | 1884 | Box 88 | | McDaniel, Robert | 1898 | Box 177 |

| | | | | | | |
|---|---|---|---|---|---|
| McDaniels, Frances | 1913 | Box 473 | McElroy, Anthony | 1841 | Box 15 |
| McDermott, F. P. | 1909 | Box 373 | McElroy, Carrie B. | 1918 | Box 604 |
| McDermott, Henry J. | 1912 | Box 449 | McElroy, John | 1878 | Box 66 |
| McDermott, James | 1895 | Box 155 | McElwee, James | 1888 | Box 109 |
| McDermott, John | 1910 | Box 398 | McEniry, Thomas | 1889 | Box 115 |
| McDermott, Joseph Arthur | 1899 | Box 185 | McEuen, Thomas | 1911 | Box 423 |
| McDermott, Margaret | 1909 | Box 373 | McEvoy, James | 1890 | Box 120 |
| McDermott, Maria | 1820 | Box 6 | McEwan, Walter | 1909 | Box 373 |
| McDermott, Michael | 1808 | Box 3 | McEwen, Louise A. | 1905 | Box 287 |
| McDermott, Sarah | 1874 | Box 54 | McFadden, Ellen | 1898 | Box 177 |
| McDevitt, Ann | 1879 | Box 69 | McFall, John Campbell | 1919 | Box 635 |
| McDevitt, Dennis | 1915 | Box 525 | McFalls, Louisa E. | 1911 | Box 423 |
| McDevitt, John | 1876 | Box 61 | McFarlan, Daniel | 1915 | Box 525 |
| McDevitt, Rebecca M. V. | 1903 | Box 249 | McFarlan, Josephine | 1858 | Box 27 |
| McDonald, Alexander | 1835 | Box 13 | McFarlan, Mary A. | 1913 | Box 473 |
| McDonald, Annie B. | 1899 | Box 185 | McFarland, Jane | 1908 | Box 350 |
| McDonald, Brunette S. | 1914 | Box 496 | McFarland, John | 1845 | Box 17 |
| McDonald, Charles J. | 1897 | Box 170 | McFarland, John M. | 1894 | Box 147 |
| McDonald, Cornelia E. | 1899 | Box 185 | McFarland, Neil | 1920 | Box 668 |
| McDonald, Flora E. | 1905 | Box 286 | McFarland, Sidney | 1890 | Box 120 |
| McDonald, H. Bowyer | 1907 | Box 328 | McFarland, Walter A. | 1915 | Box 525 |
| McDonald, Isabella | 1897 | Box 170 | McFarland, William David | 1909 | Box 373 |
| McDonald, James | 1915 | Box 525 | McFarlane, Matilda | 1873 | Box 51 |
| McDonald, John G. | 1837 | Box 13 | McFarlane, William | 1919 | Box 635 |
| McDonald, Joseph | 1897 | Box 170 | McFarran, Mary | 1915 | Box 525 |
| McDonald, Lydia P. | 1886 | Box 98 | McFerran, Rose H. | 1912 | Box 449 |
| McDonald, Paul Harding | 1909 | Box 373 | McGarvey (Garvey), Annie | 1911 | Box 417 |
| McDonald, Robert | 1899 | Box 185 | McGarvey, John | 1867 | Box 38 |
| McDonald, Sara Marie | 1918 | Box 604 | McGarvey, Patrick | 1850 | Box 21 |
| McDonald, William J. | 1915 | Box 525 | McGee, Bernard | 1899 | Box 185 |
| McDonnall, Mary | 1814 | Box 4 | McGee, Joseph F. | 1914 | Box 496 |
| McDonnell, Christopher | 1875 | Box 58 | McGee, W. J. | 1913 | Box 473 |
| McDonnell, Dennis | 1894 | Box 147 | McGee, Winnie | 1916 | Box 551 |
| McDonnell, Mary E. | 1885 | Box 93 | McGetrick, Edward B. | 1917 | Box 576 |
| McDonnell, Richard | 1906 | Box 306 | McGill, Charles | 1859 | Box 27 |
| McDonnell, Thomas | 1882 | Box 80 | McGill, Frank A. | 1885 | Box 93 |
| McDonnell, William R. | 1915 | Box 525 | McGill, Harriet J. | 1901 | Box 211 |
| McDonough, Ferdinand | 1903 | Box 249 | McGill, J. Nota | 1915 | Box 525 |
| McDonough, Maria | 1920 | Box 668 | McGill, James H. | 1908 | Box 350 |
| McDonough, Peter | 1865 | Box 34 | McGill, Jane L. | 1911 | Box 423 |
| McDonough, Sarah E. | 1906 | Box 306 | McGill, Thomas | 1901 | Box 211 |
| McDougall, Charles | 1885 | Box 93 | McGillicuddy, Eugene | 1894 | Box 147 |
| McDowell, Albert F. | 1919 | Box 635 | McGilton, James | 1892 | Box 133 |
| McDowell, Anna C. | 1910 | Box 398 | McGinley, Michael | 1905 | Box 287 |
| McDowell, Fanny G. | 1911 | Box 423 | McGinnell, Margaret | 1909 | Box 373 |
| McDowell, James G. | 1912 | Box 449 | McGinness, Annie | 1907 | Box 328 |
| McDowell, Samuel C. | 1918 | Box 604 | McGinnis, Peter | 1908 | Box 350 |
| McDowell, Woodford G. | 1904 | Box 268 | McGivern, Henry | 1883 | Box 83 |
| McDuell, John | 1866 | Box 36 | McGlue, Eliza | 1895 | Box 155 |
| McElfresh, William Henry | 1906 | Box 306 | McGlue, George T. (Sr.) | 1887 | Box 104 |
| McElhenny, Thomas J. | 1888 | Box 109 | McGlue, George T. | 1905 | Box 287 |
| McElhone, John J. | 1890 | Box 120 | McGlue, Owen | 1820 | Box 6 |

| | | | | | | |
|---|---|---|---|---|---|---|
| McGolrick, Mary A. | 1905 | Box 287 | McIntire, Alexander | 1860 | Box 28 |
| McGolrick, William | 1877 | Box 64 | McIntire, David | 1884 | Box 88 |
| McGowan, John | 1915 | Box 525 | McIntire, Edwin A. | 1907 | Box 328 |
| McGowan, Jonas H. | 1909 | Box 373 | McIntire, Frances B. | 1911 | Box 423 |
| McGowan, Michael A. | 1901 | Box 211 | McIntire, Lettie F. | 1919 | Box 635 |
| McGowan, Nicholas | 1906 | Box 306 | McIntire, Martha | 1906 | Box 306 |
| McGowan, William C. | 1919 | Box 635 | McIntire, Mary A. | 1918 | Box 604 |
| McGrann, Henry | 1889 | Box 115 | McIntire, Timothy C. | 1861 | Box 29 |
| McGrann, Henry F. | 1891 | Box 126 | McIntosh, Emma B. | 1918 | Box 604 |
| McGrann, James | 1888 | Box 109 | McInturff, Alfred R. | 1893 | Box 140 |
| McGrann, John | 1891 | Box 126 | McInturff, Maggie T. | 1920 | Box 668 |
| McGrann, Mary A. | 1918 | Box 604 | McIntyre, Bridget | 1886 | Box 98 |
| McGrath, Dennis | 1904 | Box 268 | McIntyre, Peter J. | 1920 | Box 668 |
| McGrath, Honora | 1916 | Box 551 | McIntyre, Thomas | 1891 | Box 126 |
| McGrath, James | 1911 | Box 423 | McJilton, Catherine | 1865 | Box 34 |
| McGrath, Peter | 1883 | Box 83 | McKaraher, Ann | 1849 | Box 20 |
| McGraw (Bemon), Catherine | 1825 | Box 8 | McKavett, F. | 1847 | Box 19 |
| McGraw, Eliza | 1877 | Box 64 | McKay, Gordon | 1909 | Box 373 |
| McGraw, Francis James | 1913 | Box 473 | McKay, Nathaniel | 1903 | Box 249 |
| McGraw, James | 1875 | Box 58 | McKeag, John | 1887 | Box 104 |
| McGregor, John | 1911 | Box 423 | McKean, Elizabeth R. | 1910 | Box 398 |
| McGrew, Alexander | 1916 | Box 551 | McKean, Frances M. | 1908 | Box 350 |
| McGrew, Armilda | 1906 | Box 306 | McKean, Harriet M. | 1910 | Box 398 |
| McGrew, J. M. | 1895 | Box 155 | McKean, Henry B. | 1903 | Box 249 |
| McGuigan, Alexander | 1902 | Box 230 | McKean, Joseph P. | 1882 | Box 80 |
| McGuiggan, Mary | 1874 | Box 55 | McKean, Katherine W. | 1904 | Box 268 |
| McGuillan, Mary A. | 1892 | Box 133 | McKean, Marcia V. | 1912 | Box 449 |
| McGuinn, Catherine | 1905 | Box 287 | McKean, Margaret A. | 1910 | Box 398 |
| McGuire, Anna | 1864 | Box 32 | McKean, Mary K. | 1910 | Box 398 |
| McGuire, Emily N. | 1916 | Box 551 | McKean, Samuel M. | 1869 | Box 41 |
| McGuire, Frederick B. | 1916 | Box 551 | McKee, Albert J. | 1906 | Box 306 |
| McGuire, James C. | 1888 | Box 109 | McKee, Caroline | 1889 | Box 115 |
| McGuire, Joseph D. | 1916 | Box 551 | McKee, Frances Dunn | 1920 | Box 668 |
| McGuire, Maria | 1901 | Box 211 | McKee, John H. | 1920 | Box 668 |
| McGuire, Martin | 1894 | Box 147 | McKee, John M. E. | 1916 | Box 551 |
| McGuire, Mary Elizabeth | 1893 | Box 140 | McKee, Redick | 1886 | Box 98 |
| McGuire, Patrick | 1881 | Box 76 | McKee, William | 1891 | Box 126 |
| McGunigle, Nicholas | 1821 | Box 7 | McKeehan, George Henry | 1917 | Box 577 |
| McGurk, Edward A. | 1899 | Box 185 | McKeever, Annie | 1905 | Box 287 |
| McHenry, James | 1880 | Box 72 | McKeever, Chauncey | 1902 | Box 230 |
| McHenry, Margaret | 1906 | Box 306 | McKeever, Edwin K. | 1908 | Box 350 |
| McHugh, Charles H. | 1917 | Box 576 | McKeever, Mary F. | 1900 | Box 196 |
| McIlhenny, George A. | 1892 | Box 133 | McKelden, John C. | 1886 | Box 98 |
| McIlhenny, Nellie M. | 1909 | Box 373 | McKeldin, William Henry | 1920 | Box 668 |
| McIlhenny, Oliver | 1908 | Box 350 | McKeldon, Mary | 1897 | Box 170 |
| McIlhenny, Thyrza V. | 1913 | Box 473 | McKellip, Sarah C. | 1910 | Box 398 |
| McIlvaine, Helen M. | 1917 | Box 576 | McKelway, Alexander Jeffrey | 1918 | Box 604 |
| McInerney, Dennis | 1890 | Box 120 | McKenna, Felix | 1891 | Box 126 |
| McInerney, Morgan | 1907 | Box 328 | McKenna, James | 1913 | Box 473 |
| McInesten, James | 1879 | Box 69 | McKenna, James Patrica | 1912 | Box 449 |
| McIntee, Mark | 1878 | Box 66 | McKenna, John | 1916 | Box 551 |
| McIntire, Adaline | 1885 | Box 93 | McKenna, Patrick | 1865 | Box 34 |

| | | | | | | |
|---|---|---|---|---|---|---|
| McKenney, America | 1907 | Box 328 | McKnight, William James | 1902 | Box 231 |
| McKenney, Edward | 1887 | Box 104 | McKy, Elizabeth | 1908 | Box 351 |
| McKenney, Edward T. | 1901 | Box 211 | McLain, William | 1873 | Box 51 |
| McKenney, Fanny | 1904 | Box 268 | McLanahan, George William | 1908 | Box 351 |
| McKenney, James H. | 1913 | Box 473 | McLanahan, George Xavier | 1919 | Box 635 |
| McKenney, John S. | 1895 | Box 155 | McLane, Abby K. | 1918 | Box 604 |
| McKenney, Mary | 1905 | Box 287 | McLane, Allan | 1893 | Box 140 |
| McKenney, Mary Ann | 1895 | Box 155 | McLane, Thomas | 1883 | Box 83 |
| McKenney, Mary Ann | 1895 | Box 155 | McLane, William | 1895 | Box 155 |
| McKenney, Owen P. | 1889 | Box 115 | McLaren, Ida L. | 1908 | Box 351 |
| McKenney, Robert Vincin | 1908 | Box 351 | McLaughlin, Daniel | 1897 | Box 171 |
| McKenney, Samuel F. | 1865 | Box 34 | McLaughlin, Elizabeth | 1905 | Box 287 |
| McKenney, William A. | 1913 | Box 473 | McLaughlin, Henry J. | 1894 | Box 147 |
| McKenzie, Alexander | 1904 | Box 268 | McLaughlin, Henry W. | 1915 | Box 525 |
| McKenzie, David | 1901 | Box 211 | McLaughlin, James A. | 1882 | Box 80 |
| McKenzie, Donald A. | 1920 | Box 668 | McLaughlin, James Alexander | 1854 | Box 23 |
| McKenzie, Michael | 1914 | Box 496 | McLaughlin, James B. | 1899 | Box 185 |
| McKenzie, William | 1864 | Box 32 | McLaughlin, John | 1906 | Box 306 |
| McKeon, John | 1908 | Box 350 | McLaughlin, Josephine | 1920 | Box 668 |
| McKeon, Mary | 1904 | Box 268 | McLaughlin, Mary | 1913 | Box 473 |
| McKeon, Michael | 1895 | Box 155 | McLaughlin, Mary A. | 1918 | Box 604 |
| McKerichar, Alexander | 1914 | Box 496 | McLaughlin, Mary Ann | 1860 | Box 28 |
| McKericher, Alexander S. | 1902 | Box 230 | McLaughlin, Rachel E. | 1914 | Box 497 |
| McKevit, Anna | 1894 | Box 147 | McLaughlin, Rebecca | 1915 | Box 525 |
| McKibben, Marion | 1901 | Box 211 | McLaughlin, Sarepta C. | 1914 | Box 497 |
| McKie, Margaret L. | 1911 | Box 423 | McLaws, Meta T. | 1912 | Box 449 |
| McKie, Thomas B. | 1901 | Box 211 | McLean, Andrew | 1809 | Box 3 |
| McKierman, Edward | 1918 | Box 604 | McLean, Francis | 1910 | Box 398 |
| McKim, John | 1867 | Box 38 | McLean, Honona | 1848 | Box 19 |
| McKim, Martha Moran | 1914 | Box 496 | McLean, John R. | 1916 | Box 551 |
| McKim, Randolph H. | 1920 | Box 668 | McLean, Louise A. | 1914 | Box 497 |
| McKimmie, Mareb R. | 1918 | Box 604 | McLean, Mary L. | 1901 | Box 211 |
| McKinney, Christopher C. | 1899 | Box 185 | McLean, Washington | 1890 | Box 120 |
| McKinney, Eslander L. | 1909 | Box 373 | McLean, William | 1885 | Box 93 |
| McKinney, John M. | 1918 | Box 604 | McLean, William E. | 1907 | Box 328 |
| McKinney, Robert Christian | 1918 | Box 604 | McLean, William Thomas | 1912 | Box 449 |
| McKinstry, William | 1853 | Box 22 | McLeish, Martha | 1832 | Box 11 |
| McKinstry, William G. | 1864 | Box 32 | McLeod, Alexander N. | 1918 | Box 604 |
| McKlive, Elizabeth | 1870 | Box 43 | McLeod, Alice E. | 1882 | Box 80 |
| McKnew, Elizabeth A. | 1894 | Box 147 | McLeod, Martha | 1874 | Box 55 |
| McKnew, Nathan C. | 1869 | Box 41 | McLeod, William E. | 1901 | Box 211 |
| McKnew, Rosalie B. | 1906 | Box 306 | McLeran, John E. | 1911 | Box 423 |
| McKnew, Wilbur H. | 1897 | Box 171 | McMahon, Anna | 1904 | Box 268 |
| McKnew, William H. | 1902 | Box 231 | McMahon, Elizabeth | 1902 | Box 231 |
| McKnight, Annie | 1885 | Box 93 | McMahon, James | 1905 | Box 287 |
| McKnight, Annie E. | 1910 | Box 399 | McMahon, Thomas | 1885 | Box 93 |
| McKnight, David | 1900 | Box 196 | McMannus, Patrick A. | 1911 | Box 423 |
| McKnight, George B. | 1857 | Box 26 | McManus, Edward | 1890 | Box 120 |
| McKnight, George J. | 1918 | Box 604 | McMerny, Patrick | 1882 | Box 80 |
| McKnight, Martha H. | 1873 | Box 51 | McMichael, Carrie M. | 1912 | Box 449 |
| McKnight, Mary A. | 1886 | Box 98 | McMillan, Alexander F. | 1912 | Box 449 |
| McKnight, Susan | 1919 | Box 635 | McMillan, Caroline Augusta | 1883 | Box 83 |

| | | | | | | |
|---|---|---|---|---|---|---|
| McMillan, James | 1906 | Box 306 | McPhee, Mary A. | 1893 | Box 140 |
| McMillan, James | 1920 | Box 668 | McPherson, Edla J. | 1902 | Box 231 |
| McMillan, Margaret | 1912 | Box 449 | McPherson, Elizabeth H. | 1839 | Box 14 |
| McMillan, Mary L. | 1918 | Box 604 | McPherson, Frances W. | 1907 | Box 328 |
| McMillan, Minerva A. | 1917 | Box 577 | McPherson, Henry | 1865 | Box 34 |
| McMillan, Uriah | 1881 | Box 76 | McPherson, John D. | 1896 | Box 164 |
| McMonigal, Katharine | 1918 | Box 604 | McPherson, John R. | 1898 | Box 177 |
| McMorrow, Bartholomew | 1900 | Box 196 | McPherson, Lewis Edwin | 1905 | Box 287 |
| McMurdy, Robert | 1892 | Box 133 | McPherson, Margaret T. | 1904 | Box 268 |
| McMurtrie, Daniel | 1899 | Box 185 | McPherson, Mary E. | 1898 | Box 177 |
| McMurtrie, Sarah A. | 1920 | Box 668 | McPherson, Mary E. | 1902 | Box 231 |
| McNabb, Gertrude E. | 1920 | Box 668 | McPherson, Robert L. | 1880 | Box 72 |
| McNabb, John | 1914 | Box 497 | McPherson, Robert W. | 1907 | Box 328 |
| McNair, Dunning | 1875 | Box 58 | McPherson, Theodore H. N. | 1900 | Box 197 |
| McNair, Frederick | 1901 | Box 211 | McPhilomy, Ann | 1917 | Box 577 |
| McNairy, Walter S. | 1899 | Box 185 | McPyncheon, William | 1898 | Box 177 |
| McNally, Elizabeth | 1917 | Box 577 | McQuade (Quade), Edward | 1911 | Box 423 |
| McNally, Isabella | 1910 | Box 398 | McQuade, Owen | 1876 | Box 61 |
| McNally, John | 1873 | Box 51 | McQueen, Christiana J. | 1896 | Box 164 |
| McNally, John | 1890 | Box 120 | McQueen, David | 1881 | Box 76 |
| McNally, Valentine | 1914 | Box 497 | McRee, Kate L. | 1901 | Box 211 |
| McNamara, Bridget | 1883 | Box 83 | McReynolds, George H. | 1910 | Box 399 |
| McNamara, Bridget | 1900 | Box 197 | McSherry, William | 1840 | Box 15 |
| McNamara, Catherine | 1915 | Box 525 | McSwyny, Eugene B. | 1913 | Box 473 |
| McNamara, Daniel | 1906 | Box 306 | McVary, James | 1886 | Box 98 |
| McNamara, Hamilton M. | 1917 | Box 577 | McVary, Peter | 1888 | Box 109 |
| McNamara, Josephine C. | 1917 | Box 577 | McVasy, James | 1895 | Box 155 |
| McNamara, Mary | 1915 | Box 525 | McVeagh, Emily Eames | 1916 | Box 551 |
| McNamara, Mary Blake | 1908 | Box 351 | McVeigh, Columbia | 1913 | Box 473 |
| McNamara, Matthew C. | 1914 | Box 497 | McVeigh, Jane Eliza | 1918 | Box 604 |
| McNamara, Michael J. | 1896 | Box 163 | McWhirter, Martha | 1904 | Box 268 |
| McNamara, Peter | 1879 | Box 69 | McWhorter, George T. | 1910 | Box 399 |
| McNamee, Catherine | 1911 | Box 423 | McWilliams, Clement | 1841 | Box 15 |
| McNamee, Elizabeth M. | 1913 | Box 473 | McWilliamson, Elizabeth | 1904 | Box 268 |
| McNamee, John | 1902 | Box 231 | McWilliamson, George E. | 1900 | Box 197 |
| McNantz, Mary | 1822 | Box 7 | Mead, Edward C. | 1908 | Box 351 |
| McNantz, Mary Anna | 1813 | Box 4 | Mead, Francis W. | 1913 | Box 474 |
| McNantz, Patrick H. | 1886 | Box 98 | Meade, Charles C. | 1885 | Box 93 |
| McNaught, Archibald | 1915 | Box 525 | Meade, George | 1862 | Box 30 |
| McNeal, Joshua | 1894 | Box 147 | Meade, Isabella C. | 1905 | Box 287 |
| McNeilly, Archibald | 1867 | Box 38 | Meade, Lizzie L. | 1906 | Box 307 |
| McNeir, Augusta M. | 1878 | Box 66 | Meade, Margaret C. | 1852 | Box 22 |
| McNeir, Caroline C. | 1914 | Box 497 | Meade, Richard W. | 1852 | Box 22 |
| McNeir, George A. R. | 1918 | Box 604 | Meade, Richard W. | 1897 | Box 171 |
| McNeir, Sarah J. | 1916 | Box 551 | Meader, Jane E. | 1890 | Box 120 |
| McNelly, Charles | 1901 | Box 211 | Meador, Ann C. | 1900 | Box 197 |
| McNerney, Catherine | 1919 | Box 635 | Meador, Chastian C. | 1904 | Box 269 |
| McNett, Charles M. | 1890 | Box 120 | Meads, Charles C. | 1909 | Box 374 |
| McNolan, Henry J. | 1892 | Box 133 | Meagher, Peter | 1903 | Box 249 |
| McNolan, Mary A. | 1891 | Box 126 | Means, Rachel A. | 1916 | Box 552 |
| McNulty, Martin | 1888 | Box 109 | Meany, Thomas | 1878 | Box 66 |
| McPhail, Archibald | 1822 | Box 7 | Mears, Helen Delia Elizabeth | 1917 | Box 577 |

| | | | | | | |
|---|---|---|---|---|---|---|
| Mechlin, Joseph | 1839 | Box 14 | Mellis, John | 1879 | Box 69 |
| Mechlin, Margaretta | 1853 | Box 22 | Meloy, William A. | 1905 | Box 287 |
| Medary, Thomas B. | 1885 | Box 93 | Melton, Mary S. | 1914 | Box 498 |
| Medford, Amelia | 1913 | Box 474 | Melton, Thomas H. | 1920 | Box 670 |
| Meding, Anna H. | 1886 | Box 98 | Melvin, Alonzo D. | 1918 | Box 605 |
| Meding, Caroline P. | 1895 | Box 155 | Melvin, Eliza A. | 1913 | Box 474 |
| Meding, Caroline P. | 1898 | Box 178 | Melvin, Josiah | 1868 | Box 39 |
| Medtart, Jacob | 1892 | Box 133 | Membert, Jacob J. | 1918 | Box 605 |
| Meeds, Benjamin | 1875 | Box 58 | Memmert, Charles | 1895 | Box 155 |
| Meehan, Ellen | 1903 | Box 249 | Memmert, Louise | 1879 | Box 69 |
| Meehan, John | 1906 | Box 307 | Mendenhall, William K. | 1910 | Box 399 |
| Meehan, John S. | 1863 | Box 31 | Menefee, John Wellington | 1915 | Box 526 |
| Meehan, Laura G. | 1905 | Box 287 | Menke, Meinard | 1896 | Box 164 |
| Meehan, Michael | 1893 | Box 140 | Mercer, Carroll | 1919 | Box 636 |
| Meehan, Patrick | 1913 | Box 474 | Mercer, Cora Livingston B. | 1888 | Box 109 |
| Meehan, Peter J. | 1912 | Box 449 | Mercer, William | 1892 | Box 133 |
| Meeker, Esther A. | 1896 | Box 164 | Merchant, Ella | 1916 | Box 552 |
| Meeks, Fannie A. | 1918 | Box 605 | Merchant, Lorenzo Dow | 1888 | Box 109 |
| Meeks, Frances E. | 1919 | Box 636 | Merchant, Mary | 1896 | Box 164 |
| Meeks, Samuel | 1899 | Box 186 | Merchant, Mary C. | 1918 | Box 605 |
| Meem, Margaret | 1873 | Box 51 | Meredith, David K. | 1917 | Box 578 |
| Meem, Peter G. | 1881 | Box 76 | Meredith, Edward Wilson | 1872 | Box 48 |
| Meeny, Margaret | 1879 | Box 69 | Meredith, Levi | 1917 | Box 578 |
| Megee, George F. | 1913 | Box 474 | Meredith, Mary E. | 1903 | Box 249 |
| Mehler, Herman | 1902 | Box 231 | Meredith, Philip | 1883 | Box 83 |
| Meier, John | 1887 | Box 104 | Merilion, Mary H. | 1893 | Box 140 |
| Meier, Susan S. | 1910 | Box 399 | Merillat, Stella R. | 1907 | Box 329 |
| Meigs, Elizabeth S. J. | 1915 | Box 526 | Meritt, Fountain A. | 1846 | Box 18 |
| Meigs, Grace Lynde | 1910 | Box 399 | Meriwether, Colyer | 1920 | Box 670 |
| Meigs, John Forsyth | 1883 | Box 83 | Merrell, Harvey B. | 1890 | Box 120 |
| Meigs, Louisa Rodgers | 1879 | Box 69 | Merrell, John Porter | 1916 | Box 552 |
| Meigs, Montgomery C. | 1892 | Box 133 | Merrell, Sarah Frances | 1916 | Box 552 |
| Meiners, John Henry | 1907 | Box 329 | Merriam, Helen M. | 1916 | Box 552 |
| Meiners, Ludwig A. | 1874 | Box 55 | Merrick, Henry A. | 1888 | Box 109 |
| Meinking, Adolph | 1901 | Box 212 | Merrick, Joseph I. | 1854 | Box 23 |
| Meinking, Caroline A. | 1897 | Box 171 | Merrick, Richard T. | 1885 | Box 93 |
| Meinking, Elisa | 1897 | Box 171 | Merrick, William M. | 1889 | Box 115 |
| Meinking, William | 1877 | Box 64 | Merrill, Annie M. | 1910 | Box 399 |
| Meister, Charles J. | 1918 | Box 605 | Merrill, Daniel Ford | 1904 | Box 269 |
| Mejasky, Francis | 1914 | Box 497 | Merrill, James Cushing | 1902 | Box 231 |
| Mejasky, Mercedes | 1919 | Box 636 | Merrill, Jane Hammond | 1918 | Box 605 |
| Meldon, May E. | 1876 | Box 61 | Merrill, John | 1877 | Box 64 |
| Meldrum, Margaret Gardner | 1906 | Box 307 | Merrill, Louisa L. | 1887 | Box 104 |
| Melhorn, Francis C. | 1871 | Box 45 | Merrill, Luella Bell | 1910 | Box 399 |
| Meline, J. F. | 1908 | Box 351 | Merrill, Margaret H. B. | 1902 | Box 231 |
| Meline, Louis D. | 1905 | Box 287 | Merrill, Mary E. | 1911 | Box 424 |
| Meline, Manche H. | 1910 | Box 399 | Merrill, Oliver R. | 1907 | Box 329 |
| Mell, William G. | 1917 | Box 578 | Merrill, Richard H. | 1907 | Box 329 |
| Mellen, Mary Ann | 1920 | Box 670 | Merrill, Samuel F. | 1903 | Box 249 |
| Meller, Elizabeth | 1883 | Box 83 | Merrill, Squire G. | 1895 | Box 155 |
| Melling, Rose | 1916 | Box 552 | Merriman, George B. | 1918 | Box 605 |
| Mellis, Hellen V. | 1915 | Box 526 | Merriman, Matilda R. | 1913 | Box 474 |

| | | | | | | |
|---|---|---|---|---|---|
| Merritt, Augustus E. | 1910 | Box 399 | Middleton, J. Benjamin | 1919 | Box 637 |
| Merritt, Kate P. | 1920 | Box 670 | Middleton, John W. | 1892 | Box 133 |
| Merritt, Wesley | 1911 | Box 424 | Middleton, Johnson Van Dyke | 1907 | Box 329 |
| Mertz, Della E. | 1919 | Box 637 | Middleton, Margaret H. | 1910 | Box 400 |
| Meserole, Louise C. Stone | 1904 | Box 269 | Middleton, Mary E. | 1914 | Box 498 |
| Meserve, Harry Fessenden | 1919 | Box 637 | Middleton, Richard | 1886 | Box 98 |
| Mesmer, Crescentia | 1905 | Box 287 | Middleton, Robert I. | 1894 | Box 148 |
| Messenger, Dora A. | 1917 | Box 578 | Middleton, Samuel | 1902 | Box 231 |
| Messer, George | 1894 | Box 148 | Middleton, Samuel C. | 1892 | Box 133 |
| Messer, Mary Janette | 1917 | Box 578 | Middleton, Virginia White | 1906 | Box 307 |
| Messer, William | 1906 | Box 307 | Middleton, William | 1885 | Box 93 |
| Metcalf, Francis S. | 1904 | Box 269 | Middleton, William | 1920 | Box 670 |
| Metts, Lucinda A. | 1886 | Box 98 | Miffleton, Winter B. | 1919 | Box 637 |
| Metzerott, William G. | 1884 | Box 88 | Milans, Joseph D. | 1906 | Box 307 |
| Metzger, Mary C. | 1912 | Box 449 | Milburn, George | 1872 | Box 48 |
| Metzger, Millard | 1914 | Box 498 | Milburn, J. Parker | 1874 | Box 55 |
| Meusel, Bertha | 1915 | Box 526 | Milburn, Joseph W. | 1879 | Box 69 |
| Meyer, Charles | 1916 | Box 552 | Milburn, Martha V. | 1908 | Box 351 |
| Meyer, Frank N. | 1919 | Box 637 | Milburn, Washington C. | 1891 | Box 126 |
| Meyer, George von L. | 1918 | Box 605 | Miles, Eliza | 1885 | Box 93 |
| Meyer, Henry C. | 1911 | Box 424 | Miles, Elizabeth | 1866 | Box 36 |
| Meyer, Jeannette | 1894 | Box 148 | Miles, Henry | 1822 | Box 7 |
| Meyer, John C. | 1904 | Box 269 | Miles, Henry R. | 1911 | Box 424 |
| Meyer, Louis | 1901 | Box 212 | Miles, Jonathan Chandler | 1905 | Box 287 |
| Meyer, Maria | 1911 | Box 424 | Miles, Maria | 1887 | Box 104 |
| Meyers, Charles Frederick | 1916 | Box 552 | Miles, Mary | 1873 | Box 51 |
| Meyers, William Henry | 1913 | Box 475 | Miles, Mary | 1901 | Box 212 |
| Meyns, Charles A. | 1906 | Box 307 | Miles, Sarah E. | 1920 | Box 670 |
| Michael, Perry | 1915 | Box 526 | Miley, William | 1866 | Box 36 |
| Michael, William II. | 1916 | Box 552 | Millard, Catharine C. | 1887 | Box 104 |
| Michaelis, Julius | 1910 | Box 399 | Millard, Francis | 1828 | Box 9 |
| Michaelis, Theresa | 1912 | Box 449 | Miller, Abraham | 1842 | Box 16 |
| Michel, Jane W. | 1892 | Box 133 | Miller, Adelaide G. | 1918 | Box 606 |
| Michelbacher, George M. | 1896 | Box 164 | Miller, Alexander Macomb | 1904 | Box 269 |
| Michener, Charles Byron | 1894 | Box 148 | Miller, Alice H. | 1892 | Box 133 |
| Michie, Maria Louisa | 1919 | Box 637 | Miller, Alonzo C. | 1919 | Box 637 |
| Michler, Nathaniel | 1884 | Box 88 | Miller, Ann M. | 1828 | Box 9 |
| Mickle, Addie Ruth | 1907 | Box 329 | Miller, Anna L. Offutt | 1903 | Box 249 |
| Mickle, William H. (Jr.) | 1911 | Box 424 | Miller, Anna Marie | 1909 | Box 374 |
| Mickleham, Eleanora Jefferson | 1913 | Box 475 | Miller, Annie M. | 1900 | Box 197 |
| Mickley, Matilda Ellen | 1913 | Box 475 | Miller, Annie M. | 1911 | Box 424 |
| Mickum, Sarah P. | 1891 | Box 126 | Miller, Augusta C. | 1917 | Box 578 |
| Middaugh, Ray E. | 1910 | Box 399 | Miller, Benjamin | 1882 | Box 80 |
| Middleton, Arthur E. H. | 1919 | Box 637 | Miller, Benjamin A. | 1906 | Box 307 |
| Middleton, Benjamin F. | 1863 | Box 31 | Miller, Benjamin F. | 1893 | Box 140 |
| Middleton, Catherine M. | 1900 | Box 197 | Miller, Caroline | 1908 | Box 351 |
| Middleton, Edward | 1883 | Box 83 | Miller, Caroline R. | 1916 | Box 552 |
| Middleton, Ellen R. | 1904 | Box 269 | Miller, Catharine | 1883 | Box 83 |
| Middleton, Ellida Juell | 1910 | Box 400 | Miller, Charles | 1897 | Box 171 |
| Middleton, Erasmus J. (Jr.) | 1881 | Box 76 | Miller, Charles | 1897 | Box 171 |
| Middleton, Francis G. | 1885 | Box 93 | Miller, Charles H. | 1915 | Box 526 |
| Middleton, Harriet E. | 1900 | Box 197 | Miller, Charles P. | 1892 | Box 133 |

| | | | |
|---|---|---|---|
| Miller, Charles W. | 1916 | Box 552 |
| Miller, Christian | 1903 | Box 249 |
| Miller, Cornelia | 1900 | Box 197 |
| Miller, Edward D. | 1903 | Box 249 |
| Miller, Edward G. | 1912 | Box 450 |
| Miller, Edwin | 1893 | Box 140 |
| Miller, Effie M. | 1917 | Box 578 |
| Miller, Eleanor | 1868 | Box 39 |
| Miller, Eleanor Grafton Hanson | 1910 | Box 400 |
| Miller, Eliza Ann | 1909 | Box 374 |
| Miller, Eliza Ariss | 1856 | Box 25 |
| Miller, Eliza W. | 1900 | Box 197 |
| Miller, Elizabeth | 1807 | Box 2 |
| Miller, Elizabeth A. | 1896 | Box 164 |
| Miller, Elizabeth M. | 1915 | Box 526 |
| Miller, Elizabeth Rebecca | 1917 | Box 578 |
| Miller, Enoch K. | 1910 | Box 400 |
| Miller, Ferdinand | 1908 | Box 351 |
| Miller, Francis | 1888 | Box 109 |
| Miller, Francis | 1906 | Box 307 |
| Miller, Francis | 1907 | Box 329 |
| Miller, Frank A. | 1918 | Box 606 |
| Miller, Franklin | 1898 | Box 178 |
| Miller, Frederick | 1898 | Box 178 |
| Miller, Frederick Augustus | 1909 | Box 374 |
| Miller, Frederick J. | 1909 | Box 374 |
| Miller, George | 1874 | Box 55 |
| Miller, George | 1911 | Box 424 |
| Miller, George | 1911 | Box 424 |
| Miller, George B. | 1916 | Box 552 |
| Miller, George W. | 1864 | Box 32 |
| Miller, Harriot | 1871 | Box 45 |
| Miller, Hattie Belle | 1914 | Box 498 |
| Miller, Henry | 1917 | Box 578 |
| Miller, Henry H. | 1920 | Box 670 |
| Miller, Henry William | 1909 | Box 374 |
| Miller, Isaac Smith | 1862 | Box 30 |
| Miller, Jacob | 1876 | Box 61 |
| Miller, Jacob | 1906 | Box 307 |
| Miller, Jacob B. | 1888 | Box 109 |
| Miller, James | 1805 | Box 1 |
| Miller, James | 1874 | Box 55 |
| Miller, James E. | 1903 | Box 250 |
| Miller, Jane O. | 1900 | Box 197 |
| Miller, Jesse | 1920 | Box 670 |
| Miller, John | 1870 | Box 43 |
| Miller, John | 1892 | Box 133 |
| Miller, John | 1909 | Box 374 |
| Miller, John | 1914 | Box 498 |
| Miller, John B. | 1893 | Box 140 |
| Miller, John Blake | 1915 | Box 527 |
| Miller, John F. | 1886 | Box 98 |
| Miller, John L. | 1888 | Box 109 |
| Miller, Joseph | 1916 | Box 552 |
| Miller, Julia T. | 1885 | Box 93 |
| Miller, Katharina | 1916 | Box 552 |
| Miller, Lois McE. | 1883 | Box 83 |
| Miller, Lucy R. | 1867 | Box 37 |
| Miller, Marcus P. | 1907 | Box 329 |
| Miller, Margaret | 1909 | Box 374 |
| Miller, Margaret P. Montgomery | 1914 | Box 498 |
| Miller, Maria | 1867 | Box 37 |
| Miller, Maria | 1887 | Box 104 |
| Miller, Maria Savage | 1905 | Box 287 |
| Miller, Martha | 1915 | Box 527 |
| Miller, Mary | 1864 | Box 32 |
| Miller, Mary | 1875 | Box 58 |
| Miller, Mary | 1898 | Box 178 |
| Miller, Mary A. | 1914 | Box 498 |
| Miller, Mary Ann | 1859 | Box 27 |
| Miller, Mary C. | 1879 | Box 69 |
| Miller, Mary Chess | 1891 | Box 126 |
| Miller, Mary Farnham | 1920 | Box 670 |
| Miller, Mary Luckett | 1916 | Box 552 |
| Miller, Mary M. | 1905 | Box 287 |
| Miller, May A. | 1919 | Box 637 |
| Miller, Minna S. | 1915 | Box 527 |
| Miller, Mitchel H. | 1866 | Box 36 |
| Miller, Nehemiah H. | 1889 | Box 115 |
| Miller, Ozias Smith | 1905 | Box 287 |
| Miller, Peter | 1891 | Box 126 |
| Miller, Rebecca S. | 1882 | Box 80 |
| Miller, Rezin A. | 1883 | Box 83 |
| Miller, Robert | 1837 | Box 13 |
| Miller, Robert H. | 1920 | Box 670 |
| Miller, Royal E. | 1872 | Box 48 |
| Miller, Samuel | 1857 | Box 26 |
| Miller, Stephen A. | 1916 | Box 552 |
| Miller, Stephen C. | 1910 | Box 400 |
| Miller, Thomas | 1873 | Box 51 |
| Miller, Thomas (Jr.) | 1918 | Box 606 |
| Miller, Valentine | 1891 | Box 126 |
| Miller, Virginia C. | 1892 | Box 133 |
| Miller, William | 1894 | Box 148 |
| Miller, William H. | 1902 | Box 231 |
| Miller, William J. | 1905 | Box 287 |
| Miller, William Leon | 1911 | Box 425 |
| Millett, Clarence W. | 1895 | Box 155 |
| Millett, John | 1837 | Box 13 |
| Millett, Lucy L. | 1892 | Box 133 |
| Milligan, Charles Howard | 1920 | Box 670 |
| Milligan, Patrick Francis | 1897 | Box 171 |
| Millin, Peter | 1812 | Box 4 |
| Mills, Albert L. | 1916 | Box 552 |

| | | | | | | |
|---|---|---|---|---|---|---|
| Mills, Anna V. | 1917 | Box 578 | Mirick, Anna J. G. | 1887 | Box 104 |
| Mills, Charles C. | 1895 | Box 155 | Mirick, Henry B. | 1909 | Box 374 |
| Mills, Christy | 1904 | Box 269 | Mirick, Henry D. | 1914 | Box 498 |
| Mills, Clark | 1884 | Box 88 | Mirick, Stephen H. | 1883 | Box 83 |
| Mills, Elizabeth | 1920 | Box 670 | Mirick, Ursula O. | 1865 | Box 34 |
| Mills, George A. | 1901 | Box 212 | Mishaw, John | 1909 | Box 374 |
| Mills, George G. | 1919 | Box 637 | Mister, Isaac | 1890 | Box 120 |
| Mills, Gertrude S. | 1916 | Box 552 | Mitchel, Phebe | 1866 | Box 36 |
| Mills, Hannah Cassel | 1917 | Box 578 | Mitchell, Andrew C. | 1826 | Box 8 |
| Mills, Harriet | 1904 | Box 269 | Mitchell, Annie G. | 1916 | Box 552 |
| Mills, John E. | 1891 | Box 126 | Mitchell, Catherine R. | 1919 | Box 637 |
| Mills, Kate J. | 1919 | Box 637 | Mitchell, Cormac | 1870 | Box 43 |
| Mills, Mary | 1885 | Box 93 | Mitchell, Caroline | 1890 | Box 120 |
| Mills, Mary Ann | 1895 | Box 155 | Mitchell, Dennis | 1857 | Box 26 |
| Mills, Peter | 1830 | Box 10 | Mitchell, Elizabeth Patterson | 1918 | Box 606 |
| Mills, Robert T. | 1863 | Box 31 | Mitchell, Ellen M. | 1888 | Box 109 |
| Mills, Steven Horton | 1913 | Box 475 | Mitchell, George | 1808 | Box 3 |
| Mills, Willis N. | 1919 | Box 637 | Mitchell, George | 1903 | Box 250 |
| Millson, Mary Sturman | 1897 | Box 171 | Mitchell, George C. B. | 1869 | Box 41 |
| Millward, Margaret A. | 1919 | Box 637 | Mitchell, George W. | 1865 | Box 34 |
| Milmore, George | 1914 | Box 498 | Mitchell, Harriet M. | 1871 | Box 45 |
| Milner, Alfred | 1893 | Box 140 | Mitchell, Imogene G. | 1913 | Box 475 |
| Milner, Sarah | 1915 | Box 527 | Mitchell, James | 1899 | Box 186 |
| Milnor, Susan J. | 1904 | Box 269 | Mitchell, John | 1808 | Box 3 |
| Milstead, Alonzo | 1889 | Box 115 | Mitchell, John H. | 1908 | Box 352 |
| Milstead, Barton | 1838 | Box 14 | Mitchell, John N. | 1918 | Box 606 |
| Milstead, Harrie S. | 1918 | Box 606 | Mitchell, Joseph T. | 1904 | Box 269 |
| Milstead, Margaret | 1844 | Box 17 | Mitchell, Judson | 1865 | Box 34 |
| Milstead, Thomas | 1863 | Box 31 | Mitchell, Levi | 1865 | Box 34 |
| Mimmack, Bernard P. | 1910 | Box 400 | Mitchell, Margaret E. | 1894 | Box 148 |
| Mimmack, Katharine Collins | 1919 | Box 637 | Mitchell, Maria D. | 1906 | Box 307 |
| Minahan, Delia | 1899 | Box 186 | Mitchell, Martha Ann | 1857 | Box 26 |
| Minahan, John J. | 1919 | Box 637 | Mitchell, Mary F. | 1909 | Box 374 |
| Miner, Benjamin | 1868 | Box 39 | Mitchell, Middleton | 1888 | Box 109 |
| Miner, Charles A. | 1912 | Box 450 | Mitchell, Milton C. | 1915 | Box 527 |
| Miner, George A. | 1914 | Box 498 | Mitchell, Morton | 1908 | Box 352 |
| Minnix, Catherine | 1892 | Box 133 | Mitchell, Nicholas | 1808 | Box 3 |
| Minor, Ann M. | 1860 | Box 28 | Mitchell, Richard S. | 1920 | Box 670 |
| Minor, Catharine Berkeley | 1911 | Box 425 | Mitchell, Richard T. | 1888 | Box 109 |
| Minor, Charles L. | 1889 | Box 115 | Mitchell, Sarah | 1899 | Box 186 |
| Minor, Eliza Jane | 1890 | Box 120 | Mitchell, Sarah A. | 1920 | Box 670 |
| Minor, Henry A. | 1915 | Box 527 | Mitchell, Sarah C. | 1910 | Box 400 |
| Minor, James M. | 1858 | Box 27 | Mitchell, Susan Thomas | 1908 | Box 352 |
| Minor, Jane Eliza | 1916 | Box 552 | Mitchell, Thomas A. | 1892 | Box 133 |
| Minor, Mary Virginia | 1920 | Box 670 | Mitchell, Uriah B. | 1889 | Box 115 |
| Minor, Matilda | 1912 | Box 450 | Mitchell, William | 1871 | Box 45 |
| Minor, Rebecca | 1908 | Box 351 | Mitchell, William | 1903 | Box 250 |
| Minshall, R. P. | 1905 | Box 287 | Mitchell, William | 1851 | Box 21 |
| Minster, Doris | 1904 | Box 269 | Mitford, George W. | 1918 | Box 606 |
| Minster, Hannah | 1916 | Box 552 | Mitkiewiez, Olga Hortense de | 1896 | Box 160 |
| Minturn, Benjamin G. | 1913 | Box 475 | Mix, Catharine S. | 1894 | Box 148 |
| Miranda, Bailey | 1898 | Box 174 | Mix, Catherine D. | 1902 | Box 231 |

| | | | | | | |
|---|---|---|---|---|---|---|---|
| Mix, Martha E. | 1906 | Box 307 | | Moodey, Beverly E. | 1907 | Box 329 |
| Moan, John | 1915 | Box 527 | | Mooney, Margaret C. | 1905 | Box 287 |
| Moberly, William | 1896 | Box 164 | | Mooney, Maud E. | 1913 | Box 475 |
| Mockabee, Adelia | 1917 | Box 578 | | Mooney, Michael | 1886 | Box 98 |
| Mockabee, Daniel F. | 1903 | Box 250 | | Moor, A. B. | 1915 | Box 527 |
| Mockabee, John William | 1919 | Box 637 | | Moor, William H. | 1915 | Box 527 |
| Moelich, Frederick | 1894 | Box 148 | | Moore, Adeline M. | 1906 | Box 307 |
| Moeller, Agnes | 1896 | Box 164 | | Moore, Amanda B. | 1916 | Box 552 |
| Moeller, John N. | 1910 | Box 400 | | Moore, Ann | 1894 | Box 148 |
| Moffatt, Emily | 1918 | Box 606 | | Moore, Anna V. | 1918 | Box 606 |
| Moffatt, Josiah S. | 1903 | Box 250 | | Moore, Baldwin S. | 1905 | Box 287 |
| Moffitt, Thomas | 1816 | Box 5 | | Moore, Charles O. | 1894 | Box 148 |
| Mogh, John | 1822 | Box 7 | | Moore, Clara J. | 1902 | Box 231 |
| Mohler, William H. | 1892 | Box 133 | | Moore, David | 1883 | Box 83 |
| Mohr, Magdalena Friedricka | 1912 | Box 450 | | Moore, David | 1916 | Box 552 |
| Mohun, Francis | 1879 | Box 70 | | Moore, Dorothy A. | 1905 | Box 288 |
| Mohun, Francis B. | 1893 | Box 140 | | Moore, Edwin W. | 1868 | Box 40 |
| Mohun, Philip | 1856 | Box 25 | | Moore, Eli Charles | 1903 | Box 250 |
| Mohun, R. Dorsey | 1915 | Box 527 | | Moore, Emma E. | 1914 | Box 498 |
| Mohun, Susannah E. | 1874 | Box 55 | | Moore, Frances M. | 1905 | Box 288 |
| Mohun, William | 1898 | Box 178 | | Moore, Francis H. | 1905 | Box 288 |
| Mölich, Wilhemina | 1895 | Box 155 | | Moore, George E. | 1904 | Box 269 |
| Molkow, Emil | 1920 | Box 670 | | Moore, George E. (Sr.) | 1888 | Box 109 |
| Molloy, Virginia C. | 1906 | Box 307 | | Moore, George Evertson | 1901 | Box 212 |
| Monaghan, Andrew | 1914 | Box 498 | | Moore, George F. | 1886 | Box 98 |
| Monaghan, Peter | 1885 | Box 93 | | Moore, George H. | 1901 | Box 212 |
| Moncure, Jaquelin A. | 1917 | Box 578 | | Moore, Gledstanes A. | 1895 | Box 156 |
| Moncure, Temple | 1898 | Box 178 | | Moore, Harry Burton | 1906 | Box 307 |
| Monder, George H. | 1894 | Box 148 | | Moore, Ida N. | 1904 | Box 269 |
| Monder, Natalie | 1913 | Box 475 | | Moore, James | 1848 | Box 19 |
| Mondscheim, Carl | 1904 | Box 269 | | Moore, James | 1905 | Box 288 |
| Monell, John D. | 1895 | Box 156 | | Moore, James W. | 1901 | Box 212 |
| Monell, Phoebe Ann | 1893 | Box 140 | | Moore, Johanna | 1893 | Box 140 |
| Monroe, Ann Sarah | 1913 | Box 475 | | Moore, John | 1824 | Box 8 |
| Monroe, Ellen | 1910 | Box 400 | | Moore, John | 1870 | Box 43 |
| Monroe, Hannah | 1888 | Box 109 | | Moore, John | 1885 | Box 93 |
| Monroe, Horace R. | 1870 | Box 43 | | Moore, John | 1907 | Box 329 |
| Monroe, James | 1849 | Box 20 | | Moore, John | 1915 | Box 527 |
| Montague, Edward | 1912 | Box 450 | | Moore, John B. | 1903 | Box 250 |
| Montague, W. Grattan | 1920 | Box 670 | | Moore, John G. | 1901 | Box 212 |
| Montague, William P. | 1897 | Box 171 | | Moore, John H. | 1872 | Box 48 |
| Montandon, Julian | 1851 | Box 21 | | Moore, John Massey | 1861 | Box 29 |
| Montgomery, George W. | 1841 | Box 15 | | Moore, John Wilson | 1887 | Box 104 |
| Montgomery, Henry | 1899 | Box 186 | | Moore, Joseph H. | 1915 | Box 527 |
| Montgomery, John | 1893 | Box 140 | | Moore, Joseph V. | 1905 | Box 288 |
| Montgomery, John B. | 1873 | Box 51 | | Moore, Julia B. | 1918 | Box 606 |
| Montgomery, Julia A. | 1917 | Box 578 | | Moore, Kate | 1908 | Box 352 |
| Montgomery, Robert H. | 1905 | Box 287 | | Moore, Laura M. | 1904 | Box 269 |
| Montgomery, Robert Home | 1882 | Box 80 | | Moore, Margaret | 1903 | Box 250 |
| Montgomery, Thomas | 1905 | Box 287 | | Moore, Margaret Ballard | 1915 | Box 527 |
| Montgomery, Victor F. | 1907 | Box 329 | | Moore, Maria | 1909 | Box 374 |
| Montgomery, Virginia C. | 1893 | Box 140 | | Moore, Mark William | 1913 | Box 475 |

| | | | | | | |
|---|---|---|---|---|---|---|
| Moore, Martha B. | 1917 | Box 578 | Moran, William E. | 1884 | Box 88 |
| Moore, Mary | 1884 | Box 88 | Morcoe, Edward R. | 1905 | Box 288 |
| Moore, Mary | 1891 | Box 126 | Mordecai, Alfred | 1920 | Box 670 |
| Moore, Mary | 1898 | Box 178 | Morehead, John L. | 1901 | Box 212 |
| Moore, Mary A. | 1894 | Box 148 | Moreland, Eliza G. | 1854 | Box 23 |
| Moore, Mary Ann | 1910 | Box 400 | Moreland, Eliza G. | 1864 | Box 32 |
| Moore, Mary Augusta | 1912 | Box 450 | Moreland, Enoch | 1859 | Box 27 |
| Moore, Mary I. | 1905 | Box 288 | Moreland, Enoch C. | 1920 | Box 670 |
| Moore, Mary J. | 1912 | Box 450 | Moreland, Rachel A. | 1917 | Box 578 |
| Moore, Mary Jane | 1910 | Box 400 | Morell, Wilhelm Otto Adolph | 1903 | Box 250 |
| Moore, Mary Virginia | 1918 | Box 606 | Morey, Nellie D. | 1918 | Box 606 |
| Moore, Michael | 1918 | Box 606 | Morfit, Henry M. | 1867 | Box 38 |
| Moore, Patrick | 1893 | Box 140 | Morgan, Bridget | 1882 | Box 80 |
| Moore, Richard | 1891 | Box 126 | Morgan, Carol Ethelbert | 1891 | Box 126 |
| Moore, Robert | 1888 | Box 109 | Morgan, Caroline Waugh | 1896 | Box 164 |
| Moore, Robert E. | 1888 | Box 109 | Morgan, Carolyn F. | 1914 | Box 498 |
| Moore, Sarah | 1869 | Box 41 | Morgan, Charles A. | 1918 | Box 606 |
| Moore, Sarah | 1902 | Box 231 | Morgan, Charles R. | 1908 | Box 352 |
| Moore, Sarah B. | 1900 | Box 197 | Morgan, David | 1901 | Box 212 |
| Moore, Sarah E. | 1917 | Box 578 | Morgan, Ebenezer | 1898 | Box 178 |
| Moore, Sarah R. | 1919 | Box 637 | Morgan, Edwin D. | 1883 | Box 83 |
| Moore, Stillman | 1916 | Box 552 | Morgan, Elizabeth | 1846 | Box 18 |
| Moore, Susan | 1917 | Box 578 | Morgan, Evelina P. | 1905 | Box 288 |
| Moore, Theodore T. | 1915 | Box 527 | Morgan, Francis H. | 1886 | Box 98 |
| Moore, Thomas | 1835 | Box 13 | Morgan, Frank P. | 1919 | Box 637 |
| Moore, Virginia H. | 1893 | Box 140 | Morgan, Harriet | 1912 | Box 450 |
| Moore, Vona L. | 1915 | Box 527 | Morgan, Harriet A. | 1905 | Box 288 |
| Moore, William Aken | 1913 | Box 475 | Morgan, Harriet Ann | 1892 | Box 133 |
| Moore, William M. | 1892 | Box 133 | Morgan, Henry James | 1917 | Box 578 |
| Moore, William Sturtevant | 1915 | Box 527 | Morgan, Hugh | 1904 | Box 269 |
| Moore, William W. | 1887 | Box 104 | Morgan, James E. | 1889 | Box 115 |
| Moorman, George | 1908 | Box 352 | Morgan, John | 1868 | Box 39 |
| Moorsom, Richard Lister | 1914 | Box 498 | Morgan, John | 1907 | Box 329 |
| Moqué, Alice Lee | 1919 | Box 637 | Morgan, John | 1910 | Box 400 |
| Mora, Antonio Maximo | 1897 | Box 171 | Morgan, John B. | 1871 | Box 45 |
| Moran, Alexander F. | 1905 | Box 288 | Morgan, John R. | 1889 | Box 115 |
| Moran, Alice | 1896 | Box 164 | Morgan, John R. | 1917 | Box 578 |
| Moran, Clarissa A. | 1915 | Box 527 | Morgan, Margaret A. | 1915 | Box 527 |
| Moran, Daniel | 1909 | Box 374 | Morgan, Martha | 1847 | Box 19 |
| Moran, Eliza | 1876 | Box 61 | Morgan, Mary | 1878 | Box 66 |
| Moran, Elizabeth | 1898 | Box 178 | Morgan, Mary A. | 1873 | Box 51 |
| Moran, F. Berger | 1912 | Box 450 | Morgan, Mary E. | 1909 | Box 374 |
| Moran, John | 1906 | Box 307 | Morgan, Mary G. | 1910 | Box 400 |
| Moran, John J. | 1904 | Box 269 | Morgan, Miriam | 1910 | Box 400 |
| Moran, John S. | 1896 | Box 164 | Morgan, Nannie Rebecca | 1913 | Box 475 |
| Moran, Joseph M. | 1901 | Box 212 | Morgan, Nora | 1896 | Box 164 |
| Moran, Julia May | 1913 | Box 475 | Morgan, Richard W. | 1909 | Box 374 |
| Moran, Leila R. Eliot | 1887 | Box 104 | Morgan, Robert C. | 1886 | Box 98 |
| Moran, Leonard Canter | 1816 | Box 5 | Morgan, Sarah B. | 1911 | Box 425 |
| Moran, Patrick | 1847 | Box 19 | Morgan, Ward | 1894 | Box 148 |
| Moran, Patrick | 1855 | Box 24 | Morison, Eliza C. | 1913 | Box 475 |
| Moran, Susan Catharine | 1915 | Box 527 | Morison, Elizabeth | 1867 | Box 38 |

| | | | | | | |
|---|---|---|---|---|---|---|
| Morison, Sarah J. | 1915 | Box 527 | Morrison, William C. | 1911 | Box 425 |
| Morley, Mary | 1877 | Box 64 | Morrison, William M. | 1863 | Box 31 |
| Morony, Patrick | 1868 | Box 39 | Morrisson, Lucy | 1897 | Box 171 |
| Morran, David | 1863 | Box 31 | Morrow, Honora A. | 1908 | Box 352 |
| Morrell, Abraham | 1879 | Box 70 | Morrow (Marrow), Mary | 1911 | Box 424 |
| Morrell, Charles | 1899 | Box 186 | Morrow, William | 1858 | Box 27 |
| Morrell, Edward de Veaux | 1918 | Box 606 | Morse, Catharine N. | 1881 | Box 76 |
| Morrell, John A. L. | 1879 | Box 70 | Morse, Charles H. | 1883 | Box 84 |
| Morrell, Laurette | 1899 | Box 186 | Morse, George W. | 1888 | Box 109 |
| Morrice, Lizzie | 1890 | Box 121 | Morse, John P. | 1917 | Box 578 |
| Morrill, Edward D. | 1907 | Box 329 | Morse, Laura A. | 1891 | Box 126 |
| Morrill, Henry A. | 1920 | Box 670 | Morse, Marion R. | 1920 | Box 670 |
| Morrill, James Swan | 1910 | Box 400 | Morse, Mary | 1899 | Box 186 |
| Morrill, Justin | 1899 | Box 186 | Morse, Mary S. | 1894 | Box 148 |
| Morris, Alva L. | 1884 | Box 88 | Morse, Rosa | 1899 | Box 186 |
| Morris, Charles | 1856 | Box 25 | Morsell, Elizabeth E. | 1884 | Box 88 |
| Morris, Gerard | 1857 | Box 26 | Morsell, Maria S. | 1891 | Box 126 |
| Morris, Harriet | 1878 | Box 66 | Morsell, Richard I. | 1853 | Box 22 |
| Morris, Helen I. | 1912 | Box 450 | Morsell, Samuel T. G. | 1909 | Box 374 |
| Morris, Henry | 1891 | Box 126 | Mortimer, Joseph H. | 1909 | Box 374 |
| Morris, Howard Taylor | 1919 | Box 637 | Morton, Anna Livingston | 1918 | Box 606 |
| Morris, John | 1904 | Box 269 | Morton, Ellen | 1863 | Box 31 |
| Morris, John M. | 1873 | Box 51 | Morton, Francis T. | 1920 | Box 670 |
| Morris, Lucius S. | 1901 | Box 212 | Morton, George T. | 1887 | Box 104 |
| Morris, Maggie | 1914 | Box 498 | Morton, James F. | 1858 | Box 27 |
| Morris, Martin F. | 1909 | Box 374 | Morton, Levi Parsons | 1920 | Box 670 |
| Morris, Mary Ann | 1900 | Box 197 | Morton, Mary Pittney | 1835 | Box 13 |
| Morris, Mary L. | 1919 | Box 637 | Moscrop, Henry | 1888 | Box 109 |
| Morris, Peter | 1917 | Box 578 | Moseby, Peter | 1887 | Box 104 |
| Morris, Robert | 1865 | Box 34 | Moseley, Charles | 1888 | Box 109 |
| Morris, Robert Murray | 1897 | Box 171 | Moseley, Edward A. | 1911 | Box 425 |
| Morris, Steven W. | 1906 | Box 307 | Moseley, Kate M. | 1917 | Box 578 |
| Morris, Thomas | 1876 | Box 61 | Moses, Emma Richardson | 1920 | Box 670 |
| Morris, Thomas H. | 1902 | Box 231 | Moses, Franklin James | 1914 | Box 498 |
| Morris, Thomas R. | 1920 | Box 670 | Moses, James E. | 1894 | Box 148 |
| Morris, William B. | 1885 | Box 93 | Moses, Rebecca J. McKnight | 1909 | Box 374 |
| Morris, William Judson | 1912 | Box 450 | Moses, Zebina | 1918 | Box 606 |
| Morrisett, Thomas | 1893 | Box 140 | Mosher, Anna M. | 1917 | Box 578 |
| Morrisey, Emma | 1902 | Box 231 | Mosher, Eliza | 1900 | Box 197 |
| Morrison, Abby | 1910 | Box 400 | Mosher, Eliza M. | 1877 | Box 64 |
| Morrison, Alexander | 1864 | Box 32 | Mosher, James | 1907 | Box 329 |
| Morrison, David L. | 1887 | Box 104 | Mosher, Theodore | 1878 | Box 66 |
| Morrison, Dugald Cameron | 1910 | Box 400 | Mosher, Theodore | 1912 | Box 450 |
| Morrison, George | 1899 | Box 186 | Mosher, Theron C. | 1918 | Box 606 |
| Morrison, George A. | 1883 | Box 83 | Mosheuvel, Frank H. | 1919 | Box 637 |
| Morrison, Isabella H. | 1908 | Box 352 | Moss, Annie V. | 1914 | Box 498 |
| Morrison, John P. | 1914 | Box 498 | Moss, Charles A. | 1916 | Box 552 |
| Morrison, Mary J. | 1919 | Box 637 | Moss, Jane G. | 1876 | Box 61 |
| Morrison, Obadiah H. | 1876 | Box 61 | Moss, Josephine D. | 1888 | Box 109 |
| Morrison, Robert | 1891 | Box 126 | Moss, Martha E. Owen | 1892 | Box 133 |
| Morrison, Sarah E. | 1902 | Box 232 | Moss, Philemon | 1837 | Box 13 |
| Morrison, Sarah J. | 1901 | Box 212 | Moss, Richard T. | 1893 | Box 140 |

| | | | | | | |
|---|---|---|---|---|---|---|
| Moss, William | 1869 | Box 41 | Mullen, Bridget Dehlia | 1906 | Box 307 |
| Mossell, Charles W. | 1915 | Box 527 | Mullen, Dolly | 1860 | Box 28 |
| Mossell, Cornelia | 1907 | Box 330 | Müller, August | 1885 | Box 93 |
| Moten, Alfred | 1902 | Box 232 | Muller, Charles | 1874 | Box 55 |
| Moten, Benjamin | 1878 | Box 66 | Muller, Frances Henrietta | 1906 | Box 307 |
| Moten, Kate E. | 1914 | Box 498 | Muller, Hermann H. | 1902 | Box 232 |
| Moten, Sarah | 1920 | Box 670 | Müller, John | 1885 | Box 93 |
| Mothershead, John C. | 1912 | Box 450 | Muller, John P. | 1894 | Box 148 |
| Motlow, William Goodlett | 1911 | Box 425 | Mullery, Edward | 1904 | Box 269 |
| Motter, Elizabeth A. | 1905 | Box 288 | Mullett, Alfred B. | 1890 | Box 121 |
| Motts, George | 1907 | Box 330 | Mullett, Augustin A. | 1880 | Box 72 |
| Motz, Emilie C. | 1901 | Box 212 | Mullett, Hannah | 1909 | Box 374 |
| Motz, Werner C. | 1906 | Box 307 | Mullett, Thomas B. | 1887 | Box 104 |
| Moulton, Charles B. L. | 1891 | Box 126 | Mulligan, Anna A. | 1917 | Box 578 |
| Moulton, Mary A. | 1904 | Box 269 | Mulligan, Emilie Ogston | 1914 | Box 498 |
| Mount, Celia J. | 1895 | Box 156 | Mulligan, James S. | 1890 | Box 121 |
| Mount, John | 1840 | Box 15 | Mulligan, Richard T. | 1917 | Box 578 |
| Mount, Morgan F. | 1891 | Box 126 | Mulliken, Ella T. | 1895 | Box 156 |
| Mountz, John | 1857 | Box 26 | Mullikin, Elizabeth H. | 1888 | Box 109 |
| Mountz, Marie E. | 1832 | Box 11 | Mullikin, Joseph | 1832 | Box 11 |
| Moxley, Aquilla | 1915 | Box 527 | Mullikin, Nathaniel | 1877 | Box 64 |
| Moxley, Benjamin | 1870 | Box 43 | Mullin, Catherine | 1910 | Box 400 |
| Moxley, Emily A. | 1916 | Box 552 | Mullin, John | 1898 | Box 178 |
| Moxley, Lloyd | 1896 | Box 163 | Mullin, Philip E. | 1919 | Box 638 |
| Moxley, Lucy J. | 1914 | Box 498 | Mulloy, Hannah Hopkins | 1908 | Box 352 |
| Moxon, William K. | 1863 | Box 31 | Mulloy, Henrietta M. | 1911 | Box 425 |
| Moyers, Gilbert | 1903 | Box 250 | Mulloy, James | 1906 | Box 307 |
| Moynihan, Joseph | 1882 | Box 80 | Muncaster, Harriet E. | 1920 | Box 670 |
| Mudd, Elizabeth | 1821 | Box 7 | Muncey, Emily B. | 1903 | Box 250 |
| Mudd, Jeremiah | 1815 | Box 4 | Munch, Edward C. | 1914 | Box 498 |
| Mudd, Mary | 1862 | Box 30 | Munck, Charlotte | 1905 | Box 288 |
| Mueleisen, William | 1889 | Box 115 | Munday, Fielding | 1898 | Box 178 |
| Mueller, Carl | 1888 | Box 109 | Munday, Leah | 1850 | Box 21 |
| Mueller, Carl | 1911 | Box 425 | Mundell, Mary Elizabeth | 1919 | Box 638 |
| Mueller, Charles | 1917 | Box 578 | Mundheim, Augusta | 1911 | Box 425 |
| Mueller, Christine | 1901 | Box 213 | Munn, Charles A. | 1904 | Box 269 |
| Müeller, Wilhelm | 1888 | Box 109 | Munn, Henry B. | 1910 | Box 400 |
| Mueller, Wilhelmina | 1914 | Box 498 | Munn, Orson Desaix | 1907 | Box 330 |
| Muir, Elizabeth Katherine | 1918 | Box 607 | Munn, Rachael | 1906 | Box 307 |
| Muirhead, William | 1912 | Box 450 | Munro, James | 1906 | Box 307 |
| Muirheid, Elizabeth N. | 1900 | Box 197 | Munro, Robert | 1819 | Box 6 |
| Mulcare, James Edward | 1918 | Box 607 | Munro, Sarah B. | 1874 | Box 55 |
| Mulhall, Annie M. | 1900 | Box 197 | Munroe, Fanny | 1858 | Box 27 |
| Mulhall, John | 1905 | Box 288 | Munroe, Jennie L. | 1920 | Box 670 |
| Mulhall, Mary C. | 1917 | Box 578 | Munroe, Louise S. | 1904 | Box 269 |
| Mulhollen, Henzell | 1869 | Box 41 | Munroe, Seaton | 1896 | Box 163 |
| Mullaly, Mary E. | 1917 | Box 578 | Munroe, Thomas | 1852 | Box 22 |
| Mullan, John | 1911 | Box 425 | Munson, Henry T. | 1899 | Box 186 |
| Mullan, Mary | 1900 | Box 197 | Munson, Nellie S. | 1897 | Box 171 |
| Mullany, Dennis | 1910 | Box 400 | Munson, Owen | 1868 | Box 40 |
| Mulledy, Thomas F. | 1860 | Box 28 | Munzenheimer, Gustave | 1918 | Box 607 |
| Mullen, Bernard | 1908 | Box 352 | Murdoch, John | 1820 | Box 6 |

| | | | | | | |
|---|---|---|---|---|---|---|
| Murdock, Alice S. | 1914 | Box 498 | Murphy, Patrick | 1871 | Box 45 |
| Murdock, Eleanor | 1857 | Box 26 | Murphy, Patrick | 1912 | Box 450 |
| Murdock, George | 1884 | Box 88 | Murphy, Patrick J. | 1892 | Box 133 |
| Murdock, Louise Elise | 1920 | Box 670 | Murphy, Rachel Virginia | 1908 | Box 352 |
| Murdock, Marianne | 1920 | Box 670 | Murphy, Richard | 1899 | Box 186 |
| Murdock, Mary | 1893 | Box 140 | Murphy, Richard | 1908 | Box 352 |
| Murdock, Mary C. | 1857 | Box 26 | Murphy, Richard | 1909 | Box 374 |
| Murphey, Helen Swift | 1915 | Box 527 | Murphy, Thomas | 1906 | Box 308 |
| Murphy, Ann | 1904 | Box 269 | Murphy, Thomas T. | 1919 | Box 638 |
| Murphy, Bridget | 1900 | Box 197 | Murphy, Timothy W. | 1905 | Box 288 |
| Murphy, Charles J. | 1920 | Box 670 | Murphy, William Thompson | 1913 | Box 475 |
| Murphy, Christenia C. | 1895 | Box 156 | Murray, Alexander | 1885 | Box 93 |
| Murphy, Christopher C. | 1916 | Box 552 | Murray, Annie E. | 1891 | Box 126 |
| Murphy, Daniel | 1899 | Box 186 | Murray, Bentley P. | 1909 | Box 375 |
| Murphy, David | 1907 | Box 330 | Murray, Charles F. | 1903 | Box 250 |
| Murphy, Delia | 1913 | Box 475 | Murray, Daniel | 1899 | Box 186 |
| Murphy, Dennis | 1872 | Box 48 | Murray, Emma L. | 1897 | Box 171 |
| Murphy, Edgar | 1911 | Box 425 | Murray, Florence | 1885 | Box 93 |
| Murphy, Edward | 1838 | Box 14 | Murray, Florence | 1910 | Box 400 |
| Murphy, Edward | 1904 | Box 269 | Murray, George | 1912 | Box 450 |
| Murphy, Edward | 1905 | Box 288 | Murray, Hattie (Harriet) | 1911 | Box 425 |
| Murphy, Edward V. | 1919 | Box 638 | Murray, Henry | 1906 | Box 307 |
| Murphy, Ella T. | 1916 | Box 552 | Murray, John B. | 1918 | Box 607 |
| Murphy, Ellen | 1906 | Box 307 | Murray, John R. | 1882 | Box 80 |
| Murphy, Isabella | 1907 | Box 330 | Murray, Martha E. | 1886 | Box 98 |
| Murphy, James K. | 1907 | Box 330 | Murray, Mary | 1897 | Box 171 |
| Murphy, Jennie | 1906 | Box 307 | Murray, Mary Christina | 1920 | Box 670 |
| Murphy, Jeremiah | 1911 | Box 425 | Murray, Mary M. | 1903 | Box 250 |
| Murphy, Johanna | 1910 | Box 400 | Murray, Mattie B. | 1917 | Box 578 |
| Murphy, John | 1869 | Box 41 | Murray, Patrick | 1886 | Box 98 |
| Murphy, John | 1871 | Box 45 | Murray, Robert J. | 1896 | Box 164 |
| Murphy, John | 1894 | Box 148 | Murray, Simeon H. | 1914 | Box 498 |
| Murphy, John | 1896 | Box 164 | Murray, Stuart | 1907 | Box 330 |
| Murphy, John A. | 1889 | Box 115 | Murray, Washington | 1914 | Box 499 |
| Murphy, John A. | 1905 | Box 288 | Murray, Wilhelmina B. | 1890 | Box 121 |
| Murphy, John A. | 1913 | Box 475 | Murtagh, Caroline | 1919 | Box 638 |
| Murphy, John P. | 1903 | Box 250 | Murth, Bridget | 1906 | Box 308 |
| Murphy, John Parker | 1887 | Box 104 | Muschett, Virginia M. | 1900 | Box 198 |
| Murphy, John S. | 1894 | Box 148 | Muse, Frederick | 1917 | Box 578 |
| Murphy, John T. | 1909 | Box 374 | Muse, Lindsay | 1888 | Box 109 |
| Murphy, Julia | 1900 | Box 197 | Musgrave, Frances E. | 1918 | Box 607 |
| Murphy, Kate | 1915 | Box 527 | Musgrove, Mary C. | 1902 | Box 232 |
| Murphy, Letitia W. | 1882 | Box 80 | Mushbach, George A. | 1903 | Box 250 |
| Murphy, Martin | 1846 | Box 18 | Musser, George J. | 1895 | Box 156 |
| Murphy, Mary | 1873 | Box 52 | Mussey, Caroline Lindsly | 1913 | Box 475 |
| Murphy, Mary | 1907 | Box 330 | Mussey, Reuben Delavan | 1892 | Box 133 |
| Murphy, Mary | 1908 | Box 352 | Musson, Poynton | 1903 | Box 250 |
| Murphy, Mary Jane | 1919 | Box 638 | Musson, Sarah Eyton | 1904 | Box 269 |
| Murphy, Matthew | 1906 | Box 308 | Mutersbaugh, Sarah D. | 1901 | Box 213 |
| Murphy, Michael | 1866 | Box 36 | Muth, Philip E. | 1918 | Box 607 |
| Murphy, Michael | 1903 | Box 250 | Myer, Albert J. | 1882 | Box 80 |
| Murphy, Morris | 1896 | Box 164 | Myer, Catherine W. | 1893 | Box 140 |

| | | | | | | |
|---|---|---|---|---|---|---|
| Myer, Helen W. | 1912 | Box 450 | | Nash, George J. | 1912 | Box 450 |
| Myer, Viola Walden | 1918 | Box 607 | | Nash, Michael | 1883 | Box 84 |
| Myerheffer, Peter | 1847 | Box 19 | | Nass, John | 1911 | Box 425 |
| Myers, Benjamin B. | 1833 | Box 12 | | Nater, Savilla | 1895 | Box 156 |
| Myers, Catalina Juliana Mason | 1905 | Box 288 | | Nation, Carry A. | 1911 | Box 425 |
| Myers, Charles | 1864 | Box 32 | | Nattans, Arthur | 1905 | Box 288 |
| Myers, Clement J. | 1905 | Box 288 | | Nau, Christina Amalia | 1907 | Box 330 |
| Myers, Emily | 1879 | Box 70 | | Nau, Sophie | 1909 | Box 375 |
| Myers, Emma E. | 1914 | Box 499 | | Nau, William R. | 1905 | Box 288 |
| Myers, Fred | 1903 | Box 250 | | Nauck, Arthur A. | 1894 | Box 148 |
| Myers, George Alexander | 1919 | Box 638 | | Nauck, Ernst Amos | 1914 | Box 499 |
| Myers, George W. | 1903 | Box 250 | | Nauck, Louisa M. | 1901 | Box 213 |
| Myers, John | 1900 | Box 198 | | Naughton, Bridget | 1903 | Box 250 |
| Myers, John J. | 1883 | Box 84 | | Naughton, Martin | 1909 | Box 375 |
| Myers, John P. | 1918 | Box 607 | | Naugre (Neighder), Moris | 1826 | Box 8 |
| Myers, John P. | 1919 | Box 638 | | Naumann, Caspar | 1874 | Box 55 |
| Myers, Joseph Henry | 1890 | Box 121 | | Naylor, Henry | 1871 | Box 45 |
| Myers, Marion Twiggs | 1893 | Box 140 | | Naylor, Henry Rodley | 1913 | Box 475 |
| Myers, Martha P. | 1901 | Box 213 | | Naylor, John S. | 1818 | Box 5 |
| Myers, Matthew | 1884 | Box 88 | | Naylor, Joshua S. | 1889 | Box 115 |
| Myers, Salome | 1837 | Box 13 | | Naylor, Mary Ann | 1901 | Box 213 |
| Myers, Sarah | 1892 | Box 133 | | Naylor, Mary Smith | 1910 | Box 400 |
| Myers, Virginia M. | 1878 | Box 66 | | Naylor, William | 1896 | Box 164 |
| Myers, William | 1888 | Box 109 | | Naylor, William D. | 1920 | Box 670 |
| Myers, William E. | 1905 | Box 288 | | Naylor, William J. | 1916 | Box 552 |
| Myers, William Hunter | 1910 | Box 400 | | Naylor, William O. | 1894 | Box 148 |
| Myers, William R. | 1916 | Box 552 | | Neal, Asbury | 1907 | Box 330 |
| Myers, Williams | 1898 | Box 178 | | Neal, Levi | 1866 | Box 36 |
| Naegele, Charles A. | 1872 | Box 48 | | Neal, Simon T. | 1907 | Box 330 |
| Nagle, David | 1901 | Box 213 | | Neale, Ann Elizabeth | 1852 | Box 22 |
| Nagle, Levi | 1909 | Box 375 | | Neale, Charles | 1815 | Box 4 |
| Nailor, Allison Jr. | 1908 | Box 352 | | Neale, Charles A. | 1918 | Box 607 |
| Nailor, Bettie F. | 1912 | Box 450 | | Neale, Edward F. | 1839 | Box 14 |
| Nailor, Thompson | 1886 | Box 98 | | Neale, Francis Ignatius | 1881 | Box 76 |
| Nailor, Washington T. | 1908 | Box 352 | | Neale, Isabelle P. | 1876 | Box 61 |
| Nairn, James | 1829 | Box 10 | | Neale, Jennie C. | 1891 | Box 126 |
| Nairn, John W. | 1903 | Box 250 | | Neale, Mary | 1844 | Box 17 |
| Nairn, Joseph W. | 1902 | Box 232 | | Neale, Mary E. | 1889 | Box 115 |
| Nairn, Mary | 1829 | Box 10 | | Neale, Priscilla | 1853 | Box 22 |
| Nalle, Edmund P. | 1912 | Box 450 | | Neale, Zachariah | 1816 | Box 5 |
| Nalle, James B. | 1918 | Box 607 | | Neall, Richard | 1913 | Box 475 |
| Nalle, James B. | 1919 | Box 638 | | Nealon, Mary | 1916 | Box 552 |
| Nalley, John T. | 1919 | Box 638 | | Neben, Charles | 1918 | Box 607 |
| Nalley, Rebecker | 1809 | Box 3 | | Needham, Charles Willard H. | 1915 | Box 527 |
| Nalley, William A. | 1920 | Box 670 | | Needham, George F. | 1889 | Box 115 |
| Nally, Mary A. | 1857 | Box 26 | | Needham, Henry Beach | 1915 | Box 527 |
| Nally, Richard Bennett | 1849 | Box 20 | | Neenan, John | 1879 | Box 70 |
| Naltingham, William | 1882 | Box 80 | | Neff, Benedict | 1879 | Box 70 |
| Narden, Joseph | 1882 | Box 80 | | Neff, Mary J. | 1899 | Box 186 |
| Nash, Ann | 1861 | Box 29 | | Neff, Wendelin | 1894 | Box 148 |
| Nash, Ann M. | 1891 | Box 126 | | Neff, William Erwin | 1915 | Box 528 |
| Nash, Annie E. | 1916 | Box 552 | | Negro Luce | 1806 | Box 2 |

| | | | | | | |
|---|---|---|---|---|---|---|
| Neil, Mary Thresa | 1918 | Box 607 | Neurohr, Joseph | 1905 | Box 288 |
| Neild, Harry William | 1901 | Box 213 | Neville, Andrew | 1909 | Box 375 |
| Neill, George S. | 1858 | Box 27 | Neville, Ellen | 1912 | Box 450 |
| Neilson, Daniel | 1920 | Box 670 | Nevitt, Elizabeth | 1809 | Box 3 |
| Neiman, Mary | 1838 | Box 14 | Nevitt, Frances | 1895 | Box 156 |
| Neitzey, Catherine | 1908 | Box 352 | Nevitt, Mary | 1815 | Box 4 |
| Neitzey, George | 1896 | Box 164 | Nevitt, Mary E. R. | 1913 | Box 475 |
| Neitzey, John | 1902 | Box 232 | Nevitt, Sarah C. | 1895 | Box 156 |
| Neitzey, Joseph Henry | 1896 | Box 164 | Nevius, Lucy Emma | 1915 | Box 528 |
| Neitzey, William | 1908 | Box 352 | Nevius, Lula May Fuller | 1918 | Box 607 |
| Neligan, Patrick | 1866 | Box 36 | Newbold, Adelaide | 1912 | Box 450 |
| Nelligan, John J. | 1919 | Box 638 | Newbold, Charles | 1909 | Box 375 |
| Nelson, Alexander | 1852 | Box 22 | Newbold, Frances K. | 1915 | Box 528 |
| Nelson, Anderson D. | 1911 | Box 425 | Newburn, Mary F. | 1911 | Box 426 |
| Nelson, Charles E. | 1889 | Box 115 | Newburn, Mathias | 1875 | Box 58 |
| Nelson, Charles E. | 1911 | Box 426 | Newby, Henry | 1899 | Box 186 |
| Nelson, Daniel | 1894 | Box 148 | Newcomb, Simon | 1909 | Box 375 |
| Nelson, Edward | 1917 | Box 578 | Newell, Emma Serena | 1915 | Box 528 |
| Nelson, Elias | 1850 | Box 21 | Newlands, Francis G. | 1918 | Box 607 |
| Nelson, Ellen | 1913 | Box 475 | Newlin, James B. | 1897 | Box 171 |
| Nelson, Emma G. | 1889 | Box 115 | Newman, Ann Jane | 1891 | Box 126 |
| Nelson, Mary M. | 1911 | Box 426 | Newman, Celeno V. | 1910 | Box 401 |
| Nelson, Rebecca W. | 1889 | Box 115 | Newman, Charles | 1919 | Box 638 |
| Nelson, Rebecca W. | 1892 | Box 133 | Newman, Charles P. | 1915 | Box 528 |
| Nelson, Thomas | 1916 | Box 552 | Newman, Edward A. | 1920 | Box 670 |
| Nelson, William Francis | 1875 | Box 58 | Newman, Elizabeth H. | 1855 | Box 24 |
| Nelson, William J. | 1903 | Box 250 | Newman, George John | 1916 | Box 552 |
| Nemirovsky, Ida (Hudle Malkie) | 1920 | Box 670 | Newman, John | 1920 | Box 670 |
| Nephew, Frederick D. | 1913 | Box 475 | Newman, John Andreus | 1900 | Box 198 |
| Nephuth, Andrew | 1886 | Box 98 | Newman, John C. | 1919 | Box 638 |
| Nervis, Henry | 1874 | Box 55 | Newman, Louisiana Halsey | 1901 | Box 213 |
| Nesmith, Mary Elizabeth | 1918 | Box 607 | Newman, Mary | 1915 | Box 528 |
| Nessensohn, Joseph | 1873 | Box 52 | Newman, Mary C. | 1909 | Box 375 |
| Nesseth, Maria Sophia | 1907 | Box 330 | Newman, Olivia A. | 1894 | Box 148 |
| Nessmith, Annie Virginia | 1910 | Box 401 | Newman, Thomas Albert | 1913 | Box 475 |
| Nessmith, James M. | 1919 | Box 638 | Newman, Thomas Alfred | 1888 | Box 109 |
| Nestler, William A. | 1914 | Box 499 | Newman, Walter E. | 1914 | Box 499 |
| Netherland, Thomas Henry | 1909 | Box 375 | Newman, William G. H. | 1883 | Box 84 |
| Netherland, William Moody | 1919 | Box 638 | Newman, William R. | 1895 | Box 156 |
| Nettleton, Hallett O. | 1907 | Box 330 | Newmeyer, Solomon | 1908 | Box 352 |
| Neu, Johann George | 1878 | Box 66 | Newmyer, Mose H. | 1915 | Box 528 |
| Neuburger, Anselm | 1917 | Box 578 | Newsom, Nathan C. | 1919 | Box 638 |
| Neuhaus, Joseph H. A. | 1885 | Box 93 | Newton, Albert | 1877 | Box 64 |
| Neuland, Andrew | 1914 | Box 499 | Newton, Alida S. | 1909 | Box 375 |
| Neuland, Bertha | 1914 | Box 499 | Newton, Anna B. | 1906 | Box 308 |
| Neumann, Ernst H. | 1914 | Box 499 | Newton, Benjamin | 1864 | Box 32 |
| Neumann, Julius J. | 1892 | Box 133 | Newton, Charles | 1875 | Box 58 |
| Neumeyer, Christopher | 1881 | Box 76 | Newton, Charles A. | 1916 | Box 552 |
| Neumeyer, Leopold | 1910 | Box 401 | Newton, Gabrial | 1808 | Box 3 |
| Neumeyer, Mary V. | 1919 | Box 638 | Newton, James Colbran | 1899 | Box 186 |
| Neurath, Catharine E. | 1886 | Box 98 | Newton, Joseph | 1812 | Box 4 |
| Neurath, Louis | 1883 | Box 84 | Newton, Louis E. | 1889 | Box 115 |

| | | | | | | |
|---|---|---|---|---|---|---|
| Newton, Mary E. | 1882 | Box 80 | | Nissen, Henry | 1881 | Box 76 |
| Newton, Watson J. | 1913 | Box 475 | | Nixdorff, Eliza P. | 1909 | Box 375 |
| Newton, William G. | 1896 | Box 164 | | Nixdorff, Lewis M. | 1909 | Box 375 |
| Newton, William L. | 1892 | Box 133 | | Nixdorff, Samuel | 1824 | Box 8 |
| Newyahr, Bridget | 1908 | Box 352 | | Nixon, Eliza Ann | 1897 | Box 171 |
| Nichlas, Annie | 1893 | Box 140 | | Nixon, Frank | 1909 | Box 375 |
| Nichlaus, Mary A. | 1870 | Box 43 | | Nixon, George S. | 1915 | Box 528 |
| Nicholas, Elizabeth Byrd | 1902 | Box 232 | | Nixon, James H. | 1904 | Box 269 |
| Nicholas, Philip Cary | 1900 | Box 198 | | Noack, August Wilhelm | 1891 | Box 126 |
| Nichols, Andrew W. | 1871 | Box 45 | | Noah, Jacob J. | 1897 | Box 171 |
| Nichols, Ann | 1888 | Box 109 | | Noble, Adeline M. | 1911 | Box 426 |
| Nichols, Charles D. | 1920 | Box 670 | | Noble, Alice | 1913 | Box 475 |
| Nichols, Charles H. | 1890 | Box 121 | | Noble, Alice Thomas | 1879 | Box 70 |
| Nichols, Daniel Hale | 1912 | Box 450 | | Noble, Belden | 1887 | Box 104 |
| Nichols, Eugene R. | 1920 | Box 670 | | Noble, Charles J. | 1919 | Box 638 |
| Nichols, Frank Steuart | 1920 | Box 670 | | Noble, Eliza C. | 1915 | Box 528 |
| Nichols, J. Estelle | 1907 | Box 330 | | Noble, Eric M. | 1892 | Box 133 |
| Nichols, James | 1911 | Box 426 | | Noble, Henry Bliss (Jr.) | 1889 | Box 115 |
| Nichols, John H. | 1894 | Box 148 | | Noble, Henry Bliss | 1902 | Box 232 |
| Nichols, Otway | 1903 | Box 250 | | Noble, Thomas K. | 1913 | Box 476 |
| Nichols, Rebecca S. | 1908 | Box 352 | | Noble, William Belden | 1896 | Box 164 |
| Nichols, Sallie Lathrop | 1920 | Box 670 | | Nobles, Sarah Crawford | 1920 | Box 671 |
| Nichols, Thomas | 1897 | Box 171 | | Nodine, Mary Davis | 1914 | Box 499 |
| Nicholson, Augustus S. | 1911 | Box 426 | | Noel, Edward McCandless | 1915 | Box 528 |
| Nicholson, George N. | 1905 | Box 288 | | Noerr, Martin Luther | 1893 | Box 140 |
| Nicholson, Mary A. | 1891 | Box 126 | | Noerr, William B. | 1907 | Box 330 |
| Nicholson, Mary A. | 1915 | Box 528 | | Nohe, Catharine A. | 1920 | Box 671 |
| Nicholson, Mary C. | 1914 | Box 499 | | Nohe, Charles | 1920 | Box 671 |
| Nicholson, Walter A. | 1892 | Box 133 | | Nolan, James A. | 1893 | Box 140 |
| Nicholson, William Saxon | 1906 | Box 308 | | Nolan, John | 1892 | Box 134 |
| Nickel, August | 1899 | Box 186 | | Nolen, George A. | 1875 | Box 58 |
| Nickerson, Azor Howitt | 1920 | Box 671 | | Nolen, William | 1893 | Box 140 |
| Nickerson, Lena D. Carter | 1919 | Box 638 | | Noll, Gertrude | 1911 | Box 426 |
| Nicklen, Philip Houlbrooke | 1890 | Box 121 | | Noll, Henry | 1900 | Box 198 |
| Nicolson, Alice W. | 1912 | Box 450 | | Noll, Simon | 1902 | Box 232 |
| Niebel, August | 1916 | Box 553 | | Nollner, Harry N. | 1918 | Box 607 |
| Niedfeldt, Catherine | 1891 | Box 126 | | Nolte, Elenora | 1918 | Box 607 |
| Niedfeldt, John | 1872 | Box 48 | | Nolte, Hermann | 1890 | Box 121 |
| Niehaus, Franz | 1907 | Box 330 | | Nolte, John | 1875 | Box 58 |
| Niehaus, Margaretta | 1912 | Box 450 | | Nolte, Mathias | 1911 | Box 426 |
| Niel, Elizabeth Wheelock | 1897 | Box 171 | | Noon, Martin | 1897 | Box 171 |
| Nieman, Barbara | 1888 | Box 110 | | Noonan, Cornelius | 1892 | Box 134 |
| Nierkirk, Frank S. | 1907 | Box 330 | | Noonan, Delia | 1897 | Box 171 |
| Nihill, Michael | 1888 | Box 110 | | Noonan, James | 1891 | Box 126 |
| Niland, Dennis P. | 1908 | Box 352 | | Noonan, John | 1898 | Box 178 |
| Niland, John | 1888 | Box 110 | | Noonan, James | 1877 | Box 64 |
| Niles, Edward G. | 1905 | Box 288 | | Noonan, Mathias | 1899 | Box 186 |
| Niles, Louise | 1894 | Box 148 | | Noonan, Matthew | 1916 | Box 553 |
| Niles, Mary Gordon | 1902 | Box 232 | | Noonan, Patrick | 1907 | Box 330 |
| Niles, Samuel V. | 1887 | Box 104 | | Nordlinger, Meyer | 1920 | Box 671 |
| Nimmo, Mary C. | 1889 | Box 115 | | Nordlinger, Sarah | 1909 | Box 375 |
| Nisbet, Clara | 1866 | Box 36 | | Nordlinger, Wolf | 1900 | Box 198 |

| | | | | | | |
|---|---|---|---|---|---|---|
| Nordlingher, Bernard | 1907 | Box 330 | Nourse, Isabella Lucretia | 1903 | Box 250 |
| Norman, George A. | 1894 | Box 148 | Nourse, James | 1854 | Box 23 |
| Norman, John | 1826 | Box 9 | Nourse, James B. | 1917 | Box 578 |
| Norman, John James | 1920 | Box 671 | Nourse, John R. | 1871 | Box 45 |
| Norman, Mary S. | 1888 | Box 110 | Nourse, Joseph | 1843 | Box 16 |
| Norment, Samuel | 1891 | Box 127 | Nourse, Joseph E. | 1889 | Box 115 |
| Norris, Adam | 1890 | Box 121 | Nourse, Maria L. | 1851 | Box 21 |
| Norris, Alice C. | 1907 | Box 330 | Nourse, Mary J. | 1908 | Box 352 |
| Norris, Brison | 1905 | Box 288 | Nourse, Mary R. | 1867 | Box 38 |
| Norris, Elizabeth | 1874 | Box 55 | Nourse, Michael | 1861 | Box 29 |
| Norris, Enoch M. | 1896 | Box 164 | Nourse, Rosa M. | 1903 | Box 250 |
| Norris, Hattie Scott | 1915 | Box 528 | Nourse, William | 1892 | Box 134 |
| Norris, Henry Caldwell | 1907 | Box 330 | Novel, Louise | 1908 | Box 352 |
| Norris, Henry Caldwell | 1900 | Box 198 | Nowlan, Henry James | 1899 | Box 186 |
| Norris, Howard D. | 1908 | Box 352 | Noyes, Catharine H. | 1896 | Box 164 |
| Norris, Isabella | 1902 | Box 232 | Noyes, George Enoch | 1899 | Box 186 |
| Norris, James | 1893 | Box 140 | Noyes, Isaac Pitman | 1910 | Box 401 |
| Norris, James L. | 1910 | Box 401 | Noyes, Morillo | 1907 | Box 330 |
| Norris, John | 1815 | Box 4 | Noyes, Samuel Verrill | 1886 | Box 98 |
| Norris, John L. | 1917 | Box 578 | Noyes, Thomas L. | 1873 | Box 52 |
| Norris, John R. | 1916 | Box 553 | Noyes, William | 1864 | Box 32 |
| Norris, Mary E. | 1916 | Box 553 | Nugent, Eli | 1862 | Box 30 |
| Norris, Priscilla | 1896 | Box 164 | Nugent, Jane | 1869 | Box 41 |
| Norris, William G. | 1893 | Box 140 | Nugent, Margaret | 1908 | Box 352 |
| North, Anna | 1898 | Box 178 | Nugent, Owen | 1887 | Box 104 |
| North, Willoughby | 1886 | Box 98 | Nugent, Shadrack | 1891 | Box 127 |
| Northcutt, Annie | 1898 | Box 178 | Nugent, Timothy | 1892 | Box 134 |
| Northcutt, Annie E. | 1893 | Box 140 | Nusslein, Magdalena | 1903 | Box 251 |
| Northedge, Jane | 1886 | Box 98 | Nute, Harriette N. A. | 1895 | Box 156 |
| Norton, Albert Bartlet | 1873 | Box 52 | Nutt, Arbia H. | 1919 | Box 638 |
| Norton, Charles James | 1907 | Box 330 | Nuttall, John | 1919 | Box 638 |
| Norton, Edward S. | 1917 | Box 578 | Nutter, Anna | 1910 | Box 401 |
| Norton, Emily M. | 1904 | Box 269 | Nyman, Charles E. | 1918 | Box 607 |
| Norton, Henry | 1918 | Box 607 | Nyman, Howard S. | 1918 | Box 607 |
| Norton, Hervey J. | 1876 | Box 61 | O'Beirne, Eliza | 1910 | Box 401 |
| Norton, Mary Louisa | 1913 | Box 476 | O'Beirne, Thomas | 1894 | Box 148 |
| Norton, William H. | 1912 | Box 451 | O'Brian, Joseph Henry | 1858 | Box 27 |
| Norvell, Stevens T. | 1912 | Box 451 | O'Brien, Bridget | 1917 | Box 579 |
| Norville, Anna L. | 1906 | Box 308 | O'Brien, Bury John | 1902 | Box 232 |
| Norwig, Apolonia | 1900 | Box 198 | O'Brien, Daniel | 1905 | Box 288 |
| Norwood, John H. | 1887 | Box 104 | O'Brien, Daniel S. | 1920 | Box 671 |
| Norwood, Thomas | 1908 | Box 352 | O'Brien, Ellen | 1906 | Box 308 |
| Nott, Alice | 1899 | Box 186 | O'Brien, Ellen Marie | 1917 | Box 579 |
| Nott, Andrew H. | 1913 | Box 476 | O'Brien, John | 1878 | Box 66 |
| Nott, William E. | 1897 | Box 171 | O'Brien, Joseph T. | 1903 | Box 251 |
| Nottingham, Elizabeth | 1912 | Box 451 | O'Brien, Kate | 1919 | Box 638 |
| Nottingham, William | 1882 | Box 80 | O'Brien, Katherine | 1916 | Box 553 |
| Nottingham, William W. | 1917 | Box 578 | O'Brien, Lawrence | 1854 | Box 23 |
| Noud, Ermina J. | 1910 | Box 401 | O'Brien, Margaret | 1911 | Box 426 |
| Nourse, Charles I. | 1851 | Box 21 | O'Brien, Margaret A. | 1920 | Box 671 |
| Nourse, Charles J. | 1908 | Box 352 | O'Brien, Martin | 1911 | Box 426 |
| Nourse, Charles J. | 1908 | Box 352 | O'Brien, Michael | 1890 | Box 121 |

| | | | | | | |
|---|---|---|---|---|---|---|
| O'Brien, Michael | 1901 | Box 213 | | O'Donnell, Mary | 1914 | Box 499 |
| O'Brien, Michael | 1900 | Box 198 | | O'Donnell, Michael F. | 1910 | Box 401 |
| O'Brien, Michael T. | 1915 | Box 528 | | O'Donnell, Sarah Elizabeth | 1886 | Box 98 |
| O'Brien, Rodey | 1871 | Box 45 | | O'Donnell, Thomas | 1893 | Box 141 |
| O'Brien, Rosa | 1889 | Box 116 | | O'Donnell, Thomas | 1920 | Box 671 |
| O'Brien, Thomas | 1913 | Box 476 | | O'Donnell, Thomas P. | 1917 | Box 579 |
| O'Brien, Timothy | 1909 | Box 375 | | O'Donnell, William | 1902 | Box 232 |
| O'Brien, Timothy | 1911 | Box 426 | | O'Donnoghue, Agnes | 1913 | Box 476 |
| O'Brien, William | 1820 | Box 6 | | O'Donnoghue, James | 1860 | Box 28 |
| O'Callaghan, Patrick | 1897 | Box 171 | | O'Donnoghue, Peter | 1880 | Box 72 |
| O'Connell, Daniel | 1904 | Box 269 | | O'Donnoghue, Timothy | 1859 | Box 27 |
| O'Connell, Ellen | 1914 | Box 499 | | O'Donoghue, Anna M. | 1914 | Box 499 |
| O'Connell, Margaret | 1885 | Box 93 | | O'Donoghue, B. Agnes | 1889 | Box 116 |
| O'Connell, Margaret L. B. | 1910 | Box 401 | | O'Donoghue, B. Agnes | 1891 | Box 127 |
| O'Connell, Mary | 1911 | Box 426 | | O'Donoghue, Catherine | 1919 | Box 638 |
| O'Connell, Michael J. | 1903 | Box 251 | | O'Donoghue, Cornelius | 1889 | Box 1161 |
| O'Connell, Patrick | 1861 | Box 29 | | O'Donovan, Mary E. | 1892 | Box 134 |
| O'Connell, Timothy | 1896 | Box 164 | | O'Dowd, Margaret | 1919 | Box 639 |
| O'Connell, Timothy John | 1909 | Box 375 | | O'Dowd, Richard | 1899 | Box 186 |
| O'Connell, William J. | 1894 | Box 148 | | O'Driscoll, Benedict J. | 1915 | Box 528 |
| O'Conner, Margaret A. | 1888 | Box 110 | | O'Driscoll, George | 1846 | Box 18 |
| O'Connor, Austin | 1897 | Box 171 | | O'Dwyer, John | 1874 | Box 55 |
| O'Connor, Charles | 1895 | Box 156 | | O'Farrell, Patrick | 1903 | Box 251 |
| O'Connor, Daniel | 1885 | Box 93 | | O'Halloran, James | 1874 | Box 55 |
| O'Connor, Daniel | 1908 | Box 352 | | O'Hara, Ida Caroline | 1919 | Box 639 |
| O'Connor, Daniel A. | 1914 | Box 499 | | O'Hare, Ann E. | 1902 | Box 232 |
| O'Connor, Daniel Justus | 1885 | Box 93 | | O'Hare, Christopher S. | 1890 | Box 121 |
| O'Connor, Dennis | 1870 | Box 43 | | O'Hare, Catharine | 1916 | Box 553 |
| O'Connor, Honora | 1900 | Box 198 | | O'Keefe, Patrick J. | 1920 | Box 671 |
| O'Connor, James | 1893 | Box 141 | | O'Leary, Catherine | 1903 | Box 251 |
| O'Connor, Jeannie | 1883 | Box 84 | | O'Leary, Cornelius | 1864 | Box 32 |
| O'Connor, Jeremiah J. | 1892 | Box 134 | | O'Leary, Daniel | 1897 | Box 171 |
| O'Connor, Lizzie | 1894 | Box 148 | | O'Leary, Ellen | 1877 | Box 64 |
| O'Connor, Margaret | 1900 | Box 198 | | O'Leary, Ellen | 1903 | Box 251 |
| O'Connor, Margaret | 1908 | Box 352 | | O'Leary, Jeremiah | 1916 | Box 553 |
| O'Connor, Martin | 1913 | Box 476 | | O'Leary, John | 1892 | Box 134 |
| O'Connor, Mary A. | 1910 | Box 401 | | O'Leary, Maria | 1899 | Box 186 |
| O'Connor, Michael | 1895 | Box 156 | | O'Leary, Mary | 1906 | Box 308 |
| O'Connor, Sarah L. | 1916 | Box 553 | | O'Leary, Mary | 1918 | Box 607 |
| O'Connor, Susan | 1914 | Box 499 | | O'Leary, William Bernard | 1916 | Box 553 |
| O'Connor, Thomas | 1891 | Box 127 | | O'Malley, John | 1914 | Box 499 |
| O'Connor, Timothy | 1887 | Box 104 | | O'Mara, James J. | 1918 | Box 607 |
| O'Connor, William D. | 1889 | Box 116 | | O'Mealey, William | 1909 | Box 375 |
| O'Connor, Winifred | 1917 | Box 579 | | O'Meara, John | 1848 | Box 19 |
| O'Day, Bridget | 1877 | Box 64 | | O'Meara, Sarah A. | 1917 | Box 579 |
| O'Day, James | 1916 | Box 553 | | O'Meara, William A. | 1908 | Box 352 |
| O'Day, Mary E. | 1891 | Box 127 | | O'Meara, William C. | 1908 | Box 352 |
| O'Dea, Thomas | 1878 | Box 66 | | O'Neal, Eliza J. | 1900 | Box 198 |
| O'Day, Thomas | 1888 | Box 110 | | O'Neal, James | 1849 | Box 20 |
| O'Donnell, James | 1920 | Box 671 | | O'Neal, Lewis I. | 1907 | Box 330 |
| O'Donnell, John | 1904 | Box 269 | | O'Neal, Mary A. | 1920 | Box 671 |
| O'Donnell, Mariah | 1904 | Box 269 | | O'Neal, William | 1888 | Box 110 |

| | | | | | | |
|---|---|---|---|---|---|---|
| O'Neale, Julia | 1886 | Box 98 | Ockstadt, William | 1897 | Box 171 |
| O'Neale, Timothy | 1854 | Box 23 | Odder, Michael | 1900 | Box 198 |
| O'Neil, John | 1902 | Box 232 | Oden, Anthony | 1902 | Box 232 |
| O'Neil, Mary C. | 1901 | Box 213 | Oden, Benjamin | 1857 | Box 26 |
| O'Neil, Michael | 1904 | Box 269 | Odenwald, Albert G. | 1888 | Box 110 |
| O'Neil, Michael | 1894 | Box 148 | Odenwald, Jacob | 1903 | Box 251 |
| O'Neill, Charles W. | 1897 | Box 171 | Oehmann, Sarah V. | 1917 | Box 579 |
| O'Neill, John | 1888 | Box 110 | Oehmann, Sophia | 1906 | Box 308 |
| O'Neill, John | 1897 | Box 171 | Oehmann, Valentine | 1892 | Box 134 |
| O'Neill, John D. | 1916 | Box 554 | Oeston, Yves D. M. | 1902 | Box 232 |
| O'Neill, John F. | 1919 | Box 639 | Oettinger, Carrie | 1908 | Box 352 |
| O'Neill, Margaret Melanie | 1905 | Box 288 | Ofenstein, Barbara | 1895 | Box 156 |
| O'Neill, Mary | 1876 | Box 61 | Ofenstein, Casper | 1880 | Box 72 |
| O'Neill, Mary | 1914 | Box 499 | Ofenstein, Leopold | 1881 | Box 76 |
| O'Neill, Mary A. | 1905 | Box 288 | Offley, Catharine Van R. | 1887 | Box 104 |
| O'Neill, Peter C. | 1881 | Box 76 | Offutt, Alexander | 1817 | Box 5 |
| O'Neill, Rebecca J. | 1908 | Box 352 | Offutt, Ann | 1911 | Box 426 |
| O'Neill, Robert | 1910 | Box 401 | Offutt, Edward T. | 1890 | Box 121 |
| O'Neill, Sarah Frances | 1916 | Box 554 | Offutt, Eliza A. | 1888 | Box 110 |
| O'Neill, Thomas F. | 1914 | Box 499 | Offutt, Frank V. | 1907 | Box 330 |
| O'Reiley, Maria | 1900 | Box 198 | Offutt, Hilleary L. | 1891 | Box 127 |
| O'Reiley (O'Riley), Mary | 1856 | Box 25 | Offutt, Hilliary L. | 1886 | Box 98 |
| O'Reilly, Anna | 1886 | Box 98 | Offutt, Joseph Washington | 1919 | Box 639 |
| O'Reilly, Bernard | 1865 | Box 34 | Offutt, Mary Ellen | 1894 | Box 148 |
| O'Reilly, Elizabeth | 1869 | Box 41 | Offutt, Rezin B. | 1837 | Box 13 |
| O'Reilly, Patrick H. | 1844 | Box 17 | Offutt, William A. | 1881 | Box 76 |
| O'Reilly, Robert M. | 1912 | Box 451 | Offutt, Winfield | 1916 | Box 553 |
| O'Shaughnessy, Anna P. | 1914 | Box 499 | Offutt, Zachariah M. | 1878 | Box 66 |
| O'Shea, David | 1875 | Box 58 | Ofterdinger, Theodore A. | 1883 | Box 84 |
| O'Sullivan, Dennis O. | 1883 | Box 84 | Ogden, Herbert G. | 1906 | Box 308 |
| O'Sullivan, Jeremiah | 1844 | Box 17 | Ogden, Lucy | 1915 | Box 528 |
| O'Toole, Margaret | 1911 | Box 426 | Ogilvie, David | 1805 | Box 1 |
| O'Toole, Martin | 1870 | Box 43 | Ogilvie, Walter | 1873 | Box 52 |
| O'Toole, Michael | 1890 | Box 121 | Ogle, Reazin H. | 1904 | Box 269 |
| Oakes, James | 1911 | Box 426 | Ogston, Harriet Wood | 1916 | Box 553 |
| Oates, Anna Amelia | 1919 | Box 638 | Ohl, John | 1899 | Box 186 |
| Ober, George C. | 1920 | Box 671 | Ohl, John W. | 1893 | Box 141 |
| Oberdorf, Joseph Valentine | 1861 | Box 29 | Ohm, Annie Elizabeth | 1916 | Box 553 |
| Oberheim, John | 1903 | Box 251 | Ohme, Frederick | 1864 | Box 32 |
| Oberheim, Sophie | 1892 | Box 134 | Oker, Catharina | 1903 | Box 251 |
| Oberly, John | 1899 | Box 186 | Okey, Cornelius W. | 1901 | Box 213 |
| Obermeyer, Carl C. F. G. | 1896 | Box 164 | Okey, Mary B. | 1913 | Box 476 |
| Oblinger, Wilson | 1919 | Box 638 | Okun, Gustave | 1895 | Box 156 |
| Obold, Agnes | 1911 | Box 426 | Olcott, Henry A. | 1910 | Box 401 |
| Obold, Charles M. | 1914 | Box 499 | Oldberg, Rudolph | 1878 | Box 66 |
| Obold, Francis S. | 1901 | Box 213 | Oldham, Francis F. | 1912 | Box 451 |
| Obold, Sarah J. | 1908 | Box 352 | Olds, Mark L. | 1869 | Box 41 |
| Ochsenreiter, Francis | 1884 | Box 88 | Olin, Abraham B. | 1879 | Box 70 |
| Ochsenreiter, Marie | 1920 | Box 671 | Olive, Winfield Scott | 1907 | Box 330 |
| Ockershausen, John | 1919 | Box 639 | Oliver, Annie R. | 1915 | Box 528 |
| Ockhert, August Louis | 1904 | Box 269 | Oliver, Elias | 1920 | Box 671 |
| Ockstadt, Catharina | 1901 | Box 213 | Oliver, Ella J. | 1916 | Box 553 |

| | | | | | | |
|---|---|---|---|---|---|---|
| Oliver, James B. | 1906 | Box 308 | Osborn, William McKinney | 1856 | Box 25 |
| Oliver, John E. | 1892 | Box 134 | Osborne, Edward Lee | 1919 | Box 639 |
| Oliver, Sarah Ann | 1875 | Box 58 | Osborne, Eleanora | 1901 | Box 213 |
| Oliver, Thomas | 1903 | Box 251 | Osborne, Leonard | 1837 | Box 13 |
| Olmstead, John | 1899 | Box 186 | Osborne, Teresa M. | 1903 | Box 251 |
| Olmstead, Katie H. | 1889 | Box 116 | Osbourn, Margaret | 1869 | Box 41 |
| Olmsted, Helen M. H. | 1920 | Box 671 | Osbourn, Sarah C. | 1869 | Box 41 |
| Olmsted, Hirah F. | 1918 | Box 607 | Osgodby, Thomas W. | 1858 | Box 27 |
| Olmsted, Josephine A. | 1919 | Box 639 | Osmun, Charles | 1919 | Box 639 |
| Ontrich, John H. | 1895 | Box 156 | Osmun, Little C. | 1905 | Box 289 |
| Oppenheimer, Augustus | 1915 | Box 528 | Osmun, Rachel V. | 1913 | Box 476 |
| Oppenheimer, Michael | 1886 | Box 99 | Ossinger, John | 1865 | Box 34 |
| Oppermann, Elizabeth C. | 1905 | Box 288 | Ostermayer, Bernhardt | 1867 | Box 38 |
| Oram, Joseph H. | 1902 | Box 232 | Ostmann, Bernard | 1919 | Box 639 |
| Orange, Joseph | 1916 | Box 554 | Ostrander, Elisha C. | 1910 | Box 401 |
| Orcutt, Warren H. | 1909 | Box 375 | Ostrander, Margaret A. | 1913 | Box 476 |
| Ord, James | 1810 | Box 3 | Ostrander, William H. | 1909 | Box 375 |
| Ord, Pacificus | 1900 | Box 198 | Otis, Genevieve P. | 1894 | Box 148 |
| Ordway, Albert | 1897 | Box 171 | Otis, George A. | 1881 | Box 76 |
| Ordway, Harriet | 1894 | Box 148 | Otis, Louis | 1898 | Box 178 |
| Ordway, Nancy A. | 1918 | Box 608 | Ott, Anne | 1828 | Box 9 |
| Orme, Anne | 1839 | Box 14 | Ott, David | 1820 | Box 6 |
| Orme, Dennis | 1873 | Box 52 | Ott, Joseph W. | 1907 | Box 330 |
| Orme, Elizabeth | 1863 | Box 31 | Otterback, Benjamin Louis | 1896 | Box 164 |
| Orme, Ella | 1912 | Box 451 | Otterback, Philip | 1858 | Box 27 |
| Orme, Francis M. | 1873 | Box 52 | Otterback, Rosella | 1904 | Box 270 |
| Orme, Frank D. | 1903 | Box 251 | Otterback, Sarah | 1910 | Box 401 |
| Orme, James W. | 1905 | Box 288 | Otterback, Sarah Ellen | 1896 | Box 164 |
| Orme, Jeremiah | 1859 | Box 27 | Otto, Emma L. | 1919 | Box 639 |
| Orme, William | 1882 | Box 80 | Otto, George | 1883 | Box 84 |
| Orme, William W. | 1888 | Box 110 | Oulahan, Richard | 1895 | Box 156 |
| Ormsby, David G. | 1895 | Box 156 | Ould, Henry | 1871 | Box 45 |
| Orndorff, Lunsford Gibbons | 1909 | Box 375 | Ould, Remus R. | 1852 | Box 22 |
| Orr, Elizabeth | 1827 | Box 9 | Ould, Susan Britton | 1909 | Box 375 |
| Orr, Henry | 1846 | Box 18 | Oulds, James | 1915 | Box 529 |
| Orr, John | 1828 | Box 9 | Ourand, Catharine | 1889 | Box 116 |
| Orr, John D. | 1817 | Box 5 | Ourand, Elijah | 1877 | Box 64 |
| Orr, William H. | 1869 | Box 41 | Ourdan, Edith V. | 1906 | Box 308 |
| Orrick, Georgia | 1912 | Box 451 | Ourdan, Joseph J. P. | 1874 | Box 55 |
| Orrid, Horace | 1908 | Box 352 | Ourdan, Margaret J. | 1902 | Box 232 |
| Orrid, Mary Ann | 1907 | Box 330 | Ourdan, Mary M. | 1896 | Box 164 |
| Orth, Henry | 1909 | Box 375 | Ousley, John | 1857 | Box 26 |
| Orth, J. Fred | 1920 | Box 671 | Outwater, Theron | 1915 | Box 529 |
| Ortman, Louisa | 1910 | Box 403 | Over, Andrew | 1917 | Box 579 |
| Osborn, Alfred G. | 1907 | Box 330 | Overand, Edmund D. | 1906 | Box 308 |
| Osborn, Charles D. | 1920 | Box 671 | Overand, Emma J. | 1905 | Box 289 |
| Osborn, Ellen F. | 1917 | Box 579 | Overby, William H. | 1892 | Box 134 |
| Osborn, George W. | 1915 | Box 529 | Overman, Elizabeth | 1910 | Box 401 |
| Osborn, James T. | 1915 | Box 529 | Overstreet, James T. | 1853 | Box 22 |
| Osborn, Marion | 1916 | Box 554 | Owen, Catherine E. | 1901 | Box 213 |
| Osborn, Sarah | 1917 | Box 579 | Owen, Clarence Senior | 1914 | Box 499 |
| Osborn, William McKenney | 1917 | Box 579 | Owen, Edward | 1878 | Box 66 |

| | | | | | | |
|---|---|---|---|---|---|---|
| Owen, Elisha D. | 1893 | Box 141 | Paine, Horace | 1903 | Box 251 |
| Owen, Ellen | 1887 | Box 104 | Paine, Louisa | 1917 | Box 579 |
| Owen, Fred S. | 1918 | Box 608 | Paine, Sumner | 1899 | Box 186 |
| Owen, Henritta B. | 1879 | Box 70 | Painter, John I. | 1914 | Box 499 |
| Owen, Hester A. | 1896 | Box 164 | Painter, Joseph H. | 1909 | Box 375 |
| Owen, Mary | 1806 | Box 2 | Pairo, Alice | 1908 | Box 352 |
| Owen, Owen | 1912 | Box 451 | Pairo, Charles W. | 1897 | Box 171 |
| Owen, Thomas J. | 1919 | Box 639 | Pairo, Elinor Carson | 1908 | Box 352 |
| Owen, William H. | 1904 | Box 270 | Pairo, Robert M. | 1896 | Box 164 |
| Owens, Alfred | 1919 | Box 639 | Pairo, Thomas William | 1840 | Box 18 |
| Owens, Ann Stacy | 1900 | Box 198 | Palmer, Ann | 1826 | Box 9 |
| Owens, Benjamin | 1828 | Box 9 | Palmer, Ann D. | 1894 | Box 148 |
| Owens, Benjamin | 1880 | Box 73 | Palmer, Augustus B. P. | 1916 | Box 554 |
| Owens, Fanny | 1917 | Box 579 | Palmer, Benjamin F. | 1876 | Box 61 |
| Owens, Isaac | 1833 | Box 12 | Palmer, Edmond | 1902 | Box 232 |
| Owens, James | 1891 | Box 127 | Palmer, Edward | 1911 | Box 426 |
| Owens, James Z. | 1917 | Box 579 | Palmer, Elizabeth D. | 1908 | Box 353 |
| Owens, Joseph | 1860 | Box 28 | Palmer, Fannie G. | 1909 | Box 375 |
| Owens, Louise M. | 1900 | Box 198 | Palmer, Gideon Stinson | 1892 | Box 134 |
| Owner, James. | 1848 | Box 19 | Palmer, Innis N. | 1901 | Box 213 |
| Oyster, David W. | 1893 | Box 141 | Palmer, James C. | 1883 | Box 84 |
| Oyster, George | 1848 | Box 19 | Palmer, Joseph | 1916 | Box 554 |
| P'Pool, Barney A. | 1911 | Box 427 | Palmer, Kate | 1859 | Box 27 |
| P'Pool, Oscar B. | 1911 | Box 427 | Palmer, Lee | 1871 | Box 45 |
| Pace, Kate | 1897 | Box 171 | Palmer, Lizzie M. | 1913 | Box 476 |
| Pach, Julius | 1892 | Box 134 | Palmer, Lovina S. | 1919 | Box 639 |
| Pach, Pauline | 1901 | Box 213 | Palmer, Sally | 1884 | Box 88 |
| Pack, Catharine | 1828 | Box 9 | Palmer, Samuel C. | 1914 | Box 499 |
| Packard, Mary L. | 1911 | Box 426 | Palmer, Waterman | 1882 | Box 80 |
| Paddon, Jane W. | 1912 | Box 451 | Palmer, William Bladen | 1919 | Box 639 |
| Paddon, Robert | 1894 | Box 148 | Palmer, Wilson D. | 1893 | Box 141 |
| Padgett, Helen W. | 1914 | Box 499 | Pancoast, Rachel N. | 1871 | Box 45 |
| Padgett, Joseph H. | 1903 | Box 251 | Pannell, Mary Clare | 1891 | Box 127 |
| Page, Charles Grafton | 1868 | Box 40 | Pantzerbeiter, Frederika | 1900 | Box 198 |
| Page, Christena | 1920 | Box 671 | Pantzerbieter, Henry | 1919 | Box 639 |
| Page, Daniel | 1847 | Box 19 | Parcel, John C. | 1890 | Box 121 |
| Page, Francis A. | 1890 | Box 121 | Paret, Adelia V. | 1912 | Box 451 |
| Page, Freeborn H. | 1905 | Box 289 | Parham, Theophilus S. | 1904 | Box 270 |
| Page, Horace F. | 1890 | Box 121 | Parigo, Geovanni | 1901 | Box 213 |
| Page, Maria C. | 1877 | Box 64 | Paris, Walter | 1907 | Box 330 |
| Page, Mary E. | 1909 | Box 375 | Parish, Joseph W. | 1905 | Box 289 |
| Page, Mary Irene | 1910 | Box 401 | Park, Anna M. | 1907 | Box 330 |
| Page, R. C. | 1876 | Box 61 | Park, Cassius M. | 1913 | Box 476 |
| Page, Sarah | 1901 | Box 213 | Park, Sarah J. | 1892 | Box 134 |
| Page, Thomas | 1897 | Box 171 | Parke, Ellen | 1903 | Box 251 |
| Page, Yelverton P. | 1863 | Box 31 | Parke, John G. | 1901 | Box 213 |
| Paige, Frazier | 1897 | Box 171 | Parke, Joseph Maxwell | 1890 | Box 121 |
| Paige, Hildegard Brooks | 1920 | Box 671 | Parke, Lucinda Neel | 1904 | Box 270 |
| Paige, Rosa | 1911 | Box 426 | Parke, Margaret | 1889 | Box 116 |
| Paine, Anna J. | 1918 | Box 608 | Parker, Amelia | 1906 | Box 308 |
| Paine, Eliza L. B. | 1905 | Box 289 | Parker, Anita Emily | 1903 | Box 251 |
| Paine, Halbert E. | 1905 | Box 289 | Parker, Bettie J. | 1920 | Box 671 |

| | | | | | | |
|---|---|---|---|---|---|
| Parker, Catharine A. | 1911 | Box 426 | Parrish, Mary C. | 1909 | Box 376 |
| Parker, Charles H. | 1915 | Box 529 | Parrott, Richard | 1823 | Box 7 |
| Parker, Daniel | 1846 | Box 18 | Parschal, George W. | 1878 | Box 67 |
| Parker, David | 1918 | Box 608 | Parson, John T. | 1890 | Box 121 |
| Parker, David Crawford | 1830 | Box 10 | Parson, Martha | 1900 | Box 198 |
| Parker, Ellen E. | 1878 | Box 67 | Parsons, Ann Mary | 1842 | Box 16 |
| Parker, Ellen M. | 1919 | Box 639 | Parsons, Arthur Jeffrey | 1915 | Box 529 |
| Parker, Frances Perry | 1919 | Box 639 | Parsons, Bernard | 1855 | Box 24 |
| Parker, George | 1893 | Box 141 | Parsons, Hosmer Buckingham | 1908 | Box 353 |
| Parker, George S. | 1903 | Box 251 | Parsons, James L. | 1917 | Box 579 |
| Parker, George Stanley | 1873 | Box 52 | Parsons, Joseph | 1849 | Box 20 |
| Parker, Grace Graham | 1912 | Box 451 | Parsons, Sarah Maria | 1918 | Box 608 |
| Parker, Harriet C. Webster | 1896 | Box 164 | Parsons, Sarah Rice | 1910 | Box 401 |
| Parker, Harry B. | 1911 | Box 426 | Parsons, William | 1847 | Box 19 |
| Parker, Henry T. | 1865 | Box 34 | Parsons, William | 1864 | Box 32 |
| Parker, John C. | 1904 | Box 270 | Parsons, William H. | 1917 | Box 579 |
| Parker, John E. | 1915 | Box 529 | Partello, Dwight J. | 1920 | Box 671 |
| Parker, Julia Florence | 1918 | Box 608 | Partello, William P. | 1878 | Box 67 |
| Parker, Louise | 1899 | Box 186 | Partlow, William F. | 1906 | Box 308 |
| Parker, Martha | 1917 | Box 579 | Partridge, Annie | 1905 | Box 289 |
| Parker, Mary Frances | 1918 | Box 608 | Partridge, John | 1898 | Box 178 |
| Parker, Peter | 1888 | Box 110 | Partridge, John H. | 1873 | Box 52 |
| Parker, Rebecca S. | 1887 | Box 104 | Paschall, Margaret | 1895 | Box 156 |
| Parker, Richard C. | 1903 | Box 251 | Paschall, Mary L. | 1895 | Box 156 |
| Parker, Sarah A. | 1876 | Box 61 | Passmore, Deborah G. | 1911 | Box 426 |
| Parker, Sophia A. | 1896 | Box 164 | Patch, Dan W. | 1918 | Box 608 |
| Parker, Southey S. | 1889 | Box 116 | Patch, Elizabeth | 1909 | Box 376 |
| Parker, Thomas | 1889 | Box 116 | Patch, George | 1898 | Box 178 |
| Parker, Thomas S. | 1917 | Box 579 | Patch, Joseph | 1905 | Box 289 |
| Parker, William | 1837 | Box 13 | Patchell, James L. | 1917 | Box 579 |
| Parker, William | 1890 | Box 121 | Paterson, Alexander | 1872 | Box 48 |
| Parker, William H. | 1902 | Box 232 | Patrick, Caroline E. | 1906 | Box 308 |
| Parkins, Margaret W. | 1915 | Box 529 | Patrick, Hattie E. L. | 1911 | Box 426 |
| Parkinson, Amanda Gardner | 1919 | Box 639 | Patrick, John H. | 1893 | Box 141 |
| Parkinson, Anthony | 1875 | Box 58 | Patten, Anastasia | 1888 | Box 110 |
| Parkinson, Caleb | 1916 | Box 554 | Patten, Lewis | 1872 | Box 48 |
| Parkman, Robert | 1899 | Box 186 | Patterson, Amelia C. | 1913 | Box 476 |
| Parks, Ellen | 1900 | Box 198 | Patterson, Anna Granville | 1914 | Box 499 |
| Parks, George T. | 1895 | Box 156 | Patterson, Anna Ledward | 1917 | Box 579 |
| Parks, Lucinda | 1889 | Box 116 | Patterson, Annie E. | 1901 | Box 213 |
| Parks, William G. | 1907 | Box 330 | Patterson, Bazil | 1866 | Box 36 |
| Parmelee, Julia F. | 1917 | Box 579 | Patterson, Carlile P. | 1881 | Box 76 |
| Parnell, George | 1872 | Box 48 | Patterson, Edward Hopkins | 1917 | Box 579 |
| Parnell, Rosina M. | 1910 | Box 401 | Patterson, Fannie B. | 1909 | Box 376 |
| Parris, Annie K. | 1916 | Box 554 | Patterson, Francis Gordon | 1906 | Box 308 |
| Parris, Bessie H. | 1915 | Box 529 | Patterson, Henry I. | 1887 | Box 104 |
| Parris, Joseph | 1917 | Box 579 | Patterson, James | 1916 | Box 554 |
| Parris, Julia W. | 1894 | Box 148 | Patterson, John | 1893 | Box 141 |
| Parris, Samuel B. | 1900 | Box 198 | Patterson, John B. | 1833 | Box 12 |
| Parris, Sarah Whitman | 1883 | Box 84 | Patterson, John H. | 1914 | Box 500 |
| Parrish, Caroline M. | 1912 | Box 451 | Patterson, Marie E. | 1904 | Box 270 |
| Parrish, Clara C. | 1895 | Box 156 | Patterson, Mary E. | 1916 | Box 554 |

| | | | | | | |
|---|---|---|---|---|---|---|
| Patterson, Mary J. | 1894 | Box 148 | Payson, Lewis E. | 1909 | Box 376 |
| Patterson, Raymond Albert | 1910 | Box 401 | Payson, Louise C. | 1915 | Box 529 |
| Patterson, Robert Y. | 1903 | Box 251 | Payte, Francis | 1901 | Box 213 |
| Patterson, Sarah A. | 1907 | Box 330 | Payton, Forney | 1907 | Box 331 |
| Patton, Julia Chunn | 1901 | Box 213 | Peabody, Mary D. | 1895 | Box 156 |
| Patton, Mary B. | 1881 | Box 76 | Peabody, Rose W. | 1917 | Box 580 |
| Patton, Milton M. | 1916 | Box 554 | Peabody, William L. | 1914 | Box 500 |
| Patton, William P. | 1907 | Box 330 | Peach, Emanuel C. | 1914 | Box 500 |
| Paul, Alexander | 1898 | Box 178 | Peaco, Ruth A. | 1855 | Box 24 |
| Paul, Augusta Gray | 1920 | Box 671 | Peaco, William H. | 1853 | Box 22 |
| Paul, Edward A. | 1879 | Box 70 | Peacock, Albert | 1907 | Box 331 |
| Paul, Gabriel R. | 1886 | Box 99 | Peacock, Virginia T. M. | 1906 | Box 308 |
| Paul, James W. (Jr.) | 1912 | Box 451 | Peacock, Virginia Tatnall | 1918 | Box 608 |
| Paul, Louise | 1898 | Box 178 | Peak, John | 1857 | Box 26 |
| Paul, Margaret | 1909 | Box 376 | Peake, James F. | 1883 | Box 84 |
| Paul, Sarah Gertrude | 1914 | Box 500 | Peake, John H. | 1896 | Box 164 |
| Paul, Thomas H. | 1891 | Box 127 | Pearce, Charles C. | 1916 | Box 554 |
| Paulding, Helen J. | 1910 | Box 401 | Pearce, Edward | 1865 | Box 34 |
| Pauley, Mary E. | 1910 | Box 401 | Pearce, Jessie L. | 1907 | Box 331 |
| Pavarini, Isadore | 1910 | Box 401 | Pearce, Rebecca | 1843 | Box 16 |
| Pavarini, Rosa | 1911 | Box 426 | Pearce, Sally E. | 1902 | Box 232 |
| Paxon, Marietta J. | 1919 | Box 639 | Pearce, Stanley | 1905 | Box 289 |
| Paxson, Alverta C. | 1915 | Box 529 | Pearl, Helen Kate | 1917 | Box 580 |
| Paxton, John S. | 1884 | Box 88 | Pearl, Jane B. | 1910 | Box 402 |
| Paxton, Thomas S. | 1908 | Box 353 | Pearl, Marcus | 1878 | Box 67 |
| Paxton, William E. | 1904 | Box 270 | Pearsall, Paul Spofford | 1920 | Box 672 |
| Payne, Charles H. | 1886 | Box 99 | Pearson, Aven | 1904 | Box 270 |
| Payne, Columbia Newton | 1920 | Box 672 | Pearson, Catherine | 1868 | Box 40 |
| Payne, Hattie M. | 1905 | Box 289 | Pearson, Edwin H. | 1900 | Box 198 |
| Payne, Henry | 1899 | Box 186 | Pearson, George W. | 1918 | Box 608 |
| Payne, Henry C. | 1912 | Box 451 | Pearson, Henry M. | 1896 | Box 164 |
| Payne, Hester | 1907 | Box 330 | Pearson, Joseph | 1835 | Box 13 |
| Payne, Jacob | 1849 | Box 20 | Pearson, Joseph L. | 1914 | Box 500 |
| Payne, James G. | 1910 | Box 401 | Pearson, Lawson | 1830 | Box 10 |
| Payne, James H. | 1920 | Box 672 | Pearson, Mattie J. | 1896 | Box 164 |
| Payne, Jennie Bryan | 1920 | Box 672 | Pearson, Peter M. | 1882 | Box 80 |
| Payne, John | 1882 | Box 80 | Pearson, Sinah E. | 1908 | Box 353 |
| Payne, Lavinia M. | 1907 | Box 330 | Pearson, Sven P. | 1916 | Box 554 |
| Payne, Margaret | 1915 | Box 529 | Pearson, William Gaston | 1861 | Box 29 |
| Payne, Mary | 1903 | Box 251 | Peary, Robert E. | 1920 | Box 672 |
| Payne, Mary | 1808 | Box 3 | Pease, Seth | 1819 | Box 6 |
| Payne, Priscilla R. | 1904 | Box 270 | Peck, Charles F. | 1890 | Box 121 |
| Payne, Rice W. | 1889 | Box 116 | Peck, David Brainerd | 1913 | Box 476 |
| Payne, Robert | 1883 | Box 84 | Peck, Joseph | 1809 | Box 3 |
| Payne, Robert Henry | 1908 | Box 353 | Peck, Julia Ashley | 1910 | Box 402 |
| Payne, Sarah A. | 1910 | Box 401 | Peck, Melvin Dewitt | 1901 | Box 213 |
| Payne, Stafford | 1901 | Box 213 | Peckham, Rufus W. | 1909 | Box 376 |
| Payne, Susan | 1900 | Box 198 | Pedersen, Anders | 1916 | Box 554 |
| Payne, Susan | 1914 | Box 500 | Pedrick, America G. | 1893 | Box 141 |
| Payne, William | 1913 | Box 476 | Peeples, George L. | 1911 | Box 426 |
| Payne, William H. | 1904 | Box 270 | Peerce, James F. | 1905 | Box 289 |
| Payson, Charles | 1914 | Box 500 | Peerce, Mary Eliza | 1906 | Box 308 |

| | | | | | | |
|---|---|---|---|---|---|---|---|
| Peers, Aquila | 1829 | Box 10 | | Perreard, Jean Marie | 1918 | Box 608 |
| Peet, Maria C. | 1908 | Box 353 | | Perrie, Sophia H. | 1851 | Box 21 |
| Pegg, John H. | 1867 | Box 38 | | Perrottet, Albert M. | 1883 | Box 84 |
| Peirce, Abner C. | 1851 | Box 21 | | Perrottet, Marie | 1884 | Box 88 |
| Peirce, Isaac | 1842 | Box 16 | | Perry, Alexander J. | 1913 | Box 476 |
| Peirce, Joshua | 1869 | Box 41 | | Perry, Amanda E. | 1912 | Box 451 |
| Peirce, Susan Ann | 1861 | Box 29 | | Perry, Charles | 1883 | Box 84 |
| Peitz, John Henry | 1914 | Box 500 | | Perry, Daniel | 1915 | Box 529 |
| Pelletier, Antonio | 1887 | Box 104 | | Perry, Edith | 1919 | Box 639 |
| Pelouze, Louis H. | 1878 | Box 67 | | Perry, Elizabeth A. W. | 1893 | Box 141 |
| Pelton, Elizabeth | 1895 | Box 156 | | Perry, Fred C. | 1917 | Box 580 |
| Peltz, John | 1817 | Box 5 | | Perry, George N. | 1916 | Box 554 |
| Pelz, Paul J. | 1918 | Box 608 | | Perry, Howard | 1900 | Box 198 |
| Pemont, William H. | 1877 | Box 64 | | Perry, Ida M. | 1902 | Box 232 |
| Pendergast, Margaret A. | 1903 | Box 251 | | Perry, James | 1908 | Box 353 |
| Pendleton, Charles Mason | 1919 | Box 639 | | Perry, Jennie Purcell | 1917 | Box 580 |
| Pendleton, Edward H. | 1858 | Box 27 | | Perry, Josephine A. | 1917 | Box 580 |
| Pendleton, Selina C. | 1885 | Box 93 | | Perry, Josiah | 1885 | Box 93 |
| Pendrick, John C. | 1893 | Box 141 | | Perry, Josiah B. | 1919 | Box 639 |
| Penfield, Luther | 1899 | Box 186 | | Perry, Josiah Newman | 1920 | Box 672 |
| Penhallow, Mary | 1903 | Box 251 | | Perry, M. H. | 1915 | Box 529 |
| Penicks, Sarah Janette | 1906 | Box 308 | | Perry, Mary C. | 1913 | Box 476 |
| Penington, David Frey | 1914 | Box 500 | | Perry, Mary A. | 1902 | Box 232 |
| Penn, Elizabeth C. | 1894 | Box 149 | | Perry, Mary Jane | 1908 | Box 353 |
| Penn, Samuel | 1919 | Box 639 | | Perry, Sarah | 1899 | Box 186 |
| Pennebaker, Charles D. | 1888 | Box 110 | | Perry, Seaton | 1898 | Box 178 |
| Penniman, Maria Hosmer | 1914 | Box 500 | | Perry, Susan | 1901 | Box 214 |
| Pennington, Alexander C. M. | 1918 | Box 608 | | Perry, Thomas J. L. | 1881 | Box 76 |
| Pennington, Martha Ellen | 1912 | Box 451 | | Perry, Walter S. | 1912 | Box 451 |
| Pennoyer, Mae E. | 1918 | Box 608 | | Perry, William | 1879 | Box 70 |
| Penrose, Charles W. | 1920 | Box 672 | | Perskin, Samuel | 1918 | Box 608 |
| Pentland, Andrew W. | 1917 | Box 580 | | Persons, Agnes E. | 1915 | Box 529 |
| Pentland, Elizabeth E. | 1913 | Box 476 | | Persons, Charles E. | 1905 | Box 289 |
| Pentland, Margaret Ewing | 1918 | Box 608 | | Persons, Remus Charles | 1918 | Box 608 |
| Pepper, John | 1914 | Box 500 | | Pester, Margaret | 1899 | Box 186 |
| Pepper, John P. | 1867 | Box 38 | | Peter, Charlotte B. | 1911 | Box 427 |
| Percy, Henry | 1910 | Box 402 | | Peter, David | 1812 | Box 4 |
| Percy, Henry Tucker | 1910 | Box 402 | | Peter, Elizabeth | 1821 | Box 7 |
| Perin, Clifford | 1902 | Box 232 | | Peter, James | 1808 | Box 3 |
| Perkins, Addie R. | 1908 | Box 353 | | Peter, John | 1837 | Box 13 |
| Perkins, Bertha | 1920 | Box 672 | | Peter, Martha | 1854 | Box 23 |
| Perkins, Carrie Davis | 1904 | Box 270 | | Peter, Mary | 1869 | Box 41 |
| Perkins, Julia E. | 1907 | Box 331 | | Peter, Rebecca | 1872 | Box 48 |
| Perkins, Loftus | 1897 | Box 171 | | Peter, Robert | 1807 | Box 2 |
| Perkins, Mary Ann | 1858 | Box 27 | | Peter, Robert | 1811 | Box 3 |
| Perkins, Nellie Maria | 1920 | Box 672 | | Peter, Robert | 1904 | Box 270 |
| Perkins, Sarah J. | 1893 | Box 141 | | Peter, Roberta | 1895 | Box 156 |
| Perkins, Thomas B. | 1912 | Box 451 | | Peter, Sallie | 1898 | Box 178 |
| Perlatt, John | 1905 | Box 289 | | Peter, Thomas | 1834 | Box 12 |
| Perley, Fannie A. | 1897 | Box 171 | | Peters, Clara Louise | 1912 | Box 451 |
| Perley, James | 1899 | Box 186 | | Peters, George H. | 1916 | Box 554 |
| Perley, Lucy B. | 1919 | Box 639 | | Peters, Mary | 1897 | Box 171 |

| | | | | | | |
|---|---|---|---|---|---|---|
| Peters, William J. | 1908 | Box 353 | | Phelps, Anna Mohun | 1916 | Box 554 |
| Petersen, Anna | 1871 | Box 45 | | Phelps, Cyrus Emmet | 1907 | Box 331 |
| Petersen, Anna | 1915 | Box 529 | | Phelps, Eliza | 1899 | Box 186 |
| Petersen, Carl | 1914 | Box 500 | | Phelps, James | 1899 | Box 186 |
| Petersen, Ferdinand | 1915 | Box 529 | | Phelps, James A. | 1906 | Box 308 |
| Petersen, Jane D. | 1892 | Box 134 | | Phelps, Thomas Stowell | 1901 | Box 214 |
| Peterson, Almira L. | 1906 | Box 308 | | Phelps, William Walter | 1894 | Box 149 |
| Peterson, Emily L. | 1893 | Box 141 | | Phenix, Legare | 1915 | Box 529 |
| Peterson, Henry | 1893 | Box 141 | | Phenix, Rebecca S. | 1904 | Box 270 |
| Peterson, Per Edward August | 1906 | Box 308 | | Philip, Eliza W. | 1897 | Box 171 |
| Petingale, Frances A. | 1897 | Box 171 | | Philips, Seth Ledyard | 1885 | Box 93 |
| Pettengill, Addie S. | 1901 | Box 214 | | Philips, William H. | 1920 | Box 672 |
| Pettengill, True E. A. | 1895 | Box 156 | | Phillibrown, John | 1804 | Box 1 |
| Pettibone, Elizabeth | 1872 | Box 48 | | Phillippe, Mary Alice | 1915 | Box 529 |
| Pettibone, William | 1891 | Box 127 | | Phillips, Anthony | 1913 | Box 476 |
| Pettigrew, Nellie D. | 1918 | Box 608 | | Phillips, Asa E. | 1880 | Box 73 |
| Pettit, Benjamin | 1897 | Box 171 | | Phillips, Duncan Clinch | 1917 | Box 580 |
| Pettit, Catharine Ann | 1911 | Box 427 | | Phillips, George W. | 1896 | Box 164 |
| Pettit, Charles | 1856 | Box 25 | | Phillips, Jeanett B. | 1854 | Box 23 |
| Pettit, Charles Albertus | 1912 | Box 451 | | Phillips, Jeffery | 1918 | Box 608 |
| Pettit, Charles William | 1911 | Box 427 | | Phillips, John | 1863 | Box 31 |
| Pettit, Edgar R. | 1916 | Box 554 | | Phillips, Josephine F. | 1910 | Box 402 |
| Pettit, Hannah V. | 1917 | Box 580 | | Phillips, Louie M. | 1911 | Box 427 |
| Pettit, Jessie Elizabeth | 1914 | Box 500 | | Phillips, Mary A. | 1910 | Box 402 |
| Pettit, Mary A. | 1917 | Box 580 | | Phillips, Mary F. | 1897 | Box 171 |
| Pettit, Mary Ann | 1871 | Box 45 | | Phillips, Patrick | 1915 | Box 529 |
| Pettit, Richard | 1873 | Box 52 | | Phillips, Philip | 1884 | Box 88 |
| Pettit, Smith | 1899 | Box 186 | | Phillips, Reubin Alexander | 1881 | Box 76 |
| Petty, Luther Y. | 1920 | Box 672 | | Phillips, Robert A. | 1912 | Box 451 |
| Petty, Marie M. | 1913 | Box 476 | | Phillips, Sarah Maria | 1902 | Box 233 |
| Peugh, Agnes L. W. | 1896 | Box 164 | | Phillips, Solomon | 1918 | Box 608 |
| Peugh, Amelia | 1862 | Box 30 | | Phillips, Thomas W. | 1893 | Box 141 |
| Peugh, Caroline S. | 1886 | Box 99 | | Phillips, William Hallett | 1897 | Box 171 |
| Peugh, Samuel A. | 1896 | Box 164 | | Phillips, William Rader | 1907 | Box 331 |
| Peyton, Alice | 1908 | Box 353 | | Phinny, Jennie | 1918 | Box 608 |
| Peyton, Catherine | 1899 | Box 186 | | Picard, Theodore | 1920 | Box 672 |
| Peyton, Elizabeth | 1884 | Box 88 | | Picken, Thomas | 1870 | Box 43 |
| Peyton, Pauline L. | 1910 | Box 402 | | Pickering, John Edward | 1920 | Box 672 |
| Peyton, William J. | 1888 | Box 110 | | Pickett, George | 1829 | Box 10 |
| Pfaff, Benjamin | 1912 | Box 451 | | Pickett, Harriet I. | 1897 | Box 171 |
| Pfaff, Frederick | 1886 | Box 99 | | Pickett, Theodore J. | 1918 | Box 608 |
| Pfarr, Paul | 1912 | Box 451 | | Pickford, Charles W. | 1910 | Box 402 |
| Pfeifer, Lewis K. | 1909 | Box 376 | | Pickrell, Adolphus | 1879 | Box 70 |
| Pfeiffer, Mathias | 1881 | Box 76 | | Pickrell, Ann | 1874 | Box 55 |
| Pfeil, Catharine | 1901 | Box 214 | | Pickrell, John | 1851 | Box 21 |
| Pfeil, John K. | 1908 | Box 353 | | Pickrell, Mary | 1898 | Box 178 |
| Pflueger, Ferdinand | 1867 | Box 38 | | Pickrell, Thomas | 1841 | Box 15 |
| Pflueger, George L. | 1869 | Box 41 | | Pickrell, Virginia E. | 1882 | Box 80 |
| Pfluger, George | 1892 | Box 134 | | Piepenbring, Edward | 1896 | Box 164 |
| Pfluger, Mary Barbara | 1910 | Box 402 | | Piepenbring, Maria | 1919 | Box 639 |
| Pfungst, Henry Joseph | 1920 | Box 672 | | Pier, Ewald | 1913 | Box 476 |
| Phelan, Nicholas | 1870 | Box 43 | | Pierce, Daniel T. | 1903 | Box 251 |

| | | | | | | |
|---|---|---|---|---|---|---|
| Pierce, Edwin S. | 1912 | Box 451 | Pinn, Susan | 1888 | Box 110 |
| Pierce, Franklin | 1880 | Box 73 | Pinn, Susie E. | 1897 | Box 171 |
| Pierce, Godwin | 1897 | Box 171 | Pinner, Willis | 1913 | Box 476 |
| Pierce, James S. | 1909 | Box 376 | Pinney, Aron | 1891 | Box 127 |
| Pierce, Josiah | 1902 | Box 233 | Pinyon, Josephine E. | 1910 | Box 402 |
| Pierce, Mary Parkhurst | 1913 | Box 476 | Piper, Horace | 1895 | Box 156 |
| Pierce, Minnie K. | 1919 | Box 639 | Piper, Horace L. | 1906 | Box 308 |
| Pierce, Perry Benjamin | 1905 | Box 289 | Pipes, Felix Hughes | 1918 | Box 609 |
| Pierce, Sarah E. | 1918 | Box 608 | Pippert, Mary Magdaline W. | 1886 | Box 99 |
| Pierpont, Albert | 1920 | Box 672 | Pippert, Peter | 1887 | Box 104 |
| Pierpont, Samuel S. | 1869 | Box 41 | Pirrone, Agostino | 1916 | Box 554 |
| Pierre, John A. | 1912 | Box 451 | Pitcher, David L. | 1910 | Box 402 |
| Pierson, Charles T. | 1888 | Box 110 | Pitcher, Joseph B. | 1920 | Box 673 |
| Pierson, John A. | 1902 | Box 233 | Pitchlynn, Caroline M. | 1894 | Box 149 |
| Pierson, Mariner A. | 1905 | Box 289 | Pitkin, Julia Jaggar | 1920 | Box 673 |
| Pierson, Mary | 1914 | Box 500 | Pitkin, Walter S. | 1903 | Box 252 |
| Pierson, William Henry | 1902 | Box 233 | Pitney, Ora L. | 1909 | Box 376 |
| Pierson, William T. | 1906 | Box 308 | Pitts, E. Frances P. | 1913 | Box 476 |
| Pifferling, Seligman | 1893 | Box 141 | Pitts, Edward | 1913 | Box 476 |
| Pigeon, Edmund O. | 1910 | Box 402 | Pitts, Florida | 1901 | Box 214 |
| Pigman, George Wood | 1920 | Box 672 | Pitts, George | 1816 | Box 5 |
| Pigman, Lillie Howard | 1907 | Box 331 | Pitts, Jane F. | 1893 | Box 141 |
| Pignole, Eleanor | 1809 | Box 3 | Pitts, Jane W. | 1895 | Box 156 |
| Pigott, Edward | 1849 | Box 20 | Pitzer, Frank | 1918 | Box 609 |
| Pike, Albert | 1891 | Box 127 | Pixley, Albert B. | 1908 | Box 353 |
| Pike, Luther H. | 1895 | Box 156 | Pizinger, Paulina | 1894 | Box 149 |
| Pike, Mary | 1893 | Box 141 | Plain, Benjamin K. | 1893 | Box 141 |
| Pile, Ann P. | 1910 | Box 402 | Plant, Alice A. M. | 1876 | Box 61 |
| Pile, Charlotte J. | 1917 | Box 580 | Plant, Arthur G. | 1915 | Box 529 |
| Pile, Eastmond | 1890 | Box 121 | Plant, Edward K. | 1908 | Box 353 |
| Piles, Joseph W. | 1918 | Box 608 | Plant, Ella L. | 1908 | Box 353 |
| Pilling, Elizabeth | 1909 | Box 376 | Plant, George H. | 1903 | Box 252 |
| Pilling, Elizabeth C. | 1919 | Box 640 | Plant, Henrietta P. | 1885 | Box 93 |
| Pilling, Frederic W. | 1918 | Box 608 | Plant, Horatio | 1840 | Box 15 |
| Pilling, Frederick | 1903 | Box 251 | Plater, John Rousby | 1913 | Box 476 |
| Pilling, James | 1896 | Box 164 | Plater, Mayhew | 1894 | Box 149 |
| Pilling, James C. | 1895 | Box 156 | Platt, Benjamin S. | 1915 | Box 529 |
| Pilling, John W. | 1914 | Box 500 | Platt, Lester B. | 1915 | Box 529 |
| Pilling, Mary | 1912 | Box 452 | Platt, Sherman | 1919 | Box 640 |
| Pilling, Mary Elenor | 1918 | Box 608 | Plaz, Maggie Dentelin | 1917 | Box 580 |
| Pilling, Mary Emma | 1920 | Box 672 | Pleasants, Frances | 1906 | Box 308 |
| Pillow, Mary E. | 1913 | Box 476 | Pleasonton, Clementina | 1888 | Box 110 |
| Pillsbury, John Elliott | 1920 | Box 672 | Pleasonton, Laura | 1894 | Box 149 |
| Pilson, Benjamin F. | 1911 | Box 427 | Pleasonton, Stephen | 1855 | Box 24 |
| Pilson, James H. | 1890 | Box 121 | Plitt, Theodore | 1912 | Box 452 |
| Pinchot, James W. | 1908 | Box 353 | Plowden, Edmund | 1805 | Box 2 |
| Pinion, Anna | 1885 | Box 93 | Plowden, Henrietta | 1805 | Box 2 |
| Pinion, William | 1903 | Box 251 | Plugge, Charles H. | 1915 | Box 529 |
| Pinkerton, Julia B. | 1920 | Box 672 | Plugge, Frederich W. | 1876 | Box 61 |
| Pinkney, Sophia U. | 1903 | Box 251 | Plumb, Edward Lee | 1913 | Box 476 |
| Pinn, Gertrude E. | 1919 | Box 640 | Plumb, Preston B. | 1892 | Box 134 |
| Pinn, James | 1912 | Box 452 | Plumley, Cornelia | 1919 | Box 640 |

| | | | | | | |
|---|---|---|---|---|---|---|
| Plummer, Frances H. | 1900 | Box 198 | Pool, Fannie R. C. | 1920 | Box 673 |
| Plummer, Frank E. | 1918 | Box 609 | Pool, Mary Frances | 1912 | Box 452 |
| Plummer, Henry | 1878 | Box 67 | Pool, Mary Mercer | 1907 | Box 331 |
| Plummer, Lidia T. L. | 1914 | Box 500 | Pool, Samuel Morris | 1915 | Box 529 |
| Plummer, Louisa Burleigh | 1916 | Box 554 | Poole, Charles H. | 1880 | Box 73 |
| Plunkett, Robert | 1815 | Box 4 | Poole, Emily | 1910 | Box 402 |
| Poates, Charles Edwin | 1920 | Box 673 | Poole, J. Sprigg | 1914 | Box 500 |
| Poates, William L. | 1901 | Box 214 | Poole, John H. | 1907 | Box 331 |
| Poch, Pauline | 1919 | Box 640 | Poole, Nannie Owen | 1916 | Box 554 |
| Poe, Fernando B. | 1870 | Box 43 | Poole, Nathan A. | 1900 | Box 198 |
| Poe, Florence | 1868 | Box 40 | Poole, Silas | 1917 | Box 580 |
| Poe, Francis | 1863 | Box 31 | Poor, Charles H. | 1882 | Box 80 |
| Poe, George Jr. | 1864 | Box 32 | Poor, Charlotte | 1864 | Box 32 |
| Poe, George W. | 1902 | Box 233 | Poor, John | 1825 | Box 8 |
| Poe, Toulmin A. | 1870 | Box 43 | Poor, John C. | 1905 | Box 289 |
| Poetzmann, Catharine | 1919 | Box 640 | Poore, Anna M. | 1905 | Box 289 |
| Pohler, Augustus | 1895 | Box 156 | Poore, Francis | 1875 | Box 58 |
| Pohndorff, Frederick | 1917 | Box 580 | Poore, Virginia Dodge | 1894 | Box 149 |
| Poindexter, Mary | 1920 | Box 673 | Poore, William F. | 1905 | Box 289 |
| Poindexter, William M. | 1909 | Box 376 | Pope, Alfred | 1908 | Box 353 |
| Poletti, Joseph | 1877 | Box 64 | Pope, Anna E. | 1919 | Box 640 |
| Polhemus, George W. | 1919 | Box 640 | Pope, Clara V. | 1895 | Box 156 |
| Polk, Charles Peale | 1822 | Box 7 | Pope, Eleanor | 1832 | Box 11 |
| Polk, Elizabeth | 1825 | Box 8 | Pope, Eliza | 1853 | Box 22 |
| Polkinhorn, Hannah E. | 1910 | Box 402 | Pope, Frederick C. | 1913 | Box 476 |
| Polkinhorn, Hannah M. | 1914 | Box 500 | Pope, Gustavus W. Jr. | 1902 | Box 233 |
| Polkinhorn, Martha Jane | 1893 | Box 141 | Pope, John W. | 1919 | Box 640 |
| Polkinhorn, Rachel A. | 1919 | Box 640 | Pope, Matthew | 1842 | Box 16 |
| Polkinhorn, Richard W. | 1874 | Box 55 | Pope, Sophia C. | 1915 | Box 529 |
| Pollard, Alfred F. | 1884 | Box 88 | Pope, Susan | 1884 | Box 88 |
| Pollard, Mary M. | 1918 | Box 609 | Pope, William B. | 1849 | Box 20 |
| Pollard, Missouri | 1898 | Box 178 | Pope, William T. | 1912 | Box 452 |
| Pollard, Philip | 1890 | Box 120 | Popham, Eleanor E. | 1920 | Box 673 |
| Pollet, Louise Depoilly | 1906 | Box 308 | Poppers, Leon | 1894 | Box 149 |
| Pollitt, Susan | 1837 | Box 13 | Port, John | 1893 | Box 141 |
| Pollock, Aitcheson | 1913 | Box 476 | Porter, Abby G. | 1909 | Box 376 |
| Pollock, Allen | 1837 | Box 13 | Porter, Carolyn E. | 1917 | Box 580 |
| Pollock, Cora Lee | 1910 | Box 402 | Porter, Charles | 1902 | Box 233 |
| Pollock, Emma A. | 1917 | Box 580 | Porter, Charles | 1919 | Box 640 |
| Pollok, Anthony | 1898 | Box 178 | Porter, Charles W. | 1913 | Box 476 |
| Pollok, Sarah | 1898 | Box 178 | Porter, David | 1854 | Box 23 |
| Poloni, Theresa | 1920 | Box 673 | Porter, David D. | 1896 | Box 164 |
| Pomeroy, Charles | 1891 | Box 127 | Porter, Elizabeth A. | 1886 | Box 99 |
| Pomeroy, Martha S. | 1899 | Box 186 | Porter, Elizabeth L. | 1888 | Box 110 |
| Pomeroy, Ruth E. | 1917 | Box 580 | Porter, Eugene D. | 1920 | Box 673 |
| Pomeroy, Samuel C. | 1892 | Box 134 | Porter, Evelina | 1886 | Box 99 |
| Pond, William G. | 1912 | Box 452 | Porter, Frederick | 1916 | Box 554 |
| Ponickau, Henrietta | 1899 | Box 186 | Porter, Henry | 1899 | Box 186 |
| Ponickau, Robert | 1920 | Box 673 | Porter, James | 1802 | Box 1 |
| Pons, Antonio | 1889 | Box 116 | Porter, James Jefferson | 1885 | Box 93 |
| Pook, Samuel H. | 1901 | Box 214 | Porter, John Biddle | 1915 | Box 529 |
| Pool, Benjamin G. | 1920 | Box 673 | Porter, Lucy Jane | 1912 | Box 452 |

| | | | | | | |
|---|---|---|---|---|---|---|
| Porter, Margaret | 1820 | Box 6 | Powell, Henry William | 1914 | Box 500 |
| Porter, Margaretta Biddle | 1913 | Box 477 | Powell, J. Tyler | 1920 | Box 673 |
| Porter, Maria | 1873 | Box 52 | Powell, John E. | 1918 | Box 609 |
| Porter, Mary | 1879 | Box 70 | Powell, John W. | 1902 | Box 233 |
| Porter, Mary A. | 1900 | Box 198 | Powell, Julia A. C. | 1903 | Box 252 |
| Porter, Mary L. | 1906 | Box 309 | Powell, Levin M. | 1885 | Box 93 |
| Porter, Maud T. | 1907 | Box 331 | Powell, Margaret E. | 1913 | Box 477 |
| Porter, William D. | 1864 | Box 32 | Powell, Philip | 1869 | Box 41 |
| Portner, Anna | 1912 | Box 452 | Powell, Robert J. | 1883 | Box 84 |
| Portner, Edward G. | 1918 | Box 609 | Powell, W. T. | 1903 | Box 252 |
| Portner, Robert | 1906 | Box 309 | Powell, William | 1816 | Box 5 |
| Portner, Robert | 1914 | Box 500 | Powell, William | 1895 | Box 156 |
| Ports, Albert D. | 1910 | Box 402 | Powell, William Thackara | 1910 | Box 402 |
| Ports, Susan | 1920 | Box 673 | Power, Emily Browne Alsop | 1911 | Box 427 |
| Posey, Kate | 1920 | Box 673 | Power, Frederick D. | 1911 | Box 427 |
| Posey, Luther H. | 1909 | Box 376 | Power, John T. | 1915 | Box 529 |
| Posey, Mary Iola | 1903 | Box 252 | Power, Joseph T. | 1886 | Box 99 |
| Posey, Peter D. | 1885 | Box 93 | Power, Phebe | 1895 | Box 156 |
| Posey, Richmond | 1861 | Box 29 | Powers, Edmund M. | 1900 | Box 198 |
| Posey, William A. | 1913 | Box 477 | Powers, John B. | 1900 | Box 198 |
| Post, Charles W. | 1914 | Box 500 | Powers, Katharine G. | 1916 | Box 554 |
| Post, Ella M. | 1912 | Box 452 | Powers, Mary | 1903 | Box 252 |
| Post, Frank O. | 1892 | Box 134 | Poynton, Lydia Mary | 1913 | Box 477 |
| Post, John W. (John Williams) | 1905 | Box 289 | Prather, Henry Clay | 1884 | Box 88 |
| Postley, Charles E. | 1912 | Box 452 | Prather, Jesse F. | 1905 | Box 289 |
| Postone, Fielder B. | 1856 | Box 25 | Prather, Jesse J. | 1914 | Box 500 |
| Potburg, Edwin | 1920 | Box 673 | Prather, Joseph | 1901 | Box 214 |
| Potbury, Sarah Ann | 1917 | Box 580 | Prather, Leonard B. | 1876 | Box 61 |
| Potee, George Thomas | 1890 | Box 120 | Pratt, Adam S. | 1900 | Box 198 |
| Potter, Amy R. | 1918 | Box 609 | Pratt, Arthur | 1912 | Box 452 |
| Potter, Berton W. | 1906 | Box 309 | Pratt, Cary | 1843 | Box 16 |
| Potter, Henry G. | 1911 | Box 427 | Pratt, Charles P. | 1886 | Box 99 |
| Potter, Jane E. | 1913 | Box 477 | Pratt, Electus A. | 1910 | Box 402 |
| Potter, Margaret S. | 1919 | Box 640 | Pratt, Frederick W. | 1916 | Box 554 |
| Potter, Mary A. | 1894 | Box 149 | Pratt, George Whitfield | 1909 | Box 376 |
| Potter, Sarah E. | 1910 | Box 402 | Pratt, James | 1898 | Box 178 |
| Potts, Fannie Griffiss | 1909 | Box 376 | Pratt, Lillie | 1917 | Box 580 |
| Potts, Louisa R. | 1894 | Box 149 | Pratt, Louisa Addison | 1914 | Box 500 |
| Potts, Mary Ann | 1853 | Box 22 | Pratt, Sarah J. B. | 1876 | Box 61 |
| Potts, Robert | 1913 | Box 477 | Pratt, William | 1905 | Box 289 |
| Potts, Roberta J. | 1892 | Box 134 | Pratt, William B. | 1897 | Box 171 |
| Poulton, George C. | 1913 | Box 477 | Pratt, William Thomas Cassel | 1896 | Box 164 |
| Poulton, Rosia M. | 1901 | Box 214 | Prediger, Henry F. | 1895 | Box 156 |
| Poulton, Susan | 1903 | Box 252 | Preinkert, Charlotte S. | 1907 | Box 331 |
| Poulton, William | 1874 | Box 55 | Preinkert, George | 1898 | Box 178 |
| Poulton, William Edward | 1919 | Box 640 | Preinkert, John F. C. | 1909 | Box 376 |
| Powell, Almira W. | 1888 | Box 110 | Preinkert, John F. | 1902 | Box 233 |
| Powell, Altha Mary Gibbs | 1912 | Box 452 | Preinkert, John G. | 1900 | Box 198 |
| Powell, Carrie E. | 1916 | Box 554 | Preinkert, Mary Jane | 1894 | Box 149 |
| Powell, Diana Kearney | 1905 | Box 289 | Pren, Gottlieb | 1893 | Box 141 |
| Powell, Grafton | 1865 | Box 34 | Prentice, Laura A. | 1896 | Box 164 |
| Powell, Henry S. | 1918 | Box 609 | Prentice, Nathan B. | 1906 | Box 309 |

| | | | | | | |
|---|---|---|---|---|---|
| Prentiss, Webster | 1899 | Box 186 | Probasco, Arabella McLean | 1911 | Box 427 |
| Prescott, James Lewis | 1915 | Box 529 | Probey, Annie Elizabeth | 1896 | Box 164 |
| Presnell, Henderson | 1907 | Box 331 | Probey, James K. | 1902 | Box 233 |
| Pressey, Warren E. | 1913 | Box 477 | Probey, Mary Sophia | 1896 | Box 164 |
| Preston, Benjamin | 1893 | Box 141 | Prockter, William Washington | 1878 | Box 67 |
| Preston, Ellen | 1900 | Box 198 | Proctor, Almira A. | 1919 | Box 640 |
| Preston, Emma B. | 1919 | Box 640 | Proctor, Arthur Beverly | 1905 | Box 289 |
| Preston, Erasmus D. | 1906 | Box 309 | Proctor, Charles Biscoe | 1919 | Box 640 |
| Preston, Mary | 1900 | Box 198 | Proctor, David Gill | 1903 | Box 252 |
| Preston, Mary Ord | 1917 | Box 580 | Proctor, Emma G. | 1903 | Box 252 |
| Preston, Susan P. | 1912 | Box 452 | Proctor, Frances | 1851 | Box 21 |
| Preuss, Louisa Jane | 1871 | Box 45 | Proctor, Henry | 1915 | Box 529 |
| Prevost, Sarah M. | 1901 | Box 214 | Proctor, Jane | 1899 | Box 186 |
| Price, Abel F. | 1919 | Box 640 | Proctor, Redfield | 1908 | Box 353 |
| Price, Almira Van Orsdel | 1918 | Box 609 | Proctor, Robert | 1899 | Box 186 |
| Price, Butler D. | 1919 | Box 640 | Proctor, Samuel | 1887 | Box 105 |
| Price, David M. | 1918 | Box 609 | Proctor, Sarah E. | 1905 | Box 289 |
| Price, Elmira W. | 1916 | Box 554 | Proctor, William H. | 1917 | Box 580 |
| Price, Emily Moss | 1918 | Box 609 | Prosperi, Charles B. | 1913 | Box 477 |
| Price, Emmeline M. | 1920 | Box 673 | Prosperi, Francis | 1873 | Box 52 |
| Price, Florence | 1919 | Box 640 | Prosperi, Josephine | 1912 | Box 452 |
| Price, George Thomas | 1917 | Box 580 | Prout, Mary C. | 1906 | Box 309 |
| Price, Harriet | 1917 | Box 580 | Prout, Robert | 1881 | Box 76 |
| Price, Harriet | 1917 | Box 580 | Provest, Alexander | 1871 | Box 45 |
| Price, Henry | 1902 | Box 233 | Prudhomme, Evelina M. | 1914 | Box 500 |
| Price, Hiram | 1901 | Box 214 | Pryor, Beverly | 1905 | Box 289 |
| Price, J. Clarence | 1911 | Box 427 | Pryor, Elizabeth | 1872 | Box 48 |
| Price, Jehu | 1880 | Box 73 | Pryor, Joseph | 1909 | Box 376 |
| Price, John F. | 1903 | Box 252 | Psotta, Elizabeth | 1913 | Box 477 |
| Price, Lurena P. | 1917 | Box 580 | Pugh, James E. | 1895 | Box 156 |
| Price, Morris | 1911 | Box 427 | Pugh, Sarah E. | 1920 | Box 673 |
| Price, William K. | 1919 | Box 640 | Pugh, Sarah S. | 1912 | Box 452 |
| Price, William S. | 1900 | Box 198 | Pulizzi, Louisa D. | 1842 | Box 16 |
| Price, William V. | 1911 | Box 427 | Pulizzi, Vernerando | 1852 | Box 22 |
| Prier, Dorothe | 1871 | Box 44 | Pulliam, Elizabeth G. | 1917 | Box 580 |
| Priestley, Charles Henry | 1894 | Box 149 | Pullman, Charles Lewis | 1903 | Box 252 |
| Priestley, Deborah | 1887 | Box 104 | Pulsifer, Pitman | 1911 | Box 427 |
| Primrose, Eleanora | 1915 | Box 529 | Pumphrey, Elizabeth A. | 1885 | Box 93 |
| Prince, Abraham D. | 1915 | Box 529 | Pumphrey, Ellen | 1865 | Box 34 |
| Prince, Eliza P. | 1889 | Box 116 | Pumphrey, Georgianna | 1907 | Box 331 |
| Prince, Hennie V. | 1905 | Box 289 | Pumphrey, Hannah Jane | 1912 | Box 452 |
| Prince, Mary | 1899 | Box 186 | Pumphrey, James W. | 1907 | Box 331 |
| Prindeville, Thomas | 1912 | Box 452 | Pumphrey, John | 1896 | Box 164 |
| Prindle, Parrott A. | 1861 | Box 29 | Pumphrey, James B. | 1875 | Box 58 |
| Pringle, Adelaide | 1887 | Box 104 | Pumphrey, Thomas B. | 1911 | Box 427 |
| Printz, James | 1902 | Box 233 | Purcell, John J. | 1890 | Box 120 |
| Prior, George G. | 1907 | Box 331 | Purcell, Michael A. | 1918 | Box 609 |
| Pritchard, Ellen N. | 1919 | Box 640 | Purcell, Pierce | 1815 | Box 4 |
| Pritchard, James | 1899 | Box 186 | Purcell, Sarah H. | 1911 | Box 427 |
| Pritchard, Stephen M. | 1913 | Box 477 | Purcell, Thomas | 1912 | Box 452 |
| Pritchett, Charles | 1909 | Box 376 | Purdy, John | 1881 | Box 76 |
| Pritchett, Mary Jane | 1908 | Box 353 | Purdy, Nathaniel | 1875 | Box 58 |

| | | | | | | |
|---|---|---|---|---|---|---|---|
| Purdy, Sarah C. | 1884 | Box 88 | | Quigley, James D. | 1913 | Box 477 |
| Purdy, William J. | 1890 | Box 121 | | Quigley, Mary A. | 1897 | Box 172 |
| Purks, Forrest H. | 1918 | Box 609 | | Quigley, Patrick | 1866 | Box 36 |
| Purl, Elizabeth | 1865 | Box 34 | | Quill, Ann | 1914 | Box 501 |
| Purman, James Jackson | 1915 | Box 529 | | Quill, Elizabeth | 1909 | Box 376 |
| Purnell, Margaret A. | 1905 | Box 289 | | Quill, John W. | 1918 | Box 609 |
| Purner, Johann Andreas | 1881 | Box 76 | | Quill, Lawrence J. | 1916 | Box 555 |
| Pursell, John R. | 1900 | Box 198 | | Quill, William J. | 1913 | Box 477 |
| Pursell, Mary A. | 1897 | Box 171 | | Quilter, Margaret | 1908 | Box 353 |
| Purviance, Marion | 1899 | Box 186 | | Quin, Charles | 1869 | Box 41 |
| Putney, Hester A. | 1874 | Box 55 | | Quincy, Mary A. T. | 1884 | Box 89 |
| Pyewell, Robert I. | 1908 | Box 353 | | Quinlan, Ann | 1909 | Box 376 |
| Pyle, Robert L. | 1919 | Box 640 | | Quinlan, Elizabeth S. | 1907 | Box 331 |
| Pyles, George F. | 1920 | Box 673 | | Quinlin, Tasker C. | 1837 | Box 14 |
| Pyles, Marian | 1920 | Box 673 | | Quinn, Catherine | 1911 | Box 427 |
| Pyles, Thomas E. | 1867 | Box 38 | | Quinn, Edward | 1824 | Box 8 |
| Pyne, Elizabeth A. | 1905 | Box 289 | | Quinn, Ellen | 1914 | Box 501 |
| Pywell, Robert R. | 1883 | Box 84 | | Quinn, Jeremiah | 1887 | Box 105 |
| Quackenbush, Elsie Jane | 1916 | Box 554 | | Quinn, John | 1911 | Box 427 |
| Quackenbush, Isaac | 1916 | Box 554 | | Quinn, John | 1915 | Box 529 |
| Quackenbush, John V. | 1911 | Box 427 | | Quinn, John B. | 1907 | Box 331 |
| Quackenbush, Stephen P. | 1901 | Box 214 | | Quinn, Michael | 1850 | Box 21 |
| Quade (McQuade), Edward | 1911 | Box 423 | | Quinn, Sarah J. | 1899 | Box 187 |
| Quaid, Daniel J. | 1891 | Box 127 | | Quinn, Thomas | 1906 | Box 309 |
| Quaid, Mary | 1915 | Box 529 | | Quint, Clara G. | 1896 | Box 165 |
| Quakenbush, Elizabeth A. | 1887 | Box 105 | | Quintard, Edward A. | 1903 | Box 252 |
| Qualtrough, Leila Ray | 1918 | Box 609 | | Quinter, Joseph R. | 1907 | Box 331 |
| Quast, Henry | 1918 | Box 609 | | Quirk, Patrick | 1886 | Box 99 |
| Quay, Agnes B. | 1912 | Box 452 | | Quirk, Patrick | 1894 | Box 149 |
| Queen, Charles R. | 1859 | Box 28 | | Raab, Adam | 1861 | Box 29 |
| Queen, Christiana C. | 1909 | Box 376 | | Raab, Gertrude | 1902 | Box 233 |
| Queen, Eliza | 1857 | Box 26 | | Rabbitt, Charles F. | 1906 | Box 309 |
| Queen, Eliza | 1869 | Box 41 | | Rabbitt, Samuel E. | 1903 | Box 252 |
| Queen, Elizabeth | 1835 | Box 13 | | Rabe, Henry | 1901 | Box 214 |
| Queen, Elizabeth | 1900 | Box 198 | | Rabe, Mary S. | 1920 | Box 673 |
| Queen, Elizabeth T. | 1843 | Box 16 | | Raber, Katherine M. | 1918 | Box 609 |
| Queen, John | 1841 | Box 15 | | Race, James A. | 1895 | Box 157 |
| Queen, John A. | 1864 | Box 32 | | Rackey, Lizzie | 1914 | Box 501 |
| Queen, Laura F. | 1913 | Box 477 | | Rackliffe, Sara | 1805 | Box 2 |
| Queen, Margaret | 1876 | Box 61 | | Radcliffe, George W. | 1914 | Box 501 |
| Queen, Mary | 1884 | Box 89 | | Radcliffe, Nora F. | 1907 | Box 331 |
| Queen, Mary C. | 1899 | Box 187 | | Radford, Ann | 1918 | Box 609 |
| Queen, Rosena | 1847 | Box 19 | | Radford, Mary E. Lovell | 1903 | Box 252 |
| Queen, Samuel | 1885 | Box 93 | | Radford, William | 1890 | Box 121 |
| Queen, Walter W. | 1893 | Box 141 | | Rady, Catharine | 1902 | Box 233 |
| Quick, Ellen H. | 1918 | Box 609 | | Rady, Michael | 1892 | Box 134 |
| Quick, Susan R. S. | 1897 | Box 172 | | Rady, Thomas | 1891 | Box 127 |
| Quicksall, William F. | 1920 | Box 673 | | Rae, Charles Whiteside | 1908 | Box 353 |
| Quigby, Michael | 1845 | Box 17 | | Rae, John | 1890 | Box 121 |
| Quigley, Bridget | 1912 | Box 452 | | Raebach, Kathryn H. | 1914 | Box 501 |
| Quigley, Catherine Rose | 1919 | Box 640 | | Rafferty, Michael | 1898 | Box 178 |
| Quigley, Hugh | 1907 | Box 331 | | Rafferty, William A. | 1902 | Box 233 |

| | | | | | | |
|---|---|---|---|---|---|---|
| Raftery, Patrick | 1916 | Box 555 | | Randol, Alanson Merwin | 1910 | Box 402 |
| Rafus, John W. | 1912 | Box 453 | | Randolph, Arthur Bertram | 1918 | Box 609 |
| Ragan, Elizabeth | 1884 | Box 89 | | Randolph, Cornelia P. | 1917 | Box 581 |
| Ragan, Emily Lee | 1916 | Box 555 | | Randolph, Ellen C. | 1915 | Box 529 |
| Ragan, James | 1901 | Box 214 | | Randolph, Hezekiah | 1913 | Box 477 |
| Ragan, Mary | 1914 | Box 501 | | Randolph, Sarah L. | 1878 | Box 67 |
| Ragan, Mary Matilda | 1885 | Box 93 | | Randolph, William B. | 1868 | Box 40 |
| Ragan, Raymond T. | 1920 | Box 673 | | Random, Ann | 1885 | Box 94 |
| Ragland, Frances Cecelia | 1911 | Box 427 | | Random, Benedict | 1861 | Box 29 |
| Rahm, George A. | 1906 | Box 309 | | Rank, Jesse B. | 1911 | Box 427 |
| Railey, Christiana | 1861 | Box 29 | | Rankin, Christopher | 1826 | Box 9 |
| Rainals, Augusta | 1911 | Box 427 | | Rankin, Emmeline C. | 1915 | Box 529 |
| Rainals, Henry E. | 1867 | Box 38 | | Rankin, John M. | 1918 | Box 609 |
| Raines, Cynthia F. | 1876 | Box 61 | | Rankin, John R. | 1910 | Box 402 |
| Raines, Frances Desire | 1881 | Box 76 | | Rankin, Margaret E. | 1908 | Box 354 |
| Rainey, Rosa Sewell | 1909 | Box 376 | | Ranney, Lewis H. | 1900 | Box 199 |
| Rainey, Samuel | 1865 | Box 34 | | Ransdell, Daniel Moore | 1912 | Box 453 |
| Rakemann, Joseph | 1917 | Box 581 | | Ransom, Archite Lewis | 1902 | Box 233 |
| Raley, Lillian M. | 1910 | Box 402 | | Rapine, Charlotte G. | 1835 | Box 13 |
| Ralph, William L. | 1908 | Box 353 | | Rapley, William W. | 1902 | Box 233 |
| Ralston, David C. | 1884 | Box 89 | | Rasner, Margaret | 1894 | Box 149 |
| Ralston, John | 1909 | Box 376 | | Rassbach, Hermann | 1913 | Box 477 |
| Ralston, Laura E. Dunbar | 1900 | Box 199 | | Ratcliff, Howard | 1916 | Box 555 |
| Ramsay, Francis Munroe | 1914 | Box 501 | | Ratcliff, Joseph | 1858 | Box 27 |
| Ramsay, George D. | 1882 | Box 80 | | Ratcliffe, Jane E. | 1916 | Box 555 |
| Ramsay, Mary D. | 1902 | Box 233 | | Ratcliffe, Lewis | 1849 | Box 20 |
| Ramsay, Richard H. | 1908 | Box 353 | | Rathbun, Richard | 1918 | Box 609 |
| Ramsburgh, Jesse H. | 1917 | Box 581 | | Ratrie, James | 1854 | Box 23 |
| Ramsdell, Zephor D. | 1910 | Box 402 | | Ratrie, Robert | 1869 | Box 41 |
| Ramsey, Charles Chandler | 1912 | Box 453 | | Rau, Charles | 1887 | Box 105 |
| Ramsey, Eliza Gales | 1891 | Box 127 | | Raub, George T. | 1903 | Box 252 |
| Ramsey, Frances (Fanny) L. | 1912 | Box 453 | | Raub, Jacob F. | 1906 | Box 309 |
| Ramsey, James M. | 1858 | Box 27 | | Raub, John P. | 1885 | Box 94 |
| Ramsey, Mary E. | 1881 | Box 76 | | Rauh, Gottlieb H. | 1873 | Box 52 |
| Ramsey, Matilda J. | 1918 | Box 609 | | Raum, George | 1908 | Box 354 |
| Ramsey, Virginia L. | 1896 | Box 165 | | Rauscher, Charles | 1917 | Box 581 |
| Ramsey, William R. | 1913 | Box 477 | | Rauterberg, Charles | 1892 | Box 134 |
| Rand, Charles F. | 1908 | Box 354 | | Rauterberg, Mary A. | 1916 | Box 555 |
| Rand, Louise C. | 1911 | Box 427 | | Ravenburg, Rudolph | 1914 | Box 501 |
| Rand, Stephen | 1915 | Box 529 | | Rawles, George | 1920 | Box 673 |
| Randall, Ann | 1884 | Box 89 | | Rawlings, Frank T. | 1915 | Box 529 |
| Randall, Daniel | 1851 | Box 21 | | Rawlings, Joshua | 1832 | Box 11 |
| Randall, Ephraim S. | 1908 | Box 354 | | Rawlings, Kate E. | 1916 | Box 555 |
| Randall, George Augustine W. | 1878 | Box 67 | | Rawlins, John A. | 1869 | Box 41 |
| Randall, Hagar | 1893 | Box 141 | | Rawls, Abraham | 1908 | Box 354 |
| Randall, Henry K. | 1877 | Box 64 | | Rawson, Thomas H. | 1902 | Box 233 |
| Randall, Louisa S. | 1918 | Box 609 | | Ray, Alexander | 1878 | Box 67 |
| Randall, Margaret Ann | 1883 | Box 84 | | Ray, Charles Andrew | 1912 | Box 453 |
| Randall, Martha | 1920 | Box 673 | | Ray, Eliza S. | 1888 | Box 110 |
| Randall, Nicholas A. | 1858 | Box 27 | | Ray, Elizabeth | 1914 | Box 501 |
| Randall, Richard G. | 1878 | Box 67 | | Ray, Enos | 1881 | Box 76 |
| Randle, Roderick Bolitho | 1920 | Box 673 | | Ray, George H. | 1911 | Box 427 |

| | | | | | | |
|---|---|---|---|---|---|---|
| Ray, Helena A. | 1913 | Box 477 | Recar, George | 1908 | Box 354 |
| Ray, James | 1912 | Box 453 | Reddick, James W. | 1886 | Box 99 |
| Ray, James Enos Sr. | 1912 | Box 453 | Reddick, Mary L. | 1905 | Box 290 |
| Ray, John W. | 1913 | Box 477 | Reddick, Samuel | 1891 | Box 127 |
| Ray, Josiah | 1870 | Box 43 | Reddington, Patrick | 1908 | Box 354 |
| Ray, R. C. | 1899 | Box 187 | Redfern, Eliza J. | 1896 | Box 165 |
| Ray, Sara | 1802 | Box 1 | Redfern, Jane F. | 1884 | Box 89 |
| Raybolds, Samuel H. | 1868 | Box 40 | Redfern, Joseph | 1899 | Box 187 |
| Raymond, Charles W. | 1913 | Box 477 | Redfern, Joseph Louis | 1909 | Box 376 |
| Raymond, Edward | 1897 | Box 172 | Redfern, Mary Elizabeth | 1915 | Box 529 |
| Raymond, Jane | 1865 | Box 34 | Redfield, Annie L. | 1909 | Box 376 |
| Raymond, John Underwood | 1914 | Box 501 | Redhead, Jane | 1911 | Box 428 |
| Raymond, Victoria | 1899 | Box 187 | Redhead, John | 1897 | Box 172 |
| Raynal, Alfred H. | 1919 | Box 641 | Redin, William | 1866 | Box 36 |
| Raynal, Mary | 1910 | Box 402 | Redman, Catharine | 1828 | Box 9 |
| Raynor, Edward | 1903 | Box 252 | Redman, Jacob S. | 1900 | Box 199 |
| Rea, George W. | 1917 | Box 581 | Redman, John Collins | 1909 | Box 376 |
| Rea, Hannah | 1912 | Box 453 | Redman, Mary J. | 1895 | Box 157 |
| Rea, James | 1893 | Box 141 | Redman, Sarah A. | 1884 | Box 89 |
| Rea, Julia Hammond | 1902 | Box 233 | Redman, William | 1893 | Box 141 |
| Rea, S. M. (Mrs.) | 1906 | Box 309 | Redmond, William A. | 1918 | Box 610 |
| Rea, Thomas F. | 1914 | Box 501 | Redstrake, William J. | 1894 | Box 149 |
| Read, Frances R. | 1879 | Box 70 | Redway, Hamilton K. | 1889 | Box 116 |
| Read, Isabella | 1897 | Box 172 | Redway, Roscoe E. | 1919 | Box 641 |
| Read, Jane | 1913 | Box 477 | Reece, Mary Jane | 1917 | Box 581 |
| Read, Margaret E. | 1883 | Box 84 | Reed, Angelina F. | 1904 | Box 270 |
| Read, Margaret M. | 1910 | Box 402 | Reed, Anna L. | 1912 | Box 453 |
| Read, Martha M. | 1905 | Box 289 | Reed, Brittania C. | 1916 | Box 555 |
| Read, Mary E. | 1903 | Box 252 | Reed, Bushrod W. | 1875 | Box 58 |
| Read, Robert | 1864 | Box 32 | Reed, Catherine P. | 1915 | Box 529 |
| Read, Semmes | 1920 | Box 673 | Reed, Elijah B. | 1916 | Box 555 |
| Reading, Anna W. | 1907 | Box 331 | Reed, Elizabeth Sturges | 1907 | Box 331 |
| Reading, Fannie W. | 1918 | Box 610 | Reed, Ellen G. | 1913 | Box 477 |
| Ready, Henry | 1894 | Box 149 | Reed, Emma J. | 1914 | Box 501 |
| Ready, John | 1903 | Box 252 | Reed, Ethelinda | 1886 | Box 99 |
| Ready, Thomas | 1919 | Box 641 | Reed, Frances A. | 1909 | Box 377 |
| Ream, Fanny Redlin | 1897 | Box 172 | Reed, Henry H. | 1907 | Box 331 |
| Reamer, Harriet | 1906 | Box 309 | Reed, James | 1882 | Box 80 |
| Reamer, Maggie | 1915 | Box 529 | Reed, John | 1867 | Box 38 |
| Reamer, Sarah J. | 1916 | Box 555 | Reed, John A. | 1909 | Box 377 |
| Reamey, Lazarus Lowrey | 1914 | Box 501 | Reed, Letitia | 1903 | Box 252 |
| Reaney, Annie E. | 1918 | Box 610 | Reed, Oliver H. | 1904 | Box 270 |
| Reaney, Charles H. | 1908 | Box 354 | Reed, Philis | 1849 | Box 20 |
| Reapsomer, Nellie A. | 1916 | Box 555 | Reed, Sarah Ann | 1872 | Box 48 |
| Rearden, Bella C. | 1914 | Box 501 | Reed, Sophia | 1859 | Box 28 |
| Rearden, Michael | 1879 | Box 70 | Reed, Susan | 1908 | Box 354 |
| Reardon, Bridget | 1905 | Box 289 | Reed, William F. | 1915 | Box 529 |
| Reardon, Daniel | 1902 | Box 233 | Reed, William Field | 1919 | Box 641 |
| Reardon, Dennis J. | 1912 | Box 453 | Reed, Wilson G. | 1903 | Box 252 |
| Reardon, Mary A. | 1911 | Box 428 | Reedeger, Caroline | 1866 | Box 36 |
| Reaves, Eliza | 1865 | Box 34 | Reedeger, Jerome | 1865 | Box 34 |
| Rebuschatis, Cora A. | 1919 | Box 641 | Rees, Augusta | 1911 | Box 428 |

| | | | | | | |
|---|---|---|---|---|---|---|
| Rees, Frederick | 1910 | Box 403 | Reilly, William Patrick Joseph | 1919 | Box 641 |
| Reese, Chauncey B. | 1911 | Box 428 | Reily, Albert O. S. | 1915 | Box 529 |
| Reese, John J. | 1911 | Box 428 | Reily, Barbara | 1852 | Box 22 |
| Reese, Joseph | 1883 | Box 84 | Reily, Euphemia B. | 1869 | Box 41 |
| Reese, William H. | 1912 | Box 453 | Reily, John H. | 1864 | Box 32 |
| Reeve, Anna Eliza | 1891 | Box 127 | Reily, John M. | 1870 | Box 43 |
| Reeve, Constantia | 1869 | Box 41 | Reily, James A. | 1877 | Box 64 |
| Reeves, Courtney | 1866 | Box 36 | Reily, Philip K. | 1911 | Box 428 |
| Reeves, David C. | 1917 | Box 581 | Reily, Susan W. | 1874 | Box 55 |
| Reeves, Edward H. | 1909 | Box 377 | Reily, Susannah E. | 1911 | Box 428 |
| Reeves, Isaac Stockton Keith | 1917 | Box 581 | Reily, William | 1824 | Box 8 |
| Reeves, James | 1886 | Box 99 | Reinburg, Louis | 1903 | Box 252 |
| Reeves, John Clark | 1890 | Box 121 | Reinburg, Louis G. | 1908 | Box 354 |
| Reeves, Mary A. | 1886 | Box 99 | Reiners, Gertrude | 1904 | Box 270 |
| Reeves, Rebecca | 1917 | Box 581 | Reinhardt, Charles | 1895 | Box 157 |
| Regan, Cornelius | 1915 | Box 529 | Reinhardt, Charles | 1916 | Box 555 |
| Regan, Mamie | 1920 | Box 673 | Reinhardt, John F. | 1914 | Box 501 |
| Regan, Philip | 1919 | Box 641 | Reinhardt, Mary | 1905 | Box 290 |
| Reh, Frederick | 1905 | Box 290 | Reinhart, George J. | 1919 | Box 641 |
| Reh, Henry F. | 1910 | Box 403 | Reintzel, Andrew | 1816 | Box 5 |
| Reh, Maria | 1913 | Box 477 | Reintzel, Sarah Irene | 1920 | Box 673 |
| Rehm, Dorette | 1883 | Box 84 | Reiser, Margaret | 1911 | Box 428 |
| Reich, John | 1859 | Box 28 | Reiser, William | 1912 | Box 453 |
| Reichard, Thomas J. | 1919 | Box 641 | Reisinger, Charles H. | 1905 | Box 290 |
| Reichenbach, Frederick C. | 1872 | Box 48 | Reisinger, Jacob S. | 1903 | Box 252 |
| Reid, Alexander | 1810 | Box 3 | Reisinger, John G. | 1914 | Box 501 |
| Reid, Douglas | 1916 | Box 555 | Reisinger, Julia | 1917 | Box 581 |
| Reid, Esli D. | 1914 | Box 501 | Reiss, Adelaide C. | 1902 | Box 233 |
| Reid, Fannie A. | 1911 | Box 428 | Reiss, John | 1858 | Box 27 |
| Reid, George Croghan | 1914 | Box 501 | Reiss, Mary Ann | 1887 | Box 105 |
| Reid, Henrietta | 1900 | Box 199 | Reiter, Henry | 1914 | Box 501 |
| Reid, James H. | 1880 | Box 73 | Reith, Gertrude | 1912 | Box 453 |
| Reid, John K. | 1898 | Box 178 | Reith, Pius | 1882 | Box 80 |
| Reid, Joseph | 1880 | Box 73 | Reithmüller, Ignaz | 1876 | Box 61 |
| Reid, Narina M. | 1904 | Box 270 | Reitz, John | 1849 | Box 20 |
| Reid, William | 1911 | Box 428 | Reizenstein, Herman | 1899 | Box 187 |
| Reidy, David | 1872 | Box 48 | Relay, Lena Riley | 1884 | Box 89 |
| Reidy, Elizabeth | 1893 | Box 141 | Remington, William | 1868 | Box 40 |
| Reidy, Harry J. | 1892 | Box 134 | Remy, Anton | 1908 | Box 354 |
| Reidy, Mary | 1877 | Box 64 | Renard, Mary A. | 1920 | Box 673 |
| Reidy, Maurice | 1888 | Box 110 | Renfro, George W. | 1886 | Box 99 |
| Reiley, William H. | 1891 | Box 127 | Renfro, Harry B. | 1917 | Box 581 |
| Reilly, Annie | 1894 | Box 149 | Renick, Annie C. | 1907 | Box 331 |
| Reilly, Annie C. | 1920 | Box 673 | Renick, Edward Ireland | 1900 | Box 199 |
| Reilly, Benjamin Thomas | 1892 | Box 134 | Renno, Le Roy E. | 1919 | Box 641 |
| Reilly, Cornelius J. | 1917 | Box 581 | Reno, Marcus A. | 1889 | Box 116 |
| Reilly, Edmund | 1864 | Box 32 | Renz, Andrew | 1919 | Box 641 |
| Reilly, Frances | 1917 | Box 581 | Repetti, Gaetano | 1904 | Box 270 |
| Reilly, James William | 1910 | Box 403 | Repetti, Joseph | 1888 | Box 110 |
| Reilly, Margaret Ulrica | 1899 | Box 187 | Repetti, Mary | 1902 | Box 233 |
| Reilly, Michael Joseph | 1919 | Box 641 | Reson, Mary | 1907 | Box 331 |
| Reilly, Patrick | 1904 | Box 270 | Reuter, Frederick W. | 1906 | Box 309 |

| | | | | | | |
|---|---|---|---|---|---|---|
| Reuther, Michael | 1883 | Box 84 | Rice, Elvina | 1909 | Box 377 |
| Revels, Thomas J. | 1910 | Box 403 | Rice, George W. | 1885 | Box 94 |
| Reyburn, Robert | 1909 | Box 377 | Rice, Harriet C. | 1917 | Box 581 |
| Reynolds, Alice P. | 1920 | Box 673 | Rice, Joseph A. | 1902 | Box 233 |
| Reynolds, Ann | 1906 | Box 309 | Rice, Josephine W. | 1919 | Box 641 |
| Reynolds, Christina | 1907 | Box 332 | Rice, Lorenzo | 1890 | Box 121 |
| Reynolds, Elizabeth J. | 1906 | Box 309 | Rice, Lorenzo M. | 1890 | Box 121 |
| Reynolds, Emma | 1904 | Box 270 | Rice, Margaret A. | 1920 | Box 673 |
| Reynolds, Fannie S. | 1917 | Box 581 | Rice, Margaret M. | 1897 | Box 172 |
| Reynolds, George R. | 1901 | Box 214 | Rice, Wolf | 1909 | Box 377 |
| Reynolds, John | 1893 | Box 141 | Rich, Hester | 1903 | Box 252 |
| Reynolds, Joseph | 1885 | Box 94 | Rich, Margaret S. | 1903 | Box 252 |
| Reynolds, Joseph J. | 1899 | Box 187 | Rich, Walter I. | 1899 | Box 187 |
| Reynolds, Lovell | 1893 | Box 141 | Richard, Alvan S. | 1898 | Box 178 |
| Reynolds, Lucius E. | 1897 | Box 172 | Richard, Edward | 1911 | Box 428 |
| Reynolds, Mary | 1917 | Box 581 | Richard, Emanuel | 1886 | Box 99 |
| Reynolds, Mary C. | 1903 | Box 252 | Richard, Henrietta | 1900 | Box 199 |
| Reynolds, Mary E. | 1913 | Box 477 | Richards, Alfred | 1894 | Box 149 |
| Reynolds, Mary J. | 1913 | Box 477 | Richards, Almarin C. | 1907 | Box 332 |
| Reynolds, Patrick | 1867 | Box 38 | Richards, Benjamin Sayre | 1917 | Box 581 |
| Reynolds, Patrick | 1913 | Box 478 | Richards, Catherine | 1919 | Box 641 |
| Reynolds, Rebecca | 1885 | Box 94 | Richards, Charles H. | 1894 | Box 149 |
| Reynolds, Robert M. | 1885 | Box 94 | Richards, Clara O. | 1906 | Box 309 |
| Reynolds, Thomas | 1825 | Box 8 | Richards, Cyrus S. | 1885 | Box 94 |
| Reynolds, William | 1886 | Box 99 | Richards, David | 1896 | Box 165 |
| Rhea, James | 1875 | Box 58 | Richards, Edward N. | 1909 | Box 377 |
| Rheam, Henry U. | 1909 | Box 377 | Richards, Elizabeth | 1878 | Box 67 |
| Rheam, Julia A. | 1911 | Box 428 | Richards, Harriet R. | 1882 | Box 80 |
| Rheem, Clarence B. | 1913 | Box 478 | Richards, James G. K. | 1920 | Box 673 |
| Rhees, William Jones | 1907 | Box 332 | Richards, John H. | 1881 | Box 76 |
| Rhett, Henry Johns | 1912 | Box 453 | Richards, Louisa C. | 1911 | Box 428 |
| Rhett, Thomas S. | 1894 | Box 149 | Richards, Marcelina | 1903 | Box 252 |
| Rhinelander, Frederic W. | 1905 | Box 290 | Richards, Maria W. | 1905 | Box 290 |
| Rhoades, Eunice Ida Gallup | 1899 | Box 187 | Richards, Mary A. | 1897 | Box 172 |
| Rhodes, Benjamin T. | 1905 | Box 290 | Richards, Milton V. | 1918 | Box 610 |
| Rhodes, Elizabeth | 1899 | Box 187 | Richards, Thomas A. | 1888 | Box 110 |
| Rhodes, Elizabeth R. | 1907 | Box 332 | Richards, William H. | 1918 | Box 610 |
| Rhodes, George | 1890 | Box 121 | Richards, William S. | 1917 | Box 581 |
| Rhodes, George | 1892 | Box 134 | Richards, William Vigors | 1903 | Box 253 |
| Rhodes, James | 1867 | Box 38 | Richardson, Almyne Henry G. | 1920 | Box 673 |
| Rhodes, Jane E. O. | 1892 | Box 134 | Richardson, Attrel | 1918 | Box 610 |
| Rhodes, John W. | 1913 | Box 478 | Richardson, Charles | 1888 | Box 110 |
| Rhodes, Sophia | 1895 | Box 157 | Richardson, Charles F. E. | 1895 | Box 157 |
| Ribiere, Joseph | 1894 | Box 149 | Richardson, Charlotte E. | 1915 | Box 529 |
| Ribinsky, Christana Bishop | 1910 | Box 403 | Richardson, David | 1896 | Box 165 |
| Ribuitzki, William | 1914 | Box 501 | Richardson, Edwin J. | 1910 | Box 403 |
| Rice, Annie E. | 1884 | Box 89 | Richardson, Elizabeth A. | 1914 | Box 501 |
| Rice, Augusta | 1917 | Box 581 | Richardson, Emeline M. | 1910 | Box 403 |
| Rice, Charles Edward | 1916 | Box 555 | Richardson, Ira | 1871 | Box 45 |
| Rice, Charles O. | 1914 | Box 501 | Richardson, James D. | 1915 | Box 529 |
| Rice, David Hall | 1894 | Box 149 | Richardson, James H. | 1858 | Box 27 |
| Rice, Elizabeth Huntington | 1919 | Box 641 | Richardson, Netta C. | 1917 | Box 581 |

| | | | | | | |
|---|---|---|---|---|---|---|
| Richardson, Robert | 1906 | Box 309 | Ridley, Cuthbert W. | 1908 | Box 354 |
| Richardson, William A. | 1904 | Box 270 | Riecks, Henry | 1869 | Box 41 |
| Richardson, William H. | 1920 | Box 673 | Riecks, William Henry | 1881 | Box 76 |
| Richardson, William T. | 1903 | Box 253 | Riehl, Catharina | 1916 | Box 555 |
| Richey, Minna Blair | 1919 | Box 641 | Riehl, Jacob | 1911 | Box 428 |
| Richey, Stephen Olin | 1920 | Box 674 | Riehl, Margaret | 1917 | Box 581 |
| Richey, Walter T. | 1908 | Box 354 | Ries, Carl | 1908 | Box 354 |
| Richmond, Charles | 1894 | Box 149 | Riessner, Johann Christoph W. | 1916 | Box 555 |
| Richmond, Christopher | 1804 | Box 1 | Rife, Mary C. | 1910 | Box 403 |
| Richmond, James | 1909 | Box 377 | Riffle, Joseph | 1817 | Box 5 |
| Richmond, Maria N. | 1909 | Box 377 | Rigden, Ann | 1825 | Box 8 |
| Richmond, W. B. | 1866 | Box 36 | Riggles, Anne M. | 1919 | Box 641 |
| Richold, Leopold | 1920 | Box 674 | Riggles, John | 1898 | Box 178 |
| Richter, Catherine | 1913 | Box 478 | Riggles, Thomas | 1863 | Box 31 |
| Richter, Clara M. | 1899 | Box 187 | Riggles, Thomas | 1919 | Box 641 |
| Rick, George C. | 1908 | Box 354 | Riggs, Catharine G. | 1919 | Box 641 |
| Rickenbacher, Dominick | 1909 | Box 377 | Riggs, Elisha Francis | 1910 | Box 403 |
| Rickett, George W. | 1917 | Box 581 | Riggs, George W. | 1865 | Box 34 |
| Ricketts, Frances Ann Pyne | 1902 | Box 233 | Riggs, George W. | 1881 | Box 76 |
| Ricketts, James B. | 1887 | Box 105 | Riggs, Lawrason | 1884 | Box 89 |
| Ricketts, Margaret A. | 1908 | Box 354 | Riggs, Medora | 1916 | Box 555 |
| Ricketts, Mary J. | 1892 | Box 134 | Riggs, Romulus | 1920 | Box 674 |
| Ricks, Fanny J. | 1919 | Box 641 | Riley, Agnes M. | 1903 | Box 253 |
| Ricks, John S. | 1884 | Box 89 | Riley, Ann R. | 1904 | Box 270 |
| Ricks, Susan | 1884 | Box 89 | Riley, Catherine | 1900 | Box 199 |
| Rickson, Maria | 1911 | Box 428 | Riley, Charles V. | 1895 | Box 157 |
| Riddle, Charles A. | 1899 | Box 187 | Riley, Joshua | 1875 | Box 58 |
| Riddle, James A. | 1874 | Box 55 | Riley, Laura C. | 1897 | Box 172 |
| Ridenour, Annie | 1908 | Box 354 | Riley, Louisa | 1911 | Box 428 |
| Ridenour, Charles H. | 1920 | Box 674 | Riley, Manford | 1899 | Box 187 |
| Ridenour, Elizabeth M. | 1895 | Box 157 | Riley, Margaret | 1919 | Box 641 |
| Ridenour, Upton H. Jr. | 1910 | Box 403 | Riley, Margaret J. | 1907 | Box 332 |
| Ridenour, Walter S. | 1914 | Box 501 | Riley, Mary Anna | 1914 | Box 501 |
| Rider, George F. | 1903 | Box 253 | Riley, Owen | 1908 | Box 354 |
| Rider, Joseph S. | 1889 | Box 116 | Riley, Rose E. | 1907 | Box 332 |
| Rider, Lucy | 1865 | Box 34 | Riley, Thomas R. | 1846 | Box 18 |
| Rider, Nathaniel | 1854 | Box 23 | Riley, Thomas W. | 1913 | Box 478 |
| Rider, Thomas | 1872 | Box 48 | Riley, Wade Hampton | 1913 | Box 478 |
| Ridgely, Ann C. | 1875 | Box 58 | Riley, William | 1917 | Box 581 |
| Ridgely, Lucy Ellen | 1920 | Box 674 | Riley, William R. | 1893 | Box 141 |
| Ridgely, Matilda Lydia | 1875 | Box 58 | Rinck, Emil A. H. | 1902 | Box 234 |
| Ridgely, Samuel C. | 1859 | Box 28 | Rines, Clara A. | 1918 | Box 610 |
| Ridgely, William G. | 1876 | Box 61 | Rines, Lockwood C. | 1919 | Box 641 |
| Ridgeway, Anna | 1885 | Box 94 | Ring, Emily J. | 1896 | Box 165 |
| Ridgeway, Mary M. | 1919 | Box 641 | Ringgold, Cadwalader | 1894 | Box 149 |
| Ridgley, Fanny | 1871 | Box 45 | Ringgold, Eliza Lee | 1851 | Box 21 |
| Ridgway, Catharine V. | 1894 | Box 149 | Ringgold, William J. | 1920 | Box 674 |
| Ridgway, Enoch | 1888 | Box 110 | Rinker, Mary Ellen | 1918 | Box 610 |
| Ridgway, James H. | 1880 | Box 73 | Riordan, Bartholomew | 1901 | Box 214 |
| Ridgway, James M. | 1918 | Box 610 | Riordan, D. Emmett | 1916 | Box 555 |
| Ridgway, Joseph | 1880 | Box 73 | Riordan, David | 1916 | Box 555 |
| Ridgway, Thomas Edwin | 1919 | Box 641 | Riordan, James | 1867 | Box 38 |

| | | | | | | |
|---|---|---|---|---|---|---|
| Riordan, John I. | 1920 | Box 674 | Robbins, James | 1909 | Box 377 |
| Riordan, William | 1919 | Box 641 | Robbins, Laetitia M. | 1915 | Box 530 |
| Riorden, Patrick J. | 1881 | Box 76 | Robbins, Nathaniel A. | 1913 | Box 478 |
| Ripley, Eleazer H. | 1915 | Box 530 | Robbins, Stephen B. | 1887 | Box 105 |
| Rishel, Philip E. | 1916 | Box 555 | Robbins, Thomas H. | 1912 | Box 453 |
| Rishton, Martha C. | 1892 | Box 134 | Robbins, Wilford Frederick | 1902 | Box 234 |
| Risler, Thomas H. | 1918 | Box 610 | Robbins, Willard S. | 1917 | Box 582 |
| Risley, John E. | 1912 | Box 453 | Robbins, Zenas C. | 1907 | Box 332 |
| Risque, Caroline S. | 1882 | Box 80 | Roberdeau, Issac | 1829 | Box 10 |
| Ritchie, Louis W. | 1901 | Box 214 | Roberdeau, Susan S. | 1884 | Box 89 |
| Ritchie, Maria | 1890 | Box 121 | Roberds, James Madison | 1861 | Box 29 |
| Ritchie, Thomas | 1854 | Box 23 | Roberts, Augustus L. | 1917 | Box 582 |
| Rittenhouse, David | 1917 | Box 581 | Roberts, Charles E. | 1906 | Box 309 |
| Rittenhouse, Elizabeth | 1904 | Box 270 | Roberts, David | 1908 | Box 354 |
| Rittenhouse, Ernest J. | 1917 | Box 581 | Roberts, George T. | 1918 | Box 610 |
| Rittenhouse, Helen M. | 1907 | Box 332 | Roberts, Grace | 1900 | Box 199 |
| Rittenhouse, Helen S. | 1915 | Box 530 | Roberts, John | 1909 | Box 377 |
| Rittenhouse, Henrietta | 1885 | Box 94 | Roberts, John L. | 1873 | Box 52 |
| Rittenhouse, John B. | 1814 | Box 4 | Roberts, Julia A. | 1885 | Box 94 |
| Rittenhouse, Sarah Emily | 1920 | Box 674 | Roberts, Kitcy Mobley | 1899 | Box 187 |
| Rittenhouse, Sarah M. | 1892 | Box 134 | Roberts, Mabel Constance | 1918 | Box 610 |
| Ritter, Adam | 1894 | Box 149 | Roberts, Mary Augusta | 1917 | Box 582 |
| Ritter, David Augustus | 1905 | Box 290 | Roberts, Mary E. | 1909 | Box 377 |
| Ritter, Emily I. | 1900 | Box 199 | Roberts, Mary M. | 1901 | Box 214 |
| Ritter, George | 1916 | Box 555 | Roberts, Matilda C. | 1898 | Box 178 |
| Ritter, Homer P. | 1919 | Box 642 | Roberts, Milton S. | 1920 | Box 674 |
| Ritter, John P. V. | 1916 | Box 555 | Roberts, Peter | 1869 | Box 41 |
| Ritter, Theresa | 1853 | Box 22 | Roberts, Rebecca Warren | 1917 | Box 582 |
| Rittershofer, Charles J. | 1914 | Box 502 | Roberts, Richard | 1887 | Box 105 |
| Rittershofer, Pheklee Selma | 1876 | Box 62 | Roberts, Ruth E. | 1920 | Box 674 |
| Rittue, Andrew J. | 1913 | Box 478 | Robertson, Alexander | 1805 | Box 2 |
| Rittue, Eliza Jane Todd | 1913 | Box 478 | Robertson, Catherine | 1898 | Box 178 |
| Ritz, John | 1894 | Box 149 | Robertson, Elbert | 1901 | Box 214 |
| Ritz, Justina | 1900 | Box 199 | Robertson, John | 1839 | Box 14 |
| Rivers, Eliza | 1877 | Box 64 | Robertson, John L. | 1918 | Box 610 |
| Rives, Arthur Landon | 1920 | Box 674 | Robertson, Rachel | 1853 | Box 22 |
| Rives, Grace W. | 1919 | Box 642 | Robertson, William | 1869 | Box 41 |
| Rives, John C. | 1864 | Box 32 | Robeson, Mary I. | 1910 | Box 403 |
| Rives, John C. | 1886 | Box 99 | Robeson, William H. | 1914 | Box 502 |
| Rives, Lucy | 1882 | Box 80 | Robey, Georgeanna E. | 1918 | Box 610 |
| Rives, William C. | 1919 | Box 642 | Robey, Harry N. | 1912 | Box 453 |
| Rives, Wright | 1918 | Box 610 | Robey, Helen Adams | 1919 | Box 642 |
| Rixford, Caroline L. | 1917 | Box 582 | Robey, Malvina Virginia | 1908 | Box 354 |
| Rixford, Sarah M. | 1891 | Box 127 | Robey, Nehemiah | 1899 | Box 187 |
| Rizzo, Colletta | 1902 | Box 234 | Robey, William Millard | 1917 | Box 582 |
| Roach, Catherine M. | 1903 | Box 253 | Robey, William R. | 1899 | Box 187 |
| Roach, David | 1878 | Box 67 | Robie, Edward Dunham | 1911 | Box 428 |
| Roach, Honora | 1870 | Box 43 | Robinson, Alcinda M. | 1892 | Box 134 |
| Roach, Michael | 1876 | Box 62 | Robinson, Alexander | 1889 | Box 116 |
| Roach, Sarah B. | 1906 | Box 309 | Robinson, Annie | 1919 | Box 642 |
| Robb, John | 1869 | Box 41 | Robinson, Annie C. | 1913 | Box 478 |
| Robbins, Henry A. | 1912 | Box 453 | Robinson, Annie Collins | 1894 | Box 149 |

| | | | | | | |
|---|---|---|---|---|---|---|
| Robinson, Barsine S. | 1911 | Box 428 | Robison, Anna | 1918 | Box 610 |
| Robinson, Bessie | 1917 | Box 582 | Robison, Christy | 1865 | Box 34 |
| Robinson, Betsy | 1870 | Box 43 | Roby, Adelia | 1902 | Box 234 |
| Robinson, Beverly | 1914 | Box 502 | Rocca, John B. | 1916 | Box 555 |
| Robinson, Bushrod | 1902 | Box 234 | Rocca, Paulina | 1907 | Box 332 |
| Robinson, Charles | 1918 | Box 610 | Rochat, Henry | 1880 | Box 73 |
| Robinson, Charles W. | 1873 | Box 52 | Roche, Honora | 1885 | Box 94 |
| Robinson, Charlotte | 1912 | Box 453 | Roche, James | 1893 | Box 141 |
| Robinson, Clem | 1920 | Box 674 | Roche, James E. | 1904 | Box 270 |
| Robinson, Conway | 1884 | Box 89 | Roche, John | 1901 | Box 214 |
| Robinson, Edward W. | 1902 | Box 234 | Roche, Margaret | 1907 | Box 332 |
| Robinson, Elizabeth P. Stuart | 1919 | Box 642 | Roche, Maurice | 1894 | Box 1491 |
| Robinson, Erastus R. | 1917 | Box 582 | Roche, Robert J. | 1858 | Box 27 |
| Robinson, Fielding | 1891 | Box 127 | Rochester, Anna Martin | 1905 | Box 290 |
| Robinson, Frances L. | 1906 | Box 309 | Rochester, William Beatty | 1910 | Box 403 |
| Robinson, Francis V. | 1918 | Box 610 | Rochford, John A. | 1897 | Box 172 |
| Robinson, Georgia M. | 1911 | Box 428 | Rochon, Joannes | 1907 | Box 332 |
| Robinson, Harry Arthur | 1916 | Box 555 | Rock, Alfred Mayer | 1907 | Box 332 |
| Robinson, Henry | 1918 | Box 610 | Rock, Anna M. | 1914 | Box 502 |
| Robinson, James S. | 1905 | Box 290 | Rock, George A. | 1919 | Box 642 |
| Robinson, Jane | 1878 | Box 67 | Rock, Miles | 1901 | Box 214 |
| Robinson, Jennie W. | 1913 | Box 478 | Rockar, Ferdinand A. | 1909 | Box 377 |
| Robinson, Jesse Daniel | 1917 | Box 582 | Rockett, Lucy M. | 1905 | Box 290 |
| Robinson, Jesse H. | 1912 | Box 453 | Rockett, Robert W. | 1886 | Box 99 |
| Robinson, John | 1863 | Box 31 | Rockwell, Eckley West | 1920 | Box 674 |
| Robinson, John | 1869 | Box 41 | Rockwell, Henry E. | 1882 | Box 80 |
| Robinson, John | 1908 | Box 354 | Rockwell, Julia Lee | 1918 | Box 610 |
| Robinson, John G. | 1876 | Box 62 | Rockwell, Margaret C. | 1904 | Box 270 |
| Robinson, John Hancock | 1911 | Box 428 | Rockwell, Sarah J. | 1898 | Box 178 |
| Robinson, John Marshall | 1911 | Box 428 | Rockwell, W. H. | 1915 | Box 530 |
| Robinson, Julia Sophia | 1914 | Box 502 | Rode, Jacob | 1915 | Box 530 |
| Robinson, Junius | 1827 | Box 9 | Roderick, Charlotte R. | 1901 | Box 214 |
| Robinson, Kitty | 1872 | Box 48 | Roderick, Edmund A. | 1900 | Box 199 |
| Robinson, Louisa | 1896 | Box 165 | Roderick, Frank A. | 1913 | Box 478 |
| Robinson, Manson | 1894 | Box 149 | Roderick, Virginia F. | 1914 | Box 502 |
| Robinson, Marian | 1918 | Box 610 | Rodgers, Ann Elizabeth | 1897 | Box 172 |
| Robinson, Mary E. | 1892 | Box 134 | Rodgers, Christopher R. P. | 1892 | Box 134 |
| Robinson, Mary Elizabeth | 1806 | Box 2 | Rodgers, John | 1838 | Box 14 |
| Robinson, Mary V. C. | 1914 | Box 502 | Rodgers, John | 1882 | Box 80 |
| Robinson, Mattie V. | 1912 | Box 453 | Rodgers, John F. | 1899 | Box 187 |
| Robinson, Moncure | 1892 | Box 134 | Rodgers, Julia | 1890 | Box 121 |
| Robinson, Nannie Hollingshead | 1916 | Box 555 | Rodgers, Julia Ann | 1910 | Box 403 |
| Robinson, Samuel Adam | 1913 | Box 478 | Rodgers, Minerva | 1877 | Box 65 |
| Robinson, Sarah | 1892 | Box 134 | Rodier, Maria E. | 1888 | Box 110 |
| Robinson, Sarah M. | 1920 | Box 674 | Rodrick, Walter F. | 1905 | Box 290 |
| Robinson, Snowdon W. | 1914 | Box 502 | Rodriguez, Jose Ignacio | 1907 | Box 332 |
| Robinson, Somerset | 1897 | Box 172 | Rodriguez, Mary A. | 1908 | Box 354 |
| Robinson, William | 1908 | Box 354 | Roe, Cornelius McDermott | 1807 | Box 2 |
| Robinson, William C. | 1894 | Box 149 | Roe, Eliza J. | 1920 | Box 674 |
| Robinson, William C. | 1912 | Box 453 | Roe, Francis A. | 1902 | Box 234 |
| Robinson, William O. | 1916 | Box 555 | Roelker, Charles R. | 1910 | Box 403 |
| Robinson, William Pitt | 1907 | Box 332 | Roemmele, Joseph | 1884 | Box 89 |

| | | | | | | |
|---|---|---|---|---|---|---|
| Roesch, Lothar | 1911 | Box 428 | Root, Cornelia M. | 1918 | Box 610 |
| Roeser, Carl | 1898 | Box 178 | Root, Mary E. | 1912 | Box 453 |
| Roessle, Theophilus E. | 1904 | Box 270 | Root, Zelina | 1886 | Box 99 |
| Roff, Ann E. | 1919 | Box 642 | Roper, William B. | 1873 | Box 52 |
| Roger, Johnson K. | 1872 | Box 48 | Rorebeck, Alice Gantt | 1915 | Box 530 |
| Rogers, Archibald Irwin | 1912 | Box 453 | Rorebeck, Azur Curtis | 1915 | Box 530 |
| Rogers, Austin M. | 1915 | Box 530 | Rosa, Cornelia E. | 1893 | Box 141 |
| Rogers, Bertha S. | 1916 | Box 555 | Rose, Catherine | 1916 | Box 555 |
| Rogers, Eliza B. | 1881 | Box 76 | Rose, Charles A. | 1917 | Box 582 |
| Rogers, G. Sherburne | 1920 | Box 674 | Rose, Elizabeth A. | 1911 | Box 428 |
| Rogers, James R. | 1914 | Box 502 | Rose, Frederick | 1903 | Box 253 |
| Rogers, Jane | 1887 | Box 105 | Rose, George B. | 1918 | Box 610 |
| Rogers, John D. | 1919 | Box 642 | Rose, Jane | 1830 | Box 10 |
| Rogers, John H. | 1900 | Box 199 | Rose, Joseph | 1890 | Box 121 |
| Rogers, Johnson K. | 1872 | Box 48 | Rose, Joseph A. | 1916 | Box 555 |
| Rogers, Joseph | 1900 | Box 199 | Rose, Robert | 1847 | Box 19 |
| Rogers, Lloyd A. | 1883 | Box 84 | Rose, Samuel B. | 1917 | Box 582 |
| Rogers, Mary L. | 1908 | Box 355 | Rosen, Ferdinand von | 1908 | Box 355 |
| Rogers, Thomas E. | 1911 | Box 428 | Rosenbaum, William T. | 1913 | Box 478 |
| Rogers, William P. | 1916 | Box 555 | Rosenberg, John | 1894 | Box 149 |
| Rogier, Caroline | 1898 | Box 178 | Rosenberg, Koppel | 1902 | Box 234 |
| Roginsky, Max | 1913 | Box 478 | Rosenberg, Louis | 1915 | Box 530 |
| Rohl-Smith, Carl | 1900 | Box 199 | Rosenberg, Lydia E. | 1902 | Box 234 |
| Rohr, Anna M. | 1920 | Box 674 | Rosenberg, Rosalie | 1902 | Box 234 |
| Rohr, Frederick Gustav | 1877 | Box 65 | Rosenberger, Sarah Seibert | 1910 | Box 403 |
| Rohrer, Charlotte Haight Arthur | 1917 | Box 582 | Rosenbusch, Caroline F. | 1904 | Box 270 |
| Rohrer, Karl | 1913 | Box 478 | Rosenbusch, Traugott | 1912 | Box 453 |
| Rohrer, William H. | 1914 | Box 502 | Rosendale, Henry | 1890 | Box 121 |
| Rolle, Helen M. | 1909 | Box 377 | Rosengarn, Herman | 1882 | Box 80 |
| Roller, John E. | 1918 | Box 610 | Rosenthal, Amanda | 1901 | Box 214 |
| Rolleris, Eliza | 1893 | Box 136 | Rosenthal, Babette | 1914 | Box 502 |
| Rollings, Caroline | 1886 | Box 99 | Rosenthal, Charles | 1857 | Box 26 |
| Rollings, George | 1872 | Box 48 | Rosenthal, Emil | 1900 | Box 199 |
| Rollings, Louisa J. | 1894 | Box 149 | Rosenthal, Ernestine | 1919 | Box 642 |
| Rollins, Alferd | 1907 | Box 332 | Rosenthal, Esther | 1918 | Box 610 |
| Rollins, Daniel | 1900 | Box 199 | Rosenthal, Julius | 1889 | Box 116 |
| Rollins, Edward A. | 1909 | Box 377 | Rosenthal, Sarah J. | 1917 | Box 582 |
| Rollins, Eliza | 1893 | Box 138 | Rosenthal, Sidney Emil | 1905 | Box 290 |
| Rollins, James | 1894 | Box 149 | Rosenthal, Wilhelm | 1917 | Box 582 |
| Rollins, Violette A. | 1919 | Box 642 | Rosier, Nathan | 1878 | Box 67 |
| Rollins, William Henry | 1909 | Box 377 | Rosinski, Charles | 1890 | Box 121 |
| Rollow, Malvina | 1876 | Box 62 | Rosinski, Maria | 1914 | Box 502 |
| Romaine, Robert | 1897 | Box 172 | Ross, Aairy | 1872 | Box 48 |
| Roney, John | 1893 | Box 141 | Ross, Andrew | 1822 | Box 7 |
| Ronne, Andrew C. | 1897 | Box 172 | Ross, Edward J. | 1898 | Box 178 |
| Rookard, Sarah E. | 1919 | Box 642 | Ross, Elizabeth | 1848 | Box 19 |
| Rooker, B. A. | 1860 | Box 28 | Ross, Elizabeth | 1918 | Box 611 |
| Rookstool, William H. | 1915 | Box 530 | Ross, Henry | 1866 | Box 36 |
| Roome, Edward | 1891 | Box 127 | Ross, Jane | 1872 | Box 48 |
| Roosa, Clinton D. | 1899 | Box 187 | Ross, John | 1882 | Box 80 |
| Roose, William S. | 1897 | Box 172 | Ross, John A. | 1871 | Box 45 |
| Root, Albert L. | 1898 | Box 178 | Ross, John W. | 1902 | Box 234 |

| | | | | | | |
|---|---|---|---|---|---|---|
| Ross, Julia Ann | 1899 | Box 187 | Rowley, Alice M. | 1920 | Box 674 |
| Ross, Kate | 1905 | Box 290 | Rowzee, Charles R. | 1906 | Box 309 |
| Ross, Lucy | 1898 | Box 178 | Rowzee, Greenberry | 1916 | Box 555 |
| Ross, Mary Anna | 1879 | Box 70 | Rowzee, Julia N. | 1906 | Box 309 |
| Ross, Mary Jane | 1892 | Box 134 | Roy, Eleanor M. | 1912 | Box 454 |
| Ross, Mary R. | 1916 | Box 555 | Royall, Elizabeth Coxe | 1903 | Box 253 |
| Ross, Susan | 1888 | Box 110 | Royall, William B. | 1896 | Box 165 |
| Ross, Thomas | 1893 | Box 141 | Royster, O. M. | 1914 | Box 502 |
| Ross, Travus | 1908 | Box 355 | Rozel, Ennols | 1867 | Box 38 |
| Ross, William F. | 1909 | Box 377 | Rucker, Daniel H. | 1910 | Box 403 |
| Rossiter, Catharine | 1884 | Box 89 | Rudd, Theodore M. | 1904 | Box 270 |
| Rossiter, George Ignatius | 1920 | Box 674 | Rudden, John | 1920 | Box 674 |
| Rotchford, Anna E. | 1884 | Box 89 | Rudenstein, Magnus F. T. | 1902 | Box 234 |
| Rotchford, John Francis | 1910 | Box 403 | Rudenstein, Margaret | 1905 | Box 290 |
| Roth, Ambrosius | 1871 | Box 45 | Rudhardt, Romanus | 1880 | Box 73 |
| Roth, Benedict | 1907 | Box 332 | Rudolph, Arthur F. | 1918 | Box 611 |
| Roth, John A. | 1891 | Box 127 | Rudy, Ida E. H. | 1889 | Box 116 |
| Roth, Louise S. | 1914 | Box 502 | Rudy, William Dole | 1899 | Box 187 |
| Roth, Mary A. | 1888 | Box 110 | Rue, Annie B. | 1894 | Box 149 |
| Rothchild, Theresa | 1904 | Box 270 | Ruebsam, Annie M. | 1889 | Box 116 |
| Rothert, Samuel | 1907 | Box 332 | Ruess, Irma C. | 1919 | Box 642 |
| Rothrock, Maynard W. | 1916 | Box 555 | Rueth, John M. | 1899 | Box 187 |
| Rothschild, Hannah | 1895 | Box 157 | Ruf, Alexander | 1916 | Box 555 |
| Rothschild, Louis | 1898 | Box 178 | Ruff, Albert B. | 1920 | Box 674 |
| Rothwell, Andrew | 1883 | Box 84 | Ruff, George R. | 1879 | Box 70 |
| Rothwell, Emily J. | 1916 | Box 555 | Ruff, Joanna Mather | 1847 | Box 19 |
| Rothwell, Fannie | 1919 | Box 642 | Ruff, John A. | 1891 | Box 127 |
| Rothwell, George W. | 1873 | Box 52 | Ruff, John N. | 1885 | Box 94 |
| Rothwell, James | 1889 | Box 116 | Rüfli, Frederick | 1920 | Box 674 |
| Rothwell, Richard | 1906 | Box 309 | Ruggle, Lavinia A. | 1907 | Box 332 |
| Rothwell, Richard (Jr.) | 1896 | Box 165 | Ruggles, George D. | 1905 | Box 290 |
| Rott, Gustavus Emill | 1907 | Box 332 | Ruggles, William | 1877 | Box 65 |
| Roulot, Virginia | 1892 | Box 134 | Ruhl, George | 1887 | Box 105 |
| Roumel, Peter | 1920 | Box 674 | Ruhl, James | 1893 | Box 141 |
| Rout, Thomas J. | 1908 | Box 355 | Ruland, Elizabeth | 1920 | Box 674 |
| Rouzer, George W. | 1912 | Box 453 | Rumbley, Georgiana A. | 1894 | Box 149 |
| Rouzer, Lewis D. | 1917 | Box 582 | Rumpf, Gottlieb | 1882 | Box 80 |
| Rover, Thomas A. | 1908 | Box 355 | Rumsey, James Gorham | 1874 | Box 55 |
| Rowan, Ellen | 1898 | Box 178 | Rumsey, Joseph C. | 1913 | Box 478 |
| Rowan, Hamilton | 1917 | Box 582 | Runkel, Mary B. | 1918 | Box 611 |
| Rowan, Stephen C. | 1890 | Box 121 | Runner, John H. | 1894 | Box 149 |
| Rowe, Elizabeth | 1897 | Box 172 | Ruoff, Charles H. | 1896 | Box 165 |
| Rowe, Richard H. | 1893 | Box 141 | Rupertus, Herman | 1886 | Box 99 |
| Rowell, Alfred W. | 1908 | Box 355 | Rupertus, Mary | 1917 | Box 582 |
| Rowell, Daniel M. | 1908 | Box 355 | Rupertus, Pauline | 1918 | Box 611 |
| Rowell, Dennison P. | 1918 | Box 611 | Rupli, John Jacob | 1904 | Box 271 |
| Rowland, Daniel | 1866 | Box 36 | Rupp, Edward C. | 1914 | Box 502 |
| Rowland, Frederica Leech | 1917 | Box 582 | Ruppel, Joseph | 1895 | Box 157 |
| Rowland, James Harvey | 1908 | Box 355 | Ruppert, Andrew | 1845 | Box 17 |
| Rowland, Julian S. | 1915 | Box 530 | Ruppert, Anton | 1911 | Box 428 |
| Rowland, L. Bernard | 1912 | Box 454 | Ruppert, Catherine | 1908 | Box 355 |
| Rowland, Mary Helen | 1905 | Box 290 | Ruppert, Christian | 1897 | Box 172 |

| | | | | | | |
|---|---|---|---|---|---|---|
| Ruppert, Ellen | 1914 | Box 502 | Rust, John R. | 1920 | Box 674 |
| Ruppert, Gertrude | 1904 | Box 271 | Rüth, Henny | 1886 | Box 99 |
| Ruppert, Gustav | 1910 | Box 403 | Ruth, John B. | 1883 | Box 84 |
| Ruppert, Henny | 1893 | Box 141 | Ruth, Mary Eleanor | 1892 | Box 134 |
| Ruppert, Ignatius | 1880 | Box 73 | Rutherford, Alexander | 1872 | Box 48 |
| Ruppert, John | 1881 | Box 76 | Rutherford, Andrew | 1803 | Box 1 |
| Ruppert, John M. | 1916 | Box 555 | Rutherford, Elizabeth King | 1912 | Box 454 |
| Ruppert, Kate E. | 1913 | Box 478 | Rutherford, James A. | 1893 | Box 141 |
| Ruppert, Leonora | 1893 | Box 141 | Rutherford, Mary E. | 1901 | Box 214 |
| Ruppert, Mary Dunn | 1918 | Box 611 | Rutherford, Matilda | 1908 | Box 355 |
| Ruppert, Matthew | 1919 | Box 642 | Rutherford, Robert Gedney | 1907 | Box 332 |
| Ruppert, Michael | 1890 | Box 121 | Rutledge, James McC. | 1908 | Box 355 |
| Ruppert, Sallie G. | 1891 | Box 127 | Rutledge, Samuel | 1918 | Box 611 |
| Rupprecht, Harry E. | 1911 | Box 429 | Ruttledge, Thomas W. | 1915 | Box 530 |
| Rush, Ellen | 1900 | Box 199 | Ryall, George | 1920 | Box 674 |
| Rush, Frederick | 1904 | Box 271 | Ryan, Daniel M. | 1905 | Box 290 |
| Rush, Isaac N. | 1886 | Box 99 | Ryan, Hanorah | 1874 | Box 55 |
| Rush, Richard | 1873 | Box 52 | Ryan, Harvey E. | 1907 | Box 332 |
| Rush, Richard | 1912 | Box 454 | Ryan, James | 1887 | Box 105 |
| Rushburger, Mary | 1911 | Box 429 | Ryan, James | 1899 | Box 187 |
| Rusk, Alexander | 1870 | Box 43 | Ryan, James | 1918 | Box 611 |
| Rusk, James M. | 1917 | Box 582 | Ryan, John | 1893 | Box 141 |
| Russ, Anna A. | 1918 | Box 611 | Ryan, Martha Aurelia | 1913 | Box 478 |
| Russell, Ann R. | 1893 | Box 141 | Ryan, Mary | 1836 | Box 13 |
| Russell, Charles | 1902 | Box 234 | Ryan, Mary | 1866 | Box 36 |
| Russell, Charlotte | 1851 | Box 21 | Ryan, Mary | 1872 | Box 48 |
| Russell, David McC. | 1895 | Box 157 | Ryan, Mary | 1903 | Box 253 |
| Russell, David N. | 1902 | Box 234 | Ryan, Mary F. | 1912 | Box 454 |
| Russell, Eliza Jane | 1887 | Box 105 | Ryan, Mary P. | 1904 | Box 271 |
| Russell, Ellen | 1871 | Box 45 | Ryan, Mary W. | 1906 | Box 309 |
| Russell, George | 1912 | Box 454 | Ryan, Michael P. | 1911 | Box 429 |
| Russell, Israel Cook | 1917 | Box 582 | Ryan, Patrick J. | 1887 | Box 105 |
| Russell, John D. | 1912 | Box 454 | Ryan, Richard | 1908 | Box 355 |
| Russell, John H. | 1897 | Box 172 | Ryan, Sarah E. | 1917 | Box 582 |
| Russell, Joseph E. | 1906 | Box 309 | Ryan, Stanislaus F. | 1903 | Box 253 |
| Russell, Leonidas | 1902 | Box 234 | Ryan, William | 1913 | Box 478 |
| Russell, Lilean Kendall | 1886 | Box 99 | Ryan, William F. | 1912 | Box 454 |
| Russell, Lizzie | 1920 | Box 674 | Ryan, William K. | 1896 | Box 165 |
| Russell, Lucy | 1919 | Box 642 | Ryder, Emeline | 1912 | Box 454 |
| Russell, Marion R. | 1915 | Box 530 | Ryder, William J. | 1899 | Box 187 |
| Russell, Martha L. | 1920 | Box 674 | Ryder, William P. | 1905 | Box 290 |
| Russell, Mary | 1825 | Box 8 | Rye, Ann | 1872 | Box 48 |
| Russell, Philip Gray | 1900 | Box 199 | Ryer, Mary K. | 1917 | Box 582 |
| Russell, Rachel Doherty | 1914 | Box 502 | Ryer, Mary Scott | 1917 | Box 582 |
| Russell, Samuel | 1871 | Box 45 | Ryland, William | 1846 | Box 18 |
| Russell, Sarah W. | 1919 | Box 642 | Rynex, Adela C. W. | 1898 | Box 178 |
| Russell, Thomas | 1918 | Box 611 | Rynex, Amanda V. | 1908 | Box 355 |
| Russell, Thomas F. | 1892 | Box 134 | Rynex, John M. | 1901 | Box 214 |
| Russell, William H. | 1909 | Box 377 | Rynex, William H. | 1906 | Box 309 |
| Russell, William R. | 1902 | Box 234 | Ryon, Arabella | 1895 | Box 157 |
| Russell, William W. | 1862 | Box 30 | Ryon, Clara Teel Rowland | 1909 | Box 377 |
| Rust, Elizabeth Ellen | 1912 | Box 454 | Ryon, James P. | 1899 | Box 187 |

| | | | | | | |
|---|---|---|---|---|---|
| Ryon, Percival B. | 1914 | Box 502 | Sands, Emilie A. | 1884 | Box 89 |
| Ryon, Richard J. | 1868 | Box 40 | Sands, Henrietta M. | 1893 | Box 141 |
| Ryther, Edwin A. | 1875 | Box 58 | Sands, John G. | 1920 | Box 674 |
| Sabin, Oliver C. | 1914 | Box 502 | Sands, Joseph W. | 1888 | Box 110 |
| Sachs, Magdalena Willert | 1920 | Box 674 | Sands, Lucy P. | 1902 | Box 234 |
| Sachse, Alberta | 1918 | Box 611 | Sands, Timothy | 1889 | Box 116 |
| Sackett, Martin J. | 1916 | Box 556 | Sanfellipo, Frank | 1918 | Box 611 |
| Sadler, Loren A. | 1919 | Box 642 | Sanford, Claude B. | 1920 | Box 674 |
| Sadler, Mary R. | 1919 | Box 642 | Sanford, Don Alonzo Sr. | 1915 | Box 530 |
| Sadtler, Anna Bryant | 1912 | Box 454 | Sanford, G. Washington | 1900 | Box 199 |
| Safford, Mary Joanna | 1916 | Box 556 | Sanford, George | 1838 | Box 14 |
| Sage, Harriet | 1881 | Box 76 | Sanford, John M. | 1895 | Box 157 |
| Sage, Mary E. | 1915 | Box 530 | Sanford, Louise J. | 1920 | Box 674 |
| Sahm, Justus Rudolph | 1876 | Box 62 | Sanger, William P. S. | 1890 | Box 121 |
| Sailer, Bowman | 1886 | Box 99 | Sangiorgio, Guiseppe | 1894 | Box 149 |
| Sailer, Deborah S. | 1902 | Box 234 | Sangston, Jane E. | 1902 | Box 234 |
| Sailer, Elizabeth Barbara | 1901 | Box 215 | Sanno, Euphemia R. | 1898 | Box 178 |
| Sailer, Jacob Frederick | 1882 | Box 80 | Sansbury, James A. | 1907 | Box 333 |
| Saks, Isidore | 1916 | Box 556 | Sansom, Lizzie | 1920 | Box 674 |
| Salkeld, Thomas L. | 1897 | Box 172 | Sargent, Nathan | 1875 | Box 58 |
| Salmon, Abraham M. | 1910 | Box 403 | Sargent, Nathan | 1908 | Box 355 |
| Salmon, Daniel Elmer | 1914 | Box 502 | Sargent, Rosina | 1878 | Box 67 |
| Salomon, Lewis | 1835 | Box 13 | Sariol, Thomas D. | 1915 | Box 530 |
| Salomon, Theresie | 1915 | Box 530 | Sauerland, Joseph A. | 1918 | Box 611 |
| Salsbury, Harmon L. | 1914 | Box 502 | Sauerwein, Jessie F. | 1906 | Box 310 |
| Salter, Albert T. | 1905 | Box 290 | Saul, John | 1897 | Box 172 |
| Salter, William F. | 1918 | Box 611 | Saul, Susan | 1887 | Box 105 |
| Saltmer, George Heins | 1884 | Box 89 | Saul, Teresa M. | 1915 | Box 530 |
| Samo, Theodore B. | 1882 | Box 80 | Saunders, Carrie | 1916 | Box 556 |
| Sample, James A. | 1916 | Box 556 | Saunders, David | 1888 | Box 110 |
| Sampson, Calvin T. | 1894 | Box 149 | Saunders, David I. | 1917 | Box 582 |
| Sampson, Daniel | 1873 | Box 52 | Saunders, Eliza A. | 1917 | Box 583 |
| Sampson, Elizabeth | 1910 | Box 403 | Saunders, Fenton G. | 1915 | Box 530 |
| Sampson, Joseph | 1851 | Box 21 | Saunders, Griffin | 1887 | Box 105 |
| Sampson, Nellie P. | 1910 | Box 403 | Saunders, Isabella I. | 1917 | Box 583 |
| Sampson, Sarah S. | 1908 | Box 355 | Saunders, John H. | 1905 | Box 290 |
| Sampson, Thomas | 1917 | Box 582 | Saunders, Joseph W. | 1920 | Box 674 |
| Sampson, William H. | 1899 | Box 187 | Saunders, Lorin M. | 1905 | Box 290 |
| Sampson, William T. | 1902 | Box 234 | Saunders, Lucy B. Page | 1886 | Box 99 |
| Samuel, George | 1895 | Box 157 | Saunders, Martha | 1913 | Box 478 |
| Samuels, Dorethea | 1914 | Box 502 | Saunders, Mary P. | 1905 | Box 290 |
| Sanderlin, Eliza W. | 1912 | Box 454 | Saunders, Mary P. | 1898 | Box 178 |
| Sanders, Albert | 1919 | Box 642 | Saunders, Melissa Miriam H. | 1916 | Box 556 |
| Sanders, Harriet E. | 1890 | Box 121 | Saunders, Nancy S. | 1886 | Box 99 |
| Sanders, Henry P. | 1908 | Box 355 | Saunders, Thomas B. | 1916 | Box 556 |
| Sanders, Lewis | 1846 | Box 18 | Saunders, Ulyses | 1912 | Box 454 |
| Sanders, William G. | 1845 | Box 17 | Saunders, William | 1901 | Box 215 |
| Sanderson, Edward O. | 1901 | Box 215 | Saunders, William | 1914 | Box 502 |
| Sanderson, Kate | 1909 | Box 377 | Saur, Rudolph | 1915 | Box 530 |
| Sanderson, Thomas H. | 1863 | Box 31 | Saur, William | 1916 | Box 556 |
| Sandmann, Rachel | 1898 | Box 178 | Sauter, Benford | 1912 | Box 454 |
| Sands, Benjamin F. | 1883 | Box 84 | Sauter, Mary Ellen | 1920 | Box 674 |

| | | | | | | |
|---|---|---|---|---|---|---|
| Sautter, Charles A. | 1904 | Box 271 | Schaefer, Sarah J. | 1898 | Box 177 |
| Sautter, Elise Dorothea | 1895 | Box 157 | Schaeffer, Edward M. | 1917 | Box 583 |
| Sautter, Sophia | 1905 | Box 290 | Schaeffer, Samuel F. | 1899 | Box 187 |
| Savage, Edward H. | 1913 | Box 478 | Schaer, Marie Therese | 1918 | Box 611 |
| Savage, Julia G. | 1917 | Box 583 | Schafer, Conrad | 1907 | Box 333 |
| Savary, John | 1910 | Box 403 | Schafer, Elizabeth | 1897 | Box 172 |
| Savigne, John | 1894 | Box 149 | Schafer, Emil G. | 1917 | Box 583 |
| Saville, James Hamilton | 1913 | Box 478 | Schafer, Emma E. C. | 1918 | Box 611 |
| Savoy, Samuel W. | 1915 | Box 530 | Schafer, Frank H. | 1873 | Box 52 |
| Sawtell, Samuel Allen | 1908 | Box 355 | Schafer, Frederick | 1913 | Box 479 |
| Sawtelle, Charles G. | 1913 | Box 478 | Schafer, George F. | 1892 | Box 134 |
| Sawyer, Christy | 1863 | Box 31 | Schafer, John | 1893 | Box 142 |
| Sawyer, Eunice B. | 1910 | Box 403 | Schafer, John | 1912 | Box 454 |
| Sawyer, Horace B. | 1871 | Box 45 | Schafer, Minna | 1909 | Box 377 |
| Sawyer, William C. | 1849 | Box 20 | Schafer, Peter | 1892 | Box 134 |
| Saxton, Edward | 1920 | Box 674 | Schaffer, George F. | 1909 | Box 377 |
| Saxton, James | 1849 | Box 20 | Schaffer, Milton R. | 1908 | Box 355 |
| Saxton, Joseph | 1873 | Box 52 | Schafhirt, Adolph J. | 1903 | Box 253 |
| Saxton, Matilda G. | 1915 | Box 530 | Schafhirt, Ernest F. | 1902 | Box 234 |
| Saxton, Rufus | 1908 | Box 355 | Schafhirt, Frederic | 1880 | Box 73 |
| Sayer, Charles B. | 1894 | Box 149 | Schaper, Frederick W. | 1892 | Box 134 |
| Sayer, Mary | 1893 | Box 141 | Scharf, Samuel R. | 1906 | Box 310 |
| Sayer, Susan E. | 1896 | Box 165 | Scharr, George G. | 1899 | Box 187 |
| Sayers, Archibald | 1813 | Box 4 | Schaub, Frederick | 1903 | Box 253 |
| Sayers, James | 1883 | Box 84 | Schayer, George F. | 1918 | Box 611 |
| Sayles, Henry C. | 1896 | Box 165 | Scheahan, John | 1862 | Box 30 |
| Sayles, Jane H. | 1911 | Box 429 | Scheel, Catherine E. | 1908 | Box 355 |
| Sayre, Charles Leroy | 1876 | Box 62 | Scheele, Lillian H. | 1906 | Box 310 |
| Sayre, Harriet Soper | 1898 | Box 178 | Scheer, Frank | 1920 | Box 674 |
| Sayre, William | 1879 | Box 70 | Scheer, Mary E. | 1919 | Box 642 |
| Scaggs, James F. | 1908 | Box 355 | Scheerer, George W. | 1911 | Box 429 |
| Scaggs, Sallie A. | 1907 | Box 333 | Scheifley, Jacob | 1879 | Box 70 |
| Scaggs, Selby B. | 1911 | Box 429 | Scheitlin, Bernard T. | 1877 | Box 65 |
| Scala, Francis | 1903 | Box 253 | Scheitlin, Elise | 1919 | Box 642 |
| Scallan, Robert | 1837 | Box 14 | Schelcher, Louis | 1917 | Box 583 |
| Scanlan, Patrick | 1875 | Box 59 | Schell, Charles W. | 1900 | Box 199 |
| Scanlon, John | 1894 | Box 149 | Schenck, Elizabeth H. | 1911 | Box 429 |
| Scanlon, John T. | 1907 | Box 333 | Schenck, Robert C. | 1890 | Box 121 |
| Scannell, Cornelius | 1874 | Box 55 | Schenig, Eliza J. | 1866 | Box 36 |
| Scantling, John C. | 1917 | Box 583 | Schenig, Francis | 1864 | Box 32 |
| Scarff, Thomas T. | 1885 | Box 94 | Scherer, Charles H. | 1914 | Box 503 |
| Schaad, John C. | 1883 | Box 84 | Scherer, Henry | 1868 | Box 40 |
| Schad, Bonaventura | 1858 | Box 27 | Scherger, William | 1895 | Box 157 |
| Schade, Louis | 1903 | Box 253 | Scherick, Julia C. | 1905 | Box 290 |
| Schaefer, Barbara | 1905 | Box 290 | Scheuch, Carolina | 1906 | Box 310 |
| Schaefer, Caspar | 1885 | Box 94 | Scheuch, Emily | 1895 | Box 157 |
| Schaefer, Elizabeth | 1897 | Box 172 | Scheuch, George | 1918 | Box 611 |
| Schaefer, Frances | 1895 | Box 157 | Scheuch, John | 1883 | Box 84 |
| Schaefer, Henry | 1903 | Box 253 | Scheuch, Kate | 1919 | Box 642 |
| Schaefer, John William | 1903 | Box 253 | Scheuch, Margaret | 1897 | Box 172 |
| Schaefer, Louisa C. | 1893 | Box 142 | Scheuch, Peter | 1881 | Box 76 |
| Schaefer, Mary Catherine | 1914 | Box 502 | Scheuerman, Camilla Hinke | 1915 | Box 530 |

| | | | | | | |
|---|---|---|---|---|---|
| Scheuerman, Camilla Hinke | 1918 | Box 611 | Schmidt, Susan A. | 1896 | Box 165 |
| Schickler, Elizabeth | 1914 | Box 503 | Schmidt, Wilhelm A. C. | 1895 | Box 157 |
| Schilling, Mathias | 1910 | Box 403 | Schmieg, Conrad | 1881 | Box 76 |
| Schilling, Otto | 1907 | Box 333 | Schmitt, Louise | 1915 | Box 530 |
| Schilling, Sophia | 1918 | Box 611 | Schmitz, Victoria | 1899 | Box 187 |
| Schillinger, Minnie | 1905 | Box 290 | Schmuck, Valentin | 1912 | Box 454 |
| Schimmelfennig, Sophie | 1890 | Box 121 | Schmulovitz, Barney | 1908 | Box 355 |
| Schindler, George W. | 1913 | Box 479 | Schnaidt, August | 1906 | Box 310 |
| Schio, Peter | 1858 | Box 27 | Schnebel, Louis | 1906 | Box 310 |
| Schlegel, Charles | 1908 | Box 355 | Schnebly, Daniel H. | 1859 | Box 28 |
| Schlegel, Ferdinand | 1873 | Box 52 | Schneider, August | 1919 | Box 642 |
| Schlegel, Wilhelmina | 1911 | Box 429 | Schneider, Charles | 1911 | Box 429 |
| Schlerf, George | 1916 | Box 556 | Schneider, Charles A. | 1893 | Box 142 |
| Schlett, George | 1880 | Box 73 | Schneider, Charles F. | 1917 | Box 583 |
| Schley, Anne Rebecca | 1920 | Box 674 | Schneider, Charles W. | 1907 | Box 333 |
| Schley, Winfield Scott | 1911 | Box 429 | Schneider, Christian G. | 1896 | Box 165 |
| Schlorb, Magthalina | 1851 | Box 21 | Schneider, Edward L. | 1916 | Box 556 |
| Schloss, Nathan A. | 1892 | Box 134 | Schneider, Emma V. | 1916 | Box 556 |
| Schlosser, John H. | 1874 | Box 55 | Schneider, Franz Heinrich | 1889 | Box 116 |
| Schlosser, Martin H. | 1900 | Box 199 | Schneider, Harry M. | 1920 | Box 674 |
| Schlosser, Maurice | 1900 | Box 199 | Schneider, J. M. | 1918 | Box 611 |
| Schlosser, William T. | 1898 | Box 179 | Schneider, Jane | 1903 | Box 253 |
| Schlotterbeck, Albert B. | 1917 | Box 583 | Schneider, John | 1880 | Box 73 |
| Schlotterbeck, John | 1895 | Box 157 | Schneider, John A. | 1890 | Box 121 |
| Schlotterbeck, Maria E. | 1893 | Box 142 | Schneider, John A. | 1918 | Box 611 |
| Schlueter, Julius J. | 1905 | Box 290 | Schneider, Louie | 1918 | Box 611 |
| Schlueter, Louis W. A. | 1911 | Box 429 | Schneider, Louis H. | 1896 | Box 165 |
| Schlueter, William Henry | 1912 | Box 454 | Schneider, Louise R. | 1911 | Box 429 |
| Schmalhoff, William L. | 1915 | Box 530 | Schneider, Mary A. | 1898 | Box 179 |
| Schmalholz, Theodore | 1912 | Box 454 | Schneider, Roderick R. | 1887 | Box 105 |
| Schmalzinger, Augustus | 1900 | Box 199 | Schneider, Rufina | 1906 | Box 310 |
| Schmeck, Albert B. | 1917 | Box 583 | Schnell, George | 1872 | Box 48 |
| Schmedtee, Henry | 1902 | Box 234 | Schnid, Louis | 1895 | Box 157 |
| Schmedtic, August | 1907 | Box 333 | Schnier, Rosa A. | 1887 | Box 105 |
| Schmelzle, Leo | 1891 | Box 127 | Schnopp, John A. | 1883 | Box 84 |
| Schmerz, Henry | 1888 | Box 110 | Schoellkopf, Johann G. | 1906 | Box 310 |
| Schmid, Andreas | 1881 | Box 76 | Schoenborn, August G. | 1902 | Box 234 |
| Schmid, Ernst | 1914 | Box 503 | Schoenborn, Helene | 1904 | Box 271 |
| Schmid, Mary V. | 1918 | Box 611 | Schofield, John McAllister | 1907 | Box 333 |
| Schmidt, Albert D. | 1910 | Box 403 | Schofield, Lillie M. | 1917 | Box 583 |
| Schmidt, August | 1916 | Box 556 | Schofield, Mary J. | 1907 | Box 333 |
| Schmidt, Babet | 1900 | Box 199 | Schofield, Sam T. | 1912 | Box 454 |
| Schmidt, Catharine C. | 1894 | Box 149 | Scholfield, Andrew | 1841 | Box 15 |
| Schmidt, Cathrina A. | 1886 | Box 99 | Scholfield, Joseph L. | 1848 | Box 19 |
| Schmidt, Christian F. G. | 1874 | Box 55 | Scholl, Joseph | 1902 | Box 234 |
| Schmidt, Ernest L. | 1876 | Box 62 | Scholl, Mary Elizabeth | 1915 | Box 530 |
| Schmidt, Ferdinand | 1900 | Box 199 | Scholz, Otto | 1890 | Box 121 |
| Schmidt, Katharine M. | 1915 | Box 530 | Schommer, Ada J. | 1917 | Box 583 |
| Schmidt, Louis | 1908 | Box 355 | Schönborn, Henry F. | 1896 | Box 165 |
| Schmidt, Marie | 1915 | Box 530 | Schondau, Lena | 1911 | Box 429 |
| Schmidt, Martha Keck | 1914 | Box 503 | Schoolcraft, Henry R. | 1865 | Box 34 |
| Schmidt, Rasina | 1895 | Box 157 | Schoolcraft, Mary H. | 1878 | Box 67 |

| | | | | | | |
|---|---|---|---|---|---|---|
| Schoonover, William | 1900 | Box 199 | Schwakopf, Mary | 1906 | Box 310 |
| Schott, Charles Anthony | 1901 | Box 215 | Schwan, Elizabeth M. | 1919 | Box 643 |
| Schott, Nancy | 1868 | Box 40 | Schwartz, Andrew | 1896 | Box 165 |
| Schoyer, Louis | 1902 | Box 234 | Schwartz, Bertha | 1899 | Box 187 |
| Schranduer, John | 1904 | Box 271 | Schwartz, Joseph | 1884 | Box 89 |
| Schreiber, Ernst Otto (Jr.) | 1917 | Box 583 | Schwartze, Augustus J. | 1854 | Box 23 |
| Schreiber, William | 1893 | Box 142 | Schwarz, August | 1919 | Box 643 |
| Schreiner, Ella F. | 1907 | Box 333 | Schwarz, Conrad | 1863 | Box 31 |
| Schreiner, Josephine L. | 1918 | Box 611 | Schwarz, Frank | 1893 | Box 142 |
| Schreiner, Louisa S. | 1887 | Box 105 | Schwarz, William Christian | 1896 | Box 165 |
| Schreyer, Alice Ellsworth | 1914 | Box 503 | Schweitzer, Adam | 1874 | Box 55 |
| Schreyer, George | 1914 | Box 503 | Schweitzer, Annie | 1909 | Box 378 |
| Schriver, Edmund | 1899 | Box 187 | Schweitzer, Peter | 1907 | Box 333 |
| Schroder, Frederick | 1891 | Box 127 | Schwennecker, William | 1917 | Box 583 |
| Schroeder, Anna | 1920 | Box 674 | Schwing, Louis | 1892 | Box 134 |
| Schroeder, August W. | 1918 | Box 611 | Schwing, Mary C. | 1911 | Box 429 |
| Schroeder, Charles | 1909 | Box 378 | Schwing, William | 1915 | Box 530 |
| Schroeder, Dorothea | 1889 | Box 116 | Schwinghammer, Eugene | 1891 | Box 127 |
| Schroeder, Florence V. | 1919 | Box 642 | Scipio, Celia P. | 1920 | Box 674 |
| Schroth, Charles | 1906 | Box 310 | Scofield, Laura L. | 1905 | Box 290 |
| Schroth, Frank | 1914 | Box 503 | Scott, Alfred V. | 1860 | Box 29 |
| Schroth, John B. | 1920 | Box 674 | Scott, Alice Josephene | 1914 | Box 503 |
| Schu, Hannah | 1905 | Box 290 | Scott, Amanda | 1907 | Box 333 |
| Schucking, Alfred | 1898 | Box 179 | Scott, Ann | 1871 | Box 45 |
| Schücking, Prosper L. | 1887 | Box 105 | Scott, Ann H. | 1860 | Box 29 |
| Schuh, Maria | 1918 | Box 612 | Scott, Cephas W. | 1918 | Box 612 |
| Schuler, August | 1911 | Box 429 | Scott, Charles | 1893 | Box 142 |
| Schulte, Henry | 1899 | Box 187 | Scott, Charles F. | 1905 | Box 290 |
| Schulteis, Anna Maria | 1911 | Box 429 | Scott, Charles L. | 1920 | Box 674 |
| Schulteis, Herman J. | 1889 | Box 116 | Scott, Charles P. | 1913 | Box 479 |
| Schulteis, Margaretha | 1898 | Box 179 | Scott, Charles W. | 1907 | Box 333 |
| Schulter, Augusta K. | 1892 | Box 134 | Scott, D. M. | 1904 | Box 271 |
| Schultz, Anna Maria | 1913 | Box 479 | Scott, Edward L. | 1907 | Box 333 |
| Schultz, Cornelia Isador | 1891 | Box 127 | Scott, Eleanor G. | 1909 | Box 378 |
| Schultz, John George | 1898 | Box 179 | Scott, Eliza | 1874 | Box 55 |
| Schultz, Lewis | 1917 | Box 583 | Scott, Eliza J. | 1912 | Box 454 |
| Schultzbach, John | 1898 | Box 179 | Scott, Elizabeth | 1887 | Box 105 |
| Schultze, Henry | 1820 | Box 6 | Scott, Elizabeth C. | 1861 | Box 29 |
| Schultze, John Henry | 1899 | Box 187 | Scott, Elizabeth J. | 1910 | Box 404 |
| Schultze, Sarah E. | 1901 | Box 215 | Scott, George D. | 1906 | Box 310 |
| Schulz, Charles A. T. | 1872 | Box 48 | Scott, George W. | 1871 | Box 45 |
| Schulz, Henry | 1915 | Box 530 | Scott, George W. | 1919 | Box 643 |
| Schulz, John | 1883 | Box 84 | Scott, Gustavus | 1801 | Box 1 |
| Schulz, Julius | 1915 | Box 530 | Scott, Gustavus H. | 1882 | Box 80 |
| Schulz, Robert F. | 1902 | Box 235 | Scott, Henry E. | 1888 | Box 110 |
| Schulze, Menie | 1878 | Box 67 | Scott, James A. | 1919 | Box 643 |
| Schulze, Wilhelm | 1869 | Box 41 | Scott, James W. | 1890 | Box 121 |
| Schutt, William H. | 1893 | Box 142 | Scott, Jennie H. | 1908 | Box 355 |
| Schwab, Barbara E. | 1907 | Box 333 | Scott, Jesse | 1830 | Box 10 |
| Schwab, Conrad | 1913 | Box 479 | Scott, John A. | 1897 | Box 172 |
| Schwab, George J. | 1898 | Box 179 | Scott, John Johnson | 1896 | Box 165 |
| Schwab, John George | 1903 | Box 253 | Scott, John M. | 1909 | Box 378 |

| | | | | | | |
|---|---|---|---|---|---|---|
| Scott, John T. | 1893 | Box 142 | Searight, Joseph D. | 1910 | Box 404 |
| Scott, John W. | 1883 | Box 84 | Searle, Anna F. | 1909 | Box 378 |
| Scott, Julia T. | 1908 | Box 355 | Searle, Henry | 1892 | Box 134 |
| Scott, Lewis | 1915 | Box 530 | Sears, Alice R. | 1920 | Box 674 |
| Scott, Margret | 1806 | Box 2 | Sears, Clinton M. | 1867 | Box 38 |
| Scott, Martha | 1909 | Box 378 | Sears, James W. | 1853 | Box 22 |
| Scott, Martha A. | 1894 | Box 149 | Sears, Julien | 1900 | Box 199 |
| Scott, Mary | 1806 | Box 2 | Seaton, Daniel P. | 1918 | Box 612 |
| Scott, Mary Elizabeth | 1910 | Box 404 | Seaton, Sarah F. | 1915 | Box 530 |
| Scott, Mary Ellen | 1903 | Box 253 | Seaver, Jonathan | 1864 | Box 32 |
| Scott, Mary M. | 1911 | Box 429 | Seavey, Hannah V. | 1903 | Box 253 |
| Scott, Mary M. | 1914 | Box 503 | Seawell, Molly Elliot | 1916 | Box 556 |
| Scott, Moses | 1902 | Box 235 | Seay, Mary Tilton | 1918 | Box 612 |
| Scott, Rebecca B. | 1897 | Box 172 | Seay, Samuel Jr. | 1913 | Box 479 |
| Scott, Richard W. | 1885 | Box 94 | Sebring, James E. | 1894 | Box 149 |
| Scott, Richard Marshall | 1915 | Box 530 | Sebring, Rachel | 1898 | Box 179 |
| Scott, Sabert | 1824 | Box 8 | Sechrist, Laura Debrue | 1910 | Box 404 |
| Scott, Samuel | 1892 | Box 134 | Seckendorff, Gertrude Heléne | 1913 | Box 479 |
| Scott, Sarah | 1884 | Box 89 | Sedgwick, Emma | 1905 | Box 290 |
| Scott, Sarah C. | 1919 | Box 643 | Seebode, Henry | 1894 | Box 149 |
| Scott, Upton | 1872 | Box 48 | Seek, Sarah Main | 1907 | Box 333 |
| Scott, Virginia | 1845 | Box 17 | Seeley, Eva | 1916 | Box 556 |
| Scott, William A. | 1906 | Box 310 | Seelig, Mary H. | 1874 | Box 55 |
| Scott, William A. | 1846 | Box 18 | Seely, Franklin A. | 1895 | Box 157 |
| Scott, William F. | 1916 | Box 556 | Seely, George Dallas | 1908 | Box 356 |
| Scott, William H. | 1918 | Box 612 | Seeney, Emma | 1917 | Box 583 |
| Scott, William K. | 1911 | Box 429 | Sefton, Sarah C. | 1911 | Box 429 |
| Scott, William Laurence | 1911 | Box 429 | Sefton, William Murray | 1903 | Box 253 |
| Scott, William Owen Nixon | 1917 | Box 583 | Seibel, John | 1903 | Box 253 |
| Scott, William T. | 1908 | Box 356 | Seibert, Albina | 1911 | Box 429 |
| Scriber, Columbus | 1885 | Box 94 | Seibert, Samuel Rush | 1909 | Box 378 |
| Scrivener, Elizabeth A. | 1889 | Box 116 | Seibold, Justine W. | 1899 | Box 187 |
| Scrivener, James E. | 1884 | Box 89 | Seiler, Franz William | 1876 | Box 62 |
| Scrivener, John | 1871 | Box 46 | Seiler, John A. | 1919 | Box 643 |
| Scrivener, John D. | 1909 | Box 378 | Seip, Albert N. | 1918 | Box 612 |
| Scrivener, Thomas | 1891 | Box 127 | Seip, Annie C. | 1914 | Box 503 |
| Scrivner, Mary Ann | 1868 | Box 40 | Seitz, George W. | 1912 | Box 454 |
| Scroggins, Hattie | 1919 | Box 643 | Seitz, John | 1913 | Box 479 |
| Scudder, Nancy B. | 1893 | Box 142 | Seizd, Frederick | 1848 | Box 19 |
| Scudder, William Henry | 1915 | Box 530 | Selbie, Elizabeth | 1911 | Box 429 |
| Scully, John S. | 1914 | Box 503 | Selby, Alice | 1914 | Box 503 |
| Scully, William | 1907 | Box 333 | Selby, Henry | 1805 | Box 2 |
| Seager, Eliza | 1894 | Box 149 | Selby, James C. | 1904 | Box 271 |
| Seal, William D. | 1882 | Box 80 | Selby, Joshua W. | 1915 | Box 530 |
| Sealey, Alexander | 1909 | Box 378 | Selby, Verlindo | 1815 | Box 4 |
| Seals, Charles | 1873 | Box 52 | Selden, George S. | 1864 | Box 33 |
| Seals, George W. | 1920 | Box 674 | Selden, Robert R. | 1900 | Box 199 |
| Seaman, Hannah | 1910 | Box 404 | Selden, William | 1874 | Box 55 |
| Seaman, John G. | 1889 | Box 116 | Seldner, Eva | 1911 | Box 429 |
| Seaman, Samuel Lewis | 1821 | Box 7 | Seldner, George L. | 1911 | Box 429 |
| Seaman, William Henry | 1910 | Box 404 | Seldner, Joseph Jonas | 1911 | Box 429 |
| Searcy, Robert Eastin | 1830 | Box 10 | Seldner, Lewis | 1882 | Box 80 |

| | | | | | | |
|---|---|---|---|---|---|---|
| Selfridge, Ellen Shepley | 1905 | Box 290 | Seufert, Anna J. | 1903 | Box 253 |
| Selfridge, H. Louisa C. | 1896 | Box 165 | Seufert, Francis | 1894 | Box 149 |
| Selfridge, Thomas O. | 1903 | Box 253 | Seufert, John | 1913 | Box 479 |
| Seligman, Abraham | 1890 | Box 121 | Seufferle, George J. | 1913 | Box 479 |
| Seligson, Herman A. | 1891 | Box 127 | Seufferle, William Lowndes | 1898 | Box 179 |
| Seller, James | 1801 | Box 1 | Severson, Frances Ann | 1908 | Box 356 |
| Sellhausen, Babette | 1912 | Box 454 | Severson, William H. | 1915 | Box 530 |
| Sellhausen, Emilie P. | 1914 | Box 503 | Seville, William Penn | 1913 | Box 479 |
| Sellhausen, Ernest A. | 1914 | Box 503 | Sewall, Clement | 1829 | Box 10 |
| Sellhausen, Frederich W. | 1881 | Box 76 | Sewall, Elizabeth Carroll | 1824 | Box 8 |
| Sellhausen, Philip August | 1880 | Box 73 | Sewall, Frank | 1915 | Box 531 |
| Sellman, John J. M. | 1902 | Box 235 | Sewall, Robert | 1821 | Box 7 |
| Sellner John | 1900 | Box 199 | Sewall, Thomas | 1845 | Box 17 |
| Sells Michael | 1897 | Box 172 | Seward, Olive Risley | 1909 | Box 378 |
| Seltz, Marie F. | 1908 | Box 356 | Sewell, Charles H. | 1904 | Box 271 |
| Selvey, Louisa | 1868 | Box 40 | Sewell, James B. | 1915 | Box 531 |
| Semken, Henry C. T. | 1895 | Box 157 | Sexton, Daniel Joseph | 1895 | Box 157 |
| Semken, Susan E. L. | 1900 | Box 199 | Sexton, Patrick | 1895 | Box 157 |
| Semmelbauer, Margueretta F. | 1914 | Box 503 | Seybert, Henry | 1904 | Box 271 |
| Semmes, Edmonia | 1903 | Box 253 | Seymour, Bela Newton | 1903 | Box 253 |
| Semmes, Henrietta | 1833 | Box 12 | Seymour, Emily M. | 1901 | Box 215 |
| Semmes, J. Hall | 1912 | Box 454 | Seymour, George T. | 1902 | Box 235 |
| Semmes, Joseph | 1832 | Box 11 | Seymour, Mary Catharine | 1906 | Box 310 |
| Semmes, Mary J. | 1914 | Box 503 | Seymour, Virginia C. | 1914 | Box 503 |
| Semmes, Raphael | 1846 | Box 18 | Seymour, William D. | 1855 | Box 24 |
| Semple, Estelle H. | 1916 | Box 556 | Seymour, William F. | 1889 | Box 116 |
| Semple, Letitia Tyler | 1908 | Box 356 | Shaaff, John Thomas | 1819 | Box 6 |
| Senay, Harry J. | 1915 | Box 530 | Shaaff, Mary | 1860 | Box 29 |
| Sendorff, Elizabeth | 1914 | Box 503 | Shacklett, Harriet W. | 1892 | Box 134 |
| Sener, Henry C. | 1891 | Box 127 | Shadd, Furmann J. | 1908 | Box 356 |
| Seney, James | 1907 | Box 333 | Shafer, Charles A. | 1920 | Box 674 |
| Seney, Mary | 1882 | Box 80 | Shafer, Frank B. | 1916 | Box 556 |
| Senft, William | 1912 | Box 454 | Shafer, John | 1906 | Box 310 |
| Senge, Henry | 1899 | Box 187 | Shaffer, Augustus L. | 1888 | Box 110 |
| Senkind, Conrad | 1891 | Box 127 | Shaffer, Catherine | 1897 | Box 172 |
| Senseney, Francis G. | 1891 | Box 127 | Shaffer, Edward | 1912 | Box 455 |
| Senseney, George E. | 1869 | Box 41 | Shaffer, Thomas J. | 1892 | Box 134 |
| Senter, Louisa J. | 1896 | Box 165 | Shailer, Thomas | 1882 | Box 80 |
| Sergeant, Adeline | 1876 | Box 62 | Shaler, Florence Stidham | 1918 | Box 612 |
| Sergeant, John | 1854 | Box 23 | Shaler, Sophia Penn | 1918 | Box 612 |
| Sergeon, Sylvester | 1892 | Box 134 | Shallenberger, Elizabeth | 1912 | Box 455 |
| Serpell, G. M. | 1917 | Box 583 | Shallenberger, George A. | 1902 | Box 235 |
| Serrell, John A. | 1919 | Box 644 | Shallenberger, William S. | 1914 | Box 503 |
| Serrin, Sarah A. | 1898 | Box 179 | Shamwell, Caroline Sophia | 1895 | Box 157 |
| Serrin, William | 1852 | Box 22 | Shamwell, Mary C. | 1895 | Box 157 |
| Serrin, William Durr | 1895 | Box 157 | Shanahan, Annie R. | 1902 | Box 235 |
| Service, Henry H. | 1887 | Box 105 | Shanahan, John | 1900 | Box 199 |
| Sessford, Charles Edwin | 1920 | Box 674 | Shanahan, Margaret | 1907 | Box 333 |
| Sessford, John | 1862 | Box 30 | Shanahan, Michael | 1879 | Box 70 |
| Sessford, Julia | 1866 | Box 36 | Shane, William T. | 1918 | Box 612 |
| Sesso, Saverio | 1917 | Box 583 | Shank, Charles D. | 1916 | Box 556 |
| Seuberth, John | 1869 | Box 41 | Shanklin, George | 1885 | Box 94 |

| | | | | | | |
|---|---|---|---|---|---|---|
| Shanklin, Lydia | 1899 | Box 187 | Shea, John | 1855 | Box 24 |
| Shanks, Catharine N. | 1879 | Box 70 | Shea, John | 1908 | Box 356 |
| Shanley, Patrick | 1915 | Box 531 | Shea, Mary | 1878 | Box 67 |
| Shanly, Jeffery Dillon | 1809 | Box 3 | Shea, Mary | 1910 | Box 404 |
| Shannessy, John | 1916 | Box 556 | Shea, Mary A. | 1907 | Box 333 |
| Shannon, Anna F. | 1920 | Box 674 | Shea, Mary Catharine | 1890 | Box 121 |
| Shannon, H. Georgeana | 1891 | Box 127 | Shea, Michael | 1865 | Box 34 |
| Shannon, John | 1904 | Box 271 | Shea, Michael J. | 1917 | Box 583 |
| Shannon, John H. | 1898 | Box 179 | Shea, Nicholas H. | 1917 | Box 583 |
| Shannon, Stewart | 1915 | Box 531 | Sheads, Ann Elizabeth | 1914 | Box 503 |
| Shannon, Thomas Jefferson | 1912 | Box 455 | Sheaff, Eliza | 1916 | Box 556 |
| Shannon, W. B. | 1920 | Box 658 | Sheaff, William S. | 1894 | Box 149 |
| Shannon, William A. | 1915 | Box 531 | Sheahan, Daniel | 1875 | Box 59 |
| Sharkey, William L. | 1873 | Box 52 | Sheahan, Jeremiah | 1882 | Box 80 |
| Sharp, George | 1907 | Box 333 | Sheahan, Mary | 1894 | Box 149 |
| Sharpe, Benjamin (Sr.) | 1875 | Box 59 | Sheahan, Mary | 1896 | Box 165 |
| Sharpe, Thomas | 1875 | Box 59 | Sheahan, Mary E. | 1911 | Box 430 |
| Sharpless, Henry | 1892 | Box 134 | Sheahan, Michael | 1894 | Box 149 |
| Sharretts, David E. | 1906 | Box 310 | Shearer, John A. | 1917 | Box 583 |
| Sharretts, Selma B. | 1906 | Box 310 | Shearer, Mary A. | 1903 | Box 254 |
| Shauter, Susan | 1900 | Box 199 | Sheckells, John W. | 1889 | Box 116 |
| Shaver, Lewellyn A. | 1910 | Box 404 | Sheckels, Margaret Rosalia | 1905 | Box 290 |
| Shaw, Alexander | 1872 | Box 48 | Sheckels, Mary M. D. | 1913 | Box 479 |
| Shaw, Alexander Provost | 1917 | Box 583 | Sheckels, Theodore | 1896 | Box 165 |
| Shaw, Anna Virginia | 1900 | Box 199 | Shedd, Adelaide M. | 1905 | Box 291 |
| Shaw, Annie M. | 1909 | Box 378 | Shedd, James J. | 1900 | Box 199 |
| Shaw, Edward | 1915 | Box 531 | Shedd, Samuel S. | 1913 | Box 479 |
| Shaw, Francis N. | 1854 | Box 23 | Shedd, William A. | 1906 | Box 310 |
| Shaw, Frank A. | 1914 | Box 503 | Shedd, William B. | 1874 | Box 55 |
| Shaw, Hannah M. | 1909 | Box 378 | Shedd, William P. | 1884 | Box 89 |
| Shaw, Helen L. | 1916 | Box 556 | Sheehan, Annie C. | 1919 | Box 643 |
| Shaw, Isabella | 1915 | Box 531 | Sheehan, James | 1915 | Box 531 |
| Shaw, John | 1824 | Box 8 | Sheehan, John | 1906 | Box 310 |
| Shaw, John H. | 1871 | Box 45 | Sheehy, Alice Sarah | 1910 | Box 404 |
| Shaw, Josiah | 1914 | Box 503 | Sheehy, Edward J. | 1896 | Box 165 |
| Shaw, Laura A. | 1898 | Box 179 | Sheehy, James J. | 1910 | Box 404 |
| Shaw, Lorenzo D. | 1912 | Box 455 | Sheeny, Patrick H. | 1911 | Box 430 |
| Shaw, Margaret A. | 1913 | Box 479 | Shehan, George Alexander | 1904 | Box 271 |
| Shaw, Mary Ann | 1905 | Box 290 | Shehan, Julia H. | 1904 | Box 271 |
| Shaw, Mary Ellen | 1895 | Box 157 | Shekell, Harriett | 1886 | Box 99 |
| Shaw, Mary Jane | 1907 | Box 333 | Sheldon, C. Augusta Searle | 1915 | Box 531 |
| Shaw, Nicholas S. | 1875 | Box 59 | Sheldon, Ellen H. | 1890 | Box 122 |
| Shaw, Richard A. | 1916 | Box 556 | Sheldon, George T. | 1904 | Box 271 |
| Shaw, Robert Tennent | 1879 | Box 70 | Shellabarger, Samuel | 1896 | Box 165 |
| Shaw, William H. | 1909 | Box 378 | Shellabarger, Sara R. | 1892 | Box 134 |
| Shea, Anne | 1871 | Box 46 | Shellenberger, Elizabeth | 1917 | Box 584 |
| Shea, Catharine | 1901 | Box 215 | Shelley, Josephine R. | 1906 | Box 310 |
| Shea, Cornelius | 1875 | Box 59 | Shelley, Richard | 1917 | Box 584 |
| Shea, Cornelius | 1887 | Box 105 | Shelley, Samuel S. | 1915 | Box 531 |
| Shea, Daniel | 1872 | Box 48 | Shellman, John | 1894 | Box 149 |
| Shea, Daniel | 1917 | Box 583 | Shelton, Charles F. | 1913 | Box 479 |
| Shea, Johanna | 1916 | Box 556 | Shelton, Charles W. | 1913 | Box 479 |

| | | | | | | |
|---|---|---|---|---|---|---|
| Shelton, George H. | 1920 | Box 674 | Shields, Bernard | 1873 | Box 52 |
| Shelton, Joseph G. | 1908 | Box 356 | Shields, Bridget | 1895 | Box 157 |
| Shelton, Mary | 1906 | Box 310 | Shields, Caroline H. | 1902 | Box 235 |
| Shelton, Newman | 1868 | Box 40 | Shields, Charles | 1890 | Box 122 |
| Shepard, Alice S. | 1915 | Box 531 | Shields, Charles A. | 1920 | Box 674 |
| Shepard, Clara Kibby Billings | 1910 | Box 404 | Shields, James Van Allen | 1904 | Box 271 |
| Shepard, Edwin M. | 1904 | Box 271 | Shields, James W. | 1864 | Box 33 |
| Shepard, Mida W. | 1920 | Box 674 | Shields, Josephine V. | 1905 | Box 291 |
| Shepard, Seth | 1918 | Box 612 | Shields, Margaret | 1897 | Box 172 |
| Shepard, William | 1901 | Box 215 | Shields, Margaret E. | 1915 | Box 532 |
| Shepard, William Augustus | 1899 | Box 187 | Shields, Mary B. | 1906 | Box 310 |
| Shepardson, Parmelia E. | 1900 | Box 200 | Shields, Mary L. | 1916 | Box 556 |
| Shephard, Martha E. | 1911 | Box 430 | Shields, Virginia | 1918 | Box 612 |
| Shepherd, Alexander | 1845 | Box 17 | Shill, Richard Edmund | 1893 | Box 142 |
| Shepherd, Azemia | 1915 | Box 532 | Shilling, George | 1917 | Box 584 |
| Shepherd, William S. | 1872 | Box 48 | Shimoneck, William C. | 1917 | Box 584 |
| Sheppard, Martha Virginia | 1904 | Box 271 | Shindler, A. Zeno | 1899 | Box 187 |
| Shepperd, Helen Y. | 1908 | Box 356 | Shinn, Caroline C. | 1915 | Box 532 |
| Sherbutt, Elizabeth | 1876 | Box 62 | Shinn, Luther E. | 1920 | Box 674 |
| Sheridan, Margaret | 1917 | Box 584 | Shinn, Riley A. | 1904 | Box 271 |
| Sheridan, Michael V. | 1918 | Box 612 | Shinners, Mary Jane | 1864 | Box 33 |
| Sheridan, Philip H. | 1888 | Box 110 | Shinnick, Margaret L. | 1918 | Box 612 |
| Sheridan, Thomas | 1903 | Box 254 | Shipley, Charles | 1904 | Box 271 |
| Sherier, John C. | 1918 | Box 612 | Shipley, Francis Lloyd | 1904 | Box 271 |
| Sherier, Nora T. | 1919 | Box 643 | Shipman, Caroline A. | 1915 | Box 532 |
| Sheriff, Emmeline | 1875 | Box 59 | Shippen, William | 1875 | Box 59 |
| Sheriff, George L. | 1893 | Box 142 | Shiras, Alexander | 1875 | Box 59 |
| Sheriff, Levi | 1854 | Box 23 | Shirley, Ann D. | 1873 | Box 52 |
| Sheriff, Mary L. | 1900 | Box 200 | Shirley, James R. | 1906 | Box 310 |
| Sheriff, Susan Beall | 1912 | Box 455 | Shirley, Martha L. | 1917 | Box 584 |
| Sherman, Amelia | 1901 | Box 215 | Shiverick, Elizabeth H. | 1889 | Box 116 |
| Sherman, Caroline H. | 1892 | Box 134 | Shock, William Henry | 1906 | Box 310 |
| Sherman, Frank | 1918 | Box 612 | Shoemake, Harriet | 1900 | Box 200 |
| Sherman, Gale | 1909 | Box 378 | Shoemaker, Abner C. P. | 1890 | Box 122 |
| Sherman, George | 1862 | Box 30 | Shoemaker, Abner C. P. | 1920 | Box 674 |
| Sherman, Henry C. | 1896 | Box 165 | Shoemaker, Augusta C. E. | 1908 | Box 356 |
| Sherman, Jessie G. | 1884 | Box 89 | Shoemaker, Edward | 1906 | Box 311 |
| Sherman, John | 1900 | Box 200 | Shoemaker, Elizabeth H. | 1911 | Box 430 |
| Sherman, Margaret | 1900 | Box 200 | Shoemaker, Hannah L. | 1905 | Box 291 |
| Sherman, Stephen H. | 1886 | Box 99 | Shoemaker, Isaac | 1909 | Box 378 |
| Sherratt, Samuel | 1903 | Box 254 | Shoemaker, Isaiah | 1894 | Box 149 |
| Sherrill, Charles H. | 1882 | Box 105 | Shoemaker, Laura D. | 1911 | Box 430 |
| Sherrill, Edgar B. | 1914 | Box 503 | Shoemaker, Lewis W. | 1898 | Box 179 |
| Sherrill, Marie Jennie | 1920 | Box 674 | Shoemaker, Louis P. | 1916 | Box 556 |
| Sherrill, Sarah | 1897 | Box 172 | Shoemaker, Mary | 1874 | Box 55 |
| Sherry, Conrad | 1867 | Box 38 | Shoemaker, Mary E. | 1913 | Box 479 |
| Sherwood, Jessie Randolph | 1903 | Box 254 | Shoemaker, Pierce | 1891 | Box 127 |
| Sherwood, John W. | 1918 | Box 612 | Shoemaker, Samuel | 1891 | Box 127 |
| Sherwood, Josephine W. M. | 1896 | Box 165 | Shoemaker, William Lukens | 1906 | Box 311 |
| Sherwood, Mary | 1918 | Box 612 | Shomo, Catharine A. | 1899 | Box 187 |
| Sherwood, Thomas H. | 1905 | Box 291 | Shomo, John M. | 1899 | Box 187 |
| Shidy, William | 1904 | Box 271 | Shoomaker, William | 1883 | Box 84 |

| | | | | | |
|---|---|---|---|---|---|
| Shopland, Georgianna | 1919 | Box 643 | Sibley, William J. | 1897 | Box 172 |
| Shoppell, Grace Van Buren | 1907 | Box 333 | Sibrey, William | 1895 | Box 157 |
| Shoppell, Robert W. | 1920 | Box 675 | Siccardi, Giovanni | 1916 | Box 557 |
| Short, Edward | 1894 | Box 149 | Sickel, Catharine | 1918 | Box 612 |
| Shorter, Fanny | 1853 | Box 22 | Sickel, Charles A. | 1914 | Box 503 |
| Shorter, Isaac | 1911 | Box 430 | Sickel, Mary M. Post | 1919 | Box 643 |
| Shorter, Joseph | 1910 | Box 404 | Sickels, Antonia P. | 1919 | Box 643 |
| Shorter, Maria | 1862 | Box 30 | Siddons, J. H. | 1886 | Box 99 |
| Shorter, Rachel | 1851 | Box 21 | Sides, Abigail | 1853 | Box 22 |
| Shorter, Rebecca | 1900 | Box 200 | Siebel, George H. | 1918 | Box 612 |
| Shoulters, George H. | 1907 | Box 333 | Siebert, Eliza Oothout | 1915 | Box 532 |
| Shreve, Caroline E. | 1920 | Box 675 | Siebert, Emma | 1902 | Box 235 |
| Shreve, Charles M. | 1903 | Box 254 | Siebert, Louis Philipp | 1914 | Box 503 |
| Shreve, Charles S. | 1913 | Box 479 | Siedenberg, Barbara E. | 1917 | Box 584 |
| Shreve, Elizabeth | 1895 | Box 157 | Siedenberg, Diedrich | 1874 | Box 55 |
| Shreve, James H. | 1870 | Box 43 | Sievers, Henry Louis Christoph | 1902 | Box 235 |
| Shreve, James H. (Sr.) | 1909 | Box 378 | Sievers, Maggie W. | 1919 | Box 643 |
| Shreve, John | 1822 | Box 7 | Sigel, Pauline | 1907 | Box 334 |
| Shreve, John | 1861 | Box 29 | Siggers, George William | 1919 | Box 643 |
| Shreve, Mary | 1836 | Box 13 | Siggins, John J. | 1908 | Box 356 |
| Shreve, Samuel Francis | 1886 | Box 99 | Sigmund, Ann M. | 1895 | Box 157 |
| Shreve, William O. | 1901 | Box 215 | Silance, J. Vernon | 1920 | Box 675 |
| Shriver, Abraham F. | 1878 | Box 67 | Silance, John A. | 1914 | Box 503 |
| Shriver, David H. | 1920 | Box 675 | Silence, Alice R. | 1915 | Box 532 |
| Shriver, Mary Jane | 1919 | Box 643 | Silence, Caroline A. | 1903 | Box 254 |
| Shriver, William A. | 1920 | Box 675 | Silence, Sarah A. | 1910 | Box 404 |
| Shryer, Susan | 1875 | Box 59 | Sillers, Ellen | 1918 | Box 612 |
| Shubrick, William B. | 1874 | Box 55 | Silsby, Howard W. | 1909 | Box 378 |
| Shufeldt, Robert W. | 1895 | Box 157 | Silver, Tena | 1915 | Box 532 |
| Shuffle, Edwin | 1901 | Box 215 | Silverberg, Mary | 1919 | Box 643 |
| Shufflebotham, George | 1879 | Box 70 | Silverman, Harry | 1920 | Box 675 |
| Shugert, Caroline E. | 1889 | Box 116 | Silverman, Louis J. | 1920 | Box 675 |
| Shughrue, Michael | 1916 | Box 557 | Sim, Thomas | 1832 | Box 11 |
| Shugrue, Catherine | 1904 | Box 271 | Simi, Lorenzo | 1920 | Box 675 |
| Shugrue, John J. | 1902 | Box 235 | Simkins, Elizabeth M. | 1909 | Box 378 |
| Shugrue, Margaret | 1915 | Box 532 | Simmermacher, Catharine | 1878 | Box 67 |
| Shugrue, Mary | 1907 | Box 333 | Simmes, Elizabeth James | 1907 | Box 334 |
| Shugrue, Michael | 1894 | Box 149 | Simmons, Abby S. | 1901 | Box 215 |
| Shukk, Michael | 1917 | Box 584 | Simmons, Alice | 1910 | Box 404 |
| Shuman, Anna S. | 1918 | Box 612 | Simmons, Arthur | 1908 | Box 356 |
| Shunk, Alonzo W. | 1918 | Box 612 | Simmons, Charles W. | 1887 | Box 105 |
| Shunk, Lena A. | 1911 | Box 430 | Simmons, Charles W. | 1891 | Box 127 |
| Shurtleff, Albert T. | 1903 | Box 254 | Simmons, Eliza C. | 1891 | Box 127 |
| Shuster, Elizabeth M. | 1899 | Box 187 | Simmons, Helena C. | 1905 | Box 291 |
| Shuster, Samuel D. | 1911 | Box 430 | Simmons, John Brenton | 1906 | Box 311 |
| Shuster, William M. | 1897 | Box 172 | Simmons, Mary P. | 1918 | Box 612 |
| Shute, Henry C. | 1919 | Box 643 | Simmons, Primus H. | 1919 | Box 643 |
| Shute, Samuel M. | 1912 | Box 455 | Simmons, Samuel | 1901 | Box 215 |
| Shutz, Peter H. | 1889 | Box 116 | Simmons, William | 1845 | Box 17 |
| Shyne, Michael Roche | 1860 | Box 29 | Simmons, William H. | 1890 | Box 122 |
| Shyrock, Marab T. | 1919 | Box 643 | Simmons, William H. | 1895 | Box 157 |
| Sibbald, John A. | 1897 | Box 172 | Simmons, William R. | 1871 | Box 46 |

| | | | | | | |
|---|---|---|---|---|---|---|
| Simms, Alice R. | 1918 | Box 612 | Simpson, Mattie R. | 1901 | Box 215 |
| Simms, Ann | 1858 | Box 27 | Simpson, Robert | 1916 | Box 557 |
| Simms, Anna C. | 1903 | Box 254 | Simpson, Robert L. | 1911 | Box 430 |
| Simms, Catherine Virginia | 1906 | Box 311 | Simpson, Sarah T. | 1883 | Box 84 |
| Simms, Charles Ignatius | 1920 | Box 675 | Simpson, Solomon | 1804 | Box 1 |
| Simms, Charles Neville | 1878 | Box 67 | Simpson, Winnie S. | 1905 | Box 291 |
| Simms, Clarissa | 1917 | Box 584 | Sims, Basil | 1850 | Box 21 |
| Simms, Clayton E. | 1909 | Box 378 | Sims, Dora B. | 1908 | Box 356 |
| Simms, Craven | 1815 | Box 4 | Sims, Frederick M. | 1907 | Box 334 |
| Simms, Edward | 1884 | Box 89 | Sims, John M. | 1889 | Box 116 |
| Simms, Edward | 1804 | Box 1 | Sinclair, Arthur G. | 1916 | Box 557 |
| Simms, Eleanor | 1814 | Box 4 | Sinclair, Cephas Hempstone | 1920 | Box 675 |
| Simms, Eleanor C. | 1846 | Box 18 | Sinclair, Eugenia | 1917 | Box 584 |
| Simms, Eliza M. | 1906 | Box 311 | Sinclair, John S. | 1919 | Box 643 |
| Simms, Euridice F. | 1881 | Box 76 | Sinclair, Joseph McDonald | 1913 | Box 479 |
| Simms, Giles G. C. | 1909 | Box 378 | Sinclair, Mary Jane | 1906 | Box 311 |
| Simms, Ignatius | 1849 | Box 20 | Sinclair, Richard E. | 1916 | Box 557 |
| Simms, James J. | 1899 | Box 187 | Singay, George | 1831 | Box 11 |
| Simms, John A. | 1918 | Box 612 | Singer, Myrtle Maud | 1904 | Box 271 |
| Simms, John W. | 1902 | Box 235 | Singleton, Mary B. | 1886 | Box 99 |
| Simms, Joseph A. | 1898 | Box 179 | Singleton, Otho R. | 1889 | Box 116 |
| Simms, Lucinda | 1858 | Box 27 | Sinkler, Tersa | 1898 | Box 179 |
| Simms, Mary Georgiana | 1898 | Box 179 | Sinon, John | 1862 | Box 30 |
| Simms, Mary J. | 1912 | Box 455 | Sinon, Margaret | 1907 | Box 334 |
| Simms, Richard Douglas | 1920 | Box 675 | Sinsabaugh, Robert Augustus | 1899 | Box 187 |
| Simms, Rosa G. | 1910 | Box 404 | Sinsheimer, Moses | 1920 | Box 675 |
| Simms, Sampson | 1862 | Box 30 | Sintes, Eliza | 1884 | Box 89 |
| Simms, Willie Ann | 1901 | Box 215 | Sintes, Matthew | 1884 | Box 89 |
| Simon, Anne | 1916 | Box 557 | Sioussa, Augustus T. | 1864 | Box 33 |
| Simon, Charles Christian | 1904 | Box 271 | Sioussa, Charles | 1884 | Box 89 |
| Simonds, Stephen | 1910 | Box 404 | Sioussa, Frederick | 1894 | Box 149 |
| Simonds, Susan Charlotte | 1872 | Box 48 | Sioussa, John | 1864 | Box 33 |
| Simons, Amelia M. | 1915 | Box 532 | Sioussa, Margaret | 1886 | Box 99 |
| Simons, Francis Asbury | 1895 | Box 157 | Sioussa, Mary | 1881 | Box 76 |
| Simons, John T. | 1914 | Box 504 | Sipperley, Phoebe A. | 1916 | Box 557 |
| Simons, L. Blanche | 1897 | Box 172 | Sissel, Catharine Gloyd | 1816 | Box 5 |
| Simons, Theodore T. | 1919 | Box 643 | Sisson, Anna Rebecca | 1914 | Box 504 |
| Simonton, Edward | 1919 | Box 643 | Sisson, J. Henry | 1906 | Box 311 |
| Simonton, Florida | 1878 | Box 67 | Sitgreaves, Lorenzo | 1888 | Box 110 |
| Simonton, John W. | 1854 | Box 23 | Sixbury, Maria E. | 1913 | Box 479 |
| Simpson, Angelica | 1885 | Box 94 | Sixbury, Sidney A. | 1901 | Box 215 |
| Simpson, Benjamin L. | 1888 | Box 110 | Sizer, Lucian D. | 1918 | Box 613 |
| Simpson, Benjamin L. | 1913 | Box 479 | Skeen, Caroline | 1905 | Box 291 |
| Simpson, David | 1903 | Box 254 | Skehin, Eliza | 1897 | Box 172 |
| Simpson, George Washington | 1913 | Box 479 | Skelly, Elizabeth | 1904 | Box 271 |
| Simpson, Henry K. | 1918 | Box 613 | Skelly, Joseph P. | 1918 | Box 613 |
| Simpson, James | 1909 | Box 378 | Skerrett, Margaret Love | 1906 | Box 311 |
| Simpson, James | 1909 | Box 378 | Skidmore, Samuel | 1870 | Box 70 |
| Simpson, Joel T. | 1894 | Box 149 | Skilton, Ellen L. | 1917 | Box 584 |
| Simpson, Margaret K. | 1920 | Box 675 | Skinker, William K. | 1920 | Box 675 |
| Simpson, Mary | 1907 | Box 334 | Skinkle, Kate W. | 1906 | Box 311 |
| Simpson, Mary Eliza | 1917 | Box 584 | Skinner, Aaron Nichols | 1918 | Box 613 |

| | | | | | | |
|---|---|---|---|---|---|---|
| Skinner, Annie | 1904 | Box 271 | Small, J. Henry | 1918 | Box 613 |
| Skinner, James | 1807 | Box 2 | Small, James | 1893 | Box 142 |
| Skinner, Mills | 1908 | Box 356 | Small, Jane A. | 1899 | Box 187 |
| Skinner, St. John B. L. | 1872 | Box 48 | Small, John Henry | 1909 | Box 379 |
| Skirving, Ann | 1851 | Box 21 | Smallwood, George | 1903 | Box 254 |
| Skirving, James | 1865 | Box 34 | Smallwood, Henry | 1893 | Box 142 |
| Skirving, Mary L. | 1903 | Box 254 | Smallwood, John H. | 1896 | Box 165 |
| Slack, Amelia A. L. | 1897 | Box 172 | Smallwood, Lucy | 1919 | Box 643 |
| Slack, Fannie G. | 1916 | Box 557 | Smallwood, Martha Jane | 1902 | Box 235 |
| Slack, Mary Kemble | 1910 | Box 404 | Smallwood, Moses | 1879 | Box 70 |
| Slack, William B. | 1896 | Box 165 | Smallwood, Moses H. | 1894 | Box 149 |
| Slack, William Hall | 1895 | Box 157 | Smallwood, Ophelia | 1909 | Box 379 |
| Slade, John William | 1918 | Box 613 | Smallwood, Richard L. | 1857 | Box 26 |
| Slade, William | 1868 | Box 40 | Smallwood, Ruth | 1836 | Box 13 |
| Slagle, Charles W. | 1908 | Box 356 | Smallwood, William H. | 1909 | Box 379 |
| Slamm, Jane E. | 1895 | Box 157 | Smart, Ransom | 1918 | Box 613 |
| Slarrow, Mary Gordon | 1919 | Box 643 | Smedberg, Indiana C. | 1888 | Box 110 |
| Slason, William T. | 1899 | Box 187 | Smeltzer, Clara L. | 1916 | Box 557 |
| Slater, Anna M. | 1892 | Box 134 | Smidley, Antone | 1862 | Box 30 |
| Slater, David | 1891 | Box 127 | Smillie, Thomas W. | 1917 | Box 584 |
| Slater, John | 1883 | Box 84 | Smith, Addison M. | 1910 | Box 404 |
| Slater, John S. | 1875 | Box 59 | Smith, Agnes Maria | 1888 | Box 110 |
| Slater, Luther W. | 1909 | Box 379 | Smith, Albert | 1902 | Box 235 |
| Slater, Mary | 1918 | Box 613 | Smith, Alice Hamilton | 1908 | Box 356 |
| Slater, Matilda | 1879 | Box 70 | Smith, Amzi | 1907 | Box 334 |
| Slater, Samuel Edward | 1912 | Box 455 | Smith, Ann W. | 1865 | Box 34 |
| Slater, William | 1900 | Box 200 | Smith, Anna B. | 1896 | Box 165 |
| Slater, William A. | 1919 | Box 643 | Smith, Anna B. | 1904 | Box 271 |
| Slattery, Sarah | 1878 | Box 67 | Smith, Anna E. | 1894 | Box 149 |
| Slaughter, Alfred | 1910 | Box 404 | Smith, Anna M. C. | 1891 | Box 127 |
| Slaughter, James E. | 1901 | Box 215 | Smith, Anna McC. | 1907 | Box 334 |
| Slaughter, Lillian L. | 1917 | Box 584 | Smith, Anna Tolman | 1917 | Box 584 |
| Slaughter, Teresa | 1898 | Box 179 | Smith, Anne C. | 1865 | Box 34 |
| Slayden, S. W. | 1917 | Box 584 | Smith, Annie | 1910 | Box 404 |
| Sleator, Anna E. | 1888 | Box 110 | Smith, Annie | 1911 | Box 430 |
| Slee, James Henry | 1916 | Box 557 | Smith, Annie A. | 1916 | Box 557 |
| Sleeper, Ruby E. | 1909 | Box 379 | Smith, Annie E. | 1916 | Box 557 |
| Slemaker, Ellen Gordon | 1900 | Box 200 | Smith, Anthony | 1859 | Box 28 |
| Sleman, John Bottrell Jr. | 1911 | Box 430 | Smith, Augustine Jaquelin | 1918 | Box 613 |
| Slidell, Ann C. | 1889 | Box 116 | Smith, Augustus | 1914 | Box 504 |
| Slight, Ann | 1905 | Box 291 | Smith, Benjamin | 1908 | Box 356 |
| Slight, Pringle | 1862 | Box 30 | Smith, Blanch W. | 1911 | Box 430 |
| Slingluff, Edward S. | 1920 | Box 675 | Smith, Carrie | 1901 | Box 215 |
| Slingluff, Mary Naomi | 1920 | Box 675 | Smith, Catharine | 1865 | Box 34 |
| Slivey, William F. | 1901 | Box 215 | Smith, Catharine | 1899 | Box 187 |
| Sloan, Anna Stockton | 1914 | Box 504 | Smith, Catharine A. | 1862 | Box 30 |
| Sloan, John | 1864 | Box 33 | Smith, Catharine E. | 1879 | Box 70 |
| Sloane, Robert | 1872 | Box 48 | Smith, Cecilia Young | 1909 | Box 379 |
| Slosson, Marie C. | 1910 | Box 404 | Smith, Charles | 1902 | Box 235 |
| Smackum, John P. | 1899 | Box 187 | Smith, Charles Alvin | 1908 | Box 356 |
| Small, Andrew | 1867 | Box 38 | Smith, Charles C. | 1898 | Box 179 |
| Small, Emma Holly | 1904 | Box 271 | Smith, Charles E. | 1907 | Box 334 |

| | | | | | | |
|---|---|---|---|---|---|---|
| Smith, Charles G. | 1911 | Box 430 | Smith, George Spencer | 1897 | Box 172 |
| Smith, Charles H. | 1902 | Box 235 | Smith, George T. | 1865 | Box 34 |
| Smith, Charles H. | 1906 | Box 311 | Smith, George V. | 1905 | Box 291 |
| Smith, Charles H. | 1912 | Box 455 | Smith, Georgiana | 1918 | Box 613 |
| Smith, Charles M. | 1880 | Box 73 | Smith, Hamilton | 1857 | Box 26 |
| Smith, Charles Maurice | 1900 | Box 200 | Smith, Harry F. | 1917 | Box 584 |
| Smith, Charles R. | 1904 | Box 271 | Smith, Helen L. | 1893 | Box 142 |
| Smith, Charlotte | 1906 | Box 311 | Smith, Henrietta | 1841 | Box 15 |
| Smith, Charlotte M. | 1886 | Box 99 | Smith, Henry | 1845 | Box 17 |
| Smith, Christian | 1914 | Box 504 | Smith, Henry | 1888 | Box 110 |
| Smith, Christopher McP. | 1896 | Box 165 | Smith, Henry | 1889 | Box 116 |
| Smith, Claudius B. | 1914 | Box 504 | Smith, Henry | 1891 | Box 127 |
| Smith, Clement | 1839 | Box 15 | Smith, Henry C. | 1904 | Box 271 |
| Smith, Clinton | 1905 | Box 291 | Smith, Hilary M. | 1869 | Box 41 |
| Smith, Cornelius W. | 1892 | Box 135 | Smith, Hiram R. | 1906 | Box 311 |
| Smith, Covington | 1877 | Box 65 | Smith, Isaac | 1887 | Box 105 |
| Smith, Cruger W. | 1912 | Box 455 | Smith, Isaac Canfield | 1849 | Box 20 |
| Smith, Daniel A. | 1901 | Box 215 | Smith, Israel J. | 1913 | Box 479 |
| Smith, Darius E. | 1884 | Box 89 | Smith, J. Dempster | 1895 | Box 157 |
| Smith, David | 1903 | Box 254 | Smith, J. Henley | 1907 | Box 334 |
| Smith, Dennis | 1910 | Box 404 | Smith, J. Hopkinson | 1867 | Box 38 |
| Smith, Draper C. | 1876 | Box 62 | Smith, James | 1900 | Box 200 |
| Smith, E. Goodrich | 1873 | Box 52 | Smith, James H. | 1862 | Box 30 |
| Smith, Edward | 1890 | Box 122 | Smith, James H. | 1909 | Box 379 |
| Smith, Edward S. | 1875 | Box 59 | Smith, James L. | 1903 | Box 254 |
| Smith, Edward W. | 1891 | Box 127 | Smith, James M. | 1854 | Box 23 |
| Smith, Eldridge J. | 1906 | Box 311 | Smith, James W. | 1884 | Box 89 |
| Smith, Eliza Ann | 1892 | Box 135 | Smith, Jane | 1907 | Box 334 |
| Smith, Eliza Jane | 1900 | Box 200 | Smith, Jane L. | 1885 | Box 94 |
| Smith, Eliza Williams | 1911 | Box 430 | Smith, Jasper | 1895 | Box 157 |
| Smith, Elizabeth | 1886 | Box 100 | Smith, Jeremiah | 1904 | Box 271 |
| Smith, Elizabeth A. | 1883 | Box 84 | Smith, Jeremiah M. | 1906 | Box 311 |
| Smith, Elizabeth Peyton | 1891 | Box 127 | Smith, Jesse | 1912 | Box 455 |
| Smith, Elizabeth S. | 1903 | Box 254 | Smith, Johanna | 1884 | Box 89 |
| Smith, Ella | 1909 | Box 379 | Smith, John | 1812 | Box 4 |
| Smith, Ella Leonora | 1906 | Box 311 | Smith, John | 1813 | Box 4 |
| Smith, Ellen T. | 1919 | Box 643 | Smith, John | 1814 | Box 4 |
| Smith, Emily H. | 1894 | Box 149 | Smith, John | 1857 | Box 26 |
| Smith, Fanny G. | 1857 | Box 26 | Smith, John | 1863 | Box 31 |
| Smith, Flora Green | 1917 | Box 584 | Smith, John | 1864 | Box 33 |
| Smith, Francis H. | 1906 | Box 311 | Smith, John | 1868 | Box 40 |
| Smith, Frank A. | 1907 | Box 334 | Smith, John | 1870 | Box 43 |
| Smith, Frank B. | 1905 | Box 291 | Smith, John | 1892 | Box 135 |
| Smith, Franklin Guest | 1912 | Box 455 | Smith, John A. | 1868 | Box 40 |
| Smith, Frederick | 1852 | Box 22 | Smith, John A. | 1895 | Box 157 |
| Smith, Frederick B. | 1915 | Box 532 | Smith, John C. | 1878 | Box 67 |
| Smith, Frederick S. | 1867 | Box 38 | Smith, John Casper | 1874 | Box 55 |
| Smith, George | 1885 | Box 94 | Smith, John F. | 1901 | Box 215 |
| Smith, George | 1887 | Box 105 | Smith, John H. | 1876 | Box 62 |
| Smith, George B. | 1877 | Box 65 | Smith, John Hoffman | 1907 | Box 334 |
| Smith, George H. | 1909 | Box 379 | Smith, John L. | 1873 | Box 52 |
| Smith, George S. | 1908 | Box 356 | Smith, John T. | 1918 | Box 613 |

| | | | | | | |
|---|---|---|---|---|---|---|
| Smith, John W. | 1905 | Box 291 | Smith, Reuben S. | 1907 | Box 334 |
| Smith, John Wesley | 1911 | Box 430 | Smith, Richard | 1864 | Box 33 |
| Smith, Joseph | 1877 | Box 65 | Smith, Robert Atwater | 1920 | Box 675 |
| Smith, Joseph A. | 1892 | Box 135 | Smith, Robert E. | 1915 | Box 532 |
| Smith, Joseph E. | 1911 | Box 430 | Smith, Robert L. | 1904 | Box 271 |
| Smith, Josephine | 1906 | Box 311 | Smith, Rosie E. | 1908 | Box 356 |
| Smith, Julia | 1896 | Box 165 | Smith, Sally | 1860 | Box 29 |
| Smith, Julia Maria | 1903 | Box 254 | Smith, Sally | 1884 | Box 89 |
| Smith, Katharine W. | 1897 | Box 172 | Smith, Sally | 1902 | Box 235 |
| Smith, Laurastine Cotheal | 1916 | Box 557 | Smith, Samuel | 1839 | Box 15 |
| Smith, Lemuel | 1920 | Box 675 | Smith, Samuel | 1906 | Box 311 |
| Smith, Lena D. | 1910 | Box 404 | Smith, Samuel H. | 1915 | Box 532 |
| Smith, Lewis | 1856 | Box 25 | Smith, Samuel Harrison | 1845 | Box 17 |
| Smith, Lewis | 1920 | Box 675 | Smith, Sarah | 1834 | Box 12 |
| Smith, Lewis M. | 1875 | Box 59 | Smith, Sarah | 1897 | Box 172 |
| Smith, Louisa | 1899 | Box 187 | Smith, Sarah C. | 1919 | Box 644 |
| Smith, Lucinda | 1911 | Box 430 | Smith, Sarah Catharine | 1884 | Box 89 |
| Smith, Luther R. | 1913 | Box 479 | Smith, Sarah L. | 1911 | Box 430 |
| Smith, Lydia | 1884 | Box 89 | Smith, Sina | 1912 | Box 455 |
| Smith, Lydia J. | 1918 | Box 613 | Smith, Sophia H. | 1881 | Box 76 |
| Smith, Margaret | 1895 | Box 157 | Smith, Sophia R. | 1920 | Box 675 |
| Smith, Margaret | 1911 | Box 430 | Smith, Sophia W. | 1860 | Box 29 |
| Smith, Margaret Bayard | 1909 | Box 379 | Smith, Sterling T. | 1913 | Box 479 |
| Smith, Margaret Clare | 1862 | Box 30 | Smith, Susan Virginia | 1895 | Box 157 |
| Smith, Margaret Glen | 1824 | Box 8 | Smith, Susanna | 1827 | Box 9 |
| Smith, Maria B. | 1920 | Box 675 | Smith, Susanna | 1825 | Box 8 |
| Smith, Marietta M. | 1917 | Box 584 | Smith, Susanna Duvall | 1918 | Box 613 |
| Smith, Marshall L. | 1913 | Box 479 | Smith, Thomas | 1834 | Box 12 |
| Smith, Mary | 1890 | Box 122 | Smith, Thomas C. | 1916 | Box 557 |
| Smith, Mary | 1907 | Box 334 | Smith, Thomas C. | 1918 | Box 613 |
| Smith, Mary A. M. | 1904 | Box 271 | Smith, Thomas C. | 1913 | Box 479 |
| Smith, Mary A. W. | 1902 | Box 235 | Smith, Thomas H. | 1909 | Box 379 |
| Smith, Mary F. | 1919 | Box 644 | Smith, Thomas Jefferson | 1870 | Box 43 |
| Smith, Mary J. | 1897 | Box 172 | Smith, Thomas M. | 1890 | Box 122 |
| Smith, Matilda E. | 1894 | Box 150 | Smith, Thomas R. | 1914 | Box 504 |
| Smith, Mattie W. Powell | 1918 | Box 613 | Smith, Thomas V. | 1915 | Box 532 |
| Smith, Melende H. | 1910 | Box 404 | Smith, Thomas W. | 1919 | Box 644 |
| Smith, Mina R. | 1914 | Box 504 | Smith, Thornton | 1896 | Box 165 |
| Smith, Miranda B. | 1880 | Box 73 | Smith, Verlinda | 1861 | Box 29 |
| Smith, Napoleon J. | 1909 | Box 379 | Smith, Virginia Gadsby | 1906 | Box 311 |
| Smith, Nathaniel | 1876 | Box 62 | Smith, Virginia P. | 1908 | Box 357 |
| Smith, Nellie E. | 1914 | Box 504 | Smith, Virginia R. | 1856 | Box 25 |
| Smith, Norman B. | 1889 | Box 116 | Smith, Walter | 1848 | Box 19 |
| Smith, Oliver Hampton Sr. | 1919 | Box 644 | Smith, Walter C. | 1897 | Box 172 |
| Smith, Otto G. | 1913 | Box 479 | Smith, Walter H. | 1908 | Box 357 |
| Smith, P. Curtis | 1917 | Box 584 | Smith, William | 1900 | Box 200 |
| Smith, Peter H. | 1910 | Box 404 | Smith, William | 1908 | Box 357 |
| Smith, Philemon M. | 1912 | Box 455 | Smith, William | 1883 | Box 84 |
| Smith, Philip | 1886 | Box 100 | Smith, William | 1894 | Box 150 |
| Smith, Philip Van Ness | 1886 | Box 100 | Smith, William | 1809 | Box 3 |
| Smith, Phineas W. | 1906 | Box 311 | Smith, William A. | 1900 | Box 200 |
| Smith, Randolph | 1886 | Box 100 | Smith, William F. | 1914 | Box 504 |

| | | | | | | |
|---|---|---|---|---|---|
| Smith, William H. | 1920 | Box 675 | Snowden, Philip | 1912 | Box 455 |
| Smith, William R. | 1896 | Box 165 | Snowden, Samuel | 1886 | Box 100 |
| Smith, William R. | 1920 | Box 675 | Snowden, Theresa | 1904 | Box 271 |
| Smith, William Robertson | 1912 | Box 455 | Snowden, Thomas | 1804 | Box 1 |
| Smith, William Scharf | 1897 | Box 172 | Snyder, Anne Clapham | 1920 | Box 676 |
| Smith, William T. | 1900 | Box 200 | Snyder, Benjamin P. | 1897 | Box 172 |
| Smith, Willoughby | 1893 | Box 142 | Snyder, Clarinda C. | 1897 | Box 172 |
| Smith, Zilphia | 1881 | Box 76 | Snyder, Cyrus | 1906 | Box 311 |
| Smithmeyer, John L. | 1908 | Box 357 | Snyder, Jacob | 1866 | Box 36 |
| Smithson, Alice J. | 1918 | Box 613 | Snyder, James A. | 1900 | Box 200 |
| Smithson, Bettie | 1918 | Box 613 | Snyder, Sophia C. | 1906 | Box 311 |
| Smithson, Mary Jane | 1910 | Box 405 | Snyder, William O. | 1915 | Box 532 |
| Smithson, Thomas J. | 1886 | Box 100 | Sobotka, Franz | 1901 | Box 215 |
| Smolinski, Mary Ann | 1901 | Box 215 | Soevyn, Francis | 1895 | Box 157 |
| Smoot, Ann | 1854 | Box 23 | Soh, Pom K. | 1897 | Box 172 |
| Smoot, Ann | 1898 | Box 179 | Sohl, Christian August | 1896 | Box 165 |
| Smoot, Ann E. | 1887 | Box 105 | Sohon, Gustavus | 1903 | Box 254 |
| Smoot, Charles C. | 1864 | Box 33 | Solan, Frank J. | 1914 | Box 504 |
| Smoot, Charles C. | 1901 | Box 215 | Soloman, Moses | 1886 | Box 100 |
| Smoot, Charlotte Q. | 1897 | Box 172 | Soloman, William Thomas Sr. | 1905 | Box 291 |
| Smoot, Emily | 1893 | Box 142 | Solomon, Bertha | 1920 | Box 676 |
| Smoot, John H. | 1891 | Box 127 | Solomon, Charity | 1887 | Box 105 |
| Smoot, John W. | 1908 | Box 357 | Solomon, David | 1900 | Box 200 |
| Smoot, Joseph | 1857 | Box 26 | Solomon, Minnie | 1916 | Box 557 |
| Smoot, Louisa J. | 1916 | Box 557 | Solomon, Teresa | 1909 | Box 379 |
| Smoot, Mary B. | 1857 | Box 26 | Solomons, Rachel S. | 1881 | Box 76 |
| Smoot, Mollie E. | 1894 | Box 150 | Solomons, Zillah | 1918 | Box 613 |
| Smoot, Rachel A. | 1904 | Box 271 | Somers, James W. | 1904 | Box 272 |
| Smoot, William L. | 1891 | Box 127 | Somerset, Charles | 1915 | Box 532 |
| Smootz, Sarah | 1919 | Box 644 | Somerville, Arnold | 1867 | Box 38 |
| Smyser, Isyphena E. | 1913 | Box 479 | Somerville, David | 1812 | Box 4 |
| Smyser, William Henry | 1919 | Box 644 | Somerville, Margaret | 1899 | Box 187 |
| Smyth, Fannie E. | 1908 | Box 357 | Somerville, Thomas | 1899 | Box 187 |
| Smyth, Gertrude Hastings | 1919 | Box 644 | Sommenschmidt, Charles S. | 1908 | Box 357 |
| Smyth, John Beveridge | 1906 | Box 311 | Sommer, Elizabeth | 1886 | Box 100 |
| Snead, Fayetta C. | 1889 | Box 116 | Sommer, John H. | 1881 | Box 76 |
| Snead, Julia | 1902 | Box 235 | Sommers, Adeline Virginia | 1890 | Box 122 |
| Snee, Ellen | 1897 | Box 172 | Sommers, Edward | 1914 | Box 504 |
| Snell, M. Porter | 1910 | Box 405 | Sommers, Hermann | 1903 | Box 254 |
| Snell, William B. | 1891 | Box 127 | Sommers, Joseph | 1911 | Box 430 |
| Snellenburg, Joseph J. | 1905 | Box 291 | Sommers, Lena | 1909 | Box 379 |
| Snider, Ellen M. | 1910 | Box 405 | Sondheimer, Beckie | 1909 | Box 379 |
| Sniffin, Theodore | 1900 | Box 200 | Sondheimer, Julius | 1919 | Box 644 |
| Snodgrass, Joseph E. | 1880 | Box 73 | Songer, Sarah Ann | 1881 | Box 77 |
| Snow, Alpheus Henry | 1920 | Box 675 | Sonneborn, Louis | 1918 | Box 613 |
| Snow, Dexter A. | 1906 | Box 311 | Sonneborn, Moses J. | 1917 | Box 584 |
| Snow, Ellen Lane | 1917 | Box 584 | Sonneman,, Christine | 1917 | Box 584 |
| Snow, Gertrude E. | 1898 | Box 179 | Sonnemann, George | 1909 | Box 379 |
| Snow, Louisa | 1915 | Box 532 | Sonnenschmidt, Catharine | 1881 | Box 77 |
| Snowden, Eliza | 1890 | Box 122 | Soper, George F. D. | 1906 | Box 311 |
| Snowden, Gurden | 1885 | Box 94 | Sorrel, Francis | 1916 | Box 557 |
| Snowden, Gurden | 1908 | Box 357 | Sorrell, Elizabeth | 1915 | Box 532 |

| | | | | | | |
|---|---|---|---|---|---|---|
| Sorrell, Lewis A. B. | 1898 | Box 179 | Spealman, James | 1830 | Box 10 |
| Sorrell, Mildred A. Farrell | 1920 | Box 676 | Spear, Catharine S. | 1897 | Box 172 |
| Sorrell, William T. | 1914 | Box 504 | Spear, Ellis | 1917 | Box 584 |
| Soteldo, Antonio M. | 1898 | Box 179 | Spear, Robert | 1891 | Box 127 |
| Soter, John | 1882 | Box 80 | Spear, Sarah F. | 1917 | Box 584 |
| Soter, Maria | 1889 | Box 116 | Speare, Frank A. | 1915 | Box 532 |
| Sothoron, Elizabeth C. | 1900 | Box 200 | Speare, Willis R. | 1916 | Box 557 |
| Sothoron, James T. | 1897 | Box 172 | Specht, Charles | 1917 | Box 585 |
| Sothoron, Susanna | 1835 | Box 13 | Specht, Louise Pauline | 1919 | Box 644 |
| Soule, Maurice J. | 1908 | Box 357 | Specht, Mary M. | 1918 | Box 613 |
| Soulé, John Hartley | 1911 | Box 430 | Spedden, Edward M. | 1885 | Box 94 |
| Soules, Eliza Ellen | 1915 | Box 532 | Speer, Kittie | 1905 | Box 291 |
| Sousa, Antonio | 1901 | Box 215 | Speiden, Ann | 1846 | Box 18 |
| Southard, Townsend B. | 1909 | Box 379 | Speiden, Marian | 1866 | Box 36 |
| Souther, John | 1827 | Box 9 | Speiden, William | 1861 | Box 29 |
| Souther, John Kerfoot | 1909 | Box 379 | Speiden, William R. | 1904 | Box 272 |
| Souther, Letitia | 1897 | Box 172 | Speier, Henrietta | 1900 | Box 200 |
| Southron, Maria | 1882 | Box 80 | Speir, Gilbert M. | 1912 | Box 455 |
| Southwick, George N. | 1914 | Box 504 | Speiser, John Frederick | 1854 | Box 23 |
| Southwick, Margaret J. | 1918 | Box 613 | Spellissy, Ellen | 1911 | Box 430 |
| Sowers, Zachariah T. | 1919 | Box 644 | Spelshouse, Katherine | 1918 | Box 613 |
| Spackman, Mary Dora | 1904 | Box 272 | Spence, Adolph Nichols | 1916 | Box 557 |
| Spain, Eliza T. | 1912 | Box 455 | Spence, Thomas Browning | 1918 | Box 613 |
| Spalding, Ann | 1838 | Box 14 | Spencer, Arabella | 1889 | Box 116 |
| Spalding, Archibald C. | 1885 | Box 94 | Spencer, Dan A. | 1887 | Box 105 |
| Spalding, Daniel James | 1918 | Box 613 | Spencer, Florence V. | 1914 | Box 504 |
| Spalding, Enoch | 1829 | Box 10 | Spencer, George E. | 1893 | Box 142 |
| Spalding, John | 1817 | Box 5 | Spencer, Henry C. | 1891 | Box 127 |
| Spalding, Lucy | 1893 | Box 142 | Spencer, John | 1891 | Box 127 |
| Spalding, Marcella | 1866 | Box 36 | Spencer, Louisa Vivian | 1919 | Box 644 |
| Spalding, Martin John | 1876 | Box 62 | Spencer, Mary | 1909 | Box 379 |
| Spalding, Mary | 1829 | Box 10 | Spencer, Mary Ann | 1919 | Box 644 |
| Spalding, Richard | 1833 | Box 13 | Spencer, Matilda A. | 1911 | Box 430 |
| Spalding, Sophia H. | 1915 | Box 532 | Spencer, Samuel | 1906 | Box 312 |
| Spang, Virginia E. | 1909 | Box 379 | Spengler, Ottelia | 1913 | Box 479 |
| Spangler, James B. | 1904 | Box 272 | Spensley, John | 1917 | Box 585 |
| Spangler, Walter | 1893 | Box 142 | Sperry, Andrew F. | 1911 | Box 430 |
| Spanier, Louis | 1908 | Box 357 | Spignul, William H. | 1909 | Box 379 |
| Sparhawk, Benjamin F. | 1917 | Box 584 | Spillman, Margaret | 1915 | Box 532 |
| Sparhawk, Helen G. | 1909 | Box 379 | Spindle, John Powell | 1908 | Box 357 |
| Sparks, Augustus Reuben | 1871 | Box 46 | Spindle, Lelia Ellis | 1919 | Box 644 |
| Sparks, Abigail Power | 1920 | Box 676 | Spindle, Margaret Powell | 1919 | Box 644 |
| Sparks, Sarah A. | 1893 | Box 142 | Spindle, Robert H. | 1889 | Box 116 |
| Spatz, Columba | 1895 | Box 157 | Spittell, Maria | 1916 | Box 557 |
| Spaulding, James J. | 1914 | Box 504 | Spitzer, Frederika | 1916 | Box 557 |
| Spaulding, Lilian A. | 1904 | Box 272 | Spliedt, Jacob | 1911 | Box 430 |
| Spaulding, Louis | 1912 | Box 455 | Spofford, Ainsworth Rand | 1908 | Box 357 |
| Speake, Eleanor | 1811 | Box 4 | Spofford, Ophelia M. | 1896 | Box 165 |
| Speake, Letitia | 1867 | Box 38 | Spollen (Spaulding), John | 1907 | Box 334 |
| Speake, Mary Ann | 1835 | Box 13 | Spotswood, Williams | 1867 | Box 38 |
| Speake, Rufus H. | 1867 | Box 38 | Spottswood, James M. A. | 1910 | Box 405 |
| Speaks, Lillian Alexander | 1920 | Box 676 | Spottswood, William G. | 1917 | Box 585 |

| | | | | | | |
|---|---|---|---|---|---|
| Sprague, Abigail Vance | 1907 | Box 334 | Stalcup, Mary E. | 1907 | Box 334 |
| Sprague, Frank Harris | 1908 | Box 357 | Staley, Eliza | 1895 | Box 157 |
| Sprague, Kitty | 1910 | Box 405 | Stamler, George | 1913 | Box 480 |
| Sprague, William G. | 1905 | Box 291 | Stamp, Frances | 1819 | Box 6 |
| Spranger, Gay Beatrice | 1895 | Box 157 | Stanard, Martha | 1895 | Box 157 |
| Spransy, Benjamin C. | 1918 | Box 614 | Standiford, John Harvey | 1908 | Box 357 |
| Spransy, Brower F. | 1908 | Box 357 | Standley, Elizabeth C. | 1913 | Box 480 |
| Spransy, Joseph R. | 1901 | Box 215 | Stanford, Charles E. | 1900 | Box 200 |
| Spransy, Mary Ann | 1901 | Box 216 | Stanford, Helen R. | 1909 | Box 379 |
| Spransy, Wilbur F. | 1914 | Box 504 | Stanford, Leland | 1901 | Box 216 |
| Spratt, Sarah | 1838 | Box 14 | Stanford, William | 1915 | Box 532 |
| Sprigg, Daniel Francis | 1908 | Box 357 | Stanley, Anna Maria | 1895 | Box 157 |
| Sprigg, Mary Ann | 1877 | Box 65 | Stanley, Caroline A. | 1919 | Box 644 |
| Sprigg, Violetta L. | 1883 | Box 84 | Stanley, Charles H. | 1918 | Box 614 |
| Spriggs, Benedict | 1919 | Box 644 | Stanley, David Sloane | 1902 | Box 235 |
| Springer, William McKendree | 1903 | Box 254 | Stanly, Cornelia A. | 1899 | Box 188 |
| Springman, George A. | 1883 | Box 84 | Stanly, Fabius | 1884 | Box 89 |
| Springmann, Charles E. | 1915 | Box 532 | Stanowski, Charles Fredrick | 1919 | Box 644 |
| Sproesser, Christian | 1905 | Box 291 | Stansbury, Ida May | 1892 | Box 135 |
| Sproston, Emily V. | 1905 | Box 291 | Stanton, Catherine | 1901 | Box 216 |
| Sproston, George S. | 1900 | Box 200 | Stanton, Edwin L. | 1877 | Box 65 |
| Spunogle, Eleanor | 1854 | Box 23 | Stanton, Edwin M. | 1871 | Box 46 |
| Spurgin, William F. | 1904 | Box 272 | Stanton, Ellen H. | 1887 | Box 105 |
| Squire, Linus T. | 1907 | Box 334 | Stanton, Joshua Otis | 1891 | Box 127 |
| Squire, Susan J. | 1919 | Box 644 | Stanton, Marietta E. | 1916 | Box 557 |
| Squires, Mary E. | 1910 | Box 405 | Stanton, Matilda W. | 1914 | Box 504 |
| Sroufe, Robert | 1913 | Box 479 | Stanton, Rose Ann | 1880 | Box 73 |
| St. Clair, James W. | 1892 | Box 135 | Staples, Helen E. | 1903 | Box 254 |
| St. Clair, Susan L. M. | 1883 | Box 84 | Staples, Helen M. | 1902 | Box 235 |
| St. John, Mary | 1897 | Box 172 | Staples, Lavenia V. | 1907 | Box 334 |
| St. John, Mary F. | 1885 | Box 94 | Staples, Orren G. | 1918 | Box 614 |
| Stack, John | 1920 | Box 676 | Stapleton, Daniel Casey | 1920 | Box 676 |
| Stack, Maurice John | 1909 | Box 379 | Stark, Henry | 1865 | Box 34 |
| Stackpole, Thomas | 1872 | Box 48 | Starke, Willis | 1885 | Box 94 |
| Stadtler, Gottlieb | 1896 | Box 165 | Starkes, Mattie S. | 1917 | Box 585 |
| Staff, Ada M. | 1916 | Box 557 | Starkweather, John C. | 1890 | Box 122 |
| Staffan, George | 1903 | Box 254 | Starr, John W. | 1883 | Box 84 |
| Staffan, Mary Ann | 1890 | Box 122 | Starr, William M. | 1909 | Box 379 |
| Stafford, Denis J. | 1908 | Box 357 | Stathis, Mary Carolyn | 1920 | Box 676 |
| Stafford, Frederick H. | 1920 | Box 676 | Statter, William G. | 1899 | Box 188 |
| Stafford, Ira A. | 1904 | Box 272 | Statz, John | 1877 | Box 65 |
| Stafford, John J. | 1902 | Box 235 | Staub, Jacob F. | 1892 | Box 135 |
| Stage, Myrta | 1892 | Box 135 | Staum, Christian | 1865 | Box 34 |
| Stagg, Irene Lalor | 1919 | Box 644 | Stead, Cynthia Force | 1918 | Box 614 |
| Stahel, Julius | 1913 | Box 479 | Stead, Mary Force | 1895 | Box 157 |
| Stahl, Emma | 1906 | Box 312 | Stearn, William P. | 1910 | Box 405 |
| Stahl, Harriet | 1862 | Box 30 | Stearns, Mary D. | 1906 | Box 312 |
| Stahl, Henrietta H. | 1920 | Box 676 | Stearns, Mary E. | 1918 | Box 614 |
| Stahl, John W. | 1896 | Box 165 | Stebbens, Martha E. | 1903 | Box 254 |
| Stahl, Thomas B. | 1898 | Box 179 | Stedman, Buckley | 1879 | Box 70 |
| Stailey, Eliza Ann | 1884 | Box 89 | Stedman, Clarence Augustus | 1920 | Box 676 |
| Stake, James E. | 1914 | Box 504 | Stedman, Elizabeth B. | 1901 | Box 216 |

| | | | | | | |
|---|---|---|---|---|---|---|
| Stedman, William P. | 1915 | Box 532 | Stephenson, John A. | 1919 | Box 644 |
| Steel, John M. | 1919 | Box 644 | Stephenson, Joseph White | 1918 | Box 614 |
| Steel, Thomas M. | 1900 | Box 200 | Stephenson, Margaret | 1912 | Box 455 |
| Steele, Annie M. | 1919 | Box 644 | Stephenson, Paul | 1916 | Box 557 |
| Steele, Ashbel | 1869 | Box 41 | Stepp, Mary E. | 1918 | Box 614 |
| Steele, Grace V. | 1916 | Box 558 | Stepper, Andrew | 1854 | Box 23 |
| Steele, Horatio N. | 1905 | Box 291 | Steptoe, Diana | 1909 | Box 379 |
| Steele, Isaac | 1807 | Box 2 | Steptoe, William | 1892 | Box 135 |
| Steele, Samuel | 1850 | Box 21 | Steptow, Jane Elizabeth | 1915 | Box 533 |
| Steen, Elizabeth | 1870 | Box 43 | Sterett, Samuel | 1889 | Box 116 |
| Steer, Isabella | 1892 | Box 135 | Sterling, Virginia | 1882 | Box 81 |
| Steer, Phineas J. | 1892 | Box 135 | Sterling, Virginia A. | 1913 | Box 480 |
| Steers, Marie Grace | 1917 | Box 585 | Stern, Aaron | 1904 | Box 272 |
| Steever, Edgar Z. | 1879 | Box 70 | Stern, Adolf | 1920 | Box 676 |
| Steever, Edgar Zell | 1920 | Box 676 | Stern, Betty | 1918 | Box 614 |
| Steever, Margaret W. | 1874 | Box 55 | Stern, George | 1881 | Box 77 |
| Steever, Mary Rebecca | 1908 | Box 357 | Stern, Louis | 1920 | Box 676 |
| Stefansson, Steingrimur | 1913 | Box 480 | Stern, Simon | 1890 | Box 122 |
| Steffen, Henriette | 1907 | Box 334 | Sternberg, George M. | 1916 | Box 558 |
| Steffenhagen, Henry | 1916 | Box 557 | Sterns, Charles Merwin | 1918 | Box 614 |
| Stege, Paul E. | 1913 | Box 480 | Sterrett, Samuel | 1916 | Box 558 |
| Stegmaier, Michael | 1876 | Box 62 | Stetnik, Staneslaus | 1915 | Box 533 |
| Steibel, Francis John | 1917 | Box 585 | Stetson, Maria A. | 1872 | Box 48 |
| Steiger, William T. | 1892 | Box 135 | Stettinius, John | 1834 | Box 12 |
| Stein, G. W. | 1908 | Box 357 | Stettinius, Joseph S. | 1894 | Box 150 |
| Stein, John C. | 1910 | Box 405 | Stettinius, Mary Ann | 1881 | Box 77 |
| Stein, Josephine Amelia | 1913 | Box 480 | Steuart, Margaret | 1853 | Box 22 |
| Stein, Nathan | 1918 | Box 614 | Steuart, Maria H. | 1900 | Box 200 |
| Stein, Robert | 1917 | Box 585 | Steuart, Maria H. | 1899 | Box 188 |
| Steinberg, Henry | 1920 | Box 676 | Steurnagel, Conrad | 1891 | Box 127 |
| Steinem, Isaac | 1900 | Box 200 | Steurnagel, Mary | 1891 | Box 127 |
| Steinle, Frederick | 1910 | Box 405 | Stevens, Adie Allen | 1918 | Box 614 |
| Steinle, Sabine C. | 1912 | Box 455 | Stevens, Charles A. | 1900 | Box 200 |
| Stelle, Edward B. | 1872 | Box 48 | Stevens, Charlotte E. | 1908 | Box 357 |
| Stelle, Rosa W. | 1920 | Box 676 | Stevens, Dianthia K. | 1909 | Box 379 |
| Stello, Henry | 1877 | Box 65 | Stevens, Durham White | 1908 | Box 357 |
| Stellwagen, Charles K. | 1908 | Box 357 | Stevens, Edward | 1920 | Box 676 |
| Stellwagen, Eliza S. | 1896 | Box 165 | Stevens, Eliza J. | 1909 | Box 379 |
| Stelzle, Lorenz | 1898 | Box 179 | Stevens, Ernestine H. | 1917 | Box 585 |
| Stembel, James McBride | 1907 | Box 334 | Stevens, Frederick C. (Sr.) | 1916 | Box 558 |
| Stembel, Louise Deshler | 1904 | Box 272 | Stevens, George F. | 1907 | Box 334 |
| Stemble, Roger N. | 1901 | Box 216 | Stevens, Henry E. | 1886 | Box 100 |
| Stephen, Charles H. | 1886 | Box 100 | Stevens, Ida Little | 1903 | Box 254 |
| Stephen, Virginia | 1898 | Box 179 | Stevens, Joseph T. | 1892 | Box 135 |
| Stephens, John Edmondson | 1919 | Box 644 | Stevens, Moses T. | 1908 | Box 357 |
| Stephens, Mary L. | 1902 | Box 235 | Stevens, Robert J. | 1890 | Box 122 |
| Stephens, Thomas A. | 1919 | Box 644 | Stevens, Robert William | 1910 | Box 405 |
| Stephenson, Ambrose H. | 1911 | Box 431 | Stevens, Roswell | 1897 | Box 172 |
| Stephenson, Anna E. | 1889 | Box 116 | Stevens, Samuel | 1892 | Box 135 |
| Stephenson, Emily | 1915 | Box 532 | Stevens, Sarah E. | 1920 | Box 676 |
| Stephenson, George B. | 1877 | Box 65 | Stevens, Sophia L. | 1903 | Box 254 |
| Stephenson, John A. | 1892 | Box 135 | Stevens, William | 1904 | Box 272 |

| | | | | | | |
|---|---|---|---|---|---|---|
| Stevenson, Basil | 1892 | Box 135 | Stewart, Samuel | 1919 | Box 645 |
| Stevenson, Fannie | 1919 | Box 644 | Stewart, Susannah | 1866 | Box 36 |
| Stevenson, Mary | 1865 | Box 341 | Stewart, Thomas Tyler | 1901 | Box 216 |
| Stevenson, Matilda Coxe | 1915 | Box 533 | Stewart, Thomas W. | 1904 | Box 272 |
| Stevenson, Sally W. | 1898 | Box 179 | Stewart, Walter | 1900 | Box 200 |
| Stever, West | 1908 | Box 357 | Stewart, Walter | 1901 | Box 216 |
| Steverson, John | 1915 | Box 533 | Stewart, Walter | 1802 | Box 1 |
| Steves, Homer C. | 1919 | Box 645 | Stewart, William | 1858 | Box 27 |
| Steward, John H. | 1895 | Box 157 | Stewart, William H. | 1845 | Box 17 |
| Stewart, Albert | 1916 | Box 558 | Stewart, William M. | 1875 | Box 59 |
| Stewart, Alberta | 1901 | Box 216 | Stewart, William M. | 1909 | Box 379 |
| Stewart, Alexander | 1914 | Box 504 | Stewart, William S. | 1895 | Box 157 |
| Stewart, Alice A. | 1894 | Box 150 | Stickel, Mary Elizabeth | 1919 | Box 645 |
| Stewart, Alphonso C. | 1916 | Box 558 | Stickney, Francis H. | 1906 | Box 312 |
| Stewart, Amos B. | 1908 | Box 357 | Stickney, Harriet C. | 1915 | Box 533 |
| Stewart, Ann Eliza | 1908 | Box 357 | Stickney, Jeannie Kendall | 1903 | Box 254 |
| Stewart, Anna Howell | 1905 | Box 291 | Stickney, John M. | 1908 | Box 357 |
| Stewart, Augustus | 1912 | Box 455 | Stickney, Robert Clark | 1886 | Box 100 |
| Stewart, Benjamin | 1894 | Box 150 | Stidham, William F. | 1892 | Box 135 |
| Stewart, Caroline | 1911 | Box 431 | Stiebel, Emil Adolph | 1912 | Box 455 |
| Stewart, Charles | 1897 | Box 172 | Stiebeling, Anna M. | 1909 | Box 379 |
| Stewart, D. Shriver | 1897 | Box 172 | Stiefel, Caroline | 1909 | Box 379 |
| Stewart, Daniel | 1886 | Box 100 | Stier, Ann E. | 1906 | Box 312 |
| Stewart, Daniel Webster | 1882 | Box 81 | Stier, Frederick A. | 1906 | Box 312 |
| Stewart, Edward C. | 1914 | Box 504 | Stier, Henry Joseph | 1823 | Box 7 |
| Stewart, Elizabeth | 1886 | Box 100 | Stierlin, Charles | 1902 | Box 235 |
| Stewart, Etta B. | 1907 | Box 334 | Stiles, John | 1880 | Box 73 |
| Stewart, Franklin B. | 1905 | Box 291 | Stiles, Lewis | 1848 | Box 20 |
| Stewart, George F. | 1889 | Box 116 | Stillings, Elizabeth D. | 1844 | Box 17 |
| Stewart, Henry Clay | 1898 | Box 179 | Stillson, Adelaide F. | 1916 | Box 558 |
| Stewart, Henry Clay | 1899 | Box 188 | Stinchcomb, William W. | 1889 | Box 116 |
| Stewart, Howell | 1913 | Box 480 | Stinde, Charles W. | 1886 | Box 100 |
| Stewart, Hugh | 1820 | Box 6 | Stinemetz, Benjamin H. | 1902 | Box 235 |
| Stewart, Jennie E. | 1911 | Box 431 | Stinemetz, Samuel | 1867 | Box 38 |
| Stewart, John | 1863 | Box 31 | Stinemetz, Samuel W. | 1908 | Box 357 |
| Stewart, John | 1887 | Box 105 | Stines, Katharine | 1918 | Box 614 |
| Stewart, John | 1905 | Box 291 | Stinzing, Frederick | 1892 | Box 135 |
| Stewart, John A. | 1892 | Box 135 | Stinzing, John P. | 1902 | Box 236 |
| Stewart, John A. | 1899 | Box 188 | Stites, George J. | 1916 | Box 558 |
| Stewart, John F. | 1907 | Box 334 | Stitt, Francis U. | 1893 | Box 142 |
| Stewart, Juno | 1905 | Box 291 | Stitt, Martha | 1899 | Box 188 |
| Stewart, Lucinda | 1908 | Box 357 | Stöbesand, Carl A. | 1892 | Box 135 |
| Stewart, Margaret E. | 1893 | Box 142 | Stöbesand, Elise | 1916 | Box 558 |
| Stewart, Maria | 1880 | Box 73 | Stock, Charles | 1916 | Box 558 |
| Stewart, Mary Ann | 1891 | Box 127 | Stock, Ottilie | 1911 | Box 431 |
| Stewart, Mary C. | 1917 | Box 585 | Stockdate, Thomas R. | 1906 | Box 312 |
| Stewart, Minnie E. | 1907 | Box 334 | Stocke, Charles | 1867 | Box 38 |
| Stewart, Mollie | 1920 | Box 676 | Stocker, Caroline | 1899 | Box 188 |
| Stewart, Philip | 1911 | Box 431 | Stockett, Charles Augustus | 1913 | Box 480 |
| Stewart, Rachel | 1870 | Box 43 | Stockett, George W. | 1916 | Box 558 |
| Stewart, Rachel | 1920 | Box 676 | Stockett, James | 1893 | Box 142 |
| Stewart, Samuel | 1832 | Box 12 | Stocking, Edgar B. | 1917 | Box 585 |

| | | | | | | |
|---|---|---|---|---|---|---|
| Stocking, Mary A. | 1895 | Box 157 | Storer, Dorothy H. | 1851 | Box 21 |
| Stocking, Mary H. B. | 1893 | Box 142 | Storer, Euretta S. | 1846 | Box 18 |
| Stocking, Patty Miller | 1906 | Box 312 | Storer, Frances L. | 1895 | Box 158 |
| Stocking, Sarah C. | 1919 | Box 645 | Storer, Mary E. | 1914 | Box 504 |
| Stocking, Solon Walter | 1906 | Box 312 | Storey, James | 1906 | Box 312 |
| Stocking, Wilbur F. | 1875 | Box 59 | Storm, Charles Otto | 1905 | Box 291 |
| Stockman, Andrew H. | 1903 | Box 254 | Storrs, Eliza H. | 1903 | Box 255 |
| Stockman, Hugh R. | 1885 | Box 94 | Storum, Carrie E. | 1912 | Box 456 |
| Stockton, Asher W. | 1917 | Box 585 | Storum, James | 1910 | Box 405 |
| Stockton, Elvene M. | 1917 | Box 585 | Story, Mary Elizabeth | 1890 | Box 122 |
| Stockton, Francis B. | 1858 | Box 27 | Story, Mattie A. | 1909 | Box 379 |
| Stockton, Mary Ann Edwards | 1907 | Box 335 | Story, Myron L. | 1911 | Box 431 |
| Stockwell, Mark | 1805 | Box 2 | Story, Robert | 1890 | Box 122 |
| Stoddard, Agnes E. | 1898 | Box 179 | Story, William | 1877 | Box 65 |
| Stoddard, Chauncey | 1912 | Box 455 | Stotch, Frederick W. | 1899 | Box 188 |
| Stoddard, Joseph M. | 1919 | Box 645 | Stott, Charles | 1889 | Box 116 |
| Stoddard, Pauline C. | 1918 | Box 614 | Stott, Esther Ann | 1885 | Box 94 |
| Stodder, Phylenda M. | 1892 | Box 135 | Stott, Samuel | 1883 | Box 84 |
| Stohlman, Frederick | 1916 | Box 558 | Stotts, Jennie | 1914 | Box 505 |
| Stokes, John W. | 1914 | Box 504 | Stouch, George W. H. | 1907 | Box 335 |
| Stolpp, Fredericka W. | 1899 | Box 188 | Stouffer, Charles C. | 1918 | Box 614 |
| Stone, Charles A. | 1903 | Box 254 | Stoughton, Marion C. | 1910 | Box 405 |
| Stone, Charles Henry | 1822 | Box 7 | Stout, Mary A. | 1903 | Box 255 |
| Stone, Edward E. | 1892 | Box 135 | Stoutenburgh, James D. C. | 1900 | Box 200 |
| Stone, Elizabeth Belle | 1911 | Box 431 | Stover, Charles | 1846 | Box 18 |
| Stone, Elizabeth J. | 1892 | Box 135 | Stover, Sadie M. | 1906 | Box 312 |
| Stone, Frederick William | 1919 | Box 645 | Stover, Solomon | 1880 | Box 73 |
| Stone, Garaphelia B. H. | 1899 | Box 188 | Stow, Lizzie Miller | 1919 | Box 645 |
| Stone, George W. | 1918 | Box 614 | Strahan, Charles | 1846 | Box 18 |
| Stone, Guy | 1818 | Box 5 | Strahan, Susan Hooe | 1861 | Box 29 |
| Stone, Henry | 1846 | Box 18 | Strang, Caroline F. | 1920 | Box 676 |
| Stone, Israel W. | 1918 | Box 614 | Strang, Mary W. | 1902 | Box 236 |
| Stone, John | 1870 | Box 43 | Strasburger, A. Ross | 1911 | Box 431 |
| Stone, Leonard | 1894 | Box 150 | Strasburger, Mina | 1907 | Box 335 |
| Stone, Lester M. | 1910 | Box 405 | Strasburger, Sarah | 1915 | Box 533 |
| Stone, Margaret Ritchie | 1904 | Box 272 | Strasburger, Zody | 1920 | Box 676 |
| Stone, Marvin C. | 1899 | Box 188 | Straub, Eva | 1918 | Box 614 |
| Stone, Mary F. | 1913 | Box 480 | Straub, Joseph | 1890 | Box 122 |
| Stone, Nehemiah | 1883 | Box 84 | Straughn, Martin Norris | 1919 | Box 645 |
| Stone, Rachael | 1875 | Box 59 | Straus, William S. | 1888 | Box 110 |
| Stone, Robert King | 1872 | Box 48 | Strauss, Albert C. | 1909 | Box 380 |
| Stone, Robert King | 1890 | Box 122 | Strauss, Christina | 1903 | Box 255 |
| Stone, Sarah Sophia | 1917 | Box 585 | Strauss, Flossie G. | 1916 | Box 558 |
| Stone, Sarah Sophia | 1917 | Box 584 | Strayer, Minnie W. | 1910 | Box 405 |
| Stone, Thomas | 1907 | Box 335 | Streb, Magdalena | 1905 | Box 291 |
| Stone, William J. (Jr.) | 1866 | Box 36 | Streb, Sophia R. | 1919 | Box 645 |
| Stone, William James | 1865 | Box 34 | Strecker, Helen von Eznatten | 1908 | Box 357 |
| Stone, William L. | 1893 | Box 142 | Street, Daniel Baen | 1912 | Box 456 |
| Stone, William T. | 1872 | Box 48 | Street, Jennie Harvey | 1918 | Box 614 |
| Stone, William W. | 1906 | Box 312 | Street, Peter | 1918 | Box 614 |
| Stonebraker, Daniel K. | 1909 | Box 379 | Streitberger, Henry A. | 1918 | Box 614 |
| Stoner, Elizabeth | 1914 | Box 504 | Streng, Caroline F. | 1920 | Box 676 |

| Name | Year | Box | | Name | Year | Box |
|---|---|---|---|---|---|---|
| Stretch, Joseph | 1820 | Box 6 | | Suber, Fannie | 1916 | Box 558 |
| Strickhardt, Charles | 1884 | Box 89 | | Suddards, Frances A. | 1913 | Box 480 |
| Strife, Jacob | 1901 | Box 216 | | Sudler, James K. | 1908 | Box 357 |
| Striffler, Leonhard | 1894 | Box 150 | | Sugenheimer, Salomon | 1906 | Box 312 |
| Strike, John | 1919 | Box 645 | | Sughrue, James D. | 1889 | Box 116 |
| Strobel, Clement | 1892 | Box 131 | | Suit, Samuel Scott | 1915 | Box 533 |
| Strobel, Elizabeth | 1906 | Box 312 | | Suit, Samuel Taylor | 1888 | Box 110 |
| Strobel, John G. | 1877 | Box 65 | | Suits, Margaret B. | 1914 | Box 505 |
| Strobell, John | 1867 | Box 38 | | Sullivan, Abbie | 1918 | Box 614 |
| Strobridge, Charles | 1918 | Box 614 | | Sullivan, Bridget | 1901 | Box 216 |
| Stroman, Gracie Mary | 1908 | Box 357 | | Sullivan, Bridget | 1914 | Box 505 |
| Stromberger, Julia B. | 1919 | Box 645 | | Sullivan, Catherine | 1905 | Box 291 |
| Strong, Arthur L. | 1914 | Box 505 | | Sullivan, Daniel F. | 1890 | Box 122 |
| Strong, Edward | 1881 | Box 77 | | Sullivan, Daniel J. | 1917 | Box 585 |
| Strong, Frank | 1903 | Box 255 | | Sullivan, Daniel Joseph | 1886 | Box 100 |
| Strong, Levi H. | 1898 | Box 179 | | Sullivan, Daniel T. | 1893 | Box 142 |
| Strong, Lucy Jane Williams | 1902 | Box 236 | | Sullivan, Edward J. | 1896 | Box 165 |
| Strong, Mary Ellen | 1915 | Box 533 | | Sullivan, Elizabeth | 1891 | Box 127 |
| Strong, Mary W. | 1908 | Box 357 | | Sullivan, Elizabeth M. | 1913 | Box 480 |
| Strong, Samuel | 1892 | Box 135 | | Sullivan, Ellen | 1897 | Box 172 |
| Strong, William | 1895 | Box 158 | | Sullivan, Ellen | 1911 | Box 431 |
| Strother, Benjamin | 1909 | Box 380 | | Sullivan, Ellen | 1915 | Box 533 |
| Strother, Francis M. | 1866 | Box 36 | | Sullivan, Emily F. | 1883 | Box 84 |
| Strother, Thomas R. | 1909 | Box 380 | | Sullivan, Harriett M. | 1880 | Box 73 |
| Stryker, Peter A. | 1884 | Box 89 | | Sullivan, Henry L. | 1910 | Box 405 |
| Stuard, Alice Emma | 1920 | Box 676 | | Sullivan, James | 1899 | Box 188 |
| Stuart, Abbie M. | 1912 | Box 456 | | Sullivan, Jenny | 1883 | Box 84 |
| Stuart, Donald G. | 1920 | Box 676 | | Sullivan, Jeremiah | 1895 | Box 158 |
| Stuart, Foster E. | 1912 | Box 456 | | Sullivan, Johanna | 1882 | Box 81 |
| Stuart, Harriet C. | 1911 | Box 431 | | Sullivan, Johanna | 1908 | Box 357 |
| Stuart, Henrietta | 1909 | Box 380 | | Sullivan, John | 1879 | Box 70 |
| Stuart, Jane Scott | 1914 | Box 505 | | Sullivan, John | 1888 | Box 110 |
| Stuart, Mary | 1891 | Box 127 | | Sullivan, John | 1892 | Box 135 |
| Stuart, Philip | 1830 | Box 10 | | Sullivan, John | 1902 | Box 236 |
| Stubblefield, E. C. | 1919 | Box 645 | | Sullivan, John D. | 1892 | Box 135 |
| Stueven, Charles E. | 1902 | Box 236 | | Sullivan, John T. | 1863 | Box 31 |
| Stuhmann, Mary E. | 1914 | Box 505 | | Sullivan, Katharine B. | 1906 | Box 312 |
| Stull, John | 1850 | Box 21 | | Sullivan, Margaret | 1893 | Box 142 |
| Stump, Joseph | 1905 | Box 291 | | Sullivan, Margaret | 1894 | Box 150 |
| Stumph, Eliza B. | 1912 | Box 456 | | Sullivan, Mary | 1891 | Box 127 |
| Stundan, Ellen | 1880 | Box 73 | | Sullivan, Mary | 1903 | Box 255 |
| Stuntz, Appolonia | 1902 | Box 236 | | Sullivan, Mary | 1905 | Box 291 |
| Sturges, Henrietta | 1919 | Box 645 | | Sullivan, Mary E. | 1909 | Box 380 |
| Sturtevant, Albert L. | 1913 | Box 480 | | Sullivan, Matlie | 1897 | Box 173 |
| Stutsman, Charles | 1917 | Box 585 | | Sullivan, Michael | 1897 | Box 173 |
| Stutts, Rufus A. | 1917 | Box 585 | | Sullivan, Michael | 1899 | Box 188 |
| Stutz, Emma K. | 1917 | Box 585 | | Sullivan, Michael B. | 1894 | Box 150 |
| Stutz, Frederick | 1908 | Box 357 | | Sullivan, Murtho | 1886 | Box 100 |
| Stutz, George Frederick | 1916 | Box 558 | | Sullivan, Patrick | 1872 | Box 48 |
| Stutz, Henrietta S. | 1905 | Box 291 | | Sullivan, Patrick | 1877 | Box 65 |
| Stutz, Louis F. | 1904 | Box 272 | | Sullivan, Patrick | 1915 | Box 533 |
| Styles, Hanrietta Jane | 1903 | Box 255 | | Sullivan, Patrick D. | 1905 | Box 291 |

| | | | | | | |
|---|---|---|---|---|---|---|
| Sullivan, Robert E. | 1905 | Box 291 | Swan, Caleb | 1810 | Box 3 |
| Sullivan, Rosina | 1890 | Box 122 | Swan, Jane | 1822 | Box 7 |
| Sullivan, Stephen | 1901 | Box 216 | Swan, Louise S. | 1920 | Box 676 |
| Sullivan, Thomas | 1857 | Box 26 | Swan, Martha J. | 1918 | Box 614 |
| Sullivan, Thomas C. | 1908 | Box 357 | Swan, William D. | 1910 | Box 405 |
| Sullivan, Thomas M. | 1904 | Box 272 | Swann, Edward | 1873 | Box 52 |
| Sullivan, Timothy | 1883 | Box 84 | Swann, Francis Le Roy | 1920 | Box 676 |
| Sultan, Joseph H. | 1911 | Box 431 | Swann, Kate L. | 1903 | Box 255 |
| Suman, Agnes | 1905 | Box 291 | Swann, Thomas | 1883 | Box 84 |
| Sumby, Sidney A. | 1894 | Box 150 | Swann, Thomas | 1896 | Box 165 |
| Summers, Aquila T. | 1881 | Box 77 | Swanson, Mary L. | 1917 | Box 585 |
| Summers, Edward W. | 1905 | Box 291 | Swanton, Lilian Frances | 1913 | Box 480 |
| Summers, John | 1890 | Box 122 | Swart, Anna J. | 1919 | Box 645 |
| Summers, Kizzi R. | 1881 | Box 77 | Swart, Sarah A. | 1909 | Box 380 |
| Summers, Louisa | 1877 | Box 65 | Swart, T. Barnet | 1891 | Box 127 |
| Summers, Mary Ellen | 1890 | Box 122 | Swayze, Lillian E. | 1917 | Box 585 |
| Summers, William H. | 1902 | Box 236 | Swearingen, Isabella V. | 1881 | Box 77 |
| Summerscales, Mary | 1905 | Box 291 | Swearingen, Mary E. | 1891 | Box 127 |
| Summerscales, Thomas | 1887 | Box 105 | Swearingen, Scott A. | 1913 | Box 480 |
| Summy, Ida M. I. | 1906 | Box 312 | Sweeney, Daniel | 1910 | Box 405 |
| Sumner, Charles | 1874 | Box 55 | Sweeney, Daniel | 1908 | Box 357 |
| Sumner, Helen Lewis | 1908 | Box 357 | Sweeney, Edward | 1874 | Box 55 |
| Sumner, Katharine | 1919 | Box 645 | Sweeney, Eliza D. | 1871 | Box 46 |
| Sunderland, Bryon | 1901 | Box 216 | Sweeney, Ellen | 1910 | Box 405 |
| Sunderland, Elizabeth M. | 1896 | Box 165 | Sweeney, Emma C. | 1916 | Box 558 |
| Sunderland, Emma V. Norris | 1917 | Box 585 | Sweeney, Henry M. | 1896 | Box 165 |
| Sunderland, Thomas | 1886 | Box 100 | Sweeney, John | 1898 | Box 179 |
| Supple, Margaret A. | 1890 | Box 122 | Sweeney, John | 1897 | Box 173 |
| Suraci, John | 1919 | Box 645 | Sweeney, Mary | 1852 | Box 22 |
| Susan, Graham | 1860 | Box 28 | Sweeney, Michael | 1900 | Box 200 |
| Sutcliffe, Ellner B. | 1919 | Box 645 | Sweeney, Patrick | 1886 | Box 100 |
| Suter, Henderson | 1920 | Box 676 | Sweeney, Patrick Charles | 1920 | Box 676 |
| Suter, Mary E. | 1906 | Box 312 | Sweeney, Roger | 1885 | Box 94 |
| Suter, Sarah | 1836 | Box 13 | Sweeney, William H. | 1912 | Box 456 |
| Sutherland, Edward B. R. | 1900 | Box 200 | Sweeny, George | 1849 | Box 20 |
| Sutherland, Fanny M. | 1881 | Box 77 | Sweet, Judith | 1904 | Box 272 |
| Sutherland, Lucretia A. | 1916 | Box 558 | Sweet, Parker Hall | 1887 | Box 105 |
| Sutliff, Mary E. | 1909 | Box 380 | Sweetman, Richard | 1898 | Box 179 |
| Sutton, Henry | 1900 | Box 200 | Sweitzer, Helen M. | 1914 | Box 505 |
| Sutton, John Robert | 1910 | Box 405 | Sweitzer, Nelson B. | 1898 | Box 179 |
| Sutton, Mary D. | 1917 | Box 585 | Swett, Charles D. | 1918 | Box 614 |
| Sutton, Richard | 1878 | Box 67 | Swift, Florence A. | 1916 | Box 558 |
| Sutton, Robert M. | 1910 | Box 405 | Swift, Jacque Bradley | 1914 | Box 505 |
| Sutton, William S. | 1916 | Box 558 | Swift, Joseph | 1918 | Box 614 |
| Suydam, Jennie | 1881 | Box 77 | Swift, Sarah | 1885 | Box 94 |
| Swails, Charlotte M. | 1910 | Box 405 | Swift, William H. | 1910 | Box 405 |
| Swaim, David | 1897 | Box 173 | Swiggett, William Y. | 1912 | Box 456 |
| Swaim, Mary C. | 1919 | Box 645 | Swindells, John A. | 1916 | Box 558 |
| Swain, Mary Antoinette Cheney | 1905 | Box 291 | Swindells, Martha Ann | 1916 | Box 558 |
| Swain, Moses P. | 1875 | Box 59 | Swingle, Catherine Jane | 1920 | Box 676 |
| Swain, William C. | 1916 | Box 558 | Swingle, Robert Duncan | 1905 | Box 291 |
| Swaine, Frank G. | 1914 | Box 505 | Swinton, William | 1807 | Box 2 |

| | | | | | | |
|---|---|---|---|---|---|
| Swope, Blanche M. | 1913 | Box 480 | Tallman, Katherine | 1897 | Box 173 |
| Swope, John A. | 1910 | Box 405 | Talmage, Frank De Witt | 1913 | Box 480 |
| Sword, John | 1814 | Box 4 | Talmage, Jennie DeWitt | 1907 | Box 335 |
| Sydnor, Ellen F. | 1912 | Box 456 | Talmage, T. Dewitt | 1902 | Box 236 |
| Sylvester, Elias J. | 1850 | Box 21 | Talty, David | 1915 | Box 533 |
| Sylvester, Marie F. | 1913 | Box 480 | Talty, John E. | 1892 | Box 135 |
| Symanoskie, Joseph | 1919 | Box 645 | Talty, Michael | 1890 | Box 122 |
| Symington, Mary A. | 1893 | Box 142 | Talty, Stephen | 1919 | Box 645 |
| Symons, Thomas William | 1920 | Box 676 | Taney, Augustine | 1823 | Box 7 |
| Syphax, Mary M. | 1913 | Box 480 | Tanner, Alethea | 1864 | Box 33 |
| Syphax, William | 1891 | Box 127 | Tanner, Zera Luther | 1907 | Box 335 |
| Sypherd, Thomas H. | 1916 | Box 558 | Taplet, William A. | 1899 | Box 188 |
| Syrich, Frank D. | 1915 | Box 533 | Taplin, Horatio N. | 1917 | Box 585 |
| Szemelenyi, E. | 1919 | Box 645 | Taplin, J. Corwin | 1907 | Box 335 |
| Tabbs, Barton | 1876 | Box 62 | Tappan, Catherine A. | 1918 | Box 615 |
| Tabbs, Elizabeth | 1830 | Box 10 | Tappan, Fannie M. | 1915 | Box 533 |
| Taber, Emily A. | 1919 | Box 645 | Tappan, John | 1868 | Box 40 |
| Tabler, Catherene E. | 1899 | Box 188 | Tappan, Myron A. | 1911 | Box 431 |
| Taff, Andrew F. | 1911 | Box 431 | Tappan, William S. | 1918 | Box 615 |
| Taff, George D. | 1892 | Box 135 | Tarbell, Jonathan | 1888 | Box 110 |
| Taff, Mary E. | 1910 | Box 405 | Tarlton, Lervis A. | 1866 | Box 36 |
| Taggart, John W. | 1871 | Box 46 | Tarring, Edward | 1915 | Box 533 |
| Tait, James A. | 1895 | Box 158 | Tascoe, Dennis | 1887 | Box 105 |
| Talbert, Charles E. | 1917 | Box 585 | Tashof, Sarah | 1920 | Box 677 |
| Talbert, George C. | 1862 | Box 30 | Tasker, John C. | 1891 | Box 127 |
| Talbert, George W. | 1911 | Box 431 | Tasker, Quinlin C. | 1837 | Box 14 |
| Talbert, Richard T. | 1907 | Box 335 | Tasker, Vernon C. | 1907 | Box 335 |
| Talbert (Talburt), Thomas | 1827 | Box 9 | Tastet, Nicholas | 1863 | Box 31 |
| Talbert, Tobias | 1905 | Box 292 | Tate, Elizabeth | 1884 | Box 89 |
| Talbert (Talburt), Zadock | 1826 | Box 9 | Tate, Joseph B. | 1858 | Box 27 |
| Talbot, Amelia | 1878 | Box 67 | Tate, Mary Ann Susannah | 1860 | Box 29 |
| Talbot, Joanna | 1902 | Box 236 | Tatlock, Lucy B. | 1919 | Box 645 |
| Talbot, Mary L. | 1882 | Box 81 | Tatum, Sledge | 1916 | Box 558 |
| Talbot, Robert E. | 1898 | Box 179 | Tauberschmidt, George | 1907 | Box 335 |
| Talbot, Sarah G. | 1873 | Box 52 | Tauffer, Elisabeth | 1881 | Box 77 |
| Talbott, Elizabeth | 1857 | Box 26 | Taulbutt, William | 1885 | Box 94 |
| Talbott, Robert W. | 1911 | Box 431 | Tayloe, Benjamin Ogle | 1870 | Box 43 |
| Talbott, William | 1885 | Box 94 | Tayloe, John | 1828 | Box 9 |
| Talburg, Mary | 1895 | Box 158 | Tayloe, Mary Lomax | 1913 | Box 480 |
| Talburt, Alexander | 1855 | Box 24 | Tayloe, Virginia | 1883 | Box 84 |
| Talburtt, Catharine A. | 1911 | Box 431 | Tayloe, Virginia | 1885 | Box 94 |
| Talburtt, Charles | 1821 | Box 7 | Tayloe, William H. | 1872 | Box 49 |
| Talburtt, Jennie L. | 1879 | Box 70 | Taylor, Abel | 1920 | Box 677 |
| Talburtt, Lewin | 1831 | Box 11 | Taylor, Alfred B. | 1903 | Box 255 |
| Talcott, Daniel S. | 1909 | Box 380 | Taylor, Anna R. | 1904 | Box 272 |
| Talcott, R. Barnard | 1910 | Box 405 | Taylor, Annie E. | 1887 | Box 105 |
| Taliaferro, Ella | 1896 | Box 165 | Taylor, Anson S. | 1917 | Box 585 |
| Taliaferro, Mary | 1917 | Box 585 | Taylor, Benjamin | 1857 | Box 26 |
| Tallerday, David S. | 1898 | Box 179 | Taylor, Benjamin N. | 1913 | Box 480 |
| Tallmadge, Abby L. | 1887 | Box 105 | Taylor, Bettie E. | 1903 | Box 255 |
| Tallmadge, Grier | 1887 | Box 105 | Taylor, Bridget D. | 1866 | Box 36 |
| Tallmadge, Theodore W. | 1905 | Box 292 | Taylor, Catharine | 1892 | Box 135 |

| | | | | | | |
|---|---|---|---|---|---|---|
| Taylor, Charles | 1899 | Box 188 | Taylor, Lizzie | 1903 | Box 255 |
| Taylor, Charles William | 1900 | Box 201 | Taylor, Margaret | 1903 | Box 255 |
| Taylor, Daniel Morgan | 1907 | Box 335 | Taylor, Maria Louisa | 1873 | Box 52 |
| Taylor, Diana | 1893 | Box 142 | Taylor, Maria S. | 1917 | Box 586 |
| Taylor, Edward | 1883 | Box 84 | Taylor, Mary E. | 1879 | Box 70 |
| Taylor, Edward | 1901 | Box 216 | Taylor, Mary Jane | 1872 | Box 49 |
| Taylor, Edward | 1916 | Box 558 | Taylor, Mary V. | 1914 | Box 505 |
| Taylor, Edward Thornton | 1882 | Box 81 | Taylor, Minnie C. | 1893 | Box 142 |
| Taylor, Eliza | 1874 | Box 56 | Taylor, Peter (Jr.) | 1920 | Box 677 |
| Taylor, Elizabeth | 1838 | Box 14 | Taylor, Phebe Warren | 1884 | Box 89 |
| Taylor, Elmer Ellsworth | 1914 | Box 505 | Taylor, Reuben | 1905 | Box 292 |
| Taylor, Emily F. | 1890 | Box 122 | Taylor, Richard | 1881 | Box 77 |
| Taylor, Erastus H. | 1902 | Box 236 | Taylor, Richard H. | 1886 | Box 100 |
| Taylor, Florence O. | 1916 | Box 559 | Taylor, Rose | 1901 | Box 216 |
| Taylor, Francis | 1860 | Box 29 | Taylor, Sabella B. Bryson | 1919 | Box 645 |
| Taylor, Francis F. | 1902 | Box 236 | Taylor, Samuel S. | 1888 | Box 110 |
| Taylor, Franck | 1873 | Box 52 | Taylor, Samuel S. | 1903 | Box 255 |
| Taylor, Frank | 1920 | Box 677 | Taylor, Sophia | 1868 | Box 40 |
| Taylor, Frederick | 1872 | Box 49 | Taylor, Sophia | 1890 | Box 122 |
| Taylor, Frederick S. | 1908 | Box 358 | Taylor, Stark B. | 1910 | Box 405 |
| Taylor, George | 1894 | Box 150 | Taylor, Thomas | 1906 | Box 312 |
| Taylor, George Myron | 1909 | Box 380 | Taylor, Thomas S. | 1908 | Box 358 |
| Taylor, George P. | 1907 | Box 335 | Taylor, Victoria | 1893 | Box 143 |
| Taylor, George W. | 1850 | Box 21 | Taylor, Vincent J. | 1859 | Box 28 |
| Taylor, George W. | 1920 | Box 677 | Taylor, Virginia A. | 1872 | Box 49 |
| Taylor, Georgia Gordon | 1913 | Box 480 | Taylor, William | 1867 | Box 38 |
| Taylor, Harrison | 1866 | Box 36 | Taylor, William | 1891 | Box 127 |
| Taylor, Hawkins | 1893 | Box 142 | Taylor, William C. | 1912 | Box 456 |
| Taylor, Henry | 1857 | Box 26 | Taylor, William H. | 1899 | Box 188 |
| Taylor, Henry | 1903 | Box 255 | Taylor, William K. | 1906 | Box 312 |
| Taylor, Henry C. | 1904 | Box 272 | Teachum, William K. | 1917 | Box 586 |
| Taylor, Horace A. | 1910 | Box 405 | Teagle, Edward | 1919 | Box 646 |
| Taylor, James | 1878 | Box 67 | Tebault, James D. | 1899 | Box 188 |
| Taylor, James | 1897 | Box 173 | Teepe, William H. | 1913 | Box 480 |
| Taylor, James | 1912 | Box 456 | Tegethoff, Anthony | 1902 | Box 236 |
| Taylor, James H. | 1914 | Box 505 | Temple, Catlyna T. | 1889 | Box 116 |
| Taylor, John | 1821 | Box 7 | Temple, Edward | 1892 | Box 135 |
| Taylor, John | 1822 | Box 7 | Temple, Major S. | 1902 | Box 236 |
| Taylor, John | 1849 | Box 20 | Temple, Mary J. Gunton | 1896 | Box 165 |
| Taylor, John B. | 1893 | Box 142 | Temple, Rachel C. | 1900 | Box 201 |
| Taylor, John G. | 1920 | Box 677 | Temple, William G. | 1894 | Box 150 |
| Taylor, John H. | 1871 | Box 46 | Temps, Henry Fred August | 1919 | Box 646 |
| Taylor, John J. | 1888 | Box 110 | Ten Eyck, Cynthia A. | 1909 | Box 380 |
| Taylor, John T. | 1916 | Box 559 | Tench, Thomas P. | 1852 | Box 22 |
| Taylor, John Y. | 1911 | Box 431 | Tenley, William H. | 1917 | Box 586 |
| Taylor, Joseph | 1806 | Box 2 | Tenly, Effie L. | 1919 | Box 646 |
| Taylor, Joseph Clarence | 1901 | Box 216 | Tennally, Sarah | 1822 | Box 7 |
| Taylor, Joseph P. | 1864 | Box 33 | Tennant, Christopher R. C. | 1907 | Box 335 |
| Taylor, Katharine H. | 1900 | Box 201 | Tenney, Franklin | 1896 | Box 165 |
| Taylor, Laura O. | 1885 | Box 94 | Tenney, Mary | 1875 | Box 59 |
| Taylor, Lena Maria | 1913 | Box 480 | Tenney, William H. | 1888 | Box 110 |
| Taylor, Leroy M. | 1904 | Box 272 | Tennille, Mary Sue | 1904 | Box 272 |

| | | | | | | |
|---|---|---|---|---|---|---|
| Tenny, Caroline | 1874 | Box 56 | Thomas, Charles | 1871 | Box 46 |
| Tenny, Louisa | 1885 | Box 94 | Thomas, Charles | 1878 | Box 67 |
| Tenny, Rebecca N. | 1900 | Box 201 | Thomas, Charles M. | 1908 | Box 358 |
| Terrell, Eliza | 1878 | Box 67 | Thomas, Charlotte R. | 1907 | Box 335 |
| Terrell, Harrison | 1906 | Box 312 | Thomas, Edward H. | 1916 | Box 559 |
| Terrell, James M. | 1895 | Box 158 | Thomas, Elenora | 1916 | Box 559 |
| Terrell, Wilson J. | 1912 | Box 456 | Thomas, Eliza M. | 1916 | Box 559 |
| Terrill, Jared D. | 1916 | Box 559 | Thomas, Elizabeth | 1810 | Box 3 |
| Terry, Daniel E. | 1911 | Box 431 | Thomas, Elizabeth | 1888 | Box 110 |
| Terry, Edward | 1882 | Box 81 | Thomas, Elizabeth M. | 1903 | Box 255 |
| Terry, Harriette Manning | 1916 | Box 559 | Thomas, Elizabeth R. | 1917 | Box 586 |
| Terry, John | 1916 | Box 559 | Thomas, Ellen | 1883 | Box 84 |
| Terry, Lucy | 1834 | Box 12 | Thomas, Emma E. Vreeland | 1919 | Box 646 |
| Terry, Maria P. | 1914 | Box 505 | Thomas, Eugene S. | 1909 | Box 380 |
| Terry, Martha A. | 1918 | Box 615 | Thomas, Frances L. | 1890 | Box 122 |
| Terry, Mary F. | 1915 | Box 533 | Thomas, Frances W. | 1916 | Box 559 |
| Terry, Seth A. | 1919 | Box 646 | Thomas, Francis | 1917 | Box 586 |
| Teuber, Frank | 1912 | Box 456 | Thomas, Frank | 1897 | Box 173 |
| Teulon, Emily | 1914 | Box 505 | Thomas, Frank | 1901 | Box 216 |
| Tew, William E. | 1915 | Box 533 | Thomas, Frank H. | 1907 | Box 335 |
| Thaden, Henry Bernhard | 1910 | Box 405 | Thomas, George | 1858 | Box 27 |
| Thalaker, Jefferson Grove | 1920 | Box 677 | Thomas, George H. Sr. | 1920 | Box 677 |
| Tharp, Elizabeth | 1902 | Box 236 | Thomas, George Ira | 1911 | Box 431 |
| Tharp, Henry P. | 1907 | Box 335 | Thomas, George W. | 1902 | Box 236 |
| Tharp, James | 1901 | Box 216 | Thomas, George W. | 1917 | Box 586 |
| Tharp, Walter J. | 1919 | Box 646 | Thomas, Georgine | 1892 | Box 135 |
| Thaw, Joseph | 1840 | Box 15 | Thomas, Harriet | 1918 | Box 615 |
| Thaw, Mary E. | 1919 | Box 646 | Thomas, Henrietta | 1884 | Box 90 |
| Thayer, Elizabeth | 1880 | Box 73 | Thomas, Henrietta | 1915 | Box 533 |
| Thayer, Julia M. | 1913 | Box 480 | Thomas, Henry | 1812 | Box 4 |
| Thayer, Maria W. | 1913 | Box 480 | Thomas, Henry | 1859 | Box 28 |
| Thayer, William M. | 1893 | Box 143 | Thomas, Hester | 1882 | Box 81 |
| Thayer, William Utley | 1919 | Box 646 | Thomas, Isabella | 1846 | Box 18 |
| Thecker, Mary W. | 1913 | Box 480 | Thomas, James E. | 1917 | Box 586 |
| Theilkuh, Agnes | 1890 | Box 122 | Thomas, Jenkin | 1885 | Box 94 |
| Theodore, Henry | 1910 | Box 405 | Thomas, John | 1905 | Box 292 |
| Theurer, Andreas | 1903 | Box 255 | Thomas, John A. | 1901 | Box 216 |
| Thiebaut, Regina | 1919 | Box 646 | Thomas, John Addison | 1911 | Box 431 |
| Thill, Anton | 1907 | Box 335 | Thomas, John E. | 1917 | Box 586 |
| Thom, Christopher N. | 1895 | Box 158 | Thomas, John L. | 1898 | Box 179 |
| Thom, Jennie W. | 1914 | Box 505 | Thomas, John W. | 1904 | Box 272 |
| Thom, Sarah C. | 1902 | Box 236 | Thomas, Levi | 1885 | Box 94 |
| Thom, William | 1892 | Box 135 | Thomas, Lillie Bond | 1918 | Box 615 |
| Thoma, Charles | 1859 | Box 28 | Thomas, Louise | 1919 | Box 646 |
| Thoma, Lorenz | 1862 | Box 30 | Thomas, Manson | 1872 | Box 49 |
| Thomas, Adelaide | 1904 | Box 272 | Thomas, Margaret | 1910 | Box 405 |
| Thomas, Amelia | 1849 | Box 20 | Thomas, Margaret E. | 1910 | Box 405 |
| Thomas, Ann C. | 1884 | Box 89 | Thomas, Mary Ann | 1892 | Box 135 |
| Thomas, Ann E. | 1885 | Box 94 | Thomas, Mary E. V. | 1898 | Box 179 |
| Thomas, Annie L. | 1919 | Box 646 | Thomas, Minnie Ellerbrook | 1915 | Box 533 |
| Thomas, Artemisia H. | 1920 | Box 677 | Thomas, Morgan | 1891 | Box 127 |
| Thomas, Bruce | 1913 | Box 480 | Thomas, Nona Gordon | 1890 | Box 122 |

| | | | | | | |
|---|---|---|---|---|---|---|
| Thomas, Philip | 1866 | Box 36 | Thompson, Jane | 1872 | Box 49 |
| Thomas, Philip | 1891 | Box 128 | Thompson, John | 1897 | Box 173 |
| Thomas, Richard | 1807 | Box 2 | Thompson, John | 1831 | Box 11 |
| Thomas, Rosalie Poole | 1905 | Box 292 | Thompson, John E. | 1885 | Box 94 |
| Thomas, Sampson | 1901 | Box 216 | Thompson, John Henry | 1888 | Box 110 |
| Thomas, Samuel | 1898 | Box 179 | Thompson, John S. | 1898 | Box 179 |
| Thomas, Sarah J. | 1900 | Box 201 | Thompson, John T. | 1802 | Box 1 |
| Thomas, Thomas | 1873 | Box 52 | Thompson, John W. | 1903 | Box 255 |
| Thomas, Thomas | 1873 | Box 52 | Thompson, John W. | 1901 | Box 216 |
| Thomas, William | 1859 | Box 28 | Thompson, Joseph A. | 1853 | Box 22 |
| Thomas, William Wilson | 1810 | Box 3 | Thompson, Lee | 1889 | Box 116 |
| Thomason, Charles B. | 1901 | Box 216 | Thompson, Lucy C. Daniels | 1913 | Box 480 |
| Thomason, Elizabeth B. | 1915 | Box 533 | Thompson, Luther C. | 1919 | Box 646 |
| Thomason, Ida Jane | 1919 | Box 646 | Thompson, Margaret | 1838 | Box 14 |
| Thombs, Adelia L. S. | 1908 | Box 358 | Thompson, Marie N. | 1908 | Box 358 |
| Thomfordt, Henry | 1909 | Box 380 | Thompson, Marion V. | 1905 | Box 292 |
| Thompkins, Lottie | 1895 | Box 158 | Thompson, Mary | 1919 | Box 646 |
| Thompkins, Richard | 1889 | Box 116 | Thompson, Mary E. | 1916 | Box 559 |
| Thompson, Alice Elizabeth | 1915 | Box 533 | Thompson, Mary E. | 1920 | Box 677 |
| Thompson, Ambrose W. | 1887 | Box 105 | Thompson, Mary Nichols | 1901 | Box 216 |
| Thompson, Ann | 1802 | Box 1 | Thompson, Mary V. | 1899 | Box 188 |
| Thompson, Ann Eliza | 1872 | Box 49 | Thompson, Michael | 1901 | Box 216 |
| Thompson, Anna Key | 1895 | Box 158 | Thompson, Nancy E. Little | 1911 | Box 431 |
| Thompson, Annie H. | 1920 | Box 677 | Thompson, Oliver | 1897 | Box 173 |
| Thompson, Camilla M. | 1914 | Box 505 | Thompson, Olivia A. | 1918 | Box 615 |
| Thompson, Charles P. | 1901 | Box 216 | Thompson, Oscar F. | 1916 | Box 559 |
| Thompson, D. Darby | 1913 | Box 480 | Thompson, Pauline E. | 1894 | Box 150 |
| Thompson, David A. | 1904 | Box 272 | Thompson, Rachel | 1891 | Box 128 |
| Thompson, Elbertine Mariette | 1910 | Box 405 | Thompson, Rebecca | 1904 | Box 272 |
| Thompson, Eleazar | 1905 | Box 292 | Thompson, Robert E. | 1883 | Box 84 |
| Thompson, Elizabeth | 1867 | Box 38 | Thompson, Sarah J. | 1886 | Box 100 |
| Thompson, Elizabeth | 1904 | Box 272 | Thompson, Thomas | 1891 | Box 128 |
| Thompson, Elizabeth A. | 1848 | Box 20 | Thompson, Virginia | 1914 | Box 505 |
| Thompson, Ella M. | 1906 | Box 312 | Thompson, Virginia A. | 1920 | Box 677 |
| Thompson, Ellen | 1893 | Box 143 | Thompson, W. Taliaferro | 1920 | Box 677 |
| Thompson, Ellen | 1915 | Box 533 | Thompson, William | 1858 | Box 27 |
| Thompson, Emily B. | 1894 | Box 150 | Thompson, William | 1896 | Box 166 |
| Thompson, Ernest G. | 1920 | Box 677 | Thompson, William A. | 1901 | Box 217 |
| Thompson, Frederick A. | 1898 | Box 179 | Thompson, William Baker | 1920 | Box 677 |
| Thompson, G. Tabor | 1916 | Box 559 | Thompson, William H. | 1888 | Box 110 |
| Thompson, George | 1869 | Box 41 | Thompson, William H. | 1899 | Box 188 |
| Thompson, George Henry | 1859 | Box 28 | Thompson, William P. | 1876 | Box 62 |
| Thompson, George W. | 1854 | Box 23 | Thompson, William P. | 1908 | Box 358 |
| Thompson, Gilbert | 1909 | Box 380 | Thompson, William S. | 1901 | Box 217 |
| Thompson, Harriet J. C. | 1914 | Box 505 | Thompson, Wilson H. | 1903 | Box 255 |
| Thompson, Henry | 1909 | Box 380 | Thomson, Benjamin D. | 1914 | Box 505 |
| Thompson, Henry | 1837 | Box 14 | Thomson, Charles | 1911 | Box 431 |
| Thompson, Hugh | 1873 | Box 52 | Thomson, Emma B. | 1882 | Box 81 |
| Thompson, J. Ford | 1917 | Box 586 | Thomson, Isabella | 1846 | Box 18 |
| Thompson, James | 1856 | Box 25 | Thomson, Lewis B. | 1920 | Box 677 |
| Thompson, James E. | 1898 | Box 179 | Thomson, Maria S. | 1887 | Box 105 |
| Thompson, James M. | 1901 | Box 216 | Thomson, Matilda L. | 1916 | Box 559 |

| | | | | | | |
|---|---|---|---|---|---|
| Thomson, Patrick H. | 1910 | Box 405 | Thwing, Charles | 1912 | Box 456 |
| Thomson, Sarah M. | 1874 | Box 56 | Thyson, Parthenia | 1899 | Box 188 |
| Thomson, William | 1887 | Box 105 | Thyson, Poulus | 1874 | Box 56 |
| Thomson, William | 1888 | Box 110 | Tiar, Ann B. | 1813 | Box 4 |
| Thorn, Charles G. | 1905 | Box 292 | Tibbitts, Russell D. | 1918 | Box 615 |
| Thorn, Clorinda A. | 1843 | Box 16 | Tibbs, John H. | 1912 | Box 456 |
| Thorn, Columbus W. | 1888 | Box 110 | Tichenor, Isaac S. | 1898 | Box 179 |
| Thorn, Henry | 1882 | Box 81 | Tiernan, Ann | 1903 | Box 255 |
| Thorn, Martha A. | 1914 | Box 505 | Tierney, Ann | 1888 | Box 110 |
| Thorn, Mary E. | 1909 | Box 380 | Tierney (Tierny), Hugh | 1832 | Box 12 |
| Thorn, Mary J. | 1872 | Box 49 | Tierney, Kate | 1904 | Box 272 |
| Thornburg, Claude T. | 1915 | Box 533 | Tiers, Mary M. | 1913 | Box 481 |
| Thornburg, Isaac N. | 1894 | Box 150 | Tifney, John | 1812 | Box 4 |
| Thorne, Rachel Victoria | 1920 | Box 677 | Tignor, Ezekiel | 1905 | Box 292 |
| Thorne, S. Norris | 1910 | Box 405 | Tilghman, Henry H. | 1900 | Box 201 |
| Thornley, Thomas | 1885 | Box 94 | Tilleux, Louis | 1912 | Box 456 |
| Thornton, Alexander B. | 1906 | Box 312 | Tilley, Ann | 1833 | Box 12 |
| Thornton, Anna M. | 1865 | Box 34 | Tilley, Benjamin F. | 1907 | Box 335 |
| Thornton, Anthony | 1914 | Box 505 | Tilley, Eleanor Jane | 1881 | Box 77 |
| Thornton, Clara | 1913 | Box 481 | Tillman, James L. | 1899 | Box 188 |
| Thornton, Dolly | 1844 | Box 17 | Tills, Catharine | 1900 | Box 201 |
| Thornton, Harriet | 1902 | Box 236 | Tilly, Huldah | 1899 | Box 188 |
| Thornton, John | 1887 | Box 105 | Tilston, Samuel | 1867 | Box 38 |
| Thornton, John | 1913 | Box 481 | Tilton, Alfred E. | 1877 | Box 65 |
| Thornton, Owen | 1904 | Box 272 | Tilton, Edward G. | 1861 | Box 29 |
| Thornton, Pauline | 1917 | Box 586 | Tilton, Elizabeth | 1918 | Box 615 |
| Thornton, Richard R. | 1888 | Box 110 | Tilton, Rufus N. | 1901 | Box 217 |
| Thornton, Sevilia E. | 1913 | Box 481 | Tinaglia, Ignatius | 1913 | Box 481 |
| Thornton, William | 1828 | Box 9 | Tingle, Amory K. | 1913 | Box 481 |
| Thorp, Edwina Hurlbut | 1920 | Box 677 | Tingle, Elsie J. | 1901 | Box 217 |
| Thorp, Katie R. | 1902 | Box 236 | Tingwold, Christian A. | 1895 | Box 158 |
| Thorpe, George | 1893 | Box 143 | Tinker, Ellen Maria | 1917 | Box 586 |
| Thouars, Rudolphe C. de | 1870 | Box 44 | Tinker, Mary L. | 1908 | Box 358 |
| Thouston, Caroline | 1865 | Box 34 | Tinney, Mary Ann | 1914 | Box 505 |
| Thrasher, Mary J. | 1907 | Box 335 | Tippett, Edward T. | 1895 | Box 158 |
| Throckmorton, Mary B. | 1899 | Box 188 | Tippett, Thomas A. | 1822 | Box 7 |
| Throckmorton, Rebecca Ellen | 1895 | Box 158 | Tippett, Thomas I. N. | 1855 | Box 24 |
| Thue, August | 1899 | Box 188 | Tipton, Die P. | 1894 | Box 150 |
| Thumbert, Mary Jane | 1905 | Box 292 | Tipton, Rachel I. | 1900 | Box 201 |
| Thumlert, Esther | 1873 | Box 52 | Tipton, Thomas Corwin | 1914 | Box 505 |
| Thumlert, William | 1867 | Box 38 | Tisdale, Sarah | 1887 | Box 105 |
| Thumlert William H. | 1891 | Box 128 | Tisdel, Willard P. | 1911 | Box 431 |
| Thurlow, Augusta R. | 1907 | Box 335 | Tise, Sarah Catharine | 1908 | Box 358 |
| Thurm, Herman | 1901 | Box 217 | Titcomb, William Parsons | 1910 | Box 406 |
| Thurm, Julius | 1899 | Box 188 | Tiverny, Martha J. | 1916 | Box 559 |
| Thursby, Ann | 1829 | Box 10 | Toban, Patrick | 1868 | Box 40 |
| Thursby, Ann | 1829 | Box 10 | Tobey, Thomas F. | 1920 | Box 677 |
| Thurston, Henry | 1906 | Box 312 | Tobey, Walter L. | 1910 | Box 406 |
| Thurston, Ida T. | 1920 | Box 677 | Tobin, Ellen | 1915 | Box 533 |
| Thurston, Sealina | 1906 | Box 313 | Tod, Maria W. | 1872 | Box 49 |
| Thwaites, George | 1892 | Box 135 | Todd, Albert | 1913 | Box 481 |
| Thwing, Alice | 1908 | Box 358 | Todd, Elizabeth G. | 1894 | Box 150 |

| | | | | | | |
|---|---|---|---|---|---|---|
| Todd, John P. | 1852 | Box 22 | | Torrens, William J. | 1919 | Box 646 |
| Todd, Robert S. | 1890 | Box 122 | | Torrey, Hannah M. | 1902 | Box 236 |
| Todd, Seth I. | 1841 | Box 15 | | Torrey, William A. | 1915 | Box 534 |
| Todd, Seth J. | 1874 | Box 56 | | Tossit, George E. | 1920 | Box 677 |
| Toel, Sarah C. | 1901 | Box 217 | | Totten, Anne | 1910 | Box 406 |
| Toense, John | 1907 | Box 335 | | Totten, Edward H. | 1911 | Box 431 |
| Toepfer, Caroline | 1914 | Box 505 | | Totten, Ephraim J. | 1920 | Box 677 |
| Toepfer, Fannie M. | 1910 | Box 406 | | Totten, Joseph | 1864 | Box 33 |
| Toepfer, Sebastian | 1896 | Box 166 | | Touhey, Michael | 1898 | Box 179 |
| Tolbert, Adele A. | 1910 | Box 406 | | Touhy, Martin | 1899 | Box 188 |
| Toliver, Ann | 1896 | Box 166 | | Touhy, Thomas | 1898 | Box 179 |
| Toliver, Isaac | 1914 | Box 505 | | Toumey, Francis | 1895 | Box 158 |
| Tolliver, Carrie | 1919 | Box 646 | | Toumey, Timothy | 1884 | Box 90 |
| Tolliver, William | 1894 | Box 150 | | Tousley, Orson V. | 1902 | Box 236 |
| Tolman, Edward M. | 1903 | Box 255 | | Tower, Frederick W. | 1909 | Box 380 |
| Tolman, Frances H. | 1908 | Box 358 | | Tower, George Edward | 1914 | Box 506 |
| Tolman, James P. | 1915 | Box 533 | | Towers, Chatham M. | 1908 | Box 358 |
| Tolman, William C. | 1880 | Box 73 | | Towers, Julia L. | 1920 | Box 677 |
| Tolson, Edward | 1861 | Box 29 | | Towers, Sarah | 1893 | Box 143 |
| Tolson, Jane | 1903 | Box 255 | | Towles, Henry Orme | 1905 | Box 292 |
| Tolson, Nancy | 1918 | Box 615 | | Towles, James | 1882 | Box 81 |
| Tolson, Watkins | 1897 | Box 173 | | Towles, Thomas Oliver | 1915 | Box 534 |
| Tolson, William B. | 1886 | Box 100 | | Town, John P. | 1899 | Box 188 |
| Tome, Jacob | 1898 | Box 179 | | Town, Mary L. | 1908 | Box 358 |
| Tomelty, Sarah | 1894 | Box 150 | | Towner, America E. | 1905 | Box 292 |
| Tomes, Henrietta | 1897 | Box 173 | | Towner, Oscar T. | 1903 | Box 255 |
| Tomlin, Lou Morell | 1913 | Box 481 | | Towner, Thomas B. | 1900 | Box 201 |
| Tomlinson, Bettie | 1904 | Box 272 | | Townes, John | 1802 | Box 1 |
| Tomlinson, Daniel W. | 1871 | Box 46 | | Townsend, Ann O. | 1917 | Box 586 |
| Tompkins, Catherine A. | 1915 | Box 533 | | Townsend, Ebenezer | 1897 | Box 173 |
| Tompkins, Ella Cameron | 1917 | Box 586 | | Townsend, Eddy B. | 1909 | Box 380 |
| Tompkins, Frances Henrietta | 1911 | Box 431 | | Townsend, Edward | 1893 | Box 143 |
| Tompkins, Francis Meade | 1919 | Box 646 | | Townsend, Edwin F. | 1909 | Box 380 |
| Tompkins, Laura | 1869 | Box 41 | | Townsend, Elizabeth | 1892 | Box 135 |
| Tompkins, Louise C. | 1919 | Box 646 | | Townsend, Frank C. | 1915 | Box 534 |
| Toner, Ellen | 1867 | Box 38 | | Townsend, Julia C. | 1911 | Box 431 |
| Toner, James L. | 1905 | Box 292 | | Townsend, Maria Farnam | 1911 | Box 431 |
| Toner, John E. | 1912 | Box 456 | | Townsend, Maria T. | 1911 | Box 431 |
| Toner, Joseph M. | 1896 | Box 166 | | Townsend, Rebecca A. | 1825 | Box 8 |
| Toner, Margaret E. | 1906 | Box 313 | | Townsend, Thomas Gerry | 1902 | Box 236 |
| Toomb, Robert | 1897 | Box 173 | | Tows, Coe Downing | 1915 | Box 534 |
| Toomb, Sarah J. | 1919 | Box 646 | | Towson, Dorsey E. W. | 1906 | Box 313 |
| Toomer, Nina Eliza Pinchback | 1909 | Box 380 | | Toy, James M. | 1917 | Box 586 |
| Toomey, Dennis | 1889 | Box 116 | | Toyer, Maria | 1907 | Box 335 |
| Toomey, Dennis | 1903 | Box 255 | | Tracy, Arabella S. | 1909 | Box 380 |
| Toomey, Florence T. | 1920 | Box 677 | | Tracy, James | 1920 | Box 677 |
| Toomey, James | 1891 | Box 128 | | Tracy, Mattie Flandreau | 1920 | Box 677 |
| Torbert, Elizabeth C. | 1917 | Box 586 | | Tracy, Philip A. | 1898 | Box 179 |
| Torbert, James M. | 1880 | Box 73 | | Trager, William | 1903 | Box 255 |
| Torney, Caroline Matilda | 1888 | Box 111 | | Trageser, Katharina | 1896 | Box 166 |
| Torphy, James | 1885 | Box 94 | | Trailes, Monich | 1830 | Box 10 |
| Torrens, Mary | 1919 | Box 646 | | Train, Alice Brown | 1906 | Box 313 |

| | | | | | | |
|---|---|---|---|---|---|---|
| Trankler, William W. | 1902 | Box 236 | | Truett, John H. | 1920 | Box 677 |
| Traphagen, Henry C. | 1919 | Box 615 | | Trueworthy, Burnett T. | 1913 | Box 481 |
| Trapier, Alice Pauline | 1912 | Box 456 | | Truman, Ann | 1898 | Box 179 |
| Trapier, Sarah R. | 1890 | Box 122 | | Truman, Ellen | 1916 | Box 559 |
| Trapier, Theodore D. | 1906 | Box 313 | | Truman, Sarah | 1863 | Box 31 |
| Trapp, Casper | 1877 | Box 65 | | Trumble, Carrie E. | 1910 | Box 406 |
| Trapp, John T. | 1919 | Box 646 | | Trumble, Delmer M. | 1912 | Box 456 |
| Trapp, Mary Ann | 1899 | Box 188 | | Trumbull, Annie Eliza | 1909 | Box 380 |
| Travers, Elizabeth | 1900 | Box 201 | | Trumbull, Ellen | 1920 | Box 677 |
| Travers, Elizabeth H. | 1881 | Box 77 | | Trumpf, Frederick | 1918 | Box 615 |
| Travers, James | 1884 | Box 90 | | Trunnel, Charles H. | 1904 | Box 272 |
| Travers, John | 1884 | Box 90 | | Trunnel, Christa A. | 1902 | Box 236 |
| Travers, Maria L. | 1894 | Box 150 | | Trunnel, Elizabeth A. | 1889 | Box 116 |
| Travers, Nicholas | 1851 | Box 21 | | Trunnell, Elizabeth | 1913 | Box 481 |
| Travers, Richard B. | 1912 | Box 456 | | Trunnell, John H. | 1870 | Box 44 |
| Travers, Sidney | 1853 | Box 22 | | Trusheim, Eberhard | 1914 | Box 506 |
| Travers, William R. | 1891 | Box 128 | | Trusheim, Emma R. | 1892 | Box 135 |
| Travis, Edward | 1846 | Box 18 | | Trusheim, George U. | 1918 | Box 615 |
| Travis, John A. | 1918 | Box 615 | | Truxton, Julia P. | 1920 | Box 677 |
| Treakle, Mary Jane | 1888 | Box 111 | | Tryon, William | 1919 | Box 646 |
| Tree, Lambert | 1881 | Box 77 | | Trzeciak, John | 1875 | Box 57 |
| Tree, Lambert | 1912 | Box 456 | | Tschiffely, Elizabeth Whiting | 1919 | Box 646 |
| Trego, Eliza | 1854 | Box 23 | | Tschiffely, Frederick A. | 1918 | Box 615 |
| Trenis, Benjamin F. | 1913 | Box 481 | | Tubia, Frank | 1913 | Box 481 |
| Trevitt, Constant S. | 1903 | Box 255 | | Tubman, Albert M. | 1895 | Box 158 |
| Triay, Raphael R. | 1855 | Box 24 | | Tubman, George M. | 1835 | Box 13 |
| Tricker, Lucy | 1897 | Box 173 | | Tubman, Sarah E. | 1906 | Box 313 |
| Trigg, Margaret Anne O'D. | 1915 | Box 534 | | Tubman, William | 1910 | Box 406 |
| Triguet, Etien | 1838 | Box 14 | | Tuck, Philemon H. | 1917 | Box 586 |
| Trimble, John | 1903 | Box 256 | | Tuck, Philemon H. | 1917 | Box 586 |
| Trimble, Joseph | 1885 | Box 94 | | Tucker, Beverly | 1904 | Box 272 |
| Trimble, Lucinda | 1890 | Box 122 | | Tucker, Elizabeth | 1848 | Box 120 |
| Trimmer, Louise F. | 1916 | Box 559 | | Tucker, Emma | 1876 | Box 62 |
| Triplett, Maria Louisa | 1894 | Box 150 | | Tucker, Enoch | 1869 | Box 41 |
| Triplett, Martha Lofton | 1912 | Box 456 | | Tucker, Henrietta | 1867 | Box 38 |
| Triplett, Thomas J. | 1878 | Box 67 | | Tucker, Inder V. | 1918 | Box 615 |
| Triplett, William | 1913 | Box 481 | | Tucker, James | 1865 | Box 34 |
| Tripp, Henry | 1900 | Box 201 | | Tucker, Jenifer C. | 1871 | Box 46 |
| Tripp, Ralph Wright | 1919 | Box 646 | | Tucker, John H. | 1883 | Box 84 |
| Tripp, Sarah S. | 1911 | Box 431 | | Tucker, John W. | 1872 | Box 49 |
| Troiano, Joseph | 1917 | Box 586 | | Tucker, Joseph S. | 1905 | Box 292 |
| Trook, Victoria V. | 1918 | Box 615 | | Tucker, Logan | 1912 | Box 456 |
| Trott, Emma J. | 1913 | Box 481 | | Tucker, Mary | 1910 | Box 406 |
| Trott, Frances C. | 1911 | Box 431 | | Tucker, Mary Keyworth | 1913 | Box 481 |
| Trott, Stanley G. | 1892 | Box 135 | | Tucker, Matilda | 1904 | Box 272 |
| Trouland, Anna L. | 1914 | Box 506 | | Tucker, Susannah Powell | 1911 | Box 432 |
| Troutman, Michael | 1859 | Box 28 | | Tucker, Thomas | 1857 | Box 26 |
| Trudrung, Marie A. | 1904 | Box 272 | | Tucker, Thomas Tuder | 1828 | Box 9 |
| True, Frederick William | 1914 | Box 506 | | Tucker, William E. | 1895 | Box 158 |
| True, Loring B. | 1864 | Box 33 | | Tucker, William W. | 1870 | Box 44 |
| Truell, Edwin M. | 1908 | Box 358 | | Tuckerman, Lucius | 1907 | Box 335 |
| Truesdail, Emily Larned | 1907 | Box 335 | | Tudge, Margaret | 1914 | Box 506 |

| | | | | | | |
|---|---|---|---|---|---|---|
| Tudge, William | 1911 | Box 432 | Turner, Weston B. | 1899 | Box 188 |
| Tudor, Delia | 1843 | Box 16 | Turnure, Lawrence | 1901 | Box 217 |
| Tudor, William V. | 1917 | Box 586 | Turpin, Ann | 1853 | Box 22 |
| Tuel, Winfred | 1847 | Box 19 | Turpin, William T. | 1906 | Box 313 |
| Tufts, James F. | 1920 | Box 677 | Turtle, Virginia L. | 1919 | Box 646 |
| Tull, Eliza A. | 1875 | Box 59 | Turton, George H. | 1911 | Box 432 |
| Tull, Mary E. | 1914 | Box 506 | Turton, James E. | 1913 | Box 481 |
| Tulloch, Eliza Colman | 1917 | Box 586 | Turton, W. Elmo | 1918 | Box 615 |
| Tulloch, Henry V. | 1915 | Box 534 | Turvey, Thomas | 1883 | Box 84 |
| Tulloch, Miranda B. | 1915 | Box 534 | Tustin, Septimus | 1871 | Box 46 |
| Tumelty, Hugh | 1898 | Box 179 | Tutt, Elizabeth J. | 1856 | Box 25 |
| Tumey, Catherine | 1903 | Box 256 | Tutt, Henry | 1895 | Box 158 |
| Tuner, Henry | 1896 | Box 166 | Tuttle, Adelaide M. | 1911 | Box 432 |
| Tüngel, Ernst | 1890 | Box 122 | Tuttle, Elmore A. | 1884 | Box 90 |
| Tunnicliff, Julia | 1910 | Box 406 | Tuttle, Leroy | 1894 | Box 150 |
| Tunstall, Lizzie G. | 1917 | Box 586 | Tweedale, Myra Bourn | 1913 | Box 481 |
| Tuohy, Hugh | 1906 | Box 313 | Tweedy, Eliza E. | 1916 | Box 559 |
| Tuohy, Thomas F. | 1913 | Box 481 | Tweedy, Robert | 1846 | Box 18 |
| Tuomy, Patrick | 1858 | Box 27 | Twine, Andrew | 1898 | Box 179 |
| Tupper, James B. T. | 1920 | Box 677 | Twine, Charles H. | 1875 | Box 59 |
| Turkenton, Edward | 1909 | Box 380 | Twine, David | 1894 | Box 150 |
| Turnbull, Helen | 1913 | Box 481 | Twine, William | 1891 | Box 128 |
| Turnbull, Henry | 1893 | Box 143 | Twining, William | 1885 | Box 94 |
| Turnbull, Jeannie | 1912 | Box 456 | Twombly, William | 1915 | Box 534 |
| Turnbull, Robert | 1826 | Box 9 | Twomey, Dennis | 1889 | Box 116 |
| Turnburke, James Theodore | 1903 | Box 256 | Twyman, Smith | 1913 | Box 481 |
| Turner, Alexander | 1884 | Box 90 | Tyler, Constance Adee | 1919 | Box 646 |
| Turner, Benjamin Brecknell | 1895 | Box 158 | Tyler, Emma R. | 1892 | Box 135 |
| Turner, Cornelia H. | 1916 | Box 559 | Tyler, Grafton | 1884 | Box 90 |
| Turner, Daniel | 1854 | Box 23 | Tyler, Harriet A. | 1920 | Box 677 |
| Turner, Duane C. | 1912 | Box 457 | Tyler, Harriett | 1916 | Box 559 |
| Turner, Emily | 1898 | Box 179 | Tyler, James W. | 1903 | Box 256 |
| Turner, Fanny | 1885 | Box 94 | Tyler, Jane | 1874 | Box 56 |
| Turner, George | 1901 | Box 217 | Tyler, Johnston W. | 1901 | Box 217 |
| Turner, Harriet Ann | 1901 | Box 217 | Tyler, Matilda | 1910 | Box 406 |
| Turner, Harriet V. Boardman | 1919 | Box 646 | Tyler, Nathaniel | 1918 | Box 615 |
| Turner, Henry | 1896 | Box 166 | Tyler, Nellie | 1906 | Box 313 |
| Turner, Jane A. W. | 1896 | Box 166 | Tyler, Richard K. | 1920 | Box 677 |
| Turner, John Henry | 1893 | Box 143 | Tyler, Richard Woolsey | 1909 | Box 380 |
| Turner, Julia | 1902 | Box 236 | Tyler, Sallie Robb | 1907 | Box 335 |
| Turner, Martha Jane | 1902 | Box 237 | Tyler, Sarah F. | 1918 | Box 615 |
| Turner, Mary M. | 1906 | Box 313 | Tyler, Sarah Wright | 1913 | Box 481 |
| Turner, Matthew A. | 1901 | Box 217 | Tyler, Susannah | 1913 | Box 481 |
| Turner, Nathaniel | 1882 | Box 81 | Tyler, Tamar M. | 1911 | Box 432 |
| Turner, Patience | 1807 | Box 2 | Tyler, William C. | 1907 | Box 336 |
| Turner, Sarah Ellen | 1916 | Box 559 | Tynan, John | 1894 | Box 150 |
| Turner, Steven | 1914 | Box 506 | Tynan, Mary J. | 1915 | Box 534 |
| Turner, Susan | 1906 | Box 313 | Tyne, Georgianna | 1919 | Box 646 |
| Turner, Susan Wadden | 1898 | Box 179 | Tyner, Christine | 1916 | Box 559 |
| Turner, Thomas | 1816 | Box 5 | Tyner, James N. | 1905 | Box 292 |
| Turner, Thomas B. | 1896 | Box 166 | Tyrrell, Margaret | 1912 | Box 457 |
| Turner, W. A. H. | 1916 | Box 559 | Tyson, Rachel L. | 1877 | Box 65 |

| | | | | | | |
|---|---|---|---|---|---|---|
| Tyson, William J. | 1910 | Box 406 | Utermuhle, George W. | 1855 | Box 24 |
| Tyssowski, Anthony Z. | 1920 | Box 677 | Uttz, William W. | 1916 | Box 561 |
| Tyssowski, Joseph | 1911 | Box 432 | V'Hartleben, Carl August | 1911 | Box 432 |
| Tyssowski, Thaddeus M. | 1911 | Box 432 | Vaeth, Philip J. | 1882 | Box 81 |
| Uber, Samuel | 1905 | Box 292 | Vail, Emily Jervis | 1913 | Box 481 |
| Ubhoff, Christian | 1877 | Box 65 | Vail, I. B. | 1919 | Box 647 |
| Uchesco, Michael Charles | 1915 | Box 534 | Vail, Israel Everett | 1915 | Box 534 |
| Ucker, Mary Genevieve | 1905 | Box 292 | Vail, Stephen | 1909 | Box 380 |
| Uhler, Clayton R. | 1919 | Box 647 | Valaperta, Joseph | 1818 | Box 5 |
| Uhler, Hannah Louise | 1912 | Box 457 | Vale, Jennie Griffin | 1906 | Box 313 |
| Uhler, Margaret H. | 1919 | Box 647 | Valentine, Martha H. | 1899 | Box 188 |
| Uihlein, August | 1920 | Box 678 | Valentine, Robert Grosvenor | 1917 | Box 586 |
| Ulke, Helene | 1916 | Box 559 | Valery, Ann | 1876 | Box 62 |
| Ulke, Julius | 1910 | Box 406 | Valiant, John | 1906 | Box 313 |
| Ulke, Veronica | 1894 | Box 150 | Vallandingham, Amelia | 1855 | Box 24 |
| Ullman, Tony | 1893 | Box 143 | Vallendingham, John | 1849 | Box 20 |
| Ulrich, Hannah | 1863 | Box 31 | Van Alstyne, Anna Richards | 1917 | Box 586 |
| Ulrich, John B. | 1888 | Box 111 | Van Arsdale, Ida | 1920 | Box 678 |
| Umhow, George | 1897 | Box 173 | Van Bibber, Abraham | 1807 | Box 2 |
| Umphrey, Edward | 1885 | Box 94 | Van Bibber, Henry P. | 1889 | Box 117 |
| Uncles, Isaac H. | 1904 | Box 272 | Van Buren, Abraham | 1910 | Box 406 |
| Underdue, William H. | 1913 | Box 481 | Van Buren, Annie E. | 1917 | Box 586 |
| Underhill, Harriet | 1899 | Box 188 | Van Buskirk, Peter | 1862 | Box 30 |
| Underhill, Phebe T. | 1909 | Box 380 | Van Coble, Ann H. | 1849 | Box 20 |
| Underwood, Jesse W. | 1904 | Box 272 | Van Cortlandt, Philip | 1859 | Box 28 |
| Underwood, Maria G. | 1884 | Box 90 | Van Deman, Henry E. | 1915 | Box 534 |
| Upham, Emeline C. | 1913 | Box 481 | Van Derlip, Sarah A. | 1906 | Box 313 |
| Upperman, Archie | 1906 | Box 313 | Van Deusen, Albert Harrison | 1918 | Box 615 |
| Upperman, Charles A. | 1902 | Box 237 | Van Doren, Jane A. | 1899 | Box 188 |
| Upperman, George | 1835 | Box 13 | Van Doren, John A. | 1894 | Box 150 |
| Upperman, Henry | 1845 | Box 17 | Van Dyke, Ann | 1910 | Box 406 |
| Upshur, Agnes M. | 1917 | Box 586 | Van Dyke, Celia I. | 1919 | Box 647 |
| Upshur, Annie A. | 1906 | Box 313 | Van Dyne, Frederick | 1915 | Box 534 |
| Upshur, Catherine T. | 1911 | Box 432 | Van Elstine, Mary | 1914 | Box 506 |
| Upshur, Columbia W. | 1891 | Box 128 | Van Fleet, William S. | 1910 | Box 406 |
| Upshur, Sally S. | 1872 | Box 49 | Van Horn, Eliza | 1910 | Box 406 |
| Upton, Anabella | 1893 | Box 143 | Van Horn, John F. | 1905 | Box 292 |
| Upton, Frederick E. | 1918 | Box 615 | Van Horne, Althea E. | 1903 | Box 256 |
| Upton, Martha E. | 1884 | Box 90 | Van Keuren, Sarah A. | 1913 | Box 481 |
| Upton, William Bayly | 1916 | Box 559 | Van Mater, Lou A. K. | 1911 | Box 432 |
| Upton, William Bayly | 1917 | Box 586 | Van Mater, M. Annie | 1904 | Box 272 |
| Upton, William W. | 1896 | Box 166 | Van Ness, Cornelius P. | 1853 | Box 22 |
| Upture, Mary | 1869 | Box 41 | Van Ness, Julia A. | 1898 | Box 180 |
| Urann, Mary R. | 1918 | Box 615 | Van Ness, Matilda | 1867 | Box 38 |
| Urell, Thomas E. | 1872 | Box 49 | Van Newkirk, William | 1884 | Box 90 |
| Urban, Anna M. | 1914 | Box 506 | Van Norsdall, Elmer E. | 1910 | Box 406 |
| Urich, William | 1914 | Box 506 | Van Reuth, Adolph | 1916 | Box 560 |
| Usher, John W. | 1895 | Box 158 | Van Riswich, Leander | 1906 | Box 313 |
| Utermehle, Charles W. | 1910 | Box 406 | Van Riswick, J. Thompson | 1874 | Box 56 |
| Utermehle, George W. | 1889 | Box 117 | Van Riswick, Mary | 1896 | Box 166 |
| Utermehle, Sarah | 1893 | Box 143 | Van Riswick, Olivia | 1894 | Box 150 |
| Utermoehle, Charles W. | 1883 | Box 84 | Van Sicklen, William | 1900 | Box 201 |

| | | | | | |
|---|---|---|---|---|---|
| Van Vleit, Stewart | 1901 | Box 217 | Vermillion, Avarilla | 1851 | Box 21 |
| Van Vliet, Sarah J. | 1919 | Box 647 | Vermillion, Barbara | 1850 | Box 21 |
| Van Volkenberg, Margaret A. | 1902 | Box 237 | Vermillion, Sarah | 1876 | Box 62 |
| Van Voorhies, Di W. | 1904 | Box 273 | Vernay, Adelaid C. | 1920 | Box 678 |
| Van Vranken, Mary | 1909 | Box 380 | Vernon, Charles R. | 1907 | Box 336 |
| Van Why, Marianna Matilda | 1908 | Box 358 | Vernon, Fannie A. | 1920 | Box 678 |
| Van Wyck, Elizabeth S. | 1874 | Box 56 | Vertner, Constance Kearny | 1915 | Box 534 |
| Van Zandt, Marie Wood | 1863 | Box 31 | Vest, George G. | 1904 | Box 273 |
| Van Zandt, Nicholas B. | 1864 | Box 33 | Viboud, Francois | 1904 | Box 273 |
| Vance, Ida J. | 1912 | Box 457 | Vickery, Charles W. | 1919 | Box 647 |
| Vance, Mary | 1916 | Box 559 | Viehmann, George | 1895 | Box 158 |
| Vance, Mary J. | 1910 | Box 406 | Viele, Herman K. | 1910 | Box 406 |
| Vandegrift, Redwood | 1916 | Box 560 | Vierbuchen, Peter | 1906 | Box 313 |
| Vanderbilt, George W. | 1914 | Box 506 | Viessmann, Andreas | 1912 | Box 457 |
| Vanderlehr, George | 1863 | Box 31 | Vigle, Elizabeth | 1903 | Box 256 |
| Vanderslice, Margaret A. | 1906 | Box 313 | Villard, Andra Joseph | 1819 | Box 6 |
| Vanderwerken, Gilbert | 1894 | Box 150 | Villard, Richard | 1849 | Box 20 |
| Vandeventer, Christopher | 1838 | Box 14 | Vinal, Emily M. W. | 1916 | Box 560 |
| Vandoren, Theodore J. F. | 1894 | Box 150 | Vinal, Washington Irving | 1914 | Box 506 |
| Vanfleet, Janet S. | 1919 | Box 647 | Vincent, Edward B. | 1894 | Box 150 |
| Vangender, Alexander | 1907 | Box 336 | Vincent, Sarah K. | 1913 | Box 481 |
| Vansant, John | 1902 | Box 237 | Vincent, Thomas M. | 1909 | Box 380 |
| Vansant, Mary Ann A. | 1895 | Box 158 | Vinson, Charles | 1872 | Box 49 |
| Vansant, Mary Duncan | 1918 | Box 615 | Vinson, John T. | 1903 | Box 256 |
| Vansciver, William | 1860 | Box 29 | Vinson, Webster | 1918 | Box 615 |
| Vanter, Amanda | 1899 | Box 188 | Vinton, David H. | 1910 | Box 406 |
| Varden, Alice R. | 1870 | Box 44 | Vinton, Samuel F. | 1862 | Box 30 |
| Varden, John | 1865 | Box 34 | Violland, Hardin A. | 1905 | Box 292 |
| Varden, Joseph | 1809 | Box 3 | Virnstein, Anna | 1870 | Box 44 |
| Varden, Richard W. | 1860 | Box 29 | Virnstein, Annie | 1919 | Box 647 |
| Varella, Vincenzo | 1920 | Box 678 | Vockey, Maria | 1899 | Box 188 |
| Varnell, John T. | 1910 | Box 406 | Vockey, Theodore | 1901 | Box 217 |
| Varney, Elizabeth | 1915 | Box 534 | Voegler, John | 1885 | Box 94 |
| Varnum, Jacob B. | 1874 | Box 56 | Vogel, Henry | 1898 | Box 180 |
| Varnum, James M. | 1908 | Box 358 | Vogel, Jakob | 1900 | Box 201 |
| Varnum, Joseph B. | 1875 | Box 59 | Vogel, Karl | 1918 | Box 615 |
| Vasey, Flora N. | 1918 | Box 615 | Vogelsberger, August | 1900 | Box 201 |
| Vass, Douglass | 1856 | Box 25 | Vogt, Clifford | 1907 | Box 336 |
| Vass, Douglass | 1867 | Box 38 | Vogt, John P. | 1904 | Box 273 |
| Vaughan, Gideon | 1872 | Box 49 | Vogt, Leo J. | 1906 | Box 313 |
| Vaughan, John | 1847 | Box 19 | Vogt, Sophia | 1910 | Box 406 |
| Vaughn, Elizabeth | 1903 | Box 256 | Voight, Edward | 1883 | Box 84 |
| Vaughn, Francis W. | 1913 | Box 481 | Voight, Frederick William | 1877 | Box 65 |
| Vaughn, Samuel J. | 1906 | Box 313 | Voigt, Sophia | 1915 | Box 534 |
| Vedder, Indiana | 1900 | Box 201 | Voigt, Therese | 1913 | Box 481 |
| Vedder, Nicholas | 1892 | Box 135 | Voigt, William | 1909 | Box 380 |
| Veerhoff, William H. | 1905 | Box 292 | Volk, Frederick | 1890 | Box 122 |
| Veihmeyer, Jacob | 1908 | Box 358 | Volk, Margaretha | 1892 | Box 135 |
| Venable, Caroline C. | 1911 | Box 432 | Volland, David | 1903 | Box 256 |
| Venable, George W. | 1859 | Box 28 | Vollbrecht, August | 1879 | Box 70 |
| Venable, Peter | 1864 | Box 33 | Von Bayer, C. Mathilde | 1905 | Box 292 |
| Vergnes, William | 1823 | Box 7 | Von Derlehr, Elizabeth V. | 1910 | Box 406 |

| | | | | | |
|---|---|---|---|---|---|
| Von Derlehr, Matthew Goddard | 1911 | Box 432 | Wagner, John | 1903 | Box 256 |
| von Erichsen, Paul | 1915 | Box 534 | Wagner, John A. | 1907 | Box 336 |
| Von Essen, John P. | 1873 | Box 52 | Wagner, John E. | 1916 | Box 560 |
| Von Essen, Peter | 1866 | Box 36 | Wagner, John Jacob | 1878 | Box 67 |
| von Ezdorf, Rudolf H. | 1916 | Box 560 | Wagner, John W. | 1906 | Box 313 |
| Von Hemert, Anna E. | 1919 | Box 647 | Wagner, Julius | 1896 | Box 166 |
| von Ringharz, Mary K. | 1915 | Box 534 | Wagner, Louise | 1883 | Box 84 |
| Voorhees, Elizabeth Warder | 1912 | Box 457 | Wagner, Mary M. E. | 1913 | Box 481 |
| Voorhees, Joseph H. | 1910 | Box 406 | Wahl, George | 1876 | Box 62 |
| Vosburgh, John R. | 1891 | Box 128 | Wahler, Genvefa | 1904 | Box 273 |
| Vose, James A. | 1904 | Box 273 | Wahler, Joseph | 1915 | Box 534 |
| Vose, William P. | 1906 | Box 313 | Wahling, Essee | 1907 | Box 336 |
| Voss, Hermann H. | 1891 | Box 128 | Wailes, Isaac Newton | 1862 | Box 30 |
| Vreeland, Charles E. | 1917 | Box 586 | Wailes, Mary Nannie | 1886 | Box 100 |
| Vrooman, Charles E. | 1918 | Box 616 | Wailes, Mary Victoria | 1916 | Box 560 |
| Vrooman, Gracia W. B. B. | 1911 | Box 432 | Wainwright, Charles Shiels | 1908 | Box 358 |
| Wade, Anne | 1804 | Box 1 | Wainwright, Richard | 1863 | Box 31 |
| Wade, Decius S. | 1905 | Box 292 | Wainwright, Thomas Bacot | 1851 | Box 21 |
| Wade, Edward | 1920 | Box 678 | Wainwright, Virginia A. | 1904 | Box 273 |
| Wade, Elazer | 1891 | Box 128 | Waite, Amelia C. | 1896 | Box 166 |
| Wade, James E. | 1902 | Box 237 | Waite, Mary Frances | 1906 | Box 313 |
| Wade, John K. | 1889 | Box 117 | Waite, Matthew | 1877 | Box 65 |
| Wade, John W. | 1889 | Box 117 | Waite, Morrison R. | 1912 | Box 457 |
| Wade, Patrick | 1902 | Box 237 | Wakefield, James I. | 1830 | Box 10 |
| Wade, Rufus D. | 1913 | Box 481 | Walbridge, Herman D. | 1899 | Box 188 |
| Wadleigh, Frances Ellen | 1909 | Box 380 | Walbridge, Hiram | 1872 | Box 49 |
| Wadskier, Theodore Vigo | 1898 | Box 180 | Walcott, Albert H. | 1898 | Box 180 |
| Wadsworth, Adrian | 1897 | Box 173 | Walcott, Helena B. | 1911 | Box 432 |
| Wadsworth, Alexander S. | 1851 | Box 21 | Walcott, Josephine M. | 1908 | Box 358 |
| Wadsworth, Caroline A. | 1900 | Box 201 | Waldecker, Franz | 1883 | Box 84 |
| Wadsworth, Evelyn Willing | 1886 | Box 100 | Waldecker, Louis | 1890 | Box 122 |
| Wadsworth, Hiram N. | 1896 | Box 166 | Waldecker, Paulina | 1910 | Box 407 |
| Wadsworth, Louisa J. | 1857 | Box 26 | Waldron, Charles | 1893 | Box 143 |
| Wagar, Humphrey R. | 1916 | Box 560 | Waldron, John | 1866 | Box 36 |
| Wager, Barney | 1910 | Box 407 | Walker, Alfred | 1895 | Box 158 |
| Waggaman, Daniel B. Clarke | 1919 | Box 647 | Walker, Allen | 1916 | Box 560 |
| Waggamann, Bernard | 1864 | Box 33 | Walker, Annie | 1895 | Box 158 |
| Wagner, Adolph | 1864 | Box 33 | Walker, Caroline H. | 1880 | Box 73 |
| Wagner, Barbara | 1899 | Box 188 | Walker, Charles H. | 1903 | Box 256 |
| Wagner, Catherine | 1884 | Box 90 | Walker, Charles L. | 1908 | Box 358 |
| Wagner, Charles J. | 1910 | Box 407 | Walker, Cuthbert | 1888 | Box 111 |
| Wagner, Emile | 1915 | Box 534 | Walker, David | 1828 | Box 9 |
| Wagner, Emma | 1909 | Box 380 | Walker, Diana | 1904 | Box 273 |
| Wagner, Frederick | 1873 | Box 52 | Walker, Edward | 1914 | Box 506 |
| Wagner, George | 1910 | Box 407 | Walker, Elizabeth Agg | 1890 | Box 122 |
| Wagner, George | 1914 | Box 506 | Walker, Francis V. | 1915 | Box 534 |
| Wagner, George F. | 1905 | Box 292 | Walker, George | 1803 | Box 1 |
| Wagner, George F. | 1916 | Box 560 | Walker, George C. | 1906 | Box 313 |
| Wagner, Henry | 1899 | Box 188 | Walker, George H. | 1906 | Box 314 |
| Wagner, John | 1876 | Box 62 | Walker, George W. | 1911 | Box 432 |
| Wagner, John | 1895 | Box 158 | Walker, Hall Christy | 1919 | Box 647 |
| Wagner, John | 1902 | Box 237 | Walker, Henry W. | 1912 | Box 457 |

| | | | | | | |
|---|---|---|---|---|---|---|
| Walker, Hiram | 1920 | Box 678 | | Wallace, Elizabeth | 1917 | Box 587 |
| Walker, Ida B. | 1900 | Box 201 | | Wallace, Elizabeth B. | 1887 | Box 105 |
| Walker, James | 1832 | Box 12 | | Wallace, Ellen Rebecca | 1912 | Box 457 |
| Walker, James C. | 1870 | Box 44 | | Wallace, Hattie C. | 1920 | Box 678 |
| Walker, Janet | 1890 | Box 122 | | Wallace, James | 1872 | Box 49 |
| Walker, Johannah | 1893 | Box 143 | | Wallace, James H. C. | 1912 | Box 457 |
| Walker, John | 1835 | Box 13 | | Wallace, James P. | 1899 | Box 188 |
| Walker, John G. | 1907 | Box 336 | | Wallace, M. Louise | 1912 | Box 457 |
| Walker, John L. | 1895 | Box 158 | | Wallace, Mary Key | 1864 | Box 33 |
| Walker, John N. | 1917 | Box 587 | | Wallace, Noah | 1889 | Box 117 |
| Walker, Judson | 1863 | Box 31 | | Wallace, Sarah Belle | 1916 | Box 560 |
| Walker, Lewis E. | 1880 | Box 73 | | Wallace, Theodora H. P. | 1909 | Box 381 |
| Walker, Maria Louisa | 1888 | Box 111 | | Wallace, William | 1903 | Box 256 |
| Walker, Martha A. | 1890 | Box 122 | | Wallace, William F. | 1886 | Box 100 |
| Walker, Mary | 1872 | Box 49 | | Wallach, Philip | 1889 | Box 117 |
| Walker, Mary A. J. | 1911 | Box 432 | | Wallach, Richard | 1881 | Box 77 |
| Walker, Mary D. | 1920 | Box 678 | | Wallach, Richard | 1920 | Box 678 |
| Walker, Mary E. | 1862 | Box 30 | | Wallach, Rosa | 1916 | Box 560 |
| Walker, Mary E. Chase | 1911 | Box 432 | | Wallach, William D. | 1872 | Box 49 |
| Walker, Phebe A. | 1899 | Box 188 | | Wallen, Angeline | 1886 | Box 100 |
| Walker, Redford W. | 1909 | Box 381 | | Wallen, Samuel S. | 1906 | Box 314 |
| Walker, Richard A. | 1913 | Box 481 | | Waller, Clarence H. | 1912 | Box 457 |
| Walker, Robert J. | 1869 | Box 41 | | Waller, Frances A. | 1891 | Box 128 |
| Walker, Robert J. | 1911 | Box 432 | | Waller, Leila W. | 1919 | Box 647 |
| Walker, Robert Jarvis C. | 1908 | Box 358 | | Waller, Louise | 1890 | Box 122 |
| Walker, Robert Jarvis C. | 1912 | Box 457 | | Waller, Mary | 1900 | Box 201 |
| Walker, Statira F. | 1896 | Box 166 | | Waller, Victoria A. | 1912 | Box 457 |
| Walker, Susan | 1888 | Box 111 | | Waller, Washington | 1900 | Box 201 |
| Walker, Thomas H. | 1915 | Box 534 | | Wallerstein, Nathan | 1911 | Box 432 |
| Walker, William | 1887 | Box 105 | | Wallerstein, Ricka | 1916 | Box 560 |
| Walker, William | 1893 | Box 143 | | Walling, Joseph B. | 1899 | Box 188 |
| Walker, William | 1914 | Box 506 | | Walling, Rose | 1919 | Box 647 |
| Walker, William G. | 1914 | Box 506 | | Wallingsford, George Noble | 1859 | Box 28 |
| Walker, William H. | 1874 | Box 56 | | Wallis, John H. | 1904 | Box 273 |
| Walker, William M. | 1866 | Box 36 | | Wallis, William | 1879 | Box 70 |
| Walker, William Tobias | 1911 | Box 432 | | Wallis, William Creighton | 1912 | Box 457 |
| Walker, Zachariah | 1857 | Box 26 | | Walls, George | 1850 | Box 21 |
| Walkley, Roxanna | 1912 | Box 457 | | Walmsley, Edwin | 1915 | Box 534 |
| Walks, Elizabeth P. | 1899 | Box 188 | | Walsh, Anna Louisa | 1915 | Box 534 |
| Wall, Allen | 1895 | Box 158 | | Walsh, Bridget | 1897 | Box 173 |
| Wall, Eliza | 1912 | Box 457 | | Walsh, Catherine | 1917 | Box 587 |
| Wall, Howard C. | 1909 | Box 381 | | Walsh, Edmond | 1868 | Box 40 |
| Wall, James Henry | 1914 | Box 506 | | Walsh, Francis S. | 1875 | Box 59 |
| Wall, Jennie L. | 1878 | Box 67 | | Walsh, James | 1848 | Box 20 |
| Wall, Julia | 1915 | Box 534 | | Walsh, James | 1875 | Box 59 |
| Wall, Maurice J. | 1914 | Box 506 | | Walsh, John | 1894 | Box 150 |
| Wall, Thomas | 1873 | Box 52 | | Walsh, John David Hanigan | 1916 | Box 560 |
| Wall, William | 1899 | Box 188 | | Walsh, John James | 1919 | Box 647 |
| Wall, William C. | 1876 | Box 62 | | Walsh, John M. | 1912 | Box 457 |
| Wallace, Adelaide | 1903 | Box 256 | | Walsh, Joseph | 1880 | Box 74 |
| Wallace, Albert | 1893 | Box 143 | | Walsh, Kate | 1918 | Box 616 |
| Wallace, Catharine | 1901 | Box 217 | | Walsh, Margaret | 1908 | Box 358 |

| | | | | | | |
|---|---|---|---|---|---|---|
| Walsh, Mary | 1903 | Box 256 | Ward, Henry S. | 1864 | Box 33 |
| Walsh, Mary A. | 1908 | Box 358 | Ward, Jane | 1865 | Box 34 |
| Walsh, Mary M. | 1857 | Box 26 | Ward, John B. | 1918 | Box 616 |
| Walsh, Thomas | 1913 | Box 481 | Ward, John R. | 1899 | Box 188 |
| Walsh, Thomas | 1918 | Box 616 | Ward, John W. | 1918 | Box 616 |
| Walsh, Thomas F. | 1910 | Box 407 | Ward, Joseph D. | 1865 | Box 34 |
| Walsh, William | 1904 | Box 273 | Ward, Lester F. | 1913 | Box 481 |
| Walsky, Isaac | 1886 | Box 100 | Ward, Lottie J. | 1918 | Box 616 |
| Walson, Charles F. | 1903 | Box 256 | Ward, Lucy M. | 1911 | Box 432 |
| Walter, Charles | 1904 | Box 273 | Ward, Mabel | 1914 | Box 507 |
| Walter (Walters), Daniel | 1886 | Box 100 | Ward, Margaret | 1877 | Box 65 |
| Walter, George W. | 1912 | Box 457 | Ward, Mary | 1911 | Box 432 |
| Walter, Henry | 1917 | Box 587 | Ward, Mary Ann | 1892 | Box 135 |
| Walter, Henry M. | 1909 | Box 381 | Ward, Mary E. | 1915 | Box 535 |
| Walter, Ida | 1917 | Box 587 | Ward, Mary F. | 1891 | Box 128 |
| Walter, Jacob A. | 1894 | Box 150 | Ward, Osborne | 1902 | Box 237 |
| Walter, John | 1907 | Box 336 | Ward, Samuel A. | 1915 | Box 535 |
| Walter, John (Jr.) | 1907 | Box 336 | Ward, Samuel Gray | 1907 | Box 336 |
| Walter, John L. | 1895 | Box 158 | Ward, Thomas M. D. | 1894 | Box 150 |
| Walter, Joseph | 1915 | Box 534 | Ward, Ulysses | 1868 | Box 40 |
| Walter, Olivia | 1915 | Box 535 | Ward, William | 1851 | Box 21 |
| Walter, Wilhelmina | 1887 | Box 105 | Ward, William | 1877 | Box 65 |
| Walter, Wilhelmina | 1888 | Box 111 | Ward, William | 1880 | Box 74 |
| Walter, William | 1885 | Box 94 | Ward, William H. | 1881 | Box 77 |
| Walter, William | 1906 | Box 314 | Wardell, Samuel | 1893 | Box 143 |
| Walter, William | 1916 | Box 560 | Warden, Tillie | 1896 | Box 166 |
| Walters, Anna Koster | 1917 | Box 587 | Warder, Benjamin H. | 1894 | Box 150 |
| Walters, Bernhard | 1885 | Box 94 | Warder, Eliza | 1907 | Box 336 |
| Walters, Lucien N. | 1920 | Box 678 | Warder, James | 1864 | Box 33 |
| Walther, Lena Maria | 1918 | Box 616 | Warder, John | 1897 | Box 173 |
| Waltman, Blanche M. | 1901 | Box 217 | Warder, Mary E. | 1911 | Box 432 |
| Walton, Ellen | 1900 | Box 201 | Warder, Robert B. | 1905 | Box 292 |
| Walton, Henrietta H. | 1900 | Box 201 | Warder, William | 1875 | Box 59 |
| Walton, Jessie R. | 1912 | Box 457 | Wardley, Emma | 1893 | Box 143 |
| Walton, Robert C. | 1907 | Box 336 | Ware, Effie | 1909 | Box 381 |
| Walton, Wilhelimina Binkley | 1914 | Box 506 | Ware, Ellen M. | 1906 | Box 314 |
| Walton, William B. | 1879 | Box 70 | Ware, George | 1913 | Box 481 |
| Walton, William H. | 1914 | Box 506 | Ware, Judea | 1822 | Box 7 |
| Walz, Conrad | 1876 | Box 62 | Ware, Margaret | 1894 | Box 150 |
| Wamsley, William G. | 1911 | Box 432 | Ware, Maria | 1871 | Box 46 |
| Wandel, Charles B. | 1919 | Box 647 | Ware, Mary Angeline | 1909 | Box 381 |
| Wannall, Charles | 1893 | Box 143 | Ware, Robert Benjamin | 1891 | Box 128 |
| Wannall, Mary A. | 1872 | Box 49 | Ware, Sallie | 1910 | Box 407 |
| Ward, Anna H. B. | 1901 | Box 217 | Warfield, Ella Lawrence | 1914 | Box 507 |
| Ward, Annie E. | 1892 | Box 135 | Warfield, Peregrine | 1856 | Box 25 |
| Ward, Benedict Noble | 1915 | Box 535 | Waring, Ann | 1843 | Box 16 |
| Ward, Eliza Titus | 1908 | Box 358 | Waring, Eveline | 1846 | Box 18 |
| Ward, Emily Daria | 1840 | Box 15 | Waring, Henry | 1885 | Box 94 |
| Ward, Emma H. | 1911 | Box 432 | Waring, Marsham | 1886 | Box 100 |
| Ward, Frank K. | 1893 | Box 143 | Waring, Richard M. | 1845 | Box 17 |
| Ward, Harriet Sarah | 1909 | Box 381 | Waring, Sarah | 1846 | Box 18 |
| Ward, Henry | 1909 | Box 381 | Warman, Philip C. | 1908 | Box 358 |

| | | | | | | |
|---|---|---|---|---|---|---|
| Warner, Arlon M. | 1902 | Box 237 | Washington, Peter G. | 1873 | Box 52 |
| Warner, Brainard H. | 1916 | Box 560 | Washington, Rachel A. | 1915 | Box 535 |
| Warner, Catherine Theresa | 1917 | Box 587 | Washington, Richard Bland | 1898 | Box 180 |
| Warner, Edwin F. | 1907 | Box 336 | Washington, Thomas | 1807 | Box 2 |
| Warner, George H. | 1913 | Box 481 | Washington, Warner | 1893 | Box 143 |
| Warner, Joseph Ritner | 1905 | Box 292 | Washington, William Augustine | 1810 | Box 3 |
| Warner, Lavinia | 1919 | Box 647 | Washington, William Henry | 1815 | Box 4 |
| Warren, Andrew | 1911 | Box 433 | Wasman, Charles | 1920 | Box 678 |
| Warren, Charles | 1889 | Box 117 | Wasney, Joseph | 1884 | Box 90 |
| Warren, Dora Marcella | 1917 | Box 587 | Wass, Lydia M. | 1915 | Box 535 |
| Warren, Edwardina S. | 1912 | Box 457 | Wassmann, George | 1893 | Box 143 |
| Warren, Emma Jane | 1904 | Box 273 | Wassum, John W. | 1917 | Box 587 |
| Warren, George | 1907 | Box 336 | Waterbury, Charles Dann | 1918 | Box 616 |
| Warren, Henrietta | 1920 | Box 678 | Waterman, Mary E. | 1904 | Box 273 |
| Warren, James K. | 1895 | Box 158 | Waters, Ann Maria | 1903 | Box 256 |
| Warren, Joseph | 1844 | Box 17 | Waters, Annie E. | 1914 | Box 507 |
| Warren, Julius | 1911 | Box 433 | Waters, Bernard J. | 1918 | Box 616 |
| Warren, Louisa | 1868 | Box 40 | Waters, Caroline S. | 1914 | Box 507 |
| Warren, Moses | 1872 | Box 49 | Waters, Catharine F. | 1873 | Box 52 |
| Warren, Thomas | 1914 | Box 507 | Waters, Catharine S. | 1860 | Box 29 |
| Warren, Tobias | 1882 | Box 81 | Waters, Christopher | 1894 | Box 150 |
| Warren, William E. | 1917 | Box 587 | Waters, Daniel James | 1914 | Box 507 |
| Warren, William J. | 1901 | Box 217 | Waters, Dorathey | 1852 | Box 22 |
| Warriner, William F. | 1914 | Box 507 | Waters, Elizabeth | 1824 | Box 8 |
| Warrington, Lewis | 1851 | Box 21 | Waters, Elizabeth | 1868 | Box 40 |
| Warwick, James Lawrence | 1889 | Box 117 | Waters, Elkanah | 1852 | Box 22 |
| Washburn, Ann | 1857 | Box 26 | Waters, Elkanah N. | 1908 | Box 358 |
| Washburn, Ellen M. | 1899 | Box 188 | Waters, Eugene O. | 1912 | Box 457 |
| Washburn, V. D. | 1907 | Box 336 | Waters, Flaveler | 1893 | Box 143 |
| Washington, Ann | 1896 | Box 166 | Waters, George | 1873 | Box 52 |
| Washington, Ann Matilda | 1885 | Box 94 | Waters, John A. W. | 1878 | Box 67 |
| Washington, Ann Franklin | 1895 | Box 158 | Waters, John G. | 1888 | Box 111 |
| Washington, Ann T. | 1861 | Box 29 | Waters, John L. | 1891 | Box 128 |
| Washington, Bailey | 1854 | Box 23 | Waters, Joseph G. | 1910 | Box 407 |
| Washington, Bushrod | 1876 | Box 62 | Waters, Martha | 1906 | Box 314 |
| Washington, Charles M. | 1913 | Box 481 | Waters, Mary C. | 1896 | Box 166 |
| Washington, Clement A. | 1912 | Box 457 | Waters, Mary E. | 1905 | Box 293 |
| Washington, Corbin | 1871 | Box 46 | Waters, Morris W. | 1918 | Box 616 |
| Washington, Edmund R. | 1918 | Box 616 | Waters, Robert | 1805 | Box 2 |
| Washington, Elizabeth | 1899 | Box 188 | Waters, Thomas | 1818 | Box 5 |
| Washington, Elizabeth L. | 1900 | Box 201 | Waters, William | 1860 | Box 29 |
| Washington, F. V. (Mrs.) | 1919 | Box 647 | Waters, William | 1914 | Box 507 |
| Washington, George | 1802 | Box 1 | Waters, William E. | 1903 | Box 256 |
| Washington, George | 1905 | Box 293 | Waters, Williams N. | 1891 | Box 128 |
| Washington, George Alexander | 1826 | Box 9 | Wathen, Mary Elizabeth | 1910 | Box 407 |
| Washington, Joshua | 1879 | Box 70 | Watkins, Allen | 1907 | Box 336 |
| Washington, Littleton Quinton | 1903 | Box 256 | Watkins, Benjamin | 1894 | Box 150 |
| Washington, Lucy Ann | 1898 | Box 180 | Watkins, Betty S. | 1905 | Box 293 |
| Washington, Margaret A. | 1892 | Box 135 | Watkins, Edgar P. | 1907 | Box 336 |
| Washington, Margarete | 1918 | Box 616 | Watkins, George T. | 1916 | Box 560 |
| Washington, Martha E. | 1917 | Box 587 | Watkins, Greenburg M. | 1878 | Box 67 |
| Washington, Nannie D. B. | 1920 | Box 678 | Watkins, John | 1914 | Box 507 |

| | | | | | | |
|---|---|---|---|---|---|---|
| Watkins, John Elfreth | 1903 | Box 256 | Watts, Mary Jackson | 1890 | Box 123 |
| Watkins, Lewis F. | 1890 | Box 122 | Watts, Samuel (Sr.) | 1912 | Box 457 |
| Watkins, Margaret B. | 1918 | Box 616 | Waugh, Jacob | 1821 | Box 7 |
| Watkins, Margaret J. | 1890 | Box 122 | Waugh, James B. | 1851 | Box 21 |
| Watkins, Maria E. | 1890 | Box 122 | Waugh, Warren | 1888 | Box 111 |
| Watkins, Nicholas | 1912 | Box 457 | Waugh, William B. | 1877 | Box 65 |
| Watkins, Richard J. | 1911 | Box 433 | Way, George | 1820 | Box 6 |
| Watkins, Spencer | 1907 | Box 336 | Wayland, Anna E. | 1888 | Box 111 |
| Watkins, Thomas | 1899 | Box 188 | Wayland, Annie | 1903 | Box 256 |
| Watkins, William | 1919 | Box 647 | Wayne, Francis | 1819 | Box 6 |
| Watling, John A. | 1919 | Box 647 | Wayne, James M. | 1867 | Box 38 |
| Watmough, Emmeline G. | 1904 | Box 273 | Wayne, Joseph | 1816 | Box 5 |
| Watmough, James H. | 1917 | Box 587 | Wayne, Mary J. | 1912 | Box 457 |
| Watrous, Benjamin P. | 1902 | Box 237 | Wayne, Sarah A. | 1909 | Box 381 |
| Watrous, Juliette | 1914 | Box 507 | Wayson, Edward | 1866 | Box 36 |
| Watrous, Louisa T. | 1896 | Box 166 | Wayson, Edward | 1893 | Box 143 |
| Watrous, Melinda R. | 1898 | Box 180 | Weatherby, Mary E. | 1907 | Box 336 |
| Watson, Ann Ewen | 1889 | Box 117 | Weatherly, David Jr. | 1909 | Box 381 |
| Watson, Ann P. | 1837 | Box 14 | Weaver, Augusta M. | 1917 | Box 587 |
| Watson, Charles H. | 1880 | Box 74 | Weaver, Charles | 1883 | Box 84 |
| Watson, Charles James | 1902 | Box 237 | Weaver, Clarence | 1919 | Box 647 |
| Watson, Eliza | 1897 | Box 173 | Weaver, Emma J. E. | 1913 | Box 481 |
| Watson, Elizabeth C. | 1853 | Box 22 | Weaver, Frank Joseph | 1918 | Box 616 |
| Watson, Elizabeth Love | 1886 | Box 100 | Weaver, Henry | 1893 | Box 143 |
| Watson, George | 1897 | Box 173 | Weaver, Ida | 1909 | Box 381 |
| Watson, Gillet F. | 1891 | Box 128 | Weaver, James G. | 1881 | Box 77 |
| Watson, James W. | 1862 | Box 30 | Weaver, Jessie E. | 1909 | Box 381 |
| Watson, James W. | 1920 | Box 678 | Weaver, John H. | 1891 | Box 128 |
| Watson, Jane | 1832 | Box 12 | Weaver, Lydia | 1900 | Box 201 |
| Watson, Johannas | 1888 | Box 111 | Weaver, Margaret A. | 1906 | Box 314 |
| Watson, John J. | 1886 | Box 100 | Weaver, Mary A. | 1896 | Box 166 |
| Watson, James B. | 1877 | Box 65 | Weaver, Mary H. | 1904 | Box 273 |
| Watson, Mary | 1897 | Box 173 | Weaver, Mary W. K. | 1908 | Box 358 |
| Watson, Mary E. | 1911 | Box 433 | Weaver, Michael | 1872 | Box 49 |
| Watson, Mary Eleanor | 1865 | Box 34 | Weaver, Michael C. | 1920 | Box 679 |
| Watson, Robert | 1889 | Box 117 | Weaver, Millard J. | 1911 | Box 433 |
| Watson, Samuel E. | 1887 | Box 106 | Weaver, Priscilla | 1913 | Box 481 |
| Watson, Sarah | 1910 | Box 407 | Weaver, Rebecca S. | 1898 | Box 180 |
| Watson, Sarah J. | 1915 | Box 535 | Weaver, Thomas | 1884 | Box 90 |
| Watson, Susan L. | 1900 | Box 201 | Webb, Elizabeth | 1900 | Box 201 |
| Watson, Walter J. | 1902 | Box 237 | Webb, Isabella A. | 1893 | Box 143 |
| Watt, James K. | 1898 | Box 180 | Webb, James | 1901 | Box 217 |
| Watt, Mary H. | 1919 | Box 647 | Webb, James W. | 1908 | Box 358 |
| Watters, John H. | 1917 | Box 587 | Webb, Lucy Roy | 1908 | Box 358 |
| Watterston, David | 1823 | Box 8 | Webb, Martin V. | 1911 | Box 433 |
| Watterston, David A. | 1903 | Box 256 | Webb, Rachel M. | 1901 | Box 217 |
| Watterston, Eliza H. | 1858 | Box 27 | Webb, Robert W. | 1870 | Box 44 |
| Watton, Clifford Stevens | 1912 | Box 457 | Webb, William | 1889 | Box 117 |
| Watts, Annie Elizabeth | 1905 | Box 293 | Webber, Frederick | 1908 | Box 358 |
| Watts, Charles A. | 1883 | Box 84 | Webber, Frederick N. Sr. | 1913 | Box 482 |
| Watts, Charles H. | 1917 | Box 587 | Webber, George William | 1919 | Box 647 |
| Watts, George | 1905 | Box 293 | Webel, Wilhelmina M. | 1918 | Box 616 |

| | | | | | | |
|---|---|---|---|---|---|---|
| Weber, Anna M. | 1906 | Box 314 | | Weems, Rachel A. D. | 1914 | Box 507 |
| Weber, Annie Schmidt | 1917 | Box 587 | | Weems, Rebecca M. | 1918 | Box 616 |
| Weber, Belle | 1915 | Box 535 | | Weems, Sarah Anne | 1886 | Box 100 |
| Weber, Caroline | 1874 | Box 56 | | Weide, George | 1878 | Box 67 |
| Weber, Caspar A. | 1917 | Box 587 | | Weideman, John | 1902 | Box 237 |
| Weber, Charles | 1877 | Box 65 | | Weidemann, Margaretha | 1912 | Box 458 |
| Weber, Christian Henry | 1852 | Box 22 | | Weidman, Charles S. | 1919 | Box 647 |
| Weber, Christopher | 1865 | Box 34 | | Weidman, John C. | 1887 | Box 106 |
| Weber, Jacob H. | 1902 | Box 237 | | Weidman, Julia M. | 1910 | Box 407 |
| Weber, Joseph V. | 1860 | Box 29 | | Weightman, Serena L. | 1899 | Box 188 |
| Weber, Louis F. W. | 1912 | Box 458 | | Weightman, Susan B. | 1870 | Box 44 |
| Weber, Minnie E. | 1917 | Box 587 | | Weigle, Gustav | 1886 | Box 100 |
| Weber, Philip H. | 1912 | Box 458 | | Weigle, Morris A. | 1912 | Box 458 |
| Weber, Robert | 1895 | Box 158 | | Weik, Louise A. | 1903 | Box 256 |
| Webster, Adela S. | 1912 | Box 458 | | Weil, Catharine | 1896 | Box 166 |
| Webster, Alexander Smith | 1915 | Box 535 | | Weil, George A. | 1909 | Box 381 |
| Webster, Carroll | 1918 | Box 616 | | Weil, John | 1902 | Box 237 |
| Webster, Catharine | 1905 | Box 293 | | Weil, Mort K. | 1904 | Box 273 |
| Webster, Daniel | 1882 | Box 81 | | Weilacher, John G. | 1887 | Box 106 |
| Webster, Daniel B. | 1911 | Box 433 | | Weiler, Ferdinand | 1906 | Box 314 |
| Webster, Edmund Kirby | 1911 | Box 433 | | Weinandt, George | 1885 | Box 94 |
| Webster, Ellen | 1898 | Box 180 | | Weinberger, Christian | 1898 | Box 180 |
| Webster, Ellen K. | 1881 | Box 77 | | Weiner, Clara | 1897 | Box 173 |
| Webster, Harriett | 1887 | Box 106 | | Weinheimer, William Frederick | 1915 | Box 535 |
| Webster, John | 1894 | Box 150 | | Weir, Jesse C. | 1906 | Box 314 |
| Webster, John | 1919 | Box 647 | | Weir, Lydia A. | 1899 | Box 188 |
| Webster, John T. | 1919 | Box 647 | | Weir, Mary L. | 1902 | Box 237 |
| Webster, Josephine C. | 1914 | Box 507 | | Weisenborn, Anna W. | 1919 | Box 648 |
| Webster, Margaret | 1875 | Box 59 | | Weisenborn, Augusta Louisa | 1908 | Box 358 |
| Webster, Nathan | 1874 | Box 56 | | Weisenborn, John B. | 1901 | Box 217 |
| Webster, Olevia | 1910 | Box 407 | | Weisenborn, John Henry | 1873 | Box 52 |
| Webster, Philip | 1836 | Box 13 | | Weiserborn, Maria Johanne | 1904 | Box 273 |
| Webster, Rebecca F. | 1905 | Box 293 | | Weiss, Gustav C. | 1868 | Box 40 |
| Webster, Rezin | 1870 | Box 44 | | Weiss, Konrad | 1917 | Box 587 |
| Webster, Samuel | 1865 | Box 34 | | Weiss, Leopold | 1891 | Box 128 |
| Webster, Sarah Ann | 1915 | Box 535 | | Weisser, Dora | 1917 | Box 587 |
| Webster, Sophia | 1874 | Box 56 | | Welborn, James W. | 1913 | Box 482 |
| Webster, Thomas W. | 1891 | Box 128 | | Welbourn, Isaac | 1893 | Box 143 |
| Webster, William A. | 1885 | Box 94 | | Welch, Bridget | 1871 | Box 46 |
| Webster, William H. | 1896 | Box 166 | | Welch, George B. | 1918 | Box 616 |
| Wedderburn, George C. (Jr.) | 1915 | Box 535 | | Welch, John | 1876 | Box 62 |
| Wedding, Catharine A. | 1904 | Box 273 | | Welch, LeRoy | 1893 | Box 143 |
| Wedding, Nichodemos | 1816 | Box 5 | | Welch, Martha | 1897 | Box 173 |
| Wedge, Caroline | 1907 | Box 336 | | Welch, Mary L. | 1909 | Box 381 |
| Weed, Carrie McLean | 1887 | Box 106 | | Welch, T. Douglas | 1909 | Box 381 |
| Weedon, Louisa M. | 1896 | Box 166 | | Welch, Thomas | 1905 | Box 293 |
| Weeks, Amanda | 1914 | Box 507 | | Welcker, Peter D. | 1889 | Box 117 |
| Weeks, Fannie A. | 1905 | Box 293 | | Welcker, William Paul | 1918 | Box 616 |
| Weeks, George H. | 1906 | Box 314 | | Weld, Edith M. | 1901 | Box 217 |
| Weeks, Mary E. | 1910 | Box 407 | | Wellborne, Ellie B. | 1901 | Box 217 |
| Weems, Catharine | 1915 | Box 535 | | Weller, Catherine J. | 1898 | Box 180 |
| Weems, Mary W. | 1901 | Box 217 | | Weller, Josiah Parran | 1904 | Box 273 |

| | | | | | | |
|---|---|---|---|---|---|---|
| Weller, Michael I. | 1915 | Box 535 | West, Clarissa | 1875 | Box 59 |
| Welles, Helena G. | 1915 | Box 535 | West, Evelina | 1891 | Box 128 |
| Welling, James C. | 1894 | Box 150 | West, Harriet | 1894 | Box 150 |
| Welling, Truman C. | 1920 | Box 679 | West, Henry | 1864 | Box 33 |
| Wellington, John | 1821 | Box 7 | West, J. Thomas | 1900 | Box 202 |
| Wells, Adolphus G. | 1901 | Box 217 | West, John | 1884 | Box 90 |
| Wells, Anna E. | 1892 | Box 135 | West, John Quarles | 1919 | Box 648 |
| Wells, Daniel | 1877 | Box 65 | West, John T. | 1896 | Box 166 |
| Wells, Edward L. | 1875 | Box 59 | West, Joseph | 1863 | Box 31 |
| Wells, George F. | 1911 | Box 433 | West, Maria L. | 1894 | Box 150 |
| Wells, Henry | 1897 | Box 173 | West, William H. | 1873 | Box 52 |
| Wells, Henry H. | 1900 | Box 202 | Westerfield, Elizabeth Jane | 1908 | Box 358 |
| Wells, Huylar Z. | 1917 | Box 587 | Westerfield, James | 1909 | Box 381 |
| Wells, John | 1843 | Box 16 | Westervelt, Harmon C. | 1888 | Box 111 |
| Wells, John | 1900 | Box 202 | Westnedge, Henrietta May | 1920 | Box 679 |
| Wells, Joseph M. | 1903 | Box 256 | Weston, Charles M. | 1907 | Box 336 |
| Wells, Martha A. | 1878 | Box 67 | Weston, Daniel C. | 1903 | Box 257 |
| Wells, Ralph | 1907 | Box 336 | Weston, Fred deB. | 1917 | Box 587 |
| Wells, Sallie A. | 1895 | Box 158 | Weston, Walter | 1904 | Box 273 |
| Wells, Sarah M. | 1899 | Box 188 | Wetherall, Ella J. | 1910 | Box 407 |
| Wells, Sarah W. | 1902 | Box 237 | Wetherell, Elizabeth S. | 1896 | Box 166 |
| Wells, William | 1805 | Box 2 | Wetmore, Charles W. | 1919 | Box 648 |
| Wells, William Henry | 1920 | Box 679 | Wetmore, Helen | 1887 | Box 106 |
| Welsh, James | 1914 | Box 507 | Wetty, John M. | 1906 | Box 314 |
| Welsh, John Lowber | 1905 | Box 293 | Wetzel, Elizabeth | 1881 | Box 77 |
| Welsh, Mary Ann | 1854 | Box 23 | Wetzel, Frederick | 1821 | Box 7 |
| Welsh, Thomas E. | 1886 | Box 100 | Wetzel, John W. | 1895 | Box 158 |
| Welsh, Timothy | 1910 | Box 407 | Wetzel, Margaret A. | 1906 | Box 314 |
| Wendell, Cornelius | 1870 | Box 44 | Wetzel, Philip | 1867 | Box 38 |
| Wendell, Mary | 1909 | Box 381 | Wetzel, William H. | 1906 | Box 314 |
| Wenner, Georgie G. | 1918 | Box 616 | Wetzel, Wilmer W. | 1903 | Box 257 |
| Wentworth, Maria | 1903 | Box 256 | Wetzell, Lazarus | 1897 | Box 173 |
| Wentworth, Marshall C. | 1915 | Box 535 | Wetzerick, Ida Eleanor | 1916 | Box 560 |
| Wentworth, Sophia D. | 1907 | Box 336 | Wex, Henry | 1898 | Box 180 |
| Wentz, Hannah C. | 1883 | Box 84 | Weyl, Max | 1914 | Box 507 |
| Werle, Margaret C. | 1916 | Box 560 | Weyrich, Catharine | 1902 | Box 237 |
| Werner, Bridget | 1905 | Box 293 | Weyrich, Joseph (Sr.) | 1886 | Box 100 |
| Werner, Catharine | 1874 | Box 56 | Weyss, John E. | 1903 | Box 257 |
| Werner, Charles | 1861 | Box 29 | Whalen, Frances | 1903 | Box 257 |
| Werner, Charles H. | 1879 | Box 70 | Whalen, Millard F. | 1918 | Box 617 |
| Werner, Sophia M. | 1903 | Box 256 | Whalley, Edward | 1908 | Box 358 |
| Werres, Agnes | 1909 | Box 381 | Whalley, Isabella R. | 1917 | Box 587 |
| Wertenbaker, Clark Ingersoll | 1913 | Box 482 | Whann, Margaret | 1868 | Box 40 |
| Wertz, August | 1892 | Box 136 | Wharton, Edward | 1868 | Box 40 |
| Wescott, Edward S. | 1919 | Box 648 | Wharton, Francis | 1889 | Box 117 |
| Weser, Edward | 1907 | Box 336 | Wharton, Robert S. | 1893 | Box 143 |
| Weser, Mary Ellen | 1908 | Box 358 | Wharton, William F. | 1919 | Box 648 |
| Wesley, Aaron B. | 1919 | Box 648 | Wheat, John | 1844 | Box 17 |
| West, Alonzo S. | 1918 | Box 616 | Wheat, Mary | 1859 | Box 28 |
| West, Benjamin O. | 1857 | Box 26 | Wheat, William T. | 1847 | Box 19 |
| West, Carrie B. | 1911 | Box 433 | Wheater, Alice Graham | 1916 | Box 560 |
| West, Charles E. | 1919 | Box 648 | Wheatley, Charles | 1898 | Box 180 |

| | | | | | | |
|---|---|---|---|---|---|---|
| Wheatley, Francis | 1883 | Box 84 | | Whitall, Samuel | 1855 | Box 24 |
| Wheatley, George J. | 1907 | Box 336 | | Whitcomb, David Rugg | 1908 | Box 358 |
| Wheatley, Harry Lincoln | 1913 | Box 482 | | Whitcomb, Harriet N. | 1917 | Box 588 |
| Wheatley, Ignatuis | 1849 | Box 20 | | Whitcomb, Mae W. | 1920 | Box 679 |
| Wheatley, Samuel E. | 1900 | Box 202 | | White, Albert George | 1912 | Box 458 |
| Wheatley, Walter T. | 1919 | Box 648 | | White, Ann R. | 1875 | Box 59 |
| Wheatley, William | 1918 | Box 616 | | White, Anna P. | 1920 | Box 679 |
| Wheatley, William G. | 1916 | Box 560 | | White, Annie R. | 1912 | Box 458 |
| Wheatley, William H. | 1901 | Box 217 | | White, Benjamin R. | 1896 | Box 166 |
| Wheaton, Frank | 1903 | Box 257 | | White, Charles | 1905 | Box 293 |
| Wheaton, Sarah | 1826 | Box 9 | | White, Charles A. | 1910 | Box 407 |
| Whedon, Sarah J. Belknap | 1915 | Box 535 | | White, Charles E. | 1918 | Box 616 |
| Wheelan, Adeline | 1900 | Box 202 | | White, Charles F. | 1878 | Box 67 |
| Wheelan, Florence Margaret | 1913 | Box 482 | | White, Charlotte B. | 1917 | Box 587 |
| Wheeler, Edmund G. | 1900 | Box 202 | | White, Charlotte R. | 1902 | Box 237 |
| Wheeler, Elizabeth Esther | 1914 | Box 507 | | White, Cynthia A. | 1916 | Box 560 |
| Wheeler, Ephraim | 1893 | Box 143 | | White, Dorcas A. | 1844 | Box 17 |
| Wheeler, George W. | 1864 | Box 33 | | White, Elizabeth | 1917 | Box 587 |
| Wheeler, Henry W. | 1904 | Box 273 | | White, Ellen | 1872 | Box 49 |
| Wheeler, Ignatius | 1823 | Box 8 | | White, Eva | 1895 | Box 158 |
| Wheeler, John H. | 1883 | Box 84 | | White, Fletcher | 1914 | Box 507 |
| Wheeler, John T. P. | 1892 | Box 136 | | White, George | 1884 | Box 90 |
| Wheeler, Leonard | 1817 | Box 5 | | White, George | 1896 | Box 166 |
| Wheeler, Lucy A. | 1873 | Box 52 | | White, George H. B. | 1899 | Box 189 |
| Wheeler, Mary | 1874 | Box 56 | | White, Harriet | 1873 | Box 52 |
| Wheeler, Matilda A. | 1912 | Box 458 | | White, James | 1807 | Box 2 |
| Wheeler, Robert | 1908 | Box 358 | | White, James | 1827 | Box 9 |
| Wheeler, Sarah A. | 1895 | Box 158 | | White, James | 1918 | Box 616 |
| Wheeler, Susan C. | 1898 | Box 180 | | White, James E. | 1916 | Box 560 |
| Wheeler, Theodore | 1872 | Box 49 | | White, James V. | 1910 | Box 407 |
| Wheeler, William | 1914 | Box 507 | | White, Jesse | 1893 | Box 143 |
| Wheelock, Marcus M. | 1891 | Box 128 | | White, John H. | 1889 | Box 117 |
| Wheelock, Martha | 1888 | Box 111 | | White, John R. | 1892 | Box 136 |
| Whelan, Adeline | 1900 | Box 202 | | White, Joseph M. | 1839 | Box 15 |
| Whelan, Catherine V. | 1904 | Box 273 | | White, Julia | 1917 | Box 588 |
| Whelan, Ellen | 1904 | Box 273 | | White, Kate A. | 1916 | Box 560 |
| Whelan, Thomas | 1878 | Box 67 | | White, Landonia C. | 1916 | Box 560 |
| Whelan, William | 1866 | Box 36 | | White, Margaret | 1897 | Box 173 |
| Whelan, William | 1888 | Box 111 | | White, Margaret Mitchell Kyle | 1912 | Box 458 |
| Wheless, Malone | 1909 | Box 381 | | White, Mary | 1813 | Box 4 |
| Whelpley, Louisa | 1893 | Box 143 | | White, Mary Anna | 1912 | Box 458 |
| Whetcroft, Henry | 1837 | Box 14 | | White, Mary B. | 1914 | Box 507 |
| Whetcroft, Sarah | 1838 | Box 14 | | White, Mary E. | 1910 | Box 407 |
| Whilldin, Joseph K. | 1865 | Box 35 | | White, Mary Hallisy | 1917 | Box 588 |
| Whipple, Edward J. | 1891 | Box 128 | | White, Michael | 1912 | Box 458 |
| Whisler, William | 1884 | Box 90 | | White, Nicholas | 1894 | Box 150 |
| Whitaker, Ephraim M. | 1880 | Box 74 | | White, Oliver L. | 1916 | Box 560 |
| Whitaker, Gilbert | 1865 | Box 35 | | White, Oscar W. | 1918 | Box 617 |
| Whitaker, Jesse H. | 1913 | Box 482 | | White, Rachel Louisa | 1918 | Box 617 |
| Whitaker, Laving | 1866 | Box 36 | | White, Robert | 1899 | Box 189 |
| Whitall, Lydia N. | 1862 | Box 30 | | White, Robert A. | 1912 | Box 458 |
| Whitall, Mary N. | 1879 | Box 70 | | White, Sarah A. | 1907 | Box 337 |

| | | | | | | |
|---|---|---|---|---|---|---|
| White, Susan L. | 1920 | Box 679 | Whyte, Mary E. | 1912 | Box 459 |
| White, Wesley M. | 1880 | Box 74 | Wiber, David Elmer | 1910 | Box 407 |
| White, William | 1891 | Box 128 | Wich, William George | 1919 | Box 648 |
| White, William H. | 1900 | Box 202 | Wick, George | 1913 | Box 482 |
| White, William H. | 1918 | Box 617 | Wickersham, John | 1912 | Box 459 |
| White, William J. | 1920 | Box 679 | Wickersham, Turner A. | 1915 | Box 535 |
| White, William Lee | 1910 | Box 407 | Wickware, Margaret E. | 1920 | Box 679 |
| White, William W. | 1899 | Box 189 | Widdicombe, Martha | 1917 | Box 588 |
| White, Zebulon L. | 1889 | Box 117 | Widdows, Frederick | 1893 | Box 143 |
| Whitehead, Asa | 1897 | Box 173 | Widmayer, Anna R. | 1910 | Box 407 |
| Whitehead, Josephine S. | 1899 | Box 189 | Widmayer, William G. | 1889 | Box 117 |
| Whitehead, Lucy Page | 1913 | Box 482 | Widmire, John | 1905 | Box 293 |
| Whitehead, Phebe A. | 1911 | Box 433 | Wiegmann, John P. | 1872 | Box 49 |
| Whitewood, Elizabeth | 1809 | Box 3 | Wiegmann, Lucie Caroline | 1900 | Box 202 |
| Whitford, Edward O. | 1919 | Box 648 | Wiehle, C. A. Max | 1901 | Box 217 |
| Whitford, George Amos | 1918 | Box 617 | Wiener, Jacob | 1887 | Box 106 |
| Whiting, Alice Van Doren | 1919 | Box 648 | Wigfall, Genevieve Welling | 1900 | Box 202 |
| Whiting, George B. | 1902 | Box 237 | Wiggin, Addison D. | 1905 | Box 293 |
| Whiting, Mary A. | 1919 | Box 648 | Wiggins, Margaret | 1905 | Box 293 |
| Whiting, William | 1875 | Box 59 | Wiggins, Robert | 1917 | Box 588 |
| Whitlow, Washington | 1902 | Box 237 | Wight, Otis | 1896 | Box 166 |
| Whitman, Augustine S. | 1919 | Box 648 | Wight, William H. | 1895 | Box 158 |
| Whitman, Charles Sidney | 1896 | Box 166 | Wightt, John M. | 1819 | Box 6 |
| Whitman, Harriet | 1899 | Box 189 | Wigmore, Mary Tousey | 1919 | Box 648 |
| Whitman, Mary M. B. | 1906 | Box 314 | Wilbert, Martin I. | 1917 | Box 588 |
| Whitman, Royal E. | 1913 | Box 482 | Wilbur, Fedora I. | 1918 | Box 617 |
| Whitmore, Deborah E. | 1905 | Box 293 | Wilbur, Julia A. | 1895 | Box 158 |
| Whitmore, Henrietta B. | 1914 | Box 507 | Wilbur, Mary E. C. | 1910 | Box 407 |
| Whitmore, John R. | 1891 | Box 128 | Wilcox, Adolphus D. | 1915 | Box 535 |
| Whitmore, William W. | 1903 | Box 257 | Wilcox, Clara Brown | 1919 | Box 648 |
| Whitney, Arthur P. | 1902 | Box 237 | Wilcox, George | 1907 | Box 337 |
| Whitney, Asa | 1872 | Box 49 | Wilcox, Joseph P. | 1920 | Box 679 |
| Whitney, Catharine | 1897 | Box 173 | Wilcox, Mary B. | 1905 | Box 293 |
| Whitney, Joseph N. | 1912 | Box 459 | Wilcox, Mary Emily Donelson | 1905 | Box 293 |
| Whitney, Joshua | 1871 | Box 46 | Wilcox, Mary R. | 1917 | Box 588 |
| Whitney, Leonard | 1886 | Box 100 | Wilcox, Sarah C. | 1896 | Box 166 |
| Whitney, Margaret | 1897 | Box 173 | Wilcox, William A. | 1908 | Box 358 |
| Whitney, Oscar | 1890 | Box 123 | Wild, Catherine E. | 1910 | Box 407 |
| Whitney, Sarah C. | 1884 | Box 90 | Wild, Haver | 1855 | Box 24 |
| Whiton, Albert G. | 1869 | Box 41 | Wild, John F. | 1912 | Box 459 |
| Whitridge, Katherine Whiting | 1919 | Box 648 | Wilder, Frank W. | 1919 | Box 648 |
| Whitson, William A. | 1907 | Box 337 | Wilder, Maria E. | 1903 | Box 257 |
| Whitt, Algernon Sidney | 1902 | Box 238 | Wilder, William Franklin | 1917 | Box 588 |
| Whittemore, Sarah A. | 1908 | Box 358 | Wilder, William W. | 1884 | Box 90 |
| Whitten, John | 1892 | Box 136 | Wildes, Frank | 1903 | Box 257 |
| Whittington, Granville N. | 1915 | Box 535 | Wiley, J. W. | 1917 | Box 588 |
| Whittington, Josephine B. | 1909 | Box 381 | Wilhoite, Fannie E. | 1918 | Box 617 |
| Whittlesey, Augusta P. | 1910 | Box 407 | Wilke, Auguste | 1900 | Box 202 |
| Whittlesey, Lily Camp | 1915 | Box 535 | Wilkens, Benjamin F. | 1892 | Box 136 |
| Whitton, Newton | 1910 | Box 407 | Wilkerson, James F. | 1902 | Box 238 |
| Whyte, Frederick | 1917 | Box 588 | Wilkerson, John H. | 1898 | Box 180 |
| Whyte, Joseph | 1919 | Box 648 | Wilkerson, Newman | 1897 | Box 173 |

| | | | | | | |
|---|---|---|---|---|---|
| Wilkes, Colston T. | 1835 | Box 13 | Williams, Alice V. C. | 1905 | Box 293 |
| Wilkes, Edmund | 1914 | Box 507 | Williams, Amelia S. | 1915 | Box 535 |
| Wilkes, Eliza | 1908 | Box 359 | Williams, Ann | 1873 | Box 52 |
| Wilkes, James F. | 1895 | Box 158 | Williams, Anne | 1865 | Box 34 |
| Wilkes, Kate Sydnor | 1920 | Box 679 | Williams, Annie | 1917 | Box 588 |
| Wilkes, William H. | 1914 | Box 507 | Williams, Annie L. | 1916 | Box 560 |
| Wilkie, Robert Grant | 1901 | Box 218 | Williams, Barbara | 1875 | Box 59 |
| Wilkins, Beriah | 1905 | Box 293 | Williams, Carrie R. | 1889 | Box 117 |
| Wilkins, Eliza | 1867 | Box 38 | Williams, Catherine C. | 1898 | Box 180 |
| Wilkins, Emily Jane | 1911 | Box 433 | Williams, Charles | 1858 | Box 27 |
| Wilkins, Eugene Bradley | 1905 | Box 293 | Williams, Charles | 1913 | Box 482 |
| Wilkins, Henrietta C. | 1903 | Box 257 | Williams, Charles B. | 1914 | Box 507 |
| Wilkins, John Darrogh | 1900 | Box 202 | Williams, Charles G. | 1898 | Box 180 |
| Wilkins, Laurie J. | 1911 | Box 433 | Williams, Charles L. | 1911 | Box 433 |
| Wilkins, Matilda S. | 1903 | Box 257 | Williams, Charles M. | 1864 | Box 33 |
| Wilkins, Thomas | 1909 | Box 381 | Williams, Christina | 1863 | Box 31 |
| Wilkins, William | 1908 | Box 359 | Williams, Conrad | 1902 | Box 238 |
| Wilkinson, Elizabeth | 1920 | Box 679 | Williams, Cynthia B. | 1884 | Box 90 |
| Wilkinson, James | 1903 | Box 257 | Williams, Dennis | 1885 | Box 94 |
| Wilkinson, James F. | 1909 | Box 381 | Williams, Dolly Ann | 1865 | Box 34 |
| Wilkinson, John | 1874 | Box 56 | Williams, E. Judge | 1919 | Box 648 |
| Wilkinson, John Francis N. | 1912 | Box 459 | Williams, Edgar D. | 1920 | Box 679 |
| Wilkinson, Josiah | 1903 | Box 257 | Williams, Edmund R. | 1891 | Box 128 |
| Wilkinson, Priscilla | 1857 | Box 26 | Williams, Elisha O. | 1806 | Box 2 |
| Wilkinson, Richard | 1915 | Box 535 | Williams, Eliza | 1903 | Box 257 |
| Wilkinson, Sarah F. | 1916 | Box 560 | Williams, Elizabeth W. | 1917 | Box 588 |
| Wilkinson, Walter Watkins | 1917 | Box 588 | Williams, Enoch | 1899 | Box 189 |
| Wilkinson, William | 1881 | Box 77 | Williams, Evan Robert | 1918 | Box 617 |
| Willard, Ammiel J. | 1900 | Box 202 | Williams, Fannie | 1920 | Box 679 |
| Willard, Caleb C. | 1905 | Box 293 | Williams, Fannie Thornton | 1919 | Box 648 |
| Willard, Cornelia P. | 1900 | Box 202 | Williams, Frank B. | 1890 | Box 122 |
| Willard, Henry A. | 1909 | Box 381 | Williams, Frank S. | 1901 | Box 218 |
| Willard, Lucy Parker | 1910 | Box 407 | Williams, Frederic B. | 1912 | Box 459 |
| Willard, Mae Stearns | 1919 | Box 648 | Williams, George | 1887 | Box 106 |
| Willard, Sarah Bradley | 1909 | Box 381 | Williams, George | 1916 | Box 560 |
| Willard, Theodosia | 1912 | Box 459 | Williams, George A. | 1896 | Box 166 |
| Willcox, Orlando Bolivar | 1907 | Box 337 | Williams, George B. | 1912 | Box 459 |
| Wille, Charles | 1902 | Box 238 | Williams, Georgia H. | 1906 | Box 314 |
| Willett, Ann W. | 1913 | Box 482 | Williams, Gilbert Fearing | 1919 | Box 648 |
| Willett, Edwina C. | 1913 | Box 482 | Williams, Ginevra | 1913 | Box 482 |
| Willett, James P. | 1900 | Box 202 | Williams, Hamilton J. | 1892 | Box 136 |
| Willett, Marinus | 1865 | Box 35 | Williams, Harriet | 1843 | Box 16 |
| Willett, Robert | 1904 | Box 273 | Williams, Henry H. | 1910 | Box 408 |
| Willett, Samuel L. | 1914 | Box 507 | Williams, Henry M. | 1891 | Box 128 |
| Willett, Sarah | 1875 | Box 59 | Williams, Howard H. | 1914 | Box 507 |
| Willett, Voltaire | 1869 | Box 41 | Williams, Isaiah | 1918 | Box 617 |
| Willey, America | 1888 | Box 111 | Williams, James | 1837 | Box 14 |
| Willey, Calvin | 1852 | Box 22 | Williams, James | 1850 | Box 21 |
| William, John M. | 1866 | Box 36 | Williams, James A. | 1893 | Box 143 |
| Williams, Adoniran | 1897 | Box 173 | Williams, James H. | 1914 | Box 507 |
| Williams, Albert Keith | 1901 | Box 218 | Williams, James Henry | 1904 | Box 273 |
| Williams, Alfred | 1901 | Box 218 | Williams, James M. | 1907 | Box 337 |

| | | | | | | |
|---|---|---|---|---|---|---|
| Williams, Jane | 1886 | Box 100 | Williams, Thomas Evan | 1918 | Box 617 |
| Williams, Jeremiah | 1857 | Box 26 | Williams, Thomas N. | 1915 | Box 535 |
| Williams, Jesse | 1882 | Box 81 | Williams, Thomas Owen | 1912 | Box 459 |
| Williams, John | 1841 | Box 15 | Williams, Tobias | 1865 | Box 35 |
| Williams, John | 1849 | Box 20 | Williams, Walter B. | 1912 | Box 459 |
| Williams, John | 1871 | Box 46 | Williams, William | 1882 | Box 81 |
| Williams, John | 1901 | Box 218 | Williams, William | 1897 | Box 173 |
| Williams, John (John W. Post) | 1905 | Box 289 | Williams, William D. | 1873 | Box 52 |
| Williams, John M. | 1906 | Box 314 | Williams, William Hamilton | 1901 | Box 218 |
| Williams, John S. | 1914 | Box 507 | Williams, William J. | 1908 | Box 359 |
| Williams, John W. | 1890 | Box 123 | Williams, William McKendrie | 1901 | Box 218 |
| Williams, Joseph | 1892 | Box 136 | Williams, Zadock | 1892 | Box 136 |
| Williams, Joseph | 1903 | Box 257 | Williamson, Charles A. J. | 1920 | Box 679 |
| Williams, Josephine | 1919 | Box 648 | Williamson, Collen | 1802 | Box 1 |
| Williams, Lafayette | 1897 | Box 173 | Williamson, David | 1890 | Box 123 |
| Williams, Laura Anna | 1908 | Box 359 | Williamson, George A. | 1915 | Box 535 |
| Williams, Leander P. | 1914 | Box 507 | Williamson, James | 1901 | Box 218 |
| Williams, Lemuel | 1889 | Box 117 | Williamson, James A. | 1903 | Box 257 |
| Williams, Lloyd | 1879 | Box 70 | Williamson, John Hancock | 1916 | Box 561 |
| Williams, Louisa A. | 1914 | Box 507 | Williamson, Joseph | 1868 | Box 40 |
| Williams, Louise E. | 1914 | Box 507 | Williamson, Joseph Anderson | 1898 | Box 180 |
| Williams, Lucy G. | 1911 | Box 433 | Williamson, Robert Harper | 1876 | Box 62 |
| Williams, Lucy H. | 1915 | Box 535 | Williamson, Samuel | 1880 | Box 74 |
| Williams, Maria | 1910 | Box 408 | Williamson, William | 1837 | Box 14 |
| Williams, Marial H. | 1875 | Box 59 | Williamson, William Ralph | 1920 | Box 679 |
| Williams, Marie Madeline | 1916 | Box 560 | Willian, Michael | 1915 | Box 535 |
| Williams, Marietta | 1898 | Box 180 | Willie, Sophie M. | 1902 | Box 238 |
| Williams, Martha | 1863 | Box 31 | Willige, Augustus | 1900 | Box 202 |
| Williams, Martha | 1907 | Box 337 | Willige, John Louis | 1912 | Box 459 |
| Williams, Mary | 1804 | Box 1 | Willige, Josephine Cecilia | 1905 | Box 293 |
| Williams, Mary | 1876 | Box 62 | Willis, Amanda | 1909 | Box 381 |
| Williams, Mary A. E. | 1918 | Box 617 | Willis, Caleb H. | 1870 | Box 44 |
| Williams, Mary Ann | 1852 | Box 22 | Willis, Clara | 1877 | Box 65 |
| Williams, Mary C. | 1920 | Box 679 | Willis, Edward Mott | 1913 | Box 482 |
| Williams, Mary Elizabeth | 1913 | Box 482 | Willis, Francis Ira | 1911 | Box 433 |
| Williams, Mary P. | 1917 | Box 588 | Willis, Henry M. | 1919 | Box 648 |
| Williams, Matilda W. | 1873 | Box 52 | Willis, Ida Caro | 1916 | Box 561 |
| Williams, Nellie | 1900 | Box 202 | Willis, John | 1884 | Box 90 |
| Williams, Peter William | 1893 | Box 143 | Willis, Lucy Virginia | 1913 | Box 482 |
| Williams, Polly | 1872 | Box 49 | Willis, Maria L. | 1912 | Box 459 |
| Williams, Richard P. | 1918 | Box 617 | Willis, Mary A. | 1910 | Box 408 |
| Williams, Richard W. | 1911 | Box 433 | Willis, Robert C. | 1919 | Box 648 |
| Williams, Robert | 1902 | Box 238 | Willis, Thomas | 1919 | Box 649 |
| Williams, Samuel | 1802 | Box 1 | Willison, Mary Bettie | 1896 | Box 166 |
| Williams, Sandy | 1907 | Box 337 | Willits, Jane Jerusha | 1907 | Box 337 |
| Williams, Sarah Ann | 1854 | Box 23 | Willmuth, George | 1873 | Box 52 |
| Williams, Sarah C. | 1900 | Box 202 | Willner, Ernst | 1905 | Box 293 |
| Williams, Sarah Townsend | 1876 | Box 62 | Willner, George | 1910 | Box 408 |
| Williams, Sarah W. | 1900 | Box 202 | Willoughby, Westel | 1898 | Box 180 |
| Williams, Susan | 1913 | Box 482 | Wills, David | 1916 | Box 561 |
| Williams, Susan K. | 1865 | Box 34 | Wills, Samuel | 1894 | Box 150 |
| Williams, Thomas | 1918 | Box 617 | Willson, Elizabeth K. | 1919 | Box 649 |

| | | | | | | |
|---|---|---|---|---|---|---|
| Willson, Rutledge | 1919 | Box 649 | Wilson, John H. | 1827 | Box 9 |
| Willson, Sidney Lewis | 1903 | Box 257 | Wilson, John H. A. | 1858 | Box 27 |
| Willson, William H. | 1918 | Box 617 | Wilson, John Moulder | 1919 | Box 649 |
| Wilmot, John H. | 1894 | Box 150 | Wilson, Joseph | 1826 | Box 9 |
| Wilson, Agnes | 1854 | Box 23 | Wilson, Josephine | 1919 | Box 649 |
| Wilson, Albert A. | 1907 | Box 337 | Wilson, Leah L. G. | 1876 | Box 62 |
| Wilson, Alfred M. | 1920 | Box 679 | Wilson, Leah S. | 1838 | Box 14 |
| Wilson, Alisan | 1911 | Box 433 | Wilson, Lizzie L. | 1920 | Box 679 |
| Wilson, Andrew | 1881 | Box 77 | Wilson, Lorena Sharpe | 1910 | Box 408 |
| Wilson, Annie A. | 1918 | Box 617 | Wilson, Margaret Eleanor Gale | 1844 | Box 17 |
| Wilson, Annie E. | 1916 | Box 561 | Wilson, Marie L. | 1900 | Box 202 |
| Wilson, Antonie | 1888 | Box 111 | Wilson, Martha R. | 1892 | Box 136 |
| Wilson, Cara H. | 1908 | Box 359 | Wilson, Mary | 1893 | Box 143 |
| Wilson, Charles | 1917 | Box 588 | Wilson, Mary | 1897 | Box 173 |
| Wilson, Charles Clayton | 1919 | Box 649 | Wilson, Mary | 1900 | Box 202 |
| Wilson, Charles Irving | 1913 | Box 482 | Wilson, Mary | 1910 | Box 408 |
| Wilson, Charles S. | 1908 | Box 359 | Wilson, Mary B. | 1900 | Box 202 |
| Wilson, Charles W. | 1912 | Box 459 | Wilson, Mary E. | 1892 | Box 136 |
| Wilson, David | 1900 | Box 202 | Wilson, Mary H. S. | 1900 | Box 202 |
| Wilson, David | 1897 | Box 173 | Wilson, Offa | 1835 | Box 13 |
| Wilson, Eleanor B. | 1905 | Box 293 | Wilson, Patrick | 1864 | Box 33 |
| Wilson, Eleanor C. | 1904 | Box 273 | Wilson, Paul | 1882 | Box 81 |
| Wilson, Eliza | 1884 | Box 90 | Wilson, Ralph Denton | 1902 | Box 238 |
| Wilson, Elizabeth | 1915 | Box 535 | Wilson, Richard T. | 1914 | Box 507 |
| Wilson, Emory M. | 1920 | Box 679 | Wilson, Samuel B. | 1902 | Box 238 |
| Wilson, Ephraim A. | 1903 | Box 257 | Wilson, Sarah E. | 1885 | Box 94 |
| Wilson, Ezra A. | 1898 | Box 180 | Wilson, Susan G. | 1882 | Box 81 |
| Wilson, Frederica Boyden | 1913 | Box 482 | Wilson, Theodore D. | 1896 | Box 166 |
| Wilson, Frederick T. | 1865 | Box 35 | Wilson, Thomas | 1824 | Box 8 |
| Wilson, George | 1905 | Box 294 | Wilson, Thomas | 1902 | Box 238 |
| Wilson, George B. | 1896 | Box 166 | Wilson, Thomas M. | 1882 | Box 81 |
| Wilson, George R. | 1906 | Box 314 | Wilson, William | 1869 | Box 41 |
| Wilson, Hampton | 1916 | Box 561 | Wilson, William | 1897 | Box 173 |
| Wilson, Hannah | 1866 | Box 36 | Wilson, William F. | 1917 | Box 588 |
| Wilson, Hannah | 1911 | Box 433 | Wilson, William J. | 1909 | Box 381 |
| Wilson, Harriett | 1860 | Box 29 | Wilson, Zadock | 1826 | Box 9 |
| Wilson, Harry Cornell | 1917 | Box 588 | Wiltberger, Charles H. | 1872 | Box 49 |
| Wilson, J. Henry | 1904 | Box 273 | Wiltberger, Frank H. | 1896 | Box 166 |
| Wilson, James | 1901 | Box 218 | Wiltberger, John B. | 1896 | Box 166 |
| Wilson, James Ormond | 1911 | Box 433 | Wimsatt, Ann Eliza | 1886 | Box 100 |
| Wilson, Jane F. | 1910 | Box 408 | Wimsatt, Emma C. | 1919 | Box 649 |
| Wilson, Jay Greenwood | 1909 | Box 381 | Wimsatt, Genevieve B. | 1903 | Box 257 |
| Wilson, Jeremiah M. | 1901 | Box 218 | Wimsatt, John W. | 1919 | Box 649 |
| Wilson, Jesse B. | 1920 | Box 679 | Wimsatt, Richard D. | 1906 | Box 314 |
| Wilson, Jesse H. | 1910 | Box 408 | Wimsatt, Samuel | 1837 | Box 14 |
| Wilson, John | 1876 | Box 62 | Winans, Jacob W. | 1855 | Box 24 |
| Wilson, John | 1881 | Box 77 | Winchell, Sarah R. | 1919 | Box 649 |
| Wilson, John | 1895 | Box 158 | Winchester, Mary | 1869 | Box 41 |
| Wilson, John | 1918 | Box 617 | Winchester, Robert | 1853 | Box 22 |
| Wilson, John A. | 1841 | Box 15 | Wind, Henry | 1899 | Box 189 |
| Wilson, John B. | 1890 | Box 123 | Windholtz, Rebecca | 1897 | Box 173 |
| Wilson, John C. | 1879 | Box 70 | Windholz, Carl L. | 1892 | Box 136 |

| | | | | | | |
|---|---|---|---|---|---|
| Windom, Ellen T. | 1914 | Box 507 | Wise, Henry A. | 1871 | Box 46 |
| Windsbecker, Julius | 1917 | Box 588 | Wise, Huldah J. | 1910 | Box 408 |
| Windsor, Catharine | 1880 | Box 74 | Wise, Joel | 1896 | Box 166 |
| Windsor, David A. | 1892 | Box 136 | Wise, John | 1855 | Box 24 |
| Windus, Caspar | 1896 | Box 166 | Wise, John | 1878 | Box 67 |
| Wine, Miletus J. | 1902 | Box 238 | Wise, John H. | 1871 | Box 46 |
| Wineberger, James A. | 1906 | Box 314 | Wise, Julia Caton | 1918 | Box 617 |
| Wineberger, John A. | 1917 | Box 588 | Wise, Mary A. | 1859 | Box 28 |
| Wineberger, John T. | 1902 | Box 238 | Wise, Mary Jane | 1902 | Box 238 |
| Wines, Guy W. | 1904 | Box 273 | Wise, Nellie H. | 1907 | Box 337 |
| Winfield, Arsenious A. | 1902 | Box 238 | Wise, Robert | 1901 | Box 218 |
| Winfield, Richard | 1872 | Box 49 | Wise, Samuel | 1894 | Box 150 |
| Wing, Mary M. | 1915 | Box 535 | Wise, Sarah E. | 1913 | Box 482 |
| Wingate, Daniel M. | 1918 | Box 617 | Wise, Thomas | 1915 | Box 535 |
| Wingert, Abraham | 1820 | Box 6 | Wise, Thomas W. | 1892 | Box 136 |
| Winkle, Theodore | 1901 | Box 218 | Wise, Thomas W. | 1894 | Box 150 |
| Winlock, Alice B. | 1909 | Box 382 | Wise, Tully R. | 1844 | Box 17 |
| Winn, Rebecca | 1865 | Box 35 | Wiseman, Elizabeth | 1840 | Box 15 |
| Winn, Theodore | 1890 | Box 123 | Wisner, James W. | 1913 | Box 482 |
| Winn, Timothy | 1836 | Box 13 | Wissing, Charles A. | 1918 | Box 617 |
| Winship, Margaret J. | 1898 | Box 180 | Wissner, Henry B. | 1878 | Box 67 |
| Winslow, Augusta C. | 1902 | Box 238 | Wiswell, George F. | 1892 | Box 136 |
| Winslow, Benjamin (Jr.) | 1877 | Box 65 | Witbeck, Eliza Dolson | 1918 | Box 617 |
| Winslow, Caroline | 1897 | Box 173 | Witel, John C. | 1909 | Box 382 |
| Winslow, Martha Ann | 1909 | Box 382 | Witham, Annie E. | 1919 | Box 649 |
| Winsor, William H. | 1885 | Box 94 | Witheron, Samuel H. | 1918 | Box 617 |
| Winston, Annie V. | 1914 | Box 507 | Withers, John | 1861 | Box 29 |
| Winston, Bettie | 1917 | Box 588 | Withington, Gertrude | 1914 | Box 507 |
| Winston, Sarah E. | 1920 | Box 679 | Witmer, Abraham H. | 1900 | Box 202 |
| Winston, Ulysses G. | 1920 | Box 679 | Witmer, Margaret Eliz. B. | 1879 | Box 70 |
| Winter, Elizabeth B. | 1863 | Box 31 | Wittekindt, John | 1886 | Box 100 |
| Winter, Fredericke | 1900 | Box 202 | Wittekindt, John C. | 1900 | Box 202 |
| Winter, John L. | 1902 | Box 238 | Wittenauer, Mary | 1872 | Box 49 |
| Winter, Rosanna | 1914 | Box 507 | Wittenoer, Cornelia | 1866 | Box 36 |
| Winter, William H. | 1859 | Box 28 | Witthaft, Elizabeth | 1907 | Box 337 |
| Winterhalter, Albert G. | 1920 | Box 679 | Witthaft, William | 1901 | Box 218 |
| Winters, George M. | 1879 | Box 70 | Wixom, Mary R. | 1891 | Box 128 |
| Winters, William H. | 1907 | Box 337 | Wlaker, William | 1817 | Box 5 |
| Winthrop, Alice Worthington | 1900 | Box 202 | Wohlfarth, George L. | 1901 | Box 218 |
| Winthrop, William | 1899 | Box 189 | Wolcott, Ann | 1895 | Box 158 |
| Wippermann, Dorothea | 1893 | Box 143 | Wolcott, Edward | 1884 | Box 90 |
| Wire, Ann Elizabeth | 1879 | Box 70 | Wolcott, Edward O. | 1906 | Box 314 |
| Wirt, John | 1818 | Box 5 | Wolf, Caroline H. | 1891 | Box 128 |
| Wirts, William | 1883 | Box 84 | Wolf, John | 1899 | Box 189 |
| Wise, Bridget | 1893 | Box 143 | Wolfe, Mary Eliza | 1919 | Box 649 |
| Wise, Charles B. | 1904 | Box 273 | Wolff, Bertha | 1905 | Box 294 |
| Wise, Charles B. | 1919 | Box 649 | Wolfsteiner, Anna Justina | 1914 | Box 507 |
| Wise, Charlotte B. | 1880 | Box 74 | Wolfsteiner, Jacob | 1891 | Box 128 |
| Wise, Elizabeth | 1913 | Box 482 | Wollard, Ann | 1904 | Box 273 |
| Wise, Elizabeth J. | 1871 | Box 46 | Wollard, Mary E. | 1918 | Box 617 |
| Wise, George A. | 1916 | Box 561 | Wolter, Mary M. | 1908 | Box 359 |
| Wise, Harriet Ellen | 1901 | Box 218 | Wolz, Mary C. | 1916 | Box 561 |

| | | | | | | |
|---|---|---|---|---|---|---|
| Wood, Abigail C. | 1862 | Box 30 | | Woodbury, George T. | 1898 | Box 180 |
| Wood, Alfred E. | 1920 | Box 679 | | Woodbury, Henry E. | 1906 | Box 314 |
| Wood, Andrew | 1895 | Box 158 | | Woodbury, Sallie | 1903 | Box 257 |
| Wood, Annie | 1899 | Box 189 | | Woodfield, Benjamin | 1870 | Box 44 |
| Wood, Arianne | 1894 | Box 150 | | Woodhouse, Mary E. | 1912 | Box 459 |
| Wood, Arthur Burr | 1895 | Box 158 | | Woodhull, Ellen Marian Eliz. | 1920 | Box 679 |
| Wood, Benjamin C. | 1838 | Box 14 | | Woodhull, Maxwell | 1863 | Box 31 |
| Wood, Catherine | 1891 | Box 128 | | Woodhull, Maxwell | 1895 | Box 158 |
| Wood, Charles E. | 1908 | Box 359 | | Woodland, Mary | 1886 | Box 100 |
| Wood, Charles F. | 1875 | Box 59 | | Woodley, George A. | 1891 | Box 128 |
| Wood, Edward | 1899 | Box 189 | | Woodley, Knight C. | 1898 | Box 180 |
| Wood, Elizabeth | 1906 | Box 314 | | Woodman, Francis Joseph | 1917 | Box 588 |
| Wood, Elizabeth T. | 1910 | Box 408 | | Woodruff, Ezra | 1913 | Box 482 |
| Wood, Ellen | 1885 | Box 94 | | Woodruff, Frances G. | 1919 | Box 649 |
| Wood, Frances R. | 1916 | Box 561 | | Woodruff, Henry | 1909 | Box 382 |
| Wood, Francis A. | 1917 | Box 588 | | Woodruff, Jerome B. | 1877 | Box 65 |
| Wood, Frank Ivey | 1914 | Box 507 | | Woods, Anne E. | 1911 | Box 433 |
| Wood, Franklin | 1913 | Box 482 | | Woods, Cecelia I. | 1911 | Box 433 |
| Wood, George | 1870 | Box 44 | | Woods, Charles R. | 1911 | Box 433 |
| Wood, George | 1897 | Box 173 | | Woods, Charlotte J. | 1912 | Box 459 |
| Wood, George | 1899 | Box 189 | | Woods, Elizabeth | 1919 | Box 649 |
| Wood, Gertrude L. | 1918 | Box 617 | | Woods, James S. | 1875 | Box 59 |
| Wood, Ida Ellen | 1895 | Box 158 | | Woods, Louis E. | 1915 | Box 535 |
| Wood, James | 1917 | Box 588 | | Woods, Mary F. | 1883 | Box 84 |
| Wood, James R. | 1865 | Box 35 | | Woods, Owen | 1906 | Box 314 |
| Wood, James W. | 1907 | Box 337 | | Woods, William B. | 1887 | Box 106 |
| Wood, Jane E. W. | 1915 | Box 535 | | Woodward, Amon | 1874 | Box 56 |
| Wood, Julia A. | 1912 | Box 459 | | Woodward, Anna | 1911 | Box 433 |
| Wood, Kate Adelia | 1913 | Box 482 | | Woodward, Ashby W. | 1920 | Box 679 |
| Wood, Lexious A. | 1907 | Box 337 | | Woodward, Blanche W. | 1896 | Box 166 |
| Wood, Lydia A. | 1851 | Box 21 | | Woodward, C. Virginia | 1916 | Box 561 |
| Wood, Margaret J. | 1894 | Box 150 | | Woodward, Charlotte T. | 1913 | Box 482 |
| Wood, Margaret R. | 1904 | Box 273 | | Woodward, Eliza M. | 1878 | Box 67 |
| Wood, Maria B. | 1916 | Box 561 | | Woodward, Elizabeth | 1899 | Box 189 |
| Wood, Marie Genevieve | 1917 | Box 588 | | Woodward, George T. | 1896 | Box 166 |
| Wood, Mary Cornelia | 1890 | Box 123 | | Woodward, James | 1910 | Box 408 |
| Wood, N. Elizabeth | 1913 | Box 482 | | Woodward, James Savage | 1919 | Box 649 |
| Wood, Nelson Rush | 1920 | Box 679 | | Woodward, John William | 1915 | Box 535 |
| Wood, Sarah | 1888 | Box 111 | | Woodward, Joseph Janvier | 1884 | Box 90 |
| Wood, Susan T. | 1898 | Box 180 | | Woodward, Joseph Janvier | 1906 | Box 314 |
| Wood, Thomas N. | 1917 | Box 588 | | Woodward, Maria L. | 1910 | Box 408 |
| Wood, Virginia Elton | 1909 | Box 382 | | Woodward, Mark R. | 1892 | Box 136 |
| Wood, Virginia M. | 1871 | Box 46 | | Woodward, Mary Ann | 1904 | Box 273 |
| Wood, William Henry | 1911 | Box 433 | | Woodward, Nina A. | 1912 | Box 459 |
| Wood, William P. | 1903 | Box 257 | | Woodward, S. Walter | 1917 | Box 588 |
| Wood, William W. W. | 1882 | Box 81 | | Woodward, Sabra | 1875 | Box 59 |
| Woodbridge, John Eliot | 1901 | Box 218 | | Woodward, Thomas P. | 1911 | Box 434 |
| Woodbridge, William E. | 1904 | Box 273 | | Woodward, William R. | 1905 | Box 294 |
| Woodbury, Anna Lowell | 1906 | Box 314 | | Woodward, William Redin | 1898 | Box 180 |
| Woodbury, D. P. | 1910 | Box 408 | | Woodworth, Sarah F. | 1916 | Box 561 |
| Woodbury, Edward | 1896 | Box 166 | | Woody, Edward | 1882 | Box 81 |
| Woodbury, Ellen C. de Q. | 1909 | Box 382 | | Woody, Edward T. | 1918 | Box 617 |

| | | | | | | |
|---|---|---|---|---|---|---|
| Woody, Margaret L. | 1904 | Box 273 | | Wright, John J. | 1903 | Box 257 |
| Woody, William | 1894 | Box 150 | | Wright, John Montgomery | 1915 | Box 535 |
| Woog, Edmund S. | 1910 | Box 408 | | Wright, John R. | 1906 | Box 314 |
| Woolf, Charles M. | 1912 | Box 459 | | Wright, Joseph Payson | 1900 | Box 202 |
| Wooley, Bessie L. | 1887 | Box 106 | | Wright, Julia Speir | 1912 | Box 459 |
| Woolley, Martha R. | 1866 | Box 36 | | Wright, Martha Jane | 1876 | Box 62 |
| Woolley, Mattie J. | 1920 | Box 679 | | Wright, Mary | 1886 | Box 101 |
| Woolley, Sallie | 1899 | Box 189 | | Wright, Mary Elizabeth | 1919 | Box 649 |
| Woolls, Katherine Mary | 1920 | Box 679 | | Wright, Mary J. | 1907 | Box 337 |
| Wooster, Hettie | 1915 | Box 535 | | Wright, Mary M. | 1917 | Box 588 |
| Worcester, William P. | 1910 | Box 408 | | Wright, Matthew | 1847 | Box 19 |
| Worch, Emilie | 1914 | Box 507 | | Wright, May Hayes | 1909 | Box 382 |
| Worden, Tillie | 1896 | Box 166 | | Wright, Minna | 1908 | Box 359 |
| Work, Catharine | 1896 | Box 166 | | Wright, Paul L. | 1920 | Box 679 |
| Work, Harry L. | 1900 | Box 202 | | Wright, Philo | 1886 | Box 101 |
| Work, John W. | 1893 | Box 143 | | Wright, Robert | 1898 | Box 180 |
| Wormley, Adelaide E. | 1892 | Box 136 | | Wright, Sallie | 1897 | Box 173 |
| Wormley, Anna E. | 1892 | Box 136 | | Wright, Sarah I. | 1906 | Box 314 |
| Wormley, James | 1885 | Box 94 | | Wright, Thomas H. | 1914 | Box 507 |
| Wormley, Mary Jane | 1896 | Box 166 | | Wright, Virginia | 1900 | Box 202 |
| Wormley, Matilda | 1882 | Box 81 | | Wright, Walter E. | 1913 | Box 482 |
| Wormley, Samuel | 1864 | Box 33 | | Wright, William C. | 1847 | Box 19 |
| Wormley, William | 1855 | Box 24 | | Wright, William H. | 1881 | Box 77 |
| Wormley, William H. A. | 1908 | Box 359 | | Wright, William H. | 1895 | Box 158 |
| Worrall, Alexander | 1889 | Box 117 | | Wright, William W. | 1904 | Box 273 |
| Worrell, William | 1908 | Box 359 | | Wrightson, Mary Emily | 1918 | Box 617 |
| Worthington, Charles | 1836 | Box 13 | | Wroe, Absalom | 1834 | Box 12 |
| Worthington, Charles | 1904 | Box 273 | | Wroe, Charles P. P. | 1902 | Box 238 |
| Worthington, Harriet | 1862 | Box 30 | | Wroe, Emily A. D. | 1895 | Box 158 |
| Worthington, Horace | 1908 | Box 359 | | Wroe, Everett | 1905 | Box 294 |
| Worthington, Nicholas W. | 1849 | Box 20 | | Wroe, Margaret Virginia | 1909 | Box 382 |
| Worthington, Susan | 1864 | Box 33 | | Wroe, William A. | 1908 | Box 359 |
| Worthington, William M. | 1842 | Box 16 | | Wunder, Andrew | 1906 | Box 314 |
| Wrenn, Martha Ella | 1912 | Box 459 | | Wunder, William H. | 1915 | Box 535 |
| Wricht, Henry T. | 1914 | Box 507 | | Wurdeman, August E. | 1912 | Box 459 |
| Wright, Anna M. C. | 1906 | Box 314 | | Wurdemann, Caroline M. | 1907 | Box 337 |
| Wright, Annette M. | 1911 | Box 434 | | Wurdemann, John V. | 1919 | Box 649 |
| Wright, Benjamin C. | 1911 | Box 434 | | Wurdemann, William | 1906 | Box 314 |
| Wright, Charles H. | 1873 | Box 52 | | Wurdig, Conrad | 1900 | Box 202 |
| Wright, D. Pratt | 1904 | Box 273 | | Wyatt, Culam | 1908 | Box 359 |
| Wright, Ella V. | 1917 | Box 588 | | Wyckoff, James S. | 1916 | Box 561 |
| Wright, Emma C. | 1888 | Box 111 | | Wyckoff, John W. | 1901 | Box 218 |
| Wright, Eugene Barton | 1896 | Box 166 | | Wyeth, Frances A. | 1909 | Box 382 |
| Wright, George | 1876 | Box 62 | | Wygant, Stephen | 1886 | Box 101 |
| Wright, Horatio | 1899 | Box 189 | | Wyle, Margaret | 1892 | Box 136 |
| Wright, Irvin B. | 1905 | Box 294 | | Wylie, Julia A. | 1912 | Box 459 |
| Wright, James | 1834 | Box 12 | | Wyman, Robert H. | 1883 | Box 84 |
| Wright, James H. | 1891 | Box 128 | | Wyman, Sarah E. | 1903 | Box 257 |
| Wright, James M. | 1891 | Box 128 | | Wymer, Virginia | 1880 | Box 74 |
| Wright, Jane Catharine | 1891 | Box 128 | | Wynn, James Henry | 1862 | Box 30 |
| Wright, John Essex | 1900 | Box 202 | | Wynne, Bridgett | 1906 | Box 314 |
| Wright, John Henry | 1893 | Box 143 | | Wynne, Lewis B. | 1883 | Box 84 |

| | | | | | | |
|---|---|---|---|---|---|---|
| Wynne, Mary E. | 1915 | Box 535 | York, Lewis | 1903 | Box 257 |
| Wynne, Thomas | 1898 | Box 180 | York, Lucy | 1918 | Box 618 |
| Wysill, Caroline | 1908 | Box 359 | Yost, Amos S. | 1918 | Box 618 |
| Wysong, Mary Camfield | 1917 | Box 588 | Young, Abner H. | 1860 | Box 29 |
| Wyvill, Edward Hale | 1918 | Box 617 | Young, Alexander | 1855 | Box 24 |
| Xander, Christian | 1908 | Box 359 | Young, Alexander H. | 1887 | Box 106 |
| Xander, Henry | 1897 | Box 173 | Young, Amelia | 1916 | Box 561 |
| Xander, Karl | 1918 | Box 618 | Young, Ammi Burnham | 1874 | Box 56 |
| Yager, Francis W. | 1889 | Box 117 | Young, Ann | 1871 | Box 46 |
| Yager, Geneviere | 1896 | Box 166 | Young, Ann | 1874 | Box 56 |
| Yardley, Sarah Jane | 1880 | Box 74 | Young, Ann H. | 1889 | Box 117 |
| Yarnall, Mordecai | 1879 | Box 70 | Young, Annie Roseberry | 1916 | Box 561 |
| Yarnold, Susanna F. Bray | 1918 | Box 618 | Young, Augusta Maria | 1905 | Box 294 |
| Yarrow, Anne P. Dryburgh | 1914 | Box 507 | Young, Barbara S. | 1863 | Box 31 |
| Yates, Alison S. | 1872 | Box 49 | Young, Bessie P. | 1904 | Box 274 |
| Yates, Ann B. | 1881 | Box 77 | Young, Carrington A. | 1917 | Box 588 |
| Yates, Anna M. | 1904 | Box 274 | Young, Clementina S. | 1869 | Box 41 |
| Yates, Elizabeth I. | 1917 | Box 588 | Young, Eliza | 1885 | Box 94 |
| Yates, Emily B. | 1898 | Box 180 | Young, Eliza W. | 1887 | Box 106 |
| Yates, James | 1897 | Box 173 | Young, Elizabeth | 1891 | Box 128 |
| Yates, John B. | 1890 | Box 123 | Young, Emily D. | 1881 | Box 77 |
| Yates, John F. | 1872 | Box 49 | Young, Eunice C. | 1883 | Box 84 |
| Yates, Mary | 1817 | Box 5 | Young, George A. | 1903 | Box 257 |
| Yates, Mary E. | 1894 | Box 150 | Young, George P. | 1918 | Box 618 |
| Yates, Thomas A. | 1901 | Box 218 | Young, George W. | 1867 | Box 38 |
| Yates, Thornton | 1884 | Box 90 | Young, Helen M. | 1912 | Box 459 |
| Yates, William A. | 1911 | Box 434 | Young, Ida Perry | 1920 | Box 679 |
| Yeabower, Christopher | 1867 | Box 38 | Young, Jacob | 1903 | Box 257 |
| Yeabower, S. Louisa | 1883 | Box 84 | Young, James E. | 1895 | Box 158 |
| Yeager, Morris | 1916 | Box 561 | Young, James R. | 1865 | Box 35 |
| Yeager, Thomas D. | 1908 | Box 359 | Young, James T. | 1901 | Box 218 |
| Yeates, Sarah | 1863 | Box 31 | Young, Johanna F. | 1911 | Box 434 |
| Yeates, Thomas Y. | 1914 | Box 507 | Young, John | 1816 | Box 5 |
| Yeatman, John | 1886 | Box 101 | Young, John | 1899 | Box 189 |
| Yeatman, Marinda Alice | 1917 | Box 588 | Young, John C. | 1888 | Box 111 |
| Yeatman, Medora Beale | 1911 | Box 434 | Young, John J. | 1879 | Box 70 |
| Yeatman, Robert H. | 1908 | Box 359 | Young, John M. | 1873 | Box 52 |
| Yeatman, Samuel M. | 1906 | Box 314 | Young, John M. | 1895 | Box 158 |
| Yeatman, William S. | 1901 | Box 218 | Young, John Ramsey | 1920 | Box 679 |
| Yeigh, Kate Eva | 1911 | Box 434 | Young, John Thomas | 1919 | Box 649 |
| Yerby, Everett D. | 1919 | Box 649 | Young, Joseph M. | 1883 | Box 84 |
| Yerkes, Arline Osgood | 1911 | Box 434 | Young, Joseph N. | 1918 | Box 618 |
| Yerkes, William H. | 1903 | Box 257 | Young, Lavinia | 1894 | Box 150 |
| Yerkes, William H. | 1907 | Box 337 | Young, Lucien | 1912 | Box 459 |
| Yewell, Mary Gibson | 1915 | Box 535 | Young, Manduit | 1844 | Box 17 |
| Yewell, Mary J. | 1891 | Box 128 | Young, Maria | 1904 | Box 274 |
| Yingling, David C. | 1910 | Box 408 | Young, Martha | 1849 | Box 20 |
| Yoder, Charles T. | 1916 | Box 561 | Young, Mary | 1815 | Box 4 |
| Yoder, Minerva E. | 1919 | Box 649 | Young, Mary | 1897 | Box 173 |
| Yonge, Francis Arthur | 1918 | Box 618 | Young, Mary A. | 1870 | Box 44 |
| York, John | 1876 | Box 62 | Young, Mary C. | 1885 | Box 94 |
| York, Levi | 1897 | Box 173 | Young, Matilda | 1871 | Box 46 |

| | | |
|---|---|---|
| Young, Nettie | 1916 | Box 561 |
| Young, Nicholas | 1826 | Box 9 |
| Young, Nicholas E. | 1916 | Box 561 |
| Young, Noble | 1883 | Box 84 |
| Young, Nora C. | 1896 | Box 166 |
| Young, Norris R. | 1917 | Box 588 |
| Young, Notley | 1802 | Box 1 |
| Young, Notley (Rev.) | 1820 | Box 6 |
| Young, Rebecca E. | 1920 | Box 679 |
| Young, Richard | 1879 | Box 70 |
| Young, Richard | 1887 | Box 106 |
| Young, Richard M. | 1862 | Box 30 |
| Young, Rosanna C. | 1909 | Box 382 |
| Young, Samuel | 1811 | Box 4 |
| Young, Sarah A. | 1840 | Box 15 |
| Young, Sarah C. | 1914 | Box 507 |
| Young, Susannah H. | 1913 | Box 482 |
| Young, Thomas | 1879 | Box 70 |
| Young, W. J. | 1915 | Box 535 |
| Young, Warren S. | 1917 | Box 588 |
| Young, Washington A. | 1902 | Box 238 |
| Young, William A. | 1902 | Box 238 |
| Young, William H. | 1908 | Box 359 |
| Young, William H. | 1915 | Box 535 |
| Younger, Edward Columbus | 1914 | Box 507 |
| Youngs, Amelia L. | 1920 | Box 679 |
| Youngs, Elphonza | 1905 | Box 294 |
| Youngs, Rufus B. | 1920 | Box 679 |
| Yowell, George C. | 1905 | Box 294 |
| Yulee, David | 1886 | Box 101 |
| Yundt, Elizabeth D. | 1918 | Box 618 |
| Yznaga, José M. | 1910 | Box 408 |
| Zahir, William | 1893 | Box 143 |
| Zange, Charles G. | 1906 | Box 314 |
| Zange, Margaretha | 1894 | Box 150 |
| Zanner, Alwina (Mary) | 1913 | Box 482 |
| Zanner, William | 1911 | Box 434 |
| Zanner, William F. | 1916 | Box 561 |
| Zaring, Henry F. | 1920 | Box 679 |
| Zegowitz, Joseph | 1909 | Box 382 |
| Zeh, Pauline | 1910 | Box 408 |
| Zeh, William H. | 1903 | Box 257 |
| Zeilin, Jacob | 1880 | Box 74 |
| Zeilin, Virginia | 1895 | Box 158 |
| Zeiter, Terese | 1919 | Box 649 |
| Zeller, Barbara | 1909 | Box 382 |
| Zeller, Jacob | 1881 | Box 77 |
| Zeller, Leonhard | 1910 | Box 408 |
| Zellers, George H. H. | 1917 | Box 588 |
| Zepp, Sarah Ellen | 1911 | Box 434 |
| Zerega, Giovanni M. | 1916 | Box 561 |
| Zevely, Alexander N. | 1888 | Box 111 |

| | | |
|---|---|---|
| Zglinitzke, Marie D. | 1895 | Box 158 |
| Zglinitzki, Bogislaw | 1908 | Box 359 |
| Ziemann, Carl Hugo | 1904 | Box 274 |
| Zier, Philip R. | 1915 | Box 535 |
| Zimmerman, Elizabeth | 1875 | Box 59 |
| Zimmerman, John George | 1872 | Box 49 |
| Zimmerman, John R. | 1904 | Box 274 |
| Zimmermann, Emma W. | 1919 | Box 649 |
| Zurhorst, George F. | 1919 | Box 649 |
| Zurhorst, George P. | 1911 | Box 434 |

www.ingramcontent.com/pod-product-compliance
Lightning Source LLC
Chambersburg PA
CBHW081434270326
41932CB00019B/3194